Harvard Historical Studies, Volume LXXVII

Published under the direction of the Department of History
from the income of the Henry Warren Torrey Fund

Harvard Historical Studies, Volume LXXXVII

Published under the direction of the Department of History
from the income of the Henry Warren Torrey Fund

Harvard Historical Studies, Volume LXXXVII

Published under the direction of the Department of History
from the income of the Henry Warren Torrey Fund

The House of Commons in 1624

ROBERT E. RUIGH

# The Parliament of 1624

*Politics and Foreign Policy*

Harvard University Press    Cambridge, Massachusetts    1971

# Preface

"The Monarch of Englande," wrote Sir Thomas Smith in 1565, "hath absolutelie in his power the authoritie of warre and peace, to defie what Prince it shall please him, and to bid him warre, and againe to reconcile himselfe and enter into league or truce with him at his pleasure or the advice onely of his privie counsell." [1] When, in 1624, James I took his people into his confidence, he thereby created a precedent for parliamentary discussion of foreign affairs. The historical reevaluation of that precedent is the raison d'être of this study.

Within recent years fifteen partial or complete parliamentary diaries (see Appendix B) kept by contemporary observers have been made available for scholarly research, and, in consequence, the decision-making process in the House of Commons has been clarified. The terse references in the journals of the House have been supplemented by lengthy summaries of important speeches; committee proceedings, of which we were formerly ignorant, have been described in detail. New evidence alone, therefore, warrants a reconsideration of the accomplishments of the Parliament of 1624, but it is also imperative that some of the Victorian assumptions that have influenced historical interpretations be challenged. The Whiggish predilection for injecting party politics into seventeenth-century history, for overemphasizing the constitutional importance of the House of Commons, for eulogizing heroes and

1. Sir Thomas Smith, *De Republica Anglorum,* ed. L. Alston (Cambridge: Cambridge University Press, 1906), 58–59.

vilifying Stuart inhibitors of progress and liberty must be subjected to searching criticism.

It is unfortunate, but unavoidable, that certain key words should retain modern connotations when applied to the seventeenth century. Without proper qualification, such terms as "party," "king's friends," and "antiprerogative" may be misinterpreted, and, in the interest of precision, I should like to clarify the sense in which I have employed them.

By "party" I mean a voluntary temporary association, without formal organization, of politically active individuals who share and express similar attitudes on one or more controversial issues and who tend to collect around a natural leader or patron espousing their values and policies.

By "king's friends" I mean those who, from motives of self-interest, employment, or principle, consistently support crown policy, although not necessarily to the same degree in all areas, that is, legal, economic, political, and religious.

I do not understand "antiprerogative" to imply the total destruction of the king's constitutional discretionary powers, but rather the desire, expressed in varying degrees, to confine it within statutory limits or to assure, without legal limitation, the accommodation of its exercise to the will of the nation as expressed by Parliament.

Believing, as I do, that a valid interpretation of the Parliament of 1624 must rest upon a thorough reexamination of the evidence, I have relied heavily upon primary material. While keeping in mind the main trends in English constitutional history, I have used original journals, records, and letters in an attempt to identify and define the attitudes and goals of interested cliques, factions, and personalities. The analytical framework of this study has been influenced by the need to answer several basic questions. Why was a reappraisal of English foreign policy necessary and what occasioned an appeal to Parliament? Who were the people thereby involved in the decision-making process? How was a parliamentary consensus achieved? What efforts were made to promote or impede the promulgation and effectuation of a revised foreign policy?

The answers to these questions have suggested a modification of the accepted interpretation of the comparative success of the

Commons in usurping the determination of foreign policy. They have demonstrated the importance of procedural techniques in determining parliamentary action and have clarified the extent to which the royal prerogative, in all its aspects, was compromised. They have shown the relative insignificance of party, familial, factional, economic, and regional interests in the formulation of national policy. They have emphasized the primacy of the monarchy, even when its leadership was challenged by a member of the royal family, and they have indicated the importance of extraparliamentary deliberations.

All citations of printed materials are reproduced as they were published, with the exception of the Earl of Kellie's letters where the spelling has been modernized. Manuscript references are printed utilizing modern spelling, punctuation, and capitalization. Unless otherwise indicated, all dates are given according to the Old Style (Julian) calendar, but January 1, rather than March 25, is taken as the commencement of the year.

In the discussion of patronage I have avoided multiple references to standard printed biographical sources except in such cases where I think citations are necessary to establish the identity of a member and his political affiliations.

# Acknowledgments

This study evolved from my interest in the parliamentary diaries for 1624. Professor W. K. Jordan of Harvard University has been conversant with my work from its inception and has sustained me with his encouragement and constructive criticism. He was instrumental in facilitating my research in England — research that deepened my knowledge and multiplied those friends to whom I am indebted for assistance.

Without the cooperation of directors and personnel of the archives and libraries of Britain this book could not have been written. Mr. H. C. Johnson, Keeper of the Public Records, has been a constant source of cogent advice and pertinent information in keeping with the best scholarly tradition. Sir Patrick Kingsley, Secretary and Keeper of the records of the duchy of Cornwall placed the manuscripts of that office at my disposal. Maurice F. Bond, Clerk of the Records in the House of Lords, expedited my research into the journals and legislation of the Parliament of 1624. T. C. Skeat, Keeper of Manuscripts, and G. R. C. Davis, Deputy Keeper of Manuscripts at the British Museum, copiously answered my questions about seventeenth-century manuscripts. Their help was complemented by the courtesies accorded me by their respective staffs.

The librarians and personnel of the National Library of Scotland; the National Library of Wales; the Bodleian Library, Oxford; the University of London's Libraries; the Society of Antiquaries of London; the Guildhall Library, London; the Inner Temple Library, London; the John Rylands Library, Manchester;

and the Westminster Abbey Library graciously and efficiently assisted my search of manuscripts in their collections. To them, and to their American confreres at Widener and Houghton Libraries, Harvard University, I express my appreciation.

I am obligated to the owners of private collections of manuscripts for access to their documents and permission to quote from the texts. To His Grace the Duke of Buccleuch (Montagu MSS), His Grace the Duke of Sutherland (Ellesmere and Leveson-Gower MSS), His Grace the Duke of Manchester (Manchester MSS), the Right Honourable the Marquess of Ailesbury (Hawarde MS), the Right Honourable the Marquess of Bath (Thynne and Whitelocke MSS), the trustees of the Earl of Winchilsea (Finch-Hatton MSS), the Right Honourable the Lord Sackville (Cranfield MSS), Major James More-Molyneux (More MSS), Mrs. R. A. Dyott (Dyott MS), and J. L. Jervoise, Esquire (Jervoise and Sherfield MSS), I express my appreciation for their hospitality, interest, and consideration.

Quotations from crown copyright material and the reproduction of the engraving of the House of Commons in 1624 appear by permission of the Controller of HM Stationery Office. The portraits of James I, Prince Charles, the Duke of Buckingham, and Sir Robert Phelips are reproduced by permission of the Director of the National Portrait Gallery. Citations from manuscripts in the British Museum are made by permission of the Trustees of the British Museum.

I have made extensive use of the facilities of the National Register of Archives, the History of Parliament Trust, and the Institute of Historical Research. I am indebted to H. M. G. Baillie, Assistant Secretary of the Historical Manuscripts Commission, to E. L. C. Mullins, Secretary of the History of Parliament Trust, to A. T. Milne, Secretary and Librarian of the Institute of Historical Research, and to their assistants for their efforts in my behalf.

I am grateful for the valuable aid provided by the local archivists of England: Miss E. M. Dance, Curator of the Guildford Museum and Muniment Room; P. G. M. Dickinson, Archivist of the Huntingdonshire Record Office; Felix Hull, Archivist, Kent Archives Office; P. I. King, Archivist, Northamptonshire Record Office; M. G. Rathbone, Archivist, Wiltshire Record Office; and

F. B. Stitt, Archivist, Staffordshire Record Office. Not only did they suggest additional sources of information, but they extended every courtesy in arranging for the duplication of manuscripts.

I am indebted to Miss Mary Coate and Professor J. K. Gruenfelder for providing leads to the manuscripts of the duchy of Cornwall, and to Professor T. G. Barnes for information about the diarist John Hawarde. Mr. L. C. Hector of the Public Record Office advised me about the attribution and paleography of the diary of Sir Nathaniel Rich.

Mrs. Elizabeth Read Foster and Professor Robert C. Johnson read the draft text of this book, and I am grateful for their critical appraisals and valuable suggestions.

My particular thanks are due to Harvard University, the Canada Council, and Loyola College of Montreal for the generous grants that made my research possible.

Last, but by no means least, I am indebted to my wife, Mary, for her patience, forbearance, and aid, any one of which would justify the dedication of this book to her.

R.E.R

*Columbia, Missouri*
*October 1969*

# Contents

# Illustrations

# The Parliament of 1624

*Politics and Foreign Policy*

# Introduction of 1624

## Politics and Foreign Policy

King and Commons were agreed at the opening of the Parliament of 1624 that the memory of "parliament nullities" should be buried. But, however much the Lord Keeper commended the "lex oblivionis," no one could forget that James had "broken the necks of three parliaments." Almost every speech during the debates was a commentary, either express or tacit, upon the activities of former meetings. The entire session was so fraught with mutual suspicion that it belied Coke's sanguine "Felix Parliamentum."[1]

James had had little cause to be "in love with parliaments." From the beginning of his reign they had opposed to his exalted notions of prerogative and kingcraft the doctrine that "the voice of the people, in things of their knowledge, is . . . as the voice of God."[2] The crucial dispute all through the Jacobean era involved the interpretation of the critical phrase "things of their knowledge," which the crown always interpreted strictly and the Commons in the most illimitable fashion.

More than once James had lectured the Commons on the proper place of Parliament in the constitutional structure of England. Opening the session of 1621, he again reminded them that "their

1. Cobbett, Parliamentary History, I, 1364-1365, reply of the King to the address of the Commons, Mar. 23, 1624. On the desire of all parties to forget past disagreements, see ibid., I, 1373-1381; the King's speech, Feb. 21, 1624.
2. Sir Edward Cole, The Third Part of the Institutes of the Laws of England (4th ed., London, 1670), 2.
3. Tanner, Constitutional Documents, Innes I, 280, the form of apology and satisfaction, June 20, 1604.

# Introduction

King and Commons were agreed at the opening of the Parliament of 1624 that the memory of "parliament nullities" should be buried. But, however much the Lord Keeper commended the *"lex oblivionis,"* no one could forget that James had "broken the necks of three parliaments." [1] Almost every speech during the debates was a commentary, either express or tacit, upon the activities of former meetings. The entire session was so fraught with mutual suspicion that it belied Coke's ascription *"Foelix Parliamentum."* [2]

James had had little cause to be "in love with parliaments." From the beginning of his reign they had opposed to his exalted notions of prerogative and kingcraft the doctrine that "the voice of the people, in things of their knowledge, is . . . as the voice of God." [3] The crucial dispute all through the Jacobean era involved the interpretation of the critical phrase "things of their knowledge"; which the crown always interpreted strictly and the Commons in the most illimitable fashion.

More than once James had lectured the Commons on the proper place of Parliament in the constitutional structure of England. Opening the session of 1621, he again reminded them that "there

1. Cobbett, *Parliamentary History,* I, 1404–1405, reply of the King to the address of the Commons, Mar. 23, 1624. On the desire of all parties to forget past disagreements, see *ibid.,* I, 1373–1381, the King's speech, Feb. 21, 1624.
2. Sir Edward Coke, *The Third Part of the Institutes of the Laws of England . . .* (4th ed., London, 1670), 2.
3. Tanner, *Constitutional Documents James I,* 230, the form of apology and satisfaction, June 20, 1604.

is no State or Parliament without a Monarchy." They were summoned, he said,

> To advise the King in his urgent Affairs, to give him your best Advice in such Errands as he shall ask of you, or you shall think fit to ask his Advice in. The King makes Laws, and ye are to advise him to make such as may be best for the Good of the Common-Wealth: There is another Cause also, *viz.* The House of Commons is called, for that they best know the particular Estate of the Country; and if the King shall ask their Advice, can best tell what is amiss, as being most sensible of it, and also petition him to amend and redress. You are the Authors of Sustenance also to him, to supply his Necessities; and this is the proper Use of Parliaments. Here they are to offer what they think fit to supply his Wants; and he is in Lieu hereof to afford them Mercy and Justice; and this is that I boldly say, and am not asham'd to speak it, that all People owe a Kind of Tribute to their King, as a Thankfulness to him for his Love to them; and where there is this Sympathy between the King and his People, it breeds a happy Parliament.[4]

James's ideal parliament, therefore, was a deliberative body (deriving its authority and privileges from the crown) whose primary duty was to supply the extraordinary needs of the monarchy. It was to restrict its discussions precisely to matters wherein its advice had been requested. It was to inform the King of the good or ill effects of his governance and leave the legislative initiative for the redress of grievances to the crown. If abuses existed because of the improper use of administrative and judicial authority, Parliament should petition for redress but without questioning the right of the King to those prerogatives from which grievances resulted. Moreover, royal officials were only to be held accountable in cases of malfeasance or dereliction of duty.

Never during his entire reign did James summon a Parliament that fulfilled his expectations. Indeed, since the latter years of Elizabeth's reign the House of Commons had shown resistance to domination by the royal Privy Council. It had sought on several occasions to vindicate its privileges and to restrict the inordinate use of regal authority detrimental to the subject. Dominated numerically by country gentlemen and instructed in the techniques of parliamentary procedure by a group of able lawyers, the House of Commons sought to be more than "the grand inquest of

4. *OPH,* V, 314.

the realm." By developing its legislative machinery, particularly the committee system, it attempted to remedy grievances that members presented for discussion. More and more it reflected the economic and religious views of merchants and Puritans, whose numbers increased with every session.

While James demanded subsidies as of right, the lower House reiterated the contention that the King should live of his own. Pleas of the poverty of the nation and complaints of court extravagance frequently resounded on the floor of the Commons when extraordinary supply was demanded. If the general conception of governmental finance held by the Commons was medieval, there were, nevertheless, members who saw in the embarrassment of the crown an opportunity to divest it of some of its archaic prerogatives and to secure for the Parliament a larger voice in the affairs of the realm. As early as 1572 Mr. Yelverton said: "that all matters not Treason, or too much to the Derogation of the Imperial Crown, were tolerable there, where all things came to be considered of, and where there was such fulness of Power, as even the right of the Crown was to be determined, and by Warrant whereof we have so resolved. That to say the Parliament had no Power to determine of the Crown, was High-Treason. He remembred how that men are not there for themselves, but for their Countries. He shewed, it was fit for Princes to have their prerogatives; but yet the same to be straitned within reasonable limits. The Prince, he shewed, could not of her self make Laws, neither might she by the same reason break Laws." [5]

Few Elizabethans openly subscribed to these extreme views, but in the Parliaments that met during James's reign they were not exceptional. When the crown sought to augment revenue by impositions, licenses, patents of monopoly, increased fees for governmental services, and more strict enforcement of antiquated feudal rights, it was only natural that parliament men should protest vehemently against these devices, as they did in 1610 and 1614. Admittedly, some crown rights such as wardship, purveyance, and cart taking could not be challenged on the basis of legality; precedents for their use were too strong and too ancient. More recent

5. Sir Simonds D'Ewes, *A Compleat Journal of the Votes, Speeches and Debates, both of the House of Lords and House of Commons Throughout the whole Reign of Queen Elizabeth, of Glorious Memory* (London, 1693), 176.

innovations such as impositions rested on the ill-defined prerogative of the King to regulate trade in the interests of national
welfare and defense, and the essential participation of Parliament
in granting tonnage and poundage and in defining and limiting
trade provided a firmer basis than usual to challenge the royal right
to impose.

Ordinarily Parliament contented itself with impugning the
King's right to raise extraordinary revenues by prerogative. It
was not particularly interested in assuring the financial solvency
of the crown, although it was receptive to a quid pro quo for the
abandonment of the King's feudal rights. Intransigence on the
part of both the King and the Commons ruined the negotiations
for the great contract in 1610. Subsidies for relief of the King's indebtedness were never, thereafter, seriously considered in the
House. Even in relatively prosperous times during the early part
of his reign James found it impossible to balance revenues and
expenditures. After 1620 the decay of trade and the expenses occasioned by foreign affairs made his financial condition desperate,
yet supply was never granted unless it was earmarked for specific
purposes.

Perhaps no single issue, with the possible exception of parliamentary privilege, provided a better focal point for resistance to
royal authority than did the question of revenue. It transcended
the parochial interests of lawyers, merchants, landowners, and
religious radicals. The King's continued reliance on financial
expedients — aids for the knighting of his son and the marriage
of his daughter, benevolences, forced loans, impositions, monopolies, and projects — alienated men of substance and helped speed
the coalescence of factional opposition to his program. In time this
resistance acquired some of the characteristics of those groups
most vociferous in opposing the crown. Despite its seemingly
Puritan, middle-class character, opposition to royal policies
throughout the reign was amorphous, highly individualistic, and
frequently ephemeral.

Outside Parliament as well as within its precincts James continually irritated proponents of views contrary to his own. By re-
current interference with judicial process, by applauding the
clarity and precision of Roman law, by lecturing his judges on the
proper exercise of their office, and by apparently invading the area

of legislation with his numerous proclamations, the King managed to alienate a large segment of the legal profession. Similarly, his leniency toward papists, his allowance of Sunday sports, his objection to schemes for ecclesiastical reorganization, his veto of acts promoting the reformation of morals, his strict injunctions to preachers, and his contempt for sectaries antagonized the Puritans. By levying impositions, granting licenses, and authorizing surveyorships and monopolies, James lost the support of many influential merchants. Country gentlemen, in turn, objected to patents for the discovery of defective titles and concealed wardships and the recovery of old debts, as well as to feudal aids, privy seals, and increased fees for wardships and liveries.

Sir Robert Naunton believed that Elizabeth ruled successfully by maintaining a balance among court factions. James, too, was predisposed to attempt this method of government as a result of his early experiences in Scotland, and, despite his inclination to be ruled by favorites, there is evidence that he continued the policy in England. Such a scheme could prove effective at court, but not in the House of Commons.

The oaths of allegiance and supremacy, which were required of every member, restricted attendance in the House to avowed Protestants and to those Catholics known by such unflattering epithets as "church papists," "equivocators," and "hermaphrodite Christians." [6] On those Catholics willing to distinguish between the doctrines of their church and the temporal power of the pope, the House itself imposed another qualification by requiring supervised participation in the communion service according to the rites of the Church of England. These requirements left a significant portion of the English people without a voice in the legislative assembly of the realm, and the Protestant unanimity in the House of Commons that resulted vitiated the most progressive of Jacobean policies — limited toleration.

At the opening of his first Parliament the King distinguished between political and religious Catholicism, and, although he condemned the dethroning and assassination of princes as a seditious doctrine sanctioned by the papacy, he protested his unwill-

6. Isaac Bargrave, *A Sermon Preached before the Honorable Assembly of Knights, Citizens, and Burgesses of the Lower House of Parliament: February the Last 1623* (London, 1624), 22–23.

ingness to coerce his subjects in matters of conscience. Throughout his reign, however, Parliament sought more strigent enforcement of the statutes against recusants by frequent petitions to the throne. Although the Commons understood and appreciated the motives behind the King's clemency, they remained adamant in their denial of a distinction between the politics and the religion of Catholics. As Pym explained in 1621, the penal laws were designed not to compel papists' consciences but rather to nullify their subversive activities by depriving them of their wealth. The King was deceived if he thought that leniency toward papists would win their hearts and procure his own safety. "For having gotten favor they will expect a toleration, after toleration they will look for equality, after equality for superiority, and having superiority they will seek the subversion of that religion which is contrary to theirs." [7] Early in the reign of Charles I, Sir John Eliot noticed a similar parliamentary concern for the safety of Protestantism: it "is observable in that house, as their whole storie gives it, that wher ever that mention does breake of the fears or dangers in religion, & the increase of poperie, their affections are much stir'd, & what ever is obnoxious in the State, it then is reckoned as an incident to that." [8] Necessarily, then, measures designed to alleviate the restrictions on English Catholics were instituted by executive action and were contrary to the wishes of the majority in Parliament.

Religion was not, however, the issue that ruined James's great design for a union of Scotland and England. This project, so confidently proposed in 1604, foundered on the fears Englishmen felt for the security of their social and economic positions. Whereas James envisaged "a perfect Union of Laws and Persons, and such a Naturalizing, as may make one Body of both Kingdoms, under me your King," the Commons thought that the detriment to England would outweigh the benefits accruing from common

7. *Commons Debates 1621*, II, 463. Speaking of the reception of this speech by the House, John Chamberlain wrote: "I have heard extraordinarie commendation of a neat speach made by one Pimme a recever, wherin he laboured to shew that the Kings pietie, clemencie, justice, bountie, facilitie, peaceable disposition, and other his naturall vertues were by the adverse partie perverted and turned to a quite contrarie course; and though he were somewhat long in the explanation of these particulers, yet he had great attention and was excedingly commended both for matter and manner." Chamberlain, *Letters*, II, 412, letter of Dec. 1, 1621.

8. Eliot, *Negotium Posterorum*, I, 69.

citizenship.[9] Lawyers predicted the subversion of the English
common law. Peers were reluctant to share their places in the
upper House with Scottish lords. Merchants feared the competition of naturalized Scotchmen trading on equal terms. Country
gentlemen equated the influx of impoverished northerners with
the descent of a plague of locusts. Despite explanations and plead-
ings, all that the King was able to secure from Parliament was the
repeal of statutes hostile to Scotland, and the enactment of legislation assuring the punishment of malefactors involved in border
disputes. As far as was possible, the union was implemented by
proclamations and by judicial decisions, as in Calvin's case, but
it bore little resemblance to James's dream.

However idealistic James's attitude toward the unity of the
realm, religious toleration, and the maintenance of peace, there
were other areas where his policy was static if not retrograde. His
conception of the social structure of England was essentially
medieval, and his interpretation of the English constitution was
conservative. His theory of divine right accorded well with ideas
instilled into Englishmen by Elizabethan homilies against dis-
obedience and willful rebellion. In his relations with Parliament
his claims to authority scarcely exceeded those advanced by his
predecessor. Elizabeth, too, had complained about members who
had "shewed themselves audacious, arrogant and presumptuous,
calling her Majesties Grants and Prerogatives also in question, contrary to their Duty and place that they be called unto; And contrary to the express Admonition given in her Majesties name."[10]

James was astute enough to avoid some mistakes that Elizabeth
had made, such as the arrest of a member while Parliament was
sitting, but he lacked her political finesse. Whereas the Queen
subtly threatened recalcitrant members, James made categorical
statements of his right to imprison those who abused freedom of
speech in Parliament. Whereas Elizabeth never failed to compromise when it was conducive to her interests, James frequently
allowed matters to reach an impasse where no settlement was
possible on the basis of mutual concessions. Thus, in the Bucking-

9. *OPH*, V, 185, James's speech to the House of Commons, Mar. 31, 1607; James I,
*His Maiesties Speach in the Starre-Chamber, the XX of Iune, Anno 1616* (London,
1616), unpaginated (should be pp. 12–13).

10. D'Ewes, *Compleat Journal of Elizabethan Parliaments,* 151, Lord Keeper's
speech in the Parliament of 1571.

hamshire election case, in Shirley's case, and in the debate on impositions, James appeared to have surrendered abjectly. His clemency and benevolence were not regarded as proceeding from grace and, as he had hoped, gratefully received; rather, they were viewed as the reluctant admission of parliamentary rights.

The inconsistency of James's attitude toward Parliament obscured the fundamental outlines of his policy. The proclamations that preceded the sessions of 1604 and 1621 recommended the election of grave, discreet, and able representatives, yet in 1614 royal integrity was sullied by the King's involvement in the election schemes of the "undertakers." Time and time again James professed a desire to be in love with parliaments, yet he frequently neglected their advice, convened outspoken members before the Privy Council, and once, in a solemn conclave, razed the record of their proceedings from the journal of the House of Commons.

No such ambiguity characterized the program of the parliament men. By the beginning of James's reign the three privileges — freedom of election, freedom of speech, and freedom from arrest — were thought to have attained the stature of prescriptive rights. It remained merely to define them in a way most advantageous to the Commons. Within two years of the King's accession, the lower House had vindicated its right to determine its own membership and to liberate members of Parliament arrested at the suit of a private person. The question of freedom from arrest by command of the King remained open until after James's death. Resolution of this issue was intimately involved with the determination of the limits of free speech, and it was on this latter point that King and Parliament were diametrically opposed.

Constitutional conflicts between the crown and Parliament in the early years of James's reign were primarily concerned with domestic affairs. The lengthy intervals between sessions and the traditional responsibility of the monarchy for the formulation and direction of foreign policy combined to inhibit parliamentary discussion of diplomatic questions. The King's predilection for a Spanish alliance was well known, and overtures for a marriage between the Prince of Wales and the Infanta were tendered from Madrid as early as 1605 and renewed periodically, but Parliament had little opportunity to intervene in the struggles of court factions over foreign policy. Initially the prospect of a Spanish mar-

riage alarmed those Englishmen who feared subversion of the
Protestant establishment, but after 1613 and the marriage of
Princess Elizabeth to Frederick V, elector of the Palatinate, the
conclusion of a Spanish alliance also implied a threat to England's
commitment to continental Protestantism. When in 1619 Frederick's acceptance of the Bohemian crown rallied Catholic supporters to the standard of his imperial opponent, the continuance
of English neutrality was regarded by many contemporaries as a
betrayal of the Protestant Union. Jacobean foreign policy, which
sought the pacification of Europe through Anglo-Spanish cooperation, was considered unrealistic and inimical to English interests.
Spanish attempts to negotiate an acceptable settlement of the
German problem were regarded by critics as a cloak to cover aid
to the Catholic cause.

Thus, with the advent of the Thirty Years' War support for
James's religious and foreign policies dwindled, and after 1620
the situation was further complicated by English economic difficulties. Instead of aiding financial recovery, the crown seemed to
be deepening the depression by the burdens and restrictions it
placed upon trade. Henceforth, the royal government became the
target for overt criticism enhanced and embittered by the fusion
of economic, religious, and political grievances. Disaffection was
not restricted to a few malcontents; proclamations in December
1620 and July 1621 sought to restrain "vulgar persons" from
"licentious and lavish discourse and bold censure in matters of
state." This general prohibition made the House of Commons the
obvious forum for the expression of discontent, and, as spokesman
for the multitude, it necessarily clashed with the crown.

The winter convention of 1621, assembled for the congenial
purpose of providing relief for the necessitous forces in the Palatinate, brought matters to a climax. Few, except Edward Alford,
interpreted literally the edict prohibiting discussion of affairs of
state. The inadequacy of temporary expedients for the assistance
of the Protestant cause on the Continent, when considered in the
light of diplomatic overtures to Catholic powers, invited criticism
and comment. To the Puritan party it seemed that desperate dis-
eases required desperate remedies, and, by his own admission,
James had failed to negotiate an acceptable settlement in the
interval between sessions. Yet, when the Commons demanded that

the "voice of Bellona" replace "the voice of the turtle," it was apparent to all that their action was unprecedented. On December 3 the Commons completed action on a document that not only outlined the defects they thought to be inherent in the King's policy, but presumed to "chalk out" the remedies necessary for their correction. Originally designed as a petition and finally termed "a declaration," this remonstrance clearly expressed the trepidation felt by the parliament men who favored it. The insertion of the saving clause, "no ways intending to press upon your Majesty's undoubted and regal prerogative" scarcely mitigated the force of the assertions contained in it. Experienced parliamentarians like Sir Edward Coke, Sir Robert Phelips, Sir Dudley Digges, William Hakewill, Thomas Crew, William Mallory, and Recorder Wentworth were well aware that marriages and leagues, war and peace were *"arcana imperii"* and not to be meddled with. Some justification was obviously needed for advocating a war of diversion against Spain, a Protestant match, and a select commission for the enforcement of the penal statutes against recusants. Precedents were few and not always pertinent.

In defense of their proceedings it was pretended that vague allusions in the speeches of the three lords at the commencement of the sitting had invited the Commons to express their opinions. Coke alleged that the general writ of summons conferred upon the Commons the right to "argue, debate and dispute of the estate of the kingdom." [11] This raised the disagreement between the King and Commons from the level of technicality to that of principle. It was no longer merely a question of what was proper for this Parliament to discuss; it was a question of the competence of every Parliament. In the protestation voted on December 18, the Commons claimed not only absolute freedom of discussion but also "like freedom from all impeachment, imprisonment, and molestation (other than by censure of the House itself) for or concerning any speaking, reasoning, or declaring of any matter or matters touching the Parliament or Parliament-business." [12]

11. *Commons Debates 1621*, II, 496.
12. Tanner, *Constitutional Documents James I*, 288–289, the Commons' protestation, Dec. 18, 1621. For the full implications of this protestation, see its exposition by Sir John Eliot in *Negotium Posterorum*, 3–30.

James regarded such claims as inimical to the very existence of monarchy. "Where all things are contained," he said, "nothing is omitted. So as this Plenipotency of yours, invests you in all power upon Earth, lacking nothing but the Popes to have the Keys also both of Heaven and Purgatory." [13] His attitude toward the Commons was based upon three fundamental premises: (1) the limits of free discussion in Parliament were strictly determined by the explanation of the cause of summons recited at the opening of each session; (2) parliamentary privileges were derived from royal grace and permission indicating a toleration rather than a right and inheritance; (3) punishment of the misdemeanors of members of Parliament resided in the crown.

On no issue were King and Parliament more diametrically opposed than on the question of the Spanish match. At the very opening of the Parliament in January 1621 James informed the members of the marriage negotiations with Spain, protesting his intention not to dishonor religion thereby. With this assurance the Commons seemed satisfied until, on November 26, Thomas Crew revived the controversy. Reflecting on the machinations of Spain, he pointed out that, "The common adversary is he that maintains the greate armies." In advocating a war of diversion against Spain, he emphasized the incompatibility of the Catholic and Protestant religions and intimated a desire for a Protestant match.[14]

The suggestion that "our most noble Prince may be timely and happily married to one of our own religion" was incorporated into the declaration passed on December 3. Vehement debate raged over the inclusion of this proposal. Certainly the proposition was favorably entertained by the House, but doubts remained concerning its constitutional implications. When Sir Edward Sackville inveighed against such a direct incursion upon the prerogative and predicted a "general incendiary," he was hemmed at by the members. Courtiers, such as Weston, thought it was highly presumptuous to advise the King on the marriage of his son, but Wentworth, the recorder of Oxford, pleaded that parliament must be concerned with the religion of the mother of future

13. Rushworth, *Historical Collections,* I, 48, the King's answer, Dec. 11, 1621.
14. *Commons Debates 1621,* III, 456–457.

heirs to the throne. Phelips joined Wentworth in his concern for posterity and, like him, was worried lest the suggestion of a Protestant match prove offensive to the King. No parliamentarian, least of all Coke, questioned the King's absolute right to marry his son as he wished. It was mainly for this reason that, on Heath's motion, the "petition" was resolved to be a "declaration or remonstrance." The opinions of the Commons were offered "not as directions to his Majesty but as overtures of our own." [15]

In criticizing the actions of his Commons James reserved his severest censure for their interference with the treaty of marriage. Scanning their declaration from both negative and affirmative points of view, he found that it advised the nullification of any overtures to popish princes and constrained him to negotiate a Protestant match. He felt that the very consideration of the marriage by the House "was a direct breach of our commandment and declaration out of our own mouth, at the first sitting down of this Parliament." [16] And if mere discussion was presumptuous, the remonstrance passed on December 3 was tantamount to high treason.

The Prince joined his father in condemning the proceedings in Parliament. Even before the declaration was ready for presentation, Charles had complained that his marriage was being "prostituted" in the lower House, and it was he who forwarded to the King the "false copy" of the projected petition.[17] As early as November 23 he had written to Buckingham recommending the delegation of authority from the King "to set seditious fellows fast." [18] The rigor of this course, as he admitted, exceeded that advised by the King's most trusted councillors. By November 28, the day on which one subsidy was voted, Charles was somewhat mollified: "I

15. *Ibid.*, VI, 220; II, 487–499; see also Harl. MS. 1580, fols. 166–168v, Calvert to Buckingham, Dec. 7, 1621, printed in *Commons Debates 1621*, VII, 622–625.

16. Rushworth, *Historical Collections*, I, 49.

17. *Commons Debates 1621*, II, 518; see also *ibid.*, V, 238.

18. Sir Charles Petrie, ed., *The Letters Speeches and Proclamations of King Charles I* (London: Cassell and Co., 1935), 5–6. In the text this letter is dated Friday, November 3, 1621. In Gardiner, *History of England*, IV, 250,n., it is conjectured that the date of this letter is December 3, which was a Monday, but it is obvious from the tenor of the debates as reported in the "Barrington Diary" (*Commons Debates 1621*, III, 431–438) that the letter should be dated Friday, November 23, 1621. For Buckingham's sentiments, see *Cabala*, I, 233–237, Buckingham to Count Gondomar, undated.

would not wholly discontent them: therefore, my opinion is, that the King should grant them a session at this time, but withal I should have him command them not to speak any more of Spain, whether it be of that war, or my marriage. This, in my opinion, does neither suffer them to encroach upon the King's authority, nor give them just cause of discontentment." [19]

There can be no doubt that the subsequent debates infuriated Charles and impelled him to concur with the promoters of dissolution. He was, needless to say, encouraged in this resolve by the Spanish ambassador (Gondomar), Buckingham, and the popish party. Thus, when James announced to his Council his decision to dissolve Parliament, the advocates of continuance or compromise were overawed by the weight of opinion against them. The proclamation which ended the Parliament, published on January 6, 1622, both explained and defended the King's actions and contained a reaffirmation of his constitutional principles. Rather than permit this, or future parliaments, to invade the "inseparable rights and prerogatives annexed to our Imperial Crown," James preferred to achieve his aims solely by diplomacy.[20]

Failure to secure adequate financial support for the maintenance of English forces in the Palatinate induced James to rely unreservedly on the good offices tendered by the Spanish court. Necessarily the match was regarded at Westminster as the best guarantee of the good faith of the Spanish. From the time that Digby (Bristol) received his commission to Madrid in March 1622 until the debacle of September 1623, English foreign policy was directed primarily toward concluding the marriage treaty and secondarily toward the settlement in the Palatinate. Concessions to the Spanish abroad and to the Catholics at home, together with the decline of the Protestant cause in Germany, deepened the rift between court and country. Even after the loss of Heidelberg in October 1622, James was fearful of requesting subsidies from Parliament. Although the way for a new assembly was to be smoothed by the preparation of a general pardon, the balancing

19. Petrie, ed., *Letters . . . of Charles I*, 6–7, Prince Charles to Buckingham, undated. (It can be dated November 28, 1621, from internal evidence.) This letter is also printed in *Hardwicke State Papers*, I, 456–457.

20. Tanner, *Constitutional Documents James I*, 294, the proclamation for the dissolution, Jan. 6, 1622.

of trade, the reduction of fees of crown officers, and diverse other reforms, the King would not allow the issuance of the writs.[21] The possibility of negotiating a settlement with continental Catholic powers was more alluring to James than the prospect of conciliating an unruly House of Commons bent on vindicating its privileges and insisting upon military intervention in the Palatinate.

Believing that the Spanish marriage treaty was virtually concluded, the King permitted the journey of Prince Charles and the Duke of Buckingham to Madrid early in 1623. English illusions that only the formalities of the alliance remained to be completed were quickly dispelled, and by the middle of May the Prince and the Duke had been commissioned as plenipotentiaries to renegotiate the agreement.[22] Far from the center of diplomatic effort and committed a priori to the ratification of articles agreeable to his son and favorite, James appeared to have resigned the initiative in diplomacy. Seemingly unaware of the increasing antipathy between his envoys and the Spanish court, the King, throughout the summer, endeavored to convince the Spanish ambassadors of his good faith by prompt performance of the treaty stipulations. Having virtually abdicated his authority over foreign policy, James found it difficult to recover his ascendancy after Charles and Buckingham returned from Madrid, not with the Infanta but with a burning desire for revenge against Spain. The tumultuous reception that greeted them upon their arrival was intensified by public rejoicing over their failure to secure a Spanish bride. As the courtier whose fatal influence dominated both royal father and son, the Duke of Buckingham was regarded by contemporaries as the instigator of the reversal of policy toward Spain. When, in December, the King reluctantly consented to summon Parliament, the Duke's triumph appeared complete.

Did this decision signal the end of James's reign? If, at this point, Buckingham had said, "I am the King," would he have been merely assuming a title consistent with the potential of his power? The apparent reversal of English foreign policy in 1624 lends

21. Chamberlain, *Letters*, II, 457, 460, letters of Oct. 12, Oct. 26, 1622.
22. *Hardwicke State Papers*, I, 417–419, Prince Charles to King James, Apr. 29 1623; Buckingham to King James, Apr. 29, 1623; King James to Charles and Buckingham, May 11, 1623.

credence to the contention that Buckingham had seized "the reins of government" from James's "failing hands," but power must be judged by realities and not by appearances; policy, by effects and not by intentions.[23]

What was the extent of Buckingham's power? Was it founded on other than personal attachment to the King and the Prince? Was his identification with the will of the nation merely coincidental, or did he consciously aspire to lead the popular cause? Answers to all of these questions must, in part, be sought in the Parliament of 1624. By analyzing the composition of its membership, we can arrive at some estimate of the Duke's control over the Commons. By examining its judicial proceedings, we can see Parliament being used as a private instrument to crush political opposition. By using its debates and resolutions, we can assess the extent to which Buckingham compromised royal control over foreign policy, and, from the King's reaction, we can judge the extent of the Duke's predominance. We can, then, appraise the "happiness" of the Parliament and the probable continuance of this felicity.

23. Gardiner, *History of England,* V, 184, 185; D. H. Willson, *King James VI and I* (New York: Henry Holt and Co., 1956), 425–427, 440–447.

# I  Prelude to the Session

On the morning of October 6, 1623, Prince Charles, newly arrived from Spain, departed from a London endangered by the bonfires ignited to celebrate his return. He did not hear the solemn service that was sung in St. Paul's, nor did he note, as others did, the words of the new anthem: "when Israell came out of Egipt and the house of Jacob from among the barbarous people." [1] Yet few scriptural texts could have epitomized English opinion with greater accuracy. The fear that the heir to the throne might be forcibly detained in Spain was dispelled, and the failure of the Infanta to accompany the Prince portended the abandonment of the plan for a Spanish match. [2]

Although unrestrained enthusiasm characterized his reception in London, the Prince, as he rode toward Royston, must have had some doubts about the attitude of his father; he had little to report except the monumental failure of his knight errantry. The high hopes with which he and Buckingham had undertaken the journey to Spain in the preceding spring were dashed, and the concessions wrung from the royal negotiator by the Spaniards far outweighed the advantages gained by the English. Not only was the Infanta's journey to be delayed until spring, but the restitu-

1. Chamberlain, *Letters*, II, 516, letter of Oct. 11, 1623. The Authorized (King James) Version (Ps. 114:1) differs slightly from Chamberlain's report: "When Israel went out of Egypt, the house of Jacob from a people of strange language."
2. *Cal. S. P. Venetian*, XVIII, 135, Valaresso to the Doge and Senate, Oct. 10/20, 1623. "Certainly the rejoicing on every hand has been boundless and possibly the greater because they imagine the negotiations are broken off from seeing him come without the Infanta."

tion of the Palatinate had not been accomplished. For the sake of the Spanish princess and her dowry of 600,000 pounds, a virtual toleration was to be granted to King James's Catholic subjects, to be confirmed by act of Parliament. The tutelage of future heirs to the British throne in a Catholic household, conceded to the Infanta by the terms of the marriage agreement, threatened Protestant England with a revival of popish religion. James's great plan to pacify central Europe through the joint diplomatic and military efforts of the Spanish and English crowns had, moreover, received an equivocal response at Madrid.[3]

These terms James had accepted, albeit reluctantly, but it was extremely doubtful whether he would accept with equal grace any action that jeopardized the successful completion of negotiations. Such action had, however, been secretly undertaken by the Prince when, on September 3, he had instructed Bristol, "not to deliver my proxie to the King of Spaine until I may have sufitient securitie both from him and the Infanta that after I am bethrothed, a monasterie may not rob me of my wyfe." [4] The intended suppression of this dispatch until papal approval arrived in Madrid was tantamount to a cancellation of the marriage treaty on the eve of its fulfillment; only ten days were allowed, after the official promulgation of the pope's consent, for the performance of the marriage ceremony. Charles, knowing that at least three weeks were necessary for communication between the English and the Spanish courts, may thus have been guilty of a petty act of revenge, or it may have been that he did not expect the arrival of the pope's sanction soon enough to preclude the sending of new instructions after his return to England. Adverse winds at Santander delayed his voyage for eight days and the crossing itself lasted from September 18 until October 5.[5] The lapse of so much

3. On the various versions of the marriage treaty between Charles and the Infanta Maria, see *Spanish Marriage Treaty*, 327–344.
4. HMC, *Eighth Report*, Appendix, pt. I (3 vols., London, 1907–1909), 215–216, Digby MSS, Prince of Wales to the Earl of Bristol, undated. This is quoted in full in Gardiner, *History of England*, V, 118, where the date tentatively assigned is Sept. 3, 1623. Variant versions of the same letter are printed in Halliwell, *Kings' Letters*, II, 229; *Cal. S. P. Venetian*, XVIII, 166–167.
5. John Nichols, *The Progresses, Processions, and Magnificent Festivities of King James the First* (3 vols. in 4, London, 1828), IV, 923–925. In assembling this timetable Nichols has used primarily the narratives of Sir John Finett, *Finetti Philoxenus*, and the diary of Phineas Pette, the shipwright, Harl. MS. 6279.

time partially accounted for the urgency with which Charles journeyed toward Royston.

The emotional reunion of the King with his son and the favorite preceded a lengthy appraisal of the accomplishments of the embassy to Spain. Retiring to a room apart, James conferred with the Prince and the Duke until late in the evening. "They that attended at the Door sometime heard a still Voice, and then a loud; sometime they Laught, and sometime they Chafed, and noted such variety, as they could not guess what the close might prove." [6] Buckingham, himself, later reported that a relation was made to the King of all that had passed at Madrid. "His Majesty was glad of this exact Carriage of his Son in so great a Negotiation, and told his Higness, That he had acted well the Part of a Son, and now the Part of a Father must come upon the Stage; which was, to provide with all Circumspection, that his only Son should not be married with a Portion of Tears to his only Daughter." [7]

What actually passed in these conversations was never fully revealed, but there can be no doubt that the slights, real or imagined, that Charles and Buckingham had endured in Spain were given the utmost prominence. In succeeding days a whispering campaign emphasizing the ill-treatment accorded the Prince at Madrid was begun at the court.[8] Charles, himself, considered it sheer folly that, after the Spanish "had used him so ill, they would suffer him to depart." [9]

Playing on his father's fears for his safety, Charles apparently magnified the threat of captivity in order to justify not only the concessions openly granted to the Spanish but also the necessity of his secret instructions to Bristol to withhold the proxy. This, at

6. Hacket, *Scrinia Reserata,* I, 165. Hacket says that James's decision to insist upon the restitution of the Palatinate was apparent immediately after the conference was concluded.

7. *OPH,* VI, 51, the Lord Keeper's report of the Duke of Buckingham's negotiations in Spain.

8. HMC, *Mar and Kellie,* 181–183, Thomas, earl of Kellie, to John, earl of Mar, Oct. 18, Oct. 31, Nov. 4, and Nov. 11, 1623; see also Birch, *Court and Times of James the First,* II, 435, Stuteville to Mead, Nov. 21, 1623.

9. *Cabala,* I, 289, Kensington to Buckingham, n.d. According to Kensington this "was one of the first speeches he uttered after he was entred into the ship." Kensington told the French Queen Mother that he had heard the speech with his own ears. He averred that the Prince was ill used, not in his entertainment, "but in their frivolous delayes, and in the unreasonable conditions, which they propounded, and pressed (upon the advantage they had of his Princely Person)."

least, was the impression received by the Earl of Kellie: "neither can I imagine why the Prince should have done this but out of some fear or doubt that they dealt not directly with him, but awaiting their advantage to get him once tied fast that he could take no other course and then they might make him stay their leisure and in their will to make it a match or no match." [10]

It is possible that Charles decided to stay his proxy because he was convinced that Spanish honor and interests were so far committed in the match treaty as to preclude its abandonment. He probably believed that, by departing from Spain, he would regain control of the negotiations. Rather than forego the advantages that would devolve on English Catholics, rather than risk the loss of English neutrality or aid in quelling the Dutch rebellion, rather than have his own and his sister's honor impugned, the King of Spain would be willing, in Charles's view, to assure the restitution of the Palatinate and the electorate. Moreover, if these motives were insufficient to procure Spanish compliance, the threat of war could be adduced to reinforce English demands.

War was, above all, the policy that most appealed to Buckingham. During the summer of 1623 he had grown increasingly disenchanted both with the Spanish and with the prospects for a successful treaty. His behavior in Spain had antagonized the court of Philip IV, and he had quarreled violently with the Conde de Olivares, Philip's favorite. The Infanta disliked Buckingham intensely, and her influence as the future Queen of England threatened his continuance in favor. Moreover, personal observation of the country convinced Buckingham of Spain's weakness and its inability to maintain a protracted military campaign.[11] His presence increased the friction between the Prince and the Spanish, which had become apparent as early as May 1623. When he arrived in England, Buckingham openly expressed his indignation concerning the insults that Charles had endured abroad. "It makes

10. HMC, *Mar and Kellie*, 181, Thomas, earl of Kellie, to John, earl of Mar, Oct. 18, 1623.
11. *Cal. S. P. Venetian*, XVIII, 191, Valaresso to the Doge and Senate, Jan. 2/12, 1624; see also *ibid.*, 63, Valaresso to the Doge and Senate, July 4/14, 1623; *ibid.*, 113–118, Corner to the Doge and Senate, Sept. 10/20, 1623; *Cabala*, I, 20–22, Bristol to the Bishop of Lincoln, Aug. 20, 1623 (this letter is erroneously cited in Gardiner, *History of England*, V, 114, as being from Bristol to the King); *Spanish Marriage Treaty*, 232, 251–252, 258.

him," the Earl of Kellie remarked, "more precipitate in his counsels than otherwise he would be." [12]

The dispatches to Spain that issued out of the Royston conference reflected little of Buckingham's bellicose attitude. None of the Council, with the possible exception of Carlisle and Conway, knew the contents of these letters.[13] The King, himself, wrote to Bristol alleging that both he and the Prince were content with the security which the ambassador had sent regarding the Infanta's retirement into a convent. At the same time he announced his wish that the marriage "should be upon one of the Days in Christmas, New Stile." [14] Bristol was also required to procure from Philip "a punctual Answer what Course he will take for the Restitution of the Palatinate and Electorate to our Son-in-Law; and, in case that either the Emperor or the Duke of Bavaria will oppose any Part of the expected Restitution, what Course the King will take to give us Assurance for our Content in that Point whereof we require your present Answer; and that you so press Expedition herein, that we may together receive the full Joy of both at Christmas." [15] James's conversations with the Prince and Duke had obviously convinced him that the time was propitious for joining what had been two separate treaties. The implication of the King's letter was clear: the restitution of the Palatinate was to be made a condition of the marriage. The same impression was conveyed in Charles's letter to Bristol, and, even more

12. *Cal. S. P. Venetian*, XVIII, 16–18, 20–22, Corner to the Doge and Senate, May 10/20, May 14/24, 1623; HMC, *Mar and Kellie*, 184, Thomas, earl of Kellie, to John, earl of Mar, Nov. 29, 1623; see also *Cal. S. P. Venetian*, XVIII, 146, Valaresso to the Doge and Senate, Oct. 31/Nov. 10, 1623.

13. HMC, *Mar and Kellie*, 181, Thomas, earl of Kellie to John, earl of Mar, Oct. 18, 1623. Two letters written by Secretary Conway indicate that even if he was familiar with the dispatch to Bristol, he did not consider it a serious bar to the accomplishment of the marriage. *Cal. S. P. Dom. 1623–1625*, 91, Secretary Conway to Secretary Calvert, Oct. 9, 1623; Secretary Conway to Sir Dudley Carleton, Oct. 10, 1623.

14. *OPH*, VI, 51–53, King James to the Earl of Bristol, Oct. 8, 1623; also printed in *Cabala*, II, 136. The designation of the new style of dating in this letter may indicate that James intended to make diplomatic use of the different styles of dating used in England and Spain. The Prince's proxy expired on Christmas day, but, if this date were interpreted according to the older style, it would have been possible to celebrate the marriage "upon one of the Days in Christmas, New Stile." According to this method of reckoning the proxy would not expire until January 4, 1624, new style. However, the Spanish interpreted the expiration date as Dec. 25, 1623, new style, and regarded James's wish as tantamount to an annulment of the proxy.

15. *OPH*, VI, 51–53, King James to the Earl of Bristol, Oct. 8, 1623.

strongly, in his letter to Aston: "give them all the assurance that you can think of, that I do really intend to desire this match; and the chief end of this is that we may be as well hearty friends as near allies; and, to deal freely with you, so that we may have satisfaction concerning the Palatinate, I will be content to forget all ill-usage and be hearty friends; but, if not, I can never match where I have had so dry entertainment, although I shall be infinitely sorry for the loss of the Infanta." [16]

The proposal most likely to achieve the pacification of the Palatinate question seemed to both Charles and his father to be the old scheme for a marriage between the Elector's eldest son, Prince Frederick Henry, and the Emperor's daughter. Indeed, when Charles had discussed the problem with Olivares in the preceding August, such a solution had been proposed. Its details had never been fully worked out, however, nor had the sanctions necessary for the expected restitution of the Palatinate been sufficiently guaranteed. The Prince demanded active Spanish intervention, and, according to Buckingham, asked Olivares "Whether, in case, the Emperor proved refractory, the King, his Master, would assist him [James I] with Arms, to reduce him [the Emperor] to reasonable Terms? The Conde answered negatively; because they had a Maxim of State, That the King of Spain must never fight against the Emperor." [17] Olivares had, however, invited the Prince to set down his own conditions for the restitution of the Palatinate if he would agree to the delay of the Infanta's journey to England until the spring of 1624.[18] To this Charles had

16. Gardiner, *History of England*, V, 137, quoting the letter of Prince Charles to Sir Walter Aston, Oct. 8, 1623, from *State Papers Spain*. A letter from Prince Charles to the Earl of Bristol, Oct. 8, 1623, is printed in HMC, *Eighth Report*, Appendix I, 215, MSS of G. W. Digby, Esq.

17. *OPH*, VI, 42, the Lord Keeper's report of the Duke of Buckingham's negotiations in Spain; see also Rusdorff, *Mémoires*, I, 139, John Rusdorff to the Elector Palatine, Oct. 21/Nov. 1, 1623 [*sic*]. "Buckingham aiant référé à S. M. qu'un jour, quand il parloit en Espagne de la restitution du Palatinat, et disoit que le Roi d'Espagne s'étoit obligé et avoit stipulé de joindre ses forces avec celles d'Angleterre pour le recouvrement du dit Palatinat, en cas que l'Empereur fît difficulté de le restituer. Le Comte D'Olivares avoit ri et dit tout haut, que son Maitre ne s'étoit jamais engagé avec telle promesse; il étoit bien vrai, que Sa Majesté Catholique promis de vouloir contribuer, tous les bons offices et tout ce qui lui étoit possible envers l'Empereur, en faveur de la dite restitution, mais rien d'advantage. Sur cela Sa Majesté de la grande Bretagne à écrit au Roi d'Espagne et à ses Ambassadeurs pour savoir l'intention du Roi d'Espagne."

18. *OPH*, VI, 39, Lord Keeper's report of the Duke of Buckingham's negotiations in Spain; see also *ibid.*, 53, James to the Earl of Bristol, Oct. 8, 1623.

assented and now, in October, it seemed expedient to test the sincerity of Spanish intentions and to procure a binding engagement definitely stating the extent and effectiveness of their assistance.

At the same time that he was soliciting the support of Philip IV, James was trying to induce his son-in-law to submit to a compromise by suggesting marriage between the Elector's son and the Emperor's daughter with the provision that the young Prince be brought up at the Viennese court under Protestant tutelage. James was optimistic: "The better to ensure success we have decided to induce the King of Spain to interest himself in this affair with us before proposing it to the emperor, and we feel sure he will lend a hand to bring it to a happy conclusion and also to ensure the observation of the conditions." [19]

James's overtures were secret. Few, if any, of the councillors most familiar with the Spanish negotiations were aware of the new proposals submitted to Madrid, and throughout October the King, Prince, and Duke acted in concert, excluding all others. From the moment of their return, the Prince and Buckingham maintained a constant attendance upon the King, but for some time the full import of their vigilance was not apparent. Some observers felt that James had taken negotiations into his own hands and was preventing separate access to his son and his favorite in order to give the impression of undivided counsels. Some doubts were also raised about Buckingham's continuance in favor, and it was assumed that he remained at court to prevent any machinations against him.[20]

As time passed the anti-Spanish opinions of the Duke and Prince became familiar to the court. It then became apparent that the purpose of their surveillance of the King was to preclude opposition to their policies and to strengthen the King in his resolve to secure the restoration of the Palatinate. Suffering from gout, James was in no condition to resist importunities for a diplomatic showdown. Every proposal made to the King was also known to Charles and Buckingham; every ambassador was re-

19. *Cal. S. P. Venetian*, XVIII, 158–159, King James to Frederick, the elector Palatine, Oct. 8, 1623.

20. HMC, *Mar and Kellie* 182, Thomas earl of Kellie, to John, earl of Mar, Oct. 18, Oct. 31, 1623; *Cal. S. P. Venetian*, XVIII, 137, 140–141, 142, 145, Valaresso to the Doge and Senate, Oct. 10/20, Oct. 17/27, Oct. 24/Nov. 3, Oct. 31/Nov. 10, 1623.

ceived in their presence. James's tendencies to vacillate and temporize were notorious, but the uncompromising attitude of "Baby Charles and Steenie" thwarted his inclinations and placed him under great mental stress. By November 4, 1623, the Earl of Kellie wrote: "His Majesty has been very ill, both of his gout and I think, as many others do, of his mind likewise. I can write no more what will be the conclusion of the match . . . You can not imagine how the world is possessed of the vexation his Majesty has in his mind. It may come that young folks shall have their world. I know not if that will be fit for your Lordship and me." [21]

Until a reply was received from Spain, no final decision was necessary regarding the match, and, until the end of October, the Spanish marriage still seemed possible. Charles continued to write to the Infanta, and even enemies of the match thought that it would proceed inevitably to a successful conclusion.[22] The failure of the King to communicate the state of negotiations to even his selected advisors mystified the Venetian ambassador, Valaresso, and, he thought, cast a slur upon the counselors.[23] At the same time rumors of an impending Parliament began to circulate.[24] The enthusiasm with which the Prince and Buckingham had been received on their return had not diminished; indeed, their popularity had increased, and Buckingham in particular was lionized as the hero of the hour. Even old courtiers who had no great love for the Villiers clan viewed his conduct in Spain with approval.[25]

In anticipation of the receipt of dispatches it was decided to communicate to a select number of councillors the details of the transactions in Spain. Charles and Buckingham journeyed to London, where they arrived on October 30; the King remained at Royston with only the Earl of Southampton in attendance. At

---

21. HMC, *Mar and Kellie*, 183, Thomas, earl of Kellie, to John, earl of Mar, Nov. 4, 1623.

22. Rusdorff, *Mémoires*, I, 140, Rusdorff to the Elector Palatine, Oct. 21/Nov. 1, 1623 [*sic*]; *Spanish Marriage Treaty*, 257.

23. *Cal. S. P. Venetian*, XVIII, 143, Valaresso to the Doge and Senate, Oct. 24/Nov. 3, 1623.

24. Chamberlain, *Letters*, II, 518–519, letter of Oct. 25, 1623; *Cal. S. P. Venetian*, XVIII, 143, Valaresso to the Doge and Senate, Oct. 24/Nov. 3, 1623.

25. HMC, *Mar and Kellie*, 182, Thomas, earl of Kellie, to John, earl of Mar, Oct. 18, 1623. ". . . and though I have had little cause to like well of Buckingham's love and affection to myself, yet I can not but wish him well and love him the better for his behavior and carriage at this time. It has been both for his master's honour and for the honour of the country."

St. James on the following day a junta of councillors was assembled "where the Lord of Buckingam made relation in what state they found the busines of the match at their comming into Spaine and in what state they left yt." [26] An oath of secrecy upon the Bible was imposed upon those in attendance, but as the Venetian ambassador remarked, "One may conjecture from the opinions he [Buckingham] has expressed elsewhere that he exposed the frauds practiced by the Spaniards and the hopeless state of the negotiations." [27] Significantly, no resolution was taken at this meeting because the King had not made his position clear.

The day after the council meeting Buckingham and Conway went to join James and accompany him from Royston to Theobalds where they arrived on November 7.[28] That day English couriers returned from Spain, and the following day the Prince unexpectedly left London for Theobalds, taking with him the additional dispatches that he had received from the Spanish ambassadors.[29] The information sent by Bristol from Madrid gave little cause for satisfaction. To Charles and Buckingham it must have seemed that the ambassador was deliberately evading his responsibilities. Bristol protested vehemently against deferring the desponsories until Christmas, alleging that such a procedure was "a direct and effectual revoking of them," and, as for the Palatinate, he said: "I know your Majesty hath long been of opinion

26. Chamberlain, *Letters*, II, 522, letter of Nov. 8, 1623. The date for the assembling of the Council is given as November 1 in Gardiner, *History of England*, V, 143. The date as given by the Venetian ambassador in his letter to the Doge and Senate is November 5, 1623, *Cal. S. P. Venetian*, XVIII, 149, Nov. 7/17, 1623. The October 31 date given by Chamberlain is supported by a letter from Sir George Goring to Sir Dudley Carleton, *Cal. S. P. Dom. 1623–1625*, 105, Oct. 31, 1623. The names of the twelve councillors are given in Chamberlain, *Letters*, II, 527–528, letter of Nov. 21, 1623. "I thincke I forgot to send you their names, as the Lord Keper [John Williams, bishop of Lincoln], Lord Treasurer [Lionel Cranfield, earl of Middlesex], Lord Chamberlain [William Herbert, earl of Pembroke], Lord Marshall [Thomas Howard, earl of Arundel and Surrey], the two Dukes [Ludovic Stuart, duke of Lennox and Richmond, and George Villiers, duke of Buckingham], Marques Hamilton, Lord of Carlile, Lord Belfast, Chauncellor of the Exchecquer [Sir Richard Weston], and both the Secretaries [Sir Edward Conway and Sir George Calvert], which make a full jurie."
27. *Cal. S. P. Venetian*, XVIII, 149, Valaresso to the Doge and Senate, Nov. 7/17, 1623.
28. Chamberlain, *Letters*, II, 522, letter of Nov. 8, 1623.
29. *Cal. S. P. Venetian*, XVIII, 150, 152–153, Valaresso to the Doge and Senate, Nov. 7/17, Nov. 14/24, 1623.

that the greatest assurance you could get, that the King of Spain would effectually labour the entire restitution of the Prince Palatine was, that he really proceeded to the effecting of the match; and my instructions under your Majesty's hand were, to insist upon the restoring of the Prince Palatine, but not so as to annex it to the treaty of the match, as that thereby the match should be hazarded; for that your Majesty seemed confident, they here would never grow to a perfect conclusion of the match, without a settled resolution to give your Majesty satisfaction in the business of the Palatinate." [30]

Inasmuch as he had no cause to doubt the sincerity of Spanish intentions, Bristol asked for specific orders warranting the delivery of the Prince's proxy when it should be demanded. In the meantime he promised to continue his "earnest and faithful endeavours to engage this King as far as shall be possible, both for the doing of all good offices for the Prince Palatine's entire restitution, as likewise for this King's declaration of assistance, in case the Emperor or Duke of Bavaria shall oppose the said restitution." [31] This letter, when considered in conjunction with the Elector's polite refusal to engage in any marriage negotiations with the Emperor until after the full and complete restoration of the Palatinate, brought matters to a crisis.[32] Immediately pressure was brought on James to take a stand. "His Majesty is pressed with some things which in his judgment he can not yet condescend to do; but he has chosen a number of the Council to whom he will participate his mind in these things. But in the meantime he is in much trouble in his mind. I much doubt that some would have him to embrace things much contrary to his disposition and very unfit for the nature of this time, and he so much without money as he is." [33]

Between November 11 and November 13 at least two Council meetings were held at which both the King and the Prince were

30. *Hardwicke State Papers*, I, 484–485, Earl of Bristol to King James, Oct. 24, 1623; also printed in *Cabala*, II, 137–141, where it is erroneously dated October 29, 1623.
31. *Hardwicke State Papers*, I, 488, Bristol to King James, Oct. 24, 1623.
32. *Cal. S. P. Venetian*, XVIII, 159–160, Frederick, elector Palatine, to King James, Oct. 20/30, 1623.
33. HMC, *Mar and Kellie*, 183, Thomas, earl of Kellie, to John, earl of Mar, Nov. 11, 1623.

present. The policy of joining the two treaties was confirmed
when the junta resolved unanimously not to have a match without the Palatinate.[34] This decision may have been precipitated
by recent reports regarding the partition of the Lower Palatinate.
Frederick's electoral dignity had already been transferred to the
Duke of Bavaria, but now his rich acres around the Bergstrasse
were surrendered to the Catholic archbishop of Mainz with the
connivance of the Spanish occupation forces. Grave doubts were
thus raised in England regarding Philip IV's good faith in promoting a complete restoration of the Elector's titles and territories.

The letters dispatched to Bristol emphasized the necessity of
reaching some definite agreement on the situation in Germany.
On November 13 James instructed his ambassador to procure a
written instrument from Philip outlining the aid which he was
willing to give toward the restoration of the Palatinate. At the
same time a new proxy, valid until March, was sent in order to
allow sufficient time to obtain entire satisfaction.[35] This letter
was accompanied by one from Conway ordering Bristol to return
to England if he did not receive the assurances demanded within
twenty days.[36] Two notes from the Prince on November 14 and
November 15 deprived Bristol of any discretionary power regarding the delivery of the procuration. On the fifteenth Charles
wrote: "But whatsoever answer ye gett ye must not deliver the
proxie till ye make my father & me juge of it. As for the whole
business ye must deal freelie with them, in as sivill termes as ye
will, that except that king will promise sum way under hand to
helpe my father with his armes (in case mediation fail) to restore
my brother-in-law to his honnors and inheritances, ther can
neither be marriag nor frendshippe; & as the breeding up my
nephew in the Emperor's court avoide it as handsomelie as ye can,
but I asseure you it shall never be. And if they will doe all that

34. *Cal. S. P. Venetian*, XVIII, 152–155, Valaresso to the Doge and Senate, Nov.
14/24, 1623.
35. Edward Hyde, earl of Clarendon, *State Papers Collected by Edward, Earl of
Clarendon* (3 vols., Oxford, 1767), I, 24–27, King James to the Earl of Bristol
Nov. 13, 1623.
36. HMC, *Eighth Report*, Appendix, pt. I, 216, Digby MSS, Sir Edward Conway
to the Earl of Bristol, Nov. 13, 1623.

my father desyres they may not onlie be sure of an allyance, but of a hartie sincere frendshipe. Make no replyes, suffer no delais."[37]

In the Council meetings that preceded the sending of these dispatches, the summoning of a Parliament was seriously proposed for the first time, and, although it was rejected for the moment, it was thought advisable to use the possibility of a session as a diplomatic lever to hasten a favorable decision in Spain.[38] Hopes for an early summons of Parliament were increasing in England. The Prince and Buckingham were becoming more outspoken in their animosity toward Spain and more dissatisfied with Bristol's conduct of affairs.

Gradually the King was being isolated; his inclination to negotiate was considered a sign of weakness. Buckingham told him, "he could not bear to see his reputation taken away by the Spaniards," and it was not to James alone that the Duke expressed such sentiments.[39] The Spanish ambassadors considered him an active opponent of the match and protested against his presence at their audiences. Moreover, Buckingham courted the Walloons who accompanied Don Diego Mexia, ambassador of the Archduchess Isabella. He expressed his amazement that such a brave people could endure Spanish tyranny and assured them that, if they would help themselves, they should not lack for aid.[40]

Meanwhile the Spanish ambassadors in England, Inojosa and Coloma, were relying on the project of a marriage between the Elector's son and the Emperor's daughter to meliorate the harshness of James's demands. In a stormy audience on November 15, 1623, at which the Prince and Buckingham were present, James was forced to admit that the restitution of the Palatinate had

37. *Ibid.*, 216, Digby MSS, the Prince of Wales to the Earl of Bristol, Nov. 14, 15, 1623; Gardiner, *History of England,* V, 145–147. I have accepted Gardiner's analysis of these four dispatches in preference to that which the Venetian ambassador expressed in his letters of Nov. 21/Dec. 1, Dec. 5/15, 1623 (*Cal. S. P. Venetian,* XVIII, 156–158, 167–170), although some points in Valaresso's account further illuminate the proceedings in the Council.

38. *Cal. S. P. Venetian,* XVIII, 168, Valaresso to the Doge and Senate, Dec. 5/15, 1623; see also *Cabala,* I, 222–224, for an anonymous complaint to the King against the Duke of Buckingham (tentatively dated late November 1623), which details the probable dire effects of summoning Parliament.

39. *Cal. S. P. Venetian,* XVIII, 169, Valaresso to the Doge and Senate, Dec. 5/15, 1623.

40. *Ibid.*, 156–158, 169, Valaresso to the Doge and Senate, Nov. 21/Dec. 1, Dec. 5/15, 1623; Chamberlain, *Letters,* II, 529–530, letter of Dec. 6, 1623.

never been considered a condition of the Spanish match and that it was unreasonable to expect Philip IV to take up arms against the Emperor.[41]

Again, on November 20, James wrote to Frederick offering a restitution of the Palatinate to the Elector's son providing a due submission, under convenient limitations, should first be made to the Emperor. He also suggested that the principal difficulty involved in the projected marriage of the Elector's eldest son could be evaded if his education were completed at the English court under the supervision of the Infanta.[42] As the Venetian ambassador astutely noted, James was putting forth what were essentially Spanish proposals as his own ideas. He was still maneuvering for a negotiated settlement with Philip's support, at a time when Charles had abandoned hopes of diplomatic success.[43] James was encouraged in his efforts by the English Catholics and by a faction in his Privy Council, which caused the Prince on one occasion to threaten "to remember those who have participated in the evil counsels of his father." [44]

The intransigence of the Prince and Buckingham had been increased by the arrival of a letter from the Earl of Bristol dated November 1, 1623, which announced that the dispensation was expected hourly in Madrid and that he and Aston had decided "to raise no scruple in the delivery of the said powers, but do intend when they shall be required to pass on to the nominating of a prefixed day for the Deposorio's." [45]

This news threw the English court into turmoil; it was feared that the marriage might be solemnized before the new instructions deferring the delivery of the proxy could forestall the ambassadors. The immediate reaction of the select council in England was to recommend the recall of both Sir Walter Aston and the Earl of Bristol.[46] For a time, however, cooler heads prevailed, and no

41. *Cal. S. P. Venetian*, XVIII, 156, Valaresso to the Doge and Senate, Nov. 21/Dec. 1, 1623; Gardiner, *History of England*, V, 147–148.

42. *Cabala*, II, 143–144, King James to the Elector Palatine, Nov. 20, 1623.

43. *Cal. S. P. Venetian*, XVIII, 156–158, Valaresso to the Doge and Senate, Nov. 21/Dec. 1, 1623; *ibid.*, 164, Valaresso to the Doge and Senate, Nov. 28/Dec. 8, 1623.

44. *Ibid.*, 164, Valaresso to the Doge and Senate, Nov. 28/Dec. 8, 1623.

45. *Cabala*, II, 141–143, the Earl of Bristol to King James, Nov. 1, 1623; see also Harl. MS. 1580, fols. 3–4, Sir Walter Aston to the Duke of Buckingham, Nov. 1, 1623, printed in *Cabala*, I, 30–33, undated.

46. *Ibid.*, I, 34–36, the Duke of Buckingham to Sir Walter Aston, undated. "Which

action was taken. As far as the anti-Spanish faction was concerned, Bristol's letter had a salutary effect. "His Majesty," Conway informed Buckingham, "has laid his errors home, and taken away all his excuses, but says it would be difficult, as recommended by the committee, to recal him and Sir Walter Aston." [47] "The change in the king," the Venetian ambassador reported, "arouses the hope of some good from this quarter. He now communicates to the select council what he previously kept shut up in his own breast." [48] Moreover there appeared to be hope for settlement of the Palatinate question from another quarter when Francesco della Rota arrived with proposals from the Duke of Bavaria.[49]

At the same time the select council, though not willing to flout the King's wishes, was beginning to show signs of following the lead of the Prince and the favorite. They pressed unremittingly for the assembly of a Parliament and for some definite action against Spain. In Council Charles said "that he was determined not to suffer any detriment upon three points, his honour, the kingdom and his own religion." Before the end of November the Council was considering sending Sir Robert Anstruther to the King of Denmark, and it was suspected that, under the guise of carrying the King's interest payment to the Danish court, Anstruther would propose some form of collective action in Germany.[50] On Novem-

proceeding of yours with the Earl of Bristol was so understood by the Lords of the Committee, as they took resolution once, to advise his Majestie to revoke both the Lord of Bristol, and you." See also Chamberlain, *Letters*, II, 527, letter of Nov. 21, 1623.

47. *Cal. S. P. Dom. 1623–1625*, 127, Sir Edward Conway to the Duke of Buckingham, Dec. 11, 1623.

48. *Cal. S. P. Venetian*, XVIII, 164, Valaresso to the Doge and Senate, Nov. 28/Dec. 8, 1623.

49. For Francesco della Rota's proposals, see *ibid.*, 160–162, Valaresso to the Doge and Senate, Nov. 21/Dec. 1, 1623; *ibid.*, 164–166, Valaresso to the Doge and Senate, Nov. 28/Dec. 8, 1623. The main points were a settlement based on a marriage between the Elector's son and the Duke of Bavaria's daughter and the creation of an eighth imperial elector. See also Rusdorff, *Mémoires*, I, 157–172, Rusdorff to Frederick, elector Palatine, Dec. 16/28, 1623 [*sic*]. The date should probably be Dec. 18/28, 1623. There are four other letters from Rusdorff to Frederick containing more information: *ibid.*, 177–184, same date; 190–204, Jan. 22/Feb. 1, 1624; 205–216, Feb. 5/15, 1624; 220–226, Feb. 9/19, 1624.

50. *Cal. S. P. Venetian*, XVIII, 156–157, Valaresso to the Doge and Senate, Nov. 21/Dec. 1, 1623. "The question of a parliament has also been raised in the state discussions, but this is all quenched. They proposed to send to the King of Denmark. They mention a person well disposed to the public weal, and Buckingham remarked to him he would take some good decision; but this is all quenched if not obliterated. In fine, the king remains steadfast in his old ideas, which he will never

ber 29, Sir George Goring was sent to the Netherlands with letters for the Queen of Bohemia, ostensibly excusing the Dukes of Richmond and Buckingham for their failure to appear personally at the christening of her son; again it was inferred that proposals of importance were being carried to the Dutch.[51]

Most symptomatic of the change in the state of affairs was the increasing political activity of the Prince. Formerly observers had assumed that Buckingham's influence was predominant, but now it was considered likely that Charles was the actual instigator of extreme measures.[52] Since the preceding summer, for instance, the Duke had been Bristol's declared enemy, but increasing disenchantment with the ambassador's negotiations at Madrid had converted the Prince to active hostility. "A nobleman remarked to me," Valaresso reported, "that the failures of others were to be discharged upon Bristol's shoulders and he was to be sacrificed to the common service." Charles seemed to be building a party within the court, and it was noted that he spoke with more freedom against Spain, showed somewhat less respect to the King, and gave more satisfaction to others than was usual. "He has reconciled Buckingham with some gentlemen, and especially with the lord chamberlain, with whom he had a quarrel. He is very gracious to the Earl of Southampton, who was out of favour with the king, although even he now regards the earl with a more friendly eye. Only the king holds to his first opinions, or at least has changed but little; but the opinions of the king, the prince and Buckingham seem irreconcilable." [53]

Although it was rumored that "a parlement is assuredly agreed upon," the partisans of Spain were still maintaining "that yt shold be a match, in spite of all the devills in hell, and all the puritans

abandon unless compelled, as I have said before. The Council does not dare to differ one jot from the sovereign's wishes. The prince continues in his dissimulation or stupidity, whichever it may be." See also *ibid.*, 165, Valaresso to the Doge and Senate, Nov. 28/Dec. 8, 1623; *Cal. S. P. Dom. 1623–1625*, 130, Sir Edward Conway to the Earl of Middlesex, Dec. 13, 1623.

51. HMC, *Mar and Kellie*, 185, Thomas, earl of Kellie, to John, earl of Mar, Dec. 18, 1623; *Cal. S. P. Venetian*, XVIII, 170, Valaresso to the Doge and Senate, Dec. 5/15, 1623; Chamberlain, *Letters*, II, 528, letter of Dec. 6, 1623; Sackville MS. ON 495, Sir George Goring to the Earl of Middlesex, Nov. 28, 1623.

52. *Cal. S. P. Venetian*, XVIII, 174, Valaresso to the Doge and Senate, Dec. 12/22, 1623.

53. *Ibid.*, 169, Valaresso to the Doge and Senate, Dec. 5/15, 1623.

in England." [54] But in mid-December the anxiety of the English was relieved when Killigrew returned from Spain with news that the marriage had been prevented virtually on the eve of its celebration. The Spaniards were said to be highly offended and indeed, from this time forward, they ceased active furtherance of all preparations for the Infanta's journey to England and considered the engagement annulled.[55] Although the English ambassadors continued to press for the restitution of the Palatinate, and although Charles's proxy had been renewed until March, Philip could not be brought to join with James in forcing the reinstatement of the Elector in his ancestral possessions.

As far as the Prince of Wales was concerned, the restitution of the Palatinate was the *sine qua non* of his policy, and, being dissatisfied with the Spanish tender of "good offices," he was faced with the alternative of looking elsewhere for support. His honor had been questioned by the Spanish who alleged that he had broken his written promise when he had prohibited delivery of the proxy. A break seemed inevitable, but, with the King inclined to negotiate, the question remained as to how that could be accomplished. The select council had agreed with the Prince in his demand for the Palatinate as a condition of the match. A majority of the Council were also favorably disposed toward the summoning of a Parliament.

It was an accepted conclusion that the House of Commons would be as anti-Spanish as it had proved in 1621. The main danger was that under the guise of privilege it might further impinge on the royal prerogative. Only to those who adopted the King's point of view did the risks of a Parliament outweigh its advantages; to the remainder the need for good, new laws was a paramount consideration. The increased freedom that had been granted to Catholics in the autumn of 1623 and the appearance of the titular bishop of Chalcedon as the provisional primate of the Catholic Church in England aroused fears of a popish plot. The staunchly Protestant prejudices of the commonalty were evidenced by their conduct when a house in Blackfriars collapsed

---

54. Chamberlain, *Letters*, II, 530, letter of Dec. 6, 1623.
55. *Ibid.*, 534, letter of Dec. 20, 1623; *Cal. S. P. Venetian*, XVIII, 171–173, Corner to the Doge and Senate, Dec. 7/17, 1623; *Spanish Marriage Treaty*, 264–267.

while Mass was being said on October 26.[56] To a majority of Englishmen the match negotiations were inextricably united with
the revival of Roman Catholicism. Since fears for the safety of
the Anglican Church were of primary concern to the populace,
Buckingham and the Prince undoubtedly believed that Parliament would prove tractable and would not endanger the fruition
of their policy by legalistic quibbling about the privileges of the
House. With the Council's consent to a breach confirmed by the
judgment of the whole nation through its representatives, the
initiative in foreign affairs could be snatched from the hands of
the King and exercised by the Prince and the Duke. And if war
did follow the breach, Commons would undoubtedly contribute
liberally to its support.

The complacency of the King, combined with his absence from
London, provided Charles and Buckingham with the opportunity
of influencing the Council. James seemed incapable of actively
opposing his son and favorite, and if he was vexed by their tutelage, he, nevertheless, succumbed to their influence. Although
their policy was diametrically opposed to the King's wishes, his
compliance was necessary for the convocation of a parliament.
Prior to mid-December, the Duke of Buckingham persuaded
James to leave Theobalds for Whitehall. In the ensuing days he
sat several times in Council where he was pressed to grant the writ
of summons. Before the date could be appointed, the King again
left for Theobalds, adjourning the Council meeting for two days
pending receipt of news from Spain.[57] On December 20, Conway
wrote to Buckingham informing him that packets had arrived:
"I have received two letters, one from my Lord of Bristol, of
expostulation and re-examination of things passed, already judged
and determined here, to be laid before his Majesty, the Prince,

56. Chamberlain, *Letters*, II, 520–523, letter of Nov. 8, 1623; Birch, *Court and
Times of James I*, II, 426, letter written to Rev. J. Mead, Oct. 29, 1623; see also
"The Fatal Vespers," by W. C. (London, 1623), which is reprinted in J. Morgan, ed.,
*Phoenix Britannicus* (London, 1732), 421–431. George Roberts attributes the author-
ship of "The Fatal Vespers" to Samuel Clark, pastor of Benet Finck. *Walter Yonge's
Diary*, 70, n.
57. Chamberlain, *Letters*, II, 535, letter of Dec. 20, 1623; Rusdorff, *Mémoires*, I,
156, Rusdorff to Frederick, elector Palatine, Dec. 18/28, 1623. Rusdorff states that
James did not attend the Council, but Chamberlain says that he sat several times.
*Cal. S. P. Venetian*, XVIII, 178, Valaresso to the Doge and Senate, Dec. 19/29, 1623;
HMC, *Mar and Kellie*, 185–186, Thomas, earl of Kellie to John, earl of Mar, Dec.
18 and Dec. 22, 1623.

and your Grace for better satisfaction and clearing . . . I hear not of any answer that comes; so as there is danger you will ever have chaff than corn thence, whilst you have that winnower there. The work of this day before the Prince, concludes (as I conceive by all voices) a parliament: and to objections and difficulties, good answers and provisions prepared to be offered." [58]

Knowing the King's fear of Parliament, not all of the councillors were willing to vote for its convocation. Several of the junta had achieved their position at court through Buckingham's influence, but, when the choice was clear cut between following the wishes of the King and the policy of the favorite, there was no certainty as to how they would vote. Secretary Conway was firmly Protestant, friendly with the Dutch, and unreservedly Buckingham's man.[59] The Earl of Carlisle was committed to French interests and was also the Duke's adherent. Lord Keeper Williams divined the King's intentions and molded his attitude to conform to the royal will. Since the return of the Prince, Secretary Calvert, who had conducted much of the correspondence with Spain, found himself increasingly excluded from diplomatic affairs. In addition, his religion made him suspect as the "King's popish secretary." Sir Richard Weston, too, had Catholic tendencies and, like Calvert, probably regarded the Spanish alliance as the foundation of British policy. The Earl of Arundel inclined toward peace and feared that a breach with Spain would result in war. Lord Treasurer Middlesex also opposed hostilities, not out of friendship for Spain but because of the havoc war would wreak on English trade and finance. His fiscal views were doubtless shared by his protégé, Chancellor of the Exchequer Weston. The Earl of Pembroke was anti-Spanish, pro-Parliament, and generally opposed to Buckingham. As the richest English peer and as Lord Chamberlain he was the natural leader of an independent faction. The Duke of Richmond, Marquess Hamilton, and Lord Belfast shared Pem-

58. SP 14/155/39, Sir Edward Conway to the Duke of Buckingham, Dec. 20, 1623. This letter is calendared under SP 14/155/65 in the printed calendar, i.e., *Cal. S. P. Dom. 1623–1625*, 131.
59. See the numerous letters of instructions from Buckingham and letters of information by Conway sent to Buckingham that are calendared in *ibid.*, passim; see also *Cabala*, I, 198–199, Sir Henry Wotton to the Earl of Portland, Lord Treasurer, no date. "Sir Edward Conway got the Start of you both in title, and imployment, because the late Duke of Buckingham wanted then for his own ends a Martial Secretarie."

broke's distrust of Buckingham in varying degrees. They desired
a Parliament, but not at the cost of committing themselves unreservedly to the Duke's policies.[60]

Although the Council on December 20, 1623, may have decided
on a Parliament by a majority of seven to five, there was no certainty that the King would agree to convoke it.[61] On Sunday,
December 21, a meeting was held at Theobalds, in the King's
presence, at which the final resolution may have been taken.[62] Certainly by December 24 a decision had been reached, for letters
bearing that date were sent to the Queen of Bohemia announcing
that a Parliament would meet.[63] The King had not given his consent unconditionally, however: two prospective leaders of the
Commons, Sir Edward Coke and Sir Edwin Sandys, were appointed to the commission that was to set out for Ireland on
January 12. Also named was Mr. Auditor, Francis Phelips, who
was the author of a tract, currently circulating, that vilified the
Earl of Bristol.[64] Although Coke attended the council table on

60. D. H. Willson, "Summoning and Dissolving Parliament 1603–1625," *American
Historical Review*, XLV (Jan. 1940), 279–300.
61. *Ibid.*, 299. Willson quotes from the Salvetti correspondence (Add. MS. 27,962
C, fol. 88). "Seven of the lords of the junta are servants of the parliament and
consequently against the Spanish negotiations. These are the Duke of Richmond
[Lennox], the Duke of Buckingham, the Marquis of Hamilton, the Earl of Pem-
broke who is lord chamberlain, Carlisle, Belfast [Chichester], and secretary Conway.
Five oppose them and desire to revive the treaties with Spain and do not cease to
do all they can against the calling of parliament. These are the lord keeper
[Williams], the Earl of Arundel who is grand marshall, lord treasurer Middlesex
[Cranfield], secretary Calvert, and Weston who is chancellor of the exchequer.
These men support the wishes of the king." Salvetti used the new style of dating,
and, hence, this dispatch should be dated Dec. 26, 1623/Jan. 5, 1624.
62. HMC, *Mar and Kellie*, 185, Thomas, earl of Kellie, to John, earl of Mar,
Dec. 18, 1623. "I know not whether they have concluded for a Parliament or not,
but on Sunday next they meet with his Majesty at Theobalds at which time I
think it shall be absolutely resolved." In his letter of Dec. 22, 1623, the Earl of
Kellie wrote as if the question of summoning Parliament had been decided. "Most
men think that if there be any likelihood of a breach with Spain, which I think
certainly will be, that then the Parliament will do all to the good liking and
contentment of his Majesty." (*Ibid.*, 186, Thomas, earl of Kellie to John, earl of
Mar, Dec. 22, 1623.)
63. *Cal. S. P. Venetian*, XVIII, 185, Marc Antonio Morosini, Venetian ambassador
in the Netherlands, to the Doge and Senate, Dec. 29, 1623/Jan. 8, 1624.
64. *Cal. S. P. Venetian*, XVIII, 182–183, Valaresso to the Doge and Senate, Dec.
26, 1623/Jan. 5, 1624; *APC, 1623–1625*, 157–158, 159–160, 165; Chamberlain, *Letters*,
II, 534, letter of Dec. 20, 1623. Many contemporary documents erroneously assert
that Sir Robert Phelips was a member of the commission. In Harl. MS. 3638 there
is a partial copy of the tract in question which is definitely ascribed to Francis

December 22 and expressed his willingness to obey the royal command, Sandys delayed his coming, excusing himself on the grounds
of illness in his family and community.[65] In the interim, before
they departed for Ireland, pressure was brought to bear to make
James change his mind. "The Chamberlain and the Marquis of
Hamilton, with praiseworthy liberty, protested and dissuaded the
king, acting in his own interests, as it would have provided an
unlucky beginning for the new parliament to awaken dissatisfaction, at which he is unfortunately terrified." [66] Sir Edward Coke's
cause was also taken up by the Prince,[67] but it was not until Sandys
was elected as knight of the shire for Kent that the King released
them from the necessity of going as commissioners to Ireland.[68]

The meeting of the Parliament was originally projected for
February 10, 1624, Tuesday being considered a day of good omen
by James, but when it was discovered that February 10 fell on
Shrove Tuesday and that a riot of apprentices might be expected
as a consequence, the issuance of the writs was stayed, and February 12 was substituted as the day of convocation. On December
28 James issued his warrant under the signet to the Lord Keeper
to prepare the writs for the assembling of Parliament.[69]

While the Parliament was still under discussion, Buckingham
and the Prince had begun a policy of conciliation toward the popular leaders. On November 8, 1623, Sir John Eliot, imprisoned as
the result of an affray with Captain Nutt, had written to the Duke
soliciting his favor.[70] Probably with an eye to his future services
in the Commons, Buckingham moved the Privy Council for
Eliot's release on December 23.[71] The same motivation may have

---

Phelips. See also HMC, *First Report*, Appendix (London, 1874), 59–60, Phelips
MSS, copy of the diary of Sir Robert Phelips while in Spain.

65. SP 14/158/14, Sir Edwin Sandys to Secetary Conway, Jan. 8, 1624.

66. *Cal. S. P. Venetian*, XVIII, 183, Valaresso to the Doge and Senate, Dec.
26, 1623/Jan. 5, 1624.

67. Chamberlain, *Letters*, II, 536, letter of Jan. 3, 1624.

68. *Cal. S. P. Venetian*, XVIII, 211, Valaresso to the Doge and Senate, Jan. 31/
Feb. 9, 1624; Chamberlain, *Letters*, II, 540, 543, letters of Jan. 17, Jan. 31, 1624.

69. Chamberlain, *Letters*, II, 536, letter of Jan. 3, 1624; Hacket, *Scrinia Reserata*,
I, 173, copy of a warrant of James to Lord Keeper Williams, Dec. 28, 1623.

70. *Cabala*, I, 311, Sir John Eliot to the Duke of Buckingham, Nov. 8, 1623.
Part of the reason Eliot was imprisoned in the Marshalsea was the favor shown by
Secretary Calvert to the pirate, Captain Nutt.

71. *APC 1623–1625*, 156, Dec. 23, 1623.

freed the Earl of Oxford. Oxford had languished in the Tower for twenty months as a result of a violent attack upon Gondomar's influence.[72] Although attempts were often made to liberate him, this was not finally accomplished until December 30, 1623, when the usefulness of his support had become apparent.[73] After his release, Oxford was conducted to the King for a private audience. "The honor of which busines the Duke of Buckingam takes to himself in goode reason; for having undertaken yt, he found yt more difficult than he expected, which bred a whispering that his favor and fortune declined, yt beeing observed that he had prevayled in litle or nothing since his comming out of Spaine." [74]

The Prince also was extremely gracious to the nobility, and there were many meetings at noblemens' houses.[75] In January he promoted the restitution of Lord Saye to full favor through the Lord Keeper and the Duke.[76] As a most ardent Puritan, Saye's support for the Prince's anti-Spanish policy would not be open to question. Charles also maneuvered to have the Earl of Hertford admitted to the House of Lords and restored to royal favor. But his most significant achievements resulted from his mediation between the passionate Duke and his opponents. In mid-January Buckingham had quarreled with Pembroke over the patronage for a gentleman usher's place in the Privy Chamber, but the Prince interposed and reconciled them.[77] With more than twenty seats in the Commons subject to his recommendation, William Herbert was a dangerous man to alienate. At the end of the month Charles was engaged in reconciling the Lord Keeper and the

72. Gardiner, *History of England,* V, 174; Chamberlain, *Letters,* II, 537, letter of Jan. 3, 1624.
73. Chamberlain, *Letters,* II, 537, letter of Jan. 3, 1624; Halliwell, *Kings' Letters.* II, 195, King James to the Duke of Buckingham, Apr. 18, 1623. It was feared at this time that Oxford "would provide a ringleader for the mutineers."
74. Chamberlain, *Letters,* II, 537–538, letter of Jan. 3, 1624.
75. *Ibid.,* 538, letter of Jan. 3, 1624.
76. *Cabala,* I, 88–90, Lord Keeper Williams to the Duke of Buckingham, Feb. 2, 1624, and *ibid.,* 90–91, information Williams sent to the Duke, Apr. 7, 1624; see also the letters of Lord Keeper Williams to John Packer and Lord Keeper Williams to James I, January 14, 15, 1624, printed in S. R. Gardiner, ed., *The Fortescue Papers; Consisting Chiefly of Letters Relating to State Affairs, Collected by John Packer, Secretary to George Villiers, Duke of Buckingham,* Camden Society, N. S., Volume I (London, 1871), 193–195.
77. HMC, *Mar and Kellie,* 188, Thomas, earl of Kellie, to John, earl of Mar, Jan. 14, 1624; *Cal. S. P. Venetian,* XVIII, 202, Valaresso to the Doge and Senate, Jan. 16/26, 1624.

Duke. Left to his own devices, Buckingham, by his bursts of anger, could well have destroyed any chance of a successful issue from the forthcoming Parliament.

The attempt to capture the leadership of the Parliament was coupled with the vigorous prosecution of the new foreign policy. For a time after he acquiesced in the demands for a Parliament, James seemed to capitulate entirely, passively permitting his son and the favorite to develop their program. Anti-Spanish publications began to issue from the press.[78] On December 30, 1623, Bristol was formally recalled to account for his behavior in the match negotiations.[79] Nevertheless, in spite of the wishes of his Council, James wrote to Aston expressing disappointment over the answers received regarding the Palatinate and avowing a desire to continue negotiations for the marriage. According to Valaresso, the Prince countermanded James's instructions and urged Aston to abandon such an improper office.[80] Hopes for a settlement were further dimmed when the Elector's reply to James's letter of November 20, 1623, arrived at the English court, for again Frederick refused to enter into any marriage negotiations with the imperial court or to undertake any submission until after the

78. *Certaine Reasons and Arguments of Policie, why the King of England should hereafter give over all Further Treatie, and enter into warre with the Spaniard* (London, 1624). In Morgan, ed., *Phoenix Britannicus,* there are several pamphlets printed in 1624: "Prosopopoeia. Sir Walter Rawleigh's Ghost," originally printed in 1622, was reissued in 1624, 310–324; the second part of "Vox Populi: or Gondomar Appearing in the Likeness of a Machiavel, in a Spanish (Cortes, or) Parliament," printed at Goricum in 1624, 341–368; "Robert, Earl of Essex's Ghost," printed in 1624, 441–448; see also Walter Scott, ed., *A Collection of Scarce and Valuable Tracts on the Most Interesting and Entertaining Subjects: But Chiefly Such as Relate to the History and Constitution of These Kingdoms, by Lord Somers* (London, 1809), which contains, in addition to several pamphlets about the Prince's trip to Spain, "Vox Coeli, or News From Heaven," written by S. R. N. I. and printed in 1624, 555–596. This tract, from internal evidence, seems to have been written in 1619 or 1620, but it was not published until 1624. Certain passages complimentary to the Duke of Buckingham, together with the dedication to the Parliament, lead Scott to believe that its publication was furthered by the Duke to incite opposition to the Spanish marriage. In the dedicatory letter to Parliament two main points are made: "First, For that the King of Spaine is a greater and more professed enemy to our sacred King and his royall posteritie, than either the Emperour or Duke of Bavaria, and is so to be held and esteemed of us. Secondly, That therefore to denounce warre to him, and to make it good as soon as it is denounced, is as honourable as necessary, and just as honourable for England." (*Ibid.,* 558.)

79. Gardiner, *History of England,* V, 159.

80. *Ibid.,* 159–160; *Cal. S. P. Venetian,* XVIII, 196, Valaresso to the Doge and Senate, Jan. 9/19, 1624; see also Harl. MS. 6987, fol. 210, Charles to Aston, undated (c. Dec. 30, 1623).

electoral dignity and the Palatinate had been restored to him. Preferring the alternative of war to negotiation, he suggested that the Danes and the Dutch were only waiting for some show of leadership from England before they actively espoused his cause against the Spanish-Imperialist forces.[81]

Just such offers of alliance as Frederick envisaged were being considered by the select council in England. On January 8 Conway had a long conversation with the Venetian ambassador with a view to concluding a league for the recovery of the Palatinate.[82] Similar proposals were also made to the French and Dutch ambassadors, and on January 9, Conway wrote to the Prince of Orange, accompanying an invitation to send commissioners to England with a relation of the nefarious, secret scheme, supposedly suggested by Gondomar, for the partition of the Netherlands between England and Spain.[83] The project for a French match took a new lease on life and although it had been rumored ever since the return of the Prince, it was now given semi-official sanction by the projected mission of Lord Kensington to Paris.[84] With Sir Robert Anstruther destined for northern Germany and Denmark, Sir Isaac Wake for Savoy and Venice, Lord Kensington for France, and Sir James Spens for Sweden, there was no longer any doubt as to the direction of English foreign policy. Had they been sent immediately they would have heralded the opening of a war for the recovery of the Palatinate, but it proved difficult to instruct them until Parliament had provided the revenues necessary for military action. Without definite assurances that England would actively intervene there was little hope that any of her continental

81. *Cabala*, II, 145–150, the Palsgrave to King James, Dec. 20/30, 1623.
82. *Cal. S. P. Venetian*, XVIII, 193–196, Valaresso to the Doge and Senate, Jan. 9/19, 1624. Shortly thereafter Valaresso reported "when I went to see the Prince dance, Buckingham came and whispered in my ear that in Conovel's [Conway's] embassy they had sent me their heart." *Ibid.*, 200, Valaresso to the Doge and Senate, Jan. 16/26, 1624.
83. *Ibid.*, 196, Valaresso to the Doge and Senate, Jan. 9/19, 1624; Gardiner, *History of England*, V, 174. James himself raised the Dutch question in the negotiations in 1623. The letters can be found in Halliwell, *Kings' Letters*, 177–179, King James to the Prince and the Duke of Buckingham, Mar. 15, 1623; *ibid.*, 216–217, the King to the Prince and Duke, July 21, 1623; *ibid.*, 219–220, the King to the Prince and Duke, July 31, 1623; see also HMC, *Eighth Report*, Appendix, pt. I, 215, Digby MSS, secret instructions to the Duke of Buckingham and the Earl of Bristol, July 23, 1623.
84. Chamberlain, *Letters*, II, 537, letter of Jan. 3, 1624; *Cal. S. P. Venetian*, XVIII, 196–197, Valaresso to the Doge and Senate, Jan. 9/19, 1624.

friends would commit themselves. The Dutch particularly were wary of English promises, knowing full well James's proclivity for vacillation. By February only Kensington had gone abroad, and full credence was not given to his mission.

With the King complaisant and the Council actively engaged in implementing their policy, it appeared certain that Charles and Buckingham would accomplish their objective, when, on January 14, Inojosa and Coloma succeeded in obtaining a semiprivate hearing.

The chief points advanced by the ambassadors in their audience were to send the Infanta in March and to surrender the Lower Palatinate in August; while they promised to make urgent representations for the surrender of the rest to the Palatine corresponding to the three demands made by the English ambassadors in Spain — namely efficacious offices; a limited time for restitution; and assistance in case the emperor should refuse — saying in the first instance that they would give the utmost satisfaction; to the second that they would leave the limit to the king, who should treat thereupon with the Infanta of Brussels and come to an understanding with the Duke of Bavaria; and to the third, although they ought to avoid playing the part of mediators, yet if the Palatine gave the emperor due satisfaction they would not leave anything necessary undone. They touched upon the marriage of the Palatine's son to the emperor's daughter, apparently consenting to the son being kept in England.[85]

These representations pleased James immensely and so altered the climate of opinion that, as Chamberlain remarked, "the proverb that Totnam is turnd French [is] quite chaunged into Spanish."[86] The Council was in turmoil and some that were thought to stand fast altered their opinions to side with the King. "Only the Secretary Conouel [Conway] spoke strongly in favour of breaking away once and for all from the Spanish artifices. The prince and Buckingham, who thanked the secretary for this, persevere steadfastly in their former opinion."[87] Yet it seemed to one observer that "unles God set to his helping hand we are like to be

85. *Cal. S. P. Venetian*, XVIII, 201, 207–209, Valaresso to the Doge and Senate, Jan. 16/26, Jan. 23/Feb. 2, 1624; see also Chamberlain, *Letters*, II, 539–540, Jan. 17, 1624; Gardiner, *History of England*, V, 175–176.

86. Chamberlain, *Letters*, II, 539, letter of Jan. 17, 1624.

87. *Cal. S. P. Venetian*, XVIII, 208, Valaresso to the Doge and Senate, Jan. 23/Feb. 2, 1624.

caried away by these sirens songs and suffer shipwracke in calme and faire weather." [88] Buckingham and the Prince envisaged disaster, and the Duke was so perturbed that he took to his bed. James, determined to go hunting against his physician's advice, left for Theobalds with the expectation of continuing on to Royston and Newmarket. The Prince, contrary to his plans, remained in London until the next afternoon to confer with the Duke; then he and the favorite left together to join the King.

Certainly some concerted action was needed to prevent the complete disruption of their program. Buckingham well knew that if the Spanish negotiations were revived at this juncture he stood to lose everything. Parliament could not be averted except by a prorogation, the onus of which would fall on him. If the houses did meet according to schedule and were forbidden to discuss foreign policy, the only result that could be expected would be a fruitless wrangle over privileges and a thorough investigation into those "caterpillars of the commonwealth" who had been countenanced by the favorite. Beset by the prospect of failure, Buckingham poured out his ire on those councillors whom he felt had betrayed him. Before he departed from Whitehall, he accosted Lord Belfast in the gallery and rudely inquired, "are you turned too?" [89] The Lord Keeper also felt the full weight of the favorite's wrath, so much so that he requested John Packer, the Duke's secretary, to intercede for him.[90]

For a while matters were at a standstill. The embassies to the Continent were delayed again. Nevertheless, James seemed unable to press his advantage. Beset by the entreaties of the Prince and Buckingham, who accompanied him to Newmarket, he consented to the consideration of the Spanish proposals by the select council at Westminster. But, instead of personally presiding over the junta, the King remained in Suffolk, and it was "Baby Charles" who arrived in London on January 20 to assemble the councillors. Buckingham remained behind to use his influence with the monarch. "Thus they both cooperate towards the same end, although with different functions, yet with a good understanding."

---

88. Chamberlain, *Letters*, II, 540, letter of Jan. 17, 1624.

89. *Cabala*, I, 243, Arthur Chichester to the Duke of Buckingham, Jan. 25, 1623/4.

90. *Ibid.*, I, 86–87, John Packer to Lord Keeper Williams, Jan. 21, 1624.

By the King's order the junta deliberated "how to break off the negotiations while saving their honour, and whether the satisfaction promised . . . would suffice."[91] During the frequent meetings that followed, the news leaked out that the select council was split into three factions: five for the Spanish match (the Lord Keeper, the Lord Treasurer, the Earl of Arundel, Sir Richard Weston, and Sir George Calvert); three opposed (the Duke of Buckingham, the Earl of Carlisle, and Sir Edward Conway); four neutral (the Duke of Richmond, the Marquess Hamilton, the Earl of Pembroke, and Lord Belfast).[92]

The discussions were heated, and, although a majority of the councillors preferred to end relations with Spain, they were divided as to the time and the manner. "Some desired a public declaration from the prince, possibly in order to secure their retreat in any event; some asked for detailed information about the whole affair."[93] It was considered remarkable that the anti-Spanish Earl of Pembroke "should be so backward, alledging that yf the Spaniard performed the conditions agreed on, he saw not how the King in honor could fall from the conclusion, nor himself in conscience beeing sworn to see all observed to his power."[94]

91. *Cal. S. P. Venetian*, XVIII, 210–211, Valaresso to the Doge and Senate, Jan. 31/Feb. 9, 1624.

92. Chamberlain, *Letters*, II, 541–542, letter of Jan. 31, 1624. In Hacket, *Scrinia Reserata*, I, 169, the antiwar faction is listed as "the Keeper, Treasurer, Duke of Richmond, Marquess Hamilton, Earl of Arundel, Lord Carew, Lord Belfast," but Lord Carew was not a member of the junta. The vote as reported to Maximilian, duke of Bavaria, was 8 to 4, "those in the minority being the Duke, Carlisle, Mandeville and Conway." H. G. R. Reade, *Sidelights on the Thirty Years War* (3 vols., London: K. Paul, Trench, Trubner and Co., 1924), II, 322. This also is in error since Lord Mandeville was not a member of the select committee. I cannot give any credence to Hacket's narration of the proceedings in Council, although M. Guizot, in *Un Projet de Mariage Royal* (Paris, 1863), 197–199, relies upon him almost entirely. As Gardiner has pointed out, the date Hacket assigned to the discussions is erroneous, and I can find no evidence that the questions submitted to the Council included one on war or peace. Writing more than twenty years after the event, Hacket relied heavily on the documents published in *Cabala* and although he was Williams's chaplain and had access to the Keeper's private papers, it seems to me that he embellished his narrative in a wholly unwarranted manner. Gardiner's account also does not completely fit the movements of the King, the Prince, and the Duke during the last two weeks in January, and this, in addition to his partial reliance on Hacket, has led me to amend his reconstruction of events. See also SP 14/162/52, information to the Duke of Buckingham by Secretary Conway (?), Apr. 1624, where he alleges that a war is not a consequence of the breach.

93. *Cal. S. P. Venetian*, XVIII, 211, Valaresso to the Doge and Senate, Jan. 31/Feb. 9, 1624

94. Chamberlain, *Letters*, II, 542, letter of Jan. 31, 1624; see S. P. 14/159/28, Sir

Jealousy of the Duke of Buckingham incited some members to rebel against the proposed breach with Spain. But when the final decision was taken the Prince's aversion to the match was sufficient to swing the votes of the neutrals.[95]

The resolution to reject Philip's overtures and to break off negotiations was carried to Newmarket by Richmond, Carlisle, and Conway in the closing days of January.[96] However, the question remained undecided as to whether the declaration of the rupture should be made in the Parliament or in the Council. Both possibilities were appealing. If the breach were made by the junta, Parliament would be presented with a *fait accompli,* and no extensive discussion of foreign policy would be necessary. Conversely, if the decision were left to the Commons, they would be distinctly obliged to implement the policy they advocated with financial assistance.[97] The imminence of a Parliament emphasized the need for decisive action. For the most part the elections were already over, and observers were convinced that the new House of Commons would be staunchly Protestant, anti-Spanish, and remarkably free from the influence of patrons.[98]

---

William Pelham to Secretary Conway, Feb. 12, 1624. "I heard by another way how the committee for the Spanish match were in a sort divided and of some passages betwixt the noble Duke and the Lord Chamberlain which I the more wondered at by reason I was ever of opinion with many more that the Earl favored not the Spanish cause."

95. Chamberlain, *Letters,* II, 542, letter of Jan. 31, 1624; *Cal. S. P. Venetian,* XVIII, 211, Valaresso to the Doge and Senate, Jan. 31/Feb. 9, 1624.

96. Chamberlain, *Letters,* II, 542, letter of Jan. 31, 1624, gives the date as Jan. 26, while Valaresso gives it as Jan. 30, 1624; see *Cal. S. P. Venetian,* XVIII, 211, Valaresso to the Doge and Senate, Jan. 31/Feb. 9, 1624.

97. *Cal. S. P. Venetian,* XVIII, 211, Valaresso to the Doge and Senate, Jan. 31/Feb. 9, 1624; see also Rusdorff, *Mémoires,* I, 190, Rusdorff to Frederick, elector Palatine, Jan. 22/Feb. 1, 1624.

98. HMC, *Mar and Kellie,* 191, Thomas, earl of Kellie, to John, earl of Mar, Feb. 5, 1624; *Cal. S. P. Venetian,* XVIII, 201, 211, Valaresso to the Doge and Senate, Jan. 16/26, Jan. 31/Feb. 9, 1624; Chamberlain, *Letters,* II, 542, letter of Jan. 31, 1624.

# II  Royal Patronage: A House Divided

Memories of former conflicts involving the King and his House of Commons tempered the enthusiasm of those who most eagerly anticipated the convocation of Parliament. The Venetian ambassador expected the worst, even though appearances were promising, and the Earl of Kellie was half persuaded that those who had been the chief instruments for the calling of Parliament would soon repent of it. Sir George Goring expected "strange and dangerous practices for the breaking up of this meeting," and, indeed, in January the Council heard rumors of a suspected popish plot in Yorkshire. Even an avowed parliamentarian like the Earl of Southampton mingled caution with his pious wishes: "God send the lower House may be composed of discreet and honest men or all may be naught, but I hope the best and persuade myself I have reason to do so." [1]

One ingenious and ambitious gentleman from Warwickshire was unwilling to leave the composition of Parliament to the determination of the electorate. On the same day that the writs were dispatched, Thomas Trussell wrote to Secretary Conway expressing his fears "that a new election might prove more giddy and unlearned in the causes and courses fit to be considered." He recommended to Conway's consideration a plan whereby the

1. *Cal. S. P. Venetian*, XVIII, 193–195, Valaresso to the Doge and Senate, Jan. 9/19, 1624; HMC, *Mar and Kellie*, 191, Thomas, earl of Kellie, to John, earl of Mar, Feb. 5, 1624; SP 14/159/9, Sir George Goring to Sir Dudley Carleton, Feb. 3, 1624; SP 14/159/12, information against Robert Burton of Langoll, Yorkshire, Jan. 27, 1624; SP 14/155/77, the Earl of Southampton to Sir Thomas Roe, Dec. 24, 1623.

Parliament of 1621 could be reconvened: "I make no doubt but those judges of the laws and his Majesty's council whose opinions were required in the dissolution can more easily find a means by the like proclamation to call the same members again to their proper places; and if any shall be absent by death to supply them by new choice, which they always use and may lawfully do, the former session continued." [2] It was Trussell's opinion that the Prince would not only give Conway "joyful thanks" for this advice but would also "join, second and assist" him in the prosecution of the scheme.

The possible fruition of Trussell's undertaking was thwarted by the issuance of the writs, but the return of "discreet and honest men" did not depend upon the efficacy of prayer alone. "Many aspire[d] to election with no ordinary ambition," and patrons of high and mean degree did their utmost to secure the return of their creatures.[3] Seldom before had Englishmen been so aware of the importance of parliamentary patronage. The issue was drawn between those who wished to dissolve the Spanish match and those who wished to continue it, and the vindication of the Prince's aggressive policy seemed to depend upon his success in securing parliamentary support. The results of the elections were closely watched by both foreign and domestic observers, and the rejections of recommendations were hailed as signs of freedom and independence. The Venetian ambassador's statement that "every courtier has been rejected" was somewhat less than accurate, but a more cautious appraisal by Chamberlain commended the care exercised in the choice of knights and burgesses.[4]

It may have been true "that neither noble man nor councillor can make burgesses as they have done," but attempts to do so were not lacking.[5] On December 10, 1623, more than two weeks

2. SP 14/158/6, Thomas Trussell to Sir Edward Conway, Jan. 3, 1624.
3. Cal. S. P. Venetian, XVIII, 200–203, Valaresso to the Doge and Senate, Jan. 16/26, 1624.
4. Ibid., 216–218, Valaresso to the Doge and Senate, Feb. 6/16, 1624; Chamberlain, Letters, II, 543, letter of Jan. 31, 1624.
5. HMC, Mar and Kellie, 191, Thomas, earl of Kellie, to John, earl of Mar, Feb. 5, 1624; see also SP 14/159/28, Sir William Pelham to Sir Edward Conway, Feb. 12, 1624. Pelham noted that in Lincolnshire there had "been never less laboring for particular men." He saw the issues confronting the Parliament entirely in religious terms and wished "for the good of the state that they [the Catholics] were reduced to a certain uniformity of temporal obedience and love to their King and Country."

before the writs were issued, Drew Drury wrote to Lord Zouche withdrawing a previous recommendation he had made for a burgess-ship in the Cinque Ports and instead advanced his own candidacy for a seat. By that time his former nominee, Sir John Corbet, had resolved to stand for the county of Norfolk.[6] The majority of aspirants to seats in the Commons, however, awaited the receipt of the precepts before soliciting support. Most country gentlemen were cognizant of the national issues, but they were primarily motivated by a desire to assert their prestige in their counties, advance their family and local interests, and secure domestic reform legislation. Only rarely did they seek election in more than one borough although they frequently appealed to a variety of interested parties for support.

Patronage on a grand scale was centered in the court and was more apt to be utilized in the promotion of nationwide policies. Important members of the nobility, such as the Earls of Pembroke and Southampton and Lord Zouche, exercised extensive influence, not only because of their ancestral landholdings, but also by virtue of the offices they held. Privy councillors, whether peers or not, had ex-officio power to persuade many constituencies. Naturally the patronage wielded by governmental functionaries resided ultimately in the crown, and, without doubt, the King was the most important single patron. Unfortunately royal influence is extremely difficult to trace; with few exceptions it was exerted through subordinates. Although it was reported that James was "trying his utmost to secure the return of his creatures," there is almost no evidence of his direct intervention in the elections for the Parliament of 1624.[7] Only his attempts to exclude Sir Edward Coke and Sir Edwin Sandys indicate a real concern about the membership of the Commons.

No royal proclamation preceded the Parliament of 1624, but in 1620 the King had lectured his subjects on the proper choice of representatives.

And, as to the Knightes of Shires, that they cast their Eyes upon the worthiest Men of all Sorts, of Knightes and Gentlemen that are Guides and Lightes of their Countries, of good Experience and of great In-

---

6. SP 14/155/32, Drew Drury to Lord Zouche, Dec. 10, 1623.
7. *Cal. S. P. Venetian*, **XVIII**, 200–203, Valaresso to the Doge and Senate, Jan. 16/26, 1624.

tegrity. Men that lead honest and exemplarie Lief in their Countries, doing us good Service therein; and no Bankrupts or discontented Persons that cannot fish but in troubled Waters.

And, for the Burgesses, that they make Choice of them that best understand the State of their Countries, Cities, or Burroughes; and where such may not be had within their Corporations, then of other grave and discreet Men, fit to serve in so worthy an Assembly. For we may well forsee how ill Effects the bad Choice of unfitt Men may produce, if the House should be supplied with Bankruptes and necessitous Persons, that may desire long Parliaments for their private Protections; or with young and unexperienced Men, that are not ripe and mature for so grave a Council; or with Men of mean Qualities in themselves, who may only serve to applaud the Opinion of others on whom they depend; nor yett with curious and wrangling Lawyers, who may seek Reputation by stirring needless Questions; but we wish all our good Subjects to understand theis our Admonitions, as that we noe Way mean to bar them of their lawful Freedom in Election, according to the fundamental Laws and laudable Custome of this our Kingdome, and especially in the Times of good and settled Government.[8]

Designed to insure a responsible and tractable Parliament, this proclamation, nevertheless, seemed to abjure some of the traditional rights of the crown in securing the return of its partisans. But "lawful freedom" in elections was conditioned by the "laudable customs" of the kingdom. When, in 1625, Charles wished precipitately to convene a new Parliament, the Lord Keeper told him: "It was usual in times before, that the King's Servants, and trustiest Friends did deal with the Countries, Cities, and Boroughs,

---

8. *OPH*, V, 311–312, "Proclamation Summoning the Parliament in 1621," also printed in Rymer, *Foedera*, XVII, 270–271; see also the King's proclamation touching the Parliament, Jan. 11, 1604, printed in *OPH*, V, 4–8. The proclamation of 1604 materially differs from the rough drafts of the heads of the proclamation printed in J. Payne Collier, ed., *The Egerton Papers*, Camden Society, O.S., Volume XII (London, 1840), 384–388. The document in Egerton's handwriting undoubtedly gives the clearest indication of James's views regarding elections to Parliament and its personnel. Among the significant omissions from the official proclamation are: a qualification regarding residence requirements for knights of the shire; a stipulation that burgesses and citizens be freemen of places choosing them, or, at least, residents of the county; an insistence that candidates be well experienced in the affairs and state of their respective counties, cities, and boroughs; and a statement requiring the exclusion of papists, recusants, and sectaries. This latter disqualification included those who were "vehementlye and probablye suspected to meynteyne or favour Papistrye" and "Sectaries or men of turbulent, factious, and unquiett behaviour or conversation, or disturbers of the ecclesiasticall government and peace of the Church." The King also seems to have desired the establishment of an age qualification for membership in Parliament but in this draft the age is not specified.

where they were known, to procure a Promise for their Elections, before the precise time of an insequent Parliament was publisht; and that the same Forecast would be good at that time: which would not speed, if the Summons were divulged, before they lookt about them." [9] Pious sentiments, therefore, screened actual practice, and the crown intended in no way to forego its patronage initiative. Nevertheless, it was neither customary nor desirable for the King to risk his personal credit by commanding the return of his officers. Ordinarily this onerous responsibility was delegated to the chief functionaries of the household, most of whom were privy councillors. Indeed, eligible members of the King's Council were expected to take their place in the forefront of the King's party in the House of Commons.

In 1624 seven councillors were available for service in the lower House and only one, Sir Julius Caesar, failed in his bid for a seat. The King's principal secretaries, Sir George Calvert and Sir Edward Conway, were returned for Oxford University and Evesham, Worcestershire, respectively. The Treasurer of the Household, Sir Thomas Edmondes, sat for Chichester, Sussex, and the Comptroller, Sir John Suckling, was elected by Middlesex County and the boroughs of Kingston-upon-Hull, Yorkshire, and Lich-

9. Hacket, *Scrinia Reserata*, II, 4, conversation between King Charles, Buckingham, and the Lord Keeper. Prior to the Parliament of 1604 James I informed the sheriffs that "our pleasure is that where our privy council, or any of them within their jurisdictions, in our behalf shall recommend men of learning and wisdom, in such a case their directions be regarded and followed as tending to the same which we desire, that is, to have this assembly to be of the most chiefest men in our realm for advice and good counsel." (Lansdowne MS. 94, fol. 19). During the consultations before the Parliament of 1621, Lord Chancellor Bacon addressed a letter to Buckingham (October 7, 1620) concerning four points under consideration: former and recent grievances, a proclamation particularly concerning elections, the personnel of the impending Parliament, and the preparation of commonwealth bills. "Of the four points, that which concerneth persons is not so fit to be communicated to the council-table; but be kept within fewer hands. The other three may, when they are ripe." In order to determine "what persons were fit to be of the House," Bacon, Serjeant Ranulph Crew, and the two Chief Justices, "made some lists of names of the privy councillors and principal statesmen or courtiers; of the gravest and wisest lawyers; of the most respected and best tempered knights and gentlemen of the country. And here *obiter* we did not forget to consider who were the boutefeus [i.e., firebrands or incendiaries], of the last session, how many of them are dead, how many reduced, and how many remain." (Bacon, *Works*, XIV, 115–117.) Some indication of the King's awareness of parliamentary service may be derived from his letter to Lord Chancellor Ellesmere, Aug. 18, 1614, in which he urged that the Chancery proceedings in the case of Robert Wulverstone be delayed "because he had in the Parliament house shewed himself forward in our service." (Collier, ed., *Egerton Papers*, 464.)

field, Staffordshire. The Chancellor of the Exchequer, Sir Richard Weston, was chosen at Bossiney, Cornwall, and Sir Robert Naunton was named by Cambridge University.[10]

With a nucleus of six privy councillors in the House of Commons, the King's friends seemed destined to control the Parliament of 1624. Such, however, proved not to be the case; the strength of numbers was vitiated by a lack of organization and discipline and by divided loyalties. Naunton's seat at Cambridge University was subject to royal patronage, but it was almost certainly procured at Buckingham's request. Although the King acceded to Naunton's election, he had no desire to have his anti-Spanish, Puritanically inclined councillor participate in the debates, and, consequently, Naunton's restraint, imposed in 1621 for an indiscreet conversation with a French emissary was not lifted.[11] Although Conway was Buckingham's sycophant, his connection with Evesham was of a personal nature, and his election had been procured on his own initiative. Weston was placed at Bossiney through the Prince's patronage, and it is probable that Suckling was countenanced in the Middlesex election by Buckingham, even though he appears not to have been the Duke's first choice. Probably Calvert and Edmondes owed most to James's recommendation, but the Prince was particularly solicitous regarding Edmondes's election. Normally all privy councillors, whether or not they were placed through crown influence, owed their first loyalty to the King's policies, but in 1624 their patronage alignment partially affected their service in the House.[12]

10. Suckling also appears to have solicited Great Yarmouth, Norfolk, in 1624, but he was refused the seat on the grounds that a corporation bylaw reserved it for "such onlye as are free burgesses and residents within the towne and none other." See the letter from the bailiffs of Great Yarmouth to Suckling printed in C. J. Palmer, *The History of Great Yarmouth* (Great Yarmouth, 1856), 203–204.

11. Gardiner, *History of England*, III, 391; M. B. Rex, *University Representation in England 1604–1690* (London: George Allen & Unwin, 1954), 360–361.

12. In 1624 the Prince's council recommended Edmondes to the corporations of Coventry (January 1) and St. Albans (January 31). (Duchy of Cornwall MS. "Prince Charles in Spain," fol. 34v, 37.) Prior to the Parliament of 1621 Edmondes had been nominated to the city of Chester after the original nominee, Sir Henry Carey (later Viscount Falkland), was elected knight for Hertfordshire. The letters from the Prince's council were forwarded through the Earl of Northampton and occasioned a heated controversy within the corporation. The recorder, Edward Whitby, organized the commonalty against Edmondes on the grounds that his candidacy infringed the statute of 1 H. V, which required the election "of citizens resiant, inhabiting and enfranchised." Edmondes was defeated despite the efforts of the mayor and aldermen. Subsequently overtures were made to commence a Star

Conway participated in most of the great debates on foreign policy, but spent much time in attendance upon the King. Consequently the effective strength of the privy councillors in the House of Commons was reduced to four: Calvert, Weston, Edmondes, and Suckling. Of these Calvert and Weston were the most active, but Weston's main service in promoting the bill of subsidies was as gratifying to the Prince and Buckingham as it was to the King. Edmondes diligently served the Prince's interests in the foreign policy and subsidy debates, while Suckling displayed his talents principally in the committee for trade. The councillors seem not to have acted in concert; by the latter part of the session James was complaining that he found himself "less informed at this parliament than at others from his privy councillors of the House from whom he challengeth that duty." He was fearful that questions concerning impositions, privileges of the House, and other issues that might diminish his prerogative would be allowed to come into debate, and he specifically commanded Calvert and Weston to attempt the suppression of any such motions. Calvert excused his recent absences from the House with a plea of ill health. He chided Conway for his failure to attend the Parliament, and he maintained that Edmondes and Suckling would feel themselves neglected if they were not addressed personally to implement the King's commands.[13]

Yet Calvert was so pleased with the duty and respect shown to His Majesty by the House of Commons that no guidance seemed necessary from the privy councillors to assure the success of the Parliament. To a certain extent this was true. The desire for war with Spain was so strong that the Commons were extremely chary of offending the King until after the breach had been accomplished. Hence the rather late date at which James's fears of incursions into the royal prerogative were aroused.

The seeming inactivity of the privy councillors in 1624 is in large measure attributable to the fact that the initiative in foreign policy debate had been taken from them and vested in the hands

Chamber prosecution against Whitby, but apparently nothing was done (Harl. MS. 2105, fols. 277–278, 281, Mayor and Aldermen of Chester to the Earl of Northampton, two undated letters, 1620; *ibid.*, fol. 283, Philip Mainwaring and Sir Thomas Savage to the Mayor of Chester, Jan. 23, 1621).

13. SP 14/165/4, Secretary Conway to Secretary Calvert and Sir Richard Weston, May 20, 1624; SP 14/165/11, Secretary Calvert to Secretary Conway, May 21, 1624.

of Charles, Buckingham, and their trusted agents. In the domestic sphere the councillors' role was limited by the failure on the part of the government to prepare an agenda of new legislation prior to the convention of the Parliament. All the important laws passed in 1624 were revivals of bills which had been discussed in 1621 or earlier, and, as often as not, they had been brought to the attention of the House by members who were not of the court faction.

The last important function of privy councillors, that of defending regalian rights, likewise diminished in the Parliament of 1624. The temper of the members was such that on religious and financial issues they were not prepared to compromise. Since the beginning of James's reign, moreover, arguments involving the prerogative had become increasingly legalistic and the majority of the King's privy councillors were not equipped to deal with the technicalities of the law. Thus, after the exclusion of the Attorney General in 1614, the burden of defending royal rights fell on the Solicitor and other legal officers of the crown who proved no more effective in stemming the tide of criticism. When Serjeant Hitcham tried to defend impositions in 1624, "he was interrupted by a general mislike of the House" and, on the motion of Sir Thomas Wentworth, Hitcham's speech was "rased out of the clerk's book." [14] Consequently, the effectiveness of the privy councillors in the House of Commons was not limited solely by the mediocre abilities of many of the King's advisors; it was also a result of the temper of the times and the caprices of James and his chief favorite.

Informed courtiers in 1624 were well aware of the King's reluctance to go to war, but, with the exception of Sir George Chaworth, no member of Parliament ardently opposed military involvement. The silence of the King's friends, when contrasted with the vehement expostulations of the advocates of foreign intervention, gives the deceptive impression that James was entirely devoid of support in the House of Commons. But the members themselves, whether patronized by King or courtier, were never unaware of their dependency, and, in cases where

14. Pym, fols. 68, 69, Apr. 16, 1624. Wentworth's motion is not mentioned in the *Commons Journal*, but the text of Hitcham's speech has been thoroughly obliterated in the second manuscript version of the *Commons Journal* kept by John Wright's son. fols. 146–146v.

divergences of opinion occurred, they prefaced their remarks by an appeal to the freedom of their consciences. Thus, loyalty to the monarchy was not always construed as absolute subservience to the King's wishes: in 1624 it was possible to disapprove of James's foreign policy and yet support the royal prerogative.

This necessarily complicates the identification of the King's party. Perhaps the best criterion is long occupancy of administrative or judicial office combined with frequent parliamentary service for boroughs subject to royal patronage. Lack of intimate association with Buckingham is also a factor of some importance, as is the role that individual members played in the debates. To win support for their policy Charles and Buckingham were willing to moderate or abandon the absolutist pretensions of the monarchy. Thus, their supporters in 1624 included parliamentarians who were not consistent Royalists. The King's friends, on the other hand, owed their power to the maintenance of the prerogative, and they supported it as a matter of principle and from motives of self-interest.

A traditional enclave of royal patronage was the duchy of Lancaster. Its strength was centered mainly in Lancashire, but it held properties throughout England. In 1614 the activities of its chancellor, Sir Thomas Parry, in nominating burgesses had earned the wrath of the advocates of a free Parliament. Although Parry was expelled from the House, subsequent chancellors of the duchy continued to exercise the patronage rights attendant on their dignity. In 1624 Sir Humphrey May and his subordinates made full use of those rights in Lancashire boroughs where the power of local families had not superseded that of the duchy. At Lancaster, May himself was elected, and his partner was Thomas Fanshawe of Jenkins, Essex, Clerk of the Crown. But May had also secured his own return at Leicester, partially through the influence of the Earl of Huntingdon. Less than a week after May had elected to serve for Leicester, his place at Lancaster had been given to John Selden.[15] Preston, capital of the duchy, also ap-

15. Notes of letters in reference to May's election at Leicester in 1624 are contained in HMC, *Report on the Manuscripts of the Late Reginald Rawdon Hastings, Esq., of the Manor House, Ashby-de-la-Zouche* (4 vols., London, 1928–1947), II, 63. On January 21, 1624, Sir Humphrey May wrote to Henry, fifth earl of Huntingdon, "I understand I am chosen burgess for Leicester in this parliament. I thank you for your favour, to which I am more beholding than to my own interest." Curiously

pears to have accepted nominees: Sir Edward Mosely, attorney of the duchy, and Sir William Poley, Sir Humphrey May's father-in-law. When Poley chose to serve for Sudbury in his native Suffolk, the seat at Preston went to Francis Nicholls, clerk of the Prince's Court of Wards and Liveries. Another officer, William Fanshawe, sat for Clitheroe, Lancashire. He was the brother of Thomas Fanshawe of Jenkins and was an auditor of the duchy.[16]

Outside of Lancashire it is probable that duchy influence figured in the return of several members. Huntingdon named Sir Arthur Mainwaring, Clerk of the Pipe; East Grinstead elected Sir Robert Heath, Solicitor General; Monmouth returned a Scotsman, Walter Steward; Stockbridge chose Sir Henry Holcroft; and Newcastle-under-Lyme selected Sir Edward Vere. In the absence of direct evidence it is impossible to say with certainty that the duchy exercised a decisive influence or indeed any influence at all, but it is noteworthy that when duchy properties were alienated by sale or long lease the representation of the adjacent towns changed markedly.[17]

It is apparent that in their search for places courtiers used every device at their command. In the course of several Parliaments the most powerful royal officials were frequently returned for a variety of patronage boroughs, but men of small consequence in the government sometimes represented the same constituency repeatedly. Power at court and power in the country did not always coincide. In 1624 the Master of the Jewel House, Sir Henry Mildmay, was returned for the patronage borough of Westbury, Wiltshire, but his underling, Robert Hassard, Jr., relied upon his family's power at Lyme Regis, Dorset. Thomas Fanshawe of

---

enough, the corporation of Leicester rejected the Earl's nomination of his brother, Sir George Hastings, for the other burgess-ship.

16. Fanshawe's partner at Clitheroe, Ralph Whitfield, also sounds suspiciously like a nominee. A Kentishman and a lawyer of Gray's Inn, he was made serjeant-at-law in November 1632 and King's serjeant in 1635. W. S. Weeks, in *Clitheroe in the Seventeenth Century* (Clitheroe, n.d.). 226–228, prints a letter of solicitation from William Fanshawe to the burgesses of Clitheroe, dated February 6, 1628, together with a poll list for the subsequent election.

17. Sir Henry Holcroft was also returned from Pontefract, Yorkshire, by virtue of a recommendation from the Prince's council. He may have relinquished his seat at Pontefract upon the assumption that another nomination would be equally well received, but Pontefract refused to elect the Prince's alternate candidate, Robert Mynne. Holcroft's tenure at Stockbridge was precarious; a petition against his election was denied by the House of Commons on April 9. (*CJ*, 759.)

Ware, third member of the same family to hold the office of Remembrancer of the Exchequer, used his credit with the Earl of Salisbury and his personal influence with the nearby corpora- tion of Hertford to obtain a seat. On the other hand, Sir Henry Spiller, a deputy lieutenant, justice of the peace in Middlesex and collector of recusant fines, sat for the Howard borough of Arundel, Sussex, while his son, Sir Robert Spiller, represented another Howard constituency, Castle Rising, Norfolk. The Keeper of the Tower Records, John Borough, also had strong Howard connections and was elected at Horsham, Sussex, where the Earl of Arundel and Surrey was Lord Paramount of the Manor. Sir Philip Cary, a surveyor of the customs, was chosen at Woodstock, Oxford, for the third time, although he initially obtained the seat through the recommendation of the steward of the town, Sir Thomas Spencer. Sir Edward Wardour, Clerk of the Pells, was reelected at Malmesbury in his native Wiltshire, while his compatriot in the Exchequer, William Cholmeley, was chosen at Great Bedwin in the same county. Edmund Sawyer, Auditor of the Exchequer, was returned for the royal town of Windsor where the Earl of Nottingham was the chief steward. When Sawyer's partner at Windsor died, he was replaced by another official, Sir William Hewett, a receiver of composition money for provisions for the royal household.[18]

18. Mildmay's sole connection with Wiltshire seems to have been through his brother-in-law, Edward Hungerford, who in 1624 was knight of the shire for Wiltshire. In Keeler, *Long Parliament*, 274, it is intimated that Hungerford's influ- ence may have helped Mildmay at Westbury, but, in view of the past parliamentary history of the borough and the property holdings of the Ley family, I suspect that Mildmay obtained his seat through Sir James Ley, Chief Justice of the King's Bench and member of the Prince's council. Robert Hassard died before the dissolu- tion of the Parliament and was replaced by William Wynn who was in the service of Lord Keeper Williams. The date of Wynn's return is uncertain, but on March 30, 1624, he wrote, "It is my hard fortune to be now without a place in the House, when I had one provided for me, but I was fain to relinquish the same upon my Lordship's earnest entreaty to a special friend of his that he conceived might do him good service there when occasion required." (Wynn of Gwydir Papers [Panton Group], National Library of Wales MS. 9059 E/1204, William Wynn to Sir John Wynn, Mar. 30, 1624.) As late as May 15 he was still unprovided; on that date Lord Keeper Williams wrote to the Earl of Salisbury soliciting support for Wynn at the imminent Hertford election. (L. Stone, "The Electoral Influence of the Second Earl of Salisbury, 1614–68," *English Historical Review*, LXXI [July 1956], 384–400, esp. 392.) Hassard is described by the term "courtier" in the diary of William Whiteway, Jr. (Egerton MS. 784, fol. 38, British Museum), and court news derived from his letters was incorporated in *Walter Yonge's Diary*, 71. The Thomas Fanshawe elected for Hertford was seated at Ware Park, Hertfordshire. He should not be confused

One of the results of a lucrative career at court was the acquisition of power in the counties. Thus, Edmund Sawyer, through the purchase of the manor of Heywood near Maidenhead, had established himself as a man to be reckoned with in Berkshire politics by 1628. Ordinarily the development of local power was the work of generations. Men like Sir William Uvedale, Treasurer of the King's Chamber and head of a family prominent in Hampshire affairs, were the exception rather than the rule at court. All of the constituencies he represented in the course of a long career were in his native county; in 1624 he sat for Portsmouth.

The variety of crown officers, when considered in conjunction with the multiplicity of patrons of parliamentary boroughs, makes it extremely difficult to gain insight into the real strength of the King's party in the House of Commons or to group it into meaningful categories. Many of the King's friends never figured in the debates, and, if they exerted any influence, it was entirely behind the scenes. Conversely, some of the most active protagonists of royal authority had little more than a tenuous connection with the court. It is apparent, however, that the majority of the royalist party were connected with either the financial or judicial apparatus of government.

To second the Solicitor and the officials of the Court of Wards and Liveries and the duchy of Lancaster, the King had a considerable array of legal talent at his disposal. In addition to two Masters in Chancery, Sir Edward Leech of Derby and Sir Eubule Thelwall representing Denbighshire, there were three civilians in the Commons: Dr. Arthur Duck, newly appointed King's advocate in the Earl Marshal's court, sitting for Minehead, Somersetshire; Richard

---

with Thomas Fanshawe of Jenkins. (*DNB*, XVIII, 190; Keeler, *Long Parliament*, 172; Stone, "Electoral Influence of the Second Earl of Salisbury," 392.) John Borough, the keeper of the Tower records and sometimes secretary to the Earl of Arundel and Surrey should not be confused with Sir John Burroughs, the soldier killed on the Isle of Rhe on September 12, 1627. (Birch, *Court and Times of Charles The First*, I, 273, Rev. Joseph Mead to Sir Martin Stuteville, Oct. 6, 1627.) Sir Philip Cary's partner at Woodstock in 1614 was James Whitelocke, who attributes Cary's nomination to Sir Thomas Spencer. (Whitelocke, *Liber Famelicus*, 41.) Sawyer's partner at Windsor was Thomas Woodward, Esq., who, as early as 1613, was understeward or recorder at Windsor. He was reader of Lincoln's Inn in 1623. (R. R. Tighe and J. E. Davis, *Annals of Windsor* [2 vols., London, 1858], II, 47.) Sir William Hewett was not returned until September 14, 1624, after the death of Thomas Woodward. Nevertheless, Hewett figured in the Parliament, for on May 3 he was ordered by the Commons to bring in his books in connection with the inquiry into purveyance. (Pym, fol. 86v.)

Zouche, sometime regis professor of civil law at Oxford, elected baron of Hythe; and Dr. Barnabas Gooch, vice-chancellor of Cambridge University and one of its members in Parliament.[19]

The only common lawyer of reputation to side with the King in debates over the prerogative was Serjeant Hitcham, member of Parliament for Orford, Suffolk. Most common lawyers during their parliamentary careers were aligned with the faction opposed to the court. If, however, the statements made by Robert Berkeley as member for Worcester in 1624 are contrasted with those made by Judge Berkeley when he was consulted on the question of ship money in 1635, it is evident how ephemeral opposition to the crown was apt to be. A similar change in attitude is noticeable in the case of William Noy upon his preferment to the attorney generalship.[20]

To lawyers, Parliament was frequently a forum for the display of their talents, a way station on the highroad to promotion in their chosen profession. To others whose reputations and fortunes were made outside the House, the summoning of Parliament was a cause of anxiety. Patentees like George Mynne, Clerk of the Hanaper, Sir Henry Vane of the subpoena office, and Sir Robert Mansell of the glass works found their privileges and perquisites threatened by the antimonopoly bias of the Commons. In the face

19. Sir Edward Leech appears to have been patronized upon his entry into Parliament in 1604, when he probably owed his seat at Old Sarum to the first Earl of Salisbury. In 1614, 1621, 1624, 1625, and 1628 he sat for the town of Derby. In 1626 there may have been some Pembroke influence at Derby for John Thoroughgood, the Earl's secretary, was elected along with Sir Henry Croft. Dr. Arthur Duck may have been the chancellor of the bishopric of Bath and Wells by 1623. (F. T. Colby, ed., *Visitation of the County of Somerset in the Year 1623*, Harleian Society Volume XI [London, 1876], 137.) His partner at Minehead, Somerset, was Sir Arthur Lake, son of the former Secretary of State, Sir Thomas Lake, and nephew of Arthur Lake, bishop of Bath and Wells. Duck's brother, Nicholas, was a barrister, governor of Lincoln's Inn, recorder of Exeter, and M.P. for that city in 1624 and 1625. On Gooch's elections to Parliament, see Rex, *University Representation in England*, 63–64, 102–103, 134, 136, 365.

20. Compare Robert Berkeley's speech on April 13, 1624, when he opposed the interpretation that included pretermitted customs under the statute of tonnage and poundage with his argument in the ship money case of 1637, when he supported the King's right to exact revenue without parliamentary consent. (Pym, fol. 63; *A Complete Collection of State Trials and Proceedings for High Treason* . . . , [6 vols.], 2d ed., London, 1730], I, 597–615.) As for Noy, the change in his views regarding projects and monopolies between 1621 and 1634 is little short of revolutionary. (Pym, fol. 82–82v, speech on pretermitted customs, April 28, 1624; *A Treatise of the Rights of the Crown, Declaring how the King of England may Support and Increase his Annual Revenue*. [London, 1715].)

of criticism they had perforce to rely upon support from the crown, and the King in turn required their assistance. Typical of this group of Royalists was Sir Arthur Ingram, merchant, courtier, investor in crown lands and patentee of the alum works, who in 1624 was returned for both York City and Old Sarum. He was joined in the House by his son, Sir Arthur Ingram, Jr., who represented Appleby, Westmoreland, his father's constituency in 1621. Another merchant courtier was elected at Tewkesbury, Gloucestershire: Sir Baptist Hicks, purveyor of silk and mercery to the court and creditor of the King. Sir Hugh Middleton, one of the King's jewelers and lessee of the mines royal in Cardiganshire, represented the Welsh borough of Denbigh. He was, moreover, in partnership with the King in the New River Company and in 1624 was seeking parliamentary confirmation of the company's privileges. John Jacob, who was elected at Plimpton, Devonshire, was probably the member of Parliament most intimately concerned with the defense of the prerogative. Since 1618 he had been joined with his father, Abraham Jacob, in a life patent for the collection of impositions on tobacco. He was, moreover, secretary to the Lord Treasurer and was in danger of being questioned when Cranfield's relations with the customers were being investigated.[21]

Mutual interest and identity of policy were the twin mainstays of royal patronage which, in the past, had made it of formidable consequence. The strength of the Tudor monarchs was largely due to their ability to personify the will of their subjects and to marshal their supporters to express that will in a public assembly. But in 1624 the identity between King and people was lost. In the domestic sphere the desire for strong government was in danger of being replaced by a demand for legal guarantees against oppression. In the field of foreign policy the cleavage was

21. George Mynne, member for West Looe, Cornwall, had his patent as clerk of the hanaper called in by the House of Commons after a petition was filed against it on April 23. (Pym, fol. 78; D'Ewes, fol. 111v.) Mansell's glass monopoly and Vane's patent of the subpoena office were specifically exempted from the penalties and prohibitions of the bill of monopolies by the House of Commons on May 1, 1624. (Pym, fol. 86.) For further arguments on exceptions to the bill, see Pym, fols. 71v–72, 77v. The report of the Lord Treasurer on March 11, 1624, listed Sir Baptist Hicks, Sir William Cockayne, and Sir Peter van Lore as creditors of the King in the amount of thirty thousand pounds. (Harl. MS. 159, fol. 32v.) In Keeler, *Long Parliament*, 231, it is stated that John Jacob was elected to his first Parliament in the spring of 1640. To confirm Jacob's membership in the House of Commons for 1624, see Holles, fol. 125.

complete, and the outcry for war submerged James's desire for
peace. It was possible in such a situation to use crown patronage
in contravention of the King's wishes, and to implement their
policy Charles and Buckingham were prepared to risk the consequences.

The newly won popularity of the Prince and the favorite, combined with widespread anti-Spanish sentiment, seemed to indicate
that little difficulty would be encountered in obtaining a tractable
Parliament. The Prince did his utmost to assure the return of his
partisans, but, despite his best efforts, he was frequently disappointed.[22] As Duke of Cornwall, Charles held vast properties in a
county that returned forty-four members, a county traditionally
very susceptible to outside influence. Thus, in January letters from
the Prince's council were sent to William Roscarrock, His Highness's escheator for the duchy, recommending one candidate to
each of thirteen Cornish boroughs.[23] Although Charles expected

22. HMC, *Mar and Kellie*, 191, Thomas, earl of Kellie, to John, earl of Mar,
Feb. 5, 1624; *Cal. S. P. Venetian*, XVIII, 216–219, Valaresso to the Doge and Senate,
Feb. 6/16, 1624; Chamberlain, *Letters*, II, 543, letter of Jan. 31, 1624.
23. Duchy of Cornwall MS. "Prince Charles in Spain," fols. 33–33v, the Prince's
council to William Roscarrock, Jan. 1, 1623/4. I am indebted to Miss Mary Coate
for directing my attention to the important series of patronage letters in the duchy
of Cornwall Office and for transcriptions of several documents. Subsequently Professor J. K. Gruenfelder provided me with specific references to additional duchy
manuscripts. Patronage letters are extant for the Parliaments of 1621, 1624, and the
Short and Long Parliaments. Since nominations were made in behalf of the Prince
as Duke of Cornwall, it may be that none were written from the date of Charles's
accession to the crown until the first Parliament subsequent to the birth of the
future Charles II. Patronage in Cornwall was undoubtedly facilitated by the custom of returning individual indentures for each M.P. — a practice unique in that
county. Contemporary awareness of electoral influence in Cornwall is displayed by
Sir Edward Peyton, M.P. for Cambridgeshire in 1624, in his "The Divine Catastrophe of the Kingly Family of the House of Stuarts" published in 1652 and reprinted in Sir Walter Scott, ed., *The Secret History of the Court of James the First*
(2 vols., Edinburgh, 1811), II, 435–436; see also 444. "So likewise the King by his
power, and the great Lords of the court made courtiers, burgesses, and some times
knight of the shire by letters; who hindered much the proceedings in parliament by
their vote, it being the policy of the Dukes of Cornwall in the Stannaries to have
multitude of burgesses, to make themselves potent in parliament; which now the
parliament will prevent, by providing that the representative may be equally
chosen from all parts." (*Ibid.*, II, 436.) The classic case of interference in Cornish
elections on behalf of the crown occurred in 1628 when the candidacy of Sir John
Eliot and William Coryton was opposed by royalist deputy lieutenants and gentlemen
by letters sent to candidates and electors alike. Coryton and Eliot were urged to
stand down because "his Majesty will conceive your election to be an affront to
his service." Knights of the shire acceptable to the King and county would, in the
estimation of the deputy lieutenants, be able to procure ships, salt, a magazine,
conduct money and relief from the billeting of soldiers, all of which were to be

"not to be disappointed herein," only five nominees were elected as recommended; Sir Richard Weston for Bossiney, Sir John Walter for East Looe, Sir Thomas Trevor for Saltash, Sir Francis Crane for Launceston, and William Noy for Fowey. Weston was virtually unknown to his constituents, but Walter, as the Prince's attorney, and Trevor, as his solicitor, were familiar to duchy tenants. Crane, recently sworn of the Prince's council, had served Cornish boroughs in two previous Parliaments; an East Anglian by birth, he had developed good connections in the West-Country through the marriages of his sisters. Attorney William Noy supplemented his London practice by "usurping" the stewardship of Penwith and Kerrier Hundreds, thus reinforcing his native ties. Three times previously he had represented Cornish constituencies and, like Walter and Trevor, had been included in the list of Charles's nominations in 1621.[24]

Two of the Prince's dependents were returned for towns other than those to which they had been recommended: Thomas Carey, groom of the Prince's bedchamber, son of Lord Lepington, the Prince's chamberlain, was nominated for Grampound, but returned for Helston; Sir John Hobart, son of the Prince's chancellor, Sir Henry Hobart, was presented for election at West Looe, but returned for Lostwithiel. Thus, of the thirteen designated candidates, seven were successful in obtaining Cornish seats. At least one privy councillor was among those rejected. Sir Julius Caesar, Master of the Rolls, failed in his bid for a seat at St. Ives and never sat in the Commons although his services were utilized among the learned counsel in the House of Lords. Sir John Suckling, Comptroller of the Household, was suggested for election at Camelford, and it is by no means certain that the place was denied

---

requested by petition. (Harl. MS. 4771, fol. 12v, a manuscript diary of the Parliament of 1628, Mar. 17 to May 27.)

24. Sir Francis Crane was sworn of the Prince's council in April 1623 in response to explicit instructions from Charles to his council. (Duchy of Cornwall MS. "Prince Charles in Spain," Prince Charles to his council, Mar. 28, 1623; see also Duchy of Cornwall MS. "Privy Seals, Etc. 1617–1641," fols. 41–42.) On February 13, 1624, Sir Arthur Gorge lodged a complaint before the Prince's council in which he claimed the stewardship of Penwith and Kerrier hundreds and accused Noy of usurpation. On February 18 the council deferred action because of Noy's absence; he had "gone into the western country." (Duchy of Cornwall Ms. "Acts of the Council 1622–1623.") In 1620 Noy was recommended by the Prince's council to the corporation of Fowey, but was returned by the borough of Helston. (Duchy of Cornwall MS. "Letters and Patents 1620–1621," fol. 39v, the Prince's council to William Roscarrock, Dec. 1, 1620.)

him. On January 30 the Prince's council took note of Suckling's election as knight of the shire for Middlesex and provided for the choice of Sir Francis Cottington at Camelford if Suckling had also been returned for that borough. On February 10, two days before the Parliament was scheduled to open, Cottington's indenture was sealed.[25]

The most interesting nomination made by the Prince's council was the designation of Sir Thomas Crew, serjeant-at-law, for Helston. He was the brother of Sir Ranulph Crew, King's serjeant, and had himself only attained the rank of serjeant-at-law on October 23, 1623. Crew had long been *persona non grata* with King James, and his opposition to the Spanish match, combined with his vindication of parliamentary privilege, had resulted in his inclusion on the commission of inquiry sent to Ireland after the Parliament of 1621. Now, in 1624, the bellwether of those members who had "prostituted the Prince's marriage" during the last session was recommended for a safe seat. Although Crew was rejected by the electorate, a place was found for him at Aylesbury in Buckinghamshire, a borough firmly in the control of the Packington family.[26]

The letter to William Roscarrock demonstrates several characteristics typical of crown patronage. Obviously the greatest importance was attached to the return of high governmental officials, either members of the Privy Council or eligible members of the Prince's council. Minor courtiers and household servants, recognizably dependent on the patron, also figured largely in the list of recommendations. A third group was made up of those

25. Duchy of Cornwall MS. "Acts of the Council 1622 and 1623," fol. 353, Jan. 30, 1623/4.

26. Chamberlain, *Letters*, II, 536, letter of Jan. 3, 1624, notes that "Sir Randall Crew is in speech to be speaker." I suspect that Chamberlain mistook Sir Ranulph for his brother. Particular interest seems to have centered around the election at Helston, for there is a note in Conway's letterbook (SP 14/158/8) of a letter sent to the mayor of Helston for procuring a burgess' place although the name of the candidate is not specified. Helston was distinctly a patronage borough with the Godolphins having the predominant influence. Although Sir Thomas Crew was rejected, the two members returned were acceptable to the Prince. Thomas Carey may have been viewed more favorably by the electors of Helston because of his family connections with the Trevanians and through them with the Roscarrocks. The other member, Francis Carew, was the son and heir of George, Lord Carew, privy councillor and master of the ordnance, by Thomasine, daughter of Sir Francis Godolphin. Packington influence at Aylesbury is discussed in Browne Willis, *Notitia Parliamentaria* (3 vols., London, 1715–1750), I, 110–111.

seemingly independent men of reputation whose services could prove useful in the coming session. Finally means were found to gratify the ambitions of the sons, relatives, and friends of high dignitaries.

Actual recommendations, however, do not account for the total number of the Prince's followers elected in Cornwall. Naturally some country gentlemen who had court connections or who were royalist by persuasion needed no recommendation in order to secure places. Typical of this group were Sir Robert Killigrew (Penryn), and Sir Richard Edgcombe and John Mohun (Grampound). There were also some duchy officials whose work, interests, and estates so familiarized them with the county as to virtually assure their return. Thus, the two auditors of the duchy, William Hockmore and Thomas Gewen, represented St. Mawes and Bossiney, respectively.[27]

The duchy of Cornwall, the Prince's ancient inheritance, was his patronage preserve *par excellence,* but the augmentation of his estates by the grant of additional lands and revenues in 1616, 1619, and 1620 provided new opportunities for influencing borough electorates. In 1621 Charles had tested his credit with the corporations of Chester and Pontefract, but in 1624 thirty pounds was allocated to the three messengers who carried his nomination letters throughout England. The feodaries of the Prince's honors, the stewards of his manors, the clerks of his courts, and even the Lord President of the Council of Wales were pressed into service as intermediaries through whom various corporations were in-

27. In 1624 Sir Robert Killigrew was apparently in charge of the fortifications of the Cornish castles of Pendennis, St. Mawes, and St. Michaels. See *APC 1623–1625,* 358, Nov. 12, 1624; also Harl. MS. 354, fol. 207, and *Walter Yonge's Diary,* 108. Sir Robert sat for St. Mawes in 1601, for Newport in 1604, for Helston in 1614 and 1621, for Penryn in 1624, for Cornwall in 1625, for Tregony in 1626, and for Bodmin in 1628. According to Sir James Whitelocke (*Liber Famelicus,* 41), "My worthy friend Sir Robert Kylligrew gave me a place for Helston, in the countye of Cornwall and I cawsed my brother-in-law, Henrye Bowstred, to be retorned for that place." This seat was delivered in 1614 and indicates the family interest in Cornish boroughs in this period. On the activities of Sir Richard Edgcombe and John Mohun in connection with the elections in Cornwall in 1628, see John Forster, *Sir John Eliot* (2 vols., London, 1865), II, 106–112, 275–280; see also HMC, *First Report,* Appendix (London, 1870), 51, Trelawny MSS; *ibid.,* 62, Harvey MSS. Both Thomas Gewen and William Hockmore held life patents as auditors of the duchy of Cornwall, dated July 17, 1622. (Duchy of Cornwall MS. "Enrollment of Patents Etc., Prince Charles 1620–1625," fols. 109–112.)

formed of the Prince's "care that the king and state be served of worthy and fit burgesses" and of his recommendations of gentlemen "of approved sufficiency and integrity, as befits the judgment and sincerity of him that commends them, and against whom there can be no cause of any exception." [28]

In Yorkshire the acquisition of the honors of Knaresborough and Pontefract and the manor of Beverley induced Charles to nominate one burgess to each of five corporations. The borough of Beverley, currently in the process of renegotiating its charter and the expansion of its privileges, was reluctant to offend the Prince's council and consequently acceded to the nomination of Sir Henry Vane and his replacement by Sir Henry Carey when Vane chose to serve for Carlisle. Pontefract willingly accepted Sir Henry Holcroft as its first member, but, when Holcroft elected to serve for Stockbridge, Pontefract refused to name Robert Mynne as his successor. The by-election degenerated into a contest between two Yorkshire knights, Sir John Jackson and Sir Richard Beaumont. The influence of local gentry in the former duchy towns of Knaresborough, Aldborough, and Boroughbridge also precluded the implementation of the Prince's desires. At Knaresborough Sir Arthur Mainwaring, even with the Prince's

28. Crown lands were alienated to Prince Charles by indentures and charters of January 10, 1616, February 19, 1616, October 11, 1619, February 2, 1620. Not only were the Prince's revenues substantially increased by these grants from the King, but Charles also acquired parliamentary patronage. The Yorkshire properties alone included the honor, lordship, castle, and forest of Knaresborough, the manor and town of Aldborough, the borough and bailiwick of Boroughbridge, the honor of Pontefract and the manor of Beverley. In Suffolk Charles held the honors of Eye and Clare; in Worcestershire, the manor and lordship of Bewdley; in Warwickshire, the manor of Warwick; in Devon, the fee farm of Plymouth; in Hertfordshire, the honor, castle, lordship, and manor of Hertford. Possessions in Christchurch (Hampshire), Exeter (Devon), Dorchester (Dorset), Woodstock (Oxfordshire), and Wallingford and Reading (Berkshire) provided other opportunities for patronage, but apparently no evidence survives of recommendations to these constituencies. The Prince's pretensions at Chester were based upon his hereditary earldom of Chester and his right to the fee farm of the city. (Duchy of Cornwall MS. "Charters, Prince Charles," passim; Duchy of Cornwall MS. "Letters and Patents 1620–1621," fol. 98, the Prince's council to Sir Henry Savile, Mar. 29, 1621.) The initial recommendation to Chester in favor of Sir Henry Carey was made through the Earl of Northampton, Lord President of the Council of Wales on December 17, 1620. After Carey was returned for Hertfordshire, Sir Thomas Edmondes was recommended as an alternate candidate by letters from Sir Thomas Trevor, the Prince's solicitor, to Sir Randall Mainwaring and Edward Whitby, recorder of Chester. (Harl. MS. 2105, fols. 275, 277–278.) The warrant for payment to the Prince's messengers is contained in Duchy of Cornwall MS. "Prince Charles in Spain," fol. 36v.

backing, could not challenge the influence of the Slingsbys and the Huttons. At Aldborough William Peasley, servant to Secretary Calvert, stood little chance against Christopher Wandesford; the remaining seat was already destined for John Carvill, legal representative of the town. Boroughbridge did elect one alien, Philip Mainwaring, of an established Cheshire family, but it neglected the Prince's nominee, Sir Edmund Verney, in favor of Ferdinand Fairfax.[29]

The modest success of the Prince in securing the return of his Yorkshire nominees illustrates the increasing reluctance of corporations to elect aliens in competition with entrenched members of the local gentry. Indeed, as Christopher Pepper, recorder of Richmond, noted in 1621, neither his twenty years service to the

29. The recommendation of Sir Henry Vane to Beverley was conveyed by John Cartwright, feodary of the honor of Pontefract, but the nomination of Sir Henry Carey was made directly by letter from the Prince's council to the mayor and burgesses of the town. (Duchy of Cornwall MS. "Prince Charles in Spain," fols. 34, 39v.) The proceedings in reference to the renegotiation of Beverley's privileges are entered in Duchy of Cornwall MS. "Acts of the Council 1622 and 1623: Prince Charles." Sir Henry Carey should not be confused with Sir Henry Carey, Viscount Falkland, Lord Deputy of Ireland; see W. C. Metcalfe, *A Book of Knights* (London, 1885), 168; *Visitations of Hertfordshire*, Harleian Society, Volume XXII (London, 1886), 136–137; *Cal. S. P. Dom. 1623–1625*, 554. Holcroft's recommendation to Pontefract was also conveyed via John Cartwright as was that of his prospective replacement, Robert Mynne. (Duchy of Cornwall MS. "Prince Charles in Spain," fols. 34, 39.) The franchise in both Knaresborough and Aldborough was vested in the burgage holders. In Aldborough there appear to have been nine old burgage tenants, but the number in Knaresborough was considerably larger. The Aldborough return in 1624 was signed by seven of the old burgagers; in the 1628 election at Knaresborough, Fox had twenty-two votes and Slingsby twenty, but there were apparently eighty-eight burgage houses in the borough. The purchase of blocks of burgages by local families like the Slingsbys and the Bensons tended to nullify outside influence. See W. A. Atkinson, "A Parliamentary Election in Knaresborough in 1628," *Yorkshire Archeological Journal*, XXXIV (1938–1939), 213–221. William Peasley may have been the Mr. Peasley recommended to the corporation of Southampton by Henry Sherfield when he chose to serve for Salisbury. Certainly Peasley was unknown to the electorate of Southampton, and while they were initially receptive to his nomination "yet now upon further deliberation considering the present estate of the town, needing one that is well acquainted therewith, and that if we should elect a stranger we must nevertheless send up a solicitor for the town which would be chargeable, we think it therefore more convenient to make choice of one of our own company who may supply the place of burgess and of solicitor also." (Jervoise family MS., Mayor and Aldermen of Southampton to Henry Sherfield, Feb. 15, 1623/4.) The successful candidate at Boroughbridge, Philip Mainwaring, was also recommended in 1624 to the electorate of Steyning, Sussex. This nomination by the Earl of Arundel and Surrey was refused. (H. A. Merewether and A. J. Stephens, *The History of the Boroughs* [3 vols., London, 1835], III, 1513–1514, Thomas Howard, earl of Arundel and Surrey, to the borough of Steyning, Jan. 9, 1623/4.)

borough nor nominations by Secretary Calvert and the President of the Council of the North were of any avail against the inducements offered by Sir Thomas Wharton.[30]

However much the council's letters emphasized the Prince's expectations "not to be disappointed," an awareness of the probability of rejection is apparent in the recommendations. Sir Francis Cottington's name was submitted to the corporations of Chester, Warwick, and Bury St. Edmunds in 1624, but only Camelford chose him as its representative. Chester elected their recorder in partnership with the brother of Sir Thomas Savage, while Warwick accepted the nomination of Sir Edward Conway, Jr., backed by Lord Brooke, and joined him with a scion of the Lucy family. Initially, Bury St. Edmunds had seemed receptive to Cottington's candidacy and expressed a willingness to abandon Sir Thomas Jermyn in favor of the Prince's secretary, but when Charles assumed that Cottington and Jermyn would serve in tandem he was rebuffed by the corporation who returned Jermyn and Anthony Crofts. Elsewhere in Suffolk the Prince was more successful. Francis Finch, his nominee to the corporation of Eye, was returned without incident. In Worcestershire there was a happy coincidence between the Prince's nomination and local considerations. Ralph Clare of His Highness's privy chamber was returned for Bewdley where he was lessee of the manor from the crown. However, more populous and prosperous corporations ignored the Prince's requests. Both Plymouth, Devonshire, and Coventry in Warwickshire elected their recorders, John Glanville and Sir Edward Coke, and provided them with partners from their merchant oligarchies. Plymouth slighted the nomination of the Prince's councillor, Sir Richard Smyth, just as Coventry neglected Sir Thomas Edmondes.[31]

On January 31 Edmondes was also nominated to the town of St. Albans, and a previous recommendation of John Maynard was revoked. Since Edmondes was "as yet unprovided for," the Prince interceded with the Earl of Salisbury and the Viscount St. Alban to procure his election, but the Earl steadfastly supported John Luke, and the other seat went to Sir Arthur Capel, Jr.

30. Harl. MS. 7000, fol. 41, Christopher Pepper to Sir Henry Savile, Jan. 8, 1620/1.
31. Duchy of Cornwall MS. "Prince Charles in Spain," fols. 33v, 34v–36.

Elsewhere in Hertfordshire the Prince was no more successful. He and his council assisted in the restoration of the borough of Hertford to its parliamentary franchise, but the newly revived seats went to Thomas Fanshawe and William Ashton, a nominee of the Earl of Salisbury. It may be that the election of Fanshawe served the Prince's interest, for on January 27 Thomas Fanshawe, Esq., was sworn as the Prince's surveyor general.[32]

The conflict between princely and peerage influence in Hertfordshire, if such there was, seems not to have excited mutual animosity. In fact, the Robert Mynne who was nominated to Pontefract as a replacement for Henry Holcroft was recommended "at the suit of the Earl of Salisbury to the Prince's Highness." It is apparant, therefore, that unwillingness to return Charles's nominees did not always imply opposition to his person and policies. An M.P. like John Savage of Chester could be expected, because of his brother's connections with the Prince's household, to be amenable to princely influence.[33]

The Prince's most assiduous efforts were reserved for the boroughs on or near his estates, but his close associates and adherents sat for constituencies scattered all over England. In many instances some connection can be made between a representative and the locality for which he served, either through birth, property, office, previous parliamentary service or legal employment. Oc-

32. *Ibid.*, fols. 34v, 37–38v, 40. The revocation of the Prince's recommendation of John Maynard to the borough of St. Albans on Jan. 31, 1624, may be explained by Maynard's election at Chippenham on January 21, to which borough he had been recommended by his brother Lord Maynard. In both returns filed by the contending factions in Chippenham, John Maynard's name was erased, and the name of his brother Charles substituted. Apparently this was done at the request of Lord Maynard who was under the impression that John had been elected elsewhere. Consequently, before John could gain admission to the Commons he was forced to appear before the Committee of Privileges and allege that a mistake had been made in the indentures. Sir Edward Baynton's involvement in the fraudulent alteration of the returns was not mentioned in Glanville's report from the Committee of Privileges on March 12 when, by order of the House of Commons, John's election was upheld. The Chippenham election case is treated in *CJ*, 684, 759; Pym, fols. 27v, 54v; Harl. MS. 6806 (Alford Papers), fol. 262; Glanville, *Reports*, 47–62; Hawarde, 168–169.

33. Duchy of Cornwall MS. "Acts of the Council 1622 and 1623: Prince Charles," fol. 374v, Feb. 18, 1623/4. In 1620 Sir Thomas Savage requested the corporation of Chester to elect his brother John as their representative to Parliament. (Harl. MS. 2105, fol. 285, Sir Thomas Savage to the Mayor of Chester, Nov. 12, 1620.) This recommendation by Savage was ignored, but his elevation to the Prince's council in January 1622 may have increased his influence at Chester in subsequent elections.

casionally, however, no apparent reason is evident for the return of a member. Several of the Prince's councillors procured their own election or were instrumental in promoting the return of relatives. Sir Oliver Cromwell of Hinchingbrooke, master of His Highness's game, was chosen knight of the shire for Huntingdonshire. The Prince's cofferer, Sir Henry Vane, was double returned for Carlisle, Cumberland, and Beverley, Yorkshire. When Vane chose to sit for Carlisle, a constituency he had served before, his nominated successor at Beverley was Sir Henry Carey, eldest son of Robert, Lord Lepington, the Prince's chamberlain. The comptroller of the Prince's household, John, Lord Vaughan, also had close relatives in the House of Commons: his son, Richard, represented Carmarthanshire; his brother, Henry, sat for Carmarthan borough. Sir James Ley, Lord Chief Justice and councillor to the Prince, likewise had a son in the House. Sir Henry Ley represented what was virtually the family borough of Westbury in Wiltshire. Thomas, Viscount Andover, the Prince's master of the horse relinquished his former seat at Cricklade, Wiltshire to his brother, Sir William Howard.[34]

Minor officials of the Prince's household also competed for parliamentary places. Nathaniel Tomkins, clerk of the Prince's council, was returned for Ilchester, Somerset, and Christchurch, Hampshire, and, since he preferred the latter borough, he was succeeded at Ilchester by his brother-in-law, Edmund Waller.

34. Mark Noble, *Memoirs of the Protectorate House of Cromwell* (2d ed., 2 vols., Birmingham, 1787), I, 37–50. In 1624 Cromwell was negotiating for the sale of his Hinchingbrooke estate which he had offered to the King for purchase. Cromwell prestige in Huntingdon was fading because, as he himself noted, "his creditors are pressing, and his friends begin to think him out of favour." (*Cal. S. P. Dom. 1623–1625*, 561.) At least one member of the Ley family had represented Westbury in every Parliament since 1598. On November 3, 1616, a marriage settlement was arranged by which the Westbury properties of Sir James Ley were transferred to Henry Ley, preserving a life interest to Sir James. (British Record Society, Index Library, *Abstracts of Wiltshire Inquisitiones Post Mortem Returned into the Court of Chancery in the Reign of King Charles the First* [hereafter cited as *I.P.M. Wiltshire*] [London, 1901], 268–273, inquisition taken after Sir Henry's death in 1638.) Thomas Howard, Viscount Andover and earl of Berkshire, was the second son and Sir William Howard was the sixth son of the Earl of Suffolk. (John Nichols, *The Progresses, Processions, and Magnificent Festivities of King James the First* [3 vols. in 4, London, 1828], III, 220.) The *I.P.M. Wiltshire*, 166, implies that Cricklade was entirely controlled by the Viscount Andover inasmuch as in 1633 it mentions some properties that "are held of Thomas, Earl of Berkshire, in free burgage, as of his borough of Cricklade." Thomas Howard, who bought the viscountcy of Andover from Buckingham was seated at Charleton, Wiltshire. (Chamberlain, *Letters*, II, 421, letter of Jan. 19, 1622.)

Francis Nicholls, clerk of the Prince's Court of Wards and Liveries and receiver of his revenues in the counties of Buckingham and Bedford, was returned in a by-election at Preston, Lancashire.[35]

The appearance of several of the Prince's clients as representatives of duchy towns, together with the apparent coincidence in several nominations made by the duchy of Lancaster and the Prince's council may indicate high-level collusion in the exercise of patronage, but it is likely that the initiative rested chiefly with the candidates who, in their search for places, appealed to a variety of patrons.

Most numerous of the Prince's servants sitting in the House of Commons in 1624 were the gentlemen of his privy chamber. Some of them were intimately associated with the boroughs they represented: Ralph Clare was resident at Bewdley, and Sir Edmund Verney, seated at Claydon, was well known to the electorate of Buckingham. However, some gentlemen of the privy chamber were alien to their constituencies. As already noted, Sir William Howard probably owed his seat at Cricklade to his brother, Viscount Andover. Charles Glemham of Suffolk was as little likely to be familiar to the electors of Newcastle-under-Lyme, Staffordshire, as the Essex soldier, Sir Edward Vere, whom he replaced. It is even doubtful whether the Welsh courtier, Sir Richard Wynn, was personally acquainted with the corporation of Ilchester, Somerset, despite the fact that he had served that borough in the previous Parliament. Sir Robert Carr, who succeeded the deceased John Packington, Jr., as representative for the Packington family borough of Aylesbury, Buckinghamshire, likewise appears to have had no local connections.[36]

35. In his speech prior to his execution on July 5, 1643, Tomkins attributed his conspiratorial actions to "Affection to a Brother-in-law, and Affection and Gratitude to the King, whose Bread I have eaten now above 22 Years (I have been a Servant to him 20 Years, I have been a Servant to him when he was Prince, and ever since, it will be 23 Years in August next)." (Rushworth, *Historical Collections*, V, 326; see also *Cabala*, I, 244.)

36. Clare seems to have maintained good relations with the corporation of Bewdley: "Paid to Mr. Ralph Clare, his servant for his pains in bringing the buck which he bestowed on the bailiff and burgesses 1624 00 05 00." (J. R. Burton, *A History of Bewdley; with Concise Accounts of Some Neighbouring Parishes* [London, 1883], Appendix, xxv.) Microfilms of the Verney papers preserved at Claydon House, Middle Claydon, Buckinghamshire, are on deposit in the British Museum. Only a few papers have relevance for Sir Edmund Verney's career before 1635; most of the manuscripts deal with the period between 1635 and 1715. The

Two of the Prince's minor attendants secured election in areas far afield from their native counties. Thomas Reynell, member of a family prominent in Devonshire and at court, cupbearer to Prince Charles, was chosen member of Parliament for Morpeth, Northumberland. Thomas Jermyn, Jr., who had served Prince Charles as a page during the Spanish journey, filled a vacancy created when Sir Thomas Cheeke opted to serve for Essex county instead of Berealston, Devon. Jermyn's father, Sir Thomas Jermyn, was a man of importance in Suffolk, a courtier of some note and a partisan of the Prince and Buckingham. He had represented Bury St. Edmunds in 1621 and was reelected to the Parliament in 1624 with the Prince's blessing.[37]

---

*Official Return,* 460, incorrectly assigns Vere's death to 1624. Vere was mortally wounded on August 18, 1629, at Bois le Duc. (*DNB,* LVIII, 238.) Vere's election at Newcastle-under-Lyme was nullified by the House of Commons on April 9, and Charles Glemham was returned in the subsequent by-election. See Glanville, *Reports,* 76–79, and Thomas Pape, *Newcastle-under-Lyme in Tudor and Early Stuart Times* (Manchester: Manchester University Press, 1938), 265–266. At Ilchester the high steward was Sir Robert Phelips who had succeeded to that position when his father, Sir Edward Phelips, died in 1615. Although the bailiffs of Ilchester were apt to intrigue with Sir Robert's enemies, there is no doubt that his influence dominated the borough. The election of two courtiers from Ilchester in 1624, tends to confirm the connection between Phelips and the Prince-Buckingham faction in this Parliament. In Keeler, *Long Parliament,* 402, Pembroke is credited with securing Sir Richard Wynn's return in 1621, 1624, and 1625. Defeated in the Carnarvonshire election in 1621, Wynn sought nomination at Pontefract and at Ilchester. At Pontefract he relied on the support of Lord Darcy; he had married into the Darcy family in 1618. (Evangeline de Villiers, "Parliamentary Boroughs Restored by the House of Commons 1621–41," *English Historical Review,* LXVII (Apr. 1952), 175–202, esp. 188. Sir Richard Wynn's attitude toward parliamentary service is indicated by his remark to his brother Henry (knight for Merionethshire in 1624) that "the burden need not be great, for he need not attend more than he will after his first appearance." (A. H. Dodd, "Wales's Parliamentary Apprenticeship (1536–1625)," *Transactions of the Honourable Society of Cymmrodorion* (Session 1942), 8–72, esp. 60. Sir Robert Carr is identified by Pink as a gentleman of the bedchamber to both Prince Henry and Prince Charles. After the coronation of Charles, Carr became Keeper of the Privy Purse and, on June 24, 1633, he was created Earl of Ancram, Lord Kerr of Nisbelten. (Pink Papers, English MS. 299, fol. 412, John Rylands Library.)

37. Patronage at Berealston was in the hands of the Blount family, specifically Mountjoy Blount, who was created Earl of Newport by Charles I. Mountjoy Blount was the illegitimate son of Charles Blount, earl of Devonshire, by Penelope Rich. The member originally elected for Berealston, Sir Thomas Cheeke, married Essex Rich and thus was the brother-in-law of Mountjoy Blount. Cheeke was not only returned for Berealston in 1624, but also in 1625 and for the Long Parliament. No definite connection can be established between Jermyn and the Blounts. Sir William Strode also had influence at Berealston, and it is possible, though not probable, that he may have been involved in Jermyn's nomination there. (J. J. Alexander, "Bere-Alston as a Parliamentary Borough," *Report and Transactions of the Devonshire Association for the Advancement of Science, Literature and Art,* XLI (1909), 152–179.)

From the size of the Prince's contingent in the House of Commons in 1624, it is evident that Charles and his council spared no effort in promoting the election of their partisans. Undoubtedly the most important candidates were urged to try their personal credit with constituencies other than those to which they had been nominated. Thus, in the event of double returns the way was paved for the recommendation and election of a candidate of lesser repute in those boroughs which had shown themselves most susceptible to influence. The number of the Prince's supporters who were returned at by-elections makes it apparent that the interest in patronage was sustained even beyond the actual parliamentary session. The invasion of areas of patronage not normally open to Charles lends added significance to the observation made by the Cornishman Arthur Harris: "The Prince's letters, I think, have disappointed many for some towns were before unsolicited by them." [38]

The patronage exercised by the Prince of Wales paralleled that wielded by the Duke of Buckingham. The identity of their policies and interests in the Parliament of 1624 virtually guaranteed that the servant of the one would be a partisan of the other. Yet Buckingham's influence, despite his multiple offices, is more difficult to detect with precision because most of his power had no territorial basis. During his rapid rise to his preeminent position as James's favorite, Buckingham had concentrated on building a party at court through the control of royal grants of offices, lands, and pensions. He was particularly devoted to the interests of his kindred and was instrumental in promoting their social and financial ambitions. He attempted to consolidate his position by a system of marriage alliances that united the Villiers clan with some of the most powerful families in England.

The social stratum in which his operations were most evident was the peerage, and his influence can be detected in many of the Jacobean creations.[39] The favorite's profligate brother, Chris-

38. SP 14/158/47, Arthur Harris to John Verney, Jan. 25, 1624.
39. Early in Buckingham's career, Chamberlain noted his partiality toward his relatives. See *Letters*, II, 52, letter of Feb. 8, 1617, where he writes: "I cannot but commend that Lords goode disposition in dooing goode to his kindred and frends: though some riming companions do not forbeare to taxe him for yt, as one by way of a prognostication says:

> Above in the skies shall Gemini rise,
> And Twins the court shall pester,

topher, was made Earl of Anglesey, and his half-witted brother, John, was given a seat in the House of Lords as Viscount Purbeck. William, Lord Fielding, husband of Buckingham's sister Susan, was made Earl of Denbigh and Master of the Wardrobe. Buckingham's half brothers, William and Edward, were married into the established families of Fiennes and St. John, while his half sister, Elizabeth, sealed his alliance with the Botelers. A double marriage united the Comptons and the Villiers and the first of these undoubtedly was instrumental in obtaining the presidency of the Council of Wales for William Compton, earl of Northampton. Buckingham himself had made a brilliant marriage with Katherine Manners, heiress apparent of the Earl of Rutland.[40]

Lesser kinswomen of the Duke were used as political pawns in securing the adherence of Lionel Cranfield, earl of Middlesex; Henry Montagu, Viscount Mandeville; and James, Marquess Hamilton.[41] Needless to say, under the stress of political condi-

----

George shall call up his brother Jacke [John]
And Jacke his brother Kester [Christopher]."

Charges of engrossing offices and advancing his unworthy kindred were leveled against Buckingham in the Parliament of 1626. The Duke was also sensitive to criticism regarding new creations of peerages. In 1620 this occasioned a dispute between Buckingham, the Marquess Hamilton, and the Earl of Arundel about "selling of honors and abasing auncient nobilitie, by new advancements, wherein the Lord of Buckingam tooke himselfe to be aimed at, and so tooke exceptions. (*Ibid.*, II, 286 letter of Jan. 25, 1620; Sir Simonds D'Ewes, *The Autobiography and Correspondence of Sir Simonds D'Ewes* [2 vols., London, 1845], I, 80–81, 388.)

40. Sir William Villiers married, as his second wife, Anne, daughter of Richard Fiennes, Lord Saye. Sir Edward Villiers married Barbara, daughter of Sir John St. John, of Lydiard Tregoze, Wiltshire. Elizabeth Villiers married Sir John Boteler of Higham, Bedfordshire, who was created Lord Boteler of Brantfield in 1628. Buckingham's mother was created Countess of Buckingham on July 1, 1618. She married as her second husband Sir Thomas Compton, brother of William, earl of Northampton. Throughout his life, Sir Thomas remained "a bare knight." Spencer, Lord Compton, son of the Earl of Northampton, married Mary Beaumont, Buckingham's cousin. (*Visitation of Leicestershire*, Harleian Society, Volume II [London, 1870], 29–31; Chamberlain, *Letters*, II, 105, letter of Oct. 18, 1617; 162–163, letter of Aug. 8, 1618; 402, letter of Oct. 20, 1621.)

41. In February 1619 it was rumored that Cranfield would marry Ann, widow of Lord Effingham (William Howard), but on January 8, 1620, his installation as a privy councillor was attributed partially to his marriage to Ann Brett, Buckingham's cousin, a marriage for which Cranfield "had noe great fancy." (Chamberlain, *Letters*, II, 210, letter of Feb. 6, 1619; 281, letter of Jan. 8, 1620.) Edward Montagu, son of Viscount Mandeville, married Buckingham's cousin, Susan Hill. (*Ibid.*, II, 476, letter of Feb. 10, 1623.) James, the son of James, second Marquess Hamilton, married Mary, daughter of William Fielding, earl of Denbigh, and niece of Buckingham. (*Ibid.*, II, 441, letter of June 22, 1622.) Marquess Hamilton, as a Scotsman, showed more signs of independence than most peers closely associated with Buckingham. In March 1620 it was reported that he was made a gentleman of the King's bed-

tions, the loyalty engendered by these marriages was vitiated by expediency. This is clearly evident in the case of Lionel Cranfield in the Parliament of 1624, as it had been earlier when the marriage of Frances Coke with John Villiers failed to secure the restitution of Sir Edward Coke to his former position of favor.[42]

Royal favorites of the second rank were also included in Buckingham's train; James Hay, earl of Carlisle, and Henry Rich, Lord Kensington, were recognizably subservient.[43] Kensington, whose absence from the Parliament of 1624 was caused by his employment in the renewed marriage negotiations with France, delivered his proxy to the Duke. Five other peers gave Buckingham custody of their votes: the Earls of Bath and Cumberland, Viscount Pur-

chamber without the "privity" of Buckingham. (*Ibid.*, II, 297, letter of Mar. 20, 1620.) The Earl of Kellie, however, stated that "the Marquis of Hamilton is much made of both by his Majesty and Buckingham." (HMC, *Mar and Kellie*, 80, 121, Thomas, earl of Kellie, to John, earl of Mar, Sept. 18, 1617, June 15, 1622.) The Earl of Kellie also discusses division of the spoils after the Duke of Richmond's death: the stewardship to Hamilton; the lieutenancy of Kent to the Earl of Montgomery; and the constabulary of Windsor and the reversion of the Cinque Ports to Buckingham. (*Ibid.*, 193, Thomas, earl of Kellie, to John, earl of Mar, Feb. 22, 1624.)

42. On November 9, 1616, Chamberlain mentioned the projected marriage of John Villiers to Frances Coke as the basis for Sir Edward Coke's restoration to favor. By March 15, 1617, Chamberlain was convinced that Coke's reluctance to come to terms had cost him the Lord Chancellorship. The original proposition of marriage purportedly involved a settlement of lands with an annual income of three thousand pounds plus the office of chief clerk in the Court of Common Pleas. The proposed marriage contract stipulated twenty thousand pounds ready portion, two thousand marks yearly maintenance during Coke's life, and lands with an annual value of two thousand pounds after his death. "Yf he had offered these conditions when time was, and taken occasion by the fore-head when she presented herself they might have stoode him in great stead, whereas now perhaps he doth but catch at the bald side." The marriage was celebrated on September 29, 1617, and although Coke was restored to the Privy Council in September 1617, sat frequently in the Star Chamber, and was named to numerous commissions including that for executing the office of the Lord Treasurer, he never again attained a position of eminence at court. (Chamberlain, *Letters*, II, 32–33, 64, 88–89, letters Nov. 9, 1616, Mar. 15, 1617, and July 19, 1617.) The Coventry indenture in 1624 described Coke as a privy councillor and as recorder of Coventry.

43. Both Carlisle and Kensington served the Prince and Buckingham during the journey to Spain and in subsequent negotiations for the French match. The Earl of Kellie succinctly summarized their relationship to Buckingham when he wrote: "There is but Holland [Kensington] and Carlisle great with him." (HMC, *Mar and Kellie*, 234, Thomas, earl of Kellie to John, earl of Mar, Oct. 5, 1625.) John Woodford, who appears to have been the earl of Carlisle's secretary, was elected for Tamworth, Staffordshire, in 1624. (J. C. Wedgwood, *Staffordshire Parliamentary History from the Earliest Times to the Present Day* [2 vols., London, 1919–1922], II, pt. I, 35–36.)

beck, and Lords Teynham and Noel.[44] There were, in addition, numerous other lords and bishops who were indebted to the Duke for favors received.

If Buckingham paid meticulous attention to his relations with the peerage and the principal crown officeholders, he was less careful in securing the support of the lower echelons of society. Unlike a Burghley or a Salisbury, Buckingham seems not to have openly risked his credit in promoting the election of members of Parliament favorable to his cause. Rather he seems to have relied upon the activities of his friends and satellites to assure himself of needed support. Whether this was a matter of choice is problematical. Only a few of the offices he filled had any direct connection with local politics. As high steward of Westminster or Lord Lieutenant of the counties of Buckingham and Middlesex the Duke could exert influence on parliamentary elections.[45] Certain of the lesser ports may also have been subservient to the control he exercised as Lord Admiral, but, where it existed, such influence was probably channeled through his vice admirals who were frequently men of considerable reputation in their counties. That Buckingham was not averse to employing his authority can be demonstrated by the number of nominations that he made after he secured the wardenship of the Cinque Ports, but the scarcity of direct evidence regarding the elections in 1624 forbids other than the most tentative generalizations about the nature of his patronage.[46]

44. *LJ*, III, 205.

45. Buckingham's estimate of his power as steward of Westminster is described in a letter from Rev. Joseph Mead to Sir Martin Stuteville on March 8, 1628. "There was a turbulent election of burgesses at Westminster, whereof the duke, being steward, made account he should, by his authority and vicinity, have put in Sir Robert Pye. It continued three days . . . In fine, Bradshaw, a brewer, and Maurice, a grocer, carried it from him by above 1,000 voices." (Birch, *Court and Times of Charles the First*, I, 327.) Prior to this election Sir Robert Cotton had solicited a nomination letter from Bishop Williams, Dean of Westminster. On February 12, 1628, Williams replied, "I have used heretofore to recommend to the town of Westminster one of their burgesses only and none other than was recommended unto me by my Lord Duke of Buckingham, our High Steward. I have no desire, nor is it any safety for me, to endeavor any alteration in that custom, and peradventure as the case now stands it is not feasible, and his Grace will do it immediately without moving me at all therein." (Cotton MS. Julius C III, fols. 402–402v, British Museum, John Williams, bishop of Lincoln, to Sir Robert Cotton, Feb. 12, 1627/8.)

46. Examples of Buckingham's nomination letters to the Cinque Ports are printed

Power naturally gravitated to the man who completely engrossed the King's favor. In 1620 Sir Henry Goodyere had written
to Buckingham volunteering as a candidate for "one of the many
burgesses places which will be offered to his Lordship." [47] If blank
indentures were presented to the Duke in 1620, it may reasonably
be conjectured that they were also offered in 1624 when the favorite was at the peak of his popularity. Certainly there can be
little doubt that Buckingham secured the election of his half
brother, Sir Edward Villiers, at Westminster and was instrumental
in assuring the return of Richard Oliver, his receiver general, for
Buckingham borough.[48] But the absence of other prime servants
of the Duke such as Thomas Aylesbury and John Packer, his
secretaries, Richard Graham, his gentleman of the horse, and
Edward Clark, his confidential servant, indicates that the Duke
relied for support more upon friends and allies than upon ap-
pointees.

Early in February it was rumored "that Buckingham has not
so many friends in the parliament as he hoped." However, county
as well as borough representatives were to be numbered among
his supporters.[49] By the end of James's reign court influence in
shire elections was distinctly on the wane. Consequently it cannot
be said that the adherents of Buckingham's cause who sat for
counties were his men in the same sense as the petty politicians
and favor seekers who had procured borough seats either through
his influence or in his interest. Men like Sir John and Sir Thomas
Savile, who were elected for Yorkshire, had on occasion appealed

in George Wilks, *The Barons of the Cinque Ports, and the Parliamentary Representation of Hythe* (Folkestone, 1892), 73–78. These letters deal only with Hythe,
and their editor has confused the chronological order of the first two Parliaments
of Charles I. In April 1625 Buckingham nominated Edward Clark and Sir Allen
Apsley. Clark and Sir Edward Dering were elected. In January 1626 Buckingham
nominated Sir Richard Weston, but Hythe elected Sir Peter Heyman and Basil
Dixwell before Buckingham's letters were received.

47. *Cal. S. P. Dom. 1619–1623*, 193, Sir Henry Goodyere to Buckingham, Nov. 20,
1620.

48. Richard Oliver represented Buckingham borough in 1621, 1624, 1625, and
1628. He appears to have been the Duke's receiver general as early as 1621. (HMC,
*Sixth Report*, Appendix [London, 1877], 323, 327, Graham MSS.) A "Mr. Oliver" is
mentioned in proceedings against the Duke in 1626. See also Birch, *Court and Times
of Charles the First*, I, 397, where, in a letter from Rev. Joseph Mead to Sir Martin
Stuteville, Sept. 20, 1628, Mr. Oliver and Sir Robert Pye are mentioned among the
executors of Buckingham's will.

49. *Cal. S. P. Venetian*, XVIII, 217, Valaresso to the Doge and Senate, Feb. 6/16,
1624.

to Buckingham for aid in local disputes. Undoubtedly they owed Buckingham for past favors and for anticipated preferment, but Sir John Savile was an "old parliament man" noted for his independent attitude. The alignment of the Saviles with the Duke became more conspicuous after 1625, but may, I think, be anticipated in 1624.[50]

Other county members, such as the two knights for Herefordshire, Sir John Scudamore and Sir Robert Harley, were united to Buckingham by closer ties. Both men had recently been made members of the Council of Wales. Scudamore seems to have been an avowed admirer of the Duke, and Harley had become the son-in-law of Secretary Conway. Probably neither Scudamore nor Harley owed their election to outside influence. There is some indication that the choice of members to serve for Herefordshire was largely resolved by consultation among the justices of the peace of that county.[51]

In Kent, where Sir Edwin Sandys secured the second place, no

50. Both Sir John Savile and Sir Thomas Wentworth appealed to Buckingham for support in their feud, which was initiated when Wentworth refused to vacate the office of *custos rotulorum* in 1617. Strafford, *Letters*, I, 2–4, Sir John Savile to Lord Chancellor Ellesmere, Dec. 9, 1615; Mr. Cartwright to Sir Thomas Wentworth, Dec. 26, 1615; Buckingham to Sir Thomas Wentworth, Sept. 5 and Sept. 23, 1617. S. R. Gardiner, ed., *The Fortescue Papers* . . . Camden Society, N. S., Volume I (London, 1871), 23–28, Sir Thomas Wentworth to Buckingham, Sept. 15, 1617; Sir Thomas Savile to Buckingham, Sept. (?), 1617. In 1624 Chamberlain contrasted Sir John Savile ("still the same man") with Sandys, Digges, and Phelips whom he felt had defected to the court faction. (Chamberlain, *Letters*, II, 549, letter of Mar. 20, 1624.) Although reluctant to vote large sums of money, Savile favored war with Spain, the enforcement of the penal laws against recusants, and the prosecution of Cranfield. Sir John's prevailing attitude during the Parliament seems to have been one of suspicion regarding the King's intentions. He is frequently mentioned as preferring "rather action than words," and he believed "that there were diverse and very powerful that did the House ill offices with the King, telling him we would do nothing unless we had all our desires; therefore to stop their mouths he would proceed with the subsidies." (Holles, fols. 99, 128v.) There appears to have been no contest in the Yorkshire election of 1624, but Sir Thomas Savile's nonchalant attitude toward parliamentary service offended Sir Francis Wortley, and he subsequently challeneged Sir Thomas to a duel. (Add. MS. 24,470, fols. 30–30v.) In 1625, when Sir John Savile's petition against Wentworth's election as knight of the shire from Yorkshire was debated in the House, "the major part of courtiers . . . banded mainly against Wentworth." (Eliot, *Negotium Posterorum*, I, 103.)

51. HMC, *Thirteenth Report*, Appendix, pt. IV (London, 1892), Dovaston MSS, 270, letter noting the appointment of Scudamore and Harley to the Council of the Marches of Wales, June 30, 1623. There are several undated letters from Sir Robert Harley dealing with arrangements for a parliamentary election in Herefordshire. Internal evidence indicates that these letters all refer to the same Parliament, which may be that of 1621. (*Letters of the Lady Brilliana Harley, Wife of Sir Robert Harley*, Camden Society, Volume LVIII [London, 1854], xliii–xliv.)

court influence seems discernible; indeed, Sir Dudley Digges's purported propensities toward royalism apparently helped to assure his defeat. Yet shortly thereafter Sandys was reported to have made his peace at court "with promise of all manner of conformitie," and in Parliament he was suspected of being an "undertaker." [52] The same charge of having defected to the court faction was levied against that notoriously independent knight of Somersetshire, Sir Robert Phelips, but the enthusiasm with which he seconded Buckingham in the Parliament of 1624 seems to have been based upon a temporary identity of their policies rather than upon any genuine obligation. Phelips's shift in attitude in the succeeding Parliament reveals the transitory nature of this affiliation.[53]

More mundane considerations bound Edward Montagu, knight of the shire for Huntingdon, to Buckingham's interests. Montagu's marriage in February 1623 had been the means by which his father, Lord President Mandeville, had obtained the restitution from Buckingham of ten thousand pounds which he had "loaned" to the favorite in expectation of securing the Lord Treasurer's staff in 1621. Edward's nuptials with Susan Hill, kinswoman of

52. Chamberlain, *Letters*, II, 540, letter of Jan. 17, 1624; see also *ibid.*, II, 543, 549, letters of Jan. 31, 1624, and Mar. 20, 1624. On December 26, 1623/Jan. 5, 1624, Valaresso reported that Pembroke and Hamilton had protested against the exclusion of Coke and Sandys from the Parliament, but this occurred when the suggestion was first presented to the Council. He adds, "I do not hear, however, that the king changed his mind." (*Cal. S. P. Venetian*, XVIII, 183, Valaresso to the Doge and Senate.) I suspect that Buckingham and Charles were instrumental in causing James to alter his opinion.

53. On April 14, 1624, Mr. Whistler complained that the Committee of Courts of Justice under the chairmanship of Sir Robert Phelips had heard only one complaint in six weeks of sittings: "the commonwealth groans under this extreme delay. The cause is this: that consideration is not taken of those petitions that most concern the commonwealth and that others be rejected." (Spring, 218.) It was Phelips who, on March 12, moved an exceptional address of thanks and compliment to the Prince "to assure his Highness that we shall be ready to attend upon all his princely resolutions." (*Ibid.*, 109–110; Holles, fol. 98v.) When the Commons was informed on February 27 that the Spanish ambassador had complained of Buckingham for maligning the King of Spain, "Sir Robert Phelips said, In the way that Buckingham did now run he hoped Buckingham should rather live to see many thousand Spanish heads in the sea, or lying on the ground and wished a committee to join with the Lords [to clear the Duke]." (Holles, fol. 86v.) Phelips may have had an ulterior motive in ingratiating himself with Buckingham. When the revocation of Sir Dudley Carleton as ambassador to the United Provinces was rumored in June 1624, Sir Robert Phelips was named as one of the three "sticklers" who importuned to replace Carleton at the Hague. (SP 14/168/47, Dudley Carleton to Sir Dudley Carleton, June 26, 1624.)

the Duke, were performed in the King's bedchamber and reportedly involved Buckingham's engagement to pay an additional five thousand pounds and to procure for Montagu a suitable place at court.[54]

Sir John St. John, who represented Wiltshire, was also involved in the Villiers system of marriage alliances. His daughter, Barbara, was the wife of Sir Edward Villiers, Buckingham's avaricious half brother. Moreover St. John's younger brother, Oliver, was known to be a member of the Duke's party. Partially through Buckingham's influence, Oliver became deputy of Ireland in 1616; in 1624 he was named to the Council of War. Since 1622 he had been a privy councillor, and the patent by which he was created Viscount Grandison limited the succession of this title to the children of Sir Edward Villiers.

More tenuous connections indicate that other county members were probably affiliated with Buckingham. Sir Montague Bertie, who was elected for Lincolnshire, was the eldest son of Robert Bertie, Lord Willoughby of Eresby, who was one of the four colonels appointed in June 1624 to command English troops in the Low Countries.[55] Sir William Spencer, whose suit for restitution as a deputy lieutenant in Northamptonshire was being pressed by the Earl of Exeter, found it expedient to convince Buckingham of his good intentions by all manner of conformity in Parliament.[56] Sir Richard Harrison, who represented Berkshire,

54. Chamberlain, *Letters*, II, 476, letter of Feb. 10, 1623; Gardiner, *History of England*, IV, 23–24.

55. The four colonels were the Earls of Oxford, Essex, and Southampton and Lord Willoughby. During late May and early June there was great competition for the place Willoughby ultimately secured. Dudley Carleton, writing to Sir Dudley Carleton on May 21, mentioned that the King favored the Earl of Morton, the Prince favored Sir John Borlase, and others preferred Lord Willoughby. During the period of indecision Buckingham was ill, and it was not until after he had returned to court that the appointment of the fourth colonel was made. (SP 14/165/12.) Valaresso says that Willoughby was the Prince's nominee. I suspect that Buckingham and the Prince combined their efforts to exclude the Scottish Earl of Morton from contention. (*Cal. S. P. Venetian*, XVIII, 353, Valaresso to the Doge and Senate, June 11/21, 1624; SP 14/165/12.) Willoughby later held a subordinate naval command under Buckingham and succeeded the Duke as admiral of the Rochelle expedition in 1628. He was also made a privy councillor in 1628. (Birch, *Court and Times of Charles the First*, I, 389.)

56. Sir William Spencer, son and heir of Robert, Lord Spencer, represented Northamptonshire. He had been dismissed from the deputy lieutenancy of that county at the King's command for errors committed in the Parliament of 1621. On June 6, 1624, the Earl of Exeter asked Secretary Conway to expedite, through Buckingham, his petition to the King for the restoration of Spencer "the rather because

was closely united to court interests. He was the brother-in-law of Sir Dudley Carleton, ambassador to the United Provinces, and in November 1623 he apparently used Carleton's connections with Buckingham to secure exemption from the shrievalty of Berkshire.[57]

In Cambridgeshire there was a hotly contested election between two competitors for preeminence in the county, Sir Edward Peyton and Buckingham's client, Sir John Cuts. The shire election for the Parliament of 1624 occurred on January 22 at Cambridge. Sir Edward Peyton had as his partner Sir Simeon Steward while the candidates of the opposite party were Sir John Cuts and Toby Palavicini, Esq. The undersheriff of Cambridgeshire, Ingrey, presided over the election and returned Peyton and Steward. A petition against this return was filed with the Committee of Privileges by Cuts and Palavicini and heard on March 4. At the hearing it was shown that neither the cry nor the view were sufficient to determine the majority. It was also alleged that Cuts had demanded the poll five or six times and that, for the space of a quarter of an hour, three or four hundred freeholders had loudly seconded his request. The poll was never taken. Apparently Sir Simeon Steward had convinced the undersheriff that he need not proceed after the legal time limit of the election had passed. Thereupon the undersheriff went away and the return was made by him in Sir Edward Peyton's chamber in a nearby tavern. The House of Commons invalidated this election and summoned Ingrey before them for reproof and punishment. Subsequently, on March 18, both Peyton and Cuts were elected and took their seats in the House.[58]

---

he had showed himself most forward in all things this parliament, which might tend to his Majesty's service and best pleasing, with much grief that anything should fall from him formerly which should be occasion of his Majesty's displeasure." (SP 14/167/19.) See also chap. iii, n. 52, for Spencer's association with the Earl of Southampton.

57. SP 14/154/19, Dudley Carleton to Sir Dudley Carleton, Nov. 10, 1623; see also SP 14/173/116, T. Locke to Sir Dudley Carleton, Oct. 29, 1624.

58. The legal aspects of the Cambridgeshire election case are discussed in Glanville, *Reports*, 80–86, but the facts of the election brought out at the Committee of Privileges are described most fully in Holland, fols. 26–30, 33v–34, and Earle, fol. 50. In Peyton's "Divine Catastrophe of the Kingly Family of the House of Stuarts," he alluded to his troubles with Buckingham, "A little afore this, I being *Custos Rotulorum* of the County of Cambridge, by Buckingham was put out, and Sir John

Undoubtedly the local prestige of a prospective member of Parliament counted for more than his political sentiments. A parliamentarian like John Drake of Ashe was apt to sit for Devonshire whether or not he was a Buckingham supporter. Not until after such constitutional issues as forced loans, tonnage and poundage, and the liberties of the subject had been raised in the early Parliaments of Charles I did party lines begin to have constitutional significance. The Middlesex election of 1624 clearly illustrates this fact. The contest was between Sir John Suckling, a privy councillor, Sir John Hippisley, "countenanced by the Duke of Buckingam," and Sir John Franklyn, a Middlesex landholder. Yet Sir Gilbert Gerard of Harrow-on-the-Hill was named to the prime place "though he were not present at first nor last." Suckling, a courtier of long standing, Comptroller of the Household, and owner of properties in Middlesex, managed to secure the second seat but only after a poll had disqualified those men from the mint and the stable who had been marshalled by Sir Allen Apsley in support of Hippisley's candidacy. Of the contestants Hippisley was undoubtedly least important and would not have seriously figured in the election had he not been a prime favorite of the Duke of Buckingham. Suckling's exalted position at court may have induced some electors to give him their voices, but it did not prevent Richard Bancroft and other freeholders of Middlesex from complaining that he was unduly chosen. A petition in favor of Sir John Franklyn was filed in the House of Commons by Edward Roberts, member of Parliament for Penryn,

Cuts put in, when I had that office under the broad seal; which could not legally be taken away from me, unless I had committed some fault, thereby to have forfeited the same." (Peyton's work is in *Secret History of the Court of James the First*, II, 441.) The "Divine Catastrophe" seems to have been intended as a panegyric to the Long Parliament. In it every libelous charge against the Duke of Buckingham was repeated. There is, however, in Harl. MS. 3364, "A Discourse of Court and Courtiers" written by Peyton in 1633. This treatise scarcely mentioned Buckingham and insisted that England had been free of "court comets" since the reign of Elizabeth. Peyton also alleged that favorites did good service to monarchs by increasing revenues, commanding in war, conducting embassies, and other similar pursuits. In chap. vii he contended that they might lawfully labor to advance their families and estates. Peyton listed five favorites of James who ruled the kingdom through him: the Earls of Dunbar, Montgomery, Carlisle, and Somerset and the Duke of Buckingham. ("Divine Catastrophe," 352–353.) Of the last, he said, "The Queen departed, the King sold his affections to Sir George Villiers whom he would tumble and kiss as a mistress." (*Ibid.*, 348.)

Cornwall,[59] but before it could be heard by the Committee of Privileges it was withdrawn on the grounds that the petitioners were "better informed and advised now than when their petition was first preferred." Franklyn had to wait until 1625 for his revenge, when he administered a stinging personal defeat to Suckling.[60]

The borough elections, like the county hustings, provide little definitive evidence of Buckingham's patronage. Some delineation of the Duke's coterie can be achieved, however, by pointing out affiliations that committed certain Members of Parliament to his policy. There was, for instance, a group of "inward men" who were described in contemporary letters as favorites or as associates of Buckingham. Sir George Goring, a courtier occasionally employed by Charles and Buckingham in a minor diplomatic capacity, was returned for two boroughs: Lewes in his native Sussex and Stamford in Lincolnshire. In neither instance was the influence of Buckingham apparent. Goring had previously represented

59. Roberts, like Franklyn, was of Willesden, Middlesex. Franklyn appears to have been the nephew of Roberts. (*Middlesex Pedigrees,* Harleian Society, Volume LXV [London, 1914], 3, 166; Chamberlain, *Letters,* II, 543, letter of Jan. 31, 1624.)
60. Glanville, *Reports,* 118; Chamberlain, *Letters,* II, 614, letter of May 6, 1625. "Sir John Francklin and Sir Gilbert Gerrard caried yt away in Middlesex from Master Comptroller though he were present, which was thought not so wise a part for a privie counsaillor to take the foyle in person." Middlesex electors alleged in 1621 that "they could not have access to such great persons as privy councillors." (Thomas Locke to Sir Dudley Carleton, Dec. 16, 1620, cited from Willson, *Privy Councillors in the House of Commons,* 71.) In the Kentish election for the Short Parliament of 1640, Sir Henry Vane, treasurer of the King's household, offered himself as a candidate when Sir Roger Twysden declined an invitation to stand for the knightship of the shire. Vane promised Twysden, his cousin germane, "y$^t$ if hee were knight of the shire I should serue in y$^e$ burges place w$^{ch}$ he as a pryuy counsellor would not bee destytute of, in w$^{ch}$ I could doe my country as much seruice as in this or any other, all beeing equall in y$^e$ Howse." At the time that Sir Henry Vane offered himself for election, there were already three other candidates: Mr. Knatchbul, Sir George Sonds, and Sir Thomas Walsingham. At Twysden's solicitation, Sonds and Walsingham agreed to retire "out of their affectionat respect to Mr. Treas'r." But Knatchbul who had "y$^e$ greatest vote from y$^e$ beegining" refused. At this point Sir Edward Dering, who had initially requested Twysden to seek the shire seat and who had later engaged himself to support Sir Henry Vane, was induced by George Stroude and Isaac Bargrave, dean of Canterbury, to stand for election. Twysden remonstrated with Dering for his breach of faith and then "acquainted Mr. Treas'r with all y$^e$ proceedings, who instantly resolued not to stand hymself, but writ to me w$^{th}$ all y$^e$ rest of hys friends heerabouts to set vp myself and oppose Dering." At the election on March 16, 1640, Sir Norton Knatchbul and Sir Roger Twysden were returned. (Sir Roger Twysden, *Certain Considerations Upon the Government of England,* Camden Society, Volume XLV [London, 1849], xliii–xlv.)

Lewes in 1621, and his estates in Sussex, together with his powerful court connections, were probably sufficient to guarantee his
reelection in 1624. The seat at Stamford was almost certainly
bestowed upon him by the Earl of Exeter whose interests in that
borough were predominant. When Goring chose to sit for Lewes,
he was replaced at Stamford by John St. Amand, who also had no
known association with that constituency.[61]

Sir John Hippisley, who had been supported in the Middlesex
election by Buckingham, probably owed his election at Petersfield,
Hampshire, to the support of his father-in-law, Sir Robert Norton.[62] Sir Robert Pye, auditor of the receipt of the Exchequer,
represented Bath in Somerset and his brother, Sir Walter Pye,
attorney of the Court of Wards and Liveries, sat for the borough
of Brecon in Wales. Sir Robert had long been associated with
Buckingham, and, as early as 1617, he was described as an em-
ployee of the Duke "in his most private affairs." [63] His elder
brother, Sir Walter, was linked with Brecon through his office as
Chief Justice of the great sessions for the counties of Brecknock,
Glamorgan, and Radnor, a position he had gained through Buckingham's favor, and he was elected to represent that borough in
every Parliament in the 1620's.

Another Court of Wards official, Sir Miles Fleetwood, who represented the patronage borough of Launceston in Cornwall, was
sympathetic to Buckingham's anti-Spanish policy. However, mundane rather than spiritual considerations seem to have exercised a
decisive influence in his association with the favorite. There is no
doubt that Fleetwood considered further treaties with Spain as
anathema to "religion, honor and peace," but he manifested his
greatest industry in initiating and maintaining the prosecution of
Lionel Cranfield, Master of the Court of Wards and opponent of
Buckingham. Fleetwood's patron at Launceston cannot be identified with certainty, but he was also returned for Bletchingly, Sur-

61. See the Goring letters, Harl. MS. 1580; Richard Butcher, *The Survey and
Antiquity of the Town of Stamford in the County of Lincoln and Tottenham-
High-Cross in Middlesex* (London, 1717). The preface of this work is signed by
Richard Butcher and is dated January 1, 1646.

62. Keeler, *Long Parliament*, 215–216. As early as 1618 Hippisley was referred
to as Buckingham's principal favorite. He journeyed to Spain in 1623 and in 1624
became Lieutenant of Dover Castle when Buckingham succeeded to the wardenship
of the Cinque Ports.

63. Whitelocke, *Liber Famelicus*, 55–56.

rey, a borough distinctly under Howard control. When the
Bletchingly election was contested, Fleetwood chose to sit for
Launceston, but it is noteworthy that he was named in both returns filed from the Surrey village, and it appears that his election
was not questioned.[64]

John Coke, soon to emerge as Buckingham's parliamentary
spokesman, owed his seat at St. Germans to the patronage of his
brother-in-law, Valentine Carey, bishop of Exeter. Coke had long
been associated with Fulke Greville, Lord Brooke, and it was
probably due to his influence that Coke was appointed to the
special commission for examining the state of the navy in 1618.
In this employment Coke distinguished himself; Eliot noted that
"the rest [of the commissioners] were but cyphers vnto him."

64. Spring, 44; Pym, fol. 48v; SP 14/165/1. The Bletchingly election was discussed
in the Committee of Privileges on March 18, 1624. One return named Fleetwood
and John Hawarde; another, Fleetwood and Henry Lovell. Bletchingly was an
unincorporated borough by prescription where the election was made by burgesses
who held properties by burgage tenure from Lady Elizabeth Howard, mistress of
the manor. The precept, directed to the bailiff and burgesses, was delivered to one
of the burgesses, Mr. Wright, on January 16, who gave warning of the election.
The following day seventeen of the twenty-four burgesses met and elected Fleetwood
and Hawarde. The next Sunday at church the bailiff announced that an election
would be held that Monday, and after evening prayers Dr. Harris, the minister,
read a letter from Lady Howard of Effingham recommending Sir Miles Fleetwood
and Henry Lovell. Thirty persons, both burgesses and inhabitants, elected Fleetwood
and Lovell. At the Committee of Privileges it was resolved that the bailiff of the
manor was not part of the borough corporation and that the precept need not
be delivered to him. It was also maintained that the number of electors for a parliamentary election could be restrained or abridged by custom, and, consequently, the
consent of the inhabitants was implied in the consent of the burgage holders. The
committee voted that the election of Fleetwood and Hawarde was good, and it was
upheld in this ruling by the House on March 22. Lovell was charged with a
variety of offenses: intimidating the electors who chose Hawarde, threatening the
withdrawal of an annual gift of fourteen nobles that the Lady Howard designed
for the poor of Bletchingly, being ineligible for election by reason of recusancy,
bribery, by providing 6d. for drink for his supporters, and deceitfully filing the
indenture for his own return into the crown office without the knowledge or consent
of the undersheriff. Lovell was sent to the Tower until he had satisfied the House
by his submission on April 12. He was also declared ineligible for election to
Fleetwood's vacated seat. Dr. Harris, a minister at Bletchingly who had abetted
Lovell's schemes and who had preached a sermon impugning the justice of the
Committee of Privileges, was forced to submit to the House of Commons and to
acknowledge his fault before his congregation. In the CJ (I, 753), Lovell says he
is lord of the manor in trust to my Lady Howard. (Hawarde, 224.) The election
is discussed at large in Glanville, Reports, 29–46; CJ, 745; Pym, fols. 37–37v; Earle,
fols. 91–92; Uvedale Lambert, Bletchingley: A Parish History Together with Some
Account of the Family of De Clare (London, 1922), 424–425; see also Nicholas, fol.
187. Hawarde, 224, mentions his departure from the House when the case was debated on March 22, but he makes no reference to the committee proceedings on
March 18.

Appointed Master of Requests in 1622, Coke simultaneously continued to act as navy commissioner, a position in which he was closely associated with Lord Admiral Buckingham. In the Parliament of 1624, Lord Treasurer Middlesex considered Coke, along with Sir Robert Pye and Sir Miles Fleetwood, as the chief of the Duke's agents employed against him. In September following the Parliament Coke was knighted and rumors began to circulate that he would succeed Calvert as Secretary of State, but the seals were not delivered to him until after the death of Sir Albert Morton in 1625.[65]

Other Admiralty personnel less intimately associated with the favorite sat in the Commons in 1624. The vice admiral of England, Sir Robert Mansell, represented the county of Glamorgan. Although he had been "under hatches" since the expedition against the pirates in 1620, he was preeminent among those sea captains who thronged the court (presumably at Buckingham's behest) in December 1623. Mansell, inclined to be independent, was a great favorite with the former Lord Admiral Nottingham, and his connections with Pembroke began as early as 1612. Nevertheless he was confirmed in his office as vice admiral under Buckingham and was named to the Council of War in 1624.[66]

Sir John Eliot, who had been made vice admiral of Devon through Buckingham's influence, sat for Newport in Cornwall. Eliot had labored with the burgesses of St. Germans to assure the return of John Coke from that borough, and, as yet, there were no signs of his future antagonism toward Buckingham. He was, in fact, indebted to Buckingham for his release from custody on

65. Eliot, *Negotium Posterorum*, II, 6–7. Of Coke's parliamentary employment Eliot says: "the man so chosen was Sʳ John Coke, raisd from a lowe condition to that title by the D[uke]. to him he had beene recommended by that ould courtier Sʳ ffoulke Grevill, vnder whom he had had his education as a scholler, & soe was his service & imploiment." (*Ibid.*, I, 113–114; *Lords Debates 1624 & 1626*, 61; Willson, *Privy Councillors in the House of Commons*, 96; HMC, *Twelfth Report*, Appendix, pt. I [London, 1888], 157, Cowper MSS, Valentine Carey, bishop of Exeter, to John Coke, Jan. 26, 1624.)

66. Chamberlain, *Letters*, II, 535, letter of Dec. 20, 1623; Violet A. Rowe, "The Influence of the Earls of Pembroke on Parliamentary Elections 1625–41," *English Historical Review*, L (Apr. 1935), 247; Sir Francis Nethersole, in a letter to Sir Dudley Carleton on May 6, 1624 (SP 14/164/46), discusses Mansell's project to add double decks and gun ports to two hundred merchant ships — a plan apparently not adopted by the Council of War, which probably accounted for Mansell's diminished influence in the council; see also SP 14/164/67, Thomas Locke to Sir Dudley Carleton, May 12, 1624; *Cal. S. P. Dom. 1623–1625*, 316, July 28, 1624, where warrant is given to pay Mansell arrearages due him since the expedition to Algiers.

December 23, 1623.[67] Eliot's rival, James Bagg, Jr., vice admiral of Cornwall, sat for the patronage borough of West Looe. Bagg was perhaps the most obsequious of Buckingham's supporters, and throughout this period he was doing his utmost to destroy the Duke's confidence in Eliot.[68]

A former vice admiral of Devon, Sir Edward Seymour, was elected for Callington, Cornwall, and in the Parliament was thought to have promoted the Duke's secret designs to extort ten thousand pounds from the East India Company.[69] A commissioner of the navy, Sir William Pitt, represented Wareham in Dorset, while his son, Edward, who had recently been granted the office of Teller of the Exchequer, was chosen at Poole.[70] With the exception of Coke, all of the naval personnel had some connection with the localities they represented, and it is improbable that any of them, except, perhaps, Bagg, relied heavily upon the favorite's assistance.

In one Dorset borough Buckingham's influence may have been paramount — Corfe Castle in the Isle of Purbeck. For some time Buckingham had been trying to induce the Lady Hatton to give possession of the Isle of Purbeck to her son-in-law, Sir John Villiers (Viscount Purbeck), and it may be that her nominations there were placed at his disposal. Two strangers represented the borough: Sir Peter Osborne, lieutenant governor of Gurnsey and brother of Sir John Osborne, commissioner of the navy; and Sir

67. *APC 1623–1625*, 156; *Cabala*, I, 311, Sir John Eliot to the Duke of Buckingham, Nov. 8, 1623. This letter is also printed in Forster, *Sir John Eliot*, I, 123.

68. On James Bagg, see Forster, *Sir John Eliot*, passim; Harold Hulme, *Sir John Eliot and the Vice-admiralty of Devon*, Camden Miscellany, No. XVII, 3d Ser., Volume LXIV (London, 1940), v–xiv. Hulme thinks that Bagg did not take his seat in the Parliament of 1624, but remained in the West Country on admiralty business.

69. Howell, *State Trials*, II, 1332. Sir Edward Seymour was implicated in the charges laid against the Duke of Buckingham in the Parliament of 1626, but the Duke denied that the motion in the Commons was made with his knowledge or privity.

70. It may have been the intention of Sir William Pitt to have his son Edward serve in partnership with him as M.P. for Wareham in 1624. Both Sir William and Edward wrote letters of solicitation to the mayor of Wareham, but Edward's election was blocked by a request from Sir Francis Ashley in behalf of John Trenchard. Thereupon Edward made overtures to the corporation of Poole and, with the aid of his uncles, was successful in his quest for the second seat, the first having been promised to Sir Walter Earle. (Add. MS. 29,974, fols. 74–74v, Edward Pitt to Sir William Pitt, Jan. 11, 1624; *ibid.*, fol. 72, Edward Pitt to the Mayor of Wareham, Jan. 1624; *ibid.*, fol. 76, Edward Pitt to Sir William Pitt, Jan. 15, 1624.)

Francis Nethersole, English agent at the court of Elizabeth, electress Palatine.[71]

Courtiers of all ranks formed part of the Duke's retinue. On the periphery of this group were to be found ambitious aspirants to office like Edward Nicholas who was in the process of transferring his allegiance from Lord Zouche to the Lord Admiral. Closer to the focus of power were former officials in temporary eclipse, who had enjoyed Buckingham's favor and who saw in the Parliament an opportunity to recoup their losses. These included Sir Edward Villiers, Buckingham's half brother, who, after the fall of the Treasurer, succeeded Sir Randall Cranfield as Master of the Mint. Sir Robert Naunton, privy councillor, who had been deprived of his office as Secretary of State on January 16, 1623, still enjoyed the Duke's favor and anticipated reemployment in some responsible office. There can be little doubt that Sir Edward Villiers was nominated for Westminster, and, although Naunton's letters of recommendation to Cambridge University went through the usual channels, he relied upon the favorite to secure permission from the King for his attendance in the House.[72]

71. Egerton, 784, Whiteway's Diary. Whiteway, a native of Dorset, lists the burgesses elected in the county in 1624, fols. 37–38. The fact that Osborne was unknown to him is apparent by the reference to this member as Sir Robert Osborne. He also refers to Nethersole as Francis Nethersole, Jr., but the father of our member was John Nethersole. In Browne Willis, *Notitia Parliamentaria*, II, 498–499, there is a letter from the mayor and barons of Corfe Castle to Sir John Hobart on March 10, 1603/4, notifying Hobart of his election as an M. P. for the borough at the request of Sir Edward Coke. Coke was the husband of Lady Hatton and obviously nominated in her stead. On the attempts to secure the Dorset property of Lady Hatton, see Chamberlain, *Letters*, II, 91–92, letter of Aug. 9, 1617, 239–240, letter of May 31, 1619. On Sir Francis Nethersole's connection with the Duke of Buckingham, see Gardiner, ed., *Fortescue Papers*, 214–215, Elizabeth of Bohemia to the Duke of Buckingham, Apr. 11/21, 1625, where she solicits Buckingham's influence in behalf of Nethersole "and in the meane time that his allowance and place of Agent may be continued him, which he had by your favour you did to him for my sake; and he is your true servant for it."

72. Chamberlain attributes the rapid rise of Sir Robert Naunton after 1616 to the fact that he was "of kinred to the new favorite, and so inward with his mother that he is termed her chauncellor." Chamberlain, *Letters*, II, 30, letter of Oct. 26, 1616. Even after the loss of the secretaryship Naunton retained Buckingham's favor. On June 19, 1623, Conway wrote to Cranfield raising the question of Naunton's pension (confirmed under the Great Seal, July 16): "Which the King wants dispatched; that being the only one they left undone of all that Buckingham recommended to him." (HMC, *Fourth Report*, Appendix [London, 1874], 306.) The day after the Prince and Buckingham returned to England Naunton wrote a congratulatory letter to the Duke in which he termed Charles and Buckingham "the two Angels of our Church and State." He also mentioned that he was still under restraint. (Gardiner, ed., *Fortescue Papers*, 192–193, Sir Robert Naunton to the Duke

Nearest to the Duke were crown officers like Sir Robert Heath, Solicitor General, who represented the duchy town of East Grinstead, Sussex; Sir William Beecher, Clerk of the Privy Council, who was returned for Leominster, Herefordshire; and Sir Edward Conway, Secretary of State, who sat for Evesham, Worcestershire.[73]

---

of Buckingham, Oct. 6, 1623.) On January 14, 1624 Naunton wrote to Buckingham, "For the parliament I gave your Lordship account how my Lord Keeper had acquainted me that it was his Majesty's pleasure to use my service in it, and how his Lordship had written to the university to choose me one of their burgesses, which I since understand that they have already done. And hereupon I apprehended the fitness of the time and occasion humbly to move your Grace for the timely and seasonable accomplishment of those gracious promises, which have been so often tendered and renewed unto me from his Majesty, both by your Lordship and by my Lord of Carlisle. As for any honor in parliament, my Lord, I have no other ambition there than merely to follow and observe his Majesty's directions. Only my desire and hope is, that his Majesty will not draw me out onto that stage, after all these sufferings, less than formerly I was; whom I must ever zeal to serve with a vigorous and a cheerful heart, and not with a drooping and a dejected spirit." (SP 14/158/30, Sir Robert Naunton to the Duke of Buckingham, Jan. 14, 1624.) On the question of Naunton's release from confinement in order to serve in Parliament in 1624, see Rex, *University Representation*, 360–361. I agree with her conclusion that Naunton did not sit; there is no evidence of his presence reported in the *Commons Journal* or in the diaries of the Parliament. Like Sir Edward Villiers, Naunton reaped the benefit of Cranfield's disgrace. He was apparently promised the mastership of the Court of Wards by Buckingham as early as August 1, 1624, and, although the King resisted the appointment, Buckingham was successful in his efforts on Naunton's behalf. (*Cal. S. P. Dom. 1623–1625*, 319, 327, 330, 345, 346.) The *DNB* article on Naunton is in error as to the date of his appointment as master of the Court of Wards, and this error is repeated in the Rex book on p. 365.

73. Whitelocke attributes Heath's rise in the government to Buckingham's influence. Since Heath and Whitelocke were competitors for the recordership of London in 1618, Whitelocke's evidence is tinged with malice. He credits Heath's nomination to the recordership to the fact that "the marquesse [Buckingham] whispered the king in the ear." and he also says that "This Robert Heath was the marqueses creature, and joyned in patent withe Shute for receaving of the profits of the King's Benche office for the use of the marquesse." (Whitelocke, *Liber Famelicus*, 63–69.) In Chamberlain, *Letters* (II, 180, letter of Nov. 7, 1618), Heath is also termed a Buckingham protégé, and in a letter of February 3, 1621 (*ibid.*, 337–338), his preferment to the solicitorship is attributed to "the saving of seven or eight hundred pounds a yeare to the Lord of Buckingam out of Ropers office in the Kinges Bench." Sir William Beecher was made Clerk of the Privy Council for life on January 24, 1623. (*Cal. S. P. Dom. 1619–1623*, 483.) In Eliot, *Negotium Posterorum* (I, 117), he is mentioned as the only courtier to second Sir John Coke's motion for additional supply in the Parliament of 1625. As early as 1617 Chamberlain associated Beecher with Buckingham. (*Letters*, II, 97–98, letter of Aug. 27, 1617.) Beecher, secretary of the Council of War in 1624 and 1625, attended Buckingham during the Rhe expedition. He sat for Dover in the Parliament of 1625 when he was almost certainly nominated by Buckingham, Lord Warden of the Cinque Ports. In 1626 Dover apologized to the Duke for not choosing Beecher. (SP 16/18/37, Sir John Hippisley to Buckingham, Jan. 12, 1626; see also SP 16/91/91, Sir John Hippisley to Edward Nicholas, Jan. 31, 1628, and SP 16/92/12, Sir John Hippisley to the Duke of Buckingham, Feb. 2, 1628 about recommending Beecher to Dover.

Conway, the "Duke's martial secretary," was most assiduous in soliciting burgess-ships for his relatives. From Lord Zouche he procured the nomination of his son, Thomas Conway, to the port of Rye. At Warwick he seems to have relied on the influence of his relative, Fulke Greville, Lord Brooke, to assure the election of his eldest son, Sir Edward Conway, Jr., who at the time was employed in military affairs in the Low Countries. Secretary Conway himself sat for Evesham, a borough with which he had been associated since 1621. Conway also sought election for an unnamed candidate, possibly himself, at Helston in Cornwall, and he may have helped to obtain Sir Isaac Wake's nomination to the University of Oxford. Wake, as a step toward promotion, had recently married into the Conway family, as had Sir Robert Harley, knight of the shire for Hereford. Marital ties also connected the Conways with the Pelham family of Lincolnshire, and Henry Pelham represented Great Grimsby in that county. In the cases of Harley and Pelham, Conway's influence was neither solicited nor needed, but very probably the ties of relationship helped to strengthen those of political affiliation.[74]

74. Secretary Conway's close association with Buckingham was frequently referred to by contemporaries. The Earl of Kellie called him "my Lord of Buckingham's confidant." HMC, *Mar and Kellie*, 174, Thomas, earl of Kellie, to John, earl of Mar, July 11, 1623. The appellation of the "Duke of Buckingham's martial secretary" was applied to him by Sir Henry Wotton. (*Cabala*, I, 190.) In W. R. Williams, *The Parliamentary History of the County of Worcester* ([Hereford, 1897], 141–142), it is said that Conway was elected for Evesham on November 12, 1621 (to replace Sir Thomas Diggs, deceased), in pursuance of a pledge given him when he was chosen alderman in July 1621. Doubtless it was due to his patronage that Sir Robert Harley was elected to represent Evesham in 1628. On the recommendation of Thomas Conway to the port of Rye, see the section about the Cinque Ports, chap. iii. There is no direct evidence regarding the election of Edward Conway, Jr., at Warwick. On January 10, 1624, Secretary Conway wrote, "I have sought to get you a burgess's place of the parliament and am confident I shall have one for you. So soon as the election is made I will send an express for you." (SP 84/116 [Holland], fols. 25–26, Secretary Conway to Sir Edward Conway, Jr., Jan. 10, 1624.) The secretary's anxiety about the Warwick election is evident in his letter to William Chesterman on January 31, 1624. (SP 14/158/71.) Fulke Greville, Lord Brooke had considerable influence in the borough and county of Warwick which he was willing to place at the disposal of Conway. (SP 16/523/3, Lord Brooke to Secretary Conway, Jan. 2, 1626.) Sir Isaac Wake, in December 1623, married Anna Bray, stepdaughter of Sir Edward Conway after a "wooing that hath been long adooing." (Chamberlain, *Letters*, II, 533, letter of Dec. 20, 1623.) On January 16/26, 1624, Valaresso wrote to the Doge and Senate that the embassy to Venice would be conferred on Wake: "he enjoys the good opinion of the Court and derives great advantage from his recent connection with Secretary Conowel [Conway]." (*Cal. S. P. Venetian*, XVIII, 200.) Wake assiduously attended the Parliament in 1624 "for his employment is at the stake to stand or fall as matters passe there, though he have received his letters

Two literary men, partisans of Buckingham in 1624, occupied seats in the Parliament. John Maynard, elected for Chippenham, Wiltshire, had, in November 1623, celebrated the return of Charles and Buckingham by composing a masque that offended the Spanish ambassadors. Sir Robert Cotton, who probably owed his seat at Old Sarum, Wiltshire, to the patronage of the Earl of Salisbury, found it advisable to abjure all of his previous associations with the marriage negotiations and to write a pamphlet castigating the Spanish ambassadors for a breach of diplomatic protocol.[75] Thus the muses were tuned to fulfill the commissions of the favorite and to secure the advancement of the ambitious.

---

and instructions, and lords yt handsomly alredy." (Chamberlain, *Letters*, II, 547, letter of Mar. 20, 1624.) Sir Robert Harley married Brilliana Conway on July 22, 1623. In September 1626 he was appointed Master and Worker of the Mint. (*DNB*, XXIV, 398–399; Keeler, *Long Parliament*, 203.) Secretary Conway's daughter, Frances, was married to Sir William Pelham of Brockelsby, Lincolnshire, who may be identified as the brother of the member from Great Grimsby, Henry Pelham (SP 14/159/28, Sir William Pelham [father of Henry, the member in 1624 and of Sir William Pelham] to Secretary Conway, Feb. 12, 1624.) Secretary Conway may also have had connections with John Mallet, Esq., who sat for Bath, Somerset, in 1624; in 1626 Conway, Governor of the Isle of Wight, nominated Mallet for a burgess-ship at Newtown, Isle of Wight. (SP 16/523/14, William Weld to Philip Fleming, Jan. 16, 1626.)

75. Maynard's masque is mentioned in Chamberlain, *Letters*, II, 527, letter of Nov. 21, 1623. On Maynard's election, see chap. ii, n.32. Patronage power at Old Sarum, Wiltshire, is discussed by Lawrence Stone, in his "The Electoral Influence of the Second Earl of Salisbury." The original return from Old Sarum named Sir Arthur Ingram and Michael Oldisworth. Stone considers Ingram, who was also elected for the city of York, to have been a Salisbury nominee, and it is probable, in view of the Earl's activity in this election, that Cotton, Ingram's replacement, was also Salisbury's choice. In the course of his parliamentary career, Sir Robert Cotton appealed to several patrons. He was recommended to the corporation of Thetford in 1625 by the Earl of Arundel and Surrey, and it is also probable that Howard influence accounted for his election at Castle Rising in 1628. Cotton sought a nomination to Westminster from John Williams, dean of Westminster, in 1628, and, although his request was sympathetically received, the dean's recommendation was made contingent upon the approval of the leading vestrymen. Williams also advised Cotton to make a gift of his works to the Westminster library. (Cotton MS. Julius C III, fol. 284, Mayor of Thetford to Cotton, Apr. 25, 1625; *ibid.* fols. 402–402v, John Williams, bishop of Lincoln, to Cotton, Feb. 12, 1627/8.) Cotton's "A Relation of the Proceedings against Ambassadors Who Have Miscarried Themselves, etc." is printed in *Cottoni Posthuma*, 1–9. It was written "in humble obedience" to Buckingham's command and the probable date of its composition is given as April 27, 1624. See HMC, *Third Report*, Appendix (London, 1872), 120, Duke of Northumberland MSS. See also Harl. MS. 180 for Cotton's preface to the manifesto justifying the breach with Spain in 1624. It is interesting to note that Sir Robert's son, Thomas Cotton, was returned for the restored borough of Great Marlow in Buckinghamshire. Sir Robert's services as an antiquarian were utilized in connection with the restoration of Amersham, Great Marlow, and Wendover.

More successful courtiers, however, were less intellectually inclined; their artistry consisted in subservient attendance and an ability to please. Such was Sir Clement Cotterell, elected for two boroughs in his native Lincolnshire, Boston and Grantham. Long a Buckingham supporter, Cotterell had relied on the favorite's intercession for the procurement of positions of trust and financial reward, and he had become, via this route, muster-master, groom porter, and monopolist.[76] The mere anticipation of favor was sufficient to induce some courtiers to join forces with the Duke. Just before the Parliament Sir Edward Howard, who represented Calne, Wiltshire, joined the "kindred" through marriage "chiefly upon hopefull conditions, the Lord of Buckingam professing that he will not only be an uncle but a father unto them." [77] Occasionally blood ties could prove embarrassing. Sir Thomas Bludder, who represented Reigate, Surrey, had, by his marriage with Elizabeth Brett, developed a kinship with both Buckingham and Cranfield that was to cause him some consternation in the Parliament.

(Cotton Ms. Julius C III, fols. 316–317, Francis Russell to Cotton, May 29, 1621, Jan. 20, 1621/2.)

76. Cotterell was of Wylsford, Lincolnshire. He had been appointed mustermaster of Buckinghamshire in 1616 through Villiers's influence. He was knighted at Whitehall on December 26, 1620, having been, on July 10, confirmed in the office of groomporter to the King for life. His appointment as groom-porter was the subject of a dispute between Buckingham and Pembroke in 1619. (Chamberlain, *Letters*, II, 263, letter of Sept. 11, 1619; 265, letter of Oct. 2, 1619; 275, letter of Nov. 20, 1619.) "The King cut of the difference about the groome-portership by telling the Lord Chamberlain that what right soever he had, he shold bestow yt upon him, so that one Coterell, a creature of the Lord of Buckingams placed in yt by him continues the possession without interruption." Cotterell also had a grant to oversee cards, dice, bowling alleys, tennis courts, and other such activities and to license them. (Rymer, *Foedera*, XVII, 236–238.)

77. Chamberlain, *Letters*, II, 533, letter of Dec. 20, 1623. Sir Edward Howard was a younger son of the Earl of Suffolk. In December 1623 he married Mary, daughter of Sir John Boteler and niece of the Duke of Buckingham. The marriage was celebrated at Buckingham's mansion, York House, and the Prince lodged there that evening. The "hopeful condition" in this connection was the restoration of the Earl of Suffolk to the Privy Council. (SP 14/156/3, Thomas Locke to Sir Dudley Carleton, Dec. 26, 1623.) In the Parliament of 1624 Sir Edward Howard was also returned for Wallingford, Berkshire, but he chose to sit for Calne. It may be that Howard influence both at Calne and Wallingford can be explained by their association with the constableship and stewardship of the castle and manor of Wallingford. The high steward of the Berkshire borough, Viscount Wallingford, had, moreover, married into the Howard family. For Wallingford, see J. K. Hedges, *The History of Wallingford* (2 vols., London, 1881), II, 113, 121–122. For Calne, see A. E. W. Marsh, *A History of the Borough and Town of Calne* (Calne, 1903), 66–68.

Most country gentlemen well affected to the Duke preferred to maintain a semi-independent position and solicited favors only as occasion warranted. Sir Lewis Watson, who represented Lincoln City, had been the favorite's firm friend even before Buckingham rose to power, but Watson's chief affiliations were with local families like the Montagus, Manners, and Willoughbys. John Drake of Ashe, who was elected for Devonshire, may also be categorized as an ally along with other West Country friends of the Duke such as Sir George Chudleigh (Tiverton, Devon) and Sir William Strode (Devonshire).[78]

Affiliations founded on patronage were frequently transitory; those based on popularity were even more ephemeral. In 1624 it was prudent and convenient for a member of Parliament to declare allegiance to Buckingham's policy; within a year, however, Phelips had become disenchanted with the favorite's guidance, and Eliot had abandoned his long association with the Duke to become his implacable enemy. Coke, who in 1624 had compared Buckingham with the Savior, by 1628 termed him "the grievance of grievances."

Apart from the spectacular shifts in allegiance that occurred in the early years of Charles's reign, it is apparent that Buckingham retained the loyalty of many members of Parliament. It is from evidence of continued association that I have tried to develop some conception of his coterie and, wherever possible, to show that this association was strengthened by personal ties. Yet, the continued existence of support for the Duke must be predicated on the fact that most contemporaries viewed him, not as the rapacious megalomaniac portrayed in the Commons charges of 1626, but rather as the very human politician described by the Earl of

---

78. In 1624 and again in 1626 Sir Lewis Watson was supported by Edward, Lord Montagu, for the knightship of Northamptonshire. In neither election was Watson successful. See the letters referring to these elections in HMC, *Buccleuch and Queensbery MSS* (3 vols., London 1899–1926), I, 258–260, and III, 257–263; HMC, *Lord Montagu of Beaulieu MSS* (London, 1900), 105–106. Drake entertained the Duke of Buckingham in September 1625 and again in March 1628. (*Walter Yonge's Diary*, 86, 111.) He is also mentioned, along with Chudleigh and Strode, as a partisan of the Duke in 1626. See the letter of July 1, 1626, from the commissioners of the Duke's estate to Nicholas that is cited by Hulme in *Sir John Eliot and the Vice-admiralty of Devon*, x. Drake's son, Sir John Drake, sat for Lyme Regis, Dorset, in the Parliament of 1624. He married Buckingham's niece, Elinor, daughter of Sir John Boteler. See F. T. Colby, ed., *Visitation of Devon*, Harleian Society, Volume VI (London, 1872), 94.

Kellie: "Here there is no alteration, but one man at the helm still, and I shall wish it may be so still for the good of his Majesty. Change can never be good for him nor the state, and if there has been anything amiss in this man he has had time to consider of the best; and this much I may out of my own observation say, that he has a great deal of more wit than men would believe, and that which most men complain of him is his doing so much for his friends. If it be an error it is a pardonable one, and I could wish myself so fortunate as to be one of them, for I could never have the good hope to be so well beloved with any that has been yet in favor." [79]

Obviously the disciples recruited by Charles and Buckingham in 1624 were sufficiently numerous to exert a considerable influence in the House of Commons. The direct patronage of the Prince and the Duke had, however, obligated only a fraction of the 489 members, and the experience of past Jacobean Parliaments had proven the necessity of a working majority if anything positive was to be accomplished. To compensate for the lack of a clear majority in the Commons there were several strategic steps that could be taken: presenting the foreign policy question to the Parliament in such a way as to secure maximum commitment from the Commons with a minimum of delay and investigation, reaching an understanding with the popular leaders of the House, and courting the support of independent members.

Of these, the last was most important because the effectiveness of the Commons leaders in directing the energies of the House depended upon their ability to verbalize the prejudices and opinions of the independent back-benchers. Not every member of Parliament came to Westminster with a burning desire to avenge the indignities suffered by the Prince in Spain, much less to vote the taxes required to finance a war. Sir Thomas Gerrard, elected for Liverpool, followed his conscience into the Spanish ambassador's lodgings in preference to the Commons' meeting place, St. Stephen's Chapel. Rather than compromise his religious beliefs, he risked arrest and prosecution under a bill of praemunire.[80]

Gerrard's intransigence demonstrates the major advantage en-

79. HMC, *Mar and Kellie*, 129, Thomas, earl of Kellie, to John, earl of Mar, Aug. 6, 1622.
80. Spring, 72, 93, 94, 95, 97, 113.

joyed by Charles and Buckingham in the promotion of their parliamentary program. The identification of pro-Spanish sympathies
with affection for popish religion made it practically impossible
for moderate members of Parliament to speak their minds without
risking the penalties of the recusancy laws. Then, too, the Prince
enjoyed the natural advantage of his youth and his prospective
inheritance. James was chagrined to learn that parliamentarians
and courtiers alike were prone to look to "the rising sun," and
Buckingham was not alone in paying "new respect" to the Prince's
wishes. In turn, Charles, with Buckingham's collusion, gratified
and appeased the most powerful of the popular factions by intimating a willingness to restrain the exercise of the royal prerogative in domestic affairs. The involvement of patrons like Southampton and Pembroke in the advancement of the breach with
Spain virtually secured for Charles and Buckingham the majority
necessary to implement their program.

   The apparent unanimity of the Commons in 1624 was deceptive. It was the unanimity of an overwhelmingly Protestant assembly on an issue involving religious prejudice and national
honor. The absence of discord on domestic issues was due to forbearance rather than agreement; controversial questions were
subordinated to the achievement of diplomatic disengagement
from Spain. But private interests were also served in the Parliament and the politics of clique and faction, though restrained,
frequently found expression in committee hearings and in debates
on the floor of the House. Perhaps the character and composition
of the House of Commons was affected as much by the pursuit of
private interests as by the desire to alter national policy, for the
motives that impelled men to seek election were often devoid of
concern for public welfare

# III  Other Patterns of Patronage

Early in 1624, Sir Roger Mostyn learned of the ambitions of his sons, Sir Thomas and John, to represent Flintshire in the forthcoming Parliament. Having already promised to support the candidacies of Sir John Hanmer for the single county seat and William Ravenscroft for Flint borough, Sir Roger confided his trepidations to his politically sagacious father-in-law, Sir John Wynn. Mostyn was reluctant to allow his eldest son to seek election for he feared that Sir Thomas would be drawn to live in London. "For my son John I rest wholly upon my cousin Richard Buckley's power [in Anglesey] and if it may not be had without any contesting with any country gentleman, I hold it not worth the having, and have written to him also to the same effect, though I am better pleased he should be employed in that service than his elder brother; he hath little to lose whatsoever fall thereof." [1]

1. Wynn of Gwydir Papers [Panton Group], National Library of Wales MS. 9059 E/1186, Sir Roger Mostyn to Sir John Wynn, Jan. 5, 1623/4. On August 11, 1624, Owen Wynn informed his father, Sir John Wynn, "that it is expected that Jack Mostyn should in person at Beaumaris give the gentlemen of that country thanks this assizes [for his election as knight of the shire] and remit the mise. This I hear from some out of that country. There is a decorum to be used in all things, else another time we shall be shaken off when the like occasion is offered." (Wynn of Gwydir Papers [Panton Group] National Library of Wales MS. 9059 E/1242, Owen Wynn to Sir John Wynn.) It was not, however, Sir Roger Mostyn's wish that his son should thank the gentlemen of Anglesey. His conceit was that they had no one else to fill the place. (*Calendar of Wynn (of Gwydir) Papers, 1515–1690, in the National Library of Wales and Elsewhere* [London, 1926], 205, Owen Wynn to Sir John Wynn, undated.) In the Kent county by-election in 1598 to select a replacement for Sir William Brooke, deceased, Percyvall Harte was urged to stand "for some better notification and countenance of him to the world for that he is now to make choice of another wife." His opponent in the hotly contested election was

Eventually the shire-knightship of Anglesey was negotiated for John, while Sir Thomas remained on his estates in obedience to parental command.

A year later Sir Thomas Haselrig solicited a burgess-ship from the corporation of Leicester for his son, Arthur. He asserted Arthur's willingness "to adapte himeselfe for the service of his Countrye" and his desire "to become a Scholler in the best Schoole of Christendome, for knowledge, and experience, (the parliament howse of England)." Sir Thomas opined that this was "a desire that everye father is to further in his children." [2]

These contrasting attitudes represent more than the mere passage of a year's time. Mostyn's depreciation of the value of a seat in the Commons was based upon the premise that the only gain to be derived from election was the reassertion of local prestige. His attitude was appropriate to an era in which the lower House was expected to say "aye or nay" and nothing more to the policies and demands presented for its consideration. Conversely, Haselrig's position typified the stand taken by the more aggressive gentry since the reign of Elizabeth. Far from viewing attendance at Westminster as an onerous duty, they saw it as a positive good — for both public and private reasons.

More and more, Parliament was regarded as a panacea for the ailments of the commonwealth, and the frequency of demands for its convention increased throughout the reign of James. Undoubtedly the gentry welcomed the larger role played by the House of Commons in the formation of national policy, but more important, in their estimation, was the forum it provided for the airing of public and private grievances. In some cases the consensus among members was such that alternative proposals to those advocated by the crown could be put forth, but, with rare exceptions, the coalescence of opinion in the Commons represented a negative rather than a positive approach toward government.

Local and private interests were also served by representatives

---

Sir Moyle Finch who desired the place because he had a cause depending in parliament which was on the verge of arbitrament. (Sutherland MS. D 593 S/4/19/29, Staffordshire Record Office, Sir John Leveson to the Earl of Essex, Jan. 8, 1597/8, and Percyvall Harte to Sir John Leveson, undated [Jan. 1597/8].)

2. Helen Stocks, ed., *Records of the Borough of Leicester Being a Series of Extracts from the Archives of the Corporation of Leicester, 1603–1688* (Cambridge: Cambridge University Press, 1923), 220, Sir Thomas Hasilrigge to the Mayor and Corporation of Leicester, Apr. 19, 1625.

in the lower House. Confirmation of borough charters, paving of streets, draining of fens, regulation of local officials, control of the manufacture and trade of selected materials — all were subjects of legislation initiated in the Commons.[3] Promotion of private bills for the sale or exchange of lands and confirmation of titles stimulated electoral competition already evident among the gentry. To lawyers and gentlemen alike, Parliament offered opportunities for career advancement. By assuming a "mild temper of rebelliousness," an ambitious man could bring himself to the notice of court and country — perhaps to the point of being offered royal largess and preferment in return for conformity.[4]

3. The instruction of nonresident members of Parliament presented nomination boroughs with a difficult problem. Rather than make an extended journey into the country in order to take the required oath as freeman of a borough, nominees, whenever possible, preferred to have the oath administered by commissioners in London. On December 18, 1620, for example, Lord Zouche wrote to the port of Hythe regarding the nomination of his brother, Richard Zouche, "I think it needlesse for him to be sworne a freeman of y^r Towne, and hope you will not be more strict to chose [him] that I recommend to you than you have been to others in the tyme of my Predecessors, but if you will have him take that Oathe, I pray you send hither a Commission (as other Townes that will have it soe doe) to some such gent there as you shall think fyt to minister him that Oath, that he may not have the trouble to goe to your Towne to receive it. If you desire to have anything menconed for the p—ticlar good of y^r Towne uppon which thereof by your letters, I will take Order that shalbe faithfully and carefully p—sented." (George Wilks, *The Barons of the Cinque Ports, and the Parliamentary Representation of Hythe* [Folkestone, 1892], 69–70.) In a letter [1614?] to Sir Thomas Parry, chancellor of the duchy of Lancaster, the corporation of Leicester agreed to elect his nominee providing that the candidate "maie fourthwith make his Repaire to Leicester there to take the oath of A free Burgesse of our Towne before wee proceede to our election as others heretofore have done in the like case." (Stocks, ed., *Records of the Borough of Leicester*, 148–149.) A. E. W. Marsh, *A History of the Borough and Town of Calne* (Calne, 1904), 341–342, prints a performance bond for five hundred pounds, which Edward Bayntun executed in 1658, thereby obligating himself to appear as a member of Parliament for Calne on January 27, 1659, at Westminster and "then and there to speak, do, and perform for us, the said burgesses and commons of the said borough, all such lawful and reasonable act and acts as shall be enacted and agreed upon at the said parliament as other the burgesses there assembled do or ought to do. So as the said borough, burgesses, and commons of the same be from henceforth cleared, acquitted, discharged, and saved harmless not only of all fees, wages and all other charges, losses and indemnities that by any means might happen to the said borough, burgesses and commons there by his negligence, slackness or default. That then the within written obligation to be void and of none effect or else to stand and remain in his full power and strength and virtue [spelling modernized]."

4. SP 16/522/88, Sir Fulk Greville to Lord Conway, undated. Prior to the convention of the Parliament (of 1621) the writer discussed the representation of Coventry "with one Mr. Eedes, a counsellor-at-law . . . I asked him what was the reason Mr. Hopkins (who serves for Coventry) was always so cross and violent in the parliament against the king's affairs, and what was the way to take him off. He

Whether the political consciousness of the gentry may be attributed to their increasing wealth or, alternatively, to their depressed
economic status does not alter the fact that they did predominate
in the Jacobean House of Commons. By 1620 the knights of the
shire were chosen almost exclusively from the ranks of the upper
gentry. Concomitantly, there was a decrease in the number of
privy councillors elected to represent county constituencies. In
1624 only Sir John Suckling, chosen for Middlesex, achieved this
eminence.

It is debatable whether the declining influence of privy councillors in the House of Commons is directly attributable to their
virtual exclusion from shire representation. I suggest that the authority of a parliamentary spokesman depended less and less upon
the constituency that elected him and more and more upon his
personal reputation and ability as a leader. Sir Edward Coke
preened himself on his dual election for the counties of Buckingham and Suffolk in 1628, but it was his considered opinion that
"though one be chosen for one particular County, or Borough,
yet when he is returned, and sit in Parliaments, he serveth for
the whole Realm, for the end of his comming thither, as in the
writ of his election appeareth, is generall." [5]

---

told me that he was chose by a faction in that town who had engaged him to be so in
opposition to several others that stood in competition with him; that there was
no way to alter him but by his father, Sir Richard Hopkins, with whom he would
discourse and give me a further account. This week he came to me again and told
me that Sir Richard Hopkins said he had no reason to concern himself in that
matter, for there were two puisne serjeants-at-law to him already put over his
head and called up to the bench before him, but if upon the death of any of the
ancient judges he might be preferred to be a judge in any of the king's courts he
would not only make his son go right in the king's business but several others of his
friends that went in the House of Commons as perversely as his son did." This
draft letter is undated, unsigned and without an address. I suggest that it may
tentatively be dated December 1620 because Sampson Hopkins represented Coventry
in 1614 and 1621, but never thereafter. It is unlikely that the recipient was Lord
Conway, who was not elevated to the peerage until March 24, 1625.

5. Sir Edward Coke, *The Fourth Part of the Institutes of the Laws of England:
Concerning the Jurisdiction of Courts* (London, 1644), 14; D. H. Willson, *The Privy
Councillors in the House of Commons, 1604–1629* (Minneapolis: University of Minne-
sota Press, 1940), 71–74. Willson mentions the ill-success of privy councillors in
county elections, but the leadership of the Parliaments of the 1620's was vested in
men who were not normally knights of the shire and who were frequently elected
for counties only after they had achieved prominence in national affairs. Coke was
the most widely reported and respected member of the House, yet in 1621 he sat
for a Cornish borough and in 1624 and 1625 was returned for Coventry. Sir Edwin
Sandys was listened to whether he sat for Kent, Sandwich, or elsewhere. John Glanville, John Pym, Sir Dudley Digges, and Sir Benjamin Rudyard were among the

Obviously county elections, with their uniform forty-shilling freehold franchise were more subject to negotiation and compromise than to outright domination; in shires where the influence of one family was not transcendent, the leading knights often represented the county in rotation.[6] But, with only a limited number of county seats available, those gentlemen desiring a place in the Commons were forced to apply to the boroughs. The intrusion of the gentry into the representation of the lesser towns significantly altered the patronage pattern evident in earlier Parliaments. Nominees of the peerage, and particularly of the crown, no longer were assured of election when the seat was contested by a local squire. In consequence the House of Commons became more independent and argumentative and less easily managed. But it was not always the crown or the magnates who suffered;

---

bellwethers of the House, as much so as predominantly county members like Sir Robert Phelips and Sir Francis Seymour. Nor was it merely seniority of membership that entitled a parliament man to a respectful hearing from his fellow commoners. Sir Thomas Posthumus Hoby, Edward Alford, Sir Thomas Denton, Sir Thomas Walsingham, and Richard Digges rarely, if ever, made significant contributions to the debates in the House. Alford's legalistic concern with precedents and procedures afforded him an opportunity for temporary notoriety in 1621; in 1624 he seemed merely to be quibbling. Even an ancient parliament man like Sir George More had one of his most important speeches in 1624, "interrupted with noise of some that misliked his tediousness." (Spring, 43.)

6. T. S. Bindoff, "Parliamentary History 1529–1688," in *Victoria History of the Counties of England, A History of Wiltshire* [hereafter cited as *V. C. H. Wiltshire*] (London, 1957), V, 111–169, esp. 125, refers to the case of Sir Thomas Thynne who, in the Parliament of 1604, was elected for Hindon. When one of the knights of the shire died after the first session, Thynne had himself returned for the vacant county seat. The election was disallowed by the Commons on the grounds that he was ineligible by reason of prior membership in the House. Bindoff thinks that Thynne may have so alienated the Wiltshire gentry as to preclude his future election for the shire. According to Edith Farnham's article, "The Somerset Election of 1614," *English Historical Review*, XLVI (Oct. 1931), 579–599, Sir Robert Phelips's decision to stand singly for the premier knightship of the shire in Somerset in 1614 cost him the election. The process of negotiation by which controversies in county elections were appeased is illustrated in the letters calendared in HMC, *Seventh Report*, Appendix, pt. I (London, 1879), 542, 549, in reference to the Essex election of 1604. Local prestige, which is such an important factor in parliamentary elections, is given added emphasis by legal clauses requiring tenants to vote in accordance with their landlord's desires. A. H. Dodd, in his *Studies in Stuart Wales* ([Cardiff, 1952], 177), cites such a clause in an indenture executed by John Edwards in the sixteenth century. In *The Visitation of Cornwall*, Harleian Society, Volume IX (London, 1874), 120,n., there is a reference to a Cornish deed dated June 1, 6 Elizabeth, in which John Harrys of Carnworthy, tenant of the manor of Langdon was required to give his voice "at the eleccion of the knyghts of the Shere for and with the said John Langdon and his heirs, or for and with any other person and persons at the appointment of the said John Langdon and his heirs." I know of no such indenture extant for the seventeenth century.

more frequently it was the small boroughs themselves. In many instances their independence was completely smothered in the competition for parliamentary places.[7] Boroughs, which before had been represented by one member of their corporation in partnership with a nominee, now were frequently represented by a courtier coupled with a country gentleman.

The boroughs had not lost their freedom of election entirely without their own consent.[8] Probably it was the necessity of taxing

7. In the "Interim Report of the Committee on House of Commons Personnel and Politics 1264–1832," the compilers of *Command Paper 4031* (London, 1932), 33, allege that "By the time the Stuarts came to the throne perhaps half the boroughs had acquired courage enough to retain one seat and reject the patron's demand for two. The borough member was probably less dependent upon patronage for his seat in the 17th century than either before or after that time." It is true that boroughs in the seventeenth century less frequently allowed a patron to nominate both members, but I suggest that the seventeenth century witnessed an increase in the number of solicitors for places. Consequently patronage as such did not decline, but was diffused more generally through the upper strata of society.

8. Stocks, ed., *Records of the Borough of Leicester*, 148–149. In 1614 the corporation of Leicester replied to Sir Thomas Parry's recommendations with the following saving clause: "But towchinge your honors predecessors in your place mencioned in your honors Letters may it please you to bee informed that in truth they have neyther allwaies written unto us about the Choyce of our Burgesses neyther allwaies prevayled when they did wryte. And that sometymes we have chosen both our Burgesses out of our owneselves and dwellinge in our owne towne. Howebeitt at this tyme upon due Consideracion had wee cannot but acknowledge that our wholle Corporacion have received soe manie favors from your honors hands as deserved to prevayle with us in A greater request." In 1624 the bailiffs of Great Yarmouth made use of a corporation bylaw to decline respectfully a parliamentary nomination made by the bishop of Norwich. "Whome y$^r$ L$^p$ recommends unto us and o$^r$ choyce for one of our burgesses, albeit wee have noe knowledge of; yett we p$^-$suade ourselves of his worth and sufficiency, and of further favour by his means, as in y$^r$ L$^{ps}$ lr$^-$es are remembred, in case he bee chosen. Butt so itt is, as wee su$^-$pose y$^r$ L$^p$ doe well knowe that wee have an ordenance wherto wee are tyed by oathe, so long as it abydes in force, nott to choose any for our burgesse, not being a freeman and inh$^-$itant of this towne. Yett to show our careful respect of y$^r$ L$^{ps}$ love and favour unto o$^r$ towne, wee will (if our assemblye shall thinke good to abrogate or dispense w$^{th}$ that ordenance) above all others in that kinde p$^-$ferre and reco$^-$mend hym unto their choice, whom y$^r$ L$^p$ have so worthely recomended unto us, and at our next meetyng will cause y$^r$ L$^{ps}$ l$^{-(res)}$ to be read. Howbeit, seing the choice of o$^r$ burgesses for a p$^-$liament consisting in the breasts of so many, wee cannot assure o'selves of what they shall doe when it shall by writt be putt upon them. But this we assure y$^r$ L$^p$, that, according to o$^r$ duties, and tendring the good and wellfare of o$^r$ towne wee will for o$^r$ parts with all observance further, y$^r$ L$^{ps}$ advice and good counsell." (C. J. Palmer, *The History of Great Yarmouth* [Great Yarmouth, 1856], 202–203.) On Dec. 1, 1620, the corporation of Nottingham amended its bylaws to permit the choice of nonresident M.P.'s "for the easinge of the townes chardge." In the subsequent election there were five candidates, but by 1624 there were ten suitors seeking election including Sir George Chaworth, Edward Ayscough, and John Selden. (W. H. Stevenson, ed., *Records of the Borough of Nottingham*, [4 vols., London, 1882–1889], IV, 373, 375, 387.)

local inhabitants to pay the wages of their members of Parliament that induced many corporations to accept the offers of the gentry to serve without pay. As yet, in 1624, there was little consciousness on the part of boroughs that their right to elect representatives was a marketable commodity. The techniques of corruption practiced in the eighteenth century were known, but not widely utilized. County elections provided a larger arena in which to develop political strategy, but, in the microcosm of the borough, virtually every devious device was evident.

Not many boroughs were owned outright by members of the gentry, but they were capable of offering inducements — both negative and positive — to ensure their election. They frequently became members of corporate bodies and used their influence to limit or expand the number of freemen whenever it best suited their interests. They were assiduous in their entertainment of the most important people in the town, and a buck sent to the mayor and corporation was often recompensed with added respect and consideration. Offers to prefer petitions, secure a new charter for the town, or aid in its reconstitution as a parliamentary borough sometimes helped to secure a safe seat for a local gentleman. Money bribes were uncommon, but dinner and drink were becoming increasingly indispensable as election adjuncts. A less overt form of inducement sometimes offered was the reduction or elimination of fees or services owed by the borough. If persuasion failed, coercion could be employed because the candidate usually occupied an office such as justice of the peace or deputy lieutenant. Threats, intimidation, and slander were not absent from Jacobean elections, but convenience usually dictated the means chosen. Thus, with the aid of a bailiff, one could conceal the precept, omit proper notice, alter the time and place of election or adjourn it, refuse the poll, challenge the opposition voters on precarious grounds, or, *in extremis,* file a false return.[9]

9. The influence of country gentlemen in borough corporations varied considerably. Some families like the St. Johns of Bedfordshire and the Savages of Chester held corporation appointments which they exercised personally or through deputies. Perhaps the most intimate association was that of Sir Hugh Middleton with the burgesses of Denbigh. Not only was he instrumental in obtaining their charter of incorporation in 1596, but he became their first alderman, was subsequently appointed recorder, and was their member of Parliament regularly from 1604 through 1628. He presented the corporation with a cup of silver made from bullion from his Welsh mines. See *DNB*, XXIX, 436–439. At the opposite extreme was the relation-

Even sole ownership of a borough did not guarantee that control of elections would remain unchallenged. A case in point was
Gatton, Surrey, where, since the reign of Elizabeth, it had been
conceded that the Copley family had the nomination of two par-

ship of Sir George Manners with the town of Grantham. In 1621 Sir George was
elected knight of the shire for Lincoln, but on December 3, 1620, he had written
to his servant, George Falcon, "Yf the ellection of the knights be passed, and
Grantham not chosen theyr burgesses, then commend me to Sir Thomas Ellis by
message, not shewing my letter, and lett him know, as likewise Mr. Moon and Mr.
Wyclyfe, that in regard I am a ffreeman of theyr towne, and of never a corporation
else, I shall take it very kindly att theyr hands and the townes, yf at this tyme they
will bestow a burgesses place upon me, and the more kindly for that it proceedes
from my owne motions. Postscript: Shew my letter to no man, but burne it." (HMC,
*Twelfth Report*, Appendix IV [London, 1888], 457, Duke of Rutland MSS.) In the
Pontefract and Winchelsea elections in 1624, evidence was adduced of both the expansion and the limitation of the electorate. In Pontefract it was alleged that new
burgesses were made and recusants brought in; at Winchelsea two jurats were
excluded for nonresidence. (Pym, fol. 37; Earle, fol. 102; Glanville, *Reports*, 12–24,
133–143.) Entertainments and gifts to corporations were not unusual. In 1626 Sir
Lewis Dyve presented a silver saltcellar to the corporation of Bridport, Dorset, subsequent to his election. (H. G. Tibbutt, ed., *The Life and Letters of Sir Lewis Dyve
1599–1669*, Bedfordshire Historical Record Society Publications, Volume XXVII
[Streatley: the Society, 1948], 8.) Dyve's gratitude may have been occasioned by
Bridport's refusal to elect his opponent, Edward Clark, Buckingham's nominee.
(SP 16/19/69, Corporation of Bridport to Buckingham, Jan. 28, 1625/6.) In 1628
Sir Richard Harrison sent a fat buck to the mayor and burgesses of Reading "in
parte of his love and thankes to them for their love and well wishinge to him in
his eleccion to be Knight for the shiere at Abingdon for the last Parliament." J. M.
Guilding, ed., *Reading Records* (4 vols., London, 1892–1896), II, 415. On February
15, 1628, Secretary Conway wrote to Sir Thomas Jervoise: "Your letter doth mention
some customary feast to be made to those of the town [of Andover] at the time of
the election. I pray you do me the favor to send me word speedily what is to be
done therein by me, and whether it be requisite my son be there at that time. Your
directions in all things shall be performed fully and thankfully." (SP 16/93/48, Sir
Edward Conway to Sir Thomas Jervoise, Feb. 15, 1627/8; see also SP 16/93/47, Sir
Edward Conway to the corporation of Andover, Feb. 15, 1627/8.) In 1625 "Sir Henry
Wotton stoode to be burgesse for Caunterburie, but for all the frends he could make
and though he spent almost fiftie pound in goode drincke upon his followers, yet
one Captain Fisher a muster-master won yt from him." (Chamberlain, *Letters*, 615,
letter of May 6, 1625.) Ralph Goodwin, who sat for Ludlow in 1624, and in every
succeeding Parliament until he was disabled in 1644, entertained the burgesses of
the town prior to the election for the Short Parliament. "Mr. Goodwyn appears no
less earnest, and with his Xmas Cheare hath feasted the Burgesses, and endeavours
by their bellies to gain their tongues, but it is thought the Burgesses are not well
affected towards him." (H. T. Weyman, "The Members of Parliament for Ludlow,"
*Transactions of the Shropshire Archaeological and Natural History Society*, 2d Ser.,
VII [1895], 1–54, esp. 25.) In the Bletchingly election of 1624 it was testified that
"some money, though very little, had been given" on Lovell's behalf to procure
him voices. (Glanville, *Reports*, 39.) More subtle influence was brought to bear by
Sir William Cavendish when he aided in the procurement of the charter of confirmation for Bishop's Castle. It was ordered that since " 'he only requesteth the fruit
of our love in making choice eyther of the said Sir William or of such other gent

liamentary burgesses. The investiture of one person with electoral powers was never the primary question at issue; the impediment was the recusancy of the Copley family. In 1584, and again in 1586, the lords of the Council took action to make sure that "Mrs. Coplyffe [Copley] . . . should not be allowed to influence the next election as she is known to be ill affected." In 1621 the return made by Mr. Copley, a convicted recusant, and six of his tenants was voided on the technical plea that the election was held at an improper time and place.[10] The candidates elected by one or two

---

as he shall commend to be burges for us of the next parliament,' his desire shall be 'effected when time doth serve' and that letters be written to him for assurance thereof." (HMC, *Tenth Report*, Appendix, pt. IV [London, 1885], 402, Bishop's Castle MSS, Mar. 10, 1617.) John Hampden paid the charges involved in procuring the restoration of Amersham, Wendover, and Marlow in 1624 and was forthwith elected to the Commons from Wendover. As an added inducement to secure his election at Ludlow in 1620, Richard Tomlyns mentioned that "it is not unknown unto some of my near friends among you that long since I had a purpose out of my poor estate to do some good for the town. It may be in part while I live, but sure after my decease, if it please God." See the informative series of letters from Richard Tomlyns and others to the bailiffs of Ludlow written between 1620 and 1628 and printed in Weyman, "The Members of Parliament for Ludlow," 21–23. Coercion and fraud were both evident in the Bletchingly election in 1624: Lovell threatened to procure the withdrawal of a charitable bequest made to the corporation and also, surreptitiously, filed his own return in the crown office. (Glanville, *Reports*, 29–46.) In 1628 Sir John Stawell took offense at the refusal of the freemen of Taunton to grant him their voices in the election. He "removed some soldiers that were settled, and billited them upon the mayor and others." *Walter Yonge's Diary*, 114–115. In the Canterbury election in 1624 Sir William Lovelace complained that he had been slandered by Simon Penny who spread the rumor that he "did cross himself before the French or Spanish Ambassador." (SP 14/158/67; also SP 14/159/50.) Manipulation of elections by borough officials was frequently the subject of petitions to the House of Commons. In 1624 the mayor of Newcastle-under-Lyme was charged with interrupting the poll, dissolving the electoral assembly, and making a return without warrant. At Malmesbury it was alleged that the name of Sir Edward Cecil, duly elected, "was afterwards, by corruption and abuse, rased out, and the name of Sir Thomas Hatton put in; and so the indenture returned by the sheriff." (Glanville, *Reports*, 115.) At both Gloucester and Chippenham elections were adjourned, and at Arundel the mayor refused to dissolve the assembly after the poll had been taken and the electors had departed.

10. HMC, *Seventh Report*, Appendix, pt. I, 642, Sir Francis Walsingham to Sir William More, Sir Thomas Browne, and Richard Bostock, Sept. 27, 1586; H. A. Merewether and A. J. Stephens, *The History of the Boroughs and Municipal Corporations of the United Kingdom* (3 vols., London, 1835), III, 1646–1652; *Commons Debates 1621*, II, 16, n. 1; IV, 24–25; VI, 359–360. See also Edward Nicholas, *Proceedings and Debates of the House of Commons in 1620 and 1621, Collected by a Member of that House*, ed. T. Tyrwhitt (2 vols., Oxford, 1766), I, 20. The petition against the Gatton election was filed by Sir George More who was chairman of the Committee of Privileges. No doubt this accounts for Gatton's priority among the cases considered.

resident freeholders in combination with several nonresident free-holders were seated by virtue of the Commons order to the sheriff to return them.

By 1624 the Copley preserve had been invaded by Samuel Ow-field, a Lincolnshire squire and son of a London fishmonger. With the acquisition of property at Gatton he apparently acquired a "safe seat"; except for a single intermission in 1625 he represented that constituency from 1624 through the Long Parliament.[11] When, in 1628, Copley made a last ditch attempt to recover ab-solute control of the borough by alleging that he was the sole inhabitant, the opposition, who had likewise filed a return, claimed that since 1621 Copley had joined with other inhabitants in executing indentures. Once again Copley was defeated, and his nominees ousted.

Absolute ownership of a borough was not an indispensable prerequisite for a safe seat. The lordship of a borough, such as that held by Sir Richard Fleetwood at Newton (Lancashire), Sir Robert Howard at Bishop's Castle (Shropshire), or the Packington family at Aylesbury (Buckinghamshire) virtually made their con-sent the *sine qua non* for election. Widespread property holdings, particularly in burgage tenure boroughs, also helped to guarantee the return of a preferred candidate. This type of influence was exerted by the Ducketts at Calne (Wiltshire), the Slingsbys at Knaresborough (Yorkshire), and the Cliffords at Appleby (West-moreland). Jurisdictional rights such as those vested in the Earl of Huntingdon at Leicester, or control of the markets as held by Sir William Whitmore at Bridgnorth, Shropshire, were also sig-nificant factors in influencing elections. Friendly relations with the corporation and the prestige associated with large landhold-ings in the neighborhood were probably the main reasons why

---

11. In 1625 the members for Gatton were Sir Charles Howard and Sir Thomas Crew, Serjeant-at-law and Speaker designate. Although Owfield did not sit for Gatton, he was returned by Midhurst, Sussex, as a replacement for Sir Walter Tichborne, who preferred to sit for Wootton Bassett, Wiltshire. I suspect that a deal was arranged to make sure that Sir Thomas Crew sat in the Parliament of 1625 — to have Copley, a recusant convict, agree to the return of a staunch Puritan implies the application of pressure. Patronage at Midhurst was largely controlled by the Montagu family, one of whom was the lord of the borough. On disputed elections at Gatton, see Merewether and Stephens, *History of the Boroughs*, III, 1646–1652.

some boroughs regularly returned members of the same family. The parliamentary dynasty of the Walsinghams at Rochester, Kent, was an outstanding example. Except for 1614, a member of the Walsingham family was elected to represent Rochester in every Parliament from 1597 until the end of the reign of Charles I.[12]

Continued control over borough elections depended on so many variable factors that it is extremely difficult to categorize long-term pocket boroughs. Loss of influence at court, intramural disputes within the county, changes in property holdings, friction between corporate bodies and the gentry, any of these could and did nullify patronage rights to safe seats. On occasion even the most powerful noblemen had their requests ignored. In 1621, for instance, Thomas Howard, the earl of Arundel and Surrey, recommended two members to Steyning, Sussex; they were not elected. Again on January 9, 1624, he addressed a most judicious letter to the constable and inhabitants of the town recommending Philip Mainwaring and William Gardiner, "whom I know to be every way worthy and fit for those places; and for whom I will undertake that they shall not require any parliament wages." Arundel admitted that: "It were well if the old custom were duly observed, and every borough should elect members of their own body to undergo that service. But in regard, many towns are depopulated, and some are so impovrished, as would be heavy unto them to support the *charge* incident, it hath been a usage of long continuance for most towns to make choice of such *foreigners* as were fit and worthy of the places, and herein to have recourse and respect unto the tender made unto them of able men by their chief lords; and so my ancestors have done unto your predecessors." [13] Arundel asked no more than "due consideration" of his wishes, but the borough returned neither of his candidates, preferring, instead, Sir Edward Francis and Sir Thomas Farnefold. It seems probable that Arundel's desires were more respected elsewhere. His secretary, John Borough, was elected at Horsham, Sussex, and Sir Henry Spiller and Sir Robert Spiller, father and son, respec-

---

12. In 1614 Sir Thomas Walsingham, Sr., represented Kent, and Sir Thomas Walsingham, Jr., was elected at Poole, Dorset. (*Official Return*, Appendix, Pt. I, xxxviii.)

13. Mereweather and Stephens, *History of the Boroughs*, III, 1513–1514, Thomas Howard, earl of Arundel and Surrey to the borough of Steyning, Jan. 9, 1623/4.

tively, were named members of Parliament for the Howard boroughs of Arundel, Sussex, and Castle Rising, Norfolk.[14]

The parliamentary influence of a family, whether noble or gentle, was largely determined by the aggressiveness and ambition of its leader. Some country squires never aspired to represent any other than a neighboring constituency. Sir Robert Howard was content to sit for Bishop's Castle for six Parliaments; John Duckett only represented his borough of Calne, Wiltshire, twice; Sir William Whitmore sat three times for Bridgnorth, Shropshire. Framlingham Gawdy, with extensive properties in Norfolk and Suffolk, represented Thetford in each of the seven Parliaments he attended. Ripon, Yorkshire, regularly returned William Mallory, head of a family associated with the stewardship of the borough. Sir Christopher Wray of Ashby, Lincolnshire, was elected to six Parliaments by Great Grimsby, and William Strode, Jr., who began his career in 1624, was returned by Berealston, Devon, to every Parliament until his death in 1645.

Some of these men, notably Mallory and Strode, were aggressive parliamentarians; Gawdy also kept a notebook of the debates in at least one Parliament. None of them, however, displayed the ability, ambition, and political genius that distinguished Sir Thomas Wentworth from all his colleagues. His masterly management of the Yorkshire election in 1621 sharply contrasted with the lethargic campaigns waged by those whose candidacy depended solely upon inherited position. Although he did not control a single Yorkshire borough, Wentworth parlayed his friendships and familial connections into a well-organized political machine. He relied upon Lord Clifford for a safe seat at Appleby, Westmoreland, in case he failed in his bid for a Yorkshire knightship. He anticipated the candidacy of Sir Thomas Fairfax of Walton, preempted Fairfax's intended partner, Secretary Calvert, and yet

14. HMC, *Tenth Report*, Appendix, pt. II, 127, William Stanhope to Framlingham Gawdy, Feb. 25, 1628, mentions the nomination of Sir Henry Spiller by the Earl of Arundel to the town of Thetford, Norfolk. Sir Robert Cotton was the Earl's successful nominee in 1625. (Cotton MS. Julius C III, fol. 284, The Mayor of Thetford to Sir Robert Cotton, Apr. 25, 1625.) It may be that Sir George Chaworth of Nottinghamshire, who sat for Arundel until he was expelled from the House on March 24, 1624, was also nominated by the Earl of Arundel and Surrey, although there is nothing in the diaries or contemporary letters to justify more than the probability of a connection. The contested returns from Arundel for the Long Parliament indicate that it was the practice of the Earl of Arundel and Surrey to commend candidates to the borough. (Keeler, *Long Parliament*, 66–67.)

managed to retain his friendship and support. Wentworth countered Sir John Savile's objections to Calvert's nonresidence by advising the Secretary to secure a favorable ruling from Lord Chancellor Bacon. He courted the high sheriff of Yorkshire, the Lord President of the North, and the bishop of Durham, and he invited the chiefs of his supporters to dine with him at York in a house borrowed for the occasion from his friend, Sir Arthur Ingram. He promised burgess-ships to Christopher Wandesford and Sir Henry Savile, but his Appleby seat was ultimately delivered to Sir Arthur Ingram. He marshaled his supporters like military contingents and appointed their times and places of rendezvous. He initiated a census of the Yorkshire electors and, together with Lord Darcy, asked the high constables to cause the petty constables to number the freeholders according to their political preferences. To make his ticket more appealing, he stood for the first place, but he had the order reversed in the return so that Sir George Calvert appeared as the prime knight of the shire.[15]

Enterprise, sagacity, and assiduous attention to detail were the main ingredients in Wentworth's electoral success. The same qualities that had served him well in the Yorkshire contest in 1621 were of value to him in his relations with the borough of Pontefract. Although Wentworth apparently did not figure in the restoration of Pontefract as a parliamentary borough in 1621, he maintained a paternalistic attitude toward the corporation. His estimate of his power in the borough was such that in March 1621 he imagined that he could persuade the town to annul its election and grant him the nomination of one of its members. Yet Wentworth was by no means certain that Pontefract would return him in 1624; he apparently depended heavily on Lord Clifford.

15. Strafford, *Letters*, 9, Sir Thomas Wentworth to Christopher Wandesford, Nov. 28, 1620; ibid., 10, Wentworth to Sir Thomas Fairfax, Dec. 3, 1620; *ibid.*, 10, Wentworth to Secretary Calvert, Dec. 5, 1620; *ibid.*, 8, Wentworth to Sir Henry Savile, Nov. 28, 1620; *ibid.*, 11, Wentworth to Sir Arthur Ingram, Dec. 6, 1620; *ibid.*, 13, Wentworth to Thomas Wentworth, Jr., Dec. 8, 1620; *ibid.*, 8, Wentworth to Sir Thomas Gower, Nov. 28, 1620; see also the letters to Sir Matthew Boynton, Sir Thomas Dawney, Sir Henry Slingsby, and Sir Thomas Fairfax of Denton in the same volume and the letter from Sir Thomas Wentworth to Mr. Lawson calendared in HMC, *Seventh Report*, Appendix, 674. The letter to Sir Thomas Fairfax of Denton, December 8, 1620, is also printed in G. W. Johnson, ed., *The Fairfax Correspondence* (2 vols., London, 1848), I, lix–lx. Sir George More's notes of testimony in the Committee of Privileges in 1621 are among the More-Molyneux MSS deposited in the Guildford Museum and Muniment Room, Surrey, Loseley MS. 1331/25.

When he learned that Clifford was already engaged, he expressed fear that he "should have been turned to Grass here in the Country." Nevertheless he was elected at Pontefract "nothwithstanding all [the] Labour made against [him]." [16] His partner, Sir Henry Holcroft, was also returned for Stockbridge, Hampshire, and chose to serve for that borough. Wentworth seems not to have intervened in the subsequent heated by-election at Pontefract where Sir John Jackson's candidacy was opposed by Sir Richard Beaumont. But Wentworth was an active partisan of Beaumont's cause when the Pontefract election was adjudicated by the House of Commons. Beaumont was not admitted, but Sir John Jackson sat in the House "at his peril" and the persistent petitioning of the Beaumont faction finally had the desired effect of invalidating the entire by-election on May 28.

Wentworth's enemy, Sir John Savile, had aggressively supported Sir John Jackson and was apparently triumphant; Jackson had possession, however precariously, of the burgess-ship throughout the session.[17] However, Wentworth was ultimately victorious, for in 1625 Sir John Jackson offered his support in the county elections even before any candidacy was announced. He proposed, in addition, a political alliance to control the elections at Pontefract.

A diplomatic counterproposal suggested the election of Sir Richard Beaumont as Jackson's partner if Wentworth were suc-

16. Strafford, *Letters*, 14, Wentworth to Lord Darcy, Mar. 31, 1621; *ibid.*, 19, Wentworth to Lord Clifford, Jan. 23, 1624.

17. For a discussion of the Pontefract election contest in 1624, see Glanville, *Reports*, 133–143. The double return from Pontefract was brought to the attention of the House of Commons on March 22, 1624, by Sir John Savile, *CJ*, 745. Neither the *CJ* nor Earle, fol. 102, mentions Savile's support of Jackson, although both explicitly mention Wentworth's charges that diverse recusants were brought in overnight and made freemen of the borough in order to influence the election in favor of Jackson. Pym (fol. 37), says that Savile first moved the reception of Jackson into the House and that this brought about the rejoinder by Wentworth and the subsequent referral of the matter to the Committee of Privileges. The *CJ* alone mentions that Wentworth charged the mayor of Pontefract with misbehavior, and this charge may cast some light on the doubts expressed by Wentworth earlier about his own election to the Parliament of 1624. For Glanville's report from the Committee of Privileges, see *CJ*, 751; Earle, fol. 107 (entry improperly dated as Tuesday, March 25, instead of April 1); Pym, fol. 44. Only the *CJ* mentions that Sir Thomas Wentworth preferred a further petition from Pontefract which prevented the final resolution of the case until the entire by-election was voided on May 28, 1624. (*CJ*, 714.)

cessful at the Yorkshire hustings.[18] This plan was realized: Wentworth was chosen for the county; Jackson and Beaumont, for Pontefract. Yet old enmities were not forgotten; Beaumont refused to serve. "I am much beholden to them for the Matter, but not for the Manner: I should have been willing to have kept your [Wentworth's] Place for you, or for any Friend of yours, and served in it, and yielded it up of an Hour's Warning to have done you Service; but as it is, I pray, acquaint my Kinsman that I would have him get a new Writ from Mr. Speaker, . . . that the Town may chuse another." [19] Thus by his judicious carriage Wentworth made sure of Pontefract. In 1626 Jackson offered to support any Wentworth nominee, and in 1628, despite the fact that Savile had become Baron Savile of Pontefract and steward of the honor, the mayor of the borough wrote to assure Wentworth that his good offices would "not only binde us but also our posteritie in a perpetual bond to your Worship and all yours." [20]

In his successful attempt to convert Pontefract into a family preserve Wentworth was merely following the traditional procedure adopted by many men with parliamentary ambitions. Frequently the first step toward the attainment of a successful career at Westminster was the capture of a safe seat. Such a focus of local power provided a base of operations for the extension of personal influence into county politics. In the northern counties, where borough seats were scarce, control of a parliamentary constituency was not always feasible, and dynasties tended to be established on the basis of shire elections. Competition may have been lessened somewhat by the time and expense involved in undertaking the protracted journey to London. The relative poverty of the border areas and the proportionately smaller number of noteworthy families probably facilitated the consistent return of some northern members of Parliament. Thus Sir George Dalston sat for Cumberland county in every Parliament from 1621 until he was disabled

18. Strafford, *Letters*, 25–26, Wentworth to Sir John Jackson, Apr. 6, 1625; Wentworth to Mr. Cowper, mayor of Pontefract, undated.
19. *Ibid.*, 27, Sir Richard Beaumont to Wentworth, June 9, 1625.
20. Letter of the Mayor of Pontefract to Wentworth, quoted by Evangeline de Villiers, "Parliamentary Boroughs Restored by the House of Commons 1621–41," *English Historical Review*, LXVII (Apr. 1952), 187, taken from the Wentworth correspondence in the Sheffield Public Library.

in 1643, John Lowther represented Westmoreland from 1624 through 1628, and Sir John Fenwick was elected for Northumberland from 1624 until the Long Parliament.[21]

Farther south, county representation fluctuated with increasing frequency. Notable exceptions were to be found in the counties of Warwick and Bedford. Sir Thomas Lucy of Charlcote was elected member of Parliament for Warwickshire in 1614, was reelected successively through the Short Parliament, and was chosen at Warwick borough in the autumn of 1640 despite serious illness. His brother, Francis Lucy, sat for Warwick borough from 1624 through 1628. In Bedfordshire, the families of Luke and St. John virtually dominated the county. After serving his apprenticeship in the House for Bedford borough in 1597, Sir Oliver Luke was returned for the county of Bedford in 1614 and retained his seat until he was secluded in 1648. His partner for Bedfordshire from 1624 through 1628 was Oliver St. John, eldest son of Oliver, Lord St. John of Bletsoe.

Where competing gentry were more numerous, exclusive occupancy of a shire seat was not possible. In Buckinghamshire, for instance, Sir Thomas Denton was elected to four Parliaments for the borough and two for the county. In Oxfordshire, Sir Thomas Wenman was returned for the county three times, but on five

---

21. W. W. Bean, *The Parliamentary Representation of the Six Northern Counties of England* (Hull, 1890), 17, and Keeler, *Long Parliament*, 151–152, differ widely on the date of Sir George Dalston's death. Bean says that Dalston was killed at the battle of Towton Heath near Chester in 1645; Keeler lists the date of death as being 1657, and her evidence is much more conclusive. John Lowther died in 1637, doubtless cutting short his parliamentary career. Either John or his brother Richard kept diaries of the Parliaments of 1626 and 1628 which are printed *in extenso*. (HMC, *Thirteenth Report*, Appendix, pt. VII [London, 1893], 1–74, Earl of Lonsdale MSS.) The attribution, based on a reference to the *CJ*, June 1, 1626, is inconclusive. The date of Sir John Fenwick's election to the Parliament of 1624 is not listed in the *Official Return*. Fenwick replaced Sir William Grey, who was created Lord Grey of Wark February 11, 1624. Sir George Dalston's partner as knight of the shire for Cumberland in 1624 was Ferdinand Huddleston, Esq., whose election was petitioned against on the grounds that he was ineligible by reason of twenty outlawries, some of which were after judgments. In Huddleston's defense it was said, "the nature of an outlawry is chiefly to disable the party to his own prejudice, and not to the prejudice of the commonwealth; whereas if the most sufficient knight, or esquire in the whole county, being outlawed, should thereby be made incapable to serve his country and state in parliament, it were no little prejudice to the commonwealth, so to be deprived of the possibility to be served by the worthiest persons." (Glanville, *Reports*, 125–126.) The Committee of Privileges waived the delivery of any opinion as to Huddleston's eligibility, but the House upheld his election on May 28, 1624. (*CJ*, 714.)

other occasions he sat for Brackley in Northamptonshire. Sir John Strangways of Dorset divided his service between the county and Weymouth. Sometimes county recognition was achieved only after considerable effort had been expended. John Wilde was first elected at Droitwich, Worcestershire, in 1621, but he did not secure the shire seat until the Long Parliament. Another parliamentarian of considerable experience, Sir Edward Rodney of Somerset, took his turn for the county in 1628 although he represented Wells in six Parliaments, beginning in 1621. Similarly, in Suffolk two members of Parliament, Sir Roger North and Sir Robert Crane, only departed from their usual constituencies when the shire knightship was attainable. Crane's service for Sudbury extended from 1614 through the Long Parliament, but was interrupted in 1621, 1626, and during the Short Parliament, when he represented Suffolk. From 1621 through the Long Parliament Sir Roger North sat for Eye; it was only in 1624 that he was successful in the county hustings.[22]

The inescapable result of competition for places in the House of Commons was the conclusion on the part of many country gentlemen that it was more important to be consistently returned than it was to be premier knight of the shire. Families with parliamentary aspirations like the Holles's and the Jermyns frequently sought election outside the confines of their native coun-

---

22. On May 5, 1627, Sir Richard Strode, a Buckingham nominee to Bridport in 1626, wrote to Sir John Coke, "I have been put out of the commission of the peace. I desire to be helped out of the commission for the soldiers. I am hated by Sir John Strangeways and his side great in this county, for that I complained and did discover in the last Parliament their foul corruption in the buying of burgess-ships." (HMC, *Twelfth Report*, Appendix I [London, 1888], 305.) Sir Roger North's activities in the Suffolk election of 1640 are discussed by Thomas Carlyle, "An Election to the Long Parliament," in *Critical and Miscellaneous Essays* (4 vols., Boston, 1860), IV, 400–426. In 1628 when Sir Edward Coke was elected knight of the shire for Suffolk, Edward Nuttall wrote to Sir Edward Nicholas, "Sir Edward Coke and Sir Nathaniel Barnardiston have been returned for Suffolk, but they would not have been chosen if there had been any other gentlemen of note, for neither Ipswich had any great affection for them, nor most of the country; but there were not ten gentlemen at this election." (*Cal. S. P. Dom 1628–1629*, 6.) Sir Edward Coke was also elected in Buckinghamshire and chose to serve for that county. His replacement in Suffolk was a most reluctant candidate — Sir William Spring. (See Harl. MS. 378, fol. 29v, Sir William Spring to Sir Simonds D'Ewes, Apr. 15, 1628.) In 1628 the justices of peace of Essex ordered the high constables of the county to assemble the freeholders at Chelmsford on March 4, "to give their voices for such gentlemen to be knights as shall be agreed upon by the more part of the justices of the peace of this country there assembled, for the good of our country." (SP 16/94/87, justices of the peace of Essex to the high constables, Feb. 1627/8.)

ties. Unfortunately, the success of such solicitation was beyond the control of the initiator, and thus prospective candidates were sometimes disappointed.

An awareness of the importance of a seat in the Commons influenced the peerage and the gentry alike to attempt control over more than one borough. The parliamentary family of Seymour in Wiltshire virtually had Great Bedwin and Marlborough in their pocket, so much so that in 1626 Sir Francis Seymour offered to trade a burgess-ship in Wiltshire for one in Yorkshire.[23] The Seymours, whose family head was the Earl of Hertford, were by no means unique among the peerage in dominating more than one corporation. Rarely did the gentry exercise such wide electoral control. In Cornwall the Grenvilles were credited with great influence in elections, but it was of an intangible nature, based on friendships, familial relationships, and political compatibility. The hegemony of the Godolphin family over the corporations of St. Ives and Helston was more permanent, founded upon property holdings within the boroughs and election to local magistracies.[24]

23. S. T. Bindoff, "Parliamentary History," 115–116, 127; Keeler, *Long Parliament,* 70, 71; James Waylen, *A History Military and Municipal of the Town . . . of Marlborough . . .* (London, 1854), 127–136, 465. The Earl of Hertford was lord of the borough of Marlborough, and its rents were paid to him. Marlborough continued to pay its members of Parliament at least until 1640. In 1578 and again in 1584 the parliamentary fees of the members were repaid to the corporation by the Earl of Hertford. In 1624 Sir Francis Seymour sat for Marlborough. Hugh Crompton, steward to Arabella Stuart, who, in 1610, married William Seymour, later second earl of Hertford, represented Great Bedwin in the Parliament of 1624. Another Seymour connection, Edward Kyrton, lessee of the Seymour manor of Castle Cary sat for Ludgershall. Over a considerable length of time he acted as agent for the Seymour family. For Sir Francis Seymour's offer to exchange burgess-ships with Wentworth, see Strafford, *Letters,* I, 30. Sir Arthur Ingram to Sir Thomas Wentworth, Nov. 22, 1625.

24. M. Coate, *Cornwall in the Great Civil War and Interregnum, 1642–1660* (Oxford: Clarendon Press, 1933), 24, notes that in 1640 Bevil Grenville was not sure of a borough seat in all the county. A town or two had offered to choose him if he would serve, but would not allow him to put in another candidate. The Godolphins of Godolphin appear to have had a paramount interest in the corporation of Helston. In Keeler, *Long Parliament,* 39, and *Visitation of Cornwall,* 382, Francis Godolphin, Esq., of Godolphin is listed as recorder of Helston in 1620. Yet Godolphin in 1624 sat for the borough of St. Ives where the Godolphins of Trevenage appear to have had considerable influence although the principal manor of Ludgvan Lese was held by the Paulet family. (J. H. Matthews, *A History of the Parishes of St. Ives, Lelant, Towednack and Zennor, in the County of Cornwall* [London, 1892], 42.) Of the two Helston members in 1624, Thomas Carey was recommended for a Cornish burgess-ship by the Prince's Council. His partner Francis Carew was the grandson of the Elizabethan Sir Francis Godolphin of Godolphin who died in 1608. (*Visitation of Cornwall,* 29.)

Such an arrangement transcended the vicissitudes of national politics and insured the repeated election of Godolphin candidates. Considerations of prestige gave way to concern for power. In Hampshire, Sir Thomas Jervoise sat for the borough of Whitchurch in seven Parliaments. Through the 1620's he consolidated his control over Whitchurch and extended his influence to Andover so that, by 1628, he was solicited as patron for various burgess-ships in Hampshire and Shropshire.[25]

Lawyers in particular were aware of the increasing importance of the House of Commons; the high proportion of representatives from that profession was not a factor of significance to King James alone.[26] Counselors-at-law were frequently elected burgesses in counties where they were not resident and in which they owned no property. Many recorders were returned although the title was sometimes little more than honorary. In 1624 Henry Sherfield, a London lawyer, was returned for the populous cities of Salisbury and Southampton, both of which he served as legal adviser. Even the most eminent parliamentarians did not disdain to serve the corporations that employed them in a legal capacity: Sir Edward Coke for Coventry, William Lenthall for Woodstock, Thomas Wentworth for Oxford, Sir Robert Hitcham for Orford, Christopher Sherland for Northampton, Sir Arthur Ingram for York, John Glanville for Plymouth, and Richard Digges for Marlborough.[27]

Usually a lawyer who owed his election to his professional ability was relatively free of ties to other members of the House. There were, however, cliques of representatives from families in which landed and legal fortunes were combined. Thus in the Parliaments of the 1620's Sir Edward Coke was generally accom-

25. SP 16/92/14, Secretary Conway to Sir Thomas Jervoise, Feb. 2, 1628, soliciting a burgess-ship at Andover for his son Ralph Conway. Conway's application to Jervoise may partially be explained on the grounds that the former was Lord Lieutenant of Hampshire and the latter one of his deputies.

26. Coke, *Fourth Institutes*, 47–48.

27. This list of recorders is by no means exhaustive, containing as it does the names of only the more eminent parliamentarians. One might also add such recorders as Duck of Exeter, Escott of Newport, Leeving of Derby, Pepper of Richmond, Rivet of Aldborough, Savage of Winchester, Whitaker of Shaftesbury, Southworth of Wells, Warre of Bridgewater, Towse of Colchester, Whatman of Chichester, Brakyn of Cambridge, Dyott of Stafford, Whitby of Chester, Jackson of Pontefract, and two deputy recorders: Whistler of Oxford and Taylor of Bedford.

panied by one or more of his sons; in 1624 Henry Coke represented Wycombe, Buckinghamshire. The Finch family of Kent
had three members in the House of Commons in 1624: Sir Heneage, recorder of London; his brother Francis, elected for Eye,
Suffolk; their cousin John, sometimes recorder of Canterbury, now
sitting for Winchelsea. Premier among the legal families in 1624
were the Crews. Sir Ranulph Crew was King's serjeant and sat
with the learned counsel in the House of Lords. His son, Sir
Clipsby Crew, was in the House of Commons representing Downton, Wiltshire. Sir Thomas Crew, brother of Ranulph, sat for
Aylesbury and was Speaker of the House, and his son, John Crew,
was elected at Amersham when that borough was restored to its
ancient privilege.

Undoubtedly family relationships played an important part in
determining the character of the Jacobean House of Commons;
intermarriages among the gentry multiplied the familial ties that
bound members together. Pursued vigorously to a conclusion, one
could conceivably perceive some degree of relationship existing
between the vast majority of Commons members; but, obviously,
other considerations sometimes nullified or strengthened ties of
blood. Patronage was perhaps the factor that most seriously disrupted the formation of family cliques in the lower House. Where
patronage was absent and the ties of kinship were close, the internal cohesion of such groups was strong. One suspects little
divergence of opinion among Sir Henry Poole, knight for Oxfordshire, his son, Sir Neville Poole, who sat for Cricklade, Wiltshire, and Neville's brother-in-law, Henry Poole, who represented
Cirencester, Gloucestershire. The same may be said of the St.
John coterie. A son and three brothers of Lord St. John of Bletsoe
sat in the House of Commons in 1624; of these only Sir Anthony
sat for a distinctly patronage borough, Wigan, Lancashire.[28]

28. The knight of the shire for Oxford was Sir Henry Poole of Oaksey, Wiltshire,
whose biography is given in W. R. Williams, *The Parliamentary History of the
County of Oxford, 1213–1899* (Brecknock, 1899). He should not be confused with
his relative, Sir Henry Poole, of Sapperton, Gloucestershire. Their identity is
distinguished by the indenture executed on December 18, 1612 (to which both of
them were parties) for a property settlement in consideration of the marriage
between Neville Poole and Frances Poole. *I. P. M. Wiltshire*, 148–150. The cooperation between the Poole families is evidenced by the election of Sir Neville
Poole at Cirencester in 1626. Oliver, fourth Lord St. John of Bletsoe, was summoned
to the House of Lords in 1624. His three brothers in the House of Commons were:
Sir Anthony St. John (Wigan, Lancashire), Sir Alexander St. John (Bedford, Bed-

Conversely, consideration of the closely knit family of Sir John Wynn of Gwydir, Carnarvonshire, illustrates the divisive effects of patronage. Sir John, a staunch parliamentarian and an extremely ambitious man, had three sons and a grandson in the lower House. His children had been educated to undertake careers at court. Sir Richard Wynn, currently serving the Prince and Buckingham, was elected for the patronage borough of Ilchester, Somerset. Henry Wynn, a lawyer of the Inner Temple, was returned for Merionethshire, for which seat he had been advised to stand by Sir Richard. William Wynn, in the service of Lord Keeper Williams, relinquished a certain place in the Commons at his patron's earnest entreaty, but he later secured election at Lyme Regis, Dorset. John Mostyn, Sir John Wynn's grandson, was also a member of the Lord Keeper's household, and was elected knight of the shire for Anglesey. On noncontroversial issues and on matters pertaining to Wales, these men could think and act in concert, but the same unanimity could not be evident when their patrons were at odds. After 1624 the fortunes of Sir Richard Wynn improved because of his close association with the Prince and Buckingham, but in 1625 William Wynn lost his position when the Lord Keeper was removed from office.[29]

Political embarrassment and financial losses resulting from struggles for power were a constant danger to those families who sent their sons to seek court preferment. Sometimes disaster could only be averted by a judicious change of patrons at a decisive moment. There were, however, parliamentary groups whose alliances

---

fordshire), and Sir Henry St. John (Huntingdon, Huntingdonshire). Oliver St. John, fifth baron of Bletsoe, was the eldest son of the fourth baron and was knight of the shire for Bedfordshire. He is erroneously described in the *Official Return* as Oliver, Lord St. John of Bletsoe. See *DNB*, L, 150–151.

29. The "certain place" which William Wynn relinquished at the Lord Keeper's request may have been Carnarvon borough. On December 24, 1623, William Wynn wrote to his father asking for his help in being returned for the town, but Sir Peter Mutton, Lord Keeper Williams's brother-in-law, was elected with Sir John Wynn's approval. (Wynn of Gwydir Papers [Panton Group], National Library of Wales MS. 9059 E/1204, William Wynn to Sir John Wynn, Mar. 30, 1624; *ibid.*, 1176, William Wynn to Sir John Wynn, Dec. 24, 1623; and *ibid.*, 1189, Sir William Thomas to Sir John Wynn, Jan. 21, 1624. On May 15 the Lord Keeper recommended William Wynn to Hertford borough. (L. Stone, "The Electoral Influence of the Second Earl of Salisbury, 1614–68," *English Historical Review*, LXXI [July, 1956], 384–400, esp. 392.) William Wynn was eventually returned for Lyme Regis, Dorset, as a replacement for Robert Hassard, Jr., deceased, but the *Official Return* lists no date.

were more solidly grounded. The Barringtons of Essex in the course of the early seventeenth century built up a strong network of family relationships. More than the usual amount of premeditation was involved in the construction of this entente. Sir Francis Barrington, head of the clan and long a member of Parliament had, from the first, shown an interest in church reform and better provisions for the clergy. In the 1620's this Puritanical bent was strengthened by opposition to the crown's financial policies; Sir Francis achieved great reputation as the first loan refuser of note. The marriages that he negotiated for his sons and daughters united the Barringtons with families of similar religious and political persuasions — families powerful in the counties and usually dissociated from intrigue at court. In the Parliament of 1624 Sir Francis sat for Essex, and his son, Sir Thomas, represented the Barrington borough of Newtown in the Isle of Wight. Two sons-in-law, Sir William Masham and Sir Gilbert Gerard, were elected, for Maldon, Essex, and for Middlesex County, respectively. This was the hard core of the political group that was to oppose the King so vigorously in the Long Parliament. Already friendly with the Puritanical Earl of Warwick and related to the Cromwells of Huntingdon, the Barringtons cemented their alliance with other powerful reform elements by means of economic association as well as by marriage. Thus, by 1640, Pym, Hampden, St. John, and Lytton were among those closely associated with the Barringtons, and the identity of their interests gave cohesion to the opposition in Parliament.[30]

Few families could muster as many members in the House of Commons as that headed by Sir George More, who had begun his

30. G. A. Lowndes, ed., "The History of the Barrington Family," *Essex Archaeological Society Transactions*, N.S., I (1874), 251–273; II (1894), 3–54. For Sir Francis Barrington's activities, particularly in the county election of 1604, see George Rickword, "Members of Parliament for Colchester, 1603–1683," *The Essex Review*, V (1896), 193–213; HMC, *Seventh Report*, Appendix, 542–543, Lowndes MSS. Barrington influence at Newtown on the Isle of Wight is confirmed by *ibid.*, 549, an undated draft of a letter [1640] to John Hall, "I have received a letter from Major Bull, Deputy Governor of the Isle of Wight (brought by his brother, a minister), concerning my consent for his being elected a burgess of Newtown, in the place of Mr. Serjeant Maynard." On the relationships of the Barringtons with future parliamentary leaders, see J. H. Hexter, *The Reign of King Pym* (Cambridge: Harvard University Press, 1941), 44–45, 78, 87, and the section on the Barringtons in Mark Noble, *Memoirs of Several Persons and Families who, by Females are Allies to, or Descended from the Protectorate House of Cromwell* (2 vols., Birmingham, 1734), II, 44–76.

parliamentary career in 1585. Although More's importance had declined after the death of Prince Henry, his influence in Surrey appears not to have diminished. In 1624 both knights of the shire were elected under his auspices. Sir Robert More, his son and heir apparent, had already served his apprenticeship for Guildford in 1621 and had been joined with his father in the most important Surrey magistracies. The other Surrey knight was Sir George's son-in-law, Sir Thomas Grymes, whom More had placed at Haslemere in 1621. Sir George, himself, was elected at Guildford, a constituency he had represented five times previously. Two of his grandsons, Francis Carew and Poynings More, were returned for the nomination borough of Haslemere. Of the fourteen Surrey members, therefore, five were distinctly in the More interest, yet the dominant motive for the establishment of such a powerful clique appears not to have been the independent assertion of political opinions. Neither of More's grandsons showed any political acumen, and Poynings More was notorious as a wastrel. The main efforts of Sir George in the decade between 1620 and 1630 seem to have been reserved for the repair of his family fortunes and the renewal of his influence at court.[31]

Surrey was almost unique among the southern counties in being so preponderantly influenced by a family not of peerage rank. Seemingly the Earl of Nottingham should have challenged the preeminence of the Mores, but the aged, retired Lord Admiral had virtually abandoned his formerly active role in county politics. Few shires were so devoid of influence from the nobility. Frequently the county was the arena where the peerage contended for the aggrandizement of their power.

Northamptonshire was the patronage preserve of two noble families: the Spencers and the Montagus. The traditional division

31. Among the unpublished manuscripts of Mrs. H. B. Lenthall, HMC 0185, is a letter from Sir George More to Sir Nicholas Carew dated December 12, 1620, "Many days before the receipt of your former letters I had caused the town of Haslemere to be moved for the choice of Sir Thomas Grymes and Sir William Brown who formerly served for that place." According to an entry in HMC, *Seventh Report*, Appendix, 679, the Mores received the tolls of the market of Haslemere, and this may account for some of their influence in that borough. It may be that Sir John Mill, member for Southampton in 1624, should be numbered among the More group. His first wife was Elizabeth, daughter of Sir George More, but she was dead by this time. (J. B. Burke, *A Genealogical and Heraldic History of the Extinct and Dormant Baronetcies of England, Ireland and Scotland* [2d ed., London, 1844], 356–357.)

of the county into eastern and western sections was unofficially recognized as a basis for apportioning the knightships of the shire. Edward, Lord Montagu, and Robert, Lord Spencer, heads of the eastern and western sections of the county, respectively, held conference at Boughton concerning the knights of the shire as soon as rumors of an impending Parliament began to circulate. They agreed that Sir William Spencer and Richard Knightley, members of Parliament for the county in 1621, should be reelected. On January 4, Lord Spencer reminded Lord Montagu of this understanding, but by that time Montagu had communicated with others in the east who had resolved to acquaint Spencer with their desire that the "ancient course" might be observed "to have a knight on each side for the better service of the country, without any opposition." Montagu assured Spencer that his son would be unopposed, but he asked that "your Lordship would be pleased to prevail so much with my cousin Knightley (whom I think very worthy of the place), that having had the honour already of it, he would now give way to Sir Lewis Wattson, and so the business may be carried fairly without any offence." To this suggestion Lord Spencer returned an unequivocally negative answer. He denied that it was an ancient custom to have one knight of the shire from each district, and he noted that "cousin" Knightley was by far the fittest candidate. Since both Knightley and Watson were Montagu's kinsmen, Lord Spencer urged that they be considered with "more judicious balance," and he held Montagu to the terms of the original agreement. On January 15, Sir William Spencer and Richard Knightley were reelected; Sir Lewis found a seat at Lincoln on February 2, possibly through the patronage of the Earl of Rutland.[32]

The east-west division of Northamptonshire was also apparent in the apportionment of borough seats. Of the two boroughs in the east, Peterborough was the least susceptible to Montagu influence, but it appears that Sir Francis Fane had Montagu's blessing

32. HMC, *Buccleuch and Queensbury MSS*, I, 258, Robert, Lord Spencer to Lord Montagu, Jan. 4, 1624; *ibid.*, 259–260, Edward, Lord Montagu to Robert, Lord Spencer, Jan. 1624; HMC, *Lord Montagu of Beaulieu MSS*, 105–106, Robert, Lord Spencer, to his cousin, Lord Montagu, Jan. 7, 1624. Two letters, one from Lord Montagu to the corporation of Northampton on January 7 and one from Richard Spencer to Lord Montagu on January 10, are improperly dated as referring to the election in 1624. They belong with the election letters for the Parliament of 1626. (HMC, *Buccleuch and Queensberry MSS*, I, 258–259; III, 261–263.)

in 1624. When Fane became Earl of Westmorland on December 29, 1624, he was replaced at Peterborough by Christopher Hatton, heir to extensive Northamptonshire estates, who in 1630 married Lord Montagu's niece. Higham Ferrers with its single seat had been frequently at the disposal of the Montagu family since Elizabethan times. It reelected Lord Montagu's brother, Sir Charles, who apparently made his chief residence in London.[33]

Spencer influence predominated in the western boroughs. The friendly relations subsisting between the corporation of Northampton and the Spencer family were such that in 1626 the town resolved to support Sir William Spencer's candidacy for the county seat despite his avowed desire to be excused from that service. Northampton did not confine its support of the Spencers to county elections. Richard Spencer, Lord Robert's third son, was elected by the borough to every Parliament between 1620 and 1630, having as his most frequent partner Christopher Sherland, Northampton's recorder. The other western borough, Brackley, was dominated by John Egerton, earl of Bridgwater, but here, too, the Spencers frequently found a seat available: Edward Spencer was Sir Thomas Wenman's partner in 1621, 1624, and 1625.[34]

Undoubtedly the strong Puritan tendencies of the Spencer-Knightley combine had some significance in parliamentary elec-

33. The letters written by Charles Montagu (*Ibid.*, I) indicate that he spent most of his time in London, from which place he retailed news of the court as well as business and legal advice to his brother. See also A. N. Groome, "Higham Ferrers Elections in 1640," *Northamptonshire Past and Present*, II (No. 5, 1958), 243–251.

34. HMC, *Buccleuch and Queensberry MSS*, I, 259, Richard Spencer to Lord Montagu, Jan. 10, 1626. The votes from Northampton were decisive in this election according to the observation made by Lord Montagu who supported Sir Lewis Watson for the shire seat. Sir William Spencer and Sir John Pickering were elected for Northamptonshire in 1626. Although the Spencers were on good terms with the burgesses of Brackley, it is clear that the Earl of Bridgwater exercised decisive control over the elections. In response to a request from the corporation in 1614 he nominated Arthur Terringham, Esq. "For the other place wherewith it seemeth by your letter you are willing to gratify the Lord Spencer in the behalf of my cousin, his son [William], I like very well of your course and must needs approve your discretion therein, assuring you that I shall willingly join in request unto you for the present election of him, such is my affection to the gentleman himself and to my Lord, his father. Yet I would advise you both in respect of your own and my right in that place (being as you know Lord . . . thereof) that you admit not of any continued prescription in such election wherein I purpose not to give way to equal any man's interest with my own." (Ellesmere [Brackley] MS. 574, Northamptonshire Record Office, Sir John Egerton to the Mayor of Brackley, Mar. 13, 1613/4.)

tions, but its influence was by no means decisive. Lord Montagu, too, was tainted with Puritanism, much to King James's distaste. When the county was split by political differences in 1624, it was not over religious issues but rather about the Earl of Westmorland's high-handed transfer of the quarter sessions from Northampton to Kettering. The Protestant gentry and nobility of Northamptonshire were agreed that both recusants and church-papists should be disarmed, disfranchised, and excluded from positions of responsibility; they disagreed about matters of local administration and family prestige.[35]

The parliamentary patronage exercised by peers who were Lords Lieutenant of their counties was typified by the influence exerted by William Knollys, Viscount Wallingford, in Berkshire. Despite the fact that Wallingford's power at Westminster had declined considerably since 1618 when Cranfield had supplanted him as Master of the Court of Wards, his authority in the county continued intact. Although a member of his family occasionally sat for the county in the Parliaments of the 1620's, it was in three of the four Berkshire boroughs that Wallingford's influence was paramount. As high steward of Reading in 1624, he requested the nomination of one of their members of Parliament "and both if it may be." Two nephews, Sir Francis Knollys, Jr., and Sir Robert Knollys were recommended for election. The corporation acceded to Wallingford's demand that Sir Francis Knollys have the first place, but they chose John Saunders as their second member. Both men were required to acquit Reading from the payment of any wages, fees, or duties for the performance of parliamentary service.[36] Sir Robert Knollys was not disappointed in his desire

35. HMC, *Buccleuch and Queensberry MSS,* I, 255, Sir Charles Montagu to Sir Edward Montagu, Dec. 13, 1620. "His Majesty of himself spake to my brother of you, and said he did not confer this great trust upon him only for love to himself, but of all our family, whom [sic] he thought loved him and were faithful to him, and though you smelt a little of Puritanism, yet he knew you to be honest and faithful to him." The issue of the location of the quarter sessions was referred to the Privy Council and heard on November 17, 1624. The order of the Council of that date and a subsequent rehearing of the case in December 1625 failed to resolve the controversy which materially affected Northamptonshire parliamentary elections in the late 1620's.

36. Guilding, *Reading Records,* II, 168–169, shows that in the poll four candidates were presented for election at Reading: Sir Francis Knollys, Jr., received twenty-one votes; John Saunders, Esq., sixteen; Sir Robert Knollys, nine; Sir Richard Lydall, none. Reading seems to have accepted nominations regularly. Prior to the Short Parliament of 1640, both Archbishop Laud and the Earl of Holland recommended

for a seat in the Parliament; he was chosen at Abingdon, where Wallingford was also high steward, and he continued to represent that borough in the first two Parliaments of Charles's reign. At Wallingford the Knollys influence combined with that of the Howards. Since 1621 Viscount Wallingford had been high steward of the borough, and he undoubtedly procured the return of his brother-in-law, Sir Edward Howard. Sir Edward was also named to represent Calne in Wiltshire and, preferring this borough, he was succeeded at Wallingford by Sir Anthony Forest.[37]

Undoubtedly the knights of the shire for Berkshire were chosen with the consent, and probably the approbation, of Viscount Wallingford. In counties where one family of peerage rank dominated the social structure, it was customary to consult the wishes of the head of the family before agreeing on candidates for the county election. In Hertfordshire, for instance, where William Cecil, earl of Salisbury, had succeeded to the political influence of his father, every successful shire candidate for the Parliaments between 1621 and 1628 was elected with Salisbury's support. The Earl regularly sent out letters through his secretary to the bailiffs of his Hertfordshire estates marshaling his freeholders for their appearance at the county court. One of the letters in 1624 indicates the peremptory nature of the Earl's commands: "Storie, it is my lords pleasure that you speake with all the Freeholders within the mannors of Hoddesdon Baas and Geddings and the Hundred of Broughin and Hertford and lett them knowe that

_____

candidates. See W. H. Hutton, "Two Letters of Archbishop Laud," *English Historical Review*, XLV (Jan. 1930), 107–109, where Laud's letter in answer to Reading's reply to his request for a nomination is printed. The limits of a patron's power are graphically illustrated by a marginal note next to the name of Sir John Berkeley (the Earl of Holland's candidate) in the poll list for the election held on March 12, 1640: "He is a stranger and can be no friend to the Towne."

37. Bromley Challenor, ed., *Selections from the Municipal Chronicles of the Borough of Abingdon, from A. D. 1555 to A. D. 1897* (Abingdon, 1898), 141. In July 1630 the Earl of Banbury (formerly Viscount Wallingford) resigned the high stewardship of the borough of Abingdon. Robert Knollys was member of Parliament for Abingdon in 1624, 1625, and 1626. Not only was Viscount Wallingford married to Elizabeth, daughter of Thomas Howard, first earl of Suffolk, but since 1609 two sons of the Earl, Sir Thomas Howard and Charles Howard, had held life appointments in reversion of the constableship and stewardship of the castle and manor of Wallingford. When Viscount Wallingford died in 1632 Sir Thomas Howard, who had become Viscount Andover in the reign of James and Earl of Berkshire in the reign of Charles, was elected High Steward of Wallingford. (J. K. Hedges, *The History of Wallingford* [London, 1881], 121–122.)

he would have them nowe at the Election of the Knights of the Shire to be sure to be at it and to give theire voyces furst for Sir Charles Morisone and next for Mr. William Litton whome his Lordshipp intendes to be knights of the Shire, and let this be done as speedilie as possible you cane." [38] Needless to say, Morrison and Lytton were elected.

Salisbury's influence, like Wallingford's, extended into borough elections and was not confined to the county of Hertford. From Robert Cecil, the first earl, Salisbury had inherited a crown grant of the castle and warren of Old Sarum, Wiltshire — the classic rotten borough. Here his patronage clashed with the ambitions of the powerful Earl of Pembroke and the decade of the 1620's witnessed a series of maneuvers designed, on both parts, to secure absolute control of the borough's two seats. Despite his best efforts in 1624, Salisbury was unable to prevent the return of Michael Oldisworth, one of Pembroke's secretaries. However, Sir Arthur Ingram, double returned for York City, was probably Salisbury's nominee. His replacement at Old Sarum, Sir Robert Cotton, may also have been elected under Salisbury's auspices.[39]

In Hertfordshire, Salisbury's influence in borough affairs had

---

38. Salisbury MS. General 74/9, cited from Stone, "Electoral Influence of the Second Earl of Salisbury," 384–400, esp. 385–386.

39. *Ibid.*, 384–400. Stone seems to connect Sir Arthur Ingram with Salisbury and implies that at least one seat at Old Sarum in 1624 was at the Earl's disposal. Bindoff, on the other hand, implies that Cotton was nominated by the Earl of Pembroke. Certainly in 1625 and 1626 Pembroke captured both places. (*VCH Wiltshire*, V, 124–125.) According to Stone, a compromise agreement was reached in 1628 whereby the earls divided the patronage between themselves. This ended the tendency to create new burgage tenures in Old Sarum in order to gain control of the borough. On May 29, 1624, James vetoed the bill which would have allowed the county of Durham to send knights and burgesses to Parliament. "You have too many among you already, for you have lately added more so that now you are almost five hundred in the House of Commons, and you have many burgesses that come to parliament from boroughs quite decayed as from Old Sarum where there is nothing but connies for I myself have been there and seen it. Besides consider there is no decay of you as of your noblemen in voice number; but if you will be content that those places that are quite defaced and decayed shall send no burgesses, as there is reason they should not because they have no due election by voices but the next lord or knight makes whom he pleaseth, then I will be content you enjoy the rest that are fit to send burgesses to parliament." (D'Ewes, fols. 133–133v.) In the draft proclamation for the Parliament of 1604 the sheriffs were charged not to direct any precept for electing any burgesses to any borough town within their counties "being utterlye ruined or so decayed that there are not sufficient resiants to make such choyse, and of whom lawfull election may be made." (J. Payne Collier, ed., *The Egerton Papers*, Camden Society, O.S., Volume XII [London, 1840], 385, 387; see *OPH* [2d ed.], V, 7.)

been augmented by the eclipse of Sir Francis Bacon, Viscount St. Alban. Bacon had nominated two members to the electorate of St. Albans in 1621, but by 1624 the corporation had probably turned to Salisbury in their search for a patron. Although two local squires, Sir Arthur Capel, Jr., and Sir John Luke were chosen, they were probably acceptable to Salisbury. In 1625, when Luke was reelected, a representative of St. Albans went to Hatfield to consult with Salisbury about the burgesses for the town.[40]

Prior to 1624, Hertfordshire had only two county and two borough seats with which to gratify the parliamentary ambitions of its gentry. In 1621 a movement was initiated to reconstitute Hertford as a parliamentary borough, but, owing to signs of royal displeasure, the House of Commons, on May 18, deferred action upon the application, and it was not revived during the remainder of the session. In 1624, however, when the Prince was actively canvassing the towns under his control, his council addressed a letter to Hertford suggesting that Charles was willing to give "all due furtherance to the reviveing of the said ancient priviledge of sending Burgesses to this present Parliament . . . Wee have thought good hereby to signifie unto you that if you will prepare a peticion for reviveing the said priviledge this Parliament and send it up unto us such care shalbe taken for preferring and effecting the same at such time as the Parliament shall sit as shalbe fitting without anie charge to the towne." [41]

Although the manor and castle of Hertford were once parcel of the duchy of Lancaster, they had been granted to Prince Charles

40. Stone, "Electoral Influence of the Second Earl of Salisbury," 384–400. There seems also to have been a long standing association of the Capels with the Cecil family. In HMC, *Salisbury MSS*, XVIII (London, 1940), 224, 335, there are two letters from Sir Arthur Capel of Hadham to the first Earl of Salisbury, which indicate that Arthur Capel, Jr., was in Salisbury's service in 1606.

41. DeVilliers, "Parliamentary Boroughs Restored by the House of Commons," 175–202, quoted from Hertford Borough Records, XXIII, No. 10, Prince's Council to the Mayor and Burgesses of Hertford, Feb. 9, 1624. The same letter is copied in Duchy of Cornwall MS. "Prince Charles in Spain," fols. 37v–38, and in "Prince Henry and Prince Charles: Collections," III, fol. 134, where it is dated Feb. 17, 1623/4. The HMC, *Fourteenth Report*, Appendix, pt. VIII (London, 1895) 162, lists under the date February 9, 1623/4, a letter from the duchy council to the mayor and burgesses of Hertford recommending a member for Parliament. I suggest that this refers to the letter from the Prince's Council to the Mayor and Burgesses of Hertford, dated February 17, 1623/4, nominating Christopher Vernon and Sir John Hobart. (Duchy of Cornwall MS. "Prince Charles in Spain," fol. 38v; also transcribed in "Prince Henry and Prince Charles: Collections," III, fol. 134.)

in 1619. It was thus in the interest of extending his personal patronage that the Prince undertook to forward the Hertford petition, for when the matter was reported by Glanville on May 4, 1624, the restoration of the franchise was actively opposed by Sir Humphrey May, chancellor of the duchy.[42] Nevertheless the House of Commons ordered the issuance of writs to the corporation forthwith. So confident had the Prince's council been of the borough's restoration that they had already recommended the election of Sir John Hobart and Christopher Vernon. On April 24 these recommendations were withdrawn; Hobart had been elected for Lostwithiel and Vernon "being att this present otherwise emploied for his highnes service, cannot well attend the busines of the House." The council now commended Sir William Harrington, the Prince's steward at Hertford "that he maie be elected according to his highnes' desier." [43]

In all these maneuvers little consideration was given to the Earl of Salisbury's wishes. On May 15, two days before the election, Lord Keeper Williams asked Salisbury to promote the candidacy of his servant, William Wynn, but the Earl replied that he was already engaged for William Ashton "an old servant and annuitant of his father." Moreover, Salisbury, at the solicitation of diverse townsmen, promised to make no recommendation to impede the election of Thomas Fanshawe to the second place.[44] On May 17, 240 resident burgesses assembled for the election. The names of 4 candidates were placed in nomination: Ashton, Wyllowes, Harrington, and Fanshawe. The polling lists survive and indicate that for the first seat Ashton received 103 votes; Wyllowes, 58; Harrington, 42; and Fanshawe, 19. In the contest for second place, Fanshawe, a wealthy squire seated at Ware Park, received 101 votes; Wyllowes, 86; and Harrington, 48! [45]

<hr/>

42. The honor, castle, lordship, manor, town, grange, farm, and revenues from fee farms, lands, tenements, and hereditaments of Hertford were included as parcel of "the charter of lands of £3,856,-2-11 per annum granted to the Prince his Highness, 11 Oct. 17 Jacobi (1619)." (Duchy of Cornwall MS. "Charters, Prince Charles"; Pym. fol. 87v.)

43. Letter from the Prince's council to the mayor and burgesses of Hertford, Apr. 24, 1624, quoted by DeVilliers, Parliamentary Boroughs Restored by the House of Commons," 191, from Hertford Borough Records, XXIII, No. 11. The identical letter is transcribed in Duchy of Cornwall MS. "Prince Charles in Spain," fol. 40 and in "Prince Henry and Prince Charles: Collections," III, fol. 134.

44. Stone, "Electoral Influence of the Second Earl of Salisbury," 392.

45. Ibid., 392.

No incident more graphically illustrates the primacy of local considerations in parliamentary patronage than the Hertford election in 1624. Seemingly the Prince had every reason to expect the return of his nominees; he held the manor and castle, he espoused a popular cause, and he assisted in the recovery of the borough's right to representation in Parliament. Conversely, the Earl of Salisbury was not an "inward man" in the councils of the realm even though he undoubtedly supported the breach with Spain. Personal prestige and a desire to please his friends seem to have inspired his political activities. Salisbury's wealth, his lieutenancy of the county, and the proximity of Hatfield to Hertford made the men of the borough unwilling to ignore the Earl's wishes, even when encouraged to do so by the Prince's council.

Although Salisbury was relatively undistinguished among the peerage for ability, ambition, and aggressiveness and Wallingford was definitely on the decline, the capacity of both noblemen to influence elections was virtually unaffected by their lack of eminence at court. The main issue facing the voters rarely appears to have been a matter of national importance; rather, it was a question of whose man to support. Thus the influence of the local gentry and nobility transcended political viewpoints, and members sitting for the same borough frequently were poles apart in the programs they advocated. The absence of appeals to patriotism, religion, or antiprerogative sentiments at a time when everyone was aware that issues of vital national importance were to be decided in the Parliament is dramatic evidence of a complete lack of organized party politics.

For those who wished to manage a Parliament, however, there were noblemen whose views had to be considered. Peers like the Earls of Southampton and Pembroke cut too large a figure at court and were too well versed in parliamentary procedure to be ignored. This lesson was driven home to Buckingham in 1621 when he had clashed violently in the upper House with the Earl of Southampton and his coterie. Thus, in 1624, special efforts were exerted by both the Prince and the favorite to win Southampton's support.

Like Wallingford and Salisbury, Henry Wriothesley, earl of Southampton, was a power in his county. Not only was he Lord Lieutenant and *custos rotulorum* of Hampshire, possessing vast estates obtained by his ancestors after the dissolution of the monasteries, but he had consolidated his local power by further acquisitions of office. As Keeper of the New Forest, and particularly as Captain and Governor of the Isle of Wight, large sections of Hampshire were under his immediate control. To complement this nucleus of local power, Southampton, since his youthful years, had sought eminence at court. As a result of his military experience in Ireland and the Azores he had achieved a reputation as a competent commander. By 1612 his associations with parliament men had earned him unofficial recognition as a leader of that group. His early interest in colonial ventures had probably deepened his antipathy toward Spain and enhanced the enthusiasm with which he espoused the cause of the Elector Palatine. Although he was created a privy councillor in 1619, when he least expected it, Southampton did not thereby lose his independence. His ardent support of the Protestant cause in the Palatinate and his maintenance of the privileges of the House of Lords in 1621 incurred the King's displeasure and resulted in Southampton's confinement.

During the interval between the sessions of Parliament he was searchingly questioned about his attitude toward Buckingham. Allegations of conspiracy with members of the House of Commons were leveled against him; it was contended that he not only practiced to "hinder the King's ends" but that he had planned to divert subsidies directly to the use of the Elector Palatine. Probably as a result of Lord Keeper Williams's intercession, no action was taken against the Earl, and he was released from confinement after a private conference with the King, Buckingham, and Williams in mid-July. Southampton was "wished and advised rather than enjoined and commanded" to be absent from the second session of the Parliament of 1621. Thereafter he devoted his main attention to the affairs of the Virginia Company until the return of Charles and Buckingham from Spain once more brought him into national prominence.[46]

46. For a detailed biography of Southampton, see C. C. Stopes, *The Life of Henry, Third Earl of Southampton, Shakespeare's Patron* (Cambridge: Cambridge University Press, 1922). On Southampton's association with parliament men, see Chamberlain, *Letters*, I, 358, letter of June 17, 1612; II, 384–385, letter of June 23, 1621, and 389–390, letter of July 21, 1621. There is no overt evidence of concerted action between Southampton and parliamentary leaders in the Addled Parliament of 1614, but Southampton's position on impositions and his attitude toward the bishop of Lincoln warrants, in my opinion, the assumption of communication between the

No sooner had Buckingham and Charles arrived at court than they began to woo Southampton as a prospective ally. So confident were they of the Earl's accordance with their aims that they trusted him to attend the King in their absence during late October.[47] Their confidence was not misplaced; no better "guardian" for the King could have been found. Although James had recently adopted a more benign attitude toward Southampton than he had exhibited in 1621, there was in the autumn of 1623 no danger of a rapprochement between them. James had lent his support to a faction, headed by the Earl of Warwick, which was attempting to wrest control of the Virginia Company from Southampton and his partisans. The King had announced his intention to reconstitute the government of the company under a new charter in October, and by November quo warranto proceedings were initiated in the King's Bench by which several officers of the Company were cited to appear and to exhibit the authority by which they acted. Thus, for private as well as for public reasons, Southampton was not in sympathy with the King's designs.[48]

The anticipation of proceedings in Parliament against the

---

Earl and the antiprerogative group in the Commons. See the Hastings diary of proceedings in the House of Lords, April 5 to June 7, 1614, HMC, *Hastings MSS,* IV, 230–286. The examination of Southampton in 1621 is in SP 14/121/136. There is also a version printed in Stopes, *Life of . . . Southampton,* 406–409. Letters dealing with Southampton's confinement are printed in *Cabala,* I, 57, 58, 59, 61–62. It was not until August 30, 1621, that Southampton was absolutely released from restraint; since mid-July he had been attended by his custodian, Sir William Parkhurst. Lord Keeper Williams appears to have been worried about the possible effects of Southampton's confinement on the second session of the Parliament. On August 2 he advised Buckingham to intercede for Southampton's unconditional release. "There is no readier way to stop the mouthes of idle men, nor to draw their eyes from this remainder of an object of Justice, to behold nothing but goodnesse and mercy. And the more breathing time you shall carve out between this total enlargement and the next accesse of the Parliament, the better it will be for his Majesties service." *Cabala,* I, 59, Lord Keeper to the Duke of Buckingham, Aug. 2, 1621. See also S. R. Gardiner, ed., *The Fortescue Papers . . .* Camden Society, N.S., Volume I (London, 1871), 166–167.

47. Chamberlain, *Letters,* II, 522, letter of Nov. 8, 1623. See also *Cabala,* I, 90–93, "The heads of that discourse which fell from Don Francisco, 7 die Aprilis, 1624 at 11 of the clock at night," where Southampton is mentioned as one of the popular leaders recently reconciled to the Duke.

48. On the factions in the Virginia Company, see Chamberlain, *Letters,* II, 492, letter of Apr. 19, 1623; *APC 1623–1625,* 59, 64, 97, 99, 107–108, 119, 138–139, 140, 158, 252, 254, 255. For the negotiations about the contract for the sole importation of tobacco and the proceedings against the company and its officers, see S. M. Kingsbury, *An Introduction to the Records of the Virginia Co. of London* (2 vols., Washington, D.C.: Government Printing Office, 1905), II, passim.

Virginia Company seems to have been the primary factor influencing Southampton's attitude during the elections. The men he chose to support were undoubtedly committed to the breach with Spain, but one obvious identifying characteristic among them was their close association with the Earl's government of the company. Approximately 10 percent of the members of the House of Commons in 1624 owned stock in the Virginia Company.[49] The majority supported Southampton's regime; the most prominent leaders present were Sir Edwin Sandys, Southampton's longtime associate, and William, Lord Cavendish. Three 'Virginians' of the second rank, none of whom had local connections in Hampshire, were elected for boroughs in that county. Nicholas Ferrar, deputy of the Virginia Company and a close associate of Southampton and Sandys, was returned for Lymington. Christopher Brooke, lawyer of Lincoln's Inn and one of Southampton's most active partisans, was elected both for his native York City and Newport in the Isle of Wight. When he chose to sit for York he was replaced at Newport by Sir John Danvers, scion of a family closely associated with the Wriothesleys. Danvers, too, had taken an active part in forestalling the intrigues of the Warwick faction. Since he was a native of Wiltshire and connected by marriage with the Herbert clan, the only logical explanation for his representation of Newport is the patronage of Southampton.[50]

49. For a list of shareholders, see Peter Force, ed., *Tracts and Other Papers Relating Principally to the Origin, Settlement and Progress of the Colonies in North America . . . collected by Peter Force* (Washington, D.C., 1836–1846). In 1624 Mr. [Nicholas] Ferrar compiled "the names of diverse knights, citizens and burgesses of the lower House of Commons that are adventurers and free of the Virginia Company and yet have not followed the business for sundry years." This list contains forty-nine names, but is obviously incomplete since it ends with the notation "with diverse others which we cannot upon a sudden set down." Moreover, the active members—Sir Edwin Sandys, Sir Nathaniel Rich, Lord Cavendish, Nicholas Ferrar, Christopher Brooke, Sir John Danvers, *et al.* — are not mentioned. (PRO 30/15/ 2/371, Manchester MSS.)

50. B. Blackstone, ed., *The Ferrar Papers* (Cambridge: Cambridge University Press, 1938). This contains, among other papers, a life of Nicholas Ferrar written by his brother John, who was also very active in the company. It was Nicholas Ferrar who had attested copies of the records of the Virginia Company made prior to seizure of the originals by the government. When Ferrar delivered these copies to Southampton, "The Earl, cordially embracing him, said 'You still more and more engage me to love and honour you. I accept of this your present as of a treasure. I shall value it more than the evidences of my property, because this contains the evidences of my honour and my reputation, which are more to me than wealth or life itself. They are also the testimonals of all our upright dealings in the business of the Company and the Plantation. I cannot express how much

Familial considerations and friendship also influenced South-ampton's nominations. In 1621 his son and heir, James, Lord Wriothesley, had his initiation in Parliament; at the age of fifteen he was returned for the nomination borough of Callington, Corn-wall. Undoubtedly Lord James's father was instrumental in pro-curing his election at Winchester in 1624. The Thomas Wriothes-ley, Esq., who served for Yarmouth, Isle of Wight, in 1621 and 1624 was apparently a distant relative of the Earl of Southamp-ton and was employed as his secretary. Wriothesley's partner at Yarmouth in 1624 was William Beeston who also appears to have been an intimate servant of the Earl.[51]

---

I feel obliged to you for this instance of your care and foresight.' " (Stopes, *Life of . . . Southampton*, 446, apparently cited from Peter Peckard, *Memoirs of the Life of Mr. Nicholas Ferrar* [Cambridge, 1790].) In Edward King, *Old Times Revisited in the Borough and Parish of Lymington, Hampshire* (London, 1900), 50, there is no evidence of a recommendation by Southampton for the election of a burgess at Lymington in 1624, but there is an entry in the town records allowing the expense of 6s. 1d. for a journey to Tichfield with the indenture for the Parliament, and Tichfield Abbey was Southampton's chief residence. I have found no nomination letters from Southampton to the three boroughs on the Isle of Wight but the governor's practice of nominating members of Parliament in the Isle may, I think, be inferred from the subsequent recommendations made by Secretary Conway, Southampton's successor. See the correspondence between Philip Fleming and William Weld, Conway's secretary, in SP 16/523/13, 14, and 27, Jan. 12, Jan. 16, and Jan. (?), 1626.

51. In 1624 Southampton was trying to procure for James the colonelcy of one of the four regiments of foot to be sent to the Low Countries. On May 21/31, the Venetian Ambassador reported that three of the colonels had been named, including "the Earl of Southampton's son." (*Cal. S. P. Venetian*, XVIII, 324, Valaresso to the Doge and Senate.) But on May 28/June 7, 1624, he reported, "It is certain that when Southampton desired the post for his son, and when that was refused, he had to receive it himself." (*Ibid.*, 333, Valaresso to the Doge and Senate.) James, Lord Wriothesley, died in winter quarters at Rosendale, on November 5, 1624, and Southampton himself died on November 10 at Bergen op Zoom. Southampton's advancement of his sons is further confirmed by the admission of James, Lord Wriothesley, and Thomas Wriothesley, Esq., to the freedom of Southampton on January 6, 1624. (Stopes, *Life of Southampton*, 344–345.) It is improbable that the "Thomas Risley" who sat for Yarmouth in 1621 and 1624 was the Earl's second son because he was baptized at Little Shelford, Cambridgeshire, on April 2, 1607. The most likely candidate is Thomas Wriothesley, Esq., of Cheltwood, Bucking-hamshire, who acted with the Earl in the affairs of the Virginia Company and who served as one of the administrators of his estate in 1625. (*Ibid.*, 313, 422, 437–438, 473.) There are two letters from W. Beeston to Sir Simonds D'Ewes printed in the *Autobiography and Correspondence of Sir Simonds D'Ewes* (2 vols., London, 1845), II, 166–171, Sept. 3/13, 1624, and Oct. 22/Nov. 1, 1624. It may be that Beeston was attending James, Lord Wriothesley, because the second of these letters is dated "from his excellency's campe at Rosendarl." In Stopes, *Life of Southampton*, 475–476, there is a letter from W. Beeston to Dr. Gwyn, master of St. John's College, Cambridge, dated September 20, 1625, dealing with arrangements for Thomas Wriothesley's attenance at the university.

Two sons-in-law of Southampton also sat in the 1624 House of Commons although both were able to procure their seats without his immediate assistance. Sir William Spencer, who sat for the county of Northampton, had the powerful backing of his father, Robert, Lord Spencer; Robert Wallop, who represented Andover, was the only son of Sir Henry Wallop, one of the wealthiest of the Hampshire knights. Sir Henry, an experienced parliamentarian, began his career in the House in 1597, and in 1624 he shared the constituency at Whitchurch with his close neighbor, Sir Thomas Jervoise.[52]

Southampton's influence extended beyond the mere placing of members of Parliament; he was one of the select few who understood the principles of political action. In 1621 he had been accused of holding regular meetings with his supporters before the commencement of each day's sitting. It was alleged that he not only instructed his partisans on how to vote but that he imparted directions regarding the order of business in the lower House. Neither meetings nor influence were denied by the Earl, although he repudiated implications of plotting. Among his confidants was Sir John Jephson, member for Petersfield in 1624, who informed him about Irish affairs.[53]

Knowledgeable manipulation of parliamentary procedure, which in 1621 had been so opprobrious to the government, could in 1624 prove extremely useful. Evidence of intrigue is vague and slight, being generally limited to notices of nocturnal meetings, but at least one overt act came to the attention of the House of Commons. On March 5, 1624, at a conference committee of both Houses Sir Edwin Sandys received without authorization a paper of advice penned by Southampton and Pembroke which would have pledged unrestricted financial support by the Commons to any military endeavor. This occasioned a heated controversy during which Mr. Mallory suggested that Sir Edwin Sandys deserved expulsion from the House for his imprudent behavior. After soft answers by Sandys had quieted the wrath of the members over this issue of privilege,

52. Immediately after Southampton's death, Spencer was soliciting for the wardship of Thomas Wriothesley in behalf of the Countess of Southampton. (*Cabala*, I, 96–97, Lord Keeper Williams to the Duke of Buckingham, Nov. 17, 1624.

53. Sir John Jephson is the only parliamentary informant of Southampton mentioned in Southampton's inquisition after the Parliament of 1621. (Stopes, *Life of . . . Southampton*, 406–409.) Jephson appears to have served under Southampton in Ireland during the last years of Elizabeth.

the paper was consigned to oblivion. The Commons let it be understood that no matter what the wishes of the upper House, motions for supply could only originate in the lower chamber and proceed in a parliamentary manner.[54]

Southampton's renown as a Parliament man probably exceeded that of any other peer in England chiefly because of his arrest in 1621. Of less notoriety, though with far greater power, was William Herbert, Earl of Pembroke, who in 1624 headed groups in both the Lords and the Commons. In the upper House Pembroke spoke not only as Lord Chamberlain, privy councillor, and member of the junta for foreign affairs but also as the natural leader of the moderates. His words were given added weight by the five proxies he had received from the Earls of Bedford and Derby and the Lords Darcy, Abergaveny, and Zouche.[55]

In the House of Commons the Earl's friends and clients were even more numerous; since 1612 Pembroke had quietly contrived to mold a parliamentary empire in the west of England.[56] In the

54. Spring, 84–89; Pym, fols. 18v–19v; Holles, fols. 92–93; Holland, fols. 31–33v; Rich, fols. 13v, 12v, 11v, 10v, 9v.

55. *LJ*, III, 205.

56. The Earl of Pembroke's parliamentary patronage is discussed by Violet A. Rowe, "The Influence of the Earls of Pembroke on Parliamentary Elections, 1625–41," *English Historical Review*, L (Apr. 1935), 242–256, and less specifically by Bindoff, "Parliamentary History," 111–169; Stone, "Electoral Influence of the Second Earl of Salisbury," 384–400. The letter from Sir James Bagg to the Duke of Buckingham which was edited by S. R. Gardiner in *Notes and Queries*, 4th Ser., Volume X (London, 1872), 325–326 is the chief piece of evidence for Miss Rowe's conclusions. The combined influence of the Earls of Pembroke and Hertford seems to have been decisive in Wiltshire County elections. In 1625 Sir Thomas Thynne aspired to the knightship of the shire and hoped to appropriate Sir Henry Ley as a partner, but on April 14 Ley wrote, "I received yesterday a letter from London that my Lord of Pembroke and my Lord of Hertford have taken order that all their voices go first for Sir Francis Seymour, and the other for me, if I will join with him, which appointment and agreement of their lordships I dare not dissent from." According to Sir Francis Seymour the decision of the two earls came as a complete surprise to him when he was informed of it by a letter from Mr. Kyrton. (Marquess of Bath MSS, Longleat, Thynne Papers, Vol. VIII, fol. 121, Sir Henry Ley to Sir Thomas Thynne, Apr. 14, 1625; fol. 123, Sir Francis Seymour to Sir Thomas Thynne, Apr. 18, 1625.) In 1628 Walter Long, sheriff of Wiltshire, asked Sir Thomas Thynne to stand for the knightship of the shire, "of which you shall not need to make any doubt of obtaining, for if you stand I will show you a way that you shall be sure of it." Apparently Sir Thomas declined; the successful candidates were Sir Francis Seymour and Sir William Button. (*Ibid.*, fol. 125, Walter Long to Sir Thomas Thynne, Feb. 21, 1627/8.) A letter from Sir John Hippisley to the Duke of Buckingham, Feb. 2, 1628, reveals the way in which the Earl of Pembroke tended to use his power. Hippisley begs Buckingham to "make as many burgesses as you can and to get my Lord Steward [Pembroke] to make such as shall comply with the King's occasions, and not to make Sir Thomas Lacke [?] and Dr. Turner, and

early years of James's reign Pembroke's influence even in the
Wiltshire boroughs closest to his demesnes was superseded by the
intrusive power of Robert Cecil, first earl of Salisbury. After Salisbury's death Pembroke made repeated attempts to recover the
patronage monopoly the Herberts had long enjoyed at Wilton and
Old Sarum. By 1621 he had completed the reconquest of Wilton,
but his power at Old Sarum was still challenged by the Cecils in
1624. Michael Oldisworth, his secretary, was Pembroke's nominee
for the single seat he controlled. At Wilton, where the Earl chiefly
resided and where he was lord of the manor, his majordomo, Sir
Thomas Morgan, and his cousin, Sir Percy Herbert, were elected.[57]

These two Wiltshire boroughs, both with extremely small electorates, formed the nucleus of Pembroke's patronage domain. Some
of his influence was based upon the acquisition of property rights,
even more of it on the accumulation of offices. As owner, together
with his mother, of two hundred acres of land in Shaftesbury and
as lord of that borough, Pembroke was able to procure the election
of another of his secretaries, John Thoroughgood. In Glamorganshire, where the Earl was the principal landowner, Cardiff borough was at his disposal whenever he wanted it; William Price
appears to have been his nominee for three Parliaments beginning
in 1624. The lease of the manor of Downton in Wiltshire, which
Pembroke acquired from the bishop of Winchester, ended ecclesiastical influence in that borough. Clipsby Crew of Cheshire, son
of Sir Ranulph Crew, the King's serjeant-at-law, probably owed
his seat to Pembroke. His partner was Sir William Dodington, Jr.,
one of the Wiltshire gentry, who died in the course of the Parliament and was replaced by Edward Herbert. Although Herbert

---

such like, that for their own ends neither cares for the King nor commonwealth.
These are the men that brings all to utter ruin." (SP 16/92/12.)

57. Rowe, "Influence of the Earls of Pembroke on Parliamentary Elections," 243-
244. Rowe does not mention Sir Robert Cotton as Sir Arthur Ingram's replacement
at Old Sarum in 1624. Sir Thomas Morgan is identified as Pembroke's steward
and the son of Edmund Morgan of Penllwyn-Sarth. (*Ibid.*, 244.) The Inquisition
Post Mortem of the Earl of Pembroke shows that Morgan owned property in conjunction with the Earl and his secretary, John Thoroughgood, in Hertfordshire
and Middlesex. (*I. P. M. Wiltshire*, 100.) Morgan sat for Wilton in every Parliament
from 1614 through 1628 and was knighted at Wilton when King James visited the
Earl of Pembroke on August 7, 1623. (John Nichols, The *Progresses, Processions,
and Magnificent Festivities of King James the First* [3 vols. in 4, London, 1828] IV,
888.) Sir Percy Herbert had served for another borough where Pembroke influence
was paramount, being returned for Shaftesbury, Dorset, in 1621 after the elections
of Thomas Sheppard and William Beecher were annulled.

never took his seat in the Commons in 1624, he continued to represent Downton in successive Parliaments and became one of Pembroke's prime instruments in the management of parliamentary affairs.[58]

The offices engrossed by Pembroke yielded him additional means of inducing electorates to return his candidates. No peer, with the exception of the Duke of Buckingham, rivaled him in the positions of trust he occupied. In 1621, Pembroke, as chancellor of the University of Oxford, had probably procured the return of Sir John Danvers to replace Sir John Bennet who was expelled from the House. Nominations for the 1624 election at the university almost certainly were made through Pembroke although neither candidate represented his interests. Secretary Calvert, one suspects, was the King's choice, while Sir Isaac Wake's recent association with Secretary Conway and Buckingham probably promoted his return.

Members of Parliament more closely allied with Pembroke sat for places under his jurisdiction. Sir Benjamin Rudyard, who occupied judicial office as Surveyor of the Court of Wards, was the most eminent and articulate member of Pembroke's clique. He represented Portsmouth where the Earl was Captain and Keeper of the Town and Isle. The greatest concentration of Pembroke's power was in Cornwall where he was Lord Lieutenant, Lord Warden of the Stannaries and High Steward of the Duchy Lands. Certainly association with Pembroke was propitious for the election of William Coryton as one of the county members in 1624.

58. Whiteway's Diary, fol. 37, calls Thoroughgood secretary to the Earl of Pembroke. There is a note in Conway's letterbook of a letter to Pembroke concerning a bill sent for signature granting Thoroughgood the reversion of the mastership of the Revels. James refused to grant this suit. (*Cal. S. P. Dom. 1619–1623*, 503, Feb. 28, 1623.) At Cardiff Pembroke was lord of the manor and constable of the castle. He controlled the appointment of bailiffs who made the returns. (Rowe, "Influence of the Earls of Pembroke on Parliamentary Elections," 245; W. R. Williams, *The Parliamentary History of the Principality of Wales, 1541–1895* [Brecknock, 1895], 97.) Downton, the pure burgage tenure borough, shows Pembroke influence at least as early as 1621 when Thomas Morgan was returned. On the lessees of the manor of Downtown, see Sir Richard C. Hoare, *The History of Modern Wiltshire* (14 pts. in 6 vols., London, 1822–1844), III, 13, 19, 35. On the ecclesiastical patronage at Downton before 1624, see Bindoff, "Parliamentary History," V, 111–169. Sir Clipsby Crew sat for Downton in 1624 and 1625 and for Callington, Cornwall, in 1626. In 1626 Bagg says that Crew secured his place at Callington by direction of the Earl of Pembroke to William Coryton. (Gardiner, ed., *Notes and Queries*, 325–326, James Bagg to the Duke of Buckingham, undated [Mar. ? 1626].)

Coryton was the vice-warden of the Stannaries, deputy lieutenant and *custos rotulorum* of Cornwall. Described by Sir James Bagg as "Pembroke's chief instrument" in the county, Coryton may have been instrumental in procuring burgess-ships for the Earl's supporters. Sir John Stradling of Glamorganshire, friend and tenant of Pembroke, seems to have been elected at St. Germans through the Earl's solicitation. Another Cornish member probably recommended was George Mynne who, under Pembroke, was the deputy governor of the Mineral and Battery Works. It was alleged in 1626 that five recommendations were made to Cornish boroughs by letters from John Thoroughgood, Pembroke's secretary, and that some places had sent blank indentures to the Lord Warden. Probably Pembroke's influence in 1624 did not extend to these limits inasmuch as the Prince's council had so actively canvassed the duchy constituencies.[59]

In Wales, official position combined with family relationships to augment the Earl of Pembroke's power. Sir James Perrot, the arch-Puritan who represented Pembrokeshire, was a deputy vice admiral under the Earl for the counties of Pembroke, Carmarthen, and Cardigan. In Montgomeryshire a collateral branch of the Herbert family dominated county politics. Sir William Herbert represented the county; George Herbert, the borough of Montgomery. Both were cousins of the Earl of Pembroke, and he had previously assisted them in their quests for preferment at court.[60]

Most powerful of Pembroke's relatives was his brother Philip, earl of Montgomery and sometime favorite of the King. Montgomery controlled patronage at Queenborough, Kent, to which he recommended "two of his special friends" Roger Palmer and Robert Pooley.[61] The threat of Montgomery's displeasure was

59. It is not known whether Stradling's seat at St. Germans was procured through Sir John Eliot or Valentine Carey, bishop of Exeter; but, inasmuch as Coryton and Eliot were close friends, the presumption is strongly in favor of Eliot. In "Revival of the Forest Laws Under Charles I," *History*, XLV (June 1960), 85–102, George Hammersley discusses Mynne's connection with Pembroke. A George Mynne sat for Old Sarum in 1614 and 1621. See also G. E. Aylmer, *The King's Servants: The Civil Service of Charles I, 1625–1642* (New York: Columbia University Press, 1961), 117–121.

60. The election of Perrot was challenged, but the House of Commons resolved on May 28 that Perrot's return was valid because the petition had not been presented within six weeks from the opening of Parliament. (*CJ*, 798.)

61. Rev. C. Eveleigh Woodruff, "Notes on the Municipal Records of Queenborough," *Archaeologia Cantiana*, XXII (1897), 169–185. There are notes in this article of two letters from Philip Herbert, earl of Montgomery, to the mayor and

sufficient to prevent the corporation from electing their favored candidate, one Mr. Bassett. Bassett was coerced into withdrawing to make way for the Earl's nominees.

In successive Parliaments after 1624 Pembroke's electoral influence continued to grow, and application was frequently made to him by those wishing a seat in the Commons. Those he favored were rarely distinguished, either by independence or merit, and some of his chief instruments, such as Dr. Turner, achieved their place in history as a result of the part they played in furthering Pembroke's designs. It is indicative of the Earl's canny political sense that he chose to extend his power in borough elections rather than to assert it at the county hustings. He preferred the reality of power to the prestige of notoriety. Yet not every borough where he pretended authority was willing to gratify his desires. More populous cities, such as Salisbury and Bristol, pursued their independent courses irrespective of his solicitations. To be truly susceptible to influence, boroughs required, chiefly, a limited electorate, an absence of qualified candidates, and a desire to escape the responsibility for paying the wages of their members. Many rural constituencies fulfilled all these qualifications, but none were so spectacularly grouped under the control of one official as were the Cinque Ports.

Lord Zouche, Warden of the Cinque Ports and the Ancient Towns, steadfastly maintained the prerogatives of his office despite

---

jurats of Queenborough, Kent: one dated Jan. 6, 1623/4 in reference to the withdrawal of Bassett and the recommendation of Pooley and Palmer; another relating to the parliamentary election of 1625. In 1625 Queenborough returned Roger Palmer and Sir Edward Hales. When the Earl heard of this, he wrote, "After my hastie commendacions I have just cause to make y$^e$ worst constructions of your undiscreete carriage towards me in slighting my letters which I directed unto you for M$^r$. Robert Pooley, a gent. every way able to discharge a greater trust than happily might betide him from that Corporation, if you had made choice of him according to the tenor and meaning of my sayd letters. And assure yourselves since Sir Edward Hales out of respect to mee is content to wave acceptance of that Burgesshipp w$^h$ yee would enforce upon him, if in his Roome you choose not the sayd M$^r$. Pooley for whom you see how much I am engaged, I shall consider it as a neglect and scorne doubled uppon mee, and shall most assuredly therefore whensoever your occasions shall need my furtherance bee found, Yo$^r$ friend according to yo$^r$ behavior to mee in this and in y$^e$ future, Montgomery. Whitehall, 25th of April, 1625." Apparently the Earl of Montgomery took advantage of Queenborough's desire for a new charter to help insure the return of his candidates, Palmer and Pooley, in 1626. Queenborough's charter of that year was granted with the consent of Montgomery, who was constable of the castle of Queenborough as well as Lord Lieutenant of Kent.

age, infirmity, and impending retirement. Since the late Middle
Ages the seven ports under his jurisdiction had been in a continual
state of decline, largely due to the accumulation of sand and
shingle in their harbors. Hastings was little more than a village;
Winchelsea was described as "decayed"; Sandwich and Rye had
sought rejuvenation by the importation of foreign clothworkers;
Romney and Hythe were losing their harbors; Dover alone was
thriving — mainly because it was important as an embarkation
point for the passage to the Continent. The ports as a unit had lost
their leadership in the defense of the realm, and their paramount
interest in the herring fisheries was being contested by Englishmen
and foreigners alike. As their mercantile power and wealth had
declined the influence of the Lord Warden had increased. In the
course of the sixteenth century he had established a prescriptive
right to nominate one member of Parliament for each of the ports.
His office was the intermediary through which writs and returns
were transmitted, and it was alleged by one of Zouche's servants
that until letters of recommendation were received from the
Warden it was improper for the towns to hold their elections.[62]

It was assumed that nominees of the Lord Warden would be
dedicated supporters of crown policy but, under James I, active
superintendence of patronage in the Cinque Ports seems to have
been abandoned by the crown. In 1621, Zouche, not an ardent supporter of Buckingham or the Spanish match, promised places without consulting the King, and James was forced to be content with
his lordship's appointments "not doubting but you will be careful
to nominate such as will be serviceable to his majesty and his
kingdom." [63]

With one seat in each port at his disposal, the warden thus nominated seven members, yet in 1621 Zouche listed six gentlemen
whom he had promised to recommend for election and five more
whom he had engaged to place if they failed elsewhere.[64] Irrespective of the agreement between the list and the actual returns
it appears that Zouche was instrumental in influencing eleven
elections in 1621. The pattern in 1624 is approximately the same.
Sandwich, which had had a tumultuous election in 1621,[65] tended

62. SP 14/118/21, Richard Marsh to Nicholas, Dec. 10, 1620.
63. SP 14/118/27, Duke of Buckingham to Lord Zouche, Dec. 14, 1620.
64. SP 14/118/26.
65. *Commons Debates 1621*. VII, 567–570 prints, from SP 14/119/11, a letter
from Richard Marsh to Edward Nicholas dated January 8, 1620/1. At the election

to resist the warden's influence, and Winchelsea, Hastings, and New Romney selected local gentlemen as their second members.

The patronage of Zouche in 1624, as in 1621, was based on a variety of affiliations. Richard Zouche, who was recommended to Hythe in both instances, was the Lord Warden's brother and an eminent civil lawyer. Samuel More (Hastings) and Edward Nicholas (Winchelsea) were Zouche's servants. Thomas Conway, recommended and elected for Rye, was the younger son of Secretary Conway, while John Angell, who twice sat for Rye, was the son of the King's fishmonger. Sir Peter Heyman, who had sought Zouche's commendation to Hythe in 1621, was a local gentleman, and Sir Robert Hatton also had some Kentish associations, but nominees such as Francis Fetherstonehaugh at Romney, and Sir Edward Cecil and Sir Richard Yonge at Dover seem to have had no apparent connections with their constituencies.[66]

Although two of the Cinque Ports' elections were challenged in the Committee of Privileges in 1624, only the petition involving Dover implied a curtailment of the Lord Warden's patronage power. At Winchelsea, Sir Alexander Temple tried to wrest the second seat from the control of the Finch family and, although he succeeded in having the return of John Finch invalidated, Temple was defeated in the subsequent by-election. Zouche's nom-

---

"excepcion was taken to the begynning of the letters, for my Lords nominacion as his predecessors had done." There were apparently eight candidates for the two seats. Sir Edwin Sandys carried the first place and, despite Lord Zouche's recommendation, Sir Robert Hatton had some difficulty in securing the second seat. Thirty-one electors were present: eighteen voted for Hatton, six for other candidates, and seven refused to give any voice. Hatton is described as belonging to the archbishop of Canterbury. Chamberlain, *Letters*, II, 62, letter of Mar. 15, 1617, identifies him as a steward of my Lord of Canterbury; see also SP 14/119/63, Edward Kelk to Lord Zouche, Feb. 3, 1620/1, printed in *Commons Debates 1621*, VII, 571–572, and SP 14/121/1, as printed in *ibid.*, VII, 598–599, letter of the port of Sandwich to the Cinque Ports, May 1, 1621.

66. Lord Zouche to the port of Hythe, Dec. 8, 1620, as printed in George Wilks, *The Barons of the Cinque Ports and the Parliamentary Representation of Hythe* (Folkestone, 1892), 69–70; see also Lord Zouche to the port of Hythe, Nov. 28, 1620, as printed in *ibid.*, 70–71; excerpts from the corporation records, Jan. 17, 1624, also printed in *ibid.*, 71–72; SP 14/118/33, Lord Zouche to the Mayor of Hastings, Dec. 18, 1620. Edward Nicholas was secretary to Lord Zouche and also served him as steward of certain manors and lordships in Somersetshire and Wiltshire. See SP 14/157/2. Regarding the efforts of Nicholas to secure employment with the Duke of Buckingham, see SP 14/160/14, 14/168/17, 14/174/65, and 14/175/79, Matthew Nicholas to Edward Nicholas, Mar. 2, June 21, Nov. 14, and Nov. 29, 1624. In Lord Zouche's list of nominees, Francis Fetherstonehaugh is described as "one of his Majesty's pensioners." (SP 14/118/26; see also SP 14/119/19, mayor of New Romney to Lord Zouche, Jan. 12, 1620/1.)

inee, Nicholas, was not mentioned in any report of the proceedings, and his diary indicates that he was not sufficiently concerned to attend the hearings of the Committee of Privileges. Clearly at Winchelsea only one seat was open to contest.[67]

At Dover it was traditional to elect the Lieutenant of Dover Castle as one member and to accept the Lord Warden's recommendation for the other seat.[68] In the 1624 election the situation was complicated by the dispute between Zouche and Sir Henry Mainwaring over the lieutenancy. In 1623 the warden had dismissed Mainwaring as Lieutenant of Dover Castle for such reasons as neglect of duty, fraud, keeping low company, running into debt, and absence from the castle. Mainwaring alleged that he had been displaced because he had sought employment under the Earl of Rutland in the fleet destined to bring Charles home from Spain. He actively solicited the support of the Prince and Buckingham in his campaign to secure restoration as lieutenant. Charles wrote several letters in Mainwaring's behalf, but Zouche adamantly refused to reinstate his former subordinate. His animosity toward Mainwaring was revealed by the fact that the surrender of the wardenship to Buckingham on July 17, 1624, was conditioned by the stipulation that Mainwaring was not to receive any preferment in the Cinque Ports.

With the lieutenancy vacant, Zouche made two recommendations for the Dover election: Sir Edward Cecil and Sir Richard Yonge. Mainwaring seems not to have seriously contested the election; although his name was mentioned in the proceedings, he apparently received no votes. Nevertheless the freemen of the port, who were denied a voice in the election, resolved to petition against the return of Cecil and Yonge in order to secure the restoration of their ancient privilege. In this attempt they were abetted by Mainwaring who thought that by securing election he could embarrass Zouche and thus vindicate his own conduct as lieutenant. In the Committee of Privileges on March 23, 1624, the Dover election was nullified, and this decision was confirmed by the Commons on the following day. Immediately it was rumored that

67. Glanville, *Reports*, 12–24. Nicholas in his diary made notes of Glanville's report from the Committee of Privileges, but apparently was not present when the election was considered in committee. See Nicholas, fol. 88v.

68. SP 14/117/74, William Leonard to Nicholas, Nov. 12, 1620.

Mainwaring would stand for the first place at Dover and Sir Thomas Milford for the second. Sir Edwin Sandys, "beloved of the Sandwich rabble," was thought to be laboring with the Dover freemen on Mainwaring's behalf, and an unruly election was anticipated.

Cecil and Yonge both sought reelection: Yonge, ardently; Cecil, apathetically. Cecil had been summoned to the wars in the Low Countries and, in contesting the seat again, was only interested in removing any blot from his reputation. Yonge, on the other hand, paid for the writ for a new election, suggested that Zouche conceal it until the time was propitious, and urged that Milford and Mainwaring be denied the opportunity to stand on the grounds that they were not freemen of Dover. Yonge and Cecil were returned again, apparently without incident, and Sir Henry Mainwaring's attempts to utilize the influence of the Prince and the favorite against Lord Zouche proved fruitless.[69]

The 1624 election at Rye provides an interesting insight into the local conditions that influenced the selection of candidates. Scarcely were the writs issued when Sir William Twysden offered his services to the port, and shortly thereafter the mayor and jurats of Tenderden, a corporate member of Rye, recommended the election of Samuel Short. William Angell wrote to the mayor, jurats, commons, and freemen recommending his son, John Angell, who had served for Rye in 1621. He included in his letter the persuasive argument that he would entertain a commercial representative of Rye at his own expense in order to facilitate the prosecution of port business during the sitting of Parliament. He also presumed to recommend the reelection of Emmanuel Gifford, who had been the Lord Warden's nominee in 1621. Sir Edward Conway solicited Lord Zouche's nomination of his son, and, accordingly, Sir Edward Conway, Jr., was recommended to the mayor and jurats.

69. Glanville, *Reports,* 63–70; SP 14/160/94, 14/161/32, 14/161/38, 14/161/51, and 14/162/26, Richard Yonge to Lord Zouche, Mar. 18, 23, 25, 29, Apr. 7, 1624; see also SP 14/161/39, Sir Edward Cecil to Lord Zouche, Mar. 25, 1624; SP 14/161/31, Richard Zouche to Lord Zouche, Mar. 23, 1624. On Mainwaring's efforts to enlist the Prince's aid, see SP 14/153/81, Yonge to Lord Zouche, Oct. 20, 1623; SP 14/154/9, Prince Charles to Lord Zouche, Nov. 4, 1623; SP 14/154/52, Lord Zouche to Conway, Nov. 20, 1623, and SP 14/158/41, Charles to Lord Zouche, Jan. 23, 1624. On the agreement between Buckingham and Zouche for the surrender of the wardenship of the Cinque Ports, July 17, 1624, see SP 14/170/16.

The decisive factors in the election were: the nomination by the Lord Warden and the desire to secure improvement of Rye harbor and protection against French fishing craft. Consequently Conway and Angell, who had powerful court connections, were named to represent the port.

Apparently Lord Zouche had mistaken which of Conway's sons was to be recommended to Rye — Sir Edward Conway, Jr., was also returned for Warwick borough. When he chose to sit for Warwick, Secretary Conway renewed his efforts to secure the place for his second son, Thomas Conway. Another nomination was procured from the Lord Warden and Secretary Conway apologized profusely to the corporation of Rye for the original error. As an added inducement, he stated, "I will in eavery poynt be answerable to you for his care and dillegence in serving you, and whearin he shold be slack I will myselfe execute. Your buisnes left in my hands hear by Mr. Maior I have put in execution. I have drawne my Lord Admirall to joyne with me to the King soe that I doubt not but that you will have a good ende of it to your liking." Such persuasive arguments could scarcely be ignored, and Thomas Conway was returned.[70]

The independence of the Lord Warden in the exercise of his office was reflected in the character of the ten nominees he supported. Some of them, like Conway, were mere novices whose only function was to vote as their superiors dictated. Others, such as Sir Peter Heyman, were staunchly independent in the exercise of their judgment. Some of Zouche's servants, like his secretary Nicholas, obviously molded their opinions to conform to the wishes of future patrons. It is therefore impossible to categorize the patronage in the Cinque Ports on the basis of subservience to royal interests. Perhaps the most cogent argument in support of this contention is the fact that no privy councillor represented any of the Cinque Ports during the reign of King James.

The prominence of Lord Zouche as a patron was ascribable to

70. HMC, *Thirteenth Report*, Appendix, pt. IV (London, 1892), MSS of Rye and Hereford Corporations, 163, Sir Edward Conway to the Mayor and Jurats of Rye, Feb. 24, 1624; see also *ibid.*, 162, Sir William Twysden to the Mayor and Jurats of Rye, Dec. 29, 1623, and Mayor and Jurats of Tenderden to the Mayor and Jurats of Rye, Jan. 14, 1624; *ibid.*, 162–163, William Angell to the Mayor, Jurats and commonalty of Rye, Jan. 16, 1624; *ibid.*, 163–164, Lord Warden to the Mayor and Jurats of Rye, Feb. 27, 1624; *ibid.*, 163, Sir Edward Conway to the Mayor, Jurats and commonalty of Rye, Feb. 7, 1624.

his tenancy of the wardenship and not to his personal power as a peer. His independence was guaranteed mainly by his preoccupation with the affairs of the ports and by his reluctance to become embroiled in disputes over foreign policy. Age and infirmity had lengthened his absences from court and his influence in the Parliament of 1624 was virtually nullified by his retirement from the upper House. As far as it was in his power, Zouche tried to sustain his position. When he dispatched his proxy to Pembroke on February 6, 1624, he remitted to the Earl's protection the rights and immunities of the Cinque Ports and the jurisdiction of the Lord Warden's office. He entrusted to Pembroke the "disposing of my voice for the good of God's church and my country." [71]

Not all royal servants were so fortunate as to be on the periphery of court intrigue. John Williams, bishop of Lincoln and Lord Keeper of the Great Seal, was intimately involved in the formulation of religious and foreign policy, the administration of justice, and the management of Parliament. The retention of his integrity in the performance of any one of these delicate services was a task of monumental proportions. It was his misfortune to become entangled in situations in 1623–1624 where no compromise was acceptable; a choice had to be made between the contradictory policies advocated by the King and Buckingham. As a result, expedience triumphed over probity, and survival became his motive for political action.

As a divine, Williams was undoubtedly familiar with the biblical warning against attempting to serve two masters, yet he pursued this course of action despite the widening rift between James and his favorite. Perhaps the King was partially responsible for the Lord Keeper's ambivalent behavior; it was purportedly in response to his urging that Williams first catered to Buckingham's whims and sought preferment through his influence. The deanery of Westminster, the bishopric of Lincoln, a privy councillorship, and custody of the great seal were the rewards garnered by this "court comet" in slightly more than a year. In addition, he became a personal and parliamentary advisor to the Duke and a confidant and favorite of the Countess of Buckingham.[72]

71. SP 14/159/18, Lord Zouche to the Lord Chamberlain, Feb. 6, 1624.
72. Hacket, *Scrinia Reserata*, I, 39–41 discusses the reasons that impelled Williams to seek preferment through Buckingham. His comments are purportedly based on an actual conversation with Williams at Bugden. Apparently Williams was reluctant

Like so many of Buckingham's creatures, Williams had few ties with his official associates. In the contest for favor and power, jealousies between ministers of government were rampant. When Cranfield was made Lord Treasurer, the Lord Keeper warned Buckingham: "Let him hold it but by your Lordships favour, not his own power, or wilfulnesse. And this must be apparent, and visible: Let all our greatnesse depend (as it ought) upon yours, the true original. Let the King be Pharaoh, your self Joseph, and let us come after as your half-brethren." [73]

The dispensing of royal largess through the favorite emphasized the vertical alignment of the King's official family. To James, Buckingham was undoubtedly of value as a pleasant companion

---

to solicit favors from Buckingham because "he saw his Lordship was bred in a great Error, he was so ready to cast a Cloud suddenly upon his Creatures, and with much inconstancy to root up that which he had planted." Yet when Williams was at Royston in attendance upon the King during one of Buckingham's absences from court, "The King abruptly, without dependance upon the Discourse on foot, asked him, 'When he was with Buckingham?' Sir, (says the Doctor) I have had no business to resort to his Lordship. But wheresoe'er he is, you must presently go to him upon my Message, says the King. So he did that Errand, and was welcom'd with the Countenance and Compliments of the Marquess, and invited with all sweetness to come freely to him upon his own Addresses. Who mark'd rather from whom he came, then to whom he was sent: And gather'd from the King's Dispatch, That His Majesty intended that he should seek the Marquess, and deserve him with Observance. From henceforth he resolved it; yet not to contaminate his Lordship with Bribery, or base Obsequiousness, but to shew himself in some Act of Trust and Moment, that he was as sufficient to bring his Lordship's good Ends to pass, as any whom he employed, both with readiness to do, and with judgment to do well." Compare with Gardiner, ed. *Fortescue Papers*, 158–159, Lord Keeper Williams to John Packer, Aug. 11, 1621. Williams's letter to Buckingham soliciting the deanery of Westminster is printed in Hacket, *Scrinia Reserata*, I, 44, where it is dated March 12, 1619, instead of 1620. The competition for the lord keepership is discussed by Hacket, *ibid.*, I, 51–52. The chief aspirants to the office were Sir Henry Hobart, Sir James Ley, and Sir Lionel Cranfield, as well as the Earl of Arundel. For Williams's advice to the Duke concerning the Parliament of 1621, see *ibid.*, I, 49–51, and *Cabala*, I, 65–66, the Lord Keeper to the Duke of Buckingham, Dec. 16, 1621. The tenor of the Lord Keeper's relations with the Countess of Buckingham is indicated by the letter printed in Hacket, *Scrinia Reserata*, II, 25, the Countess of Buckingham to Williams, Oct. 12, 1625. "I Must not forget my Promise to your Lordship: I have had large Conference with my Son about you. And he tells me that the King is determin'd to put another into your Place. But for his own part he says he is in Love, and Charity with your Lordship: And that he thinks that your Lordship will leave the Place better than you found it; and that you have done the King good service in it. For the rest I shall give you better Satisfaction when I see you next, than I can do by Letter. In the mean time, I am sorry there should be any unkindness betwixt your Lordship, and him that is so near to me, and that wisheth you both so well."

73. *Cabala*, I, 82–83, the Lord Keeper to the Duke, Oct. 14, 1621. For a discussion of the acrimonious disputes between Cranfield and Williams in 1622, see Hacket, *Scrinia Reserata*, I, 103–107; *Calendar of Wynn Papers*, 167–168, 169.

and a buffer against the troublesome suits of indigent courtiers. To suitors, Buckingham was the agent through whom preferment was achieved; the viceroy to whom primary allegiance was due. The Duke's encouragement of rivalries between his adherents assured his security by preventing the consolidation of an effective ministerial coalition against him. Thus, at a critical moment when the favorite's opinions diverged from those of his royal master, the mutual animosities among the Duke's subordinates virtually nullified the possibility of concerted opposition. Identity of interest and policy in 1624, for instance, indicated agreement between the Lord Keeper and Lord Treasurer Cranfield, but an alliance failed to materialize because of longstanding antagonisms between them. Mutual distrust prevented them from acting in concert even when both were subjects of their patron's displeasure. Ultimately each relied upon his individual resources to protect his interests.

Perhaps the most significant factor in the political isolation of the Lord Keeper was the departure of Charles and Buckingham from England. From the outset, Williams was not convinced of the wisdom of a royal embassy to Madrid, and his letters to the Duke in the spring of 1623 were replete with warnings of the dangers inherent in so hazardous a mission. "If things prove well, you need no Counsel, your Adventure will be Applauded, and great Note cast upon your Wisdom and Resolution. But if the Health, Entertainment, and the principal business of His Highness, nay if any one of the Three should miscarry, You cannot in your Wisdom and great Experience in this Court, but certainly know, that the blame will be laid upon you. And therefore for Gods sake prepare your self accordingly by Mature Deliberation to Encounter it. My Lord; for fear others will not, I will tell you the Truth. If I Offend you with my Trusty Care; I am sure your good Nature will blow it over before we meet again. But in sooth all the Court, and the Rabble of people lay this Voyage upon your Lordship. The King would seem sometimes, as I hear, to take it to himself (and we have Advis'd him so to do by Proclamation) yet he sticks at it, and many times casts it upon you both." [74]

Tactless admonitions such as these were unlikely to be acceptable to His Grace, but when the offense was compounded by ap-

74. Hacket, *Scrinia Reserata*, I, 116–117, the Lord Keeper to Buckingham, Feb. 25, 1623.

parent dilatoriness in implementing the commitments made to the Spanish, by uninvited interference in the rancorous quarrel between the Duke and the Earl of Bristol, and by sealing grants solicited by competitors of Buckingham, the rift between the Lord Keeper and his patron widened. Despite repeated protestations of loyalty and compliance, Williams heard disquieting rumors about his impending disgrace; Lord Mandeville reported that it would be the first action undertaken by the Duke upon his return to England.[75]

Not until the closing days of January 1624 was the Lord Keeper

75. *Ibid.*, I, 148–149, lists three main reasons for Buckingham's displeasure with the Lord Keeper: the revelation by Williams to the King of the names of the Duke's retainers at Wallingford House who urged Buckingham in 1623 to break the match treaty; the Lord Keeper's attempted mediation of the Buckingham-Bristol dispute; and Williams's continued support of the match negotiations with Spain. Hacket also cites a number of occasions in the latter part of 1623 when the King seemingly complimented Williams to the discredit of Buckingham. (*Ibid.*, 168.) The change in Williams's attitude toward Bristol as a result of the latter's quarrel with Buckingham is dramatic. On February 25, 1623, Williams wrote to the Prince, "I thank God heartily that you have in Your Company the Earl of Bristow, who for Advice and Counsel upon the Place, is, in my poor Opinion, inferior to none in His Majesties Dominions." (*Ibid.*, I, 116.) In June Williams was concerned about the confirmation of reports that Bristol had been relieved of all employment in the negotiations. (*Ibid.*, I, 135–136.) By September Williams wrote to the Duke: "Now that I understand by Sir John Hipsley how things stand between your Grace and the Earl of Bristol; I have done with that Lord, and will never think of him otherwise, than as your Grace shall direct. Nor did I ever write one syllable to that effect, but in contemplation of performing true service to your Grace." (*Cabala*, I, 84–85, Lord Keeper to the Duke of Buckingham, undated.) In reference to grants the Lord Keeper admitted in a letter to the Duke of Buckingham on April 4, 1623, that "the Great Seal walks somewhat faster than usual, which is an Argument that it was not my Lord of Buckingham only, that set it agoing." (Hacket, *Scrinia Reserata*, I, 118–119.) By September Williams was apologizing for exercising his discretion in the sealing of grants. (*Cabala*, I, 84–85, Lord Keeper to the Duke of Buckingham, undated.) Among those who informed the Duke of Williams's activities in 1623 was Tobie Matthew. (Goodman, *Court of James I*, II, 270–272, Tobie Matthew to Buckingham, Mar. 29, 1623.) The letters of Charles and Buckingham during their absence in Spain are full of importunities for the speedy fulfillment of the religious conditions they had agreed to. In their letter to King James on August 20, 1623, they noted that the Marquis Inojosa had forwarded to Spain an unfavorable report of the proceedings in England. (Halliwell, *Kings' Letters*, II, 225–226.) On August 30 the Lord Keeper wrote to the Duke informing him of the course held with English recusants. He was reluctant to grant everything the Spanish demanded, and he managed to prevent the publication of two general commands to the judges and bishops not to execute the recusancy laws until the Infanta had been in England for six months. Williams's true opinions were expressed in his remarks on the appearance of the bishop of Chalcedon: "If you were shipped (with the Infanta) the onely Councel were to let the Judges proceed with them presently, hang him out of the way, and the King to Blame my Lord of Cantuar: or myself for it." (*Cabala*, I, 79–81.) The attitude of many Englishmen toward religious concessions to the papists was cogently expressed in a letter (or speech) forged for the occasion and attributed to the archbishop of Canterbury, George Abbot, which appeared in

in dire jeopardy of losing his office. By that time he had cast his lot with those in the Council who had voted against the summoning of parliament and in favor of continued negotiations with Spain. In exasperation Buckingham vented his spleen on Williams, describing him as "a man odious to all the world," calling for his resignation, and requesting the intercession of the Prince to procure it.[76] The Lord Keeper's attempts to effect a reconciliation were requited with a cool reply written by Buckingham's secretary, John Packer, who asserted that his lordship "doth not seek your ruine (as some other had related) but onely will hereafter cease to study your fortune, as formerly he hath done: and withal added

---

July 1623. Specifically the letter inveighed against a toleration established by proclamation and complained against what the King had "done in sending the Prince into Spain without consent of your Council, the Privity and Approbation of your People." This letter was at once disavowed by Abbot, and an unsuccessful search was instituted to discover the author. The letter of Canterbury (that is, the forgery) is printed in Rushworth, *Historical Collections*, I, 85, and *Cabala*, I, 13–14, where it is erroneously attributed to the archbishop of York. Gardiner, *History of England*, V, 72, n., says that the letter must have been in circulation before the end of July. This is corroborated by a letter from Henry Rogers to Sir John Scudamore, July 23, 1623. "This is certain that the King proposed some fortnight before to his Council a toleration of popery, and that Papists might execute places of judicature. Whether the delivery of the ports was proposed is uncertain, or what more than I have expressed. The Council desired time to confer with the judges, and the answer was made the middle of the last week in Theobalds by my Lord Grace [Canterbury] to whom Lennox, Hamilton, Pembroke, Carlisle, Conway stuck stoutly. The speech of my Lord's Grace I have sent you. That passage of punishing those who drew the Prince into Spain was resolutely maintained by Marquis Hamilton." (Add. MS. 11,043, fol. 67.) On the estrangement between Buckingham and Williams, see also Henry Wharton, ed., *The History of the Troubles and Tryal of the Most Reverent Father in God, and Blessed Martyr, William Laud, Lord Arch-Bishop of Canterbury* (London, 1795), 8. On October 3 Laud noted in his diary that the Lord Keeper was very jealous of Buckingham's favor. By December 14, Laud was having nightmares about the Lord Keeper and on the fifteenth he noted that Williams had strangely forgotten himself to Buckingham, "and I think was dead in his affections." On December 27 Laud wrote, "I was with my Lord Duke of Buckingham. I found, that all went not right with the Lord Keeper, etc." (*Ibid.*, 8.) By January 11, 1624, there was so much animosity between Williams and Laud that they quarreled in the withdrawing chamber, a controversy which Laud later recounted to the Duke. Archbishop Abbot in his narrative considered Laud an intriguer against the power of Williams. See Thomas Frankland, *The Annals of King James and King Charles the First* (London, 1681), 216. Laud's biographer, Peter Heylin, credits him with giving intelligence to the Duke of a conspiracy between Cranfield and Williams. (Peter Heylin, *Cyprianus Anglicus or the History of the Life and Death . . . of William Laud* [London, 1671], 107.) Clarendon also mentions the plot between the Lord Treasurer and the Lord Keeper. (Edward, Earl of Clarendon, *The History of the Rebellion and the Civil Wars in England* [Oxford, 1839], I, 17.) I cannot, however, find any conclusive primary evidence of collusion between Cranfield and Williams. *Cabala*, I, 88–90, Lord Keeper to the Duke of Buckingham, Feb. 2, 1624.)

76. *Ibid.*, 88–90.

the reason, that your Lordship hath run a course opposite to him, which though he had cause to take ill at your hands, yet he could have passed it over, if it had been out of conscience, or affection to his Majesties service, or the Publique good, but being both dangerous to your countrie, and prejudicial to the cause of religion (which your Lordship above all other men should have laboured to uphold) he thought, he could not with reason continue that strictnesse of friendship, where your Lordship had made such a separation, especially having divers times out of his love to you, assayd to bring you into the right way, which once you promised to follow; but the two last times you met in Councel, he found, that you took your kue just as other men did, and joyned with them in their opinions, whose aim was to tax his proceedings in the managing of the Princes businesse." [77]

The return of Williams to the "right way" was smoothed by Charles, who recognized his value as a parliamentarian. On February 2 the Lord Keeper (at the Prince's suggestion) dispatched another letter of explanation and apology to the favorite, begging for "an assurance of your Graces former Love." A temporary rapprochement was effected, due largely to royal mediation, after which Williams rendered valuable service in promoting the breach with Spain. He never, however, regained Buckingham's full confidence, and he was continually harassed by the fear that "your Grace intended to sacrifice me this Parliament to appease the dislike of immunities exercised towards the Catholiques." [78] Despite his efforts to avoid impeachment, as late as April 25 the wits of the town were saying that "My Lord Treasurer cannot go without his Keeper." [79]

77. *Ibid.*, I, 86–87, John Packer to the Lord Keeper, Jan. 21, 1624.
78. *Ibid.*, I, 88–90, Lord Keeper to the Duke of Buckingham, Feb. 2, 1624. On February 6, Laud noted that Buckingham "told me of the reconciliation the day before made with the Lord Keeper." (Wharton, ed., *The History of the Troubles and Tryal of . . . William Laud*, 10.) On February 18, it was made clear that Buckingham's favor to Laud had been one of the chief causes of the estrangement between Williams and the Duke. According to Hacket (*Scrinia Reserata*, I, 159), Williams made a collection of documents dealing with the relaxation of penalties against recusants, "and stitched [them] up into one Book, every Leaf being signed with the Hands of Sir George Calvert, and Sir Edward Conway, principal Secretaries to his Majesty. If it be asked to what end was that provided, it was to shew he had a Brest-Plate, as well as an Head-Piece. It was to defend his Integrity against any Storm, that dark Days might raise about the Spanish Matters."
79. SP 14/163/50, Sir Francis Nethersole to Sir Dudley Carleton, Apr. 25, 1624. According to Hacket (*Scrinia Reserata*, I, 190), Williams realized that his fall was

Subsequent to his removal from office in 1625, Williams informed Sir John Wynn that nothing had happened which he had not foreseen and, since the death of King James, assuredly expected.[80] The Lord Keeper's foresight undoubtedly impelled him

foreshadowed by Cranfield's disgrace. "The Keeper knew he had deserved no ill; yet he trusted not to that, for he knew likewise how a Judge that hears many Causes, must condemn many, and offend many . . . He had made the Prince his fast Friend before; who was so ingenious that when he had promised Fidelity, there was no fear that he would start; chiefly because he sought to lay hold on his Highness upon no other Conditions, than to mortifie those spiteful accusations (if any such hapned) with his Frown, that durst not stand the Breath of Truth." On March 1 Secretary Calvert delivered a message from the King to the Commons "that he had received notice of some informations against the Lord Keeper and that there were more to come in; to which though he knew he would be ready to give answer, yet His Majesty's desire was that we should not suffer any aspersions to be cast upon him unless for matter of corruption wherewith he assured himself he could not be charged. The general silence shewed this to be no welcome message, but it caused no debate at this time." (Pym, fols. 12–12v.) According to Hacket (*Scrinia Reserata*, I, 191), thirty-seven frivolous petitions against the Lord Keeper were dismissed by the House of Commons' committee on one day. Four petitions of considerable consequence remained: a scandalous petition by one Morley, a woodmonger, which was eventually dismissed by the House of Lords, and its author and printer severely punished; a complaint by the Lady Darcy that she had been denied justice by the Lord Keeper when she tried to vindicate her right to present to a benefice in the gift of her minor son; Grise's petition which alleged the denial of an original writ of covenant; and a complaint by Joan Thomas charging the Lord Keeper with corruption in the issuance of a decree for the sale of lands to satisfy the debts of Sir Anthony Thomas. Lady Darcy's petition was reported by Sir Robert Phelips on May 7 and, after some small discussion in which Brooke defended the Lord Keeper and Perrot and Gwynn [*sic* — Glynn?] aggravated his offenses, the matter was dropped, and the House turned to the reading of the Lady Darcy's bill. (Earle, fol. 175.) Hacket (*Scrinia Reserata*, I, 192–194), has a full discussion of the issues at stake in Lady Darcy's case, but Pym's report is best. (Pym, fols. 75–77v.). Hacket also attributes the instigation of Morley's petition to Buckingham and maintains that John Howson, bishop of Oxford, was instrumental in spreading the petition among the peers in the upper House. His conduct is accounted for by his ,dissatisfaction over a decision Williams had rendered in a case between the bishop and Sir Henry Martin about demesne lands in Bray parish, Berkshire. The proceedings on Morley's petition are most fully reported in *Lords Debates 1624 & 1626*, 34–46, 60. In the debates both Buckingham and the Prince seemed eager for the vindication of the Lord Keeper. The report on the Grise and Thomas petitions was not made until May 26 and 27. No action was taken on Grise's complaint, and the matter remained *in statu quo* without prejudice to either party. In the Thomas affair the Lord Keeper was cleared of bribery, and the justice of his decree was vindicated. However, the sequestrations and injunctions in consequence of the decree were condemned as unjust. (Nicholas, fols. 227v–228v, and 232v–235; see also *Calendar of Wynn Papers*, 192, 193, 196.)

80. Wynn of Gwydir Papers [Panton Group], National Library of Wales MS. 9060 E/1379, Williams to Sir John Wynn, Dec. 1, 1625; see also *ibid.*, 1376, William Wynn to Sir John Wynn, Nov. 7, 1625. "The cause of his [Williams] remove was only the malice of the Duke towards him, who (when he could not by the means of the parliament displace him) used all his power with the King and made it his suit to effect his purpose, wherein with much ado, great unwillingness of the King,

to exhaust his patronage powers in 1624 in order to establish a
nucleus of support. His political acumen must also have convinced
him of the absolute necessity of an understanding with the Duke
if he was to escape the hue and cry of a House of Commons bent
on prosecution; in comparison with the number of members of
Parliament mustered under Buckingham's banner, the Keeper's
partisans were almost negligible.

Too many of the places at the disposal of the government were
solicited from the King, the Prince, and the Duke to allow Williams much freedom of action in securing the election of his
adherents. He had, perforce, to rely mainly on friends and relatives in his quest for seats. Only in his episcopal see of Lincoln
could he exercise any direct patronage. William Boswell, elected
at Boston, was his secretary and commissary of the bishopric. John
St. Amand, who replaced Sir George Goring at Stamford, seems
also to have been one of the keeper's secretaries. His election, like
Goring's, was probably procured through the Earl of Exeter, who
virtually controlled the borough.[81]

---

and grief of most of the Lords, he at length prevailed." See also D'Ewes, *Autobiography*, I, 281, which likewise ascribes Williams's fall to the malice of the Duke.
Rushworth, *Historical Collections*, I, 198, attributes Williams's loss of office to his
carriage toward Buckingham at the Parliament at Oxford "where the Bishop told
the Duke in Christchurch, upon the Dukes rebuking him, for siding against him,
That he was engaged with William Earl of Pembroke, to labor the Redress of the
Peoples Grievances, and was resolved to stand upon his own Legs. If that be your
resolution (said the Duke) Look you stand fast, and so they parted; and shortly
after that he was sequestred, though the Seal was not disposed from him till the
Thirtieth of October." Confirmation of this interpretation is contained in Sir Arthur
Ingram's letter to Sir Thomas Wentworth on November 7, 1625. "He [Buckingham]
was, and is possessed, that there were four in the higher House, that upon any
Complaint that should come up of him to them, that they with all their Strength
would set it forwards there. He is likewise possessed, that there was diverse combined against him in the lower House. For them in the higher House, it was my
Lord's Grace of Canterbury, my Lord Keeper, my Lord Marshal, and my Lord
Chamberlain. For them of the Lower House, he doth conceive, there were many,
who had their Conferences with these four Lords and others, that were depending
upon them; among which, you are not altogether free." Strafford, *Letters*, I, 28.

81. The identity of William Boswell, Esq., who sat for Boston is by no means
certain. It is clear that there was a William Boswell in the service of the Lord
Keeper as secretary and that he received, on behalf of the Lord Keeper, papers
relating to the Spanish treaties. (B. Dew Roberts, *Mitre & Musket, John Williams
Lord Keeper, Archbishop of York, 1582–1650* [London: Oxford University Press,
1938], 55; *Cal. S. P. Dom. 1623–1625*, 171.) See also *Cal S. P. Dom 1619–1623*, 375,
476, where William Boswell is identified as secretary to the bishop of Lincoln and
commissary of the bishop. A William Boswell was sworn as clerk of the Council
extraordinary on November 13, 1622. (*APC 1621–1623*, 353.) The *DNB*, V, 440, has
an article on Sir William Boswell (knighted 1633), who is identified as secretary
to Sir Dudley Carleton, ambassador to the Hague. It may be that all of this data

Another main source of Williams's meager strength was Wales. To a certain extent he could rely upon the provincial pride of Welshmen who rejoiced at the eminence of their countrymen at Westminster, but this empathy was of little use in a crisis. There were, after all, other Welsh families like the Trevors and the Vaughans who occupied offices of trust and power. In North Wales Williams had more reliable assets. John Mostyn, member of Parliament for Anglesey, was currently in the Lord Keeper's service. Sir Peter Mutton, who sat for the borough of Carnarvon, owed his place to directives sent from court and was further obligated by his marriage to the Lord Keeper's sister.

The numerous Wynn clan of Gwydir was tied to the Lord Keeper by favors, service, friendship, and marriage. Although the support of Sir Richard Wynn, elected at Ilchester, Somerset, could not be counted upon, Williams could almost certainly rely upon the loyalty of Henry Wynn who sat for Merionethshire. William Wynn, too, was commended to at least one constituency by the Keeper, and may have ultimately secured a burgess-ship at Lyme Regis through his recommendation.

Letters from the Council of Wales were one of the chief means by which Welsh elections were influenced, and the Lord Keeper had been careful to find places for his Welsh servants on the council. He was also fortunate in having his good friend, Sir James Whitelocke as Chief Justice of Chester. Williams had much obliged Whitelocke in 1621 by taking into his service Richard Oakley. During the Parliament in 1624 Oakley, a lawyer and secretary to the Lord Keeper, represented Bishop's Castle, Shropshire.[82]

---

relates to one person depending upon whether William Boswell left the Lord Keeper's service subsequent to his disgrace. See Birch, *Court and Times of Charles the First*, II, 158, Mr. Pory to Sir Thomas Puckering, Jan. 12, 1631/2; see also *The Autobiography of Thomas Raymond*, Camden Society, 3d Ser., Volume XXVIII (London: the Society 1917), Appendix II, "Life of William Boswell." John St. Amand, elected at Stamford, was admitted to Gray's Inn on March 12, 1625. The notice of his admission identifies him as one of the secretaries of the Lord Keeper. (Joseph Foster, ed., *The Register of Admissions to Gray's Inn, 1521–1889* [London, 1889], 176.) St. Amand's return was dated March 1, 1624. He replaced Sir George Goring who chose to sit for Lewes, Sussex. Goring was primarily a Buckingham adherent, yet he seems to have been on extremely good terms with the Lord Keeper. In October 1625 Goring was said to be "a vehement suitor to the duke in his [Williams] behalf." (Birch, *Court and Times of Charles the First*, I, 59–60, Rev. Joseph Mead to Sir Martin Stuteville, Oct. 29, 1625.)

82. Whitelocke, *Liber Famelicus*, 89–90; see also Pym, fol. 77, for Oakley's action in behalf of the Lord Keeper during the Darcy hearing. For additional data on

It is probable that the influence of Williams in the House of Commons would be seriously underestimated if one relied upon the evidence of his direct patronage alone. He was no defender of the high prerogative; in 1621 he had recommended compromising the dispute over privileges and hence had gained a reputation as an advocate of the *via media* between court and country. As a moderate he was more acceptable to the antiprerogative faction in the Commons than any other Buckingham adherent. Indeed, the Duke suspected that Williams's contacts with the popular leaders in the lower House were too numerous and too dangerous for his own safety. Naturally the Lord Keeper fervently denied any conspiracies with members of Parliament; whatever influence he had in the Commons he attributed to his judicial office. Lawyers who wished to practice in either the Chancery or the Star Chamber would naturally be chary of offending the Lord Keeper. Two members of the Commons in 1624, both Masters in Chancery, fell precisely into this category: Sir Eubule Thelwall, representing Denbighshire, and Sir Edward Leech, a burgess from Derby town.[83]

---

Oakley, see H. T. Weyman, "The Members of Parliament for Bishop's Castle," *Transactions of the Shropshire Archeological Society,* 2d Ser., X (1898), 33–68.

83. For the Lord Keeper's advice to Buckingham concerning the Parliament of 1621, see Hacket, *Scrinia Reserata,* I, 49–51. In Gardiner, *History of England,* IV, 52, n., the authenticity of Hacket's report is discredited. When he was under fire in 1625, Williams on three separate occasions specifically denied any conspiracies with parliament men. (Hacket, *Scrinia Reserata,* II, 17–18, 20, 24.) His most extended defense is in his "Reasons to Satisfy your Most Excellent Majesty Concerning my Carriage All This Last Parliament" (Aug. 14, 1625). "First negatively, That I did nothing disserviceably to your Majesty, or the Duke. For first, I never spake at Oxford with any of the stirring Men, as was untruly suggested to your Majesty, excepting once with Philips, with the Privity, and for the Service of the Duke. And with Wentworth at his first coming to Town, and before his coming to the House. Who promised (and I do verily believe he perform'd it) to carry himself advantageously to your Majesty's Service, and not to joyn with any that should fly upon my Lord Duke. The rest are all Strangers to me: and I never spake with any one of them concerning any Parliamentary-matters. Secondly, I did cross the popular way, more than any of the Council; which I durst not have done, if I had intended to run along with them." Williams denied knowing Sir Francis Seymour by sight, and he seemed reluctant to name any of his acquaintances. However, he identified several members of the Duke's coterie, including Sir John Eliot, Sir Thomas Crew, Sir William Strode, Sir Nathaniel Rich, and, of course, Lord Conway and Sir John Coke. As to his influence over members of the legal profession Williams stated, "I had much less at this time by reason of the Paucity of the Lawyers, who were in the Circuit." (Hacket, *Scrinia Reserata.* II, 17–18.) Williams was understandably wary of admitting associations with the leaders of the popular party, but in 1621, for instance, he had solicited Selden's release from imprisonment. On this occasion he told the Duke, "My Lord, The man hath excellent Parts, which may be diverted from an Affectation of Applause of idle

In the House of Lords, Williams could probably rely upon some support from his fellow bishops, but too many of them owed their appointments to Buckingham to afford the Lord Keeper any sense of security. As had proven the case in so many other prosecutions, Williams's support in both the Lords and the Commons was apt to evaporate in the face of any sustained campaign against him.[84]

The ends served by patronage in the Parliament of 1624 varied from the enactment of a private bill, to the protection of a minister, to the formulation of foreign policy. It may, I think, be doubted whether an analysis of patronage is the key to understanding the Parliaments in the seventeenth century. Perhaps it would be better to concentrate on identifying family cliques or mercantile and professional relationships. But however homogeneous the interests of merchants and lawyers seem when considered in retrospect, it must be remembered that this concert of opinion largely developed during the sessions of the House, and the policies advocated by these groups were usually negativistic. Merchants like Abbot and Bateman, Neale and Sherwill could agree that the crown's fiscal policy was restraining trade, but they failed to find a satisfactory positive solution to the problem, and, when their individual interests were threatened, they were as parochial in their viewpoints as the most provincial squire. Lawyers, too, varied widely in their opinions. Common lawyers could agree that their profession needed protection from the prerogative courts, but, over issues like the royal right to impose, to levy ship

---

People to do some good and useful Service to His Majesty. He is but young, and this is the first Offence that ever he committed against the King." Subsequently the Lord Keeper gave Selden the registership of the College of Westminster and "procured a Chapman that gave him 400£ for his Right in the Place: A Courtesie which Mr. Selden did never expect from the Giver, and was repaid with more Duty and Love then the Giver could ever have expected from Mr. Selden." (*Ibid.*, I, 69.) See also Selden's letter to Sir Robert Cotton on September 25, 1626, in Birch, *Court and Times of Charles the First*, I, 152: "My Lord of Lincoln remembered you, especially when I was with him the last week at Bugden. There he lives finely within doors and without, and deserves the love and honour of good men." See also Pym, fol. 77: "Mr. Selden began to strain some reasons so far in justifying my Lord Keeper that he was interrupted."

84. In Hacket, *Scrinia Reserata*, I, 63–65, it is specifically mentionel that three bishops were particularly beholden to Williams for their preferment: Laud of St. Davids, Carey of Exeter, and Davenent of Salisbury. "Salisbury and Exeter were Men of faithful Acknowledgment in all their life." See also Gardiner, ed., *Fortescue Papers*, 159–160, Lord Keeper Williams to John Packer, Sept. 1, 1621.

money, or privy seals, they were as far apart as Sir Edward Coke and John Finch. And, in the final analysis, neither merchants nor lawyers could have hoped to give voice to their grievances without either the acquiescence or the support of the back-benchers from the country gentry.

Does patronage enable us to make sense of a Parliament? Seemingly it was infinite in its variety and purpose, yet it must be remembered that it was largely in the hands of the gentry and the nobility and thus, generally speaking, reflected the identifying interests of those social groups. This is not to deny that the purposes of patronage frequently bore little relation to the issues at stake in the Parliament. Doubtless the Seymour nominees spent as much time in securing the passage of the bill concerning the Earl of Hertford's lands as they did in informing themselves on national issues and debating them.

The control of one or two seats by a single patron was of little significance in the total parliamentary picture. The control of many seats was no more significant if the places were distributed with no design in mind. But the efficient utilization of patronage in the hands of a powerful peer like the Earl of Pembroke presaged the Parliaments of the eighteenth century. The control of parliamentary boroughs enabled the patron to determine his policy in advance of Parliament and to choose candidates who would be completely subservient to his wishes. Thus the initiative was transferred to the patron; in the past it had always been vested in the crown. In the course of the seventeenth century patronage began to mean more than the manifestation of an individual's local power, and when the nominees of patrons became cohesive groups, well versed in parliamentary tactics, the days of subservience to regal authority were numbered. The pattern for future Parliaments was "chalked out" by Buckingham and Charles in 1624 when they marshaled their forces to oppose the King.

# IV  *Parlementum Pium, Doctum et Foelix?*

The select council's rejection of Spanish overtures in January 1624 emphasized the need for an immediate decision regarding the role of Parliament in the determination of foreign policy. Some members of the junta were reluctant to accept responsibility for their advice to break off negotiations without the concurrence of the remainder of the Privy Council or Parliament.[1] Prince Charles was distrustful of both Council and Parliament. He was afraid that a thorough investigation into the negotiations with Spain would be embarrassing, and he wished only to request aid from the Commons for the recovery of the Palatinate. This policy was unlikely to prove attractive to the people, and, in order to "draw on an engagement," Lord Keeper Williams suggested that Parliament be asked to advise the King whether the Palatinate should be reconquered directly or by a war of diversion. Having gauged the anti-Spanish sentiment of the nation, he perceived that the Commons would prefer a Spanish war, and he believed that by thus phrasing the question an investigation into the failure of the marriage negotiations could be avoided. This expedient was commended by the Prince; Williams was commanded to acquaint Buckingham with it and solicit his opinion.[2]

The favorite, however, was quite prepared to compromise the royal prerogative by having the breach with Spain made in Parliament. He alleged that such a course would bind the Commons

1. Chamberlain, *Letters*, II, 542–543, letter of Jan. 31, 1624.
2. *Cal. S. P. Venetian*, XVIII, 211, Valaresso to the Doge and Senate, Jan. 30/Feb. 9, 1624; *Cabala*, I, 90, Lord Keeper to the Duke of Buckingham, Feb. 2, 1624.

to support their advice with subsidies, but his foes were convinced that he wished to involve Parliament in his own salvation.[3] Distrustful of the Duke's ascendancy over the Prince and unwilling to credit him with instigating a breach which they themselves desired, Buckingham's enemies hoped "with his blood [to] wash away the stain of so many failures." When Pembroke was advised to support Buckingham as an enemy of the Spaniards and to avoid inquiring into and punishing his actions, the Earl replied that "they must consider internal foes before external ones, and they must punish those who err seriously so that everything may take place not only without detriment but to the advantage of the chief object, which means leaving to parliament the dissolution of the treaty with Spain." [4]

The paramount question — war with Spain — also concerned Buckingham's satellite, the Earl of Carlisle, in the advice he tendered to the King about parliamentary affairs. During a recent illness he had "been visited by divers Gentlemen of quality, who are Parliament-men, none of those popular, and plausible Orators, but solid, and judicious good patriots, who fear God, and honour the King. Out of their discourses I collect, That there are three things, which do chiefly trouble your people. The first, that for the subsidies granted, the two last Parliaments, they have received no retribution by any bills of Grace. The second, that some of their Burgesses were proceeded against after the Parliament were dissolved. And the third, that they misdoubt, that when they shall have satisfied your Majesties demands and desires, you will neverthelesse proceed to the conclusion of the Spanish match."

To overcome these suspicions and objections Carlisle suggested:

First let your Majesties enemies see, that the Lion hath teeth, and clawes.

2. Next, imbrace and invite a strict, and sincere friendship, and association with those whom neighbourhood and alliance, and common interest of state and religion have joyned unto you.

3. And last of all, cast off, and remove jealousies, which are between your Majestie and your people.

3. *Cal. S. P. Venetian*, XVIII, 211, Valaresso to the Doge and Senate, Jan. 30/Feb. 9, 1624.
4. *Ibid.*, 216, Valaresso to the Doge and Senate, Feb. 6/16, 1624.

Your Majestie must begin with the last, for upon that foundation, you may afterwards set what frame of building you please. And when should you begin (Sir) but at this overture of your Parliament by a gracious, clear, and confident discovery of your intentions to your People. Fear them not (Sir) never was there a better King, that had better subjects, if your Majestie would trust them. Let them but see, that you love them, and constantly rely upon their humble advice, and readie assistance, and your Majestie will see, how they will tear open their breasts, to give you their hearts, and having them, your Majestie is sure of their hands, and purses. Cast but away some crums of your Crown amongst them, and your Majestie will see those crums will make a miracle, they will satisfie many thousands. Give them assurance that your heart was alwayes at home, though your eyes were abroad; invite them to looke forward, and not backward, and constantly maintain, that with confidence you undertake, and your majestie will find admirable effects of this harmonious concord. Your Majestie as the head directing, and your people as the hands and feet, obeying and co-operating for the honour, safety, and welfare of the bodie of the State. This will revive, and reunite your friends abroad, and dismay, and disappoint the hopes of your enemies, secure your Majesties person, assure your estate, and make your memorie glorious to posterity.[5]

The good effects to be expected from the passage of new laws undoubtedly was that part of Carlisle's letter which the King found most congenial. There was no need for the government to prepare a legislative agenda in 1624; bills which had passed in 1614 and again in 1621 could be revived for speedy enactment. This would gratify his subjects and need not displease James, for on numerous occasions in the previous Parliament he had recommended passage of remedial legislation "against Informers, against the Abuse of Supersedeas, against Monopolies, against Recusants, and for Limitation of Suits." [6] It was not on domestic issues primarily that a clash was to be expected between prerogative and Parliament, and of this the King was well aware.

Carlisle had maintained that upon the firm foundation of an agreement with his people James could "afterwards set what

---

5. *Cabala*, I, 269–270, Earl of Carlisle to King James I, Feb. 14, 1624. Harl. MS. 1580 contains the original letter in fols. 193–196; see also *Cal. S. P. Venetian*, XVIII, 217, Valaresso to the Doge and Senate, Feb. 6/16, 1624.

6. *OPH*, V, 448. For James's attitude toward legislation in the Parliament of 1621 see *Commons Debates 1621*, II, 247, 305, 309, 535; III, 34, 41, 365; IV, 145, 153–155, 174, 203, 345, 394; V, 39, 54–55, 187, 200, 289, 293, 396; VI, 53, 236, 410; VII, 610, 615.

frame of building" he pleased, but the King realized the difference between rejecting the advice of the junta for foreign affairs and scorning counsel requested of Parliament. Unsolicited advice offered by the Commons in 1621 had led to a dissolution; it would be infinitely more dangerous to renege on an offer to cooperate with the Lords and Commons in the determination of foreign policy. It was for this reason that "the king fears too greatly the prejudice to his prerogatives and detests committing so much authority to the parliament." [7] It was for this reason that the propositions which the King was prepared to make at the commencement of the session remained a secret, and that he sent his secretary to the Spanish ambassadors seeking a clarification of the King of Spain's answer of January 5, 1624 (N.S.), concerning the restoration of the Palatinate. To James, Parliament was a diplomatic lever, an instrument that could be used to extort better conditions from the Spanish, but it was a weapon of dubious utility. The necessity of uniquivocally accepting or rejecting its advice could only be delayed temporarily.[8]

Inclement weather forestalled the opening of Parliament on February 12; half of the members had not yet arrived at Westminster.[9] Since the preceding weekend, James had been at White-

7. *Cal. S. P. Venetian,* XVIII, 211, Valaresso to the Doge and Senate, Jan. 30/Feb. 9, 1624.

8. On the secrecy of the King's intentions see *ibid.,* 216, Valaresso to the Doge and Senate, Feb. 6/16, 1624, and 220, Valaresso to the Doge and Senate, Feb. 13/23, 1624. In Gardiner, *History of England,* V, 182, the Salvetti newsletter of Feb. 13/23, 1624, is cited. On the request to the Spanish ambassadors, see the letter of Inojosa to Philip IV of Feb. 9/19, 1624, PRO 31/12/31, Spanish Transcripts; S. P. Foreign (Spain) 94/30, undated reply of the Spanish ambassadors, fol. 158.

9. D'Ewes attributes the original postponement to bad weather. (D'Ewes, fol. 59.) Valaresso agrees (*Cal. S. P. Venetian,* XVIII, 220, Valaresso to the Doge and Senate, Feb. 13/23, 1624), but the Venetian ambassador mentions the possibility of precautions against a Catholic gunpowder plot and also the suspicion that fresh letters were expected from Spain. Wright says that "it was generally known the day before that his Majesty (for the better dispatch of the term businesses whereof the said 12th was the last day) had resolved to adjourn this parliament until Monday after and that a commission under the Great Seal of England was prepared for that purpose." (Braye MS. 73, fol. 2.) Hacket (*Scrinia Reserata,* I, 173) erroneously says that the Duke of Richmond and Lennox died on the twelfth, and he cites this as the cause of the delay. As far as attendance in the House of Commons is concerned, Sir James Perrot reported on March 18 that 439 members had received the sacrament on February 29, and 20 more in the interim, leaving only 12 still to receive. (*CJ,* I, 739.) D'Ewes, fol. 86v, gives the same figures and lists the total membership as 471 knights and burgesses. Valaresso reported on February 27/March 8, "Many of the gentlemen who intended to keep away, fearing that this parliament would fare like the others, are now arriving every day to take part, induced by the hope of such a

hall, but mystery still obscured the tenets of his impending opening speech. However, a recent reissue of a proclamation to banish Catholic clergy from Ireland was considered by some as an attempt on the King's part "to insinuate himself into the affections of his subjects . . . and improve his position with the parliament." [10] To the Spanish ambassadors, who protested against the edict, James denied all responsibility for its publication and promised to suspend its enforcement. He probably expected some reciprocal concessions from the Spanish.

On the morning of the thirteenth, when Inojosa and Coloma came to thank the King for his clemency, they had no new concrete proposals to offer on the question of the Palatinate. Consequently they contented themselves with further invectives against Buckingham and were immensely gratified at the hearing their criticisms received. Although hampered by diplomatic decorum, they tried to break the alliance between Charles and Buckingham by begging the Prince to say if he had any complaint against Philip IV so that they might remedy it and by placing the blame for the failure of the marriage entirely on the favorite. This attempt to sow dissension failed; Charles appeared somewhat mollified, but the ambassadors feared that he was merely disguising his animosity.

Inojosa and Coloma were well aware that, in the absence of countervailing proposals from Spain, James would be left powerless before the combined influence of the Prince and the Duke who were intent on having their policy ratified by Parliament. Knowing the King's distrust of Parliament, the ambassadors intensified his fears by warning him that the secret oaths which he had taken in favor of the Catholics in July 1623 were being printed in order to make him odious to his subjects.[11] Ever sensitive to "Puri-

---

good beginning." (*Cal. S. P. Venetian*, XVIII, 233, Valaresso to the Doge and Senate.) According to my count, 481 M.P.'s representing 51 countries (90 members) 201 boroughs (387 members); and 2 universities (4 members) were eligible to sit in Parliament in 1624. This does not include 8 burgesses from the reconstituted boroughs of Hertford, Amersham, Marlow, and Wendover.

10. *Cal. S. P. Venetian*, XVIII, 217, Valaresso to the Doge and Senate, Feb. 6/16, 1624. The text of the proclamation dated January 21, 1624, is printed in *ibid.*, 218–219.

11. PRO 31/12/31, Spanish Transcripts, letter of Inojosa to Philip IV, Feb. 13/23, 1624. The Venetian ambassador reported this audience. (*Cal. S. P. Venetian*, XVIII, 227, Valaresso to the Doge and Senate, Feb. 20/March 1, 1624.)

tan sedition," James took alarm and in the ensuing days renewed efforts were made by the government to suppress the political libels pouring from the London presses. The Lord Keeper recommended the issuance of a proclamation to prohibit the publication or sale of any book not approved by an authorized person, a course which he asserted "would be neither offensive nor inconvenient." [12] Ultimately this expedient was adopted in the proclamation against seditious popish and Puritanical books and pamphlets, which was authorized at Nottingham on August 15, but, for the time being, it remained the responsibility of the Privy Council to punish those who had offended in print.

By February 16, the day to which Parliament had been prorogued, James had probably decided which proposals he would offer in his initial address, but the untimely death of the Lord Steward forced another postponement of the opening ceremonies. Finally, on Monday the nineteenth, the Lords and Commons assembled in the upper House to hear a royal oration, the tenor of which was influenced by the King's prejudices, and by the advice of Buckingham, the Council, and the Spanish ambassadors.

The necessity of having a good understanding with his people, which had been urged on the King by those who favored the assembling of Parliament, was diffused through the entirety of James's speech. "Never soldiers," he said, "marching the deserts and dry sands of Arabia where there is no water, could more thirst in hot weather for drink, than I do now for a happy end of this our meeting. And now I hope that after the miscarriage of three parliaments this will prove happy." In order to amend the misunderstandings prevalent among his subjects, the King explained his attitude toward the responsibilities of a monarch. In two ways could the King show his love to his realm: "the one, his constant government; the other, his behavior towards the representative body of his kingdom." Although he admitted that there were abuses, he reminded his subjects that "you enjoy the fruits of my government, living in peace, when all the neighbor countries are in war."

At that moment, however, the King's good governance was not the central issue, and James well knew it. Relations with Parlia-

---

12. *Cal. S. P. Dom. 1623–1625*, 163–164, CLIX, nos. 39, Secretary Conway to Lord Keeper Williams; 40, Lord Keeper to Secretary Conway, Feb. 15, 1624.

ment were critical and here the King apparently reappraised his policy. "The proper use of a parliament," he said, "is, according to the writ, *Nobiscum super arduis negotys tractare et concilium vestrum impendere:* to confer with the King, as governor of the kingdom, and to give their advice in matters of greatest importance concerning the state and defense of the King, with the church and kingdom." Seemingly James had adopted Coke's definition of parliamentary function, and, in his synopsis of the proceedings concerning the two treaties with Spain and the Prince's journey to Madrid, he had opened the door for parliamentary determination of foreign policy. By allowing his secretaries to exhibit diplomatic correspondence and by commanding Charles and Buckingham to relate their experiences, James appeared to have surrendered his absolute prerogative in matters pertaining to foreign relations. So much the Duke had hoped for and the Commons desired, yet a cautious listener would have been aware that James expected advice rather than commands.

However much he urged haste in their deliberations, he made it quite clear that the business of the Parliament was consultation, not determination. He cautioned them to avoid "law quirks, tricks and jerks" and to "use your lawful privileges and freedom." "Do what you ought," he said, "and no more, and I had rather enlarge your privileges than alter or take them away. Shew your trust now reposed in me and assure yourselves I will not be curious except you give me just occasion." To allay the Commons' suspicions of his pro-Catholic sympathies James was careful to point out that he had "never made at any time any public or private treaty in that kind without a direct reservation of *salus reipublica* and the cause of religion. Only I thought it fit some time to wink and connive and not go on so rigorously as at other times."

Coupled with the King's disavowal of religious toleration was an appeal to the affections of his Protestant subjects. He promised not to limit the session "to hours and days; your hearts must limit you. If you be earnest, yourselves will think it long till it be effected, but this remember that delays bring destruction and this business requires expedition. Consider with yourselves the state of Christendom, my children and this my own kingdom. Consider of these, and upon all give me your advice." Again, at the close of his speech, James reiterated his good intentions, invoked the bless-

ing of God on the proceedings of the Parliament, and requested
"you that are the representative body of this kingdom [to be] my
true glasses to shew me the hearts of my people." [13]

Doubtless the majority of the Commons would not have agreed
with the Lord Keeper's comparison between "his Majesty's grave
sentences" and Aeschines' orations, but it was generally admitted
that the King had made a plausible, gracious and comfortable
speech which "eased the hearts of many good and loyal subjects."
James's maladroit admission of having been deluded in the negotiations with Spain was interpreted by parliament men as a confession of the futility of past treaties and an absolute referral of
the course of future action to their consideration.[14] When, in re-

13. Harl. MS. 159, fols. 10–12v. I have used the text of the King's speech from
D'Ewes collection of separates because I think it has greater vitality. It does not
differ materially in either sense or verbiage from any other printed or manuscript
text of the address that I have seen. For James's protestation on the subject of the
articles of the Spanish match which he made in July 1623, see M. A. Tierney, ed.,
*Dodd's Church History of England* (5 vols., London, 1839–1843), V, Appendix, cccxxi–
cccxxii, text printed from William Prynne, *Hidden Works of Darkness Brought to
Public Light* (London, 1645), 47; see also *Hardwicke State Papers*, I, 429–431, Sir
Edward Conway to the Duke of Buckingham, July 23, 1623

14. Harl. MS. 159, fol. 12v, Lord Keeper's speech, Feb. 19, 1624. For reactions to
the King's speech, see *ibid.*, fols. 10, 12v; Chamberlain, *Letters*, II, 546, letter of
Feb. 21, 1624; *Cal. S. P. Venetian*, XVIII, 226–229, Valaresso to the Doge and Senate,
Feb. 20/Mar. 1, 1624, and 231–234, Feb. 27/Mar. 8, 1624. The comparison between
Valaresso's reactions in his reports of February 20 and February 27 is very instruc-
tive. On the twentieth, when he enclosed the substance of the King's speech with his
dispatch, he termed the leading ideas of the oration as "fine and good" and the
speech as a whole "one of substance rather than show." But by the twenty-seventh
he credited James with having "said more than he meant as he spoke as if he were
carried away . . . The speech shines the more by contrast with the one delivered
to the last parliament, as then they called felony what is now submitted to the
free discussion of the present assembly." Valaresso's opinion has been echoed and
amplified by modern historians who insist that the submission of a question on
foreign policy to the judgment of the Parliament implied the abdication by the
King of his prerogative rights. If Sir Francis Bacon's account of Henry VII's speech
to his Parliament in 1490 may be credited, however, there was good precedent for
James's actions. In calling for a war against Charles VIII of France, Henry told
the members of Parliament: "In this great Business, let me have your advice, and
Aid. If any of you were to make his Son Knight, you might have aid of your
Tenants by Law. This concerns the Knighthood and Spurs of the Kingdom, whereof
I am Father; and bound not only to seek to maintain it, but to advance it. But for
Matter of Treasure, let it not be taken from the Poorest Sort; but from those, to
whom the Benefit of the War may redound. France is no Wilderness: and I, that
profess Good Husbandry, hope to make the War (after the beginnings) to pay for
itself. Go together God's Name in and lose no time; for I have called this Parliament
wholly for this Cause." White Kennet, *Complete History of England*, I, 602. Bacon
himself had in 1620 drafted a proclamation for the forthcoming Parliament, which
would have explained the foreign policy considerations that caused the writ of
summons to be issued. In a significant paragraph he wrote: "For although the

sponse to the Lord Keeper's injunction, the Commons returned to
their House to elect a speaker, the conviction that the King had
renounced his sovereignty over diplomacy was reinforced by a
privy councillor's nomination of Sir Thomas Crew for the speaker-
ship. Crew was known to his contemporaries to be "relligious and
of an humble spiritt," but also, to be "a very waspe, if he be
angred." Time and again he had irritated the King by his remarks
on impositions, parliamentary privileges and the Spanish match
and, for his temerity, had been haled before the Privy Council
after the Addled Parliament and sent on a commission to Ireland
after the ill-fated winter session of 1621. The government's recommendation of Crew to be presiding officer in the lower House
substantiated James's professed desire for a good understanding
with the Commons.[15]

making of war or peace be a secret of empire, and a thing properly belonging to
our high prerogative royal, and imperial power: yet nevertheless, in causes of
that nature which we shall think fit not to reserve but to communicate, we shall
ever think ourselves much assisted and strengthened by the faithful advice and
general assent of our loving subjects." (Bacon, *Works*, XIV, 124–128.) James's
attitude toward Bacon's plan is revealed in Buckingham's letter of October 19, 1620.
"I have shewed your letter and the proclamation to his Majesty, who expecting
only, according as his meaning was, directions therein for the well ordering of the
elections of the burgesses, findeth a great deal more, containing matter of state
and the reasons of calling the parliament: whereof neither the people are capable,
nor is it fit for his Majesty to open now unto them, but to reserve to the time
of their assembling, according to the course of his predecessors, which his Majesty
intendeth to follow: the declaring whereof in the proclamation would cut off the
ground of his Majesty's and your Lordship's speech, at the proper time." (*Ibid.*,
XIV, 128.) It is significant that James did not object to the discussion of foreign
policy in a Parliament summoned for that purpose — a Parliament constituted of
the wisest and best-informed elements of society. He did, however, object to the
publication of matters of state for the vulgar multitude. That he was consistent in
maintaining this point of view is indicated by his later proclamations of December
24, 1620, and July 26, 1621.
    15. S. R. Gardiner, ed., *The Fortescue Papers* . . . Camden Society, N.S., Volume
I (London, 1871), 209–210, Lord Keeper Williams to John Packer, Feb. (?), 1625.
In 1618 James had categorically rejected Thomas Crew as a recommended candidate
for the recordership of London. He told the aldermen to "spare him [Crew] and
take any other in the Kingdom." (Whitelocke, *Liber Famelicus*, 67.) It was not
until after the return of the Prince from Spain that Crew received any court
preferment. Chamberlain (*Letters*, II, 506), mentioned that on July 12, 1623, Crew
would not accept the favor of being made serjeant-at-law, but on October 25, 1623,
he listed Crew among those who were inducted into the order on the twenty-third.
(*Ibid.*, II, 518.) *DNB* is obviously in error in assigning the date of September 1624
for Crew's serjeancy. Hacket (*Scrinia Reserata*, I, 110–113) attributed the creation
of serjeants to the intercession of the Lord Keeper and also printed the speech
of the Lord Keeper on that occasion, assigning to it the erroneous date of May 6,
1623. Crew was nominated as Speaker by Sir Thomas Edmondes, who was Treasurer
of the King's Household. (SP 14/159/60.) Hacket (*Scrinia Reserata*, I, 176) gives

Elected to the chair by a "general acclamation in the House (*nemine contradicente*)," Sir Thomas Crew soon gave evidence that he merited the confidence accorded him by both court and country.[16] When he was presented to the King on February 21, his oration impressed the clerk of the Parliament, Henry Elsynge, as the best delivered since the reign of Henry VIII. "It consists not in verbal praises, but is real, fit for the times, and well beseeming the dignity of a Parliament." [17]

Moderation was, indeed, the keynote of Crew's speech: he was judicious in his formal commendation of the King's peaceful accession, his preservation from the Gunpowder Plot, and his care of "true religion." He preserved a discreet silence on the subject of the Spanish match and tactfully left it to God in his due time to "restore the distressed Princess, her husband, and royal issue to that inheritance which is now possessed by the usurping sword of their enemies." His most caustic criticisms were directed against the Catholics, whom he regarded as the disturbers of the peace and concord so ardently desired by all loyal subjects. Again his appeal was subtle; nothing specific was said about the doctrinal differences dividing Christendom but opprobrium was heaped on the political tenets of Catholicism.

To make England, like Jerusalem, "a city of unity within itself," Crew proposed, in the name of the Commons, that the "good laws for establishing of religion may be confirmed, and that the generation of locusts, the Jesuits and seminary priests, which were wont to creep in corners and now come abroad, may by the execution

---

this character study of Crew: "He was warm in the Care of Religion, and a Chief among them that were popular in the Defence of it; A great lover of the Laws of the Land, and the Liberties of the People; Of a stay'd Temper, sound in Judgment, ready in Language; And though every Man, it is suppos'd, hath some equals in his good Parts, he had few or no Superiors. This was the Character which the Lord Keeper gave of him to the King, whereupon he was pointed out to this Honorable Task." Edward Nicholas thought that Sir Thomas Crew was the ablest Speaker known for years. (SP 14/165/61, [Edward Nicholas to John Nicholas], May 29, 1624.) Sir John Eliot agreed with this estimate terming Crew "a great master of the Lawe, & in his studies, religion had a share to a great name & reputation. his life & practice answear'd it. & his elocution was most apt for the imploiment he sustain'd." (Eliot, *Negotium Posterorum*, I, 47.) Early in 1625 Lord Keeper Williams stated, "Sir Thomas Crewe hath been a very good servaunt to the Kinge in this last Session, and very ready (upon all occasions) to serve my Lord Duke." Gardiner, ed., *Fortescue Papers*, 209–210.

16. Braye MS. 73, fol. 3–3v.

17. Henry Elsynge, *The Manner of Holding Parliaments in England* (London, 1768), 174.

of those good laws, as with an east wind, be blown into the seas."
For the perfecting of harmony between James and his people,
Crew advocated that "the bills against monopolies, informers, and
concealers may now be passed and receive strength with a general,
liberal and royal pardon . . . with release of old debts and such
other things, which will be good to your subjects and no diminution of revenue or derogation to your prerogative."

Other advice tendered by the Speaker to the King was trenchant
and pertinent. James was reminded that "parliaments are the best
way of supply of your Majesty's wants. That which proceeds from
them is your subjects' loves and loyalty; other courses of benevolence come from them heavily and unwillingly." No direct challenge was offered to the monarch's right to prerogative taxation,
but the implication was clear that concord between King and
people could be maintained only if the ancient parliamentary
forms were observed. The "fundamental common laws" were likewise not forgotten by Crew, who stated that they, like truth, were
the daughter of time. Again the meaning was clear: the approved
customs of the nation provided the surest support and operational
framework for royal government.

The question of parliamentary privilege, so inflammatory in
1621 and already probed by the King as a possible source of contention in this present Parliament, could not be avoided by the
Speaker, but, again, his tact was equal to the task of serving two
masters. In his formal petition he requested, as an "humble
suitor," confirmation of the Commons' "ancient privileges . . .
with your gracious favor according to ancient precedents." [18]
Enough emphasis was thus placed on royal grace to please James,
yet, by implication, a prescriptive right was asserted to liberty of
speech and freedom from arrest.

The aspirations of the moderates for a Parliament *"foelix, doc-
tum et pium"* were much encouraged by the equanimity displayed
in the initial addresses by the King and the Speaker, but there
could be no certainty that the good auspices would prove propitious. Immediately after prayers were concluded on the first day
of business, it became apparent that the Puritan element in the
Commons was determined to make itself heard. Mr. Snelling, a
burgess for Ipswich, moved the consideration of a bill against the

18. Harl. MS. 159, fols. 13–15v, Speaker's speech, Feb. 21, 1624.

profanation of the Sabbath which, although it had been preferred regularly since 27 Elizabeth, had never become law and was viewed by James as contradictory to his declaration regarding allowable Sunday sports. The reading of this act was followed by Sir James Perrot's motion that all members be enjoined to receive communion as a requirement for admission to the House according to the precedent established in the last two Parliaments. Assented to with *"una voce,"* the enforcement of this order and the certification of members was entrusted to a committee of five including Perrot and his fellow Puritans, Sir Francis Barrington and Sir Edward Giles.

Speaking in favor of Perrot's proposal, Sir Edward Cecil proceeded to even greater extremes. He wanted the House to imitate the example of the Low Countries and to proclaim a solemn day of fasting and humiliation as necessary preparation for the consideration of the great business before the Parliament. He also moved that the King be petitioned to have the fast made universal, and, being seconded by such worthies as Sir William Strode, Sir William Bulstrode, Sir George More, and Sir Edward Wardour, the motion was approved by the House. Secretary Calvert and Sir Richard Weston (privy councillors with pronounced Catholic sympathies) were ordered to accompany Cecil when he presented the petition to the King.[19]

At the outset, then, the Puritans had seized the initiative and, capitalizing on the religious fervor of the majority, had engaged the Commons to advocate measures distasteful to the King. Thus, the temper of the House was not conducive to calm deliberation

19. Spring, 5–7; *CJ*, 671, 715–716. The *Commons Journal* mentions "Mr. Secretary" as one of the committee to petition the King. Pym (fols. 4–4v) gives Mr. Secretary Conway. Braye MS. 73 (fols. 4v, 5) gives the text of the order of the House together with the names of the committee; Wright and Holles (fol. 81) both list Mr. Secretary Calvert. Sir William Strode moved "that some of the worthy persons about the Speaker's chair may be sent to petition this of the King: Saying farther that some did think that some persons disaffected to our religion were among us, but he could not think so, because they would be discovered now by blushing to hear of such a motion." (Spring, 6–7.) The importance attached to religion is illustrated by Sir Edward Cecil's letter to Sir Dudley Carleton on February 21, 1624: "And although his Majesty doth give us leave to advise him concerning the business of Spain and the marriage, yet we will first begin with the setting religion into his joints that hath been put out of joint by this Spanish treaty. And in that design we will give his Majesty our best advice for that is that which must set all business right for that the Spaniard did us all the harm by advancing his religion so far as he did which gave his spite here so much credit as hath cast us so far behind." (SP 84/116, fols. 147–148 [Holland].)

on issues involving war and peace; for the moment religious en-
thusiasms reigned supreme. However, the victory of the Puritans
was more apparent than real. A temporizing answer from the King
that he would advise with his bishops enervated the proposal for
a national fast. The bill for the Sabbath had likewise to receive
the King's approval, and the sacramental test imposed on the
members of Parliament was, considering the oaths of supremacy
and allegiance, merely symbolic of conformity.

When the House turned from religion to organization, the
hysteria subsided somewhat. However, the reading of a Puritan
measure, which made profane swearing punishable by fine or
pillory and whipping, was intruded into the consideration of the
agenda and the nomination of standing committees. Nevertheless
the ascendancy of "old parliament men" and lawyers over the
Commons was confirmed. The select committee for returns and
privileges, whose presiding officer was John Glanville, was dominated by a majority of experienced parliamentarians, contained
no privy councillors, and was subsequently reinforced by the recruitment of Selden and Noy.[20] The powerful grand Committees
for Grievances, Trade, and Courts of Justice were chaired by Sir
Edward Coke, Sir Edwin Sandys, and Sir Robert Phelips, respectively. These chairmen, who were neither courtiers nor precisians,
guided the House as no demagogue could, and, in the course of
the session, were to be as effective as the privy councillors in removing obstructions to a rapprochement between King and Commons.

The expedition with which the Commons acted on legislation
they fervently supported was replaced by extreme caution when
parliamentary privileges or financial commitments were involved.
A mere request from the Lords for a conference to hear Buckingham's relation stirred extensive debate among the members. Edward Alford, whose meticulous attention to procedural minutiae
had already been evidenced in former Parliaments, aroused fears
by suggesting that a joint conference with the Lords might lead
the Commons into an ill-considered and unwanted financial ob-

20. The Committee of the Whole for Grievances was moved by John Delbridge,
that for Trade by Sir Edward Coke and that for Courts of Justice by Sir Robert
Phelips. The select Committee for Elections and Privileges was proposed by Sir
John Strangways. (*CJ*, 671–672, 716–717.) Three variant lists of members of the
Committee of Privileges are to be found in *CJ*, 671, 716, and Braye MS. 73, fols. 5v–6.

ligation. This difficulty was overcome through the wisdom and tact of Sir Edward Coke and Sir Humphrey May. Coke suggested that a "meeting" be substituted for a "conference" and that no member should "move questions or offer to confer," and May asserted that a committee of the whole would technically avoid the danger of official action.[21]

No amount of formal courtesy and thanks for the "good correspondency" exhibited by the Lords could, however, obscure the fact that the lower House was jealous of its privileges and of its prerogative of taxation. It had learned from bitter experience that subsidies granted prematurely resulted in quick dissolutions, and, however predisposed it might be to favor the policy for which money was requested, it was reluctant to make grants without redress of grievances and the enactment of remedial legislation. This accounts for the haste with which the most popular bills were passed; the acts against the profanation of the Sabbath and for punishment of swearing and cursing were engrossed without commitment on the second day of the session in order to facilitate their passage in the Lords. It was not held fit to clog or alter the Sabbath bill and the Speaker, himself, asserted that it would be a pity if the act against swearing "should now receive any dash or delay by a new committee." [22]

Coupled with the engrossment of these measures was the first reading of an act for repressing popish recusants, which was designed to restrain foreign travel and support of continental seminaries and to increase the stringency of economic penalties imposed upon English Catholics. Thus, by the time they assembled to hear Buckingham's narrative, the Commons had imperiously proclaimed their hatred of Catholicism and their belief that England's security was dependent upon the maintenance of the "true religion."

What the members assembled at Whitehall on February 24 heard from the Duke of Buckingham was an exercise in apologetics rather than a systematic review of past negotiations with Spain. Documents were produced, but they were carefully selected to justify the points made in the relation. Those treaties and dis-

21. Spring, 11; Braye MS. 73, fol. 7v.
22. Spring, 17–18.

King James I

Charles, Prince of Wales

George Villiers, Duke of Buckingham

Sir Robert Phelips (1586[?]–1638)

patches that would prove embarrassing to the Prince and the Duke because of the concessions contained in them were not available for inspection. Nothing was specified concerning the secret oaths for the remission and ultimate repeal of penal laws against Catholics; nothing was precisely indicated regarding Catholic nurses or the education of future heirs to the throne; nothing was hinted about Charles's demand for a carte blanche while he was negotiating at Madrid. The entire purpose of the narrative, ostensibly to bring the English "from darkness to light," was to give added luster to the shrewd and candid proceedings of the Prince and the Duke and to contrast them with the effrontery, mendacity, and duplicity of the Spanish and the naïveté of the Earl of Bristol.

The scope of Buckingham's oration extended from Weston's return from Brussels in September 1622 to the receipt of Philip IV's last answer on the restitution of the Palatinate in January 1624. Within these limits, the Duke attempted to prove the necessity of the journey to Spain and the good results accomplished, to fix responsibility for the failure to conclude the treaties for the match and the Palatinate, and to exculpate the Prince of Wales and himself from all blame.

Weston's failure to negotiate a suspension of arms in the Palatinate was attributed, not to Protestant intransigence, but to the secret machinations of the Spanish. Buckingham thus predisposed his audience to accept uncritically the identity of the Archduchess Isabella's diplomacy with that of her nephew, Philip IV, and to discount her responsibilities as plenipotentiary for the Emperor Ferdinand. The contrast, then, between Weston's pessimistic reports from Brussels and Bristol's roseate assurances that the Spanish really desired an accommodation in the Empire seemed to necessitate some decisive diplomatic response from the English. For this reason Endymion Porter was sent to Madrid with a specific demand for armed assistance for the recovery of the Palatinate.

When Porter returned with "a Dispatch fraught with Generalities, without any one Perticular or Certeintie at all," Charles "thereupon took his Resolution to go in Person to Spayne, and gave himselfe these reasons for that Enterprize; he saw his Fathers Negotiation playnelie deluded; matters of Religion gayned

uppon and extorted; his Sisters Cause more and more desperated."
Thus, if one was prepared to believe Buckingham, the restitution
of the Palatinate was always the primary consideration, and the
match was subordinated to it.

Although the Duke admitted that during the early part of the
marriage negotiations at the Spanish court Charles had refused to
consider a simultaneous treaty of alliance, he always "intended
[it] to go hand in hand with the Treatie of the Mariage." Well
aware that the Prince had made the restoration of the Palatinate
the condition for the delivery of his proxy, Buckingham attempted
to establish Spanish responsibility for the inextricable association
of the two treaties. Letters of Olivares and Philip IV were produced to establish this point. It was alleged that Olivares had
offered Charles "a blanke Paper to set down his own Conditions
for the Restitution of the Palatinate," in order to prevent him
from returning to England before the consummation of the marriage. The Spanish junta of divines, at Olivares's prompting, had
likewise recommended a delay in the Infanta's departure until all
things were accommodated. Yet promises of armed assistance for
the recovery of the Palatinate, first made to Bristol in October
1622 and since renewed to Charles by the offer of a "blank," were
subsequently disavowed by Olivares who maintained as "a Maxim
of Estate, That the King of Spayne must never fight against the
Emperor." It was upon this provocation that Charles protested to
Olivares: "Look to it, Sir, for if you hold your selfe to that, there
is an end of all, for without this you may not rely uppon either
Marriage or Friendship, for I must (as I am required) retourne
to my Father, and acquaint him with your Resolution in this
point; Look for neither Marriage nor Friendship without Restitution of the Palatinat." Thus, the Spanish, by their failure to
honor their promises, were responsible for the Prince's refusal to
allow his espousal to the Infanta.

Buckingham deftly avoided divulging the embarrassing pro-
visos in the Spanish marriage treaty by relegating it to a secondary
role, by treating it only in the most general terms, and by emphasizing the clash of personalities and ideologies involved in the
negotiations. He salved English honor by "proving" that the
match was first proposed by Spain. He likewise established that it
was considered at Madrid as a diplomatic subterfuge with which

to entertain James and prevent English intervention on the Continent.

Every Spanish maneuver during the negotiations was castigated as a trick and a delusion which continued to beguile Bristol even after Buckingham had penetrated their artifices. It was Bristol who placed the most benign construction on Spanish proceedings, who was chiefly responsible for religious concessions, who urged Charles to remain at Madrid, who palliated the clogged dispensations, who asserted that "oaths" were mere punctilios, who altered the temporal article for the payment of the portion, who insisted that the restitution of the Palatinate should be mediated after the marriage, who prefixed a day for the espousals, and who cast an unnecessary aspersion on the honor of Philip IV and the Infanta by allowing them to proceed with arrangements for the marriage. The Spanish, however, had ambitions as world conquerors, wished to foment rebellion in England by insisting on toleration for the Catholics, assisted the downfall of Heidelberg, and connived at the transfer of the electorate. They repeatedly solicited the conversion of Charles, dictated his conversations with the Infanta, made exorbitant demands exceeding those which contented Philip II, and so dishonored Charles by their neglect that Buckingham found it necessary to beg the Condessa Olivares "to procure her Lord to vouchsafe now and then to look upon his Highnes."

Conversely, Charles, seconded by Buckingham, acted with the utmost probity, sagacity and heroism. No rock of ages was a more secure bulwark to the English faith than the Prince. Unconcerned over his own fate, he had urged his father to forget him if he were detained and "to reflect with all his Royall Thoughts uppon the Good of his Sister, and the Safetie of his own Kingdomes." He had offered to bind himself with conditions exceeding those used in the marriage treaty between King Philip and Queen Mary, and he had volunteered an English fleet to expedite the Infanta's journey. It was true that he had taken an oath not to revoke his proxy, but it was equally true "that when he first heard that Clause read he stumbled at it." It was, therefore, capable of being ignored as "a matter of meer Forme; and altho' essentially of no bynding Power, yet usually thrust into every such Instrument."

A Prince so ingenuous, dignified, and amiable could scarcely have been expected to discover the insincerity of the Spanish at the outset of negotiations; Buckingham reserved this role for himself. Within four days after his arrival in Madrid, he had come to the conclusion "that theis People never intended either Match or Restitution, and soe wished his Highnes fairlie at Home again." It was the Duke who protested against the indignities offered to the Prince's royal person. It was Buckingham who forced the Spanish to deliver the dispensation they were concealing. It was he who opposed Bristol over the private articles sworn to by the Prince and who revealed Olivares's overwhelming influence in the junta of divines and the council of state. It was also Buckingham who asserted that no toleration could be "thrust upon the Estate in England but by Consent of Parliament," and who exposed Gondomar's duplicity and earned his undying enmity. It was the Duke who undertook everything that could be done to speed the Prince's return.

Now it remained for him to warn Parliament of warlike preparations in Spain and to solicit, in his master's name, the advice of the members. Reminding his audience that alliance with Spain implied the education of the Palsgrave's son in the Emperor's Catholic court with no guarantee of Spanish armed assistance to recover the Palatinate, he put the question whether it was sufficient *"super totam materiam,* for his Majestie to relie upon with anie Safetie, as well for the Marriage of his onelie Sonne, as for the releife of his onlie Daughter? Or that, theise Treaties set aside, his Majestie were best to trust to his own Strength, and to stand upon his own Feet?" [23]

23. Rymer, *Foedera*, XVII, 106–123; see also D. M. Loades, ed., *The Papers of George Wyatt, Esq.*, Camden Society, 4th Ser., Volume V (London, 1968), 207–222. On Buckingham's early discovery of Spanish duplicity, compare Rymer, *Foedera*, XVII, 109, with Halliwell, *King's Letters*, II, 174–176, Prince Charles and the Duke of Buckingham to King James, Mar. 10, 1623, "To conclude, we find the Condé Olivares so overvaluing of our journey, that he is so full of real courtesy, that we can do no less than beseech your majesty to write the kindest letter of thanks and acknowledgment you can unto him: he said, no later to us than this morning, that, if the pope would not give a dispensation for a wife, they would give the infanta to thy son's baby, as a wench; and hath this day written to the cardinal Ludovico, the pope's nephew, that the king of England hath put such an obligation upon this king, in sending his son hither, that he intreats him to make haste of the dispensation, for he can deny him nothing that is in his kingdom. We must hold you thus much longer to tell you, the pope's nuncio works as maliciously and as actively as he can against us, but receives such rude answers, that we hope he will soon be weary on't: we make this collection of it, that the pope will be very loath to grant a dispensation, which, if he will not do, then we would gladly have your directions how far we may engage you in the acknowledgment of the pope's special power;

Although the utmost publicity had been accorded to the Duke of Buckingham's relation, no cognizance of it could be taken by either House of Parliament until the official reports had been made by the Lord Keeper in the upper chamber and by Weston and Cottington in the Commons. This did not occur until the twenty-seventh, but there could be little doubt regarding the response to the favorite's emotional tirade. "The indignation that his speech produced was such that nothing was heard for a long time but outcries, confusion and cries of war." Such, at least, was the impression received by the Spanish ambassadors who felt it incumbent upon themselves to protest to James against Buckingham's "false and cunning proceedings." An audience at Hampton Court on February 26, which they solicited for this purpose, proved to be a tactical error from the Spanish point of view. The edge of their invective against the favorite was blunted by the Prince's involvement in the delivery of the narrative; it was one thing to accuse Buckingham of misrepresentation, quite another to give the lie to the heir apparent to the crown.

The presence of both the Prince and the Duke at the audience disconcerted the ambassadors. Their resentment of insults to Philip IV was real enough, but their accusations were generalized and they were obliged to except Charles from responsibility. The ambassadors' charge that Buckingham's statements merited imprisonment and execution was more likely to increase the favorite's popularity with the House of Commons than to result in his incarceration. Even their specific indictment that Buckingham had misrepresented naval preparations in Spain could be turned to his credit. "He had heard it said," Buckingham asserted, "that when a powerful King armed himself it was a minister's duty to induce his King to do the same." He claimed, moreover, that he had spread the report to get money from Parliament.

Although appearing to regret that the Spanish ambassadors had just cause to complain, James was not interested in either acquitting or condemning his favorite. He was willing to comply with the ambassadors' request that all diplomatic correspondence relating to the two treaties should be laid before Parliament in order to correct misapprehensions caused by the Duke's relation, but he

---

for we almost find, if you will be contented to acknowledge the pope chief head under Christ, that the match will be made without him."

made it clear that his main objective was still the receipt of the King of Spain's unequivocal promise of the restoration of the Palatinate.[24]

James's proclivities for a negotiated settlement of the Palatinate question were as well known to the members of the Commons as to the representatives of the Spanish crown. Consequently, their credulous reception of Buckingham's assertions was attended by some doubts about the future consequences. The Duke's revelations had opened the floodgates of anti-Spanish and anti-Catholic popular prejudices, but there was no guarantee that the expression of those prejudices in Parliament would not be regarded as an infringement of the royal prerogative.

To some parliamentarians the whole issue turned on the definition of privilege; others were content to confine their remarks within the limits of accepted parliamentary procedure until such time as prerogative matters were presented for discussion. Thus, prior to the report of Buckingham's relation, no direct references were made to Spanish perfidy, but severe measures against the Catholics were expedited. On February 25, the act for the better repressing of popish recusants was given a second reading and passed to engrossing — despite the objections of Sandys and Pym who maintained that the bill was defective and, in some provisions, evidently contrary to a similar bill which had been submitted for consideration. To a majority of the House, commitment implied delay, and they were in no mood to be diverted from their defense of the Protestant religion.[25] Proceeding to ever more drastic measures, the House next adopted Sir William Strode's motion recommending the dismissal of recusant servants of members of Parliament upon pain of sequestration from the House for failure to comply. Notice of this order was to be intimated to the Lords, and a committee of fifteen was appointed to

24. PRO 31/12/29, Spanish Transcripts, Inojosa to King Philip IV, Feb. 26/Mar. 7, 1624; see also PRO 31/12/31 of the same date.

25. In Spring, 23, Pym and Sandys are named as recommending the commitment of the bill. Pym (fol. 7) discusses the exceptions to the bill, but he does not attribute them to any particular person. The date, February 26, assigned in Pym is incorrect. See *CJ*, 673, 718. The Braye MS. 73, fol. 10, lists a committee of six (Sir Edward Coke, Sir Nathaniel Rich, Sir Thomas Trevor, Sir Heneage Finch, Sir Robert Heath, and John Pym) appointed "to peruse this bill after it is engrossed and to compare it with the former copy which passed the house last meeting in parliament." See also Holland, I, fol. 1v.

draft it. They were also to consider further measures to be taken against recusants including the revival of the provisions requested in the petition concerning religion presented in 1621.[26]

The appointment of a committee did not, however, allay the anti-Catholic hysteria which now gripped the Commons. Mr. Dyott, burgess of Stafford, related a graphic tale of the insolences perpetrated by the titular bishop of Chalcedon who went abroad publicly in the northwestern counties baptizing and confirming English Catholics and ordaining priests. Christopher Brooke was convinced that ordination in England was designed to defeat the law and that crafty papists, who played "the Fox as well as the Lion" were intent on disturbing the peace of Parliament. His sentiments were echoed by Wentworth, the recorder of Oxford, who averred that all seminary priests were traitors and that the land was full of traitors and treason.

The suggestion that the papists were conspiring against the peace of Parliament increased the excitement of the members to fever pitch. On the following morning, February 26, Sir John Jephson voiced his fears for the safety of the House. It would be an easy matter for the papists to cut "all our throats if but some of them should attempt to set upon us in the House with weapons and armour and so seize the person of the Prince and murder what Lords and Commons they thought good." He moved that the Lord Mayor of London be solicited to provide a guard of two hundred men to assure the safety of Parliament. Military commanders, like Sir Edward Cecil and Sir Robert Mansell, supported the motion, as did that ardent Puritan, Richard Knightley, who wished to disarm the papists throughout the country. Mr. Drake confirmed the suspicions of the House by asserting that a kinsman of his, recently perverted by the Jesuits, had been ordered to provide himself with a headpiece, a coat of mail, and a case of pistols. It required the best efforts of privy councillors and courtiers to

26. *CJ* 673–674, Feb. 25, lists a committee of fifteen appointed to draft a message to the Lords concerning recusants. There is also a second version, *ibid.*, 718. The Braye MS. 73, fol. 10v, lists only thirteen members, omitting the names of Christopher Brooke and Richard Dyott. This committee seems not to have reported as ordered, and it was not until April 1 that Sir Robert Phelips revived the idea "that a select committee may be appointed to consider a proposition that hath slept; that a petition may be framed to his Majesty that a proclamation be for the removing the recusants from the city and care had of them in the country by the governors." (Spring, 165; Holland, I, fol. 74v.)

allay the fears of the Commons and cause the abandonment of the motion. Sir Humphrey May, chancellor of the duchy of Lancaster, and Sir Thomas Jermyn convinced the members that the presence of a guard implied cowardice and that, if protection were needed for Parliament, the order should originate with the Lords.

Shame prevented the Commons from requesting a guard, but they remained alert for any signs of popish conspiracy. As late as March 8, Sir John Packington directed their attention to the possibility of another gunpowder plot. He had kept vigil and had detected "diverse men and women going in and out, [and] a noise of people coming from under the Painted Chamber." His servant had seen a "gentleman-like" man with two spades concealed under his cloak. Twice Packington informed the Lord Keeper of his suspicions and a privy search of the building was instituted. Although no proof of a plot was discovered, Sir Robert Cotton and Mr. Borough insisted on having their premises searched in order to clear themselves of the imputation of guilt.[27]

Safeguarding the kingdom from the designs of the papists occupied the thoughts of most of the "godly" members of the House of Commons, but some few were aware of danger from another source. The memory of the privileges dispute in 1621 was still fresh; some who were now sitting had suffered for their forensic indiscretions after the last dissolution. The thought that the King might again call for the Journal of the House of Commons may have induced Mr. Mallory to move, on February 25, "that no man's name be entered into the clerk's book nor anything but orders." Sir James Perrot followed with a motion for the appointment of a committee to examine the clerk's book of entries every Saturday in the afternoon. This was ordered, and among the nine appointed were Pym, Alford, Seymour, Mallory, Rich, and Perrot — all staunch defenders of parliamentary privileges.[28]

27. *CJ*, 673–674, 718, Feb. 25, 1624; Spring, 30–31; Pym, fol. 7v; Holles, fol. 83v; *CJ*, 719; Holland, I, fol. 3v, Feb. 26; Earle, fol. 57.

28. Braye MS. 73, fol. 9v; *CJ*, 673, 718. Mallory's motion is noticed in neither version of the *Commons Journal* nor in Braye MS. 73. Pym (fol. 6v) omits mention of Perrot's motion, but says that Mallory's proposal was ordered. In Spring, 22, both motions are mentioned, but there is no indication whether either was adopted. Nicholas (fol. 20v) attributes both proposals to Mallory. Holland (I, fol. 1) lists only Perrot's motion together with the subsequent order and the names of the committee. Apparently Mallory's motion was not adopted because its implementation would have changed the character and content of the entries in the *Commons Journal*. On March 12 the Committee for the Survey of the Clerk's Book asked for

Up to this point the attitude of the Commons on the question of privilege was negative and defensive, but on the morning of February 27, Sir John Eliot demanded a positive declaration of parliamentary liberties. Old parliament men must have been startled by his brashness. Sir John had just obtained writs of privilege staying the prosecution of two suits against him at the Exeter assizes. As vice admiral of Devon, he was purportedly a partisan of Buckingham who had secured his release from prison the preceding December. Although he had served in the Addled Parliament, Eliot had not participated in any of the heated debates that characterized that ill-fated session. Moreover, his absence from the assemblage of 1621 scarcely qualified him to appear, in 1624, as the spokesman for parliamentary privilege. It is difficult to attribute Eliot's speech to any motive other than personal ambition. Neither Buckingham nor the Prince wanted their projects endangered by a wrangle between King and Commons, yet there is no doubt that Eliot had prepared for this moment in advance and assumed that his proposals would win the approval of a majority of the members.[29]

Eliot's main theme was the necessity for harmony between King and Parliament. He saw in the sessions of 1614 and 1621 a departure from the ancient practice that had made former Parliaments a sanctuary to subjects and a magazine to their princes.

---

instructions regarding their power to amend the entries in the *Journal*. The matter was left doubtful, and an inspection of both versions of the *Commons Journal* manuscripts has convinced me that the committee made no alterations or erasures in the text. (*CJ*, 683, 734.)

29. Forster, *Sir John Eliot* (2 vols., London, 1865), I, 135–143, prints large quotations from Eliot's speech, which is published in its entirety in Eliot, *Negotium Posterorum*, I, 130–139. Forster attributes the resistance offered to Eliot's proposals to private communication between Buckingham, Alford, and Phelips. Harold Hulme, in *The Life of Sir John Eliot 1592 to 1632: Struggle for Parliamentary Freedom* (New York: New York University Press, 1957), 49, n., unequivocally rejects Forster's contention on the grounds that no evidence exists of contacts between the favorite and parliamentary leaders. I have found no evidence connecting Alford with Buckingham, but there are definite indications of a link between Phelips and the Duke; see chap. ii, n. 36, and chap. vi, n. 37. There are many indications that Eliot's speech was prepared in advance for delivery at an appropriate time. Pym, who heard the speech, noted that it was delivered "with much earnestness and preparation." (Pym, fol. 8v.) The survival of a manuscript copy of the speech in Eliot's hand and among his papers is another indication of its premeditation. Few separates of speeches in 1624 are extant, other than those attributed to the King, the Prince, the Duke, or members of Parliament acting in an official capacity. Another copy of Eliot's speech is contained in Society of Antiquaries of London MS. 301, fols. 1–10v.

He refused to admit that prerogative and privilege inevitably clashed, and he insisted upon the constitutional legitimacy of both. "ffor the Kings prerogative noe man may dispute against it, it being an inseperable adiunct to regalitie . . . ffor the priviledges of Parliam^t they have beene such & soe esteemed, as neither [to] detract from the hono^r of the kinge nor lessen his authoritie, but conduce to the libertie of this place, that wee may heere freely treate and discourse for the publique good of the kingedome . . . by w^ch opinions are plainelie delivered, difficulties beaten out, & truth resolued vpon; whereas otherwise men, fearinge to displease will blanch those propositions that may haue question and silence theire vnderstandings in matters of most importe." [30]

Eliot could not comprehend how parliamentary privilege could be any diminution or derogation of regality for "the business is the Kings, the kingdome is the Kings, the resolucons rest whollie in y^e Kinge, and wee are only called hither by the Kinge, either vpon the generall affaires of the kingedome or the speciall propositions of his Ma^tie and therein but to deliberat and consult, not to conclude, w^ch onlie does facilitat his Ma^ts. resolutions, & ease him in the consideracon, leaving the end still to himself." [31]

With this definition of the province of parliamentary discussion, the King would have had no quarrel. Had representatives of the shires and boroughs been content merely "to deliberate and consult, not to conclude," James would, indeed, have been in love with parliaments. But Eliot would not have been content with idle and fruitless discussion, however free. The measures he called for to avoid future misunderstandings made it clear that the cure rested largely with the King: "if either his Ma^tie would reiect the Whispers of our enemies, or not beleeve them," there could be no doubt that prerogative and privilege could coexist harmoniously.[32] To prevent misinformation from reaching the King's ears, Eliot recommended the imposition of a general oath of truth and secrecy upon the members of the Commons, but, at the same time, he wanted a definitive statement of all the privileges and liberties incident to the Parliament presented in a petition and remonstrance for royal approval.

30. Eliot, *Negotium Posterorum,* I, 134.
31. *Ibid.,* 135.
32. *Ibid.,* 138.

The hidden barb in this oration of judicious commendation was the assumption by Eliot that the Commons would again insist that their privileges were matters of right, not of grace. His strategic sense may have convinced him that the time was ripe to strike for parliamentary liberties. The natural leaders of the prerogative faction — the King, the Prince, and the favorite — were divided over policy, and an isolated monarch could perhaps be pressured into making concessions fundamentally at variance with his theory of government.

The reaction that Eliot doubtless expected from old Parliament men failed to materialize for "diverse were afraid this motion would have put the House into some such heat as to disturb the great business." No one questioned the desirability of asserting the rights of the Commons, but only Sir Francis Seymour agreed that the time was seasonable. To remove all restraints upon parliamentary action, he moved the reentry into the *Journal* of the protestation made in 1621 with the further proviso that "if any of our members should offend, to take order they might be punished in the House and not [be] subject to any other punishment." He also requested testimony from those who had been penalized after the last Parliament as to the cause of their punishment.

Disagreement with Eliot and Seymour over the need for immediate action placed the other defenders of privilege in the embarrassing position of maintaining the status quo. It proved unnecessary for any privy councillor to leap to the defense of the royal prerogative and, indeed, no crown officer participated in the debate. Fearful that the privileges issue would cause the dissolution of Parliament before it fairly began, Edward Alford, Sir Robert Phelips, and Sir Edward Coke joined in urging the submission of the matter to a committee. Alford advocated the preparation of a bill declaratory of the privileges of the House, assent to which would be petitioned of the King at a later date, but Coke and Phelips, both of whom had been imprisoned in 1622, recommended even milder measures. According to Phelips, "this meeting was a miracle, which since the Prince had wrought we ought in gratitude to him (next under God) to cast off all distractions and jealousies and to rest upon his mediation, and for the present only to appoint a committee to consider what is needful to be done to express our duty to the King and secure the liberty of the subject." Coke agreed that matters past should be forgotten, but provision should be made "that nothing done might be prejudicial in the time to come." Even the Puritan parliamentarian, Sir James Perrot, concurred in this opinion and consequently the House contentedly buried the whole dispute in committee.[33]

Undoubtedly the House of Commons in 1624 hoped to establish a precedent for free speech on issues involving war and peace, but it can scarcely be maintained that at this point the precedent was a *fait accompli*. It was essential not only that foreign affairs be submitted to the Parliament for discussion but that the conclusions hammered out in the debates be accepted by the King as a policy directive. Had James unequivocally rejected the advice of the Lords and Commons, the committee appointed to conserve the privileges of the House would undoubtedly have reported forthwith. As it was, when James implied that he was not partisan in his attitude toward foreign affairs and was not personally involved in approval of Buckingham's relation, the Parliament was thrown into consternation and the archbishop of Canterbury was so chagrined that he took to his bed. Frequent reassurances by the King that he would not have asked the advice of the Parliament to "put a scorn upon it" were not sufficient to allay the suspicions of the members. What was demanded, and what James unsuccessfully resisted, was the establishment of a precedent for parliamentary participation in foreign policy acknowledged by public and formal royal declarations and enshrined in the statutes of the realm. The achievement of this goal required moderation and forbearance and, above all, time. Eliot would have avowed the principle of free speech and risked its exercise; the Commons preferred de facto rather than de jure liberties.[34]

33. Pym, fols. 8v–9; *CJ*, 720; Rich, fols. 18–20; Nicholas, fols. 28v–29v; Earle, fols. 31v–32; D'Ewes, fols. 64v–65. The committee were: Sir Edward Coke, Sir Robert Phelips, Sir Edwin Sandys, Sir Francis Barrington, Mr. Mallory, Mr. Alford, Sir Dudley Digges, Sir John Eliot, Sir Nathaniel Rich, Sir James Perrot, Sir John Savile, Sir Francis Seymour, Sir Henry Poole, Sir Humphrey May, and Sir Walter Earle.

34. The action of the Parliament in 1624 *in toto* constituted a precedent for parliamentary intervention in foreign affairs. But the King's invitation to advise on the treaties, taken by itself, was insufficient to establish the right by usage. Mere promises, as Sir Francis Seymour noted, did not constitute guarantees in the matter of privilege. "For so much he [the King] had said before yet had some been punished." (Holles, fol. 84.) Certainly 1624 did not see the end of imprisonments for antiprerogative speeches in the House of Commons, including some directly related to foreign policy.

As soon as the storm over privileges had been allayed, the members settled down to hear Weston's reprise of the Duke of Buckingham's relation. Implicit in the report was a sense of urgency; allusions were made to naval preparations in Spain and to the dispatch from Madrid of Padre Maestro [Fray Diego de Lafuente] with new propositions regarding the Palatinate. Yet when Weston had concluded, the Solicitor, Sir Robert Heath, moved the adjournment of the debate until the following Monday so that "we might better meditate upon it, and pray for God's assistance." [35]

This motion may provide a key to the parliamentary strategy that Buckingham and the Prince hoped to employ. Simultaneously with the Commons, the Lords had been hearing the Keeper's report of Buckingham's narrative, and, after some delay occasioned by a motion to clear the Duke from the charge of having aspersed the honor of the King of Spain, it was moved by Buckingham himself to proceed immediately to the debate of the "great business." From a tactical point of view initial discussion of the treaties in the House of Lords had two advantages: the presence of the Prince and Buckingham and the power of their faction would render the debates more susceptible to control, and a resolution by the Lords on an advice to the King would serve as a guiding principle to the House of Commons.

When discussion commenced in the afternoon, it became apparent that there was considerable divergence of opinion among the lords as to the nature of the central issue. The King had insisted upon the recovery of the Palatinate as the fundamental goal to be pursued, and, for a time, the debates proceeded upon the assumption that the treaty for the restitution of the Palatinate should be considered first. With the support of such peers as Hamilton, Pembroke, and the Lord Keeper, the Prince repeatedly emphasized the primacy of German affairs. This tended to divert attention from his journey to Madrid and to focus it upon Spanish perfidy during the earlier negotiations for a cessation of hostilities in the empire. Personal motives undoubtedly influenced Charles to adopt this course of action; a resolution to recover the Palatinate by war would automatically nullify the match treaty without any embarrassing inquiries into its terms.

To those who tended to see the question in religious, rather

35. Pym, fol. 9v.

than political or dynastic, terms, the recovery of the Palatinate by treaty was of secondary importance. The bishops of Durham, Bristol, and London conceived of the Elector's restoration as a religious crusade, and the latter prelate averred that he would "spende himselfe to the uttmost fartheing all his estate and . . . had he his feete as a harte he woulde be in the hedd of the troupe." But the archbishop of Canterbury, alarmed by the prospect of a Catholic toleration in England, wanted to debate the match first and to inquire into negotiations for it dating back to the days of Prince Henry.

Lay peers with Puritan tendencies, like Lord Brooke, were no less convinced that the safety of religion was the major issue. For them the recovery of the Palatinate was not a simple matter of bargaining between the powers concerned; instead, it depended upon the marriage alliance between England and Spain. Thus the two treaties were inextricable, and the restitution of the Palatinate was contingent upon the consummation of the match. The ineptitude of the Prince's parliamentary tactics was exposed when he finally conceded that the two treaties could not be considered separately. This concession tacitly implied the abandonment of the King's plan for the recovery of his son-in-law's ancestral domain because it focused attention exclusively on Spain. As Lord Sheffield put it, the alternatives were either to win the Palatinate by sword or by treaty. He recommended the former course, but "Not by sending forces into the Palatinate, but by way of diversion."

Once it had been decided to consider the treaties jointly, the Lords moved quickly toward a decision. Early on the following day the consensus was that the King should be advised to abandon both pacts with Spain. The archbishop of Canterbury pressed for an immediate resolution upon this point; Charles approved, and urged consideration of "what you wyll doe after; for Spayn wyll loose noe tyme." At this point the moderates took alarm: Pembroke, Hamilton, and the Lord Keeper were well aware of the sensitivities of the Commons and to them the "good correspondency" of the two houses was all important. A Lords' vote on a resolution which implied war might be interpreted as an insult to the Commons, particularly since they would be expected to vote the required subsidies. It was essential that the Commons not be

presented "with a leadinge opynion." Although the Lords Saye
and Sheffield thought it "fytt to come to a resolucion and passe
by vote what we wyll delyver at the conference to the Commons,"
the questions, when they were finally put, were phrased in the
delicate terminology suggested by Pembroke and Hamilton:

1. Whether in this conference the Lords intend to have with the
Comons touching the advyse you are to gyve to the K[ing] your
Lordshipes doe conceave there is a necessitye to treat of this match and
the Palat[inate] together?

2Q. Whether the Lords that shalbe of the Comittee to confer with
the Commons shall delyver unto them that your Lordships are of
opinyon that His Majeste relye not uppon any further treatises, except
their Lordships shall heare from them better reasons at the conference.[36]

Both questions passed unanimously.

Fortified by their common participation in the Sacrament and
welded together by Dr. Bargrave's exhortations enjoining concord
and **unity** in defense of true religion, the Commons met on March
1 to debate the "great business." [37] The initial speaker, Sir Benjamin Rudyard, was an admirable choice for that role. As Surveyor
of the Court of Wards and Liveries, Rudyard's dependence on the
crown was unmistakable, yet not so pronounced as that of a privy
councillor. A skilled orator, noted for meticulous preparation of
his speeches, he had the reputation of a moderate Parliament man
who saw in that institution a means of harmonizing the apparently

36. *Lords Debates 1624 & 1626*, 4–12.
37. The Commons took the sacrament at St. Margaret's Church in Westminster
on February 29, 1624. The sermon was preached by Isaac Bargrave and was printed
at the request of the House. (Isaac Bargrave, *A Sermon Preached before the
Honorable Assembly of Knights, Citizens and Burgesses of the Lower House of
Parliament: February the Last 1623* [London, 1624].) "The Altar is the proper seat of
reconciliation, Matt. 5:24 and that Holy Sacrament, as it is the best Pledge of God's
Love to us, so of our Communion, one with another. Believe it, Christians, the main
axiom and anvil of popish Policy; the very axle whereon they wind about the whole
body of their Machiavellism in England, is our division and dissention; themselves
have bragged, that there is no way so ready to convert a Lutheran, as by the
passion of a Calvinist; no means so prompt to make a Protestant a Papist, as by the
opposition of a Puritan. Thus they endeavor to destroy us (as we destroyed their
invincible Navy) by sending fire, even the fire of dissention in the midst of us.
O let us beat down this policy of the world, with the wisdom of the Spirit: away
with these distracting names of Lutheran, Calvinist, Puritan, etc. We are all the
children of the same father, who hath begotten us in the love of one Mediator, and
Sanctified us by one and the same Spirit." (*Ibid.*, 34–35.)

conflicting interests of King and subject and of advancing the reformed religion. As a dedicated Protestant, Rudyard could be relied upon to denounce the aims of Catholic Spain. Moreover, his keynote address signified to all present that an alliance had been concluded between the parliamentary forces of the Earl of Pembroke, Rudyard's patron, and those of the Duke of Buckingham.[38]

Rudyard's address was based upon the well-warranted premise that his auditors were already convinced of Spanish diplomatic tergiversations in the negotiations for the treaties. By a subtle shift of emphasis, however, he directed the attention of the House to the marriage compact as the more dangerous of the two instruments. It was under the pretense of a dynastic alliance that Spain was able to delude James and England, snatch the Palatinate, persecute continental Protestants, threaten the United Provinces of the Low Countries, and promote Catholic conspiracy in the British Isles. Thus, from the outset, Rudyard prepared his audi-

---

38. Rudyard's dependence upon Pembroke cannot be doubted. Throughout his parliamentary career, from 1621 up to and including the Long Parliament, he represented boroughs with which the Earls of Pembroke were intimately associated. Although Rudyard was native to Hampshire, he spent most of his adult life at court or on his Berkshire estates. In 1621, 1624, and 1625 he represented Portsmouth where Pembroke was captain of the castle. Rudyard's own Hampshire properties, located near Basingstoke, were not near enough to Portsmouth to warrant an assumption of his preponderant "interest" in that borough. In 1626, when he gave up Portsmouth to his "brother" Sir William Harrington, Rudyard was worried lest he had missed his opportunity for a seat because "all of my Lord's letters were sent out before." (Quoted by Violet A. Rowe in "The Influence of the Earls of Pembroke on Parliamentary Elections, 1625–41," *English Historical Review*, L [Apr. 1935], 243, Rudyard to Sir Francis Nethersole, Feb. 1626.) Nevertheless he was returned for Old Sarum, Wiltshire. It was also through the influence of the Earl of Pembroke that Rudyard had originally obtained preferment in the Court of Wards. (Chamberlain, *Letters*, II, 263, letter of Sept. 11, 1619.) The circumstances of his initial address lead one to believe that Rudyard's performance on March 1 was preconcerted. This conjecture is given confirmation by the fact that in the Parliament of 1624 he made three major addresses, each of which opened the debate on a matter of critical importance: foreign policy or supply. In 1625 he also spoke for the court and on that occasion disavowed any collusion between himself and the crown about parliamentary affairs. "I doe heer solemnlie protest, that, as heertofore I did never speake with K[ing], prince or favorit, of Parliament business, soe w^th our present K[ing], I never had the honor to speake fourtie words of any purpose what soever." (Eliot, *Negotium Posterorum*, I, 68.) Understandably Rudyard omitted any reference to the Earl of Pembroke or to privy councillors in the House of Commons. Describing Rudyard's qualifications as an orator, Sir John Eliot termed him a "great artist" who "at such times, & in such services, did speake, never but premeditated, w^ch had more shew of memorie then affection, & made his words less powerfull then observd." (*Ibid.*, I, 66, 75.)

ence to equate the cause of the Protestant religion with national security and reason of state. Because James had tendered concessions for the Catholics to Spain with the reservation *salus reipublica,* means were at hand to disavow the treaties on the grounds that they threatened the safety of the commonwealth. It was unthinkable, considering the revelations made by the Duke and the Prince, that the marriage negotiations should continue; the only acceptable alternative was a breach with Spain.

It was in considering the consequences of the disavowal of the treaties that Rudyard exceeded the instructions which James had delivered in his opening address. "If we break off the treaty," Rudyard said, "we must make good the breach; we must maintain it, and the likliest way is by a war, which is the manlier and more English way, and though we have no war presently, yet it is fit we should presently provide as if we had one." This course entailed the conclusion of alliances with continental Protestant princes, the dispatch of additional garrisons to Ireland, the repair of English fortresses, the commissioning of the navy, and the sending of assistance to the Dutch. As for the recovery of the Palatinate, it was a perplexing question fit to be relegated to a secondary role. If His Majesty saw fit to undertake a war for its recovery, Rudyard advised making "it near hand by way of diversion to save charges, whither every younger brother that hath but 20 pounds in his purse and his arms may go stocked for a profession and course of life, and where the Low Countries no doubt will be willing and ready to assist us for their own interest, which is the motive of all states." [39]

Many of the suggestions offered by Rudyard echoed the policies already implemented by the Prince and the Duke. Diplomatic representatives to continental powers were awaiting dispatch pending the action of the Parliament; the navy and coastal fortresses were being considered for repair and rebuilding; Dutch envoys had recently arrived to negotiate an alliance. More to the point, Rudyard accepted the war desired by Charles and Bucking-

---

39. SP 14/160/8, Rudyard's speech, Mar. 1, 1624. All three of Rudyard's major speeches in the Parliament of 1624 are printed in J. A. Manning, ed., *Memoirs of Sir Benjamin Rudyerd, Knight* (London, 1841), 79–82, 83–86, although two of them are taken from imperfect copies. Pym (fols. 10v–11v) and Earle (fols. 33–36) are the diarists who apparently had access to transcripts of Rudyard's speech of March 1; verbatim reports are entered in their manuscripts.

ham as a foregone conclusion and, although he did not name the enemy, he left no doubt that the Spanish would be the main target of attack — in the Low Countries on land, and wherever encountered at sea. He discounted the possibility of direct intervention in the Palatinate just as he had rejected the probability that treaties with Spain would secure its restoration. Yet, if James had been mistaken in assuming that unilateral negotiations with Madrid would force the Emperor and the Duke of Bavaria to disgorge their ill-gotten gains in the Palatinate, Rudyard and his parliamentary compatriots were no less mistaken in believing that a predominantly naval war against Spain would accomplish the desired goal. Nevertheless, they were tempted to consider the Catholic powers of Europe as a unity under the hegemony of Spain, who, by virtue of leadership in the Counter-Reformation, dynastic relationships with the Austrian Hapsburgs, disciplined armies, and a limitless supply of American treasure, could dispose of central European territories at will.

In the opinion of one observer, Rudyard had "acquitted himself so well that he spoiled all those that would needs be heard after him." [40] This, however, overstated the case. His speech was inimical to calm, lengthy deliberation of the two treaties; it stimulated the oratory of those who considered war inevitable and desirable and wished to stampede the Commons into agreeing with their aims. Thus, when Sir George More maintained "that one thing at once is fit to be handled that all may proceed with deliberation" and that the question of the match should be considered first, he was "interrupted with noise of some that misliked his tediousness" and hastily concluded his remarks.

The Commons were more in accord with the sentiments of Sir Robert Phelips who advocated action rather than words, and who considered it axiomatic that a treaty was "Spain's best army and with it and under the security of that they have gotten more, and especially the House of Austria, than ever was gotten by them otherwise, by Charles V or any of their princes." In his estimation the marriage negotiations had cost England the loss of her friends and reputation abroad, the allegiance of many of her subjects at home, and almost her obedience to God. As for the Palatinate, he lamented its loss and the distress occasioned thereby to

40. SP 14/160/33, Dudley Carleton to Sir Dudley Carleton, Mar. 5, 1624.

Princess Elizabeth, "but if we talk of revenge, yet whither should we look but towards him that hath wounded us. Spain is the great wheel that moves the whole frame of that business. They cannot, they will not restore it us. It concerns Austria and Rome too much to part with it, and all these depend on Spain. For Spain and Rome are like the twins that laugh and weep and live and die together. There is no hope to gain it by treaty. Then we must war for it, or something better than it. Spain must be the enemy." [41]

Sir Robert Phelips had the rare political gift of synthesizing the opinions and desires of many of his fellow members. He absolved them of responsibility for the loss of the Palatinate and allowed them to commiserate with the Elector Palatine and his people without the necessity of directly intervening to redress their grievances. Involvement in central Europe would be neither practicable not efficacious, yet the Palatinate "or something better than it" could be secured by attacking Spain. By identifying the Spanish menace, Phelips encouraged his auditors to focus their antipathies and to equate self-interest with magnanimity. He put the sword of divine vengeance in the hands of Englishmen and pointed it at the diabolical heart of Catholic conspiracy in Madrid.

For a time the House was carried away by the emotional impact of Phelips's address. A sense of urgency pervaded the Commons, and immediate measures to secure the safety of religion at home seemed crucial. Sir Francis Seymour insisted that the King be petitioned to enforce all penal laws against Catholics. Sir Robert Harley also was worried about domestic enemies "who lie in our bosoms and are not distinguished nor known of us but are familiar and conversant in all our companies and councils." Sir John Eliot advanced his own particular scheme to employ a bad means to a good end: not doubting that the King himself desired war, Eliot advised the House to concur and to finance hostilities by taking "from the Papists by way of mulct or fine all the moneys due by law." Sir John Strangways agreed and wanted Catholic recusants disarmed as well. Even those not immediately alarmed by domestic sedition recommended quick action. Seymour hoped that the

---

41. Spring, 43–44. A comparison of the manuscript diaries has convinced me that Spring contains the most detailed, accurate, and colorful report of the Commons debate on the advice to the King and therefore I have cited this manuscript in preference to others.

treaties could be nullified by unanimous consent; Phelips and Eliot wanted action rather than words; General Cecil advocated attack before Spain seized the initiative; Sir Thomas Belasyse, Sir Thomas Jermym, Sir Robert Hitcham, and William Coryton urged expedition in the nullification of the treaties. Even the Lords, by requesting a conference for the following afternoon, incited the Commons toward an immediate decision.[42]

Considering the temper of the House, it was difficult to restrain the war fever and restrict the debate to the questions originally propounded by the King. Experienced parliamentarians like Pym quickly realized that the discussion was getting out of hand, and he moved the appointment of a committee to collect the opinions of the House and prepare for a conference with the Lords. It remained, however, for Sir Dudley Digges and Sir Edwin Sandys to restore equilibrium to the proceedings. Digges not only advocated a committee of the whole to discuss the business in the afternoon, but he acquainted the members with the special qualifications of their body: "There be common lawyers that can advise by precedents; civil lawyers who could properly speak to the point of oaths and contracts; and country gentlemen that could speak of the means of the maintenance of wars and the present estate of the country thereunto." Sir Edwin Sandys went further; he reminded the Commons that "the King hath propounded unto us what it is we should advise of, and that it is fittest to hold us exactly to those prescribed propositions for this time. That which the King requires is to advise him whether it be fit to continue either or neither of the treaties. A short substance, a long consequence; let that be the limits of this day's business." [43] Like Digges, he insisted upon the necessity of supporting documentation; opinion without reason did not deserve the name of advice and was not sufficient for the resolution of great affairs.

Thus, when the committee met in the afternoon, the tone of the debate had altered significantly. After Digges had outlined the many ramifications involved in the annulment of the treaties, Dr. Gooch, vice-chancellor of Cambridge University, injected the first dissentient opinion opposed to the hue and cry for war. On both moral and practical grounds he objected to military action. The

42. *Ibid.*, 45, 60, 46, 50.
43. *Ibid.*, 50, 51.

recovery of the Palatinate was impossible, and it was "time lost to treat of impossibilities, and a course ill-beseeming a wise council to undertake." As for the justice of such a war, although the Elector Palatine had suffered depredations by the Spaniards, "what justice is there for us to quarrel with him? Our friend's cause is no just cause for us." With considerable courage Gooch pointed out that as far as he could learn "the provisions necessary for war are not with us for one day's good service." No wonder that "here he was taken off; the noise did interrupt him." [44]

For the remainder of this day's debate members vied with one another in suggesting cogent reasons to support the abandonment of the treaties. With his usual display of erudition, Sir Edward Coke dissected the marriage treaty between Philip II and Mary Tudor and pointed out that if English interests were thus secured when their religion was the same as that of the Spanish, "how much more is it now necessary to be wary in treaties and capitulations with them." [45] Christopher Brooke emphasized reason of state. If, by continuing the treaties, the Low Countries were devoured by Spain, "we should not only lose their assistance and friendship but be subject to the mischiefs of their powers and shipping to annoy us." [46] Sir Edward Wardour recalled Spanish diplomatic duplicity in Tudor times, and Sir George Chudleigh and Richard Hutton recapitulated reasons excerpted from the Duke's relation. Ultimately the materials for debate were exhausted, and Sir Thomas Jermyn moved "that an order may be made to thrust the word treaty out of the House for every man is weary to hear of it." [47] Without a dissenting voice the Commons resolved to recommend the dissolution of the treaties at a conference with the Lords and to empower a select committee to collect reasons in support of their advice.

The apparent unanimity of the House of Commons was deceptive; the fervor of patriotism had not only confirmed the judgment of the anti-Spanish faction, but had influenced "those that, by the consideration of the whole charge of war like to rest upon their shoulders, were wavering and ready to advise the continuance of

44. *Ibid.*, 55, 56.
45. *Ibid.*, 57.
46. *Ibid.*, 58; D'Ewes (fol. 71v) attributes this speech to Mr. Brakyn, but Earle (fol. 40) and Pym (fol. 13) agree that it was delivered by Christopher Brooke.
47. Spring, 61.

the treaty of restitution." [48] Although they came prepared to speak their minds, they were overawed by the impassioned harangues of Rudyard, Phelips, and others and were content to join with the rest in advising a breach with Spain.

The collection of reasons to support their resolution was entrusted to a committee of twelve experienced parliamentarians and privy councillors under the leadership of Sir Edwin Sandys. His views, delineated in his *Europae Speculum,* guaranteed that adequate attention would be paid to the imminent danger of religious subversion.[49] Policy, however, dictated that the political implications of religious divergence should be emphasized, and, when the committee reported on the following morning, it was the inordinate demands of the Spanish that were unequivocally castigated. They had not been content with conditions which would have satisfied other Catholic monarchs, but had insisted upon a general connivance or toleration for Catholics. Spain had made English recusants her temporal clients, had insulted Prince Charles by urging his conversion, had oppressed the Protestants abroad during the negotiation of the treaties, and had forcibly dispossessed the Elector Palatine of his territory and dignities.[50]

48. SP 14/160/33, Dudley Carleton to Sir Dudley Carleton, Mar. 5, 1624.
49. *CJ,* 724, Mar. 1, 1624. Originally printed without the author's permission, *Europae Speculum* quickly went through three editions before it was ordered burned by the High Commission at Sandys's request. Five subsequent editions appeared before 1640. The book attempts to analyze the policies that contribute to the strength of the Roman church; pp. 40–45 deal at large with the power redounding to the pope by virtue of his authority to dispense with regulations governing forbidden degrees in royal marriages and to legitimize base issue. (Sir Edwin Sandys, *Europae Speculum, or a View or Survey of the State of Religion in the Western Parts of the World* [London, 1673].)
50. Spring, 66–67; Pym, fol. 14v. The commons' reasons, with subsequent additions suggested by the Lords and approved by Parliament for delivery to the King, are printed in *OPH,* VI, 87–91. These reasons, which were not intended to be published until the King thought fit, repeatedly emphasized the religious issues involved in the negotiations with Spain and the danger thereby occasioned to the Protestant religion. The King's reaction to them may be inferred from a letter which the Marquis Inojosa wrote to King Philip IV on March 7/17, 1624. "Buckingham gave the King a paper in which the laws that had been decreed had been set down. The King threw it into the fire saying you wish to kill me." (PRO 31/12/29, Spanish Transcripts.) In all probability this report refers to the reasons, since, to my knowledge, it was the only paper delivered at the audience on March 5 to which the King could take exception. According to Spring, the King thanked the delegation for deleting religion from the motives that prompted the general advice; see p. 83. No laws had been passed by the entire Parliament, so Inojosa's reference to them must be in error. The Venetian ambassador asserted, furthermore, that "the King removed from the arguments for the rupture of the marriage one that too deeply wounded the Catholic religion, while the prince deals very tactfully with

The approval of these reasons was the signal for Sir Robert Phelips to rehearse once more the devious devices by which English innocence had been gulled by Spanish machinations. While James's fleet assisted in the suppression of the Barbary pirates, Spain implemented its aggressive designs by seizing the Palatinate and, under color of subsequent negotiations for a cease-fire and restitution, consented to the alienation of the Elector's titles and property. Phelips played upon the fears and prejudices of the Commons; Digges moved them to humble thankfulness to God, the King, and the Prince "for delivering us from Egypt, from the house of bondage."

More skeptical and experienced, Sir Edward Coke requested, "that the Lords may be moved to join with us in a petition to the King that upon the receipt of the reasons and advice from the Lords and us he will be pleased to declare himself as soon as is possible that he accepts of this advice, and that it be published." Coke had, indeed, raised the lid on Pandora's box full of parliamentary jealousies and suspicions. He and his collaborators knew that consultation and deliberation availed nothing if the King could not be bound to implement their advice, and it was by the suggestive persuasion of a joint petition from the Lords and Commons that he hoped to overcome the King's antipathy to war. His recommendations were accepted, and he was empowered to announce them to a conference committee of both Houses. Thus flattery, cajolery, reason, and pressure were the devices which the Commons were prepared to utilize in convincing the King of the expediency of their policy.[51]

By the time that the conference committee of the two Houses met on March 2, the Lords had outstripped the Commons in their consideration of the consequences of a breach with Spain. On Buckingham's motion, they had established a munitions committee to investigate the status of English and Irish defenses and report on the military supplies available for war. Suppression of the transportation of iron ordnance was mooted and the Lord Admiral's order prohibiting the sailing of four ships of the East India Company was confirmed. Ostensibly designed to keep gunpowder,

---

the Catholic lords, and both put a bridle on the zeal of the Puritans." (*Cal. S. P. Venetian*, XVIII, 249, Valaresso to the Doge and Senate, Mar. 12/22, 1624.)

51. Spring, 68.

experienced mariners, and money from leaving the country on the eve of war, this mandate provided Buckingham with additional bargaining power in his dispute with the East India Company over the booty from Ormuz. Whether his blackmail of the merchants was designed to enrich his own coffers or whether it was intended, as he later alleged, to help provide the navy with the monetary sinews of war is debatable. But one incontrovertible fact remained: money was a prime necessity for the implementation of the favorite's policy. This was the ultimate reality beneath the persiflage about Spanish dissimulation and insults to English honor.

For the moment, however, the Lords were more interested in concerting their opinion with the Commons and in confirming their convictions with additional data. As more and more of the nefarious Spanish practices came to light they dropped their tentative approach to the dissolution of the treaties and resolved to acquaint the Commons with a categorical imperative that negotiations with Spain should cease.[52] The unofficial channels of communication between the Lords and Commons may have influenced the decision of the peers; the Lord Keeper intimated to the barons and prelates that he understood that the Commons were resolved to advocate a breach. The desire for close correspondence, therefore, explains the restatement of the Lords' position to conform more closely with the advice of the Commons. Further, learning unofficially that the Commons would not offer reasons for their opinion at the conference, the Lords agreed to include in their statement only the general allegations, moved by Sheffield, that the treaties were inimical to the King's honor, the safety of the state, and the security of religion. Moreover, the coincidence of motions in the upper House, by Southampton and the Prince, and in the lower House, by Sir Robert Phelips, for the appointment of subcommittees to digest reasons is prima facie evidence of further collaboration — particularly since it was done in the absence of due notification of intention.[53]

With such preparatives it was understandable that the conference itself was a mere formality. Virtually the only thing with which the Commons were unacquainted was the information,

52. *Lords Debates 1624 & 1626*, 14–19; *CJ*, 723; *OPH*, VII, 72–83, 253–256.
53. *Lords Debates 1624 & 1626*, 17–18; *CJ*, 725.

communicated by the Lord Keeper, that negotiations for a marriage alliance had first proceeded from Spain, that armed assistance had been promised for the recovery of fortress towns in the
Palatinate and that the Prince, when threatened with detention
in Spain, had heroically urged his father to forget him and "to
bend all his affections upon his sister." As for the advice to be
proffered to the King, what Sir Edward Coke said was all too true:
"My Lords you have prevented us, and that very largely, for we
must walk upon the same ground and foundation." The only
significant addition offered by the Commons was that the King
would be petitioned to make an official declaration of the dissolution of the treaties "at his good leisure and due time (but our
suit is, that it would be with all speed)." The concurrence of the
Lords with this opinion was a foregone conclusion, as was the
agreement of the Commons to the nomination of a subcommittee
for the collection of reasons in support of their advice.[54]

The work of the subcommittee, twenty-four from the Lords and
forty-eight from the Commons, was peripheral to the issue at hand.
The recommendations of Parliament had been determined, and
it was therefore fundamentally important that they be communicated to the King. Buckingham and the Prince had urged haste,
but no one seemed more conscious of the danger of delay than
the Earl of Southampton. Even before the conference committee
had met he had recommended that the King be informed of the
advice "To nyght, if possible: that impossible, but to morrowe or
as soone as yt is possible." [55] The obvious channel of communication with the court was through Prince Charles and the Duke of
Buckingham. There was, however, good reason to fear that the
King would not give way to their persuasions for an early audience since Parliament had "begun to meddle a little deeper in
that matter of the match than does well satisfy his Majesty." [56]

Many observers of English politics were convinced that the
Prince and the Duke had formed an alliance with the Puritan
faction which would alienate them from the King. The Spanish
ambassador's list of those who counseled the Duke of Buckingham
seemed to verify this conclusion: in addition to the Earls of Car-

54. Harl. MS. 6799, fols. 183–185.
55. *Lords Debates 1624 & 1626*, 18.
56. HMC, *Mar and Kellie*, 194, Thomas, earl of Kellie, to John, earl of Mar, Mar.
4, 1624.

lisle, Dorset, and Bridgwater, it included the Earls of Oxford, Warwick, and Southampton.[57] It is significant that no Commoner was mentioned among the Duke's confidants — significant not because Buckingham lacked contacts in the lower House, but rather because they were not regarded by contemporaries as being of

57. PRO 31/12/29, Spanish Transcripts, Don Carlos Coloma to King Philip IV, Feb. 27/Mar. 8, 1624. As early as the autumn of 1623 Sir Francis Bacon detected signs of a rapprochement between Buckingham and the Puritans. In his notes for conferences with the Duke he wrote, "There are considerable in this state three sorts of men. The party of the Papists which hate you, The party of the Protestants, including those they call Puritans, whose love is yet but green towards [you] and particular great persons, which are most of them reconciled enemies, or discontented friends: and you must think there are a great many that will magnify you and make use of you for the breaking of the match or putting the realm into a war, which after will return to their old bias." (Bacon, *Works*, XIV, 442.) In another undated letter to Buckingham, written before the assembly of Parliament, Bacon counseled the favorite, "to maintain yourself firm and constant in the way which you have begun; which is, in being and shewing yourself to be a true and sound Protestant . . . And because I would have your reputation in this point complete; let me advise you that the name of Puritans, in a Papist's mouth, do not make you to withdraw your favor from such as are honest and religious men (so as they be not of turbulent and factious spirits, nor adverse to the government of the Church), though they be sometimes traduced by that name. For of this kind is the greatest part of the body of the subjects, and besides (which is not to be forgotten), it is safest for the King and his service, that such men have their dependence upon your Grace (who are intirely the King's) rather than upon any other subject." (*Ibid.*, 448–449.) An anonymous diatribe against Buckingham intended for delivery to James tends to confirm Buckingham's overtures to the Puritans, "The Parliament so much urged, they say, is to be a marrying his Mightinesse unto the Common Weal, that as your Majestie is his good Father, It may be his Mother, and so he stand not only by the King, but by the People, and popular humour, that he hath lately so earnestly courted, and especially from those who are noted to be of the most troubled humour." (*Cabala*, I, 222.) This document is undated, but because it mentions the suspension carried by Peter Killigrew to Spain in mid-November 1623 and because it was written before the convening of Parliament had been finally determined, I have tentatively ascribed it to late November 1623. During the audience of the Spanish ambassadors on February 26, "Buckingham complained that Hinojosa had said in Spain that he was the head of the Puritan party. Hinojosa said that what he had written to Spain was that out of spite to the marriage, although hated by the Puritans and Archbishop of Canterbury, he was now beloved and united to them." (PRO 31/12/29, Spanish Transcripts, Inojosa to Philip IV, Feb. 26/Mar. 7, 1624.) Irvonwy Morgan, in his book *Prince Charles' Puritan Chaplain* (London: George Allen and Unwin, 1957), maintains that in 1624 "there was a group in Parliament who were prepared to help the Duke to manage the House if he was prepared to be guided by them. This group was the Parliamentary wing of the Puritan-Scottish alliance, and are the men whom Eliot denominates as the Duke's 'friends' in his *Negotium Posterorum*." (*Ibid.*, 124–125.) Morgan claims that the leadership of this clique was vested in Lord Saye and John Preston, the Prince's chaplain. In my opinion his conclusions regarding Preston's parliamentary influence are founded on extremely tenuous evidence, most of which is derived from Hacket. Two of his major weaknesses in this work are, in my estimation, his elastic use of the designation Puritan and the subservient role he ascribes to the Duke of Buckingham during the period of his supposed Puritan alliance.

primary importance. Despite its self-consciousness, the House of
Commons was not regarded as the vital element in the political
life of the realm. With the exception of some few privy councillors whose official duties included diplomatic correspondence, none
of the leaders of the House were fully informed on current negotiations. State Papers that were exhibited to the Parliament were
communicated first to the House of Lords; only upon request were
they shown to a select committee of the lower chamber. Politicians of the Jacobean era could describe this Parliament as the
Prince's or the Duke's Parliament, but under no circumstances
would they attach an appellation to it associated with the names
of Coke, Phelips, Sandys, Digges, or any other leader of the
populace.

There was, however, a decided ambivalence in the contemporary attitude toward the House of Commons, and this was reflected in the outlook of both the Prince and the Duke. The
anachronistic conception of the dependence of the various factions
of the Commons upon select peers was very persistent, and, by
virtue of their dignity and prestige, the Lords could influence the
lower House by leading opinions and persuasive suggestions. However, the power of the purse held by the knights and burgesses
insured that careful attention would be paid to their views. A
restive or recalcitrant House of Commons could nullify the unanimous efforts of the Lords. Consequently, in the interval between
the joint resolution of the two Houses and their audience with
the King on March 5, Buckingham was confronted with a difficult
political problem. He had to continue the Commons' real sense
of participation in the advice to King James, attempt to engage
them unequivocally in its implementation, and at the same time
persuade a reluctant monarch to receive favorably the recommendations tendered by a deputation from his Parliament.

At the Prince's suggestion, Buckingham was empowered by the
conference committee of March 2 to solicit access to the King.[58]
It seems probable that he had anticipated this office and had already received a negative reply from the King predicated on the
plea of ill health. When, on the second, James again postponed

58. SP 14/160/33, Dudley Carleton to Sir Dudley Carleton, Mar. 5, 1624. Carleton
was present at this conference. "The next day in the afternoon both Houses met at
Whitehall, where, although I am far from being a parliament man I got entrance
among others that had as little to do in the assembly as myself."

the audience indefinitely, Buckingham's apprehensions vented themselves in a wrathful letter:

Notwithstanding of this unfavorable interpretation I find made of a thankful and loyal heart in calling my words crude catonic words, in obedience to your commands I will tell the House of Parliament, that you, having been upon the fields this afternoon, have taken such a fierce rheum and cough, as not knowing how you will be this night, you are not yet able to appoint them a day of hearing, but I will forbear to tell them that, notwithstanding of your cold, you were able to speak with the King of Spain's instruments, though not with your own subjects. All I can say is, you march slowly towards your own safety, those that depend of you. I pray God at last you may attain to it, otherwise I shall take little comfort in wife or child, though now I am suspected to look more to the rising sun than my maker. Sir, hitherto I have tied myself to a punctual answer of yours. If I should give myself leave to speak my own thoughts, they are so many that, though the quality of them should not grieve you coming from one you willfully and unjustly deject, yet the number of them are so many that I should not give over till I had troubled you; therefore I will only tie myself to that which shall be my last and speedy refuge, to pray the almighty to increase your joys and qualify the sorrows of your Majesty's

[humble slave and dog<br>
Steenie] [59]

The Duke was on the horns of a very real dilemma. The Commons had made it plain that they desired speedy action, and yet the King was temporizing while he attended the whispered insinuations of Archdeacon Carondelet, emissary of the Spanish ambassadors. How long would the Commons remain quiescent? This was the question that troubled Buckingham. The importance he attached to parliamentary affairs was evidenced by his continued attendance at Westminster despite the frustrating replies received from James at Theobalds. It was essential that the good correspondence between the two Houses be maintained and, consequently, when the conference committee for the compilation of

59. Harl. MS. 6987, fols. 196–197; see also *Hardwicke State Papers*, I, 460, for a variant reading, and Lucy Aikin, *Memoirs of the Court of King James the First* (3d ed., 2 vols., London, 1823), II, 371–372, the Duke of Buckingham to James I, Mar. 2. Although undated in the manuscript, it is clear from internal evidence in the letter that it was written on the evening of March 2, 1624. The King's excuses were conveyed to the Conference Committee of the Lords and Commons by Buckingham on March 3, 1624; see Pym, fol. 17; *CJ*, 727; SP 14/160/33, Dudley Carleton to Sir Dudley Carleton, Mar. 5, 1624.

reasons met on March 3, both the Prince and the Duke were in attendance. Obviously Buckingham expected his irascible letter to extort immediate compliance from the King, but, when consent to an audience was not forthcoming, he left parliamentary affairs in the Prince's charge and hurried off to Theobalds on the morning of March 4 to solicit a hearing.

Meanwhile the conference committee on reasons continued to be amused by further revelations of diplomatic intrigue. Whether consciously programmed or not, the relations made to the joint committee on March 3 and 4 were ideally designed to contribute to the Commons' self-esteem. Three members of the lower House — Sir Robert Cotton, Sir Isaac Wake, and Sir Richard Weston — disclosed the secrets of negotiations with the Spanish dating back to 1612. Cotton revealed the counterfeit overtures instituted by the Spanish ambassador, Gondomar, which were intended to frustrate the possibility of an Anglo-French marriage alliance. Wake recounted a dismal tale of Spanish treachery toward the Duke of Savoy, a tale which obviously paralleled what England could have expected had the match negotiations proved successful. Weston laid bare the Hapsburg triangle of intrigue — Madrid, Vienna and Brussels — which frustrated any bona fide solution of the German problem.[60] Indeed, the Chancellor of the Exchequer was congratulated by the archbishop of Canterbury, the Prince, and the Earl of Pembroke for his "first discovery" of Spanish dissimulation.

During his attendance at the committee, the Duke of Buckingham emphasized the Spanish threat to the Low Countries and disclosed how they had attempted to thwart English aid to the Dutch by arousing James's acquisitive desires for the crown of the Netherlands. More significantly, Buckingham outlined for the Commons the logic of his own policy. Speaking of the Spanish, he said, "their end is sovereignty, their dominion is dispersed so as they are forced to keep many garrisons, those garrisons cannot be maintained without money; to provide money the Indies are necessary, and to keep the Indies they must be masters of the sea, wherein England and the Low Countries do only impeach them." [61]

60. Harl. MS. 159, fols. 25–25v; Pym, fols. 15–17; *CJ*, 728; D'Ewes, fols. 74v–77v; Holles, fols. 90–92; Spring, 75–80, 89–90; Rich, fols, 18v, 17v, 16v, 15v, 14v.
61. Pym, fols. 16–16v; *CJ*, 727; Holles, fol. 91; Spring, 80. "He took occasion to speak of the vast ambitions of Spain after the western monarchy, which in part,

In a few sentences the Duke had synthesized the prejudices and purposes of the majority of the Commons and had logically demonstrated the vulnerability of the enemy. Whereas previously he had emphasized the need for immediate defensive preparations because of impending attacks from Spain, now he initiated an aggressive plan of naval warfare.

Doubtless his auditors were aware that the Duke had powerful private as well as public motives for advocating such a course of action but, for the moment, they chose to ignore them. Buckingham proposed a cheap war against a feared and hated enemy; it would be fought in an arena and with weapons with which the English were thoroughly conversant and confident of their own superiority. The expenses of the war would be disbursed at home, and promised not only future security for England and her colonies but immense booty as well. That a large part of the loot would be the perquisite of the Lord Admiral was of minor consequence, as was the fact that in a land engagement the Duke could not pretend to superiority of command. Nor were the Commons disinclined to avenge the Spanish insults and injuries that rankled in Buckingham's bosom; the majority of the members had already evinced opinions of anti-Catholic xenophobia.[62]

By March 4 the apparent unanimity of the Lords and Commons was such that it seemed inadvisable to delay further. The Prince's motion to have subcommittees of both Houses prepare the final draft of the reasons was approved, and, with the aid of eight Lords and sixteen members of the Commons, the Earl of Pembroke and Sir Edwin Sandys penned the manifesto in support of the Parlia-

---

and a great one, they had effected; but what remained must be gotten with arms, arms maintained by money, money with the Indies, the profit of the Indies must come by sea and if the King and the Low Countries joined they shall be masters of the sea and Spain's monarchy will have a stop." In a conversation with the Venetian ambassador on January 2, 1624, Buckingham had made two striking points: "that without going to Spain one would never believe her weakness . . . and in three years he hoped to show what England could do." (*Cal. S. P. Venetian,* XVIII, 191, Valaresso to the Dodge and Senate, Jan. 2/12, 1624.)

62. *Cabala,* I, 222–224, To the King, *ab ignoto* (my date, late Nov. 1623; see n. 57, above). "They say, our Great Duke hath certainly a brave desire to War, but in that also, he hath some great end of enriching himself, which he too well loveth, being carried away with that sweet sound, how Nottingham gained yearly during that sicknesse 40,000£ by his Admirals place but what his Majestie gained they find not in the Exchequer or Kingdome. Somewhat also they fear this his Graces precipitate humour and change of humour, hath of pride, to shew his power as great here, as is Olivares his there, as also of revenge against him in particular."

ment's advice. Concurrently news arrived from court that the King had agreed to receive the deputation from Parliament on the following day.

It was at this climactic juncture that the Lords committed a tactical blunder. Assuming the hearty concurrence of the Commons, the Earl of Southampton moved that if "occasion be offred, then those that delyver this advyse may have power to add, that yf this breakes of the treaty . . . his Ma$^t$ need not doubte but wee wylbe ready with our persons and our estates to be assistant." [63] The Lords embraced this suggestion; Lord Saye insisted that the Commons be acquainted with it, and, on Pembroke's motion, this responsibility was delegated to the subcommittee for drafting the reasons. The resolution was duly transmitted by the Earl of Southampton to his friend, Sir Edwin Sandys, who reported it to the House of Commons on the morning of March 5.

While the Lords nervously awaited the final Commons approval of the advice to the King, the members of the lower House indulged in a heated debate about the privileges of their chamber. Member after member arose to condemn the effrontery of the committee in receiving an unwarranted proposal. Oddly enough, it was the most illustrious representatives of the so-called "country party" who divided sharply over the issues involved in the proposition. Edward Alford asserted that the subcommittee had exceeded its authority and had endangered the liberties of the House. In his estimation, grievances should be redressed before supply could be granted. Moreover, the Lords should not be allowed to engross the thanks due to the Commons, who, after all, had sole and undoubted right to levy subsidies.

Opposed to him was the redoubtable Sir Robert Phelips, who alleged that the subcommittee was obliged to transmit to the

---

63. *Lords Debates 1624 & 1626*, 20. It may be argued, I think, that Southampton's motion was undertaken with Buckingham's connivance although the Duke was absent from the Lords at the time. Harleian MS. 6987, fol. 202, is a memorandum prepared by Buckingham for the speech delivered by James on March 5. Among the points he suggested for inclusion was "First to give them thanks for their uniform offer of assistance in their advice." The words "assistance in their" have been crossed out in the manuscript. This implies that Buckingham was anticipating a financial commitment by the Parliament and that, when it failed to materialize, the three words were deleted. The manuscript is undated but a comparison of its tenets with the speeches delivered by the King during 1624 establishes its connection with James's oration of March 5. It is printed in *Hardwicke State Papers*, I, 467–468.

Commons any proposition, no matter how improper, that had
been communicated to it during the exercise of its functions. He
acknowledged "that without righting the Kingdom there is little
hope of help, but yet speedy and necessary things must have their
priority." The engagement for financial support he did not consider dangerous since "the words were advisedly meditated on and
was in effect no more than had formerly fallen into the meditation
of this House upon consideration of the consequence of our advice."

In effect, members were asked to choose between defending the
privileges of the Commons and expediting a declaration of war.
Some, like Sir John Savile, feared that a general engagement would
imperil "all our estates, for who shall be the judge of our abilities?" Others, like Sir Heneage Finch and Sir Francis Seymour,
deplored the implication of contract inherent in a motion to make
supply contingent upon acceptance of advice. John Glanville
maintained "that to provide for war before it be propounded to
us is to christen a child before it was born, and saith that if the
King should move such a question it were a fair answer to say
that they did not presume to advise upon the means of maintaining a war till he propounded it." The impending delegation to
the King, he felt, was no excuse for hazarding the privileges of
the House. This sentiment was echoed by Mr. Mallory, who asserted that "if the committee have exceeded their authority . . .
it were fit they were put out of the House."

Those who favored the proposition maintained that a precedent
had been established by Sir James Perrot's motion of June 4, 1621,
which pledged the estates and lives of the Commons to the defense
of the Palatinate, but few echoed Sir William Beecher's statement
"that modesty in some cases is little less than treachery." Sir Edward Giles wanted to empower the deputation to promise subsidies if the King raised the question, but most M.P.'s agreed with
Christopher Wandesford and Sir Dudley Digges that matters
should proceed "in a parliamentary way." The apologia for the
temerity of the subcommittee reached its climax when Sir Edwin
Sandys excused his actions although he still insisted that "the consequence of the advice is war and the King must not be discour-
aged but encouraged to it." When Sir Edward Coke placed his
tremendous prestige at the disposal of the subcommittee and miti-

gated their offense, the wrath of the Commons was placated, but not to the extent that they were willing to approve of the Lords' suggestion. It was ordered that the "papers sent from them be sent back and that this be not so much as spoken of." [64]

Significantly, no member of the Privy Council had participated in the debate over privilege. Conway and Calvert could scarcely support an engagement to finance a war which their master was loath to declare. Yet Sandys, Coke, Digges, and Phelips were all willing to risk privileges which they had jealously guarded in preceding Parliaments. Some credence was thereby given to the royalist argument that the privileges of Parliament were all too often the refuge of vested interests. Leaders of the Commons were apparently not reluctant to establish dangerous precedents as long as they contributed to the achievement of their ultimate goals. Perhaps this explains why some "patriots" reversed their attitude toward the liberties of the Commons after they had accepted executive positions in the government. As viewed by crown officers, pleas for the liberties of the subject and the due process of Parliament often became an excuse for obstruction and greed rather than a guarantee of the citizen's security.

The willingness of the Commons to compromise their most fundamental beliefs in order to obtain their ends was further evidenced by their acquiescence in the decision of the subcommittee to omit any reference to religion in the presentation of their advice to the King. Obviously designed to make their resolution more palatable to James, this deletion occasioned little protest in either Lords or Commons. Except for Sir Robert Harley's expostulation that the principal reason for the breach of the treaties was left out, all discontent over the omission seems to have been expressed in private.[65]

---

64. Spring, 84–88; Nicholas, fols. 49–52v; Holles, fols. 92–93; Pym, fols. 18v–19v. Rich, fols. 13v, 12v, 11v, 10v, 9v, has the most extensive report of this acrimonious discussion. Although he did not participate in the debate, Rich seems to have been interested in ameliorating the dispute. On fol. 1v of his diary there is a draft of an answer to the Lords: "That the House of Commons have taken into consideration the proposition made by their Lordships. They are well content that their Lordships have been before them in a verbal [declaration], but they shall in convenient time according to the common usage be before them in a real expression of their true and hearty affection to cooperate with such his Majesty's designs as shall follow upon his resolution." I have omitted Rich's deletions in this draft. For Perrot's motion, see *Commons Debates 1621*, II, 428.

65. *CJ*, 729; HMC, *Buccleuch and Queensberry MSS*, III, 232.

Even the delegation from the Commons appointed to carry the advice to Theobalds was carefully chosen to avoid offending James. The twenty-four members who joined with the Lords were a nicely balanced combination of privy councillors, royal officials, dependents of the Prince and of Buckingham, military leaders, sons of peers, and senior country gentlemen. Sir Edward Coke, who had acted as spokesman for the Commons in the conference committees, and Sir Edwin Sandys, who had chaired the committee debate on the treaties and drafted the reasons, were eliminated from participation in the audience, probably because of the King's antipathy toward them.

As far as was possible the two chambers of Parliament had smoothed the way for the presentation and acceptance of their unanimous advice to nullify the treaties, but there was one critical source of discord which they had failed to consider. They were recommending—indeed, hoping to determine — future foreign policy, but they remained blissfully ignorant of immediate diplomatic developments. They were, in a sense, marching backward into the future, for, not being cognizant of contemporary negotiations, they had advised a course of action based upon antiquated evidence. In their treatment of foreign policy they had adopted the legalistic procedure of arguing from precedent, and it was all too evident that current developments would necessitate more expedient decisions.

London, for a brief moment, had become the diplomatic capital of Europe, yet Parliament seemed almost isolated from this maelstrom of Machiavellian intrigue. The Prince, the Duke, the Secretaries of State, and selected privy councillors were incessantly involved in international bargaining and politesse, but only such secrets as were conducive to the accomplishment of their aims were revealed to the Parliament. Nothing was mentioned of the overtures that had already been made to the Venetians, the French, and the Dutch for a league to assist in the recovery of the Palatinate. Nothing was whispered of the groundwork being laid for a French match by the unofficial embassies between London and Paris. Nothing was rumored of Denmark's and Sweden's purported willingness to put thousands of troops at the disposal of the Elector Palatine or of the arrival of an emissary from Count Mansfeldt.[66] Nothing was hinted of a joint Dutch-English naval venture against the Spanish treasure fleet.[67] Most significantly, nothing was reported about Bavaria's attempts, seconded by France and Venice, to arrange an accommodation in Germany which would exclude the Spanish from participation.[68] Nor was anything intimated regarding new Spanish concessions on the restitution of the Palatinate and electoral dignity.[69]

There was much private speculation by individual members in

66. *Cal. S. P. Venetian*, XVIII, 193–197, Valaresso to the Doge and Senate, Jan. 9/19, 1624; also, 214–215, 218, 221, 225, 227, 233, 245, 250, 257.

67. Even before the Dutch were officially invited to send commissioners to England to negotiate a defensive and an offensive alliance, it appears that they had received proposals from the Prince and Buckingham to launch a joint naval expedition against Spanish commerce in the name of the King and Queen of Bohemia. Some of the difficulties and alternatives are outlined in the letters written by Sir Dudley Carleton to the Duke of Buckingham on December 13 and 18, 1623, and Jan. 24, Feb. 16, Apr. 16, 1624, and printed in *Cabala*, I, 334–345. Two of these letters (Jan. 24 and Feb. 16) are erroneously ascribed to the year 1625, but from internal evidence it is clear that they were written in 1624. On March 12/22, 1624, Valaresso wrote to the Doge and Senate, "They have not yet begun negotiations with the Dutch ambassadors, the true reason being that the necessary basis must first be settled by parliament. They are sorry for the delay both because they are not without fears about the issue and because they might still have time, by deciding soon, to attack or stay the treasure fleet this year, now at Havana." (*Cal. S. P. Venetian*, XVIII, 250.)

68. For references to Francesco della Rota's proposal, see chap. i, n. 49. Few of the ambassadors on the scene believed that the Bavarian representations were seriously intended, although the French and Venetians particularly were content to second della Rota's efforts in order to discomfort the Spanish. (*Cal. S. P. Venetian*, XVIII, 202, 204–205, 212, 218, 231.) When Valaresso learned that della Rota had been dismissed, he lamented, "I could have wished they had known the art here of keeping the negoiations hanging on, so as to complete their preparations and render Bavaria more suspect to the Spaniards, or even to win him over entirely and separate him from them. (*Ibid.*, 239.) The main point which caused a rupture in Bavarian-English negotiations was whether or not the heir to the Elector Palatine should be educated in a Catholic court subsequent to his marriage into the ducal house of Bavaria. James himself was accused of ambivalent attitudes; sometimes he appeared to take the Bavarian proposal seriously, but he was accused of bad faith in revealing them to the Spanish ambassadors as a device to extort further concessions from Madrid. See also SP 14/160/58, Dudley Carleton to Sir Dudley Carleton, Mar. 10, 1624.

69. After the delivery of Philip IV's "last answer" in January 1624, Spanish concessions were more anticipated than concrete. The impending arrival of Padre Maestro portended conciliatory overtures from the Spanish, which increased James's hopes for a peaceful solution and aroused the fears of the Elector's partisans. Apparently some attempts were being made by the Spanish to resolve the German question for on March 6/16, the Venetian representative at Vienna reported that the Spanish were pressing for an imperial diet and offering to give up Frankendale if the Duke of Bavaria would restore Mannheim and Heidelberg. (*Cal. S. P. Venetian*, XVIII, 246–247, Marc' Antonio Padavin to the Doge and Senate.)

connection with these occurrences, but most of it was based upon fear or hope. The very thought that a new emissary would arrive from Spain was sufficient to render the Puritans disconsolate, just as the extraordinary reception accorded the Dutch commissioners made them jubilant. The majority of contemporaries judged by externals. They were gratified by the wave of anti-Spanish popular prejudice which made London streets unsafe for Inojosa and Coloma and forced them to mount a guard at their official residence. At the same time, most parliamentarians suspected that the sentiments of the populace were not wholeheartedly shared by the King and that his public expressions of reliance upon the will of his people were a ruse devised to extort better conditions from the Spanish. The knowledge that emissaries from Madrid were in almost daily communication with the King strengthened the fears of the Commons, for had not James admitted that the guile of Gondomar had deceived him in the past?

Indeed, the King was listening to the complaints and blandishments of the agents of Spain. Don Francisco Carondelet, on March 2, gave James his own biased report of proceedings in the House of Commons and remonstrated vigorously against parliamentary and private insults offered to the Spanish emissaries.[70] The same evening James instructed his secretaries of state to investigate the ambassador's grievances, and he further commanded them to check anti-Spanish enthusiasm in the House of Commons. Upon Calvert's and Conway's recommendation, James directed his attorney to draft a general proclamation "to forbid all misbehaviors, insolences or contempts against all ambassadors, agents and public foreign ministers." [71]

Although he was prepared to placate Inojosa and Coloma, James had hoped that they would offer constructive proposals instead of

70. PRO 31/12/29, Spanish Transcripts, account of the audience of Don Francisco Carondelet, archdeacon of Cambray, at Theobalds, Mar. 2/12, 1624. Specifically Carondelet protested against the warlike disposition of parliament which had caused the appointment of the Lords' Committee on Munitions and against motions in the House of Commons to finance hostilities by seizing the property of English Catholics. He further protested against insults to the Infanta and indignities committed against the ambassadors and threatened to transmit to Madrid a request for recall of the mission.
71. SP 14/160/15, Earl of Kellie to Secretaries Conway and Calvert, Mar. 2, 1624; SP 14/160/17, Secretaries Calvert and Conway to the Earl of Kellie, Mar. 3, 1624. The proclamation forbidding affronts to foreign ambassadors was issued on Mar. 8, 1624.

complaints. More and more the King was finding himself the prisoner of time; circumstances were forcing him into partnership with Parliament. Madrid was three weeks away; Westminster only hours. In the absence of Spanish concessions, the only feasible alternative for James was to temporize. To rebuff Parliament was unthinkable; not only would this inevitably lead to another fruitless dissolution, but it would deprive the King of his most valuable diplomatic lever.

Buckingham was well aware that, for the moment, time was on his side. Once the King had consented to meet the delegation from the Lords and Commons, the battle was half won, and all problems were refined into the single task of accommodating the King's answer to the wishes of the petitioners. A memorandum was prepared by the favorite listing conciliatory promises to be made in the royal address:

That you did not mean to put a scorn upon them, to call for their advice, and then to reject it, if they pay no real assistance with it.

First to give them thanks for their uniform offer of (assistance in their) advice.

Then to take notice of their careful proceedings in the Lower House.

That you do not desire to engage them in their gift till you be declared anent their advice.

And if you be engaged into a war by their advice you mean not to hearken to a peace without first hearing them.

And that they may see your sincere dealing with them you will be contented that they choose a committee to see the issuing out of the money they give for the recovery of the Palatinate in case you accept their advice.

Then to show them that this is the fittest time that ever presented itself to make a right understanding between you and your people, and you assure yourself that their behavior will so continue as they have begun towards you that they shall see by proofs how far you will be in love with parliaments for making of good laws and reforming of abuses.[72]

72. Harl. MS. 6987, fol. 202, a memorandum by Buckingham of points to be included in the King's speech of March 5. Gardiner, *History of England*, V, 192, n. 3, concludes that this undated memorandum was sent to the King on March 3, 1624, possibly as an enclosure in the letter in which Buckingham expostulates against royal delays in granting an audience. I prefer to believe that it was presented at Theobalds by Buckingham personally on March 4. See nn. 59, 63, above.

All of these suggestions were incorporated in the reply James delivered after the archbishop of Canterbury, in the name of both Houses, tendered the advice to discontinue the treaties. But the salutary results doubtless expected by Buckingham were debilitated somewhat by the King's equivocations. He reiterated his reluctance "without Necessity, to embroil myself with War," even though he reaffirmed his determination "not to enjoy a Furrow of Land in England, Scotland, or Ireland, without Restitution of the Palatinate." He hinted that he had lately "had no small Hope given me of obtaining better Conditions for the Restitution of the Palatinate, and that even since the sitting down of the Parliament." He insisted that his conscience and honor must be satisfied before he would even consider hostilities, and he reminded his auditors of the financial difficulties under which the crown labored. James complained that he had "had the least Help in Parliament of any King that ever reigned over you this many Years," and lamented his own indebtedness, the poverty of his prospective allies, the necessities of Ireland and the navy, and the demands of the Palsgrave's household. He promised that his insolvency would be confirmed by a detailed report from the Lord Treasurer, but his most important vow was conditional: "If, upon your Offer, I shall find the Means to make the War honourable and safe, and that I resolve to embrace your Advice; then I promise you, on the Word of a King, that although War and Peace be the peculiar Prerogatives of Kings, yet, as I have advised with you in the Treaties on which War may ensue, so I will not treat nor accept of a Peace, without first acquainting you with it, and hearing your Advice; and therein go the proper Way of Parliament, in conferring and consulting with you." [73]

The Earl of Kellie, an inward man at court, considered the King's oration wise and judicious and reported that, "This answer of his did much satisfy a great number of the House and many others that has heard of it." [74] There were in the speech things to content the Commons, particularly the concession that revenues were to be managed by treasurers appointed by the lower House. This had been privately mooted among some members as a con-

73. The King's speech to the deputation of the Lords and Commons on March 5, 1624. I have quoted from the version printed in *OPH*, VI, 92–96.
74. HMC, *Mar and Kellie*, 195, Thomas, earl of Kellie, to John, earl of Mar, Mar. 11, 1624.

dition of their assistance, and it obviously had been championed by Buckingham as a means to assure their engagement to support a war. Conversely, several points raised in the oration aroused suspicion; some observers at court made inquiries to determine just what "new hopes" had been given to the King for the immediate restitution of the Palatinate, and they were finally forced to conclude that these rested only on the unstable assurances of Francesco della Rota.[75] Consequently, when Parliament convened on the morning of March 6, a great deal of uncertainty prevailed as to the nature of the King's answer.

The Lords, expecting an immediate report, were chagrined at the absences of the archbishop of Canterbury and Lord President Mandeville, both of whom had been key figures in the delegation sent to Theobalds. A rumor circulated that the King's remarks were unsatisfactory, and the peers were reluctant to engage in any business until they were assured to the contrary. So profound was their distrust that it was only by a majority of eleven that they agreed to read further bills, and it was ordered that a committee should confer with the Commons in order to determine the true text of the King's oration.[76]

That afternoon the notes taken by various peers and commoners were digested, and, chiefly on the basis of the Lord President's minutes and information supplied by Buckingham, a subcommittee of six "composed" James's reply. With extreme nicety the subcommittee agreed "that nothing be reported but *in verbis conceptis*," and in both the Lords and Commons on March 8 the speech was read and the members allowed to take copies. Sir Heneage Finch, who reported the speech in the House of Commons, was loud in his praise of the King's oratorical ability "Where Matter and Words contend for Superiority, and are so woven to-

---

75. SP 84/116, fol. 186 (Holland Correspondence), Dudley Carleton to Sir Dudley Carleton, Mar. 1, 1624; *Cal. S. P. Venetian*, XVIII, 250, Valaresso to the Doge and Senate, Mar. 12/22, 1624. In a conversation with Buckingham, Valaresso elicited the following information, "he was not satisfied with the king's reply to the deputation, although he thought it necessary for the king to know what help his people would give before taking up an enterprise of such importance . . . He added perhaps the most remarkable thing of all, telling me that the king certainly was master but the prince also had his share, as if they would carry through to completion the work begun, whether the father desired it or no; this point requires consideration as well as secrecy." See also *ibid.*, 248; SP 14/160/58, Dudley Carleton to Sir Dudley Carleton, Mar. 10, 1624.
76. HMC, *Buccleuch and Queensberry MSS*, III, 232.

gether, that the Loss of a Word loseth the Sentence," but behind the flattery lurked the motive of closing loopholes and avoiding misinterpretations which would allow either King or Parliament to escape their responsibilities.[77]

The issues laid bare before the Commons were two, one of major and one of minor consequence. Of incidental importance was James's desire to be convinced of the moral necessity of war; much more significant was the question of monetary support for the commencement of hostilities. The King had alleged his poverty as a cause of his reluctance to declare against the treaties. On March 11, the Lord Treasurer in the upper House, and the Chancellor of the Exchequer in the lower, concerted their efforts to prove the validity of the King's contention. In the service of their master they contrived to justify the indebtedness contracted by James since 1619. Their report said nothing whatever about the King's personal estate or domestic expenditures; it was confined to disbursements and receipts relating to foreign affairs. Since Michaelmas 1619, some £661,670 had been spent upon extraordinary embassies, the voyage against the Algerian pirates, the Prince's journey to Spain, the defense of the Palatinate, and the maintenance of the Palsgrave's household. Receipts from the two subsidies granted in 1621, from various "voluntary" contributions and from impositions on wine and hops, had yielded only £371,640, leaving a net indebtedness of £290,030.[78]

By remaining silent on James's domestic expenditures, the Lord Treasurer skillfully implied that, were it not for foreign entanglements, the King could live of his own. This implication was reinforced by Cranfield's assertion that Ireland was on the verge of paying its own way and that expenditures for the navy had been

77. *CJ*, 679, 731. Copies were allowed because Sir John Eliot averred that there were "Since our Return from Theobalds many strange Reports concerning their Reception." (*Ibid.*, 731.)

78. Sackville MS. ON 7890, Lord Treasurer's report to the House of Lords, Mar. 11, 1623/4. The manuscript copies of the Treasurer's report are frequently incomplete and usually disagree as to the period of time covered, the nature of disbursements and receipts, and the figures involved. Generally speaking, they do agree that the King's payments totaled £661,670 and that the debt remaining was £290,030. None of the reports I have consulted balance. Among the best are those in Horne, fol. 63v, and Harl. MS. 159 fol. 32v. I have compared these with those contained in SP 14/160/63, Robert Cotton to Thomas Cotton, Mar. 11, 1624, and the diaries Earle, Pym and Spring, as well as *Lords Debates 1624 & 1626* and *CJ*, 682; see also F. C. Dietz, *English Public Finance 1485–1641* (2d ed., 2 vols., London: Frank Cass and Co., 1964), II, 204–205, n.

retrenched by £20,000 per annum at the same time tonnage was increased. He also reminded his auditors that the imposition on wines was to end with this Parliament and that, moreover, a war would seriously curtail the King's customs revenues and terminate the Spanish trade.[79] To the consternation of some of the peers, the Lord Treasurer concluded with the assertion that it was feasible both to relieve the King's necessities and to provide the sinews of war.

Such a report was scarcely consonant with the Prince's wishes, and when Lord Spencer asked how it would be possible to pay the King's debts and finance a war as well, Charles hastily explained that "The meaning is that the King cannot without your helpes . . . but your supplye for the mayne to have prioritye to this." Thus at the outset he sacrificed James's desire to be free of debts to the greater design of military involvement. His suggestion was eagerly commended by Southampton, who wanted to expedite matters by communicating this welcome news to the House of Commons. "Yf to leave yt wholly to them," he said, "yt wyll ask much tyme in debate." He urged, "that we doe somwhat to stirr upp them." [80]

In dealing with this motion for a conference, the Lords realized that they were on touchy ground because supply could only move from the Commons. If a message were sent immediately, the lower House might take umbrage at the pressure exerted by the peers; if it were delayed, its efficacy might be nullified. The archbishop of Canterbury wanted to postpone the message until the morrow in order that the Lords could be informed as to the reception of the King's speech in Commons, and so that "every pryvate man may move his frend that expedicion is fytt." Despite the caution of Hamilton, Wallingford, Montagu, and the archbishop, it was decided to send an immediate message when Buckingham asserted that "The present tyme the best, for the Prynce hathe authority from the King, yf any thing be mistaken, to explaine the same. This wyll take away jealousies."

The original draft of the message craving a meeting "to avoyde all mistakinges that may aryse" irritated the Treasurer and occa-

79. *Lords Debates 1624 & 1626*, 23–25; *CJ*, 682.
80. *Lords Debates 1624 & 1626*, 25–27. The Prince said, "Present relief in the Kinges estate is not expected by the Kinge."

sioned a clash with the Prince when Cranfield inquired, "wherin he mistooke?" Charles was forced to concede that the Treasurer was not mistaken, and so the word in the message was changed to "doubts." The debate ended with Cranfield still insisting "This debte to be thought on, but the buissines nowe in hand to have prioritye." [81]

Despite the fears expressed in the upper House, the Commons had no doubts about the financial report submitted to them. While the Lords were arguing about priorities, their parliamentary colleagues in the lower chamber blithely ignored the King's indebtedness in their debate on a motion for assistance. Even though the opening speaker, Sir Benjamin Rudyard, held "it fit that to relieve his Majesty and sweeten him towards us, we should make him a proportionable present for his own particular," his suggestion received scant attention from the House.

In fact Rudyard's entire keynote oration lacked the vigor and forcefulness necessary to channel the debate effectively. It was pervaded by a fear that King and Commons would clash again and that the dissolution of 1621 would be repeated. "I am afraid," he said, "if this Parliament fail, it will be the last of Parliaments; if it go well, it will be the beginning of many and of much good hereafter." Excessive love of the liberties of the Commons would, he maintained, stifle them: "we may blow up the house without gunpowder; we may do it with our own breath." Now, when the King had professed a desire to be in love with Parliaments and the Prince was the initiator of their assemblage, a golden opportunity presented itself to gratify both father and son and benefit King and commonwealth.

Rudyard spoke as if war were a foregone conclusion, and he asked his listeners not to be alarmed at "the vast charge of undertaking a great war presently." He expected Spain to make the initial assault, and so he reiterated his earlier recommendations which entailed assisting the Low Countries, securing Ireland, refurbishing English defenses, and equipping the fleet. To implement this plan he called for a joint committee of Lords and Commons "in the nature of a Council of War, of some expert members of both Houses and to call others to assist them . . . in these particulars." However, he would not venture to estimate the

81. *Ibid.*, 27.

amount of revenue necessary even though he considered provision for the general defense of the realm and relief of the King's necessities to be imperative.[82]

Almost immediately, Rudyard's most constructive suggestion was discarded by his compatriots. Few members were willing to delegate the financial prerogative of the House of Commons to a Council of War composed of experts. As a result, therefore, of neglecting or discarding Rudyard's concrete proposals, the ensuing debate was diffuse and disorganized until a consensus could be obtained on at least one issue. Not all members agreed that war was inevitable. Sandys, for instance, maintained that the restoration of the Palatinate must be categorically denied by the King of Spain before a legitimate *casus belli* existed. War, as a future contingency, might ensue, but in the meantime Parliament could devote itself to the redress of grievances and the making of good laws which would enable Englishmen to support the charge of military action.[83] The old parliamentary tradition that the redress of grievances must precede supply epitomized one segment of opinion in the House of Commons and stimulated Sir James Perrot's demand that a committee be constituted to investigate the state of the King and the kingdom.

Others, who had no doubts about the certainty of war, disagreed in their approach to it. Sir George More, Sir Edward Coke, and John Glanville thought it fundamental that the war be justified and were prepared to have this incorporated in a parliamentary resolution. The mere thought of war made Sir Edward Coke feel seven years younger, and he stated as an axiom that "war . . . with Spain is England's best prosperity." [84] His desire to resolve

82. Pym, fols. 25–25v; see also Harl. MS. 6799, fols. 201–201v; Earle, fols. 70–72v.
83. Spring, 104; see also Pym, fol. 25v; Earle, fol. 74; *CJ*, 682, 732–733.
84. Spring, 105. The debates of March 11 on a general motion for assistance to the King are treated extensively in the *Commons Journal* and by most diarists. In the majority of cases, however, some speeches are omitted, and frequently some are treated so briefly that they may be misinterpreted. The two versions of the *CJ* give the most comprehensive list of speakers, but the speeches are often fragmentary and must be supplemented by reference to other diaries. (*CJ*, 682–683, 732–734; Spring is most detailed in his treatment on pp. 101–108.) Both Pym and Earle give complete copies of Rudyard's opening speech. Thereafter Pym occasionally summarizes arguments without indicating who promoted them (fols. 25–26); this is also characteristic of D'Ewes (fols. 80–82). Earle (fols. 70–76) omits short speeches of minor consequence as does Nicholas (fols. 67–71v). Holles (fols. 95v–98) lists many speakers, but is extremely sketchy regarding the tenets of their remarks. Hawarde's entries (pp. 199–203) are also abbreviated. Jervoise (p. 45) devotes a paragraph to

on the necessity and justice of war by a vote of the Commons was a dangerous encroachment upon the royal prerogative and was recognized as such by Solicitor Heath and by Sir Heneage Finch, recorder of London. For a declaration of war in the House of Commons there was no precedent, and Coke, who ordinarily wallowed in legal lore, well knew it. In this instance, therefore, the efforts of the "King's friends" in preventing the establishment of a dangerous precedent were successful.

Others who favored war were content to leave the moral issues to the King's decision. Sir Edward Cecil "was so transported with an imaginary success of the war as to hope that with an army we might pass through Spain and fetch the Infanta, which was presently answered with a negative acclamation of the House, 'No, no.' " [85] Mr. Wentworth, the recorder of Oxford, predicted dire results for England unless immediate measures were taken to aid the Low Countries. Christopher Brooke, Esq.[86] and Sir Robert Mansell advocated an estimate of defensive expenditures so that a particular offer of assistance could be made to the King. All of these views, whether for redress of grievances, moral justification, specific military action, or particular supply, were minority opinions.

The great question to be resolved was what type of general resolution promising financial assistance would induce the King to annul the treaties. Royal officials and privy councillors alike recognized that, at present, a specific demand for money was untimely. Distrust of the King was too profound. Sir Henry Mildmay, Master of the Jewel House, recommended a general offer of assistance conditional upon the King's declaration. Sir Edward Conway reinforced this motion, as did Sir Robert Heath and Sir Robert Phelips. The consensus of the House, therefore, favored a general declaration, but opinions differed as to its phraseology. Mr. Coryton revived consideration of the earlier proposition submitted to the House by the Earl of Southampton. Others, like Sir Henry Mildmay and Sir Edward Cecil, referred to the declaration

---

Rudyard's speech and is silent on other details of the debate. In the ensuing paragraphs I have relied most heavily upon Spring.

85. Pym, fol. 25v.

86. D'Ewes, fol. 81v. D'Ewes erroneously attributes this speech to Mr. Brakyn; compare with Spring, 104.

made in 1621. Sir Henry Anderson and Sir Dudley Digges advocated a flat statement promising that the House would make good
its advice, and this Sir William Strode desired should be done in
conjunction with the Lords. Sir Robert Harley supported this
proposal with the condition that it be done "in a parliamentary
way."

Finally, Sir Heneage Finch attempted a synthesis and moved
"that the question that shall be put to pass among us should be
to this effect: that when the King shall declare himself to follow
our advice we will be ready to assist him and make it good with
our bodies and goods to the uttermost." [87] When Mr. Alford excepted against the indefinite word "uttermost," and Sir Edward
Coke preferred "persons and abilities" to "bodies and goods," Sir
Thomas Jermyn warned the House against quibbling and moved
"that the resolution of our abilities in a parliamentary way may
be concluded."

Immediately after the House had voted "that in pursuit of our
advice we will be ready (upon his Majesty's declaration to dissolve
both treaties) to assist his Majesty with our persons and abilities
in a parliamentary course," a message was received from the Lords
requesting a meeting for the purpose of clearing doubts about the
Treasurer's report.[88] What they heard from the Prince at the conference was an amplification of his earlier statement to the Lords,
obviously intended to stimulate the generosity of the Commons.
Complacent in the knowledge that they had already passed a resolution for general assistance, the Commons committees were, nevertheless, pleased to have the Prince condone their deferring of
the King's debts to later consideration. They were also delighted
by the Prince's assertion that the King would in the future convene Parliament frequently. Even more promising was the Prince's
engagement to remember any expeditious efforts in behalf of

87. *Ibid.*, 107; see also SP 14/160/89, Dudley Carleton to Sir Dudley Carleton, Mar.
17, 1624. Carleton says, "Mr. Secretary Calvert cast in a restriction to the general
offer of their lives and fortunes, that it was to be understood and expressed to be
by a parliamentary way which was followed and embraced by the House." Neither
the *Commons Journal* nor the diaries mention Calvert in connection with this
stipulation.

88. Spring, 107. The text of the address to the King was drawn by a committee
composed of Sir Edward Coke, Sir Humphrey May, Sir Thomas Jermyn, John
Glanville, Sir Robert Heath, Sir Edwin Sandys, John Coke, Sir John Savile, Sir
Heneage Finch, Sir Nathaniel Rich, Sir William Fleetwood, and Sir Benjamin
Rudyard. (*CJ*, 683.)

war: "when time shall serve hereafter," he told them, "you shall not think your labors ill bestowed." [89]

Consequently, when the Prince's remarks were reported by Secretary Calvert on the morning of March 12, it was considered an opportune moment to reopen the question of financial assistance. Sir Thomas Edmondes, a privy councillor, wondered how anyone could resist the Prince's request for expedition and insisted that a message of thanks should be sent to him with an assurance of tender concern for his interests.[90] Sir Robert Phelips wanted something "real" as well as "complimental"; to an address of thanks and acknowledgement to the Prince he wanted to append an assurance "that as soon as his Majesty shall have declared the treaties broken we will then express ourselves in some particular manner for his assistance." Secretary Conway likewise dealt plainly: "that there was no way in that resolution which we took yesterday to give satisfaction. The Prince would not have laid himself so open if his expectation had rested in general . . . We must offer him [the King] somewhat real and individual, but under those conditions to which he hath bound himself." [91]

Oddly enough, it was a Buckingham supporter, Sir John Eliot, who impeded this drive for a specific grant to the King. "He did not doubt that upon a general declaration of our intents the King would receive no satisfaction, but now conceives it to be better than the particular, because particular subsidies cannot so fully answer the charge of a war as an engagement to assist to the whole war. The war may hold when the subsidies are gone." [92] The House concurred in Eliot's opinion, and the same committee which had been appointed for drafting the resolution of general assist-

89. SP 14/160/65, speech of Prince Charles, Mar. 11, 1624; Harl. MS. 159, fol. 31v, erroneously dated Mar. 15. See also Horne, fol. 62v where the report differs radically from others in that he purports to give a speech of the Lord Treasurer at the same conference. Horne is in error because the Lords had ordered that no one but the Prince should speak at the conference. (LJ, III, 256.)

90. SP 14/160/68, speech by Sir Thomas Edmondes, Mar. 12, 1624; CJ, 683, 734.

91. Pym, fols. 26v–27; CJ, 683, 734; Spring, 109. Phelips even revived consideration of the King's debts although he admitted "that it was first necessary to relieve the Commonwealth to enable it to that." (SP 14/160/89 Dudley Carleton to Sir Dudley Carleton, Mar. 17, 1624.) "Sir Robert Phelips (who is much fallen in his credit with the parliament) proposed a question, what they should say if his Majesty were not satisfied with their offer which consisted only of general terms: which question was very ill taken by the House."

92. Spring, 110.

ance was empowered to draw up a message of thanks to the Prince. When the Solicitor reported from the committee prior to their departure to meet the Lords, it was stipulated by the Commons that no alterations in the substance of the address to the King could be entertained by them.

On the afternoon of the twelfth, therefore, forty-eight members of the committee from the Commons submitted the draft of their resolution to twenty-four peers. Almost immediately it was referred for approval to an extraordinary session of the Lords. Only their desire for "good correspondency" prevented the peers from rejecting the resolution of the lower House. Buckingham believed that the Commons had engaged themselves irrevocably, but the Lord Treasurer was resentful of the insult to the upper House implied in the restriction on amendment. The Lords, he maintained, had joined in the advice to dissolve the treaties, and he felt that they were entitled to be consulted about means to implement that advice. He wanted the question thoroughly debated and resolved in the upper chamber.

The Prince, however, was willing to forgo the privileges of the Lords: "Yf we propound for the substance," he said, "yt wyll (as by experience we fynde) distaste them." He recommended that the substance of the Commons' resolution remain intact, but when Buckingham wanted an exposition of the phrase "parliamentary way," Charles modified his position to accord with that of the favorite. Even this desire was abandoned when Southampton called the attention of the peers to the Commons' jealousy regarding their fiscal privileges. When Lord Mandeville asserted that "The Kinge [was] more propper to gyve them cause to alter the substaunce than wee," all resistance ceased, and the Lords agreed to the Commons' resolution with the minor proviso that they be included in the preamble to the offer.[93] A copy of the declaration was delivered to the Prince who was apparently empowered to ask the King to receive a deputation from Parliament. Undoubtedly, therefore, Charles acquainted his father with the terms of the general offer of assistance when he made arrangements for the reception of the committees at Whitehall on March 14. It was also Charles who suggested that the archbishop of Canterbury deliver

93. *Lords Debates 1624 & 1626*, 29–31.

the preamble to the general offer, and the text of it was approved by both Houses on the morning of the thirteenth.[94]

It seems probable that the King had no foreknowledge of Archbishop Abbot's preface before its delivery on Sunday afternoon because he immediately picked a hole in its complimentary texture. Abbot had unwittingly assumed that the King was inclined to break with Spain, and he mightily offended James by attempting to reinforce his resolution. The statement to which the King took exception was: "Hence we do exceedingly rejoice that your Majesty hath been pleased to shew yourself sensible of the insincerity of that people with whom of late you have had a double treaty and of the indignities which have been offered to the blessed Prince, your son, and royal daughter, and that your kingly heart is kindled with an earnest desire to make reparation unto her noble consort and herself of the Palatinate, their patrimonial possessions, which is agreeable to justice, the laws of God and men." [95]

As far as James was concerned, the archbishop's assertion destroyed the constitutional position of the monarchy. He had asked Parliament for advice, not dictates. He had not declared himself, despite his permission to his servants, to expose diplomatic relations with Spain. "Buckingham," he said, "made a relation unto you by my commandment, which you are to judge upon, but I never yet delivered my judgment upon that. When Jupiter speaks he useth to join his thunder to it; and a King should not speak except he maintain it by action."

Having dismayed the archbishop, James proceeded to deflate the Lords and Commons. With perhaps unconscious irony he thanked them for their large offers of assistance which "I hold to

94. *Ibid.*, 31–32. Charles was apparently somewhat offended by the Commons' refusal to allow the Lords to amend the substance of their general offer of supply even though he manifested a desire to keep good correspondency with them. When the question was raised in the Lords on the thirteenth as to whether the archbishop's preamble should be submitted to the Commons for approval, the Prince opposed its transmission and appears to have been the only one who voted in the negative when the question was put.

95. Harl. MS. 159, fol. 29. Chamberlain (*Letters*, II, 548–549, letter of Mar. 20, 1624) writes that "they are very suspicious, for having made large offers for the maintenance of the warre if the King wold declare himself, he is not willing to come to that point, but striking out warre, inserts for the great busines in hand, which is subject to divers interpretations." This statement undoubtedly refers to an amendment made in the declaration presented by the parliamentary deputation on March 14.

be more than millions of subsidies, and indeed it is an ample reward for that trust and freedom which I have used with you." But having the hearts of his subjects without the help of his neighbors and allies would avail nothing, "and except particular means be set down it will neither be a bridle to the adversary of that cause nor a comfort to my friends who shall join with me." For the "great business" he asked five subsidies and ten fifteenths, and for his "crying debts" he requested one subsidy and two fifteenths annually until they were paid. If these conditions were met, he was prepared to follow the advice of his Parliament. He dismissed their stipulations that supply must be levied in a parliamentary manner by leaving it to their "wise considerations." Since he had committed these revenues to treasurers appointed by the House of Commons, it was immaterial whether the money raised was "done by subsidies or otherwise. For, to me it is all one, and no hurt to the Kingdom, being done in parliament and in a parliamentary manner." He did, however, suggest that too great a levy would overburden the subject and too small an impost would not be sufficient to maintain a war.

The King was prepared to leave taxation to Parliament, but he would brook no interference with his conscience or his honor. He asserted that he had already given consideration to the moral problems involved in a declaration of war, "but if any scruples shall remain with me I will acquaint you with them, and not only seek but follow your advice."

To sugarcoat this bitter pill, the King announced his intention to summon Parliaments frequently and "to make this a session with the passing of as many good laws as in convenient time may be prepared. And at Michaelmas, or within few days after, to have a new session, and another in the spring." He also repeated his promise not to agree to any future peace treaties without the consent of Parliament.[96] The King's professed love for Parliaments scarcely seemed apparent to his auditors, for his remarks "struck a great amazement amongst those of the committee, and put them to such a silence that there was not heard so much as one 'God save the King,' who put off his hat to them and went his way." [97]

---

96. Quotations from the King's speech are taken from Harl. Ms. 159, fols. 29v–31v, and from Horne, fols. 63–63v.

97. SP 14/160/89, Dudley Carleton to Sir Dudley Carleton, Mar. 17, 1624. The

Perplexity, dismay, and frustration were conjoined in the reception given the speech by the Prince and the Duke. Charles "was so inwardly troubled as he spake not a word that night" and Buckingham "wept at it." By evening, however, they had recovered their equanimity and "at the prince's instigation Buckingham entered the king's chamber, and shut in there by the prince he kneeled before the king, asking for some milder interpretation of the reply given to Canterbury, and finally he obtained a favourable statement which he took to the parliament on Monday." [98]

Acting promptly to forestall any disruption of parliamentary proceedings, the Duke moved for a conference "with the Commons about the K[ing]s aunswere yesterday. For that there be some mistakeing, which the K[ing] hathe gyven the Pr[ince] leave to explayne." [99] Despite the fact that the archbishop of Canterbury was absent (he having again taken to his bed as a result of his humiliation by James) committees of the Lords and Commons met to agree on the report of the King's answer. It is doubtful whether the notes taken by the members of the lower House were consulted because these reporters had been reluctant to "avow their notes publicly." [100] Apparently a text of the King's speech was read by Sir John Davies, and editorial comment upon it was offered by the Prince and the Duke. Two major "misinterpretations" were corrected: that the King had disavowed Buckingham's and the Prince's relation of the Spanish business; and, that the King was not satisfied in his conscience to break the treaties and declare war.

Buckingham hastened to explain the reasons which had induced James to allow the reinterpretation of his oration. The King was

---

King's reaction is graphically (and probably erroneously) described by Maycote in a letter to Lord Zouche, "but of how small esteem soever my lines may seem yet these enclosed words must needs be of worth because they came out of a King's mouth, and yet no sooner born but they were metamorphized into meat and so (at sennight old) all eaten up again by the father, who went cursing and swearing away towards Theobalds again the last Monday, and would neither hear the Prince, nor parliament speak a word." (SP 14/160/92, Mar. 18, 1624.)

98. SP 14/160/90, Sir Robert Cotton to Thomas Cotton, Mar. 17, 1624; *Cal. S. P. Venetian*, XVIII, 255, Valaresso to the Doge and Senate, Mar. 19/29, 1624. "The reply given by the king displeases the prince and Buckingham extremely; when they heard it they turned pale and the prince never uttered a word the whole day."

99. *Lords Debates 1624 & 1626*, 33.

100. SP 14/160/81, Edward Nicholas to John Nicholas, Mar. 17 (?), 1624. In the *Cal. S. P. Dom. 1623–1625*, this letter is calendared under the probable date of March 15. Since it contains remarks made by the Prince on the seventeenth, it could not have been written before that date.

chagrined by the intention of Parliament "to draw him so suddenly and so far into an engagement and declaration of war," but had been assured by the Duke that Englishmen perceived that now was the strategic time to end Spanish dreams of world conquest. The present pope was pro-French and averse to Spanish designs in Germany and the Valtelline. Therefore, if James "would be pleased (with his confederates) to take this present occasion there would be no doubt but that he should be able to make the King of Spain well contented to sit down with his own in quiet." Moreover, Englishmen were opposed to a Spanish match, realizing that the conditions demanded by Madrid were prejudicial to the Protestant cause and contrary to the consciences and customs of the people. When the King objected that similar capitulations would be demanded by other Catholic monarchs, Buckingham had convinced him that this was impossible because the concessions to Spain had depended upon unique circumstances such as the ineffectuality of Aston and Bristol, the presence of the Prince in Spain and his affection for the Infanta, the promised dowry of £600,000, and the prospective restoration of the Palatinate. He had "propounded further to the King that his Majesty might stop the mouth of France or any other if he would but give way to his people to petition to his Majesty that out of the experience of the inconveniency arising by this treaty his Majesty would be pleased not to yield to any such conditions with any other popish princes; and for France, if they should urge such conditions, his Majesty might do the like for their subjects, the Protestants commonly called the Huguenots there, and this the King liked very well."

Finally, the Prince intimated that the King had definite knowledge that the Spanish never meant to carry out the obligations which they had assumed in the treaties, and he promised that in good time this intelligence should be made public.

Nothing certain appears to have been said at the conference about the discrepancy between the King's demand for immediate payment of his debts and the Prince's assertion on March 11 that his father was willing, for the present, to forgo consideration of his necessities. The King had, however, been perturbed by Parliament's failure to name a particular sum in their offer of assistance, but his doubts had been allayed by Charles's assertion that an

214 The Parliament of 1624

engagement of "their persons and abilities was more by far than six subsidies and twelve fifteenths, for there was no end of this proffer." [101]

By the afternoon of March 15 some agreement had been achieved in the conference about emendations to be made in the King's reply. Thereupon "the Duke moved it might be fair written and in wide lines; he would carry or send [them] to the King." [102] This was obviously a concession to the Commons' reluctance to accept corrections in a royal pronouncement without adequate security that they were authorized. The lower House also needed reassurance on two more major points: the King's willingness to annul the treaties; and, his commitment of a future revenue grant to war preparations. It seems probable that the Duke of Buckingham had already taken action designed to content the Commons and had petitioned James: "to send me your plain and resolute answer, whether, if your people do resolve to give you a royal assistance, as to the number of six subsidies and fifteenths, with a promise after, in case of necessity, to assist you with their lives and fortunes; whether then you will not accept it, and their counsel, to break the match with the other treaties; and whether or no, to bring them to this, I may not assure some of them underhand, because it is feared, that when your turns are served, you will not call them together again to reform abuses, grievances, and [for] the making of laws for the good government of the country." [103]

101. Holles, fol. 101; SP 14/160/81, Edward Nicholas to John Nicholas, see n. 100, above. It is extremely difficult to determine precisely what was said at the conference of the Lords and Commons on March 15. Report was not made of this and succeeding conferences until March 17, and consequently there is a tendency to garble the events and speeches. I have relied mainly upon SP 14/160/81, Edward Nicholas to John Nicholas ca. Mar. 17, 1624, and Harl. MS. 159, fol. 32. Direct quotations are from Nicholas, but the remarks I attribute to the Duke of Buckingham. Nicholas purports to give the statements of the Prince; Harl. MS. 159 attributes essentially the same arguments to the Duke of Buckingham, as does SP 14/160/79, the explanation of certain passages in the King's last speech of March 14, by the Prince and the Duke of Buckingham to the Committee of Both Houses on the fifteenth of the same, 1623. Those points which can be ascribed to a conference later than that held on March 15 I have deferred considering. In this I have been guided by the brief remarks in Holles, fols. 101–101v.
102. HMC, *Buccleuch and Queensberry MSS*, III, 234; compare with SP 14/160/81. Official sanction was given to the interpolations made by the Prince and Buckingham in the King's speech of March 14. These "explanations and interpretations" were incorporated by Henry Elsynge, clerk of the Parliament, into the text of the oration he transcribed on the Parliament Roll of 21 James I. (C65/186.)
103. Harl. MS. 6987, fols. 200–201, undated letter of the Duke of Buckingham to James I, printed in *Hardwicke State Papers*, I, 466–467. Gardiner, *History of*

Buckingham had counseled the King against wavering between the Spaniards and his own subjects and warned him against seeking to derive advantage from both. It was with the intention of getting James to resolve on a consistent course of action that the Duke went to court on the morning of the sixteenth, taking with him Sir George Goring as a witness to the King's pronouncements.[104] On the seventeenth he was again in his place in the Lords, having attained the object of his mission. Meanwhile, anxiety about the King's response to amendments in his speech had increased tension in Parliament to fever pitch. When the Lords requested a conference with the Commons to hear Buckingham's report, a mass exodus took place in the lower chamber, "Diverse running out to the place of conference before those of the committee." [105] When order was finally restored by the serjeant-at-arms, and the committees were properly dispatched, the Lord Keeper read the King's letter of explanation sealed with his privy signet:

First, that he was resolved both in his conscience and honor to make an instant war.

That he did desire to confer with them for the manner of that war.

That he did refuse to demand any subsidies for his debts and desired that his former demand of one subsidy and two fifteenths might be added to the great business of the war, and so to make six subsidies and twelve fifteenths.

---

*England*, V, 198, n., maintains that this letter must have been written before March 20 when the Commons offered less than six subsidies and perhaps even before the fourteenth of the month, when the King adopted the sum of six subsidies in his reply to the parliamentary offer of assistance. I think that this letter was written on March 15. I find no conclusive evidence that the specific sum of six subsidies, and twelve fifteenths totally allocated to a war effort, was mentioned before March 17. Harl. MS. 159, fols. 29v–31, gives the text of the King's speech of March 14 with the explanations by the Prince and the Duke interspersed. In reference to the demand by the King for particular aid "the Prince said that the Duke of Buckingham *in his absence* had moved this doubt to the King. Whereupon the Duke affirmed that speaking with the King about it, his Majesty was pleased to say that if we would add one subsidy and two fifteenths to make up six subsidies and twelve fifteenths for the war he was well content to quit what he asked for his own necessities." [Italics mine.] Buckingham left for court with a draft text of the King's speech on the morning of March 16. By the following morning he had returned, and the King's answer (including the figure of six subsidies and twelve fifteenths for the war) was read to a conference committee. This letter must, therefore, have been written prior to the sixteenth and after the fourteenth, when Buckingham was with the King at Whitehall.

104. D'Ewes, fol. 86; Horne, fol. 63v.
105. Holles, fol. 102.

He wished that the Commons might be spared, and that the moneys might not be levied by an ordinary parliamentary course but by some other speedy course now, and to be made parliamentary.

He declared that the Emperor had done his son [*sic*] the most wrong, and other princes were but collateral, and that the war there would be most comfortable for religion, and the confederates, and most honorable for him.

That he would have one session at Easter, another at Michaelmas, and another at the spring.

He justified that the Lord of Canterbury did mistake his meaning, and did add to his speech without any just cause of such construction, and therefore he saw no cause as yet to make the Spaniard the capital enemy.[106]

In addition, both Buckingham and the Prince asserted that the King was satisfied in conscience and honor that he might undertake a war, and Charles further promised that if "you will grant the King's desire I will engage myself that he will follow your advice and declare himself so to you." [107]

Now that all interpretations were reconciled, expedition again became the order of the day, and the Solicitor immediately reported the King's speech in the lower House. As before, it was read, and members of the House were allowed to take copies. Again this significant procedural innovation was employed to prevent the wide latitude of interpretations that would result from an oral report. Discussion was postponed until the following Friday in order to enable members to familiarize themselves with the King's concessions and demands. So intent were the Commons upon achieving their objectives that Sir Robert Phelips proposed a motion "that no Man may depart the Town, without special Leave of the House, till this Business be ended." [108]

Debate on a particular motion for supply, which occupied the Commons on March 19 and 20, was the climax of the session. The issues were drawn, the moment of decision had arrived, and the participants were "so warie and cautious on all sides as yf they were to treat with ennemies." [109] Every conceivable device had

---

106. Earle, fol. 89–89v.
107. Harl. MS. 159, fol. 32; *CJ*, 738.
108. *CJ*, 738.
109. Chamberlain, *Letters*, II, 548, letter of March 20, 1624.

been utilized to allay the fears of the Commons, even to the point of intimating that a petition requesting restrictions on the religious activities of a future royal consort would be favorably entertained. However meticulously the groundwork had been laid, the House of Commons remained virtually untrammeled in their discussion of a money grant. In the final analysis the Prince and the Duke were relegated to the role of spectators while the debate was in progress, and the poverty of a policy which sought to manage Parliament from a focus of power in the House of Lords was all too apparent. The tremendous prestige of the Prince of Wales could only be exerted by delegates and "undertakers" whose allegiances were influenced by the temper of the audience, the demands of the King, and the dictates of individual conscience. As Charles was to realize in the future, there was a real danger that his champions in the lower chamber would sacrifice the prerogatives of the crown in order to facilitate the immediate fruition of his aggressive designs.

Sir Benjamin Rudyard, Surveyor of the Court of Wards, again acted as spokesman for the crown. In many respects his address was a masterpiece of compliments, vagueness, and ambiguity. He assured the House that the explanations of the King's last speech were a sufficient basis for further action, but admitted that the King's monetary demands were excessive. He urged that the entire sum should be "presently declared (to give a countenance and a lustre to the action)," but maintained, paradoxically, "that we may so limit it in time, and qualify it in payment, that it shall be no greater burden to the subject than if it were not granted till our next session after Michaelmas or the other in the spring." Nevertheless, he asserted that the security of Ireland required four thousand troops; assistance to the Low Countries demanded ten or twelve thousand men; naval preparations necessitated the equipping of ten royal ships and twenty merchantmen; and the forts needed repairing and provisioning. Unless all this were done, he warned, "we may be overrun before Michaelmas."

The discrepancy between the immediate need for military preparations and the lengthy delay in levying revenues may be explained by Rudyard's attempt to serve two masters: to implement promptly the warlike aims of the Prince and the Duke and yet calm the fears of those members who were convinced of the poverty

218 The Parliament of 1624

of the country and the economic disaster that war would entail. This contradiction Rudyard sought to resolve by insisting that the Commons make a present declaration acceding to the King's entire demands. This, he emphasized, was "a point of extraordinary consequence." What he implied was that a parliamentary engagement to the extent of six subsidies and twelve fifteenths would allow the King to anticipate future revenue and provide royal creditors with adequate security for their loans. That such an engagement might jeopardize future conventions of Parliament Rudyard did not choose to acknowledge, perhaps because he distinguished between a declaration of particular aid and specific subsidy bills. Nor did he presume to suggest a specific sum for enactment during this session, preferring instead to advocate "such a round offer as may be worthy" the King's declaration.[110]

It could not be denied that the Commons were astonished at the magnitude of the King's demands, which Sir Edward Coke estimated to total £900,000.[111] They were certainly not prepared to enact a subsidy bill that would grant the entire sum, and they awaited some motion from a privy councillor or a courtier that would provide an index of immediate requirements. In this vital debate the same "general division of the House into speakers and hearers" prevailed and in each of these categories there were subdivisions representing diverse opinions.[112] Approximately 40 of the 481 members participated in the debate, and of these a significantly large proportion were privy councillors or royal officials closely dependent upon the court.[113]

110. The copy of Rudyard's speech I have used is in Earle, fols. 92–94. It is also in Pym, fols. 32–33v. The speech is printed in Rudyard's *Memoirs*, 83–86, with variations that tend to obscure Rudyard's meaning.

111. *CJ*, 743; Spring, 136–137; Earle, fol. 97. Sir Edward Coke estimated each subsidy at seventy thousand pounds, each fifteenth at thirty thousand pounds and each clerical subsidy at twenty thousand pounds. He apparently assumed that the total grant to the King would include six subsidies and twelve fifteenths from the Commons, plus six clerical subsidies from the convocation.

112. SP 14/161/30, Sir Edward Conway, Jr., to Sir Dudley Carleton, Mar. 23, 1624.

113. The privy councillors who spoke on March 19 were Sir Thomas Edmondes, Treasurer of the Household; Sir Richard Weston, Chancellor of the Exchequer; Sir Edward Conway, Secretary of State. Important royal officials who spoke on the same day were: Sir Benjamin Rudyard, Surveyor of the Court of Wards; Sir Robert Mansell, vice admiral of England; Sir Henry Mildmay, Master of the Jewel House; Sir John Walter, the Prince's solicitor; Sir Henry Vane, cofferer of the Prince's household; Sir Edward Wardour, Clerk of the Pells; and Sir Robert Heath, Solicitor General. On March 20 Sir Thomas Edmondes spoke again together with another privy councillor, Sir George Calvert, Secretary of State. Among the royal

Essentially it devolved upon the privy councillors to promote and elaborate the propositions put forward by Rudyard: to secure passage of a resolution or order engaging the Commons to supply the entire six subsidies and twelve fifteenths subject to the limitations conceded by the King, and, on the basis of this stipulation, to proceed to the enactment of a subsidy bill sufficient to defray military expenditures anticipated before Michaelmas, 1624. Chancellor of the Exchequer Weston, Secretary Conway, Comptroller of the Prince's Household Vane, and Solicitor General Heath all ardently advocated this procedure.[114] It was, however, a course of action fraught with peril. Constitutionally it implied that future Parliaments, or at least future sessions, could be bound by the decision of this present convention. Moreover, the mere size of the levy was without precedent and exceeded anything that had been granted during the Elizabethan war with Spain. Finally, such a resolution included no guarantees that the money would be expended in accordance with parliamentary wishes.

A more moderate proposal was championed by another privy councillor, Sir Thomas Edmondes, Treasurer of the Household. It was his desire that Parliament should levy a sum estimated to be sufficient for immediate needs (he suggested three subsidies or £300,000) and engage itself by a general resolution to provide future supply as occasion warranted. This proposal had the merit of being in accordance with past precedents, guaranteeing future summons of Parliament, leaving the crown's direction of foreign policy intact, and providing the House of Commons with a manageable estimate of tax requirements.[115]

A third solution to the problem of supply was suggested by Sir John Savile of Yorkshire and represented an alternative to schemes

---

officials who spoke were: Sir John Coke, commissioner of the navy and Master of Requests; Nathaniel Tomkins, clerk of the Prince's council; Sir Henry Mildmay and Sir Robert Heath. On both occasions when he spoke, Sir Henry Mildmay saw fit to assure the House that "he speaks not as a courtier or in regard of dependency but as a lover of his country." (Spring, 133, 143.) Most diarists give detailed attention to the speeches of Rudyard, Edmondes, Weston, Conway, Mansell, Mildmay, Walter, Vane, Calvert, Heath, and J. Coke. It must be noted also that powerful support was given to the efforts of the court spokesmen by such members as John Glanville, Sir Heneage Finch, John Pym, and Christopher Brooke.

114. CJ, 740–743; Spring, 123–139; Nicholas, fols. 89–95v; Earle, fols. 95–98; Holles, fols. 103–108; Pym, fols. 33v–34v.

115. CJ, 740; Spring, 124–125; Nicholas, fol. 90v; Earle, fol. 94v; Holles, fol. 103v.

supported by the court. For Savile, all difficulties could be surmounted by proper procedure; he advised the Commons to "handle first the thing to be done and the necessity of it, the charge it will ask, and the means to raise that charge." [116] Behind Savile's banner ranged those "who wished this order for the better perfecting and establishing of our councils; and perchance there wanted not [those] who in this variety affected delay, or an opportunity of crossing that in some privative or subordinate question which they would not oppose in the main." [117]

The enthusiast, the bellicose, the penurious, the suspicious, the conservative, the patriot, the Puritan, and perhaps even the pacifist seconded Savile's motion for reasons peculiar to themselves. Ostensibly it gave precision and direction to a debate that had been floundering in a sea of generalities; it required only that the work be known so that the charge could be levied. The attractive simplicity of this suggestion did, however, conceal a major constitutional innovation because the determination of military objectives and campaigns was beyond the province of the House of Commons. It could be pretended that this royal prerogative had been relinquished to Parliament. Indeed, Rudyard's speech had opened the door to such an interpretation by citing four specific purposes for which taxation was to be levied. Consequently, the Commons found no difficulty in exceeding these limitations in the heat of a discussion about war.

From considerations of defense they transferred their attention to projects of offense. "Let us remember," said Sir John Eliot, "that the war with Spain is our Indies, that there we shall fetch wealth and happiness." [118] That Spain was the enemy, none chose to deny although they were well aware that the King preferred a campaign on the Continent. As Sir Francis Seymour put it: "War is spoken of and an army, but where and against whom is fit to be known. If in the Palatinate (as the King seems to imply) the charge is too great and it hath been far from our thoughts. But we must

116. Spring, 125; *CJ*, 741; Nicholas, fol. 91; Earle, fol. 94v; Holles, fol. 104.
117. Pym, fol. 33v. Pym lists Edward Alford, Sir Arthur Ingram, and Mr. Mallory among those who seconded Savile's motion. Of these three I believe Sir Arthur Ingram was the most likely to have opposed war because of his affiliation with the Lord Treasurer and his life office as Comptroller of the Customs of the Port of London.
118. Spring, 124; *CJ*, 740; Earle, fol. 94; Holles, fol. 103v.

leave that to the King." [119] Yet not all parliament men were content to abdicate direction of the war. So eminent an authority as Sir Edward Coke said, "if the King will make a war and require no aid he may do it where he will, but if he demand aid he must be advised." Coke's aims were unmistakable; he hoped "to live till he see the King of Spain lose his Indies." [120] And his sentiments were echoed by William Neale who stated that, if the Palatinate were not surrendered soon, the Spanish fleet would be swept from the seas.[121]

Thus, every parliamentarian with his own concept of strategy eagerly espoused Savile's method of procedure, and it was not until the following day that the tide of opinion was turned against those who advocated direction of a war. Only then did the "inconveniencies" involved in public deliberation of military action nullify the desires of the Commons to name the enemy and plan the attack.

As was to be expected, privy councillors had tried to avoid any incursions into the royal prerogative, but the success of their efforts was guaranteed by the speeches of those who distinguished sharply between Parliament's role in financing a war and the power of the executive to direct it. The caveats and doubts introduced by members like Christopher Brooke, Sir Thomas Posthumus Hoby, Sir George Chudleigh, Sir Thomas Jermyn, and Sir Heneage Finch were answered by an ameliorative explanation offered by John Coke, commissioner of the navy. "That the work, which is the first thing considerable, is not to be understood where the war shall be or what it shall be. This must proceed from the King. But he thinks the King in his speech looks farther. He propounds the breach of the treaties, forsees a war will follow, and to provide for that is the work, as appears by the particulars propounded by the King, whereof the three first have no dependency with the war of the Palatinate, and the last but a little. But the general aim and the necessity is apparent to be a war with Spain." [122] Thus, with a quasi assurance that war with Spain was intended, the Commons abandoned their strategic overtures. As

119. Spring, 128; *CJ*, 741; Nicholas, fol. 91v; Earle, fol. 95v; Holles, fols. 104v–105; Pym, fol. 34.
120. Spring, 144–145; Nicholas, fol. 97v; Earle, fol. 99v; Holles, fol. 109.
121. Spring, 147; Nicholas, fol. 101.
122. Spring, 141; Nicholas, fol. 96v; Earle fol. 99; Pym, fol. 35.

Sir Edwin Sandys summed it up, "The King hath designed the particulars of this year's work, not in what place we must have war and where to fight, but to relieve the Low Countries, to strengthen our state and friends, and this is not particularly to determine a war but to be prepared for it." [123]

Along with the allure of the constitutional innovations implied in Savile's motion was the charm of its consonance with past precedent. It dealt with concrete figures, not in terms of binding future sessions but in terms of an actual subsidy bill presently to be enacted. It mentioned no vague assurances of future support. Consequently, its very familiarity encouraged members to name specific sums they would be willing to give contingent upon the performance of definite conditions. Again it seemed as if royal warrant, as well as past precedent, had licensed the Commons to designate limitations, for James himself had introduced considerations of time and quantity into the levy of taxation. It was, indeed, understood that subsidies would not be exacted unless the treaties were annulled. It was further agreed that all moneys were to be collected and expended by parliamentary commissioners. However, these concessions promised by the King and the Prince by no means satisfied the appetites of all members of Parliament.

Generally speaking, members of the landed gentry were opposed to large numbers of subsidies, realizing, as they did, that the greatest burden of taxation would fall upon their estates. Sir Francis Seymour was willing to contribute only one subsidy and two fifteenths, and many of his compatriots thought that two subsidies and four fifteenths were quite sufficient.[124] When John Glanville, the recorder of Plymouth, moved the passage of an act for four subsidies and eight fifteenths, he was squelched by Sir Thomas Belasyse, who reminded him that "Subsidies come not in so easily as Fees." Again, when Sir Henry Vane wanted an order of the House authorizing the collection of the King's entire demand, he was answered by Mr. Alford, who asserted that he had

123. Spring, 144; Earle, fol. 99.
124. Spring, 128; Nicholas, fol. 91v; Earle, fol. 95v; Holles, fols. 104v–105; Pym, fols 34, 35v. The *CJ*, 741, states that Seymour proposed two subsidies and two fifteenths, but all of the diaries (except Spring) give the figure as one subsidy and two fifteenths. Sir Christopher Hilliard and Sir Thomas Belasyse suggested two subsidies; Sir George More, Sir George Chaworth and William Mallory all supported a levy of two subsidies and four fifteenths. Pym, fol. 35v, gives two subsidies and two fifteenths as Mallory's suggestion.

never heard of the like procedure. All motions to expedite proceedings and to arrive at a determinate sum tended to excite resistance. Without adequate deliberation, as Sir Charles Morrison
averred, "The Country will say, 'We and our Money soon
parted.' " [125]

Generally speaking, the conditions parlimentarians wished to
attach to the grant of supply fell into three categories: those contingent upon special circumstances associated with the reversal of
foreign policy; those which dealt with particular considerations
influencing assessment; and those which followed the traditional
pattern of redress of grievances before supply. Sir James Perrot's
motion for an accompanying petition to the King to annul all
foreign treaties prejudicial to religion, Sir John Savile's proposal
that funds be earmarked for the four defensive purposes stipulated
by the King, William Mallory's demand that Parliament's advice
to James be incorporated into the subsidy book, Sir Henry Vane's
motion that taxation should terminate with the cessation of hostilities, and Sir Robert Phelips's proposal that a declaration of war
precede the collection of revenue — all of these reflected the historical situation that had engendered them.

Sir Francis Seymour's demand for the double assessment of
papists, Sir Edward Coke's relinquishments of fifteenths, Sir Henry
Poole's desire to secure the aid of the Scots, the moneyed men, and
the papists, Sir Dudley Digges' request that the Cinque Ports be
charged, and Sir George Chudleigh's exemption of the poorer sort
from severe levies — all of these related to the incidence of taxation.[126]

Desire for redress of grievances generated a universal craving
for what John Glanville termed a Parliament of "laws and subsidies." William Mallory fulminated: "if I were not in expectation
to meet here again I would not give a farthing." [127] Nathaniel
Tomkins opened the flood gates for specific requests when he
asked for the passage of bills of grace, the concession of a liberal
general pardon, and the redress of grievances, especially that concerning concealed titles. This provided the signal for Sir John

125. *CJ*, 742–743; Spring, 135, 136; Holles, fols. 106v, 107v; Nicholas, fols. 94,
95v; Earle, fol. 96v.
126. *CJ*, 740–744; Spring, 123–151; Nicholas, fols. 90–104; Earle, fols. 92–100;
Holles, fols. 103–110v; Pym, fols. 32v–36.
127. Earle, fol. 95v; Nicholas, fol. 93; Holles, fol. 105v; Spring, 130; *CJ*, 741.

Savile to demand an end to pretermitted customs and for Sir Edward Coke to suggest a petition soliciting the passage of the bills concerning informers, process of supersedeas, and writs of certiorari. However, these premature motions were circumvented by Sir William Herbert's reminder that the subsidies were not designed to relieve the King's necessities, and so he could scarcely be expected to make concessions to his subjects. Moreover, John Glanville pointed out that to complain of two or three grievances now would effectually vitiate a subsequent petition against abuses.[128]

The Commons' exploration of the ramifications of the problem of supply ultimately led them to reject unorthodox methods of procedure. Unwilling to supervise the war and no less unwilling to commit themselves to a specific engagement for six subsidies and twelve fifteenths, they adopted Edmondes's moderate solution which coupled an immediate specific grant with a general promise of future support. The success of this proposal was guaranteed by the nearly unanimous desire of the Commons to secure a breach with Spain. Only one member, Sir George Chaworth, disclaimed any concern for foreign affairs and his "most Catholic and apostolic Roman speech" excited a spate of verbal pyrotechnics and ultimately occasioned his expulsion from the House.[129]

128. Spring, 147–150.
129. SP 14/161/30, Sir Edward Conway, Jr., to Sir Dudley Carleton, Mar. 23, 1624. Dudley Carleton wrote to Sir Dudley Carleton on March 28, "they have picked a hole in Sir George Chaworth's election and expelled him the House, no man pitying him because of a foolish and preposterous speech or two made by him against the whole stream of the House in the point of breaking the treaties and entrance into war." (SP 14/161/49.) Sir Francis Nethersole contemptuously referred to Sir George Chaworth as *stilus veteranus* and likewise implied that he might have held his seat in the House by possession "had he not lost the good will of his judges." (SP 14/161/36, Sir Francis Nethersole to Sir Dudley Carleton, Mar. 25, 1624.) In his apologetic narrative Chaworth stated: "Daily did I attend in court and Parliament, and was told by all that I was bound to the King, who had sworn to them that had [he] been in the House of Parliament he would have spoken just my words. But all were not of his good mind; for when they could do me no harm with him, they irritated an old challenge against me, of my mis-election in the town for which I served (which was Arundel), and after I had sat in the House 6 weeks an old challenge was revived to that place, and though I had 16 witnesses to clear and justify my election, yet the committee entered to the hearing the cause, but just at sunset, and being then darkish (before Easter), they made it such a work, and in one quarter of an hour, without so much as hearing one witness for me, or more than one witness against me, they sentenced my election void; nay, they, to make sure I should not be in, allowed another's election to be good in my room, and did not order a new writ for a new election, as is just and usual, so powerful was the very humor of the Duke in that House at that time." Loseley MS. 1327/9,

Actually, nothing in Chaworth's address smacked of Catholicism, but his reluctance to see the peace broken, his contemptuous disregard of the Low Countries, and his abandonment of the Commons' pretensions to administer a money grant were so contrary to the general tenor of opinion as to appear reactionary and Romanist.[130] Paradoxically, Chaworth's pacific remarks may have expedited deliberations in the Commons because the reception accorded his speech made it quite clear that halfway measures

---

Guildford Museum and Muniment Room, Guildford, Surrey, fols. 52–52v; see also A. J. Kempe, *The Loseley Manuscripts* (London, 1835), 481–482.

130. The full text of Chaworth's speech is incorporated into his apologetic narrative. (Loseley MS. 1327/9, fols. 50–51v; see also *CJ*, 742; Spring, 132; Nicholas, fol. 93; Earle, fol. 95; Pym, fols. 34–34v; Holles, fol. 105v; Chamberlain, *Letters*, II, 550, letter of Mar. 20, 1624. The speech was at least partially motivated by Chaworth's disappointment at not being awarded an English peerage subsequent to his return from his embassy to Brussels in 1621. During 1622 and 1623 Chaworth repeatedly solicited a viscountcy of England and procured the intercession of the Archduchess Isabella and the Spanish ambassadors on his behalf. Immediately after the return of Buckingham from Spain, Chaworth requested the Duke's assistance and at Hinchingbrooke received a promise of support. When Buckingham failed to honor his promise, Chaworth was advised by the Spanish ambassadors and Secretary Calvert to bring matters to an issue. The method he used was his speech of March 19, which so incensed Charles, Buckingham, and Carlisle "that they labored my commitment or command from court." During the Easter recess, while he was attending the King, Chaworth was attacked by Buckingham because of his remarks in Parliament, but James admonished the Duke, "By the wounds, you are in the wrong! for he spake my soul; therefore speak no more of this matter I charge you." (Loseley MS. 1327/9, fols. 42, 42v, 47v, 51v–53.) SP 14/160/69, is a manuscript copy of two speeches erroneously attributed to Sir George Chaworth and given the tentative date March 12, 1624. As far as I can determine from my search of the *Commons Journal* and the manuscript diaries of the Parliament, Sir George Chaworth did not participate in the debate on a motion for general assistance which occurred on *March 11*. The only possible way of assigning a date to this state paper is by a singular reference to the Lord Treasurer's report regarding the King's indebtedness. There is, however, an ambiguous sentence in the speech advocating war which implies that a motion for general assistance had already been passed: "witness the free offers for money which this High Court of Parliament hath made to our King for the maintenance of war." In any event, both speeches could not have been delivered by the same man because they contradict each other on the advisability and strategic advantages of war. Neither speech mentions a specific grant of supply, but that advocating peace states "that if it shall by a general assent be thought behoovfall for our King and Commonwealth to enter into a preparation of war, first to provide that our King's Majesty's debts may be so well discharged that his revenues and customs may come clear to his own coffers; then to cast up by account what moneys the charges of war will yearly require, and lastly to provide that present money may always be in a readiness to defray all expenses that war shall exact." I have reluctantly concluded that neither of these speeches were delivered on the floor of the Commons in 1624. I have compared the manuscript with the text and reports of all speeches that can be authenticated and have been unable to ascribe them to any member of the House of Commons.

would not be tolerated. Mr. Wentworth, the recorder of Oxford, who rebutted Chaworth, identified war with Spain with the safety of religion and asserted that any sacrifice was justified. "He would have men free in giving though for his part he hath more children than acres," and would be content to eat from wooden spoons and drink from earthern vessels "so that God who is our strength, his honor may be maintained and the Kingdom righted." Sir John Walter, the Prince's solicitor, also repeated the refrain of austerity and sacrifice: "let our pride of clothes be abated, our great portions to our children, our back and belly lose rather than suffer so just occasions to want assistance . . . Regard not then vanity or pride but God and religion etc." [131]

However much religious passion stimulated the willingness of the Commons to contribute, however much mercantile competition with Spain excited "western men" to advocate war, it remained the province of the recognized leaders of the House to define the terms of the subsidy grant. Although £300,000 as a manageable figure had been suggested before Solicitor Heath rose to speak, it was he who constructed a formula for contribution asceptable to the majority. The £300,000 he digested into three subsidies and three fifteenths, two-thirds of which should be collected about May and the remainder about Michaelmas in time for the opening of the second session of Parliament. He successfully blocked the move to accord the recusants the "honor" of paying double and urged that, despite the poverty of the country, fifteenths should not be omitted lest this form of revenue be lost to the King through disuse.[132]

It took some time for the tenets of Heath's remarks to win general agreement, but when his basic propositions were revived by Sir Heneage Finch at the Committee of the Whole on March 20, they were adopted by a veritable chorus of speakers. Consequently, when the sum of three subsidies and three fifteenths was

131. Spring, 132–134; Nicholas, fols. 93–93v; Earle, fol. 96; Holles, fols. 105v–106; Pym, fol. 34v; *CJ*, 742.

132. Spring, 137–138; *CJ*, 743; Nicholas, fols. 94v–95; Earle, fol. 97v; Holles, fols. 107–107v; Pym, fol. 34v. SP 14/161/8 (which is calendared under the probable date March 20, 1624, as an abstract by Solicitor General Heath of the transactions between the King and Parliament relating to the breach of the treaties, and the demand and grant of subsidies) should be identified as notes prepared for the speech which Heath delivered on March 19. Obviously Heath made minor emendations in his remarks due to the exigencies of the debate.

put to the question, it was passed *nemine contradicente,* subject to the conditions that it be levied within one year after formal declaration to dissolve the treaties, that it be dedicated to the support of an impending war and the defensive projects outlined by the King, and that it be paid into the hands of parliamentary committees or commissioners appointed during the present session.

The apparent unanimity of the Commons in their grant did not imply contentment with the results of their labors. Sir Francis Nethersole reported to Sir Dudley Carleton that, on the evening of March 20, he had met only one man who was confident that the offer of the Commons would satisfy the King.[133] Even among the members appointed to draft a declaration acceptable to James there were those who had grave reservations about the value of their efforts. Sir John Savile was still disgruntled: "He had formerly wished that they might make the King a good sword. Now it is said the King only best knows how to use his sword. But for the money, he mislikes not the sum; he only thinks that we reckon without our host and it will be too little etc. The King hath heretofore said that we are the mirror through which the subjects may see him, but surely we are the mirror through which he may see his subjects. To say to the people that our own stewards or committees shall have the money and see it expended, that is no security nor satisfaction to them, only the satisfaction will be in the right ordering and employment of the money." [134] Mr. Alford echoed Savile's doubts about the role of parliamentary treasurers, and, in typical fashion, engineered the appointment of Sir Robert Cotton and John Selden to search precedents to determine whether the treasurers were to be nominated solely by the Commons and whether peers so named were liable to account in the lower House.[135] Inquiries were also undertaken to determine how former English kings had dissolved diplomatic relations and annulled treaties with foreign powers.

133. SP 14/161/36, Sir Francis Nethersole to Sir Dudley Carleton, Mar. 25, 1624.
134. Spring, 148; Nicholas, fol. 101v; Holles, fol. 110. Savile agreed with an earlier speech of Phelips in which he announced his apprehensions regarding the promised security: "That the money shall touch none of those honorable fingers who dispose of the King's revenue. By nature he was no doubtful man, yet that particular, though it somewhat moved him, did not captivate him. He had observed in story the fruit of such grace to be rendered nothing worth." (Pym, fol. 35v.)
135. *CJ,* 744; Pym, fol. 36.

On Sunday the committee appointed for that purpose hammered out the draft of a declaration of the Commons' willingness to contribute three subsidies and three fifteenths in support of a war likely to ensue upon announcement of the breach of the treaties with Spain. Apparently upon its own authority the committee incorporated into the declaration an assurance to His Majesty "that if he were engaged in a real war we would assist him, and humbly desire him to rest confidently assured of it." [136] To this liberty taken by the committee the House had no objection, but serious doubts were entertained as to whether the King's verbal declaration that the treaties were no longer in force was sufficiently binding. Christopher Brooke called for a public declaration "or manifest to the world," while others desired a proclamation or some such instrument passed under the Great Seal. Still other members suspected that the King would temporarily discharge the treaties in order to secure the promised subsidies and presently resume them upon "new hopes." To avoid this, they requested the addition of the word "final" in the text of the instrument, but the phrase "public declaration for the utter dissolution and discharge of the two treaties" was judged equally conclusive and more acceptable since it implied no preclusion of future negotiations for the restoration of the Palatinate.[137]

When these amendments had been made in the declaration, it was submitted to the Lords for their approval. Most of the more than twenty Catholic peers entitled to sit in the upper chamber appear to have absented themselves from the Parliament of 1624, and, on this particular occasion, only the Earl of Rutland remained in his place to vote "not content" when the Commons' declaration was put to the question. Despite the importunity of the Prince and Buckingham, and "belike upon some promise made to his confessor," Rutland remained adamant in his opposition, and, consequently, the Lord's concurrence to the offer was indicated by the words with "a full and cherefull consent." [138]

136. D'Ewes, fol. 95v.
137. SP 14/161/36, Sir Francis Nethersole to Sir Dudley Carleton, Mar. 25, 1624; Holles, fol. 111v. SP 14/161/19, declaration by Parliament to the King, Mar. 23, 1624.
138. SP 14/161/36, Sir Francis Nethersole to Sir Dudley Carleton, Mar. 25, 1624; *Lords Debates 1624 & 1626*, 39; SP 14/161/18, Nicholas's notes of proceedings of the Lords and Commons preceding the joint declaration of the Parliament to the King, March 23; see also SP 14/161/30, Sir Edward Conway, Jr., to Sir Dudley Carleton,

Once agreement had been reached with the Commons, the pace of events accelerated. Since the King was about to depart from Westminster, Buckingham moved that the Parliament remain in session during the afternoon of March 22. He was provided with a fair copy of the declaration and empowered to solicit an audience. Immediately after the noon recess the Duke returned with the news that James had agreed to receive a delegation of twenty-four Lords and forty-eight Commons on the following morning. He also revealed that he had exceeded the limits of his commission by showing "his Majesty the draft to make sure that he might be satisfied with it, for which transgression of order he craved pardon, his intention being good."

Ostensibly the Duke desired to avoid a repetition of the embarrassment heaped upon the archbishop of Canterbury at their last access, but, by the Lords and Commons alike, Buckingham's overtures were interpreted as an indication of the reception likely to be accorded their offer. Surprisingly enough, James had not quibbled at the size of the grant or the conditions under which it had been offered, but had taken exception instead to the defense of the "true religion of almighty God" as a pretext for war. This he believed had been unadvisedly included "in respect of the help he hopeth to have from diverse Catholic princes in this war to be undertaken for the liberty of Christendom, which notwithstanding he doubteth not but his enemies will endeavor to draw to be esteemed a war of religion, and therefore he would be careful to give them no color of ground for it." The King had also observed the omission of particular care for his own estate in the offer of subsidies, but the Duke assured him that "in due time we would take it into consideration" and with this answer James was temporarily contented. With alacrity both Lords and Commons agreed to expunge religion from the motives for war, but their silence about particular assistance in relieving the King's debts portended ill for the royal exchequer.[139]

A last-minute postponement kept the parliamentary delegation assembled to attend the King waiting until the afternoon of the

---

Mar. 23, who is in error about the reasons for Rutland's opposition to the grant of particular aid.

139. SP 14/161/36, Sir Francis Nethersole to Sir Dudley Carleton, Mar. 25, 1624; *Lords Debates 1624 & 1626*, 40; *CJ*, 746.

twenty-third. Perhaps the plea of ill health by which James deferred the audience was genuine, but undoubtedly he was still hoping that the Spanish ambassadors would appear with concessions on the German question that would avert the necessity for war. The expected arrival of Padre Maestro from Madrid afforded the King some grounds for new hopes, but time was against him. The silence of the Spanish envoys, the importunities of the Prince and Buckingham, and the chauvinism of Parliament relentlessly forced James toward his moment of decision.

The answer he returned to the Parliament's offer of three subsidies and three fifteenths was replete with self-justification and reflected the attitude of a dejected and dispirited man. Its overtones were pessimistic, but it was not without perceptive passages and categorical imperatives. Although he thankfully accepted the parliamentary offer, James warned his subjects that it was only "sufficient for the present entrance into the business, though a great deal short of what I told you it would require." When considered in conjunction with a general offer of future assistance, however, James asserted that this particular levy was adequate for present purposes and warranted his declaration. "I declare unto you," he said, "as I am willing to follow your advice in the annulling and breaking of these two treaties, both of the match and the Palatinate, so, on the other part, I assure myself that you will make good what you have spoken, and that in what you advise me unto you will assist me with your wisdom, moneys and forces, if need require."

The strong implication that the King was undertaking a contractual obligation to initiate war was reinforced by his explanation of his previous hesitancy, and by his reiterations of unequivocal commitment to the vigorous prosecution of future hostilities. He made it quite clear that performance would not be lacking on his part so long as the Commons lived up to their obligation to provide financial support.

Thus far James's answer must have contented the committee exceedingly, but, when he discussed the theater of operations, his views diverged from those of many of his auditors. He restated his conviction that the recovery of the Palatinate, one way or the other, was his primary objective. "Further, this I dare say, as old as I am, if it might do good in the business I would go in mine own person and think my labor and travel well bestowed, though with my labor I should lose my life. Think me, then, unworthy to reign over you if I shall spare any means possible for the getting of it." Again he said, "I am old but my only son is young, and I will promise for myself and for him both, that no means shall lose use that may recover it." He protested his good faith regarding the commitments he had made concerning the parliamentary collection and expenditure of subsidies, even to the point of calling for the notes of his last speech so that no doubts could remain about what had been conceded. He made it crystal clear, however, that he would brook no parliamentary interference in the prosecution of the war: "Yet I desire you to think that I must have a faithful and secret council of war, and which must not be ordered by a multitude, for so my designs may be discovered beforehand and I shall purpose nothing that the enemy will not know as well as I. Whether, therefore, I shall send 2,000 or 10,000, whether by sea or by land, north or south, by diversion or otherwise by invading the Bavarian or the Emperor, that must be in the council of mine own heart, and that you must leave to the King. But every penny bestowed shall be in the sight of your own committees; their hands only shall be in the bag; yet how much shall go out, or how little, must be in the power of the King, whose war it is, whose stewards they are."

At the same time James could not resist calling attention to his own necessities. Since, as a result of military action, his charges would increase and his customs revenues diminish, he expected that the next session of Parliament would honor Buckingham's promise of monetary support. Again the emphasis upon contract was unmistakable: "I have broken the neck of three parliaments together, but I hope to deserve so well of you, and you of me, that this will prove a happy parliament." In conclusion James invoked the blessings of God upon their martial endeavors and dubiously expressed his hopes that war would prove successful in securing the restoration of the Palatinate and vindicating his own reputation.[140]

140. Horne, fols. 64–65. I have used Horne's text of the King's speech because his version is more vigorous than that contained in other manuscripts or printed copies which I have consulted. In my opinion there are no significant differences in meaning apparent in the variant copies, but on two points the emphasis in Horne's text is more precise: the King's insistence that future Parliaments would

The King's oral declaration of the annulment of the treaties so delighted his audience that it obscured for a moment the full implications of his speech. The archbishop of Canterbury immediately requested allowance for popular demonstrations of joy, but these were not officially permitted because James "thought it not fit in regard the war was not yet begun and so what the success might be not known, and to rejoice before a victory were presumptous before it and contemptible without it." [141]

It was more difficult for the King to prevent unofficial notification of the breach of treaties to the diplomatic corps. Within hours the news had reached the Venetian and French ambassadors, and messengers had been dispatched to Sir Dudley Carleton at the Hague and Lord Kensington at Paris.[142] Nor were the Spanish ambassadors kept in ignorance although, for the time being, no official communication was sent to them. On the evening of the

---

assist him with money as well as with their wisdom, counsel and forces; and James's categorical retention of the spending power over the grant of three subsidies and three fifteenths. James was apparently quite pleased at the reception accorded his speech. He told the Lord President (Mandeville) on the evening of March 24 that "he thought never any speech of his had been so well taken." (SP 14/161/36, Sir Francis Nethersole to Sir Dudley Carleton, Mar. 25, 1624.) On March 23, Richard Yonge, member of Parliament for Dover, wrote to Lord Zouche: "My Lord, this afternoon the King did bravely declare himself to both Houses of Parliament that he would dissolve both treaties for the marriage and for the restoring of the Palatinate and sent us all cheerfully away." (SP 14/161/32.) A later reaction was chronicled by Ferdinando Fairfax, member for Boroughbridge, Yorkshire, who wrote to his father, Sir Thomas Fairfax, on March 27: "The King's declaration on Tuesday last, in the afternoon, was very full and satisfactory to our desires; but, being of that consequence, it was thought fit the committees of both Houses should confer their notes, and make it perfect, which, being afterwards presented to the King, they were a little mistaken; and, thus amended, our hopes grew cooler as it was read." G. W. Johnson, ed., *The Fairfax Correspondence* (2 vols., London, 1848), I, lvi–lvii.

141. Harl. MS. 159, fol. 34v; SP 14/161/36, Sir Francis Nethersole to Sir Dudley Carleton, Mar. 25, 1624.

142. *Cal. S. P. Venetian*, XVIII, 260–261, Valaresso to the Doge and Senate, Mar. 24/Apr. 3, 1624; SP 14/161/36, Sir Francis Nethersole to Sir Dudley Carleton, Mar. 25, 1624. There are two undated State Papers, 14/162/52 and 53, which are minutes of advice from Sir Edward Conway to the Duke of Buckingham concerning dispatches to be sent abroad about the King's declaration of the breach of the treaties. Both of these documents must have been prepared during the recess of Parliament. SP 14/162/52 has particular reference to the dispatch for Madrid, which had been completed by March 31. (See SP 14/161/61, Sir Francis Nethersole to Sir Dudley Carleton, March 31, 1624.) SP 14/162/53 deals specifically with a dispatch to France and with military preparations to be undertaken immediately. It mentions the dispatch of a commission to be sent to Paris, ostensibly to authorize Kensington and Carlisle to treat of a marriage. Such a commission was sent to Theobalds for the King's signature on March 31.

twenty-third, amidst bonfires and bell ringing, fireworks and artillery salvos, the London mobs pelted the Spanish embassy with stones and insults, causing Inojosa to complain to the King against the impudence occasioned by "hatred and heresy." [143]

Once their elation over the dissolution of the treaties had subsided, members of Parliament began to have second thoughts about the King's speech. They had anticipated, and even emphatically assumed, that the end of negotiations would bring immediate war with Spain, but, to their dismay, James had scarcely hinted that such an eventuality was likely to occur. Only his oblique reference to a war of diversion implied a military clash with the Spanish. Moreover, the Commons suspected that the King did not contemplate any official action beyond his verbal pronouncement of March 23.

As far as the Prince and Buckingham were concerned, a certain amount of progress had been made, but their problem remained essentially the same. Until the Commons actually passed a bill of subsidy, military preparations remained little more than paper projects. No recourse, therefore, was left to them but to continue their policy of placating the Commons and simultaneously influencing the King to make concessions. Implicitly both King and Parliament were suspicious; explicitly both claimed to be acting with the utmost candor and good faith. With each concession made by the King, however, the demands of the Commons increased, and the stakes of the game changed. Prior to the declaration they had called for an end to diplomatic entanglements with Catholic powers; subsequent to the declaration they insisted upon the redress of domestic grievances and the enforcement of the penal laws against papists as the price of their cooperation.

The sensitivity of Charles and Buckingham to the wishes of the lower House was illustrated on numerous occasions in the remaining days before the Easter recess. On the morning of March 24, Buckingham informed the Lords, and subsequently the Commons, that the King, "Was determined, with all Expedition, to send into Spaine, and to give notice to him, [Philip IV] that, at the Petition and Advice of his Subjects in Parliament, he was

---

143. PRO 31/12/29, Spanish Transcripts, the Marquis Inojosa to King Philip IV, Mar. 24/Apr. 3, 1624; SP 14/161/36, Sir Francis Nethersole to Sir Dudley Carleton, Mar. 25, 1624; *Lords Debates 1624 & 1626*, 49.

resolved to break off both the Treaties, and declare so much here to the Ambassadors." [144] On the following day, well aware that the Commons were discontented at the lack of publicity accorded the King's declaration, the Duke moved to have two members of each house join with the Secretaries of State in drafting a manifesto announcing and justifying the breach with Spain. This concession he had implored of the King on bended knee, and it was, with alacrity, adopted by the Lords and Commons who named the Earls of Pembroke and Southampton, and Sir Richard Weston and Sir Edwin Sandys, to draft the document during the vacation. Buckingham was not so successful in gratifying the King; when he intimated once again that James expected recompense to be made to him in the subsidy act, the suggestion was greeted with silence.[145]

The interval of parliamentary recess from March 26 until April 1 was likewise a period of furious activity on the part of the Prince and the Duke. Now that the match with Spain had been abandoned, Charles sent word to Kensington to open formal negotiations with France for a royal marriage, and commissions were prepared for the Earl of Carlisle and Lord Kensington which would authorize them to conclude a military as well as a marital alliance. Assurances were also conveyed to the Dutch ambassadors, who had audience on March 29, that money and men would be dispatched to the Low Countries as soon as terms could be agreed upon. It was intimated, moreover, that the Prince and Buckingham were not averse to English participation in a combined naval expedition against Spain and that they would use their utmost endeavors to overcome the King's objections. Indeed, on March 30, Buckingham made a posting journey to Chatham purportedly to inspect the defensive preparations of the fleet, but with the additional purpose of considering "which of the ships are fittest . . . to be employed further." [146]

Most significant for the success of their parliamentary program was the duty incumbent upon the Prince and the Duke to secure performance of the assurances they had conveyed to the Parlia-

144. *CJ*, 750; *Lords Debates 1624 & 1626*, 48.
145. *CJ*, 750; Pym, fol. 43; SP 14/161/36, Sir Francis Nethersole to Sir Dudley Carleton, Mar. 25, 1624; *Lords Debates 1624 & 1626*, 49.
146. SP 14/161/61, Sir Francis Nethersole to Sir Dudley Carleton, Mar. 31, 1624.

ment concerning official notification of the breach of the treaties. For that reason they were present when the Spanish ambassadors presented the credentials of Padre Maestro to the King on March 29. However, James's statements to the ambassadors fell far short of the unequivocal declaration sought by Charles and Buckingham. "The King said that the only thing which had been done was not to admit the proposals of Spain for the arrangement of the affairs of the Palatinate. It was not his intention to declare a war against Spain. That it was his intention to write to Philip IV informing him of what had taken place and that he reckoned with him [Philip] to help him to have the estates of his son-in-law returned to him." [147] Reluctantly Charles and Buckingham confirmed this interpretation of the consequences of the breach of the treaties.

In the ensuing days the memorial which Sir Walter Aston was to deliver at Madrid was drafted and redrafted. After reciting at length James's pious and peaceable overtures, the dispatch blamed the Spanish by implication for the rupture of negotiations and complained of their dilatoriness in offering suitable conditions for the restoration of the Palatinate. They had left James no option but to consult with his Privy Council and, finally, his Parliament: "Upon right deliberation, with unanimous opinion, no man dissenting, they have given us their faithful advice to dissolve both the treaties, as well of the marriage, as of the Palatinate. To which we have given our consent, having not found any example that any king hath refused the counsel of the whole kingdom composed of faithful and loving subjects. So that we are to seek the right of our son-in-law, and grandchildren, as God shall open us ways. Wherein we hope we shall not find any so unjust arms, especially those of that king, as to oppose us." [148]

147. PRO 31/12/29, Spanish Transcripts, letter of Marquis Inojosa to King Philip IV, Mar. 29/Apr. 8, 1624. James also told the Dutch ambassadors on March 29 that he was "not resolved as yet to enter into war." (SP 14/162/46, Dudley Carleton to Sir Dudley Carleton, Apr. 11, 1624; this document is located in S P 84/117, fols. 31a–31b2 [Holland correspondence], although it is calendared as above.)

148. S. P. Foreign (Spanish) 94/30, fols. 166–167, King James to Sir Walter Aston, Apr. 6, 1624. There is a variant copy of this letter in fols. 168–169 that concludes "and we rather expect that that King will assist us than be contrary to our so just claim." The wording was altered as in the dispatch quoted. See also fols. 172–175, which are Conway's notes, apparently prepared for the draft of this letter. The Venetian ambassador reported on Apr. 2/12, "With the intimation of the breaking off of the negotiations they proposed to send Grisli to Spain any day, a

According to James's interpretation, the temporary end of negotiations with Spain did not preclude their resumption. Aston was instructed to "boldly assure those whom you think proper to satisfy that his Majesty is bound no further than to advise with them [Parliament], but not to rest upon their advices, except their advices concur with his Majesty's wisdom and piety to guide all things according to the greatest reason and best for the public good."[149] Again James drew that fine distinction between his relations with the Spanish and the Emperor that was never recognized as legitimate or valid by parliamentary advocates of war. As far as he was concerned, he had committed himself to warfare on the Continent which could only be ended by parliamentary acceptance of the conditions of peace. He considered Spanish troops employed in Germany in the same light as English troops used in the Low Countries, and thus a direct confrontation between Spain and England was not inevitable. Consequently Spain, once a principal in the negotiations for the restoration of the Palatinate, was relegated to the role of a third party in the war undertaken for its recovery. Therefore, if Philip IV wished to intervene and use his diplomatic influence to reinstate Frederick, James was obliged only to ask advice of Parliament on the question of reopening negotiations. Conversely, only a direct attack on England by Spain would justify a declaration of war.

So successful had Charles and Buckingham been in extorting concessions from the King that they undoubtedly believed he could be forced into hostilities with Spain by a *fait accompli*. However, for the immediate accomplishment of this purpose they needed money. Summer was approaching and unless preparations were undertaken soon nothing could be ventured during the regular campaigning season. The Lords' Committee on Munitions had accomplished little heretofore, but now the Prince stimulated it to renewed activity.[150] And on April 1, when Parliament recon-

---

decision which matures with the usual slowness, the king showing his customary repugnance, and he has many times read and re-read his letter to the King of Spain, constantly extenuating and mitigating its terms." (*Cal. S. P. Venetian*, XVIII, 266, Valaresso to the Doge and Senate.)

149. S. P. Foreign (Spanish) 94/30, fol. 180, Sir Edward Conway to Sir Walter Aston, Apr. 8, 1624.

150. *LJ*, III, 278. In Harl. MS. 6799, fol. 218, there is a document dated Mar. 15, 1624, dealing with projected defensive preparations apparently to be discussed in Parliament. It may be that the Lords' committee on munitions was the body

vened, Buckingham presented a scheme for expediting military action. After assuring the Lords and Commons that he had seen the letters written to the King of Spain and was present when James informed the Spanish ambassadors of the dissolution of the treaties, the Duke gave intelligence of naval preparations in Spain and the collection of an invasion fleet at Dunkirk. Provision for defense was of critical importance and "to advance that service in due time he had tried his own credit, and the credit of the officers of the navy, but found them both not sufficient to furnish such a sum as was necessary for the work . . . That he had therefore propounded this to the consideration of the Lords and that they upon deliberation had lighted on this expedient: that some moneyed men might haply be found out who would undertake to furnish the moneys upon assurance given by the two houses of Parliament of being reimbursed out of the first subsidy by them promised to be granted." [151] Despite the fact that Sir John Eliot vouched for

intended to deal with these problems. In the *Cal. S. P. Dom. 1623–1625*, 195, there is a statement by John Coke, commissioner of the navy, which refers to the present supply of gunpowder and the terms of the government's contract with Mr. Evelyn. The revelation of the shortage of powder by Coke on Mar 21, 1624, was probably instrumental in initiating charges against Lord Treasurer Cranfield in the House of Lords on April 2.

151. SP 14/162/12, Sir Francis Nethersole to Sir Dudley Carleton, Apr. 3, 1624. The scarcity of ready money to implement Buckingham's anti-Spanish policy caused him to consider a wide variety of revenue projects during 1624. As early as March 10 the Spanish ambassador reported that "Buckingham has proposed that the English Catholics should pay a certain sum every year to help the King against the King of Spain and not be persecuted." (PRO 31/12/29, Spanish Transcripts, Marquis Inojosa to King Philip IV, Mar. 10/20, 1624.) Apparently the idea was still alive on April 9 when the Venetian ambassador wrote that the English Catholics had submitted to Buckingham's consideration a petition which they intended to present to the Prince, and that the Duke "wanted them to add a declaration and practically a renunciation of all dependence upon Spain, which seemed very hard to the Catholics." (*Cal. S. P. Venetian*, XVIII, 275, Valaresso to the Doge and Senate, Apr. 9/19, 1624.) By means of an action in the Court of Admiralty against the East India Company for their depredations at Ormuz, Buckingham managed to extort ten thousand pounds "as a full satisfaction for all tenths, duties, fees or other rights due him from the company by virtue of his office of Lord Admiral of England." (*Cal. S. P. Colonial, 1622–1624*, 271, Apr. 28, 1624.) On May 21 the Venetian ambassador reported, "Buckingham, by a generous and much admired act, has devoted his portion of the booty from Ormuz to provisioning the royal ships, to prevent delay, although he will obtain repayment in another way." (*Cal. S. P. Venetian*, XVIII, 325, Valaresso to the Doge and Senate, May 21/31, 1624.) Hacket, in *Scrinia Reserata*, 202–206, gives details of two schemes which were mooted in 1624 as projects to make money. He asserts that Dr. Preston, chaplain to Prince Charles and leader of the Puritan faction, proposed the seizure of the lands of cathedral chapters and the devotion of this income to the payment of the King's debts, the prosecution of the war, and the gratification of the Duke's friends.

the truth of Buckingham's information, and despite assurances "that the money should be expended by the commissioners of both Houses to be appointed," the Commons excused their compliance with the Duke's request on the grounds of "the thinness of the House" and quietly let the matter drop.[152] Danger was not so imminent as to warrant tampering with established constitutional procedures.

Buckingham had hoped that his mere assertion would be accepted by the House of Commons as proof positive that the treaties had been abandoned, but such did not prove to be the case. The Commons were worried because the manifesto stating the reasons for the break with Spain had not been published, and in the closely knit circle of the court it was well known that no courier had been sent to Spain. Until such time, therefore, as some official action had been taken, the subsidy bill remained in abeyance. Instead, the House turned its attention to the danger of subversion at home, and, on April 1, began consideration of a petition

---

Ostensibly this would have pleased the Puritans and avoided the necessity of demanding further subsidies from Parliament. Hacket's tale is recapitualted in Morgan, *Prince Charles' Puritan Chaplain*, 126–131. Such a scheme may well have been proposed, but the allocation of the revenues to the purposes suggested by Hacket is scarcely credible. According to Daniel Neal, *History of the Puritans: or, Protestant Nonconformists; from the Reformation in 1517 to the Revolution in 1688* (5 vols., London, 1822), II, 124, 173–176, the income from the disbanded cathedral chapters was intended for the support of the lesser clergy. The second scheme Hacket mentions can be assigned a definite date because he prints a letter from Lord Keeper Williams to the Duke of Buckingham of October 21, 1624. In this note Williams advised against massive sales of crown lands and among the reasons he gave was that it could not be undertaken until after the "next Session of Parliament is dissolved; for otherwise it will undoubtedly serve as an Excuse for not Granting Subsidies." (Hacket, *Scrinia Reserata*, 202.) Peter Heylin, *Cyprianus Anglicus or the History of the Life and Death . . . of William Laud* (London, 1671), 118–119, states that in May of 1624 Buckingham was considering "whether the great endowments belonging to the Hospitals founded in the dissolved house of Carthusian Monks (commonly, but corruptly, called the Charter-House) might not be inverted to the maintenance of an Army for the present Wars, as well for his Majesties advantage, as the ease of the Subject." Heylin maintains that Laud dissuaded Buckingham from taking this step, but it must be noted that a bill was preferred in the Parliament of 1624 confirming the trust established by Thomas Sutton. It is interesting to note that one of the reasons attributed to Laud in dissuading the Duke was that "He liked not any inversions or alienations of that nature, lest being drawn into example, the Lands of Colledges or Cathedral Churches might in like manner be employed unto secular uses." (*Ibid.*, 118.)

152. SP 14/162/12, Sir Francis Nethersole to Sir Dudley Carleton, Apr. 3, 1624. The fact that Sir John Eliot claimed that he had "Had the Sight of those Letters of the Duke of Buckingham," indicates that in 1624 he was numbered among the favorite's inner circle. (*CJ*, 752.)

against Catholic recusants. Many of the members who followed Mr. Delbridge in demanding enforcement of the penal laws had not made significant contributions to the great debates on foreign affairs, but now they gave voice to their Puritanical predispositions and regarded James's reception of a petition against recusants as a touchstone of his intentions toward Spain.

Intermittently for three days the Commons debated the text of their petition, but essentially it was a revision of the instrument presented in 1621. To fit the circumstances of 1624, the seven pleas of the petition were preceded by a preface that plumbed the depths of the Commons' anti-Spanish and anti-Catholic prejudices. After alluding to James's "princely resolution, upon our humble petition, to dissolve the two treaties," the document commenced its invective against "those incendiaries of Rome, and professed engines of Spain, the priests and jesuits." It inveighed against the boldness and insolence of English recusants because of the foreign patronage accorded them. It asserted that "great preparations are made in Spain fit for an invasion, the bent whereof is as probable to be upon some part of your Majesty's dominions, as upon any other place," and it lamented the discouragement caused patriotic Englishmen by the seditious combinations of their falsehearted countrymen.[153] Ostensibly the remedies suggested by the Commons were designed to show their alacrity in guarding against domestic subversion and to elucidate once again their conviction that Rome served the interests of Spain. Thus by advocating persecution of the Catholics the lower House hoped, with the King's compliance, to widen the breach with Madrid and provoke open warfare.

With each succeeding Jacobean Parliament, the Puritan faction in the House of Commons had grown stronger. In debating the petition they were covering familiar ground so the vocal Protestant (if not Puritan) majority did not feel impelled to discuss their demands at length. There was almost universal agreement that priests and Jesuits should be expelled from the realm by proclamation and that the penal laws against recusants should be strictly enforced. No dissent was encountered by a motion to prevent the resort of Catholics to ambassadors' chapels, and it was generally

153. *LJ*, III, 289, proposed petition from the two Houses of Parliament to the King against popish recusants, Apr. 3, 1624. This petition is reprinted in Tierney, ed., *Dodd's Church History of England*, V, Appendix, cccxli–cccxliii.

conceded that papists should be disarmed and discharged from offices of trust in their counties. Additional strictures were suggested by Sir Robert Phelips, who moved the expulsion of recusants from the environs of London, and a provision preventing their access to court and city and limiting their movements to within five miles of their residences was incorporated into the petition.

The Commons took cognizance of an even knottier problem when they sought to include "justly suspected" as well as convicted recusants within the penalties of the law. Pym had strongly urged action against "real recusants," and even that legal oracle, Sir Edward Coke, thought that just suspicions could be given sufficient definition to warrant prosecution. Extreme as these measures were, they secured the sanction of the House, but Sir Robert Harley's motion for a day of humiliation was quietly dropped, and Sir Thomas Posthumus Hoby's request to name the Catholic "ringleaders" in the body of the petition was deferred for separate consideration.

However, one clause in the text gave the Commons cause for optimism. Solicitor Heath, who was instrumental in drafting the petition, moved that the King be requested that, "by the engagement of your royal word unto them, that, upon no occasion of marriage, or treaty, or other request in that behalf, from any foreign prince or state whatsoever, you will take away or slacken the execution of your laws against the popish recusants." Obviously Heath had been instructed by the Prince and Buckingham who hoped to use this promise as a bargaining point in the marriage negotiations with France. Consequently the lower House expected powerful representations to be made by the Prince to secure a favorable reply to their petition.[154]

154. Reports of the debates on the petition against recusants tend to be sketchy. For proceedings in the House of Commons on April 1, 1624, *CJ*, 751–752, is perhaps the best account. Supplementary material may be obtained by reference to Holles, fols. 115v–116; Pym, fols. 44–45; Spring, 164–166. Debates in the Committee of the Whole, chaired by Sir Edward Coke on April 2, 1624, are most fully reported in Spring, 168–169. Rich (PRO 30/15/1/2, 168 [Manchester MSS]) and Pym (fols. 47–47v) report the meeting of the subcommittee on April 2, 1624. The *CJ* lists the forty-eight members appointed to the committee to confer with the Lords. One of those mentioned — Sir Robert Hardwicke — is obviously a clerical error since no member by that name was returned to the House of Commons in 1624. I am inclined to think that Sir Robert Hatton (steward of the archbishop of Canterbury) was the person nominated. According to Sir Francis Nethersole, the Commons'

At noon on April 3, forty-eight of the Commons carried the petition up to the Lords who postponed consideration of it until the following Monday because of the lateness of the hour. It was suspected, however, that they delayed in order "to acquaint his Majesty therewith underhand to the end that, if he can be drawn to grant the substance, the form of the petition may be made such as he can like, being indeed not liked as it is now by very many in the lower House though their voices were marked in the general approbation." [155] The King's reaction was even more precipitate than expected. As soon as he was informed of the proceedings in Parliament, he wrote to Conway: "I Doubt not but you have heard what a stinging Petition against the Papists the Lower House have sent to the Higher House this Day, that they may jointly present it to me: You know my firm Resolution not to make this a War of Religion. And seeing I would be loth to be Conny-catch by my People, I pray you stay the Post that is going into Spain, till I meet with my Son, who will be here to morrow Morning. Do it upon Pretext of some more Letters ye are to send by him; and if he should be gone, hasten after him to stay him, upon some such Pretext, and let none living know of this, as ye love me: And before Two in the Afternoon to morrow you shall without fail hear from me." [156]

Doubtless when the Prince arrived at court it demanded all of his tact to pacify his father's wrath. James had given repeated assurances to the Spanish ambassadors that he projected no persecution of Catholics, and Buckingham and Charles had been party to these promises. Lately, however, the King had detected signs of dissimulation in the Prince. Immediately before the recess Charles had voted for the passage of an act to reinforce the penal statutes against recusants and to prevent their evading forfeitures by conveying their estates to trustees.[157] Now the Prince seemed to have

---

petition was drafted by Solicitor Heath, and he presented a copy to Nethersole to forward to Elizabeth of Bohemia. (SP 14/162/12, Sir Francis Nethersole to Sir Dudley Carleton, Apr. 3, 1624).

155. SP 14/162/12, Sir Francis Nethersole to Sir Dudley Carleton, Apr. 3, 1624.

156. King James to Secretary Conway, Apr. 3, 1624. The letter appears in Arthur Wilson's "The Life and Reign of James the First, King of Great Britain," printed in Kennet, *Complete History of England*, II, 780; see also Rushworth, *Historical Collections*, I, 140–141.

157. SP 14/161/36, Sir Francis Nethersole to Sir Dudley Carleton, Mar. 25, 1624.

cast aside all restraints and joined the Puritan hue and cry against papists.

Expedience was probably the reason Charles used to excuse his actions. He apparently convinced the King that the House of Commons would not act on the subsidy bill unless they were promised a favorable hearing for their petition. Moreover, the Prince's prestige and power in the House of Lords were so great that the objectionable portions of the petition could be mitigated or omitted completely. In the final analysis, a moderate petition favorably received by the King would be an ideal diplomatic lever to use against French demands for concessions to the Catholics. After a lengthy conference, therefore, James revoked his previous instructions to Conway:

Pardon me the breaking of this hour, for it is a fault I seldom commit, but my son's being here and a number of people that came with him so plied me with business as I had never leisure till now to write unto you. My son will inform you as he finds the lower House inclined in this business that you may advertise me accordingly. I mean whether they will go on with the subsidies according to their promise and trust to my wisdom and discretion in answering their petition, or if they will make it in effect, a condition *sine qua non,* though not say it plainly. I hope you will likewise do all you can to discover this for if I may be sure that they mean to keep their promise to me, let the packets go on, otherwise it were no reason I should be bound and they leap free and leave me naked and without help; though I have commanded my son to acquaint you with what he can discover yet knows he not of these my private directions unto you. All this I must commit to your secrecy, discretion and diligence. The short and the long is that if I may be sure that their passing of the subsidies will not depend upon my answer to their petition, let the post go, post haste post, but if they will not move without first having their will in that, no reason they should break their promise and I still be bound.[158]

Until Conway was confident that the House of Commons would not insist upon the precise wording of their petition, the dispatch to Spain was delayed. Meanwhile, the Prince began his campaign

158. SP 14/163/30, King James to Secretary Conway. This letter is calendared with the probable date of April 22, but I am convinced that April 4 should be the date assigned. Obviously the post referred to was the dispatch ending negotiations with Spain. The Venetian ambassador and Dudley Carleton certify that Grisley left on April 9. See *Cal. S. P. Venetian,* XVIII, 276, Valaresso to the Doge and Senate, Apr. 9/19, 1624; SP 84/117, fol. 31a–31b2, Dudley Carleton to Sir Dudley Carleton, Apr. 11, 1624.

in the Lords to qualify the demands of the lower House. Immediately on the morning of April 5, he moved the consideration of the petition and launched an attack on its preface. Although, at the outset, the clerical lords, such as the archbishop of Canterbury and Lord Keeper Williams, were heartily in favor of the pugnacious language used by the Commons, they changed their opinions when it became clear that Puritan peers like Lords Brooke and Saye agreed with Charles. Originally the Prince had objected to the asperity of the preface, but, when he perceived that the Lords were inclined to support him, he proposed that the preface be omitted and replaced by an innocuous introduction.

When the clauses of the petition were debated point by point, the Prince made every effort to eliminate inflammatory phraseology and to avoid novelty. He approved of the conventional demand for a proclamation against Jesuits and seminary priests, but he objected to the passage requesting the disarming of recusants legally convicted or vehemently suspected. "I am perswaded," he said, "and have some cause to knowe yt, that the King wyll doe yt himselfe . . . but we not to urge him at this tyme, and he will doe yt the sooner." In general it was Charles's contention that the onus of fomenting a Catholic persecution could be evaded if no new restrictions on papists were permitted. He agreed with Pembroke who said, "Our meaninge is to make noe noyse of newe lawes, or addicions." In the final analysis, the Prince maintained that the entire Commons' petition could be condensed into two clauses: the first calling for the due execution of existing penal statutes; the second asking that no benefits redound to domestic Catholics from future negotiations with foreign princes. In consequence, a subcommittee was appointed to redraft the petition in accordance with the Prince's wishes, and, on the morning of April 6, the lower House was requested to give its sanction to the abridgement.[159]

Undoubtedly the Commons were aware of developments in the Lords because their conference committee was not empowered to make alterations in the petition without authority from the House. Although the committees were assured that the Prince had been so careful "that he would have their very words used as far as

159. *Lords Debates 1624 & 1626*, 56–57. The best report of the Lords's debates on the petition against recusants is in *ibid.*, 53–57.

might be," it was abundantly clear that in the process of "contraction" significant deletions had been made. Virtually the only point that remained intact was that requesting no connivance for English Catholics as a result of future treaty negotiations, and this was reinforced when the archbishop of Canterbury asserted, with tears of joy, that Charles had sworn a solemn oath that "whensoever it should please God to bestow upon him any Lady that were popish, she should have no further Liberty, but for her own Family, and no Advantage to the Recusants at home." [160] Undoubtedly this promise was regarded by the Prince as a sufficient incentive for the compliance of the Commons with the Lords, but discontent over the emasculation of their petition caused the lower House to disregard temporarily the Lords' request for a small subcommittee to collate the petitions. Instead, the Commons empowered their own drafting committee to compare the documents and to make recommendations. This began the process of ameliorating the intransigence of the fractious Puritans in the lower chamber in order to secure the cooperation of the Lords in presenting the petition.

It was fortunate for the Prince and the moderates that some of the demands in the Commons' original petition exceeded the limits of legal practice. Despite the remonstrances of members such as Perrot, Phelips, and Coke, the difficulty of bringing the "justly suspected" recusants within the confines of the law remained insuperable. As Sir Edwin Sandys pointed out, "If a man be suspected, it is truly or not. If truly, convict him, and then he is liable to the law. If not, acquit him, and punish him not upon an erroneous supposition of probability."

It took some time before Glanville's contention that the Commons should "Take what we can, if not what we would," bore fruit. When the committee for comparing petitions reported on April 7, the clause demanding the disarming of all popish recusants, convicted or justly suspected, remained among their recommendations; also supported were provisions requiring notification of the King's pleasure by proclamation and the designation of a certain and speedy day for the departure of the Jesuits and seminary priests. A heated debate raged in the House over the pro-

160. Spring, 177; *CJ*, 756.

priety of demanding a proclamation which the privy councillors had objected to as prejudicial to the King's military aims and offensive to prospective Catholic allies. The overwhelming majority, however, insisted that the petition should be answered "by proclamation as in like cases and upon like occasions hath been used."

Debate upon the inclusion of "justly suspected" recusants was not nearly so spirited. Already plans were germinating for an alternative method of dealing with those Catholics who occupied positions of trust. Knights and burgesses had been ordered to make presentment of all suspected Catholics in county offices and now Sir John Eliot asserted that their removal could be accomplished more easily through the Prince's intercession than by public demands in a petition. Thus, when the Lords' and Commons' committees met in conference on April 10, the spirit of compromise was in the air. Without argument the Lords agreed to a speedy and certain day for the expulsion of priests and Jesuits, and with almost as much alacrity the Commons withdrew their insistence upon a proclamation. The disarming of recusants was referred to due process of law "according to former acts and directions of state in the like case." [161]

When manifest agreement had been reached upon the text of the petition, the Prince revealed another of his motives for expediting its completion. He reminded the Commons of their promise of three subsidies and three fifteenths, and he urged them to begin prompt consideration of a revenue bill so that he could inform the King of their good faith when he solicited a hearing for their petition. Undoubtedly the Prince assumed that catering to the religious passions of the Commons was the readiest way to loosen their purse strings. To a certain extent his assessment of the dominant motives in the Commons was correct, but by the time the petition was engrossed some of the religious fervor of the lower House had been diverted into the indictment of the Lord Treasurer. There remained, moreover, the nagging doubt that the treaties were not finally dissolved. Even though a committee was

161. Spring, 179–180, 185; Holles, fol. 122. The text of the petition as it was finally agreed upon and presented to the King on April 23 is printed in *LJ*, III, 298, and reprinted in Tierney, ed., *Dodd's Church History of England*, V, Appendix, cccxliii–cccxliv.

appointed to consider a preamble to the subsidy bill, many members concurred with Edward Alford who desired "a full and public declaration before we pass the bill."

Buckingham, particularly, was sensitive to the suspicions of the Commons. In the conference committee on the petition on April 3, he had repeated his assurances that the treaties were really dissolved, and on April 9, Solicitor Heath was ordered to prepare a written memorandum of the Duke's declaration for insertion into the *Journal*. Even this was not regarded as sufficient evidence; when Sir Francis Seymour wanted to know whether the House considered public declaration of the breach to have been made, it was resolved upon the question in the negative.[162]

After long delay, during which Conway tested the temper of the Commons concerning their petition, the letters to Spain were sent. This, too, was communicated to the House by Secretary Calvert, but it stirred no response from the members. Inexorably the need for money and the pressure of time drove Buckingham to take decisive action. The fleet was preparing for sea, commissions for the Council of War were awaiting signature, and Count Mansfeldt had arrived from the Continent with a project for a campaign in the Palatinate. The Prince, by his religious concessions and his tactful procedure in Parliament, had instigated consideration of the subsidy bill and the Duke believed that the opportune moment had arrived to expedite its enactment. On April 16 he wrote to James: "The cause of my troubling you so soon with a letter is, that there is a jealousy raised in the lower House how that yet the two treaties are not absolutely broken off. The Prince, Hamilton, Pembroke, Doncaster and myself, who have all seen your dispatch to the King of Spain, think, if that were showed to them, that it would fully content them. We all like wise think there is nothing in it but what they may well see; and because on Tuesday they pass the bill of subsidies, I think it will not be amiss it be read to them, which if your Majesty like and allow of, I will call for it of the Secretary, and tomorrow morning read it to them.[163]

162. Nicholas, fol. 138; *CJ*, 760–761.

163. Harl. MS. 6987, fol. 217, the Duke of Buckingham to King James (April 16); Halliwell, *King's Letters*, II, 253–254. The reference in the letter to the passage of the subsidy bill probably refers to the projected date for its consideration. At the actual time the bill was passed (May 21), Buckingham was convalescing after a dangerous illness. In fact the last day on which he was present in Parliament was

Consequently on the morning of the seventeenth Buckingham, by the King's command, informed a committee of the Commons of the precise details of James's letter to Philip IV dissolving the treaties. Apparently the King had not allowed copies of his dispatch of April 6 to be displayed because Buckingham spoke from notes "which the Prince affirmed to be so exact as he thought it scarce differed in a word." [164] The intent of Buckingham's tactics became clear when he said he "hoped that the House of Commons would take all this for a sufficient declaration, as he understood they did by the beginning of their petition to his Majesty, and would not now expect the publication of the manifest." [165] Obviously James had refused to publish any document which implied aggressive intentions against Spain until such time as the Spanish had precipitated a war. Yet the Commons were reluctant to accept a peaceful breach of negotiations as a sufficient declaration, and until they had publicly acknowledged their contentment with the King's action no revenues could be collected. The period of a year within which three subsidies and three fifteenths were to be levied was to commence on the date that the Commons ratified the breach of the treaties.

In order to induce the Commons to concede his interpretation that the preamble to the petition against recusants officially acknowledged the end of negotiations, Buckingham once again warned of imminent peril to England. Letters from Ireland describing the threat of immediate rebellion were read, and it was asserted that, in Brussels, measures were being concerted to dispatch a Catholic Irish regiment to head the insurrection. Finally, to stimulate the Commons to grant the money needed to avert this impending calamity, Buckingham revealed that the King had ordered his learned counsel to begin consideration of a liberal general pardon.[166]

After this meticulous and persuasive preparation by the Prince

---

April 24. James's dispatch to Sir Walter Aston at Madrid signifying the end of the treaties was read to a conference committee of the Lords and Commons by the Duke of Buckingham on April 17. (*CJ*, 769; Pym, fols. 70–71.)

164. SP 14/163/2, Sir Henry Goodyere to Sir Dudley Carleton, Apr. 18, 1624.
165. SP 14/163/3, Sir Francis Nethersole to Sir Dudley Carleton, Apr. 18, 1624.
166. *CJ*, 769–770; SP 14/163/2, Sir Henry Goodyere to Sir Dudley Carleton, Apr. 18, 1624; SP 14/163/3, Sir Francis Nethersole to Sir Dudley Carleton, Apr. 18, 1624; SP 14/163/16, Dudley Carleton to Sir Dudley Carleton, Apr. 19, 1624.

and the Duke, Solicitor Heath, on the morning of April 20, moved for the hastening of the subsidy bill. At once it became apparent that the Commons were in no mood to expedite action. There was "general apprehension that these three subsidies might go the same way the two given at the last convention of parliament did if the bill of subsidy went thus on winged feet, and other bills of grace on leaden ones." [167] Some members were reluctant to act because no date had been assigned for the petition against recusants, and Sir Francis Seymour again revived the question of the declaration dissolving the treaties by demanding that it be enacted in the bill. The dilatoriness of the House was only overcome by Secretary Conway's reminder that immediate action was necessary to prevent great danger and that the bill itself was not to be passed at the first reading.[168]

That afternoon, in the committee for preparing the bill of subsidies, the House first discovered the difficulties involved in the constitutional changes they sought to initiate. After resolving to have the dissolution of the treaties expressed in the act, an argument developed over whether it should be "declared" or "enacted" and whether it should appear in the preamble or in the body of the bill. "To determine this dispute up stood Sir Edward Coke, who having made a very grave preamble that as the making, so the dissolving, of treaties with foreign states belonged to kings and sovereign princes only as an unquestioned part of their prerogative, concluded in some choler, flinging the bill of subsidy out of his hands, But I am no parenthesis man, nor no preamble man, and therefore I pray let us have it at the beginning of the body of the bill — And therefore we do humbly beseech your Majesty that it may be enacted, etc.[169]

Ultimately the Commons' desire to have the breach with Spain promulgated in some official document caused them to insert it into the bill of subsidies. Again it was Secretary Conway who quieted the unruliness of the House by pointing out that the sincerity of the King's intentions was patent, as evidenced by the imminent departure of Sir Isaac Wake and Sir Robert Anstruther and by significant progress with the Dutch commissioners.

167. SP 14/163/50, Sir Francis Nethersole to Sir Dudley Carleton, Apr. 25, 1624.
168. Earle, fol. 152.
169. SP 14/163/50, Sir Francis Nethersole to Sir Dudley Carleton, Apr. 25, 1624.

By April 22, when the subsidy bill had its first reading, the Prince and the Duke were ready with new proofs of their desire for good correspondence with the Commons. Buckingham informed the Commons' committees that, at the Prince's instigation, he had repeatedly solicited audience from the King for the reception of the petition against recusants. By using the argument of the preparation of the subsidy bill, he had prevailed upon the King to grant access to the committees of Parliament on April 23. He had also reassured the King that nothing had been intruded into the revenue act which derogated from his honor. He further acquainted the members, on the Prince's order, that the Lords had passed the important act concerning certiorari. As a quid pro quo, therefore, he requested that the subsidy bill be given speedy consideration. The report of this conference so contented the House that they resolved to give the bill a second reading on April 24.[170]

Before further deliberations on the revenue act occurred, circumstances had conspired to allay many of the fears that had jeopardized the continuance of Parliament. A tacit permission to allow the impeachment of the Lord Treasurer implied that Parliament would not be dissolved to protect royal officers. The nomination of the Duke of Buckingham, the Marquess Hamilton, the Earl of Pembroke, Sir Richard Weston, and Sir Edward Conway as commissioners to negotiate an alliance with the Dutch was considered a guarantee that substantial aid would be sent to the Low Countries.[171] Appointment of a royal Council of War was taken as good evidence that defensive preparations were really intended. The lionizing of Count Mansfeldt by the Prince and Buckingham and the agreement which James concluded with the German captain signified a long-term commitment to military action against Spanish and imperial forces in the Palatinate.[172] The dispatch dis-

170. *CJ*, 772–773; Earle, fols. 156–156v; SP 14/163/50, Sir Francis Nethersole to Sir Dudley Carleton, Apr. 25, 1624.
171. *Cal. S. P. Venetian*, XVIII, 293, Valaresso to the Doge and Senate, Apr. 23/May 3, 1624; SP 14/163/3, Sir Francis Nethersole to Sir Dudley Carleton, Apr. 18, 1624. On April 17, six thousand men in four regiments were promised to the Dutch to be maintained by James in their service until the end of the war. English expenditures were to be reimbursed after the treaty of peace, secured by English occupation of cautionary towns.
172. SP 14/163/16, Dudley Carleton to Sir Dudley Carleton, Apr. 19, 1624; SP 14/163/48, Dudley Carleton to the Queen of Bohemia, Apr. 24, 1624 (note that this letter is misdated April 15). (*Cal. S. P. Venetian*, XVIII, 293–296, Valaresso to the Doge and Senate, Apr. 23/May 3, 1624.) Mansfeldt, by letters patent, was granted

solving the treaties had been sent to Sir Walter Aston for delivery to Philip IV, and the return of the courier was expected daily.[173] Concurrently, the Spanish ambassadors in London had compromised their embassy by becoming officially involved in a breach of diplomatic decorum.

The climax of these auspicious occurrences was provided by James himself when, on April 23, he received the petition against recusants presented by a parliamentary deputation. Not only did he appear to grant everything that the Lords and Commons had requested, but he repeatedly protested that he would have taken action against the Catholics upon his own initiative. He promised the much desired proclamation against Jesuits and priests and the strict enforcement of penal laws against Catholic laymen. He asserted that resort to ambassador's chapels would be prevented and that the disarming of recusants would be accomplished by due process of law. He exceeded the Commons' expectations when he vowed that he would prevent the education of recusants' children in foreign seminaries. Even on the matter of future treaty stipulations James was conciliatory, if equivocal. He congratulated his petitioners for having "given me the best advice in the world; for it is against the rule of wisdom, that a king should suffer any of his subjects to be beholding and depend upon any other prince than himself," but he did not categorically promise to reject future concessions to Catholics. "Assure yourselves," he said, "that, by the grace of God, I will be careful that no such condition be hereafter foisted in upon any other treaty whatsoever." [174]

The instant this speech was concluded the audience "gave demonstration of their joy by acclamations and wishings of safety and happiness to his Majesty." [175] Further proof of their contentment came on the following morning when the Commons expeditiously committed the subsidy bill. Indeed, when Solicitor Heath

---

the command of ten thousand foot, three thousand horse, and six guns with payment to begin on May 1. See also *ibid.*, 303–304, Valaresso to the Doge and Senate, Apr. 30/May 10, 1624.

173. S. P. Foreign (Spanish) 94/30, Sir Walter Aston to Sir Edward Conway, Apr. 25, 1624, see fols. 202–204. Grisley arrived from Madrid on May 6. SP 14/164/44, Dudley Carleton to Sir Dudley Carleton, May 6, 1624.

174. James's speech given on April 23, 1624, is found in numerous manuscript copies. It is printed in *LJ*, III, 317, and in Tierney, ed., *Dodd's Church History of England*, V, Appendix, cccxlv–cccxlvi.

175. SP 14/163/48, Dudley Carleton to Elizabeth of Bohemia, Apr. 24, 1624.

capped the climax by revealing the tenets of the general pardon, Sir John Eliot was so moved that he proposed that thanks be rendered to the King, the Prince, and God, in that order, but the House cut him short, preferring action to words.[176]

Very quickly the harmony between King and Commons began to dissolve. Some agreed with Sir Dudley Digges who thought that with the second reading of the subsidy bill the bell had "twice tolled for the end of this session." [177] However, the difficulties involved in agreeing upon the exact text of this unique piece of legislation afforded some occasion for delay. Many new questions demanded determination: "(1) Whether the Council of War should be named. (2) How many of them should join in the warrant. (3) The form of the oath to which they and the treasurers were to be sworn. (4) The number of the treasurers, and the men. (5) For the collectors to make payment to them and their acquittance to be a discharge, and how that acquittance might be enrolled for their better security. (6) How the account should be passed. (7) The place for the collectors to make payment. (8) Whether the treasurers should be charged one for another." [178] By the end of the first committee meeting on the afternoon of April 24 agreement had been reached on only two points: the nomination of eight treasurers, and the designation of the Chamber of London as the place of deposit. To those who yearned for the immediate commencement of hostilities it seemed as if the bill of subsidies was once more "asleep."

The knights and burgesses, however, were reluctant to blame themselves for delays; Richard Knightley informed the Duke that the responsibility lay with the court. The subsidies were hindered because the King still maintained contact with the Spanish ambassadors and had not issued his promised proclamation against Jesuits.[179] On April 29, Solicitor Heath was urged to make un-

176. SP 14/163/50, Sir Francis Nethersole to Sir Dudley Carleton, Apr. 25, 1624; Pym, fols. 79v–80. The provisions of the general pardon were discussed by the Privy Council, at the King's command, on April 21. They are listed in SP 14/163/22 and 46.

177. D'Ewes, fol. 113.

178. Pym, fol. 79v.

179. Gardiner, ed., Fortescue Papers, 196–197, Sir Richard Knightley to the Duke of Buckingham, undated. At the time this letter was written, Richard Knightley had not been knighted. See HMC, Second Report, Appendix (London, 1874), 61, where the document is calendared as a letter of Mr. Richard Knightley to the Duke of Buckingham. The HMC and Gardiner tentatively date this letter in May 1624,

official inquiries to determine when the King proposed to end the session and when he would publish the proclamation. Two days later Secretary Conway returned from court with information that the Attorney General had been commanded to draft a proclamation and that the Recorder and Lord Mayor of London had been instructed to prevent the assemblage of Catholics at foreign embassies. Conway pleaded with the Commons to expedite the subsidy bill because all military preparations were interrupted pending the assessment of taxes.

Doubtless there were those in the Commons who exploited the difficulties inherent in the subsidy bill in order to extend the life of the Parliament. Day by day important legislation was being passed and sent to the Lords, and day by day the great Committees for Grievances, Trade, and Courts of Justice were preparing briefs that demanded remedial action from the King. As early as April 29 an unprecedented motion had been introduced which proposed that all "bills and businesses now on foot to stand *statu quo* as they are now left to be found at the beginning of the next sessions." Although it was warmly supported by "diverse great parliament men" like Sir Edwin Sandys, Edward Alford, and Sir Robert Phelips, the motion was defeated because it would bind the hands of posterity and "the King might upon that ground stay all our good bills from passing and say they should rest till another session when more were ready."

New precedents caused the Commons considerable trouble in relation to the subsidy act itself. By May 11 it was proposed that the subsidies should be paid in the usual manner with treasurers

but I have assigned the date April 29. The Venetian ambassador says that Buckingham did not leave London for Windsor until Wednesday, April 28. (*Cal. S. P. Venetian*, XVIII, 301, Valaresso to the Doge and Senate, Apr. 30/May 10, 1624.) Nethersole says that, on the afternoon of April 29, Solicitor Heath was requested to tell the King "that the House doth much long for the coming forth of the proclamation against priests promised by his Majesty." And he further reports that on the morning of May 1 Secretary Conway informed the Commons that the Attorney General had been instructed to draft the proclamation. (SP 14/164/46, Sir Francis Nethersole to Sir Dudley Carleton, May 6, 1624 [note, the portion of this letter referred to was actually written on May 1].) The proclamation itself was dated at Greenwich, May 6, 1624, and allowed those who held orders of the see of Rome until June 14, 1624, to depart the realm. See *Cal. S. P. Venetian*, XVIII, 321; *Cal. S. P. Dom. 1623–1625*, 239. Nethersole, writing on May 15, reported "The Papists . . . laugh at the proclamation against their priests, now they are sure the Parliament will be ended before their day come." (SP 14/164/86, Sir Francis Nethersole to Sir Dudley Carleton.)

nominated by the House "because nothing was like to be done with it in that for which it was given." This, and a subsequent motion "to give one subsidy now, another next sessions and a third at a third meeting," was rejected.[180] By May 14 the committee preparing the bill had encountered so many difficulties "that diverse wished they had kept the old way of paying their moneys into the Exchequer." [181] It was due chiefly to the arduous efforts of legal antiquarians like Coke, Selden, and Noy that the knotty problems occasioned by the Commons' desire to control the expenditure of money were solved. From the reigns of Richard II, Henry IV, Henry V, and Edward IV they dredged up legal and parliamentary precedents to justify their present action. It was in these ill-reported committee debates that revolutionary action was quietly undertaken by the House of Commons in 1624.

When the subsidy bill was reported by Solicitor Heath on the afternoon of May 14, it not only declared and enacted that the two treaties were utterly dissolved, but it contained limiting clauses that presaged the specific appropriation bills passed by Parliament a century later. The treasurers and the Council of War were nominated; both were bound by oath and made accountable to Parliament. The specific purposes for which money was to be expended were designated: "the defense of this your Realm of England, the securing of your Kingdom of Ireland, the assistance of your neighbors the States of the United Provinces and other your Majesty's friends and allies, and for the setting forth of your royal navy." [182] It was expressly provided that coat

180. D'Ewes, fols. 114v, 115, 120; Nicholas, fol. 202.

181. D'Ewes, fol. 121v. At the committee on May 13 and 14 the question of criminal responsibility of the Commons' treasurers and councillors of war who misemployed subsidies was debated. According to Earle, fol. 182v, some of the members were so afraid that the money would be misdirected that they wanted guilty officials charged with treason. It was no wonder that Sir Edwin Sandys said on April 24 that he would "rather be sent to the Tower or pay 500 pounds than to be one of the treasurers, for by it we make him obnoxious to the displeasure of the King and this State, and he hopeth none sitting here hath deserved so ill for he must neglect all his own affairs and be tied to a continual residency here." (Nicholas, fol. 173v.)

182. *Statutes of the Realm*, IV, Part II, 1247–1262. The unorthodox provisions of the bill are chiefly in sections 1 and 36 through 44. Debates on the subsidy bill are badly reported. The best account is contained in Earle, fols. 162, 166, 169v–170, 179–179v, 181–182, 183v–184v, and Nicholas, fols. 173–174v, 191, 202–203v, 205, 214, 220, 247–247v. Valuable information may also be obtained from Sir Francis Nethersole's letters to Sir Dudley Carleton, Apr. 25, May 6, May 24, and June 2. It is difficult to assign responsibility for the various radical provisions incorporated

and conduct money for troops intended for foreign service must be defrayed by this grant and not charged upon the counties. Any arrearages due before the beginning of this Parliament, even if they had been incurred in connection with the designs mentioned in the act, were not regarded as legitimate expenditures. Treasurers and councillors of war who deviated from the terms of their commission were punishable by either Lords or Commons, depending upon the social status of the offender.

Considering the strictures contained in the act, it was scarcely remarkable that Secretary Conway expressed alarm for his own safety. He knew that King and Commons were at cross purposes regarding the theater of military operations, and he pointed out that the King was already engaged to spend more than half the expected revenue on projects unlikely to be sanctioned by the Commons. Consequently, no sooner had the bill been reported from committee than Solicitor Heath made a last attempt to mitigate the strictness of its clauses. He moved three alterations which were requested by the King and the Prince. The first was a mere matter of form: the word "oppression" instead of "indignities" was preferable in describing the offensive actions of the Palsgrave's adversaries. More significant was the King's request to have the recovery of the Palatinate designated as one of the purposes for which money was provided. Thirdly, James wished to qualify assistance to the Low Countries by the limitation "as a means to recover the Palatinate." All of these innovations were utterly disliked by the members and categorically rejected on the

---

in the 1624 subsidy bill. The designation of specific funds for specific purposes arose naturally from the King's speeches on the need for defense and from the medieval precedents searched by Selden, Coke, and Noy. Sir Edward Coke appears to have been instrumental in naming the treasurers and the Council of War in the body of the bill and in prescribing oaths of office. (Nicholas, fol. 173.) Phelips must be credited with insistence that councillors of war have a commission under the great seal. (Earle, fol. 166.) Taken in combination, Coke's and Phelips' provisions converted the King's Council of War into a body responsible to the House of Commons. By incorporating the names of the councillors in the bill, the Commons seemingly limited the King's power to dismiss his officials. Phelips also appears to have been responsible for section forty-four of the bill, which was designed to prevent the levy of additional military charges upon the counties. (Nicholas, fol. 191.) This section was so vague that the Council of War on June 23, 1624, consulted the judges to determine whether coat and conduct money and the cost of arms was to be defrayed by the subsidies or levied on the counties. See SP 14/168/30, minutes of a meeting of the Council of War, June 23, 1624. Pym must be credited with initiating a compromise whereby guilty Lords were to be punished by the upper House and commoners by the lower House. (Earle, fol. 181v; Nicholas, fol. 203v.)

grounds that they were out of order and that "what was proposed was clean contrary to the intent of the House."[183]

Accordingly, the bill was passed to engrossing without any additions or alterations. Indeed, the Commons were so conscious of the bargaining power inherent in their financial prerogative that they delayed passage of the subsidy bill until the last possible moment and practically extorted, through the Prince's intercession, a week's extension of the session. On May 21 the bill finally passed the Commons, but it was not sent up to the Lords until the twenty-fourth.[184] By that time it was too late for the peers to do anything but register a feeble protest against possible infringement of their powers of judicature. The bill was so lengthy and so little time was allowed them that only the preamble and the conclusion were considered on the second reading. Within two days of its referral, the Lords passed it.

With the acceptance of the grant by James on May 29, the plans of Buckingham and Charles seemed to be on the verge of fruition. By virtue of cajolery and concession they had at last been assured of the money they needed to commence operations. But, in his remarks on the subsidy bill, James implied that their triumph was not complete and that, notwithstanding their alliance with the Commons, he meant to have his way. He gave thanks for the subsidies in the names of his "grandchildren" to whom they were given and "after this proceeded to give assurance that the money should be wholly employed to the use it was given . . . and insisted particularly and largely upon the recovery of the Palatinate (although that be not specified in the act)."[185] Moreover, he had already concluded agreements which portended no direct hostile action against Spain. Nor was he so delighted at the successful conclusion of the session that he conceded all of the Commons' desires; he vetoed the bills for restraining vain and unlawful sports on the Lord's day and for the better suppressing of popish recusants. He reflected unkindly upon his lay subjects by his excessive praise of the clergy who had given him four subsidies for

183. Earle, fols. 184–184v; SP 14/164/91, Dudley Carleton to Sir Dudley Carleton, May 17, 1624.
184. SP 14/165/34, Sir Francis Nethersole to Sir Dudley Carleton, May 24, 1624. Nicholas, fol. 214, says that the subsidy bill passed the lower House without dissent.
185. SP 14/167/10, Sir Francis Nethersole to Sir Dudley Carleton, June 2, 1624; D'Ewes, fol. 130; OPH, VI, 337–341.

his own use, and he alluded once again to the promised supply of his particular wants at the next session of Parliament. No doubt James in his innermost convictions would have agreed with the Earl of Kellie who wrote: "This parliament is such a one as I have not seen the like, but that which I most dislike is, there is not that harmony betwixt the King's Majesty and the Prince as I could wish; not that the Prince has done anything unbeseeming him to the King's Majesty, but that out of a desire to have all things go well and that there may be no stay of moneys he has been a little more popular than was fitting for him, which his father and some of the best and wisest sort here thinks will sometime meet him if ever it shall please God that he come in his father's place and that he come to govern these people." [186]

186. HMC, *Mar and Kellie*, 201–202, Thomas, earl of Kellie, to John, earl of Mar, May 22, 1624.

# V The Spanish Reaction: Conspiracy against Buckingham

In the spring of 1624 the Duke of Buckingham had reached the pinnacle of his popularity. Describing the favorite's good fortune, Sir Edward Conway, Jr., wrote: "I think that never before did meet in one man to have so much love of the King, Prince and people." [1] By displaying considerable dexterity in personal diplomacy, the Duke had managed to retain the King's favor while he acted as a parliamentary instrument for the breach of the Spanish treaties. Not even Elizabeth's Essex had been so universally applauded and courted, and, undoubtedly, this led Buckingham to misinterpret his role in affairs. The disillusionment, which in 1625 caused him to describe himself as a servant of Parliament, had not yet sapped his confidence; in 1624 he thought of himself as the architect of English destinies. [2]

As long as harmonious relations between King and Parliament remained intact, the power base from which the favorite operated was unassailable; but Buckingham, like the Lilliputian ministers, actually walked a tightrope. The concord between James and his

---

1. SP 14/161/30, Sir Edward Conway, Jr., to Sir Dudley Carleton, Mar. 23, 1624; see also James Howell, *Epistolae Ho-Elianae: The Familiar Letters of James Howell* (4 vols., Boston: Houghton, Mifflin & Co., 1907), II, 48, Howell to his father, Dec. 10, 1624. "I am now casting about for another fortune, and some hopes I have of employment about the Duke of Buckingham. He sways more than ever, for whereas he was before a favourite to the King, he is now a favourite to Parliament, people and city, for breaking the match with Spain."

2. See Buckingham's statement to the Parliament of 1625 in Eliot, *Negotium Posterorum*, II, 60–71.

legislature was artificial, based upon parliamentary forbearance and royal concession, and the dissolution of it was virtually inevitable. The identity of interests and perspectives needed for continued harmony were lacking, and charm and affability were poor substitutes that, at best, could accomplish little more than a temporary rapprochement between James and his people.

While the armistice lasted, any attempt to displace Buckingham seemed almost foredoomed to failure, but such endeavors were not lacking. Opposition to Buckingham and his adherents came from the ranks of the discontented, the ambitious, the overconfident, the desperate, and the dedicated. Whether from principles of patriotism or personal aggrandizement, the Duke's enemies ceaselessly conspired against him — individually and in cliques and factions. Of their threat to his power he was constantly aware, ever vigilant for the first symptoms of revolt. Jacobean politics were so intensely personal that even an unintentional slight could lead to prolonged estrangement between erstwhile political allies. It was the chief business of a favorite, second only to the retention of the King's good graces, to make sure of the undivided loyalty of his partisans.

Since preferment at court was principally channeled through the favorite, there was a tendency for all opposition groups to define themselves negatively. They were against Buckingham and his entourage, rather than for any particular policies or principles. The court, then, tended to be split against itself, with patronage factions forming around those most in favor with the King. Each "great one," the focus of his particular coterie, maneuvered to displace his rivals for power and calculated his success in terms of personal advancement and the ability to gratify increasing numbers of satellites. These court cabals could frequently result from religious attitudes or diplomatic alignments, and, in the struggle for power, financial and political support was often solicited from foreign sources. On domestic issues, competitors for royal favor differed little in the degree to which they supported the King's prerogative in pursuance of their predatory economic projects.

It was axiomatic that the seventeenth-century king ruled through division — pitting one court faction against another — thus preventing the ascendancy of any interest inimical to his own.

The fundamental pattern of James's rule was dichotomous. On the one hand, his appointments to ministerial office balanced religious interests and political affiliations; on the other, he had a decided propensity for favorites, which vitiated his role as arbiter among factions. His apparent subservience to Buckingham in 1624 threatened the integrity of his rule and led contemporary observers to the erroneous conclusion that the King was devoid of influence and power.

The preeminence that Buckingham enjoyed as a result of his popularity and his political alliance with the Prince afforded him a golden opportunity to consolidate his position. Those who opposed him, no matter what their convictions or motives, were immediately and contemptuously identified with Spanish interests. Partially by design, partially by accident, a campaign was begun to eradicate Spanish influence and discredit its English allies. By the end of summer, Sir Robert Phelips congratulated the Duke for having "dissolved and broken the Spanish partie, and rendred them without either the means, or the hope of ever conjoyning in such sort together again, as may probably give the least disturbance or impediment to your Graces waies and designs." [3] Phelips's congratulations were premature; although some formidable antagonists were silenced, the destruction of Buckingham's enemies was not completed in 1624. It may, indeed, be said that the political hatreds occasioned by Buckingham's decision to scrap the King's peaceful foreign policy plagued him until his assassination.

No one doubted in 1624 that a Spanish party actually existed. Contemporaries spoke of it as if it were monolithic in structure, and they assumed that every Catholic, and every crypto-Catholic, was a member of the group. Its vital center was the Spanish embassy, its directors were Inojosa and Coloma, and its agents were the communicants and sympathizers who occupied positions of trust and who frequented the ambassadors' house. Those who refused to dissimulate their beliefs were easily identifiable, and their influence could be nullified by neglect, or, if need be, by prosecution. A Catholic member of the House of Commons, like Sir

3. *Cabala*, I, 264–266, Sir Robert Phelips to the Duke of Buckingham, Aug. 21, 1624.

Thomas Gerrard, posed no threat. Once identified, he was hunted and harried until he sought sanctuary in the Spanish embassy.[4]

A greater danger originated with those who distinguished between religious beliefs and political allegiance — those whose sympathies predisposed them to prefer a Spanish alliance and whose political power could be formidable when joined in a bloc. Their alliances were not limited by the bounds of faith, and more mundane motives conditioned their objectives. Among Buckingham's enemies, the Earl of Arundel, Thomas Howard, exemplified this group. Virtually unassailable because of his distinguished peerage, a political power because of his office as Earl Marshal, a Catholic sympathizer classified by the church as a schismatic, Arundel was a dangerous opponent; but for him the revival of Howard power and prestige was probably of more consequence than the attainment of any political or religious objective. As long as he was isolated he was powerless, and for Buckingham it became a matter of policy to exclude the Earl from preferment and to prevent his alliance with his coreligionists in office.[5]

4. On Wednesday, March 3, 1624, Sir John Jephson informed the House of Commons that Sir Thomas Gerrard, elected burgess for Liverpool, had taken neither communion nor the oaths required. It was ordered that Gerrard be summoned. By March 8 a petition had been received from him alleging ill health and requesting a new election at Liverpool. This concession was denied on the grounds that no warrant could be granted except upon certification of incurable illness. Christopher Brooke informed the Commons that he had been told that Gerrard was a recusant. As a result the House peremptorily ordered Gerrard to appear on the following morning to take the oaths and communion. When he failed to keep the appointment, the serjeant-at-arms was ordered to search for him. By March 12 his servant had been arrested and interrogated, and on the following day a committee was appointed to draw a bill of praemunire against Gerrard. Finally on March 18 the serjeant-at-arms reported that he had information that Gerrard was with the Spanish ambassador at Ely House. Although the bill against him was ordered reported out, it seems not to have passed the Commons. (*CJ*, 676, 679, 680–681, 685, 686, 725, 731, 732, 735, 736, 739; Pym, fols. 15, 21, 23v, 28v.) On April 27 Sir Thomas Gerrard was among those presented as recusants by the House of Commons to the Lords. (*CJ*, 776.)

5. Clarendon describes Thomas Howard, the earl of Arundel and Surrey, as "A man supercilious and proud who lived always within himself and to himself, conversing little with any who were in common conversation. He lived towards all favorites and great officers without any kind of condescention; and rather suffered himself to be ill treated by their power and authority (for he was always in disgrace and once or twice prisoner in the Tower) than to descend in making any application to them." (Edward, earl of Clarendon, *The History of the Rebellion and civil Wars in England* [6 vols., Oxford, 1839], I, 69.) Arundel seems to have thought highly of Weston, whom he describes in a letter to Cranfield as without equal in the King's service. When in 1621 he received a false report of Weston's death, Arundel solicited Cranfield's cooperation to obtain Weston's place for Sir Richard Tichborne, scion of an eminent Hampshire Catholic family. (Sackville MS.

The same suspicion accorded Arundel was directed at lesser court functionaries with Catholic tendencies. Of these, Sir George Calvert, "the King's popish secretary," occupied the most sensitive post, and his important role in Spanish negotiations was gradually reduced to one of little consequence. Sir Richard Weston, Chancellor of the Exchequer, was another official who demanded close observation, as was Sir Francis Cottington, the Prince's secretary. Weston was notoriously pro-Spanish in his sympathies, had been recommended for diplomatic assignments by Gondomar, and was friendly with one of the current Spanish ambassadors, Coloma. Cottington had been temporarily reunited with the Roman church during an illness in Spain in 1623 and was likewise considered a Spanish partisan. All of these courtiers were overt members of the Spanish party, but they were politicians first, calculating with precision the relative advantages or disadvantages of opposition or adherence to the favorite.

There were also officials untainted by commitment to the

---

ON 91, on deposit at the Historical Manuscripts Commission, Earl of Arundel and Surrey to Lord Treasurer Cranfield, Aug. 20, 1621.) According to Dudley Carleton, Arundel joined with Cranfield on March 12 to urge the Lords to make a particular offer of supply to the King in preference to the general engagement proposed by the Commons. "The Prince told them that seeing all the rest of the Lords were of a contrary opinion it must not be their two voices that should hinder the common resolution. It is reported that the said two Lords went afterwards to St. James to excuse what they had said . . . and the Prince is said to be very sensible of the proceedings of some, who, according to their custom in the last parliament, have their intelligences and underhand combinations to hinder all good resolutions, to the end their own actions may not be looked into, which they fear more than anything else in the world." (SP 14/160/89, Dudley Carleton to Sir Dudley Carleton, Mar. 17, 1624; see also *Lords Debates 1624 & 1626*, 30.) On April 2 the Venetian ambassador reported "The Lord Treasurer is almost openly trying to oust Buckingham, assisted secretly by the Earl of Arundel." (*Cal. S. P. Venetian*, XVIII, 264–268, Valaresso to the Doge and Senate, Apr. 2/12, 1624.) By May 1 the Earl himself was under attack in the House of Commons because of a petition preferred by York Herald. Although Buckingham was not mentioned as a promoter of this complaint, the amount of interest stirred by it suggests that Arundel was in danger of losing his marshal's office. Sir Francis Nethersole reported that the hearing "drew a full committee to the Star Chamber and amongst them all my Lord his friends of whom notwithstanding he had no great need in this business. . . . So that the committee was generally satisfied my Lord had made no fault, and so it is to be presumed the House will be also." (SP 14/164/46, Sir Francis Nethersole to Sir Dudley Carleton, May 6, 1624.) It is noteworthy that, when the Council of War was named and commissioners were appointed to treat with the Dutch, the Earl of Arundel was excluded from employment in either body. "My Lord Marshal is said to take it ill that he is left out of all; but there are others left out as well as he who heretofore thought they deserved well enough to be trusted, and yet say nothing." (SP 14/162/56, Dudley Carleton to Sir Dudley Carleton, Apr. 14, 1624.)

Catholic cause who, nevertheless, seemed well disposed toward continuing negotiations with Spain. From motives of policy, economy in government, loyalty to their aging master, and personal security, courtiers like Lord Keeper Williams, Lord Treasurer Cranfield, and the Earl of Bristol ventured to oppose Buckingham's schemes. For Cranfield and Bristol, the commitment was decisive and brought them into implied association with the Spanish party; for Williams, involvement was covert, indecisive, and fraught with implications of conspiracy, espionage, and expedience. Least tinged with Spanish affiliations was the Earl of Pembroke, Lord Chamberlain, most potent of Buckingham's adversaries. It is doubtful which he desired more ardently, the breach with Spain or the disgrace of Buckingham, but his willingness to conspire against the favorite was obvious.

It was, therefore, opposition to the Duke which provided the only cohesive bond in the nebulous faction termed the Spanish party. Certainly the Catholic crusading fervor of the Spanish ambassadors was lacking in the Anglican prelate, John Williams, and the fear that actuated men like Calvert and Cottington bothered the Earl of Pembroke little, if at all. The vindication of his reputation sought by the Earl of Bristol had little relevance for a timeserving courtier like Sir Richard Weston. Thus any alliance dedicated to the overthrow of Buckingham was almost certain to be beset by centrifugal tendencies caused by the disparate interests of its tentative participants. It is doubtful whether any of Buckingham's opponents seriously meditated combined action.

Even before it had been resolved that Parliament should meet, Buckingham had been warned by Lord Bacon against "particular great persons, which are most of them reconciled enemies, or discontented friends." Many of them would magnify Buckingham and make use of him "for the breaking of the match or putting the realm into a war, which after will return to their old bias." According to Bacon, it was indispensable for the Duke's reputation that some striking evidence of his continued favor be produced, and he repeatedly advised the "advancing or depressing of persons" as a course worthy of commendation. "It is not to be forgotten," he said, "that as long as great men were in question, as in my case, all things went sweetly for the K[ing]. But the second meeting, when no such thing was, the rack went higher."

That Buckingham's enemies would seek an opportunity to assail him was a foregone conclusion as far as Bacon was concerned, and he feared that "the battery will be chiefly laid on the Prince's part, if they find any entry." Since the Prince was generally thought to be impressionable, it would be "good to have sure persons about him, or at least none dangerous." Bacon even seems to have considered candidates for debasement — possibly Sir Francis Cottington or Sir Henry Vane. At any rate he considered it politic for Buckingham "to be author of some counsel to the Prince that tasteth of religion and virtue, lest it be imputed that he entertains him only in pleasures, like a Pe. Ga[vaston]." Retention of the Prince's friendship was vital: "The way to have the King sure unto you is to keep great with the Prince."

Bacon was no Cassandra; he did not prophesy doom for Buckingham if England remained on good terms with Spain. He thought that a prudent king like James would retain Buckingham as a useful counterpoise against Spanish influence even if the match were concluded. Nevertheless, he urged the Duke to continue his anti-Spanish efforts, not doubting that the Protestants, and particularly the Puritans, would support him. Discretion, however, demanded that consideration be given to valuable alliances, and Bacon hinted that it would be expedient to mend relations with the Earl of Pembroke. The recruitment of the Chamberlain's followers to Buckingham's forces outweighed, in Bacon's estimation, the possible threat of Pembroke's ambitions: "for his person not effectual; but some dependances he hath which are drawn with him. Besides he can take no reputation from you." [6]

6. Bacon, *Works*, XIV, 442, notes for conferences with the Duke of Buckingham, undated; *ibid.*, 442–447, contains notes of four conferences between Bacon and Buckingham prior to the commencement of Parliament. The first of these is undated; the second, dated December 17, 1623; the third and fourth, dated January 2, 1623/4. It cannot be ascertained with certainty whether these conferences ever took place, but there is independent evidence that Bacon had personal interviews with Buckingham after the latter's return from Spain. See *ibid.*, 442, letters from Bacon to Buckingham, Nov. 25, 1623. There are also two letters extant from Bacon to the Earls of Southampton and Oxford in which he solicits their aid in securing his readmission to the House of Lords. Possibly this request had the prior approval of Buckingham. It is certain that late in January 1624 the Duke interceded for Bacon in his suit to be granted the arrearages due to the crown from his half brother, Sir Nicholas Bacon. (*Ibid.*, 443–446.) Bacon also urged Buckingham to use Lord Belfast and Lord Grandison for Irish affairs, and he twice commended the Earl of Montgomery as "an honest man and a good observer." Bacon's query, "Can you do nothing with Naunton?" implies a belief that Naunton would prove a useful parliamentary spokesman for Buckingham. (*Ibid.*, 444, 446.)

It did not require the perspicacity of a Bacon to recognize that the most immediate threat to Buckingham's ascendancy originated in the Spanish legation. The rift between the Duke and the ambassadors had continually widened since his return from Spain, and their attacks upon him had gained in virulence as the diplomatic options open to them declined in number. Late in 1623 there was still time for the envoys to prevent the summoning of Parliament by offering acceptable terms for the restoration of the Palatinate. Even in January 1624 concessions would have materially affected the political situation. Parliament might have been prorogued; even if it had met, foreign relations need not have been its primary concern.

Failure to offer James proposals which he would consider as a basis for further negotiations limited the alternatives which the Spanish ambassadors could pursue after the commencement of Parliament. One option was to let events take their course and assume that nothing effectual would be accomplished in the session. Another alternative was to foment discontent within Parliament and revive the disputes over the exercise of the King's prerogative, which had disrupted three previous conventions. A third choice was to wage an intensive campaign to discredit the favorite whom the ambassadors considered to be the prime mover in aggressive designs against Spain.

In their estimates of Buckingham's strength Inojosa and Coloma were probably deluded by the disagreements which had rocked the Council for Foreign Affairs just prior to the assembly of Parliament. When, in January, it appeared that only Carlisle and Conway were resolute supporters of the Duke, the ambassadors must have been optimistic about their chances of dethroning him. Indeed, they discovered that the majority of councillors were favorably disposed toward Spain, and, when they disclosed to Pembroke their plans to oust Buckingham, he advised them to hasten the return of the Earl of Bristol.[7] All the makings of a formidable conspiracy seemed to be at hand: Buckingham had alienated Lord Keeper Williams and Lord Belfast by public criticism; the Marquess Hamilton and the Earl of Pembroke were on the point of negotiating with his enemies; Lord Treasurer Cranfield categori-

7. PRO 31/12/29, Spanish Transcripts, the Marquis de la Inojosa to Philip IV, Jan. 29/Feb. 8, 1624.

cally opposed the fiscal implications of his foreign policy. All of this discontent could be brought into focus by the revelations expected when the Earl of Bristol returned from Madrid with the "true" account of negotiations at the Spanish court.

Within a month this situation had deteriorated, and Spanish prospects of success rapidly faded. Lack of money delayed Bristol's departure from the Escorial; and the Prince was instrumental in reconciling Pembroke and Buckingham; lesser lights such as Williams hurried to submit in order to retain their places. And so the strategic moment for attack was lost. Of critical importance in the salvation of Buckingham was the steadfast support of the Prince, but his security was immeasurably increased by the assistance he received from Parliament.

It was well known that, since his return from Spain, Buckingham had mended some political fences by wooing popular peers such as Oxford, Southhampton, and Saye, but most contemporary observers miscalculated the Duke's support in the House of Commons. The reaction to his speech dealing with negotiations in Spain corrected any misapprehensions and undoubtedly forced some of Buckingham's covert enemies to reappraise their political alignments. Who could have foreseen that the same House of Commons which, in 1621, had attacked Buckingham's clique of monopolists would, in 1624, rally round and hail him as the savior of the nation? [8] Certainly not the Spanish ambassadors who fondly imagined, when they protested against Buckingham's conduct at an audience on February 26, that their remarks would remain confidential. It was with considerable chagrin that they learned on the following day that Buckingham had appealed to the Lords for justification and had, in the process, exaggerated the threats made by the ambassadors. If their parliamentary informants told them that Pembroke and Hamilton had joined the bishops and the Puritan and popular peers in promoting Buckingham's acquittal, the ambassadors must have realized that they had played into the hands of their enemy. Their only recourse was to protest feebly against Buckingham's breach of diplomatic confidence and to mitigate the force of their charges by ameliorative explanations. Meanwhile, with the full support of Parliament behind him,

8. Spring, 35; Clarendon, *History of the Rebellion,* I, 7.

Buckingham could say with self-righteous smugness, "I desyre only my justificacion and approbacion, noe revenge." [9]

One benefit did redound to the Spanish envoys from their ill-advised diatribe against the favorite; a secret channel of communications to King James was contrived. Don Francisco de Carondelet, archdeacon of Cambray and chaplain to Ambassador Coloma, was employed to transmit a letter from the Spanish ambassadors defining the charges leveled against Buckingham's parliamentary conduct. On February 29 he appeared at Hampton Court, but, instead of seeking access through the Lord Chamberlain, he made his request to the Earl of Kellie, Groom of the Stole. Kellie brought Carondelet to the King, but he was cautious enough to notify the Prince about the audience, and Charles was present during the conversations.

James defended his favorite against the charge that he had aspersed Philip IV and his ministers, and he pointed out that intelligence of naval preparations in Spain had been derived from Sir Walter Aston's dispatches. On his own account, the King complained that some of the Spanish recriminations were based upon false information, and, after the end of the audience, he sent Kellie to Carondelet with the request that the ambassadors delay their dispatches to Madrid until misunderstandings could be corrected.[10]

Since the return of Charles and Buckingham from Spain, Inojosa and Coloma had complained bitterly and frequently that constant surveillance of the King had prevented private conversations. Indeed, since mid-January they had protested that spies had been hired to watch the Spanish embassy.[11] Consequently they were not slow to take advantage of the new avenue of unofficial access to James. On March 2 Carondelet returned to Theobalds

9. *Lords Debates 1624 & 1626*, 2, 3; *Cal. S. P. Venetian*, XVIII, 241, Valaresso to the Doge and Senate, Mar. 5/15, 1624. Speaking of the charges against the Duke, Valaresso concludes "in short it only damages the Spaniards themselves while benefiting Buckingham, who by this action is established strongly under the protection of parliament and no other way could have served his interests better. I am assured that the ambassadors became aware of their mistake and afterwards repented bitterly."

10. HMC, *Mar and Kellie*, 195, Thomas, earl of Kellie, to John, earl of Mar, Mar. 11, 1624; PRO 31/12/31, Spanish Transcripts, fols. 98–100v, Carondelet's relation of his audience, Feb. 29/Mar. 10, 1624.

11. PRO 31/12/29, Spanish Transcripts, the Marquis de la Inojosa to Philip IV, Jan. 13/23, 1624.

and spoke privately with the King for an hour and a half. Purportedly he came to inform James that the ambassadors could no longer delay their dispatches, but, in reality, he came to increase the King's suspicions of Parliament, to threaten the recall of the ambassadors, and to determine whether James had tempered his demands for assistance in securing the restitution of the Palatinate. Carondelet repeatedly emphasized that the religious and military designs of Parliament were at odds with the King's desires, but James, who was using parliamentary deliberations as a diplomatic weapon, did not appear overly alarmed at the militant attitude of that body. Certainly he was not prepared to consider the implications inherent in Carondelet's remarks: that Parliament must be dissolved to preserve peace and the regal authority. Instead of modifying his position, James insisted that further negotiations depended upon the arrival of Padre Maestro with conciliatory proposals from Madrid, and he complained at length about the stupidity of the Spanish in failing to complete the treaties while Charles was in Spain.[12]

Although James was prepared to facilitate negotiations, it became increasingly difficult to maintain contact in the face of parliamentary and popular demonstrations of anti-Spanish prejudice. James was forced to proclaim his protection of the ambassadors' persons and their household, and when rumors began to circulate that Padre Maestro would be hanged if he set foot in England, the King, at the ambassador's solicitation, granted him safe conduct and sent a messenger to Calais to accompany him across the Channel. Even at court vigilance against Spanish intrigues was increased, and the Earl of Kellie incurred the high displeasure of the Prince and the Duke for his part in the secret audiences of Carondelet. Consequently, on March 9, when the archdeacon again appeared at Hampton Court, Kellie referred him to the Lord Chamberlain as the proper official to conduct him to the King.

Ostensibly Carondelet came to compliment James on his mild and judicious reply to the parliamentary request to annul the treaties, but he hinted that Spanish intransigence was weakening

12. PRO 31/12/29, Spanish Transcripts, the Marquis de la Inojosa to Philip IV, Mar. 3/13, 1624, enclosing Carondelet's account of his audience at Theobalds on March 2/12, 1624. See also PRO 31/12/31, Spanish Transcripts, fols. 102v–107v.

and that the ambassadors solicited the King's views on how relations might be improved. James's reply left no doubt that he blamed the Spanish for their dilatoriness, and he pointed out that he was virtually alone in his desire to continue amity between the two nations. In dealing frankly with Carondelet, James made it abundantly clear that the previous tactics of the ambassadors were unlikely to succeed. He encouraged no hope of Parliament's dissolution. In fact he indicated that unless concessions were forthcoming from Spain he would be forced to follow the advice of Parliament. He also intimated that the alliance between the Prince and Buckingham was too firm to be broken. Although he complained that "the devil had gotten into Buckingham," it was clear from his remarks that the same demon inhabited Charles. He told Carondelet flatly that the Prince had returned with the conviction that Spain could be conquered and, further, that he had been so incensed at the ridicule accorded his love for the Infanta that he was disposed to undertake war to avenge the insult.[13]

All that Carondelet derived from the interview was a clarification of the alternatives facing the ambassadors. If the King would not dissolve Parliament, if the entente between Charles and Buckingham could not be broken, and if they continued in Parliament's good graces, the scope of the envoys' initiative would be seriously curtailed. The one vulnerable area which could be explored was the relationship between the King and his favorite. James had already expressed annoyance with Buckingham's aggressive plans. Annoyance might be turned to suspicion and, abandoned by the King, Buckingham would be left to the mercies of his secret enemies.

But as yet there were no public symptoms of a rift between James and the Duke. When, on March 21, a parliamentary deputation came to His Majesty to present the declaration of both Houses, exonerating Buckingham of the charges made against him by the Spanish ambassadors, James responded by eulogizing the conduct of his servant. The greatest fault that Buckingham had committed "was his desiring this justification from others towards me." The King was disposed to trust his "disciple and scholar trained and tutored" by himself. This trust had been vindicated

13. PRO 31/12/31, Spanish Transcripts, fols. 122v–125v, Carondelet's relation of his audience of March 9/19, 1624.

by the testimony of the Prince and confirmed by the correspondence between the accounts of negotiations which Buckingham had delivered to the King and to Parliament. "Faith, diligence and discretion," were the qualities attributed to Buckingham in his role as extraordinary envoy to Spain. Obedience to his master had earned him the ill will of those who had opposed the journey initially and the hatred of those who were now dissatisfied with its results. That this same service had won the unanimous approval of Parliament caused James to render thanks to both Houses and implied (according to their interpretation) his approbation of the Duke's parliamentary leadership.[14]

While Parliament was obsessed with its campaign to force James into hostilities with Spain, Inojosa and Coloma were watching events and meditating a personal attack on Buckingham. From four paid parliamentary informants, each of whom garnered one-hundred pounds for his efforts, the ambassadors gleaned information about proceedings in the Lords and Commons.[15] Occurrences in the latter part of March merely confirmed their belief that the removal of Buckingham was indispensable to the achievement of their aims. On the twenty-third James accepted the offer of three subsidies and three fifteenths and promised to annul the two treaties. Knowing the King's propensity for negotiation, the ambassadors were not greatly disturbed, but, when Padre Maestro arrived on the twenty-fourth bereft of his commission and papers, it seemed as if no opportunity remained for useful bargaining. Indeed, when Maestro was presented at court, he refused to reveal whether he had been empowered to make new concessions, despite persistent importunities on the part of James, Charles, and Buckingham. In the few moments he had alone with the King, Padre

14. Harl. MS. 159, fols. 24v–25. SP 14/161/10 is an account of the same audience written from memory by Edward Nicholas. The address presented by the Lord Keeper and the King's reply are considerabley abbreviated in this report, but do not vary appreciably in content. There is also a printed account in *OPH*, VI, 111–114. James dwelt at length on the expenses incurred by Buckingham during his embassy in Spain, "he hath given an ill example to ambassadors in time to come because he went this long and great journey upon his own charges (at which the Lords laughed heartily) . . . I am ascertained he spent in that journey 40 or 50,000 pounds and for it never yet made me any account or demand, nor ever will." Harl. MS. 159, fol. 25.

15. PRO 31/12/29, Spanish Transcripts, Don Carlos Coloma to Juan de Ciriza, Mar. 31/Apr. 10, 1624. In the same letter Coloma states that "Buckingham has constantly offered 10,000 pounds to anyone who discloses our correspondents, but in vain up to the present time."

Maestro was only "able to tell him that the sin which the Spanish Ministers and all the Spaniards were guilty of was that the love and veneration which they bore to the son of so great a King did not reach so far as the subject Buckingham. The King ought to judge this for much might be said on the subject." [16]

To make sure that James was informed of all their charges against Buckingham, the ambassadors once again took advantage of their secret channel of communications. During the audience of March 29, Inojosa distracted the attention of the Prince and Buckingham while Coloma gave a note to James requesting private access for Carondelet. In pursuance of the King's secret instructions, Carondelet arrived at Theobalds on the morning of March 31, but the Earl of Kellie informed him that the audience had been delayed until 8 A.M. on the following day because "it was late already and he could not enter the palace unseen as it had been agreed." [17] At dawn on April 1 new instructions were

16. PRO 31/12/29, Spanish Transcripts, Friar de Lafuente to Philip IV, Mar. 30/Apr. 9, 1624. In my text I have consistently referred to Lafuente as Padre Maestro, a name commonly associated with him in contemporary correspondence. I have not dealt at length with the theft of Lafuente's commission and papers, which were taken from him near Abbeville in France. In the letter he wrote to Philip IV, Lafuente stated that he believed his assailants came from the Castle of Amiens and that they were commanded by one Sergeant Bayer. After his arrival in England, it was alleged that responsibility for the robbery could be attributed to Buckingham. See PRO 31/12/29, Spanish Transcripts, Diego de Lafuente to Philip IV, Mar. 21/31, 1624 (from Calais); see also PRO 31/12/29, the Marquis de la Inojosa to Philip IV, Mar. 29/Apr. 8, 1624, and Carondelet's relation of his audience, Apr. 1/11, 1624. Carondelet asserted "that the Dutch tried to throw Father Lafuente into the sea, by orders of Buckingham it was said; the King knew already how his dispatches were robbed from him. The King asked whether they thought that Buckingham was the author of this attempt. The Archdeacon answered in the affirmative but said it could not be proved." On April 5 the Earl of Kellie repeated a rumor that the robbery was contrived by one of the King's envoys to France: "either Kensington or Sir Edward Herbert, and if it proves so it will not do [sic] well with them, for his Majesty is mightily offended at it." (HMC, Mar and Kellie, 197, Thomas, earl of Kellie, to John, earl of Mar, Apr. 5, 1624.) See also SP 14/162/12, Sir Francis Nethersole to Sir Dudley Carleton, Apr. 3, 1624. "Padre Maestro casteth some suspicion upon my Lord Kensington in the relation how he was robbed of his papers."

17. PRO 31/12/29, Spanish Transcripts, Carondelet's relation of his audience at Theobalds, Apr. 1/11, 1624 (enclosed with a letter from the Marquis de la Inojosa to King Philip IV, Apr. 2/12, 1624). See also PRO 31/12/31, fols. 164v–176v. The Earl of Kellie was censured for his role as intermediary between the King and the Spanish envoys. On April 5 he wrote "for though I have suffered a little out of no error of mine but of that which no man of worth or spirit could have done otherwise, yet I hope his Highness is sufficiently persuaded of my integrity every way, and I beseech your Lordship be persuaded that I am every way right in that matter, I thank God, and that I defy all that the most malicious can do against me."

communicated to Carondelet and, with the utmost secrecy, he was led to the King's apartment by a trusted Catholic emissary. While the Earl of Kellie remained in the antechamber to prevent eaves-dropping, Carondelet delivered his diatribe against Buckingham.

Undoubtedly James had granted the audience in the expectation of receiving the proposals that Padre Maestro had refused to discuss on the twenty-ninth, but Carondelet quickly disabused the King of that notion. He pleaded ignorance of the envoy's instructions, but he asserted that, if Maestro's papers had not been stolen from him, he would have spoken to the King of "several matters which would have pleased and interested him." After considerable sparring between the King and the archdeacon about a mutual lack of good faith, James frankly told Carondelet "that he found the Prince so cold that there was no hope of his marrying the Infanta." Of that Carondelet said he was well aware, and he offered to prove that negotiations were already under way to secure a French bride for the Prince. When James categorically denied that official overtures had been made to France, Carondelet asserted that Kensington had actually communicated a proposal of marriage on Buckingham's authority.

Taking advantage of the King's astonishment, Carondelet then proceeded to list further offences of which Buckingham was guilty. He described "James' position as that of a King without power or authority, and who had only the name of a King: that he was, as it were, a prisoner and besieged; his servants were creatures of Buckingham and did not dare speak without his leave; that he was like King John of France a prisoner in Windsor, or Francis I at Madrid." He suggested that "the King ought to ascertain whether parliament had met with any other object but to serve Buckingham's interests. He had favored everyone who had incurred James' displeasure, like Oxford, and others who were even worse than him." Whoever spoke most violently in the House of Commons was considered the most elegant: "the only thing one heard was that the King had grown old, and that it would be a great happiness if the Prince reigned instead, with Buckingham whom they called the Lords' friend." To cap the climax, Carondelet asserted that the favorite had thought of forcing James to

(HMC, *Mar and Kellie,* 197, Thomas, earl of Kellie, to John, earl of Mar, Apr. 5, 1624.)

retire to a country house, and abandon the exercise of "Kingcraft." In response to these heinous charges, the King merely blushed and sighed, but did not show any annoyance. He said that he had suspected that Buckingham wished to make himself popular and that, if what Carondelet had told him was true, he would have the Duke's head cut off.[18]

Because of his unofficial status Carondelet was not bound by the rules of diplomatic decorum. Many of the charges that he leveled against Buckingham were based on nothing more substantial than rumor and hearsay. The Spanish ambassadors had had a full armory of personal indictments to hurl against the favorite since the preceding autumn, but, until James pronounced the dissolution of the two treaties, Inojosa and Coloma had forborne from accusing the Duke of seditious conduct. True, they had complained about his bad manners in intruding himself into diplomatic conferences, and they had protested against his narration to Parliament as slanderous, but they had treated him as an enemy of Spain, not of England. With Carondelet's denunciation, however, the attack shifted; the loyalty of Buckingham to his master was questioned. Even in early April the ambassadors were unwilling to admit official cognizance of this change in strategy, although it was widely suspected in England that Padre Maestro had been sent for no other purpose than to defend Bristol and attack the favorite.

Taking advantage of the Prince's and the Duke's preoccupation with parliamentary affairs, the Spanish ambassadors sent Padre Maestro to Theobalds on April 3 to add fuel to the fire of James's suspicions. Secretary Conway, Buckingham's sentinel, was dismissed from attendance, and for three hours the King and Padre Maestro talked privately. Most of the conversation was about the Palatinate — inconclusive and recriminatory — but Bristol, Buckingham, and the impending persecution of Catholics were also treated. As for the Palatinate, James reiterated his insistence upon a promise of armed intervention by the Spanish if the Emperor refused to effect restitution within a reasonable time. Yet James was using the last weapon in his arsenal — the letter signifying the disavowal of negotiations was awaiting dispatch — and the Spanish

18. PRO 31/12/29, Spanish Transcripts, Carondelet's relation of his audience, Apr. 1/11, 1624; see also PRO 31/12/31, fols. 164v–176v.

had made no concessions worthy of the name. In fact, the diplomatic initiative appeared to have been regained by the Spanish. The seeds of suspicion sown by the ambassadors had taken root, and James confided to Padre Maestro that if what the ambassadors had communicated to him was true, "Buckingham was the greatest villain in the world, a greater traitor than Judas, for Judas had only had charge of the purse, while he had trusted Buckingham with his life and honor, and it annoyed him greatly to think he could not intend so wicked an act without the Prince knowing something about it." [19]

With the groundwork laid for the overthrow of Buckingham, the Spanish envoys began exploring the possibilities of recruiting support among court dignitaries. About Lord Treasurer Cranfield they had no doubts since his very survival was in jeopardy unless Buckingham fell.[20] He was, however, an ally of dubious utility; a parliamentary majority backed by the Prince and the Duke were intent upon his impeachment. As long as Cranfield retained his favor with the King, he could be useful in stiffening James's resolve not to wage war, but it was only a matter of time until access would be denied him on the pretext that he was suspect.

How many conspiratorial overtures were made to courtiers by the Spanish ambassadors it is impossible to say with certainty. Contemporaries vehemently suspected that the Earl of Arundel was involved in a cabal against the favorite, but no proof is extant. It is extremely improbable that Hamilton and Pembroke were approached because of their conduct in Parliament and their imminent involvement with the Dutch. Weston and Calvert were more likely candidates: Calvert was discontented because of neglect; Weston was jeopardized by his association with the Lord Treasurer.

Documentary evidence of Spanish intrigue survives in only one instance. Late in the evening of April 5, Don Francisco Carondelet invited Lord Keeper Williams to participate in a conspiracy against

19. PRO 31/12/29, Spanish Transcripts, Friar de Lafuente to Philip IV, Apr. 4/14, 1624.
20. On March 1/11 the Marquis de la Inojosa was already aware of the danger liable to be incurred by Lord Treasurer Cranfield if he continued his policy of disagreement with Prince Charles. He had been told by an informant that the Prince had threatened to overthrow Cranfield if he persisted in advocating the continuance of the treaties with Spain. (PRO 31/12/29, Spanish Transcripts, Marquis de la Inojosa to Philip IV, Mar. 1/11, 1624.)

the favorite. "He had heard that the Duke had pusht at me [Williams] in Parliament, and intended to do so again, when he had done with the Treasurer, and therefore shewed, that if I would joyn to set upon him with the King, there was a fit occasion."

Assuming the Keeper's compliance, Carondelet proceeded to reveal the discourse he had made to James on April 1. Naïvely enough he even described the means by which he had procured private access to the King and proudly exhibited for Williams's inspection a remonstrance against Buckingham which he had drawn up incorporating the tenets of his oral invective. He also tried to convince the Keeper that the Spanish were genuinely interested in meeting James's demands. He stated that money had been appropriated in Spain to satisfy the claims of the Duke of Bavaria and that he had offered James assurance of the restitution of the Palatinate by negotiation within three months. Futhermore, "because the people were so distrustful of the Spaniard, the King might fortifie himself at home, and assist the Hollanders with men or money at his pleasure. And the King of Spain should not be offended therewith."

Having demonstrated the tolerance and good faith of Philip IV, Carondelet proceeded to prove the estrangement between Buckingham and his monarch. Quoting the King directly, Carondelet contended that James really desired the Duke's downfall. He had admitted that Charles "was strangely carried away with rash, and youthful Councels, and followed the humour of Buckingham, who had he knew not how many Devils within him." The King had also conceded "That he had good cause to suspect the Duke of late, but he had no servant of his own, that would charge him with any particular." Moreover, on at least two occasions he had told the Spanish envoys "to get him any ground to charge him with popular courses, or to increase a suspition of it, and he would quickly take a course with him." [21] Obviously it was the archdea-

21. Harl. MS. 7000, fols. 151–152v. "Heads of that Discourse which fell from D. Fr. 7mo die April 1624 at 11 of the clock at night." Printed in *Cabala,* I, 90–93. I have assigned April 5 as the appropriate date for this composition on the basis of internal evidence. The document refers to Carondelet's last access (April 1), "which was some 4 dayes ago," and it also mentions "That he [James] desired Don Francisco, and the Embassadours (and renewed this request unto them by Padre Maestro two days ago,) to get him any ground to charge him [Buckingham] with popular courses." Padre Maestro saw the King at Theobalds on April 3. Gardiner, *History of England,* V, 211, n., discusses this conference between Carondelet and

con's intention to convince Williams that his own self-preservation and his loyalty to the crown enjoined his participation in the plot to discredit Buckingham. That he would thereby promote the interests of Spain was of incidental importance.[22]

---

Williams and tries to integrate it with Hacket's narrative of the Lord Keeper's "discovery" of the Spanish plot against Buckingham. According to Gardiner, "What had to be accounted for was, how Carondelet came to confer with Williams on such secret matters; what was his end in 'desiring this conference.'" In opposing Tierney's doubts about Hacket's veracity, Gardiner ignores the motive which is patently asserted in the document and which I have cited above. Although Gardiner is willing to challenge Hacket's authority for dates and places, he is unwilling to admit that Hacket fabricated anecdotes about the Lord Keeper's espionage system or Carondelet's morality. He maintains that Buckingham went to Theobalds "to feel his ground with the King, whilst Williams remained in London, to probe Carondelet's secret to the bottom." (*Ibid.*, 210.) The Duke was absent from the House of Lords on April 6 and 7, but there is no reason to conclude that he was ignorant of the scandalous accusations which Carondelet had made. I suggest that the main reason Buckingham went to Theobalds was to expedite Grisley's departure for Spain with the dispatch dissolving the treaties.

22. Carondelet was right in assuming that self-preservation was a powerful motivating force in the Lord Keeper's actions. Early in the parliamentary session (March 1) Williams had procured the King's intercession with the House of Commons in his behalf. The House was "desired not to be too ready to take all complaints (except they be for corruption) for as for matter of judgment and decree it is impossible for him or any judge to give account of all the decrees he makes and the proofs and reasons conducing and moving him thereunto." (Spring, 49.) In the lower House at least three petitions against Williams were fully treated by the Committee for Courts of Justice chaired by Sir Robert Phelips. "Upon the hearing of Grimsditch's complaint against the Lord Keeper the Committee resolved that so frivolous and idle a matter should not be presented to the House to divert them from better business." (SP 14/160/91, Edward Nicholas to John Nicholas, Mar. 18, 1624.) Two important petitions delivered by Joan Thomas and the Lady Darcy were of a more serious nature. Although both were in the hands of the Committee by March 17, no action was taken until late April. The Lady Darcy alleged that the Lord Keeper did unduly (in the minority of her son) present Dr. Graunt to a parsonage which belonged to her child and caused that she should not have a writ of *quare impedit* whereby to try her right by law. Proceedings on this complaint were heard in a very full committee hearing on April 21. The best reports are in Pym, fols. 75–77v; Earle, fols. 153v–156; Holles, fols. 137v–138v. Sir Edward Coke was inclined to find the Lord Keeper culpable, but he was ably defended by the Prince's solicitor, Sir John Walter, who said that, "He had no desire to break great men or to cast shame into their faces." Also, "Mr. Selden began to strain some reasons so far in justifying my Lord Keeper that he was interrupted." (Pym, fol. 77.) The problem of law in Lady Darcy's case was so obscure and technical that she was left to procure a private bill which passed the House of Commons on May 14. (Earle, fol. 183.) The petition of Joan Thomas was not heard until May 8. It alleged bribery against the Lord Keeper in passing a decree in Chancery which made her lands liable for the payment of a debt incurred by her son, Sir Anthony Thomas. The best report of proceedings is contained in Earle, fols. 177–178v. Ultimately, on May 27, the Lord Keeper was cleared by the House of Commons of the charge of corruption and bribery. (Earle, fol. 196.) Sir Francis Nethersole, in his letter to Sir Dudley Carleton of May 24, 1624, implies that by that date the Commons had already taken official action to clear Williams; "the House made no great matter of it and

The Lord Keeper returned a noncommittal answer to Carondelet's enticements. He promised to "deal by way of counsel with the Duke to be temperate, and moderate," but he disavowed any intention of opposing his friend and patron because it would prejudice his reputation as an honest man. Then, as soon as the archdeacon had departed, Williams wrote an account of their conversation and dispatched it to Buckingham.

Reflection on what had passed must have convinced Carondelet that he had acted rashly. He had apparently promised to deliver a copy of the charges against Buckingham to the Lord Keeper, but when he appeared at Williams's lodgings on the following day he excused himself by alleging that the Marquis Inojosa had the document in his custody. The real motive behind this visit was distrust of the Lord Keeper: "He [Carondelet] was very inquisitive if I had already, or intended to impart, what he had told me the night before in secret, to any man." He emphasized the need for security measures because "The King had charged him and the Frier [Padre Maestro] to be very secret." With belated caution Carondelet tried to disavow any official involvement of the Spanish ambassadors in the conspiracy against Buckingham by pretending that he had made overtures to Williams without their knowledge. Indeed, he made an ingenuous attempt to deny that a plot existed by asking the Keeper to show him "some way, how the Duke might be won unto them, and to continue the peace." This suggestion was implicitly contradicted by his commendation of the courage and resolution of the Lord Treasurer who was currently under attack in Parliament.

When Williams seemed more receptive to the idea of mediation

---

so his Lordship is now safe for this session, which will make men wary how they meddle with him at the next." (SP 14/165/34.) Earle, fols. 187v–188, includes a very interesting list of the petitions delivered to the three grand committees in 1624. By far the greater proportion of them deal with Chancery matters. In the Lords, action on a scandalous petition by Morley, a woodmonger, began on March 19. Ultimately the Lord Keeper was vindicated, and both Morley and Waterhouse (who penned the petition) were censured by the upper House. (*Lords Debates 1624 & 1626*, 34–39, 41–47, 60.) Hacket (*Scrinia Reserata*, 190–194) deals at length with the petitions preferred by Morley and Lady Darcy. He implies that the Duke of Buckingham instigated the Keeper's troubles. "Popular Favor continued a while with the Duke, and now he was St. George on Horseback, let the Dragon take heed, that stood in his Way. The Earl of Middlesex was removed, and he that presided over the great Accounts, did now stand for a Cipher. The Lord Keeper perceived his turn was next; although he wanted not fair Words, and fair Semblance from the Contriver." (*Ibid.*, 190.)

between the Spaniards and Buckingham than he did to the prospect of intrigue against the favorite, Carondelet must have realized that his efforts were in vain. Obviously, he could not believe that the Lord Keeper was as disinterested as he pretended. The intelligence which had been communicated was too valuable not to be utilized by Williams, no matter how much he protested his preoccupation with matters of his own court and the pulpit. In fact, by the end of the conference, Carondelet expressed doubts about the trustworthiness of James himself. He asked Williams "if they might rely upon the King, whom onely they found peaceably addicted; otherwise they would cease all mediation, and prepare for War." Implicit in his query was the suspicion that James's censures of Buckingham were mere dissimulation.[23]

23. Harl. MS. 7000, fol. 113, is endorsed "Bishop of Lincoln's relation of speeches passed between his lordship and Don Francisco 11 April 1623 [sic]." This paper is actually headed "Don Francisco 11 April 1623 [sic]" and is in the Lord Keeper's handwriting. This is printed in *Cabala*, I, 77–78, with the date April 11, 1622, and in Gardiner, *History of England*, V, 212–213, n. Gardiner's version is taken from Birch's transcripts. (Add. MS. 4164, fol. 280.) On the basis of internal evidence and logical probability, I have concluded that the date should be April 6, 1624. It defies reason to assume that a conspirator would wait four days (at a minimum) before he tried to be certain of the good faith of a doubtful ally. It must also be remembered that the first words of the document are: "He was very inquisitive if I had already or intended to impart what he had told me in secret, *the night before* to any man." (Italics mine.) It is quite clear from Hacket's narrative (*Scrinia Reserata*, 195) that he was familiar with both of the documents printed in *Cabala*, and that he apparently accepted the dates April 7 and 11 as genuine. On p. 198 he says, "The Copy of the main Paper, scratch'd in some places with Don Carlo Colonna's Hand (for the Keeper knew his Writing) was not brought him till four Nights after. He had enough of their Brewing at the first running; for he kept Don Carondelet till 2 of the Clock in the Morning, and let him not part, till he had squeez'd him dry." The paper corrected with Coloma's hand was shown by Carondelet during the first conversation, but it was apparently never delivered to Williams, for at the second audience an excuse was offered by the archdeacon for his failure to produce it. Yet Hacket says that "the Lord Keeper after the Good Night given to Francisco, retired to his own Thoughts, and poured the whole Conference out of his Memory into his Papers, as if Francisco had stood by to dictate every Line . . . He digested the severals into a Method, and confected an Antidote for every Poyson, Christal-clear Answers, well weighed in Judgment, to Gag the Spanish ill Framed Jealousies, and as demulcing as shortness of time would permit, to make all sweet with the Old King. He saw no Sleep that Night with his Eyes, nor stirr'd out of the Room till about 7 in the Morning he had trimm'd up a fair Copy of all the Proceedings, which he presented to the Prince in St. James's, and told him he had the Viper and her Brood in a Box." According to *Cabala*, I, 90–93, the first conference with Carondelet ended after eleven o'clock at night, and Williams completed his letter to Buckingham at 2 A.M. I have been unable to discover any document in which Williams attempted to answer the charges. Certainly Hacket prints none. (*Scrinia Reserata*, 199.) Despite the fact that Hacket's veracity has been challenged on several occasions, his narrative has gained credit by repetition. Among modern historians who have accepted his version uncritically are

The psychology of the King not only troubled Carondelet, but was also a matter of some concern to Inojosa and Coloma. They knew the royal reputation for devious and quixotic behavior and were never quite certain that they were not being duped. They conceived preservation of his regal authority to be the primary motive behind James's actions, and, having warned him of the threat to his prerogative, they resolved to convey the impression that they were merely dispassionate observers of the impending political upheaval. Consequently, the ambassadors did not press their accusations against Buckingham after the initial charges had been leveled by Carondelet and Padre Maestro. They relied upon James's instinct for self-preservation to do their work for them, and it was not long before Cottington appeared with a message expressing bewilderment at the ambassadors' silence and requesting additional converse with either of their emissaries.[24]

Anticipating an opportunity to widen the rift between the King

---

H. R. Trevor-Roper, *Archbishop Laud* (2d ed., Hamden, Conn.: Archon Books, 1963), 61–62, and D. H. Willson, *King James VI and I* (New York: Henry Holt and Co., 1956), 463,n.12. In 1828 John Nichols, in his *The Progresses, Processions, and Magnificent Festivities of King James the First* (3 vols. in 4, London, 1828), IV, 961,n., 962,n., tried to reconcile Hacket's relation with verifiable fact. He identified six types of errors in Hacket's story, but nevertheless attempted to link it with an event described by John Chamberlain in his letter to Sir Dudley Carleton on January 17, 1624. "On Sonday [January 11] the Venetian ambassador had audience, the French on Monday [January 12], and the Spaniards were with the King the morning before he went [Tuesday, January 13], and that so privatly that none were admitted, till toward the later end and after a full howres audience and more, the Prince was called, and somwhat after him the Duke of Buckingam. What passed is not knowne, but they were observed to come out very sad, and presently the Duke went to his bed, so that the Prince went not with the King (as he meant to have done, his cariages beeing called backe) but taried till the next afternoone when they went both together." (Chamberlain, *Letters*, II, 539, letter of Jan. 17, 1624.) It was at this audience that the Spanish ambassadors delivered Philip IV's "last answer" on the Palatinate question, which seemed to promise hope of restoration through negotiations. This fact alone was enough to deject Charles and Buckingham. It is interesting to note that Hacket considered an apologia necessary for his revelations about Lord Keeper Williams's espionage activities. He says that, "This passage so memorable hath pluck'd on a Prolix Narration for divers Reasons": to reveal a secret "likely to be buried for ever"; to explain why the Spanish match was never revived; to account for the naval expedition to Cadiz in pursuance of Buckingham's revenge; and to demonstrate how Williams saved Buckingham and prevented the dissolution of Parliament. According to Hacket, "The Keeper had Content enough, that the Duke triumphed over those Foes, whom he had vanquished for him." (Hacket, *Scrinia Reserata*, 200.) The effect of this "invention" is to lionize Williams and to charge the Duke with ingratitude because, simultaneously, Hacket accuses Buckingham of engineering the Lord Keeper's removal.

24. PRO 31/12/29, Spanish Transcripts, the Marquis de la Inojosa to Philip IV, May 5/15, 1624.

and his favorite, Inojosa and Coloma briefed Padre Maestro for an audience scheduled to take place at Theobalds on April 19. However, the Prince's presence at court on that day threatened the privacy of the undertaking so the interview was deferred until the twentieth. The friar began by lodging the usual complaints about the difficulties of securing access to James, reiterating the assertion that the King was virtually imprisoned in a network of Buckingham's spies, informers, and sycophants. He dealt at length with the dangerous alliance which the Duke had contrived between himself and a Puritan Parliament and condemned his betrayal of state secrets such as the projected Anglo-Spanish treaty against the Dutch and the secret articles in the marriage compact stipulating parliamentary confirmation of the abrogation of the religious penal laws within three years. Padre Maestro called for the dissolution of Parliament "which was the Duke's arm to weaken the royal authority and ruin the Catholics."

None of this was news to James; he had heard it all before from a variety of sources. Probably he expected more concrete details about the plot which Carondelet had disclosed: the confinement of the King to a country house and the usurpation of his authority by the Prince supported by Buckingham's Parliament. With this subject Padre Maestro did not deal. Tactically it was unwise for the Spanish to accuse the Prince of a conspiracy against his father; it was much better to suggest that Buckingham was aiming at self-aggrandizement. Consequently, when Padre Maestro dealt with the Duke's intrigues against royal authority, he revealed a plot that involved the extinction of the very House of Stuart. He insisted that Buckingham single-handedly had contrived to ruin the Spanish match. On the very day that he had received assurance that a marriage would be arranged between his daughter and the son of the Elector Palatine, Buckingham had obliged Prince Charles to revoke his proxy. He had screened his intentions to prevent any marriage for the Prince by instituting negotiations in France, but he had guaranteed their futility by inducing Charles to swear a public oath that no alleviation of the penalties against recusancy would be considered as a condition in a marriage treaty with a Catholic princess. His ultimate objective, therefore, was the replacement of the House of Stuart by the dynasty of Villiers.

To an attentive King, Padre Maestro described the malignant

growth of Buckingham's ambition. The symptoms had already appeared during the journey to Spain and were expressed in the contemptuous behavior of the Duke toward the Prince. Conde-scension was the least of the faults in his attitude toward "niño Carlo"; he had remained seated while the Prince stood, appeared undressed in the royal presence, and was guilty of obscene and scandalous speeches and gestures. He had profaned the Escorial by procuring harlots for his amusement. He had repeatedly broken his word and was never of the same opinion two days consecu-tively. Worst of all, he had incited the Prince to break his vows to the King of Spain. And yet these were but the first signs of Buckingham's megalomania — his vain-glorious appetites had been whetted by the popular adulation lavished upon him since his return.[25]

Into Padre Maestro's invective were infused all the poisonous rumors that had been collected by the Spanish ambassadors. Some of the aspersions laid upon Buckingham derived their authority from Conde Olivares himself, and, on his orders, had been com-municated to Inojosa in October 1623 to await the strategic mo-ment for their publication.[26] The purported marriage compact between the Elector Palatine's son and the Duke's daughter had been common gossip in the courts of Westminster, Paris, and Madrid.[27] From this mélange of charges Padre Maestro concocted a persuasive tale of intrigue far more insidious than Carondelet's outright allegations of sedition. No longer did implications of complicity in Buckingham's designs besmirch the Prince's repu-tation; his filial devotion to his father was unquestioned. Now he was portrayed as a dupe, victimized by his own virtue of loyalty to a false friend. If, however, Buckingham's true objectives were revealed to Charles, doubtless he would be reconciled to the King's policy of continued amity with Spain. In recommending this tu-torial office to James, Padre Maestro intended to use him as a

25. *Ibid.*, Friar de Lafuente to Philip IV, May 10/20, 1624; see also PRO 31/12/31, fols. 211–219.

26. PRO 31/12/29, Spanish Transcripts, Juan de Ciriza to the Marquis de la Inojosa, Sept. 25/Oct. 5, 1623.

27. *Ibid.*, Marquis de la Inojosa to Philip IV, Sept. 4/14, 1623; *Cal. S. P. Venetian*, XVIII, Appendix 629, Alvise Corner (Venetian ambassador in Spain) to the Doge and Senate, Oct. 6/16, 1623; M. A. E. Green, *Elizabeth Electress Palatine and Queen of Bohemia*, revised by S. C. Lomas (London: Methuen & Co. 1909) 231–232, Elizabeth to her father, James I, May 28, 1624.

cat's-paw to effect the isolation and destruction of Buckingham.

The King's credulity did not extend to a belief that Buckingham intended to establish his progeny on the throne of England. He likewise denied the allegation that the Duke was trying to prevent the Prince's marriage, but he did betray anxiety about the favorite's popularity. The working agreement between Buckingham and the parliamentary Puritans alarmed James, who was convinced "that the Puritans did not wish for a King, but that everyone should be equal." In fact he expressed a desire to dissolve Parliament and "send them all to the devil." [28]

Having experienced Buckingham's unstable temperament, James was prepared to believe that he had transgressed the limits of decorum. Mere accusations, however, were not enough, and, as far as the King was concerned, the burden of proof rested on the Spanish ambassadors. He continually begged for more details and the names of persons who would confirm the charges. Always his criticisms of his son and his favorite were prefaced by expressions of doubt concerning the veracity of the charges; if what was said of the Duke was true, there was not a worse man in the world, and the Prince had no sense of honor if it was true that he had seen and consented to Buckingham's conduct in Spain.

Although the King was reluctant to accept common fame as sufficient proof, Padre Maestro was unwilling to reveal his sources and produce witnesses. No revelations were made about the overtures to the Lord Keeper; neither the Lord Treasurer nor the Earl of Arundel were indicated as possible informants. Even Secretary Calvert, whom the Prince had forbidden to communicate with the Spanish ambassadors and who was in danger of prosecution for his pro-Spanish activities, was not mentioned as a willing collaborator.[29] Only the Earl of Bristol, whose return was expected daily, was conceded to be avowedly hostile to Buckingham.

28. PRO 31/12/29, Spanish Transcripts, Friar de Lafuente to Philip IV, May 10/20, 1624; see also PRO 31/12/31, fols. 211–219.

29. PRO 31/12/29, Spanish Transcripts, Marquis de la Inojosa to Philip IV, Apr. 4/14, 1624. "The King told Calvert to take him any paper or message of the Spanish Ambassadors and when the Prince heard it he prohibited it." Dudley Carleton wrote on April 24, "I hear a shrewd whispering as if Mr. Secretary Calvert were in some doubtful terms with the King and Prince, and that, among other things brought against him, he is called to an account for a reason alleged by himself almost a year since at the Council board for his not sending away to your Lordship the letters appointed by the King touching the business of the siege of the Dunkirkers in Scotland; namely, that he had shewed them to the Spanish

The Spanish ambassadors had good reason to conceal their partisans; James's reputation for dissimulation was such that they could never be sure that he was acting in good faith. He might, indeed, be acting in Buckingham's behalf, seeking out the Spanish pensioners in order to destroy them. The gracious answer which James returned to the parliamentary petition against recusants, the promises made to Mansfeldt, the negotiations with the Dutch, and the later sequestration of the Earl of Bristol from the court belied the opinions he expressed privately to the emissaries of Philip IV. He did, nevertheless, continue to solicit information from the Spanish embassy.

The climax came on April 24 when Inojosa and Coloma went to court to seek an explanation for military preparations in England. They were no longer convinced that James's assurances of peaceful intentions were true. They knew that the Commons were beginning consideration of the subsidy bill which would finance a war. Moreover, James had just given fresh evidence of his duplicity; his private engagement to the ambassadors to protect the English Catholics had been nullified by his public promise to enforce the laws against recusants.

Anger and frustration betrayed the Spanish ambassadors into rash action. Convinced of the pusillanimity of the King and foreseeing that he would continue to compromise his principles under

---

Ambassadors and at their request forborne the sending them away." (SP 14/163/47, Dudley Carleton to Sir Dudley Carleton, letter dated Apr. 15, but it should be dated Apr. 24, 1624 [later letter corrects this error, see SP 14/164/7]). On May 3 Dudley Carleton noted that the "process framing against Mr. Secretary Calvert is deferred for the present by means of a bold accusation of my Lord of Buckingham made by the Spanish Ambassador." (SP 14/164/7.) The Lord Treasurer, on the day after the plot against Buckingham became public information, became suspect. Sir Francis Nethersole wrote, "My Lord Treasurer is vehemently suspected to have had a hand in this plot, and it hath been noted for an argument thereof that he was very merry this morning after his dejection a few days since." On April 30 Chamberlain noted, "For a fortnight together he had often accesse to his Majestie and much private conference, by the meanes (as is said) of the Lords of Kelly, Holdernes, and Annan: and on Saterday last [April 24] was long with the King before he was up: but that afternoone he receved a message by the Prince, not to come in the Kings presence any more till he had cleered himself." (SP 14/163/50, Sir Francis Nethersole to Sir Dudley Carleton, Apr. 25, 1624; Chamberlain, *Letters*, II, 555, letter of Apr. 30, 1624.) In the Commons Sir Robert Phelips, particularly, was worried about the espionage and influence of the Spanish ambassadors. On March 11 he asserted that "some in this House in a secondary manner within an hour or two convey what here is done unto the Spanish Ambassador." (Earle, fol. 76; *CJ*, 683.) Again on March 20 he expressed anxiety about those who advised the King to oppose the designs of Parliament. (Pym, fol. 35v.)

pressure from the Prince, the Duke, and the Parliament, the ambassadors tried to avert this catastrophe through the artful use of terror. The groundwork had been laid by the insinuations of Carondelet and Padre Maestro, but now official credence was given to the accusations against Charles and Buckingham. Under a "pretext of zeal & particular care of his person" Inojosa and Coloma disclosed to James "a very great conjuration against his person and Royall Dignity, and it was, That at the beginning of the Parliament, the Duke of Buckingham had consulted with certain Lords, of the arguments and means which were to be taken touching the breaking and dissolving of the Treaties of the Palatinate and Match; and the consultations passed thus far, That if his Majesty would not accomodate himself to their councels, they would give him a house of pleasure whither he might retire himself to his sports, in regard that the Prince had now years sufficient to, and parts answerable for the government of the Kingdom." [30]

30. *Cabala*, II, 152–155, "A Memorial to the King of Spain by Sir Walter Aston, Ambassador in Spain, August 29, 1624." This document is endorsed with the place and date, Madrid, August 5, 1624. The charges made by the Spanish ambassadors at their audience at Whitehall on April 24, 1624, climaxed the plot against Buckingham and hence have been the subject of much historical discussion and distortion. Perhaps the most persistent misrepresentation has been Hacket's contention that these accusations were secret and were only disclosed as a result of Lord Keeper Williams's espionage activities. Every contemporary source that I have consulted confirms the conclusion that, within a matter of hours after the audience, the gist of the charges was known throughout London. In my discussion of the entire Spanish conspiracy against the favorite, I have relied upon contemporary evidence rather than upon that developed by later biographers and historians whose recollections were clouded by time and distorted by affection or political circumstances. In my opinion, the best accounts are contained in PRO 31/12/31, Spanish Transcripts, the Marquis de la Inojosa to Philip IV, May 5/15, 1624, fols. 201–211, and Friar Diego de Lafuente to Philip IV, May 10/20, 1624, fols. 211–219; *Cal. S. P. Venetian*, XVIII, 299–303, Valaresso to the Doge and Senate Apr. 30/May 10, 1624; 307–312. Valaresso to the Doge and Senate, May 7/17, 1624, 316–318, Valaresso to the Doge and Senate, May 14/24, 1624; SP 14/163/50, Sir Francis Nethersole to Sir Dudley Carleton, Apr. 25, 1624; SP 14/164/46, the same to the same, May 1 and 6, 1624; SP 14/164/12, Dudley Carleton to Sir Dudley Carleton, May 3, 1624; Rusdorff, *Mémoires*, 293–294, Rusdorff to Frederick, elector Palatine, Apr. 26/May 6, 1624; 295–297, Rusdorff to Frederick, elector Palatine, May 2/12, 1624; PRO 31/3/58, French Transcripts, Comte de Tilliers to M. de la Ville aux Clercs, Apr. 26/May 6, 1624, fols. 93v–95; May 4/14, 1624, fols. 98–100 and 102v; Chamberlain, *Letters*, II, 554–557, letter of Apr. 30, 1624; Horne, fol. 67 (written May 19, 1624). I have weighed this evidence in connection with the accounts detailed by observers (some of them contemporary) who wrote at a later date. The classic account is given by Hacket (*Scrinia Reserata*, I, 195–200). Other narratives are printed in Arthur Wilson's "Life and Reign of James First, King of Great Britain," in Kennet, *A Complete History of England*, II, 782–784; Rushworth, *Historical Collections*, I, 144–145; Sir William Sanderson, "Aulicus Coquinariae" reprinted in Sir Walter Scott,

The ambassadors reckoned without the royal conscience. Undoubtedly they hoped that James would dismiss his favorite without judicial process, but the King's justice demanded verification of the accusations, particularly since the alleged plot reflected on the Prince's conduct. To his continued solicitation for the disclosure of their informants, Inojosa and Coloma turned a deaf ear. Instead they asserted that there were Lords of the Privy Council who "could give sufficient evidence hereof if they were examined on their oath." The official nature of the Spanish representations compelled the King to take action even though he was dissatisfied with the hesitancy of the plaintiffs to pursue the prosecution.

After the ambassadors had departed, James sent Cottington to their residence with a request for a formal statement of charges against Buckingham. It may be that this request resulted from a stormy conference in which James informed the Prince and the Duke of the Spanish accusations. The agitated King was reported to have accused Buckingham of ingratitude and with having wrenched the royal will to suit his own purposes. The Spanish ambassadors heard that the Duke was reduced to despair, but that he was resolutely defended by the Prince, who exaggerated the number of his enemies and asserted that Buckingham would willingly lock himself in the Tower to prove his fidelity.

Other reporters of the conference claimed that both the Prince and the Duke were astonished, but not excessively perturbed, at the boldness of the Spanish emissaries. Buckingham was credited with sufficient perspicacity to perceive the contradictions inherent in the Spanish accusations. If any design to coerce the King were projected, it must be either with the Prince's knowledge or without it. The filial obedience of Charles precluded the assumption of his complicity in a conspiracy, and it was impossible that the Duke "should ever hope to effect such a matter by the affections of the people or parliament which are so much addicted to His Highness that nothing but tearing in pieces could befall him that should adventure upon such an action." [31]

---

ed., *The Secret History of the Court of James the First* (Edinburgh, 1811), II, 275–279. There is another manuscript account in the Salvetti letters, Add. MSS. 27,962 C, Salvetti Correspondence, 1623–1625, fols. 145–146, letter of May 7/17, 1624, and fols. 248v–249v, letter of Apr. 30/May 10, 1624.

31. SP 14/164/12, Dudley Carleton to Sir Dudley Carleton, May 3, 1624.

Contradictory descriptions of the King's behavior circulated through London as rumors of the Spanish conspiracy spread. The Venetian ambassador suspected that James had privately encouraged Inojosa and Coloma to lay their charges, but he also reported current gossip that the King had wept copiously when he was informed of the plot. Some courtiers asserted that the King considered the indictment of no consequence and would never have told Charles and Buckingham about it if he had believed it. Whatever his conduct, James learned from his conversation with the Prince and Buckingham that it was virtually impossible to break their alliance. Bringing the charges into the open had landed him in "a peck of troubles; for the Prince and my Lord of Buckingham will not let him rest till they have satisfaction against the ambassador." [32]

Certainly the continued freedom of Buckingham protended ill for Inojosa and Coloma; it implied that the King was unwilling or powerless to confine his favorite. True, the Duke had not accompanied James and Charles to Windsor for the celebration of the garter ceremonies. Presumably he absented himself from court voluntarily, pending his vindication, and came to Windsor only after persistent importunity by both King and Prince. In the meantime he commissioned Sir Robert Cotton to investigate precedents of proceedings against ambassadors, who had broken the rules of diplomatic protocol. Buckingham's friends and sycophant did not appear unduly worried about the charges aimed against him. Indeed, it was reported that Parliament longed to take notice of the affair.

Even Spanish partisans considered the ambassadors' actions imprudent, and, despite a certain amount of bravado, Inojosa and Coloma soon realized the folly of their decision. For a time they debated the wisdom of complying with the King's request for a written statement of charges, but, on the advice of one of their incognito informants, they ordered Padre Maestro to prepare the document. The paper sent to Windsor contained no reference

32. *Cal. S. P. Venetian*, XVIII, 300–301, Valaresso to the Doge and Senate, Apr. 30/May 10, 1624; see also Horne, fol. 67; Rusdorff, *Mémoires*, 293–294, Rusdorff to Frederick, elector Palatine, Apr. 26/May 6, 1624, and 295–297, Rusdorff to Frederick, elector Palatine, May 2/12, 1624; SP 14/164/12, Dudley Carleton to Sir Dudley Carleton, May 3, 1624; HMC, *Mar and Kellie*, 199, Thomas, earl of Kellie, to John, earl of Mar, May 5, 1624.

whatsoever to the conspiracy to usurp the King's authority. In fact, it was little more than a written recapitulation of the charges Padre Maestro had leveled against Buckingham during the audience of April 20. Instead of helping the ambassadors' case, it tended to undercut it. Inojosa's revelations had reinforced Carondelet's denunciation of the Duke, Prince, and Parliament for conspiring to depose the King; Padre Maestro's invective had charged Buckingham with disparaging the Prince and inhibiting his marriage. The contradiction was self-evident.

Nevertheless, having a document in hand, James resolved to proceed judicially. Even though Padre Maestro had written that the accusations were "such as cannot be made clear and manifest by any legal process," he had counseled James to "search the opinion of the more moderate in the Parliament . . . [and] enquire of those that are returned from Spain who it was that gave the first occasion of enmity?" It was incumbent upon James to free his "vassals from fear or distrust, without which they will not say, nor dare say anything." [33] By April 26 the procedural details for proof had been worked out; on that day Charles wrote to Buckingham:

Steenie:

I send you here enclosed the interrogatories that the King thinks fit should be asked concerning the malicious accusations of the Spanish ambassador. As for the way, my father is resolved (if you do not gainsay it and show reason to the contrary) to take the oaths himself and to make Secretary Calvert and the Chancellor of the Exchequer to take the examinations in writing under their hands that are examined; thus much is by the King's command.

Now for my opinion, it is this: that you can incur no danger in this, but by opposing the King's proceeding in it, to make him suspect that you have spoken somewhat that you are unwilling he should hear of, for I cannot think that any man is so mad as to call his own head in question by making a lie against you, when all the world knows me to be your true friend, and if they tell but the truth I know they can say but what the King knows that you have answered to all the world, which is, that you think, as I do, that the continuance of these treaties with Spain might breed us much mischief. Wherefore

33. PRO 31/12/29, Spanish Transcripts, Marquis de la Inojosa to Philip IV, May 5/15, 1624. The paper which Padre Maestro prepared and sent to Windsor was written in Latin. There is a copy in SP 94/30, fols. 220–222v, and it is printed in *Cal. S. P. Venetian*, XVIII, 384–387. SP 14/164/8 and SP 14/164/9 are translations of Padre Maestro's information, and it is printed in *Cabala*, I, 217–222.

my advice to you is, that you do not oppose, or show yourself dis-contented, at the King's course herein, for I think that it will be so far from doing you hurt, that it will make you trample under your feet those few poor rascals that are your enemies. Now, sweet heart, if you think I am mistaken in my judgment in this, let me know what I can do in this, or anything else to serve thee, and then thou shall see that all the world shall daily know more and more that I am and ever will be

> Your faithful, loving, constant
> friend
> Charles P.[34]

Undoubtedly this letter was a source of great comfort to Buck-ingham because it virtually allowed him to seize the initiative from his enemies. Instead of isolating the Duke, the Spanish am-bassadors had increased their own vulnerability to ostracism and disgrace. In fact, as they were to learn, on the very day that they had attacked the favorite a countercoup had deprived them of one of their most formidable allies; by the King's command the Earl of Bristol was forbidden to appear at court.[35]

With his overt enemies neutralized (Bristol by sequestration and Middlesex by impeachment), Buckingham was unlikely to be sabotaged by more timorous opponents. Watchful waiting became the order of the day. Lord Keeper Williams, on April 26, con-veniently took to his bed, being "suddenly taken with a violent fever." In his letter requesting Buckingham to procure authoriza-tion for a deputy to act in his place as presiding officer of the Lords, Williams stated that he was "so weary of this unworthy and unthankful world" that he would not regret dying. He was quickly revived by the Duke's reply, written by Conway, which expressed fears that the Lord Keeper's contempt for the world masked "some private occasion of discontent." His Grace, however, condescended to thank Williams for his "advertisement concerning Padre Maestro" and assured him that his affection and industry would not go unrewarded. The compensations for espionage proved a panacea for the Keeper's ills; the license for his absence from the Lords was not required.[36]

34. Harl. MS 6987, fol. 211, Prince Charles to the Duke of Buckingham, Apr. 26, 1624, printed in Halliwell, Kings' Letters, II, 231–232.
35. SP 14/163/43, Secretary Conway to the Earl of Bristol, Apr. 24, 1624.
36. SP 14/163/56 Lord Keeper Williams to the Duke of Buckingham, Apr. 26, 1624; SP 14/163/57, Secretary Conway to Lord Keeper Williams, Apr. 27, 1624.

A desire for disengagement was not unique in court circles. Secretary Calvert, under threat of prosecution, officially expressed a wish to resign his office to Sir Dudley Carleton. Early in April overtures had been made by Calvert's servant, and, by the end of the month, the terms of the succession to the secretariat had been agreed upon. Agents were commissioned to acquaint Buckingham with the contract "in some tender language which might not be interpreted as if he [Calvert] were weary of his place," but the Spanish attack upon the favorite diverted attention away from Calvert and both prosecution and resignation hung in abeyance.[37]

Sir Francis Cottington, the Prince's secretary, was also in danger of being consigned to political limbo. As early as the autumn of 1623 it was rumored that he was "like to be discarded from the Princes service," and, although he was given minor employment in reporting the Duke of Buckingham's relation to the House of Commons, his Spanish-Catholic sympathies made him suspect. Increasingly in the early months of 1624 Cottington inclined toward the King's position and concurred in his conviction that the Spaniards "were fully resolved to gratify his Majesty in the business of the Palatinate." As a result he became a trusted intermediary between James and the Spanish ambassadors which, at this critical juncture, earned the Duke's displeasure. Ultimately Buckingham's enmity was to cost Cottington his office and a three-year intermission in royal favor.[38]

---

Conway was writing for the Duke of Buckingham. The attendance roll of the House of Lords indicates that Williams was not absent on either April 26 or 27. (*LJ*, III, 320–321.)

37. SP 14/164/7, Dudley Carleton to Sir Dudley Carleton, May 3, 1624, and 14/164/72, May 13, 1624, where Secretary Conway is described as doubting the genuineness of Calvert's intention to resign. He credited Calvert with "a design to bring the King to take notice that he is excluded from business and therefore desires to be rid of his place, which when the King shall know, may, perchance, set all again where it was two years since; but at least bring them to a partition of provinces, which is a thing his colleague has pressed my Lord of Buckingham unto diverse times." On June 26, Dudley Carleton reported, "As for the business betwixt Mr. Secretary Calvert and your Lordship, Mr. Secretary Conway tells me plainly that the success thereof is like to be according as they can dispose of my Lord of Bristol. If he stand, and come again in credit, Calvert will not out upon any terms in the world; if he fail, Calvert will be easily persuaded and they must try what can be done with the one before they can tell what to say to the other." (SP 14/168/47, Dudley Carleton to Sir Dudley Carleton, June 26, 1624.) Calvert's desire to retire from the secretaryship was first noticed in SP 14/162/13, Dudley Carleton to Sir Dudley Carleton, Apr. 4, 1624; see also SP 14/162/25, Apr. 6, 1624.

38. Chamberlain, *Letters*, II, 517, letter of Oct. 11, 1623; Clarendon, *History of the Rebellion*, I, 40.

Desertion by their partisans soon convinced the Spanish ambassadors of the advisability of retreat. Rumors began to circulate
that Inojosa and Coloma disclaimed any direct charge against
Buckingham. "for any present plot or conspiracy, and say that all
they did was only to counsel his Majesty to a timely prevention of
that danger which might ensue upon the course his Highness and
your Grace now ran with both Houses." [39]

Sir Robert Cotton's "A Relation of the Proceedings against
Ambassadors Who Have Miscarried Themselves," which appeared
on April 27, warned the Spanish envoys of the probable consequences of their action. Cotton counselled the Prince and Buckingham to refer the matter to Parliament and "leaving it so to
their advice and justice, to depart the House." A delegation from
both chambers, led by the Lord Keeper and the Speaker of the
Commons, would then repair to the ambassadors to require the
delivery of a formal charge and the nomination of witnesses. If
this request were refused, the Parliament would declare the innocence of the Prince and the Duke by a public act. The King
would be petitioned to arrest the Spanish envoys and dispatch a
complaint against them to Madrid requiring justice according to
the law of nations. In the event Philip IV denied or delayed redress, amity and friendship with Spain should be dissolved and
open warfare declared.[40]

Fortunately for Spanish interests, Cotton's recommendations
were not followed. James had already indicated his displeasure
with the reference of a former complaint against Buckingham to
the Parliament, and he was not about to let the Lords and Commons use this incident as a pretext for an immediate declaration of
war. Rumors circulated among the diplomatic corps that the
Prince had informed the upper House of the malicious offices of
the Spanish ambassadors and had requested the peers' advice. Inasmuch as no official record of this communication survives, it

39. Harl. MS. 1580, fol. 443, Sir George Goring to the Duke of Buckingham, Apr.
28, 1624; Cal. S. P. Venetian, XVIII, 300–301, Valaresso to the Doge and Senate,
Apr. 30/May 10, 1624; SP 14/164/46, Sir Francis Nethersole to Sir Dudley Carleton,
May 1 and 6, 1624.
40. Cotton, Cottoni Posthuma, 1–9, "A Relation of the Proceedings Against
Ambassadors who have Miscarried Themselves, Etc." There is a copy of this in
Harl. MS. 830, fols. 211–217. HMC, Third Report, Appendix, 120, calendars a
notice of another copy of this document in the manuscripts of the Duke of Northumberland and gives the date as April 27, 1624.

must be inferred that the Prince was using his influence subrosa to prevent further attacks upon the favorite and to vindicate his reputation. James had reserved the judicial decision for himself; for Charles to have appealed to Parliament would have given credence to the Spanish calumnies.[41]

Although many courtiers were amazed at the temerity of Inojosa and Coloma in accusing Buckingham and Charles of plotting a coup d'etat, few were prepared to take the charges seriously. When copies of the paper that Padre Maestro had submitted were circulated in London, it was noted with satisfaction that the most heinous allegations were omitted. The enumeration of trivial impeachments of Buckingham's conduct and character weakened the Spanish case, which was regarded by many as inconsequential and frivolous.[42]

An apparent feeling of security, however, did not betray Buckingham and his minions into relaxation of their vigilance. On April 28 the Duke departed for Windsor, ostensibly to attend the garter ceremonies, but in reality to test his credit with the King. The same evening Sir George Goring, one of Buckingham's closest confidants, informed him of the latest developments in London. Rumors were circulating that the Earl of Bristol had landed and was proceeding post haste to Windsor to join in the attack. The Lord Treasurer was still writing dispatches to court, and Goring advised Buckingham to "have an especial care by your command to such as may watch all minutes for 'tis reported he gathers fresh strength." As for the Duke himself: "All your faithfulest servants humbly and heartily beg that your Grace will be pleased to keep close and near his Majesty till he come to this town, for such mischiefs as these have no appearance of security but by committing greater, and you must expect them. Your least item by any of your meanest servants for any passage here will be sufficient to keep these wheels in their right motion." [43]

41. SP 92/10, Savoy Correspondence, Sir Isaac Wake to Secretary Conway, Apr. 29, 1624 (calendared under the number 14/163/72); Cal. S. P. Venetian, XVIII, 300–301, Valaresso to the Doge and Senate, Apr. 30/May 10, 1624. Neither the Lords Journal nor Montagu's "Diary" [H.M.C., Buccleuch and Queensberry MSS, III] mentions any parliamentary action in reference to the plot against Buckingham.
42. SP 14/164/12, Dudley Carleton to Sir Dudley Carleton, May 3, 1624. "Padre Maestro produced a memorial against him for his carriage in Spain; containing, if all be true that I hear, a great number of most frivolous allegations and such as would rather move laughter than otherwise if I should repeat them."
43. Harl. MS. 1580, fol. 443, Sir George Goring to the Duke of Buckingham,

Having consolidated his support in the city, it was incumbent upon Buckingham to reestablish himself in favor with the King before the judicial inquiry into his conduct. The Spanish ambassadors heard that he was extremely doubtful about his reception at court and that he had taken "leave of his wife and mother saying he would return as he was born, or having vanquished his enemies." They were also informed that the King, in the presence of the Prince and Cottington, had charged Buckingham with all the offenses alleged in Padre Maestro's indictment. For more than two hours the Duke was kept on his knees before a furious King and was soundly berated for his arrogation of regal authority in his dealings with Parliament. Purportedly James's wrath had included his son whose attempts to excuse Buckingham were countered with verbal castigation.[44]

Undoubtedly Inojosa exaggerated the gravity of the rift between James and Buckingham in order to justify himself in the eyes of Philip IV. If James's anger flared, it was easily appeased by Steenie's grace, beauty, and address. In fact, within a matter of weeks an ailing Buckingham could congratulate himself on being trusted "as absolutely as ever, largely expressed in this, that you have no conceit of my popularity; otherwise, why should you thus study to endear me with the upper and lower House of Parliament, and so consequently with your whole kingdom?"[45]

That James was predisposed to believe in Buckingham's innocence cannot, I think, be doubted. The procedure used to establish that innocence virtually dictated the verdict. The Lords of the Privy Council, examined under oath, could reveal nothing without incriminating themselves, either by direct involvement

Apr. 28, 1624. I have supplied the Earl of Bristol's name in the text of this letter, it being purposely obliterated in the manuscript. The quotation is as follows: "This night one that holds near intelligence with that party assured me that [the Earl of Bristol] was landed and crossed over the country with all expedition to Windsor and resolves to kiss his Majesty's hands without a forerunning demand for that end, and that questionless was his resolution whensoever he should set foot on this land."

44. PRO 31/12/29, Spanish Transcripts, Marquis de la Inojosa to Philip IV, May 5/15, 1624.

45. Harl. MS. 6987, fol. 136, the Duke of Buckingham to King James, undated. From internal evidence I have assigned a tentative date of June 1, 1624, to this letter. The King, prior to the prorogation of Parliament, left Buckingham at Greenwich, apparently with an injunction to join him at Theobalds. By the first of June, James was at Theobalds, but Buckingham had retired to Newhall as a better place for convalescence. This letter is printed in Halliwell, *Kings' Letters*, II, 245–246 and in *Hardwicke State Papers*, I, 461–462.

in a conspiracy or by concealing evidence of it. In both cases they would be liable to disgrace and dismissal, and possibly in jeopardy of imprisonment and execution. Had they been granted a full pardon prior to their examination, the privy councillors would still have been reluctant to disclose information. No ambitious courtier would risk offending the heir apparent merely to confirm the suspicions of an ailing monarch. And, in the final analysis, the prospective witnesses were selected as well as suborned; neither Lord Treasurer Cranfield nor the Earl of Bristol were required to testify. Not without reason did the Spanish ambassadors believe that Buckingham "was cleared by those who were his confederates, as guilty as himself." [46]

During the King's sojourn at Windsor, Inojosa and Coloma requested another audience, intimating that Philip IV had recalled them to Madrid. Their appointment was deferred until May 3, the day after the King examined his councillors under oath. Consequently the Spaniards were prevented from inventing new charges or adducing new evidence.

Over the protests of the Earl of Pembroke, who challenged the legality of the proceedings, James charged his councillors "to declare all they should know of the pretended treason though guilty themselves." Precisely what questions were directed to the Lords is not known with certainty, but apparently they were based upon Padre Maestro's libel and chiefly concerned with Buckingham's parliamentary activities. Whether the Lords' depositions were taken individually is problematical; at least one observer stated that "nothing at all was discovered and not one that could say the least thing that might smell of any conspiracy or treason in the

---

46. SP 94/30, fols. 278v–279, Lord Nithisdale, his relation of the discourse between the Spanish ambassadors and himself, written May 20, 1624, and printed under the endorsed date May 22, 1624, in *Cabala*, I, 247–249. It is noteworthy that it was on April 24 that Lord Treasurer Cranfield "receved a message by the Prince, not to come in the Kings presence any more till he have cleered himself." (Chamberlain, *Letters*, II, 555, letter of Apr. 30, 1624.) On May 3 Dudley Carleton wrote: "it was wished my Lord Treasurer (who hath been commanded from the King's presence this sevennight) might have taken his oath with the rest; for the general opinion will needs have it that he is someway or other at the end of this business and that he hath had correspondence with the Ambassador." (SP 14/164/12, Dudley Carleton to Sir Dudley Carleton, May 3, 1624.) As for Bristol, the Venetian ambassador summed up the prevailing opinion when he reported: "I hear further that the duke has induced the king to refuse Bristol admittance to his presence, a point that would be of great consequence if true." (*Cal. S. P. Venetian*, XVIII, 305, Valaresso to the Doge and Senate, Apr. 30/May 10, 1624.)

Duke of Buckingham. Hereof they framed a kind of a manifest, all desiring the King, in conclusion, that something might be done for repairing the honor of the Prince, and their satisfaction." [47]

A fragmentary state paper which can be ascribed to the inquisition at Windsor may be a collective answer to the queries put by the King. It maintains, in refutation of the Spanish charges, that the question concerning the breach of the two treaties "was demanded and resolved by the Council before there was speech of a parliament." It also contends that there was no need of a plot in Parliament to break the match since that treaty was ended when the espousals were deferred before the commencement of the session. Furthermore, all questions concerning the treaties put before the Parliament were "the question of his Majesty." "And the proposition of that question to the Parliament was not propounded for equity or reason of granting it, but because the infallible counsel coming from them, they should be bound to be maintainers of it." As for Buckingham, the King's absolute power to promote and demote his servants was undoubted, but due process of law should be observed, "and it hath been ever a reason of the law to ground trials upon accusations formed, and offers and proofs formally exhibited." "Therefore reason and equity require that the accuser should have good fame, a person, life, and estate which may be liable and subject to reparation and punishment if he fail of the proof." Clearly the diplomatic immunity of the ambassadors should not protect them from the just vengeance of a blameless victim and an outraged nation.[48]

In the opinion of Buckingham's partisans, the interrogation of the Council had cleared him of all aspersions, and, in consequence, considerable pressure was exerted on James to initiate proceedings

47. SP 14/164/12, Dudley Carleton to Sir Dudley Carleton, May 3, 1624; SP 14/164/46, Sir Francis Nethersole to Sir Dudley Carleton, May 1 and 6, 1624; *Cal. S. P. Venetian*, XVIII, 307–309, Valaresso to the Doge and Senate, May 7/17, 1624; Horne, fol. 67.

48. SP 14/163/78, this document is calendared under the date April 30 and titled "Answers to certain interrogatories delivered at Windsor." Since the questions, according to the Prince's letter of April 26, were intended for the Council and since the Council was sworn on May 2, I suggest that this is the more appropriate date. The paper is a fragment containing the answers to five (unstated) interrogatories. Internal evidence emphatically suggests the association of this document with the inquisition at Windsor. I have compared it with the questions the Duke asked of himself in the Parliament of 1625, with Dr. Turner's interrogatories put in 1626, and with the articles presented against Buckingham by the Earl of Bristol on May 1, 1626. None of these inquiries correspond with the paper in question.

against the ambassadors. When they appeared at Theobalds on
May 3, "it was publicly observed that the King grew much out of
patience upon a very small staying for them after they were sent
for." James's patience was tried even further when "the Ambassadors disavowed the part of the accusation touching the removal of the King from the government, leaving it upon Don
Francisco — Archdeacon of Cambray and priest to Don Coloma."
However, this denial did not prevent them from reiterating other
accusations against Buckingham, despite the Prince's attempts to
exonerate him. Inojosa even offered to allow Cottington to read
his dispatches in order to prove that no aspersions had been cast
on the Prince's honor and that only the Duke had been traduced.
More substantial evidence was demanded by the King who spoke
"rounder language to the Ambassadors than every man expected."
He refused to grant them permission to return to Madrid without
the customary formalities of leave-taking. He admitted that he
had been solicited to place them under arrest, but he assured them
that he considered the person of an ambassador sacred and had no
intention of following the example of what had been done with
the Queen, his mother.[49]

Although they were relieved from the fear of arrest and public
prosecution, this audience revealed to the ambassadors the delicacy
of their position. Obviously James, as an impartial judge, could no
longer communicate with Buckingham's accusers. At the same
time, the Prince, confident that the charges could not be proved,
was unwilling to let the proceedings lapse, and it was rumored
that he had procured the King's promise to prevent the ambassadors' departure.[50] Consequently the Spanish diplomats remained
in London as powerless and unwilling observers of intensified
preparations for war.

Widespread circulation of Padre Maestro's indictment against
Buckingham, combined with popular suspicion that the interrogation of the Privy Council had not plumbed the depths of the
"conspiracy," may have caused the Duke to pen his own justification. His apologia, probably written during his convalesence in
early May, attempted a point-by-point refutation of the Spanish

49. SP 14/164/46, Sir Francis Nethersole to Sir Dudley Carleton, May 1 and 6,
1624; PRO 31/12/29, Spanish Transcripts, Marquis de la Inojosa to Philip IV, May
5/15, 1624.
50. SP 14/164/12, Dudley Carleton to Sir Dudley Carleton, May 3, 1624.

libel. Buckingham vented his scorn on calumnies that could not be cleared by judicial proofs and alleged that they were "forged, partly by Jesuits and their factions at home, and partly by corrupt ministers and emissaries abroad." He was equally contemptuous of anonymous "witnesses" who preferred "not the safety and honor of their Prince and country before the fear or respect of any person whomsoever." His innocence had been attested by the oaths of the Privy Council, by the continued friendship and support of the Prince, and by the approbation of Parliament which had styled him "redeemer of his country." This act of redemption, particularly, was the source of the ambassador's complaint: "the original sin and root of all treasons and offenses laid to my charge is that, by eating the forbidden fruit in Spain, mine eyes have been opened to discover the evil as well as the good, and so to trust them no further than they deserve."

Buckingham readily acknowledged that he had been instrumental in the reversal of English policy toward Spain, but he alleged royal warrant for all his actions and disclaimed ultimate responsibility for the course of events. "I confess ingeniously," he wrote, "that what I do amiss proceedeth from my own precipitation and error, and what I do well is by my master's wisdom and instruction." He ridiculed the Spanish contention that his was an overweening power: the journey to Madrid had been suggested by Charles and approved by the King; the negotiations in Spain had been conducted under the Prince's direction; the summoning of Parliament was James's absolute prerogative; and the same councillors who, in January, had been receptive to Spanish proposals for the restitution of the Palatinate had, in March, unanimously voted for the dissolution of both treaties. In the Duke's view, the enmity of Spain was not by his procurement; it was not a necessary consequence of the cessation of negotiations. This was a Spanish interpretation which made English subservience the price of amity and allowed no choice except submission or hostility.

Buckingham had no difficulty in rebutting several of the Spanish allegations. He challenged the ambassadors to disprove the truth of his narrative of the negotiations in 1623, and he recapitulated the essence of his "Relation to Parliament" in order to demonstrate the rectitude of his actions. He credited the Prince with the penetration of Spanish artifices, and acknowledged himself to be a loyal servant rather than the dominant partner in their relationship. It was on the Prince's instructions that he had disclosed the terms of the secret Anglo-Spanish treaty about the partition of the Netherlands. Moreover, Buckingham denied responsibility for the revocation of the Prince's proxy or that he had entertained overtures for a marriage between his daughter and the son of the Elector Palatine. All correspondence received from Elizabeth of Bohemia had been read by Charles, and he had been present when her secretary had received audience.

If it was a relatively simple matter for Buckingham to falsify accusations of conspiracy with the Prince and the King and Queen of Bohemia, it was much more difficult to remove the onus of popularity and Puritanism which he had acquired in the course of the Parliament. Of all the Spanish charges, this was the one most likely to achieve credence with James and inflame his suspicions. Buckingham was at pains, therefore, to point out the monarchical tenets of English Protestantism. "The religion we profess binds our consciences more firmly to obey, honor, support and defend our kings against all their enemies than Popish religion can do." The Duke expressly denied any association with "factious Puritans, which are now no considerable number amongst us" and took refuge behind the unanimity expressed in the parliamentary resolutions to dissolve the treaties. It was absurd, in his estimation, to stain the entire Parliament with the hateful name of Puritanism in order to make it odious to the King. The aim of the Spaniards was merely to set "factions amongst the members of both houses, as well as with the head" and to accomplish the dissolution of Parliament before it could provide for England's defense.

In vindicating the loyalty and allegiance of Parliament, Buckingham paid due attention to its constitutional importance: "and have not our greatest and wisest kings heretofore referred treaties of leagues, of marriages, of peace and war, and of religion itself to the consultations of their parliaments? Those, then, that take upon them to undervalue this high court do but expose their own judgments to censure and contempt, not knowing that parliaments, as they are the honor and support, so they are the handmaids and creatures of our kings, inspired, formed and governed by their power."

In his apologia Buckingham displayed considerable critical acumen. With lofty disdain he refused to answer charges of personal misconduct, alleging that to do so might besmirch the Prince "who best knoweth the truth in these things they object, and if there had been cause should have called me to an account." It was his purpose to apologize no further "than may concern the interest of that cause which through my sides they have labored to wound." His judicious essay was designed to alleviate the King's fears of deposition without sacrificing the goodwill of parliamentarians. By emphasizing English Protestant unanimity, Buckingham discounted the threat of seditious factionalism and dared the Spanish ambassadors to produce substantive evidence of a conspiracy.[51]

With virtually every avenue of approach to the King sealed off, Inojosa and Coloma were driven to rash expedients in their attempts to reestablish contact. On the pretext of visiting a returned ambassador, the Spanish envoys sought permission to speak with the Earl of Bristol, who was under house arrest in St. Giles. Confident that the King would summon Bristol to his presence, the ambassadors hoped to use him as an intermediary to reopen discussions on the Palatinate and as an ally against Buckingham. Thus, on May 6 and 7, after the interviews had received the King's approval, Padre Maestro, Inojosa, and Coloma held discussions with the Earl. The talks convinced Inojosa and Coloma of Bristol's intense antipathy toward the favorite, but beyond this they accomplished nothing. Bristol needed fresh concessions on the Palatinate as bait in order to procure access to the King; without a private audience, he was powerless. Only on the basis of personal influence could he hope to destroy Buckingham's credit. However, the vigilance of Bristol's opponents prevented the King from conceding a private audience. Indeed, by the end of the month Bristol realized that he was prejudicing his own case by his asso-

---

51. Stowe MS. 182, fols. 38–45v. "The Duke of Buckingham's Answer to the Spanish Ambassador's Information Etc.," printed in *The Connexion: Being Choice Collections of Some Remarkable Passages in King James His Reign* (London, 1681), 129–175. Stowe MS. 182 is endorsed as follows: "These I transcribed from the original written by Mr. Attorney Cookes own hand." Although many copies of Padre Maestro's charges are extant, so far as I know this manuscript of Buckingham's answer is unique. It must have been composed subsequent to the interrogation of the Privy Council on May 2 because the writer asks "why the honor done me in their answer should not give both his Majesty and the world satisfaction on my behalf." (*Ibid.*, fol. 39.)

ciation with the Spanish. When Padre Maestro again sought to use him as a tool, he was told that, "he should apply to those most acceptable to him [James] as I conceived personal exasperations had been in great part the cause of the disordering of the affairs; and therefore it would be wisdom particularly to apply to the Duke." [52]

As even Buckingham's overt enemies defected from their cause, the Spanish ambassadors had to rely upon written communications to solicit a hearing from the King. The arrival of couriers from Spain early in May gave them an excuse to demand an audience, but unrelenting pressure from their opponents prevented the realization of their desire. Even James's curiosity about the new concessions for the restitution of the Palatinate could not induce him to grant the Spanish emissaries a personal interview. In response to representations from his Council, the King sent Secretary Conway to inform Inojosa that he must disclose his informants and prove his charges against Buckingham before he could be permitted to leave the country. Furthermore, any new diplomatic overtures must be communicated through the secretaries of state before he would receive the ambassadors. With this demand Inojosa and Coloma refused to comply. Despite successive visits by messengers from the King, Buckingham, and the Countess of Buckingham, they declined to reveal any part of their instructions, claiming that they would be misrepresented in the process of transmission. Repeatedly Inojosa requested license to depart, but, when the Master of Ceremonies, Sir Lewis Lewkenor, attempted to provide a ship without authorization, he was sent to the Tower for his presumption. [53]

As May wore on, the isolation of the Spaniards became more complete, and the case against them was strengthened. Sir Francis Nethersole, member for Corfe Castle and secretary to the Queen of Bohemia, demanded that he be examined under oath in order

52. PRO 31/12/29, Spanish Transcripts, Marquis de la Inojosa to Philip IV, May 21/31, 1624; SP 94/30, fol. 236, the Earl of Bristol to Secretary Conway, May 5, 1624; *Cal S. P. Dom. 1623–1625*, 235, Secretary Conway to the Earl of Bristol, May 5 and 6, 1624; SP 94/30, fols. 238–240, 242, Earl of Bristol to Secretary Conway, May 6 and 7, 1624; *Cal. S. P. Dom., Addenda, 1580–1625*, 666, the Earl of Bristol to Secretary Conway, May 28, 1624.

53. PRO 31/12/29, Spanish Transcripts, Marquis de la Inojosa to Philip IV, May 21/31, 1624; SP 14/164/86, Sir Francis Nethersole to Sir Dudley Carleton, May 15, 1624; SP 14/164/92, Thomas Locke to Sir Dudley Carleton, May 17, 1624.

to exonerate himself and his patroness of any involvement in marriage negotiations with Buckingham. On May 28, Elizabeth herself wrote to her father to protest against the aspersions laid on her character. Even Catholic peers like Lord Nithisdale thought it advisable to reveal what they knew of Spanish machinations in order to avoid suspicion.[54]

All this did not keep the public from attaching sinister connotations to the continued presence of Inojosa and Coloma. Rumors circulated in early June of secret conclaves between the King and the ambassadors held at the Earl of Arundel's country houses. In reality, however, James continually resisted their importunities, using parliamentary business as his principal excuse for not conceding an audience. Even after the session had ended, he categorically refused to see Inojosa and even contrived a plan to avoid speaking to Padre Maestro.[55]

The lengthy impasse, created when the Spanish envoys refused to substantiate their charges against Buckingham or reveal their diplomatic instructions, deprived Philip IV of effective representation in London at a critical juncture and contributed materially to the implementation of the Prince's aggressive foreign policy. Buckingham's physical presence was not required to counteract Spanish influence; indeed, the King's sympathy for his ailing favorite may have stiffened his resolve not to listen to the insinuations of the Duke's adversaries. Consequently, throughout May, Inojosa and Coloma could do nothing to avert calamity. Instead of separating the King and his favorite, they had made themselves

54. Green, *Elizabeth . . . of Bohemia*, ed. Lomas, 231–232, Elizabeth to her father, King James, May 28, 1624; SP 14/164/46, Sir Francis Nethersole to Sir Dudley Carleton, May 1 and 6, 1624; SP 94/30, fols. 278v–279, Lord Nithisdale, his relation of the discourse between the Spanish ambassadors and himself, May 20, 1624. Nithisdale was about to depart for France on a confidential mission in connection with the religious conditions in the marriage treaty between Prince Charles and Henrietta Maria. See his letter to Buckingham, June 22, 1624, printed in *Cabala*, I, 249–251.

55. *Cal. S. P. Venetian*, XVIII, 343–344, Valaresso to the Doge and Senate, June 4/14, 1624. Valaresso had heard that the Earl of Bristol had met James at the Earl of Arundel's country house. He did not believe this report, but he did credit a rumor of secret meetings between the King and the Spanish ambassadors. Nethersole, on June 7, reported the same rumors in connection with Lord Treasurer Cranfield and Sir Arthur Brett, but he discounted them all as idle talk. (SP 14/167/28.) In the same letter Nethersole discusses the Spanish solicitation for an audience and the King's excuses for denying it. On June 14 Secretary Conway informed Buckingham that the King had devised a plan to avoid speaking to Padre Maestro. (SP 14/167/59, Secretary Conway to the Duke of Buckingham, June 14, 1624.)

opprobrious to the entire English nation and exposed James to the overwhelming influence of their antagonists.

During May circumstances inexorably militated against Spanish interests: the proclamation against Jesuits and seminary priests was issued, the rigging of the navy was begun, twenty thousand pounds was borrowed and sent to Mansfeldt, the Earl of Carlisle was commissioned to arrange an alliance and a marriage treaty with France, Sir Isaac Wake was dispatched to continental Catholic powers to solicit aid, and, most important, an agreement with the Dutch was concluded. Thus, by early June James was irrevocably committed to an indirect, covert military confrontation with Spain. When the colonels were named and the drums beaten for volunteers to serve in the Low Countries, it was too late for the Spanish ambassadors to become conciliatory. Indeed, no importance seems to have been attached to Philip IV's formal reply to James's letter breaking off negotiations. No one seemed to care whether the Spanish declared war or expressed peaceful intentions. By June 15, when Philip's letter leaving the initiative to James was received, plans were practically completed to expedite Inojosa's departure and to make representations to Madrid complaining of his conduct.

Immediately after the ending of Parliament the Marquis Inojosa had peremptorily informed James that "if he might not be admitted to have audience he knew not why he should stay longer here, and therefore desired to be gone." The imperious terminology in which this request was couched aroused the King's ire, and, on June 5, he sent Cottington and Conway to let Inojosa know "that his Majesty expected not to have been pressed by him in that manner considering that he had just cause to send a complaint of him to his master whensoever he went hence, but that since he urged him to it, his Majesty let him know that he had made himself unfit to have any more audiences and that if he had a mind to be gone his Majesty would give order for a ship to carry him away." [56] It was even asserted that if Don Carlos de Coloma persisted in avowing the accusations against Buckingham he need not tarry to await the coming of another Spanish diplomat.

Matters were thus brought to an issue, and in the ensuing days

56. SP 14/167/28, Sir Francis Nethersole to Sir Dudley Carleton, June 7, 1624.

arrangements were completed to waft Inojosa across the channel on a merchant ship — a decided mark of disrespect. This insult was compounded when Inojosa was required to pay for the coaches used to transport his company to the seaside, and no gifts were given him at his departure. By the time that the Marquis left England on June 26, diplomatic relations had degenerated to the level of petty insult and revenge. Only the King's flag and colors borne by a naval lieutenant prevented Inojosa from being ambushed by the Dutch. For his part, the ambassador "left a foul stink behind him in Exeter House, which at parting seems he made no more esteem of them than a jakes. All the furniture, all the rooms of the house, so beastly abused that we wish him here again with his Spanish troop to thrust their noses into it." [57]

The repercussions of the "Buckingham plot" continued to be felt even after the expulsion of Inojosa. Sir Walter Aston, the English ambassador at Madrid, had informed the Spanish ministers of the malicious practices of their diplomats long before he had received James's official letter of protest. It was not until August 29 that Aston's memorial was presented to Philip IV. After describing the machinations of Inojosa and Coloma, Aston asserted that James "would and could by the Law of Nations, and the right of his own Royall Justice, proceed against them with such severity as their offence deserved . . . but . . . he would leave the reparation hereof to the justice of their King, of whom he would demand and require it."

Thus, in the final analysis, James insisted upon treating the conspiracy against Buckingham as a plot contrived by private individuals not sanctioned by public authority. He did not mingle "the correspondence and friendship he held with your Majesty, with the faults and offences of your Minister." [58] As far as the King of

---

57. SP 14/168/48, Dudley Carleton to Sir Dudley Carleton, June 26, 1624.
58. *Cabala*, II, 152–155, a memorial to the King of Spain by Sir Walter Aston, ambassador in Spain, Aug. 29, 1624 (endorsed with the date Aug. 5, 1624); see also Howell, *Familiar Letters*, II, 12–15, James Howell to Sir John North, Aug. 26, 1623 [*sic*]. The actual date on which this memorial was presented to Philip IV is problematical. On July 17 Aston wrote to Buckingham, "I am now busy in preparing for my audience upon his Majesty's commands touching the Marquis of Inojosa and Don Carlos. I am taking forth diverse copies of my memorial intending to speak with all the Lords here of the Council before they shall meet touching that business." (Harl. MS. 1580, fol. 44–44v.) Lunardo Moro, the Venetian ambassador in Spain reported on August 4/14, 1624, "The Ambassador [Aston] performed the office verbally and also presented a very diffuse memorial . . . One thing causes

England was concerned, a private action should not be allowed to impede the progress of amicable diplomatic relations. Ultimately, the entire incident faded into insignificance. Despite Aston's efforts to implement Buckingham's revenge, "The Conde of Olivares with a strong and violent hand hath delivered the Marquis from an exemplary punishment which would certainly have been inflicted upon him had he been left unto the Council of State, and without care either of the King his master's honor or engagements has saved the Marquis and left the envy of it upon his Majesty if the King our master will so please to understand it." [59]

Doubtless in the autumn of 1624 Buckingham was little interested in the punishment of Inojosa. What need had he for reprisals when the more important victory had already been won, when Spanish influence at the court of St. James had been effectively nullified in the preceding April? The incompetence of the ambassadors had not only assured the absence of an effective deterrent to the realization of his foreign policy goals, but had also removed from the London scene a focus for the conspiratorial activities of his domestic enemies. Thus, assisted by the ineptitude of his foreign adversaries, by luck in the timing of circumstances, and by a considerable degree of political sagacity, Buckingham and his aides were able to isolate his opponents and destroy or discredit them one by one.

---

surprise, that the King has only just remonstrated here, and he has probably only done this in order to satisfy the prince and Buckingham in appearance, but really to open further negotiations and to make sure of the friendship of this crown, about which he is very doubtful. They have not yet made any reply to the remonstrances, but I understand that the ministers for the most part severely blame the action of the ambassadors, declaring it contrary to his Majesty's intentions." (*Cal. S. P. Venetian*, XVIII, 413, Lunardo Moro to the Doge and Senate, Aug. 4/14, 1624.)

59. Harl. MS. 1580, fols. 52–52v, Sir Walter Aston to the Duke of Buckingham, Oct. 20, 1624.

# VI  The Stifling of Opposition—Cranfield

Lionel Cranfield, earl of Middlesex and Lord Treasurer of England, preferred an open challenge to Buckingham's power instead of abject subservience to his wishes. It is true Cranfield may have been left with no other alternative since Buckingham and the Prince seemed resolved to ruin him even before they returned from Spain, but it is equally true that he forfeited the possibility of reconciliation by his actions in the early months of 1624. This was certainly a reversal of form for the Lord Treasurer; his previous relations with the favorite had been amicable to say the least.

Although he had been introduced into court circles by the late Earl of Northampton, Cranfield owed his rapid preferment to the Duke alone, and his alliance with the favorite had been cemented by his marriage in 1621 to Ann Brett, a cousin of Lady Buckingham. Cranfield's letters to the Duke reveal the close cooperation that existed between the two, although they implied doubts about the continuance of Buckingham's commitment to a policy of retrenchment and financial reform. On July 28, 1621, he asked Buckingham to procure the King's grant of the manor of Cranfield and ended his letter, "As for myself, my debt is so great to your Lordship, that whatsoever I have shall be ever at your command." And shortly after assuming the treasurership he wrote, "I will spare no person, nor forbear any course that is just and honourable to make our great and gracious master to subsist of his own. The pains and envies shall be mine, the honour and thanks your Lordship's. Wherefore be constant to him that loves and honours you." On December 4, 1621, Cranfield again assured the Duke that if the King, the Prince, "and your Lordship continue constant and will back me, I will perfect the work." [1]

Within a year Buckingham's constancy was wearing thin. With pensions whittled down, grants blocked, and the Mastership of the Irish Wards inexplicably delayed, Buckingham felt his patronage power stinted. The inevitable result was a growing coolness between himself and a treasurer irretrievably dedicated to a sound fiscal policy.[2] Aggravating the situation was the fact that Cranfield had won the approval of James by his financial reforms. The importunity of suitors for the King's bounty had been abated by Cranfield's insistence that all prospective grants required the approval of the Treasurer before they were presented to the King. Thus the royal Nimrod was freed from the pressure of business and left with more leisure to pursue the stag.

Coincidentally with the growing tension between the Duke and Cranfield came the rumor that the King had found a new favorite. On September 4, 1622, the Earl of Kellie wrote to the Earl of Mar, "It has been concealed here by some men that his Majesty should begin to love and favor one young man called Brett. He is a groom in his bedchamber, and cousin germane to my Lord of Buckingham. I think I may swear that it was neither in the King's mind nor in the young man's conceit." Nevertheless, by October 30, Kellie admitted, "Something there is in it, but for myself I can not understand it, neither do I think that it shall prove as many men think it will do because they would have it so." [3]

Buckingham, too, thought "there was something in it," and, although Brett was his cousin germane, he was also the brother-in-law of Lionel Cranfield. Undoubtedly court gossips magnified the rumors in an attempt to break the Buckingham-Middlesex coalition. The storm over the new aspirant to royal favor should

1. Goodman, *Court of James I*, II, 206, Lionel Cranfield to the Duke of Buckingham, July 28, 1621; 209, Lionel Cranfield to the Duke of Buckingham, Oct. 12, 1621; 215, Lionel Cranfield to the Duke of Buckingham, Dec. 4, 1621; see also *Cabala*, I, 266–267, Earl of Middlesex to the Duke of Buckingham, undated.

2. Sackville MS. ON 7580, Buckingham to Cranfield, Nov. 14, 1622. Cranfield was probably delaying the grant in pursuance of the letter of the Council to the King, Oct. 12, 1622, which recommended holding Irish grants in abeyance until the commissioners had reported. See *APC 1621–1623*, 331–332, and *Cabala*, I, 75–76.

3. HMC, *Mar and Kellie*, 133, Thomas, earl of Kellie, to John, earl of Mar, Sept. 4, 1622; 140, Thomas, earl of Kellie, to John, earl of Mar, Oct. 30, 1622.

have been allayed by his disappearance from the English court. On February 20, 1623, the Earl of Kellie reported, "Before they [the Prince and the Duke] parted from his Majesty, Mr. Brett of the bedchamber did desire leave of his Majesty to travel and is going to France." [4] But Buckingham also was absent from the source of power and patronage, while Cranfield remained close to the throne, and for a suspicious nature such a situation bore watching. The favorite was well aware of the King's vacillating affections and his penchant for dissimulation, and he knew that James had agreed to the Spanish venture reluctantly and against his better judgment. Moreover, from a variety of correspondents, including Cranfield, Buckingham quickly learned of the storm of criticism unleashed by the departure of the Prince. In his own defense he wrote, "From the beginning I foresaw that this my attendance on his Highness would draw upon me much censure of the vulgar, yea, and from persons of the wiser sort, but I chose rather to despise any inconvenience which might that way grow unto me than to suffer in mine own heart the least unwillingness to obey my master or to serve his Highness or my country." [5]

Some courtiers, hopeful of Buckingham's eclipse, tried to widen the purported breach between the favorite and the King and to break the monolithic structure of the Duke's patronage empire. On March 30 Cranfield wrote, "I assure your Lordship that the evil spirits that were very active at Christmas to divide your Lordship and me are not yet quiet but have been more busy than ever since your departure." [6] The Duke's creatures assiduously informed him of court intrigue, and reports implicating the Lord Treasurer were frequent, damaging, and seemingly authenticated by Cranfield's failure to communicate every detail of his activities to Buckingham. As early as March 29, Tobie Matthew was retailing the schemes of the Duke's enemies and advising him to return.

4. *Ibid.*, 151, Thomas, earl of Kellie, to John, earl of Mar, Feb. 20, 1622/3. See also Chamberlain, *Letters,* II, 479, letter of Feb. 22, 1623. "Younge Mounson who stoode once to be a favorite was knighted likewise by the Lord of Buckingams meanes and sent to travell. The same order is taken for Brett of the bed-chamber."

5. Sackville MS. ON 8834, Buckingham to Middlesex, Mar. 25, 1623. For James's attitude toward the Spanish journey, see Edward, earl of Clarendon, *The History of the Rebellion, and Civil Wars in England, Begun in the Year 1641* (London, 1839), I, 17–29. Part of Clarendon's information seems to have been derived from Cottington whose advice was asked by James.

6. Harl. MS. 1581, fols. 93–94, quoted by Tawney, *Cranfield*, 234, Cranfield to the Duke of Buckingham, Mar. 30, 1623.

The King, contrary to his promise to grant no petitions in his favorite's absence, was being persistently importuned by avaricious courtiers. The Duke of Richmond had secured his suit of the coals and "my Lord Treasurer also hath been very careful not to lose his time." [7]

Cranfield's awareness of the intrigues of his enemies may have induced him to strengthen his relationship with Buckingham. Before Sir George Goring joined the Prince and the Duke at Madrid, he was instructed by Cranfield to acquaint Buckingham with the Treasurer's private business, which may have involved the projected marriage of his second daughter, Elizabeth, to Lord Mountjoy. The Duke's "generous consent" to Cranfield's plans portended the continuance of harmonious relations between the two, but persistent reports of the Treasurer's double-dealing aroused Buckingham's suspicions. On July 9, Sir George Goring informed Cranfield of the circulation of "a report that my Lord Duke of Buckingham should have many ill offices done him of late by some great men, of which number your Lordship was nominated for one in a high kind. This I know hath been reported with some circumstances which now I cannot send you, but to say certainly that my Lord Duke understands so much I cannot, though I verily believe he either doth or must considering where it is already." Chancellor of the Exchequer Weston, who was suspected of being Cranfield's adherent, received a similar warning from Goring.[8]

For the time being the Duke apparently took no notice of the gossip, but in a brief note to Cranfield, penned in late July, he stated, "I hope you do not think if I have been slow in writing

7. Goodman, *Court of James I*, II, 270, Tobie Matthew to the Duke of Buckingham, Mar. 29, 1623.

8. Sackville MSS ON 9453, Sir George Goring to Middlesex, May 25, 1623; ON 8861, Goring to Middlesex, July 9, 1623 (incorrectly dated by Tawney [234, n.3] as May 9, 1623); *Cabala*, I, 202–203, Sir Richard Weston to Buckingham, July 17, 1623. Goring's references to Cranfield's private business are contained in his letter of May 25 and are very enigmatic. Moreover, the manuscript has been damaged and cannot be transcribed in its entirety, but I believe that the implications are clear that Cranfield was soliciting the Duke's approval for the marriage of his second daughter, Elizabeth, to an unnamed "young Lord" who was presently in Madrid. Inasmuch as the Captain of the Guard (Lord Kensington) was also acquainted with the affair and because Buckingham added a postscript in his letter of July 29 (?), assuring Cranfield that "Jack Hippisley will tell you my opinion concerning my Lord Mountjoy," I think it likely that Mountjoy was the intended bridegroom. (Sackville MS. ON 2457, Buckingham to Middlesex [July 29, 1623].)

that any court practices have been the cause of it. If you give this bearer [Sir John Hippisley] leave to speak with you he can acquaint you with all. I have given him directions to do it." [9]

Meanwhile more damaging reports of Cranfield's nefarious activities were being directed to Madrid. In an undated letter (probably July 1623) the Lord Keeper informed Buckingham of the creation of the Viscountess Maidstone. He told the Duke that the land offered in exchange for the peerage had been sold to the Lord Treasurer, and that he [Williams] had "stayed the Patent until I was assured your Lordship gave way thereunto." Buckingham was notified that the Lord Keeper and the Marquess Hamilton were watching events at court: "If we did know, but upon whom to keep a watchful eye for disaffected reports concerning your service, it is all the intelligence he and I do expect." On August 1, 1623, Turpyn informed the Duke that his sister, Lady Denbigh, did not receive as much money from the wardrobe as she had hoped, "which my Lord Treasurer seemed to sleek with an excuse to his Majesty's satisfaction, but nothing to her redress." [10]

Cognizance of the rift between Cranfield and Buckingham was apparent in court circles at both Madrid and Westminster. On August 20 the Earl of Bristol, already at odds with the Duke, wrote to thank Cranfield for some unspecified good offices in his behalf; "I desire you should understand me as a person very obligeable by your courtesy, and one that you may remember have ever loved and concurred with you in your public ends." And, on September 1, Sir John Hippisley informed the Duke that the Earl of Southampton "hath offered his son to marrie with my Lord Treasurers Daughter, and tells him this reason, that now is the time he may have need of friends, but it is refused as yet." [11]

While Buckingham was hearing reports that the Treasurer was

9. Sackville MS. ON 2457, Buckingham to Middlesex [29 July 1623]. I have tentatively dated this letter July 29 because it was sent in the custody of Sir John Hippisley who arrived at Cranborne on August 10. See Halliwell, *Kings' Letters*, II, 224, James I to the Duke of Buckingham, Aug. 10, 1623.

10. *Cabala*, I, 78–79, Lord Keeper Williams to the Duke of Buckingham [July, 1623]. Elizabeth Finch was created Viscountess Maidstone on July 7, 1623. (*Cal. S. P. Dom. 1623–1625*, 9.) Goodman, *Court of James I*, II, 302–303, R. Turpyn to the Duke of Buckingham, Aug. 1, 1623. See Sackville MS. ON 7571, Buckingham to Cranfield, June 18, 1622, where Buckingham refers to Turpyn as "my cousin."

11. Sackville MS. ON 210, Earl of Bristol to Middlesex, Aug. 20, 1623; *Cabala*, I, 316–317, Sir John Hippisley to the Duke of Buckingham, Sept. 1, 1623.

making the most of his absence, he was being pressed by Cranfield to hasten the negotiations and to secure the payment of the dowry in cash.[12] That Cranfield had no high hopes for the success of the Spanish venture may be inferred from his remark "that the voyage was foolishly undertaken and now must be maintained with prodigality." [13] Despite his doubts, the Treasurer seems to have done his utmost to defray the necessary expenses of the Spanish journey. Even James admitted this when he wrote to Charles and Buckingham, "The treasurer likewise made that money ready, which my baby desired. I must bear him witness, he spares not to engage himself, and all he is worth, for the business." [14]

The extravagance of the Prince must have appeared to Cranfield to be both deplorable and unnecessary. By December 22, 1623, he had paid out £ 44,477 for the Spanish venture and £ 3,370 6s. was still due the Prince. In addition, Buckingham was alleged to have spent £ 28,656 of his own. Finally the naval squadron which escorted Charles home added £ 52, 226 to the cost of the expedition.[15] And while he was demanding money for the expenses of the embassy to Spain, the Prince was not reluctant to further the requests of his adherents. Moreover, he was quick to take offense when their demands for pensions were delayed or refused outright.[16]

12. Tawney, *Cranfield*, 225. James too was eager for the payment of the dowry. Halliwell, *Kings' Letters*, II, 216–217, James to the Prince and Duke, July 21, 1623. "Be sure to bring her with you, and forget not to make them to keep their former conditions anent the portion, otherwise both Baby and I are bankrupts for ever." See also Gardiner, *History of England*, V, 133.

13. Goodman, *Court of James I*, I, 324. Goodman thought that this statement was consistent with Cranfield's attitude and personality, but he doubted the authenticity of the attribution on the grounds "that such words were never objected against him." (*Ibid.*, 325.)

14. Halliwell, *Kings' Letters*, II, 193, James to the Prince and Duke, Apr. 10, 1623.

15. HMC, *Fourth Report*, Appendix (London, 1874), 276–277. F. C. Dietz, *English Public Finance 1558–1641* (2d ed., 2 vols., Frank Cass & Co., 1964), II, 197 and 197, n.20; *Cal. S. P. Venetian*, XVIII, 8, 34, Valaresso to the Doge and Senate, May 2/12, 1623, and May 30/June 9, 1623. Valaresso first estimated the cost of the fleet at thirty thousand pounds and later gave the charge as two hundred pounds a day. Compare Sackville MS. ON 7890, Lord Treasurer's report, Mar. 11, 1624.

16. HMC, *Fourth Report*, Appendix, 277, 287; see also Goodman, *Court of James I*, II, 301, E. Clark to the Duke of Buckingham, Aug. 1, 1623; *Cal. S. P. Dom. 1619–1623*, 565, Secretary Conway to the Lord Treasurer, Apr. 22, 1623. In forwarding a recommendation by the Duke of Buckingham of a petition by Endymion Porter to James I, Secretary Conway wrote "Your Lordship knows whose he was and whose he is. His Majesty will expect an answer from you, either to give a warrant for passing the suit, or else a reason why you do it not. And for all respects I

Forewarned of the animosity felt by Charles and Buckingham, Cranfield and his colleagues devised a plan to ameliorate their wrath. Since they were well aware that the Lord Treasurer would be the principal target of the favorite's displeasure, it was agreed that a major effort should be made to vindicate Cranfield's conduct of affairs. The personable Earl of Carlisle was commissioned to test the sentiments of the Prince and the Duke and prepare the way for reconciliation. The Duke of Richmond and Lennox, who had benefited by some of the financial transactions that occurred during Buckingham's absence, made a personal appeal to the King to intervene on Cranfield's behalf. Richmond also promised to inform the Prince and Buckingham that they were more beholden to the Treasurer than to any other subject of the King.[17]

By the time that Charles and Buckingham arrived at Royston replete with excuses and explanations regarding their failure to bring back the Infanta, Cranfield found himself under attack from another quarter. Two suits preferred by Sir Henry Mildmay, Master of the Jewel House, were opposed by the Treasurer as being contrary to the King's interests, and in retaliation Sir Henry indiscretely vented his spleen upon Cranfield. For his temerity Mildmay was suspended from office and was not restored to the King's good graces until he had made submission to Cranfield and procured his intercession with James. Doubtless it was politic of the Treasurer to show compassion to a subordinate when he himself felt need of it from Charles and Buckingham.[18]

Cranfield may have met briefly with the Prince and the Duke during their sojourn in London, but he did not accompany them to Royston. On the evening of October 6 the Duke of Richmond

wish you may find it convenient, to cut off further disputes, and to preserve me from importuning of you." (Sackville MS. ON 86, Secretary Conway to Middlesex, Nov. 11, 1623.)

17. Sackville MS. ON 8884, Duke of Richmond and Lennox to Middlesex, Oct. 8, 1623.

18. *Cal. S. P. Dom. 1623–1625*, 87, Middlesex to Secretary Conway, Oct. 2, 1623. In an undated letter, probably Oct. 2, 1623, Sir Henry Mildmay wrote to Cranfield: "I protest nothing was uttered by me with premediated malice, but upon occasion in free discourse those things carelessly fell from me which I am now heartily sorry for." (Sackville MS. ON 8914.) See also Sackville MS. ON 85, Conway to Middlesex, Oct. 3, 1623; Chamberlain, *Letters*, II, 517, letter of Oct. 11, 1623; *Cal. S. P. Dom. 1623–1625*, 100, Sir Richard Yonge to Lord Zouche, Oct. 20, 1623. By November 3 Sir Henry Mildmay had procured a reference from the Duke of Buckingham to the Attorney General on his behalf. (*Cal. S. P. Dom. 1623–1625*, 106.)

dispatched a hasty note advising Cranfield to come to court. By October 8, Richmond no longer considered Cranfield's presence vital, but by the twelfth the portents were once more unfavorable. That day Cranfield received a letter from the Duchess of Richmond which noticed the Lord Keeper's departure for Royston on the eleventh and repeated the rumor current in London that Buckingham had commanded his presence. Once again Cranfield was advised to appear at court. The Treasurer's anxiety must have been increased by the brief note which the Earl of Carlisle sent on October 12. It gave no account of conversations with Buckingham and pleaded the excuse of "his Majesty's service" for Carlisle's delay in coming to London. In fact his report was to be deferred "three or four days longer." [19]

At best, the combined efforts of the King and his courtiers seem to have effected merely an uneasy truce between Buckingham and Cranfield. On October 25 the Treasurer wrote to Conway to express his gratitude for the secretary's wish to facilitate a rapprochement. Cranfield acknowledged his indebtedness, but alleged that he had left nothing undone to express his friendship and that he was "grieved that his Grace is causelessly jealous of him, and condemns him unheard, without letting him know what he is charged with." [20]

In the interim between the return of the Prince and the opening of Parliament, Cranfield participated in the frequent meetings of the select council for Spanish affairs. Any reconciliation that may have been effected in the autumn of 1623 was annihilated by the Treasurer's adamant opposition to the bellicose projects of the Prince and the Duke. Buckingham found that Cranfield took his cue from the King's mind just as other men did. The Treasurer

19. Sackville MS. ON 299, the Duke of Richmond and Lennox to Middlesex, [Oct. 6, 1623]; *ibid.*, ON 8884, the Duke of Richmond and Lennox to Middlesex, Oct. 8, 1623; *ibid.*, ON 8930, the Duchess of Richmond and Lennox to Middlesex, Oct. 12, 1623; *ibid.*, ON 102, the Earl of Carlisle to Middlesex, Oct. 12, 1623. There is a strong implication in the Duchess of Richmond's letter that Lord Keeper Williams would make his peace with the Prince and Buckingham at Cranfield's expense. Williams's awareness of the Duke's displeasure is indicated by his letter to Conway on October 10, the day before his departure for Royston. (*Cal. S. P. Dom. 1623–1625*, 92.)

20. *Cal. S. P. Dom. 1623–1625*, 102, Middlesex to Conway, Oct. 25, 1623. On Dec. 4, 1623, Conway wrote to Cranfield "Your noble friend indeed the Duke of Buckingham [is] well in his health and you very well in his understanding." (Sackville MS. ON 981.) See also *Cal. S. P. Dom. 1623–1625*, 99, Sir Richard Weston to Conway, Oct. 19, 1623, regarding Weston's efforts to regain Buckingham's favor.

was well aware of James's antipathy to Parliament and was one of the five who voted against the convocation of that assembly.[21] More than any other minister, he knew that the ordinary revenues of the crown were insufficient to maintain a war, and, after the experience of 1621, he was convinced that any assistance offered by the House of Commons would be accompanied by demands for redress of grievances and a diminution of the royal prerogative. All through the summer of 1623 Cranfield had hoped for the Infanta's portion as the solution to the King's bankruptcy. Now, not only was there no dowry, but the expenses of an unsuccessful embassy were to be compounded by the costs of a pointless war.

Cranfield's candid criticisms wounded the vanity of Buckingham and Charles, but the Prince's honor as well was questioned in the discussions that were held in mid-January 1624. During consideration of the sincerity of Spanish intentions, one of the commissioners pointedly asked Charles whether, when he swore to the marriage treaty in Spain, it had been agreed that the restitution of the Palatinate was to precede the nuptial ceremonies. After a confused silence, Charles replied that "in such matters he had no will but his father's." The majority of the councillors were disposed to accept the Prince's contention that he was free of engagement unless the Palatinate were surrendered "and that which was in his own Breast, must alone direct him how to use his Freedom." Cranfield, however, seems to have expressed a dissident opinion. Whether Charles wished to marry the Infanta or not, it was his duty to do so "for reason of state and the good that would thence redound to all Christendom." He suggested that the Prince "ought to submit his private distaste therein to the general good and honour of the kingdom." Charles retorted that Cranfield should "judge of his merchandises, if he would, for he was no arbiter in points of honour." [22] Undaunted, Middlesex voted against the breach with Spain.

There is no doubt that the Prince and Buckingham were highly offended at the checks given their policy by the votes of the select council. Whether they were more offended with Cranfield than with the other councillors who had opposed them is problematical, but there is some evidence to indicate that, in December 1623

21. See chap. i, n. 61.
22. Gardiner, *History of England*, V, 177, 229. Hacket, *Scrinia Reserata*, I, 169.

and January 1624, Cranfield was putting his house in order in expectation of an attack.[23] There is no hint of a reconciliation between the Treasurer and the favorite, but the late date on which the charges were first introduced in Parliament seems to indicate that an immediate impeachment was not contemplated. Certainly the Prince and the Duke were his "small friends," but if Cranfield had not risked further offending them, it is doubtful whether the Parliament would have been the instrument used to disgrace him.[24] His activities were being observed, however, and the Venetian ambassador noted, on March 19, "In the upper house suspicion has constantly increased against some noblemen, already opposed to the general welfare, who have taken courage from the king's resolutions, while he has perhaps received some from them. The lord treasurer is considered the worst of these, and after him the Lord Keeper, both creatures of Buckingham, but now estranged if not his enemies." [25] And, on March 26, Valaresso wrote, "The Lord Treasurer, a most sorry minister, has not ceased the worst offices with the king, and I know that among other things he told him that he should avoid making a declaration, because thereby he would subject himself to the parliament and cease to be a king.[26]

23. Sackville MS. (Kent Archives Office, U 269, Cranfield correspondence 1624), Middlesex to James I, undated. According to his own account Cranfield, in January 1624, "understood by Mr. Chancellor [Weston] of a private whispering amongst those that wish me ill that I had taken 500 pounds of the farmers for dispatching their warrant about the petty farms, whereupon presently I sent for Jacob and questioned him about it, who at first denied there was any such matter, but the next day came to me again and told me that he and his partners had charged 500 pounds of the 1,000 pounds I had of them for my 4/32 parts upon the account of the petty farms, whereupon I being very angry that they had cozened their partners and thereby dishonored me, he desired me to rest contented and they would instantly rectify it again." Subsequently Cranfield demanded from Jacob an antedated letter (June 27, 1623) confirming the sale of his four shares in the great farm to Jacob, Wolstenholm, Garroway, and Abbot. See also OPH, VI, 240–241. In his preface to the charges against Cranfield, Sir Edward Coke observed "That it is a blessed Thing of those that love Parliaments; and that surely this Lord, of all others, loved them not; because he cast himself into dark Mists, when he should meet them . . . This argues much Guiltiness." (OPH, VI, 144.)

24. SP 14/156/3, T. Locke to Sir Dudley Carleton, Dec. 26, 1623. This letter indicates that Cranfield offended Buckingham, not only in the Council, but also by his refusal to pass certain grants which the Duke had solicited. See particularly Sackville MSS. ON 39 A and 39 B, Middlesex to Buckingham, Jan. 24, 1624, in which Cranfield explains his reasons for the denial of Lord Mordaunt's suit.

25. Cal. S. P. Venetian, XVIII, 256, Valaresso to the Doge and Senate, Mar. 19/29, 1624.

26. Ibid., 262, Valaresso to the Doge and Senate, Mar. 26/Apr. 5, 1624.

On April 2, the archbishop of Canterbury reported the Lords Committee for examining the stores and ammunition for war. The day before, he noted, some speeches had passed in the committee which concerned the honor of a Lord of that House,[27] and the Treasurer had requested that examinations upon oath might be taken to clear his name. This is the first hint of the forthcoming prosecution of Cranfield. On the same day, the Venetian ambassador wrote: "The Lord Treasurer is almost openly trying to oust Buckingham, assisted secretly by the Earl of Arundel." [28]

Thus, in early April, the battle was joined between Middlesex and the favorite. Factors favoring the Treasurer were not lacking, but, when weighed against the forces opposing him, they scarcely portended success. The reluctance of the King to abandon his lifelong pacifism was notorious, and in early April the declaration dissolving the two treaties was still awaiting dispatch. The King's pacific attitude was Cranfield's greatest asset; if James could be confirmed in that policy, the efforts of the Prince and the Duke would have been in vain. Moreover, the Treasurer had proven his value as a minister of finance during a time of economic crisis, but proof of service was not alone a sufficient guarantee of royal favor. So far as James was concerned, Cranfield was a valuable, though not a personable, servant. His plebeian origins, his candid and often irritating outbursts of criticism, and his haughty demeanor alienated the King no less than the sycophants of the court.

Doubtless the Treasurer was aware of his personal shortcomings and knew that he could never replace Buckingham in the King's affections. He did, however, have a close relative who might win James's esteem. On March 24, the Earl of Kellie reported the return of Arthur Brett "who is come here without the Duke of Buckingham's consent." [29] Whether Brett's arrival at Chelsey

---

27. *OPH*, VI, 121. There are many accounts of Cranfield's trial, the most authoritative being those contained in C65/188, Parliament Roll 21 James I, Part III, and *LJ*, III. I have used the account printed in *OPH*, VI, 132–311, which includes the depositions omitted in Cobbett, *Parliamentary History*, I, 1411–1478, and in Howell, *State Trials*, II, 1183–1254.

28. *Cal. S. P. Venetian*, XVIII, 268, Valaresso to the Doge and Senate, Apr. 2/12, 1624.

29. HMC, *Mar and Kellie*, 197, Thomas, earl of Kellie to John, earl of Mar, Mar. 24, 1624; SP 14/161/36, Sir Francis Nethersole to Sir Dudley Carleton, Mar. 25, 1624; Chamberlain, *Letters*, II, 553, letter of Apr. 10, 1624.

House was actually instigated by Cranfield is open to question. The Lord Treasurer ultimately acknowledged that Buckingham had some cause for suspicion, but, according to Brett's own testimony, sheer poverty forced him to return to the shores of England. This, at least, was the excuse which he pleaded when he was under examination by Attorney General Coventry.[30] A somewhat different motive was revealed in a letter from Brett to Cranfield in 1623: "And though your Lordship's desires, I know, prevent all my own wishes of advancing my fortune or content, yet there is one of my contents so ambitiously desired that it hath neither modesty nor power to dissemble itself; which is, that by your Lordship's mindfulness of me you will be pleased to hasten me to that felicity of seeing and serving your Lordship where I am fittest to shew myself." [31]

Buckingham was not disposed to consider competitors for royal favor lightly, irrespective of whether he could prove that they were being seconded by his adversaries. Even without Cranfield, Brett posed a threat to the Duke's ascendancy, for the prospective favorite was a pawn that could be used by his foes.[32] Who knew

30. *Cal. S. P. Dom. 1623–1625*, 335, Earl of Middlesex to Buckingham, Sept. 5, 1624; *ibid.*, 310, examination of Arthur Brett, July 23, 1624.

31. Sackville MS. ON 244, Arthur Brett to Lord Treasurer Cranfield, Oct. 15/25, 1623.

32. After Cranfield's fall, the mere whisper of an impending match between Brett and the recently widowed Duchess of Richmond was considered sufficient basis for the prediction of great alterations at court. (Chamberlain, *Letters*, II, 560, letter of May 13, 1624.) Even before this the Earl of Arundel was supposedly implicated in a conspiracy with Cranfield to displace Buckingham by means of Brett. (*Cal. S. P. Venetian*, XVIII, 268, Valaresso to the Doge and Senate, Apr. 2/12, 1624.) But the most dangerous plot of all never became a matter of public knowledge. According to Brett's own testimony, he had an interview with the Duke in which he requested Buckingham's intercession for his restoration to royal favor and relaxation of the restrictions placed on his movements. Buckingham refused the former request, blamed him for coming to England, "and said he was no longer the King's servant and might live where he pleased." (*Cal. S. P. Dom. 1623–1625*, 310, examination of Arthur Brett, July 23, 1624.) Brett then resorted to London and the Venetian ambassador reported on June 4/14 that he was much seen at court. (*Cal. S. P. Venetian*, XVIII, 343, Valaresso to the Doge and Senate, June 4/14, 1624.) It must have been at this time that overtures were made to Brett from adherents of the Earl of Pembroke. In an undated letter to his sister, the Countess of Middlesex, Brett revealed the texture of the conspiracy. "Dear Sister: Concerning the first beginning of that with my Lord Chamberlain, you must know of my brother Henry, for I cannot resolve you; but as much as I understand, Mr. Valentine and one Mr. Corrington moved my brother that if I would they thought that his Lordship would present me to the King, and to that purpose Mr. Valentine and my brother consulted that Mr. Corrington should move his Lordship therein as from me, and if my Lord Chamberlain pleased to undertake it

what alliances might be secretly forming around the person of an
attractive and ambitious young courtier? Consequently, precautions were taken to isolate him from the center of political power.
The Earl of Carlisle appeared with a royal command ordering
Brett back to France, and, when compliance was refused, he was

---

they assured Mr. Corrington that I should be ruled by his Lordship. And Mr.
Corrington having moved my Lord told me that his Lordship took it very kindly
that I would address myself unto him, and desired a day or two respite to think
of it, with an assurance by Mr. Corrington that if he undertook it he would not
shrink from me, but if he perceived anything to the contrary that he could not
conveniently do it; and assured me upon his honor neither to reveal it, or any ways
to prejudice me therein, and after that my Lord had considered of it sent me word
by Mr. Corrington that he could not undertake it. His reason was in respect that
he perceived the Prince to be so much for his Grace; and again promised (as
before) not to prejudice me, but to do me all the good office he could. This is all,
and more I know not. Your assured loving brother, Arthur Brett." (Sackville MS.
ON 245.) Disappointed with Pembroke's active participation in his schemes, Brett
intended to present himself personally to the King at Chertsey, but was prevented
by the Countess of Middlesex who informed her husband, who in turn notified
Buckingham. Finally, in mid-July Brett appeared in Waltham forest and seized
the bridle of the King's horse as he was hunting "but his Majesty roughly drove him
away, threatening to have him hanged." His essay to recover royal favor ended with
imprisonment in the Fleet where he was examined on July 23 by Attorney General
Coventry. He refused to name any as cognizant of his intentions except Sir Thomas
Darell and Benjamin Valentine. Pembroke was not implicated, and, when no
further information could be elicited, Brett was released (August 30) on condition
not to approach within ten miles of the court. (See Brett examination; Cal. S. P.
Venetian, XVIII, 401, July 16/26, 1624; Cal. S. P. Dom. 1623–1625, 332, Secretary
Conway to Attorney General Coventry, Aug. 30, 1624.) The smoldering enmity between the Earl of Pembroke and the Duke of Buckingham was never effectively
extinguished by the reconciliation between the two courtiers that was engineered
by the Prince in January 1624. Pembroke's realistic assessment of the political and
personal alliance between the Prince and the Duke caused him to dissimulate his
animosity and cooperate with them in promoting the breach with Spain. But
apparently, by September 1624, Pembroke had become distrustful of Buckingham's
negotiations with France. The Earl of Montgomery, Pembroke's brother, who was
eager to accompany Buckingham to Paris, was instrumental in suggesting a basis
for reconciliation that was ardently seconded by Sir George Goring, Buckingham's
creature. On October 4, 1624, Goring wrote "I find that there is a desire of a treaty
between my sweet young lady your daughter and my Lord Montgomery's son, who is
like by his brother's allowance to prove a good English freeholder if not the best.
By the gross of what I gather I see plainly a passionate desire of a true and real
friendship with your Grace and concurrence in all your courses . . . Give me leave
my best Lord to conclude with this my petition (I dare not presume to call it a
counsel) that you please not to neglect this overture of my Lord Chamberlain's
friendship. He is worthy of you every way if you may be sure of him, as I hope
now you may." (Harl. MS. 1580, fol. 445, Sir George Goring to Buckingham, Oct.
4, 1624.) Negotiations, however, broke down, and Pembroke remained antipathetic
toward the Duke through the Parliament of 1626, during which he was implicated
in fomenting Buckingham's impeachment. Peace was finally made between these
powerful peers by virtue of the very marriage alliance suggested in October 1624.
(Birch, Court and Times of Charles I, I, 132–133, letter to the Rev. Joseph Mead,
July 21, 1626.)

enjoined not to come within forty miles of London or of the court.[33] Thus the Lord Treasurer was deprived of a potent weapon in his fight for survival.

Unless Cranfield could be assured of continued royal support, he was doomed. His enemies were legion; his rapid rise from shop-keeper to earl was resented by the ancient nobility. Officers in numerous governmental departments were alienated by the curtailment of their profiteering. A host of courtiers were antagonized by the elimination or diminution of their pensions. Customs farmers were incensed by increased rents. Merchants in London and the outports were offended by impositions on wines and sugars and composition for grocery. Country gentlemen resented Cranfield's activities in connection with the Benevolence of 1622 and his behavior as Master of the Court of Wards. A powerful faction in the Virginia company was aggrieved by the Treasurer's attitude toward the proposed tobacco monopoly. As Sir John Saville succinctly put it: "whereas other men much faulty have had yet some friend speak some good of them, he never heard of anyone speak of any virtue or goodness in the Treasurer." [34]

At any other time Cranfield's efforts to supplant Buckingham might have evoked some support in the House of Commons, but, with the nation in the grip of anti-Spanish hysteria, his few friends found it expedient to remain silent or to work behind the scenes. There can be little doubt that the attack on the King's minister was both premeditated and coordinated in the Lords and Commons. It has been suggested by Professor Tawney and Mrs. Prestwich that Sir Edwin Sandys laid the groundwork for the charge in the House of Commons in reporting the Committee for Trade on April 2.[35] This time corresponds precisely with Abbot's report of the committee for munitions in the House of Lords, and this would argue that Buckingham envisaged a concerted attack. So he did, but his main instrument in the Commons was not Sir Edwin

33. *Cal. S. P. Dom. 1623–1625*, 310, examination of Arthur Brett, July 23, 1624.
34. Spring, 225; see also *OPH*, VI, 141, where, in opening the charges against Middlesex, Sir Edward Coke said, "In their Inquisition they met with, what they scarce ever found before, many great Exorbitancies and heinous Offences, against a Member of this House, the Earl of Middlesex, the Lord Treasurer; and they found him guilty after a strange Manner; for, in all their House, not one Man said No, but concluded against him *Nemine contradicente*."
35. Tawney, *Cranfield*, 239–240; Menna Prestwich, *Cranfield: Politics and Profits Under the Early Stuarts* (Oxford: Clarendon Press, 1966), 441.

Sandys but Sir Miles Fleetwood, who on April 5 charged Cranfield with innovation and gross corruption in his administration of the Court of Wards.

The Sandys report of April 2 dealt generally with causes for the decay of trade. Only a small portion of it, that dealing with impositions, reflected on the Treasurer, and it was noted in the report that Cranfield had sent his own copy of the new book of rates to the committee.[36] The new impositions upon wines and the composition for grocery taken from the outports came in for some criticism, but the only suggestion that this was to redound to the Lord Treasurer's detriment occurred after the report was finished. Chancellor of the Exchequer Weston denied knowledge of the new book of rates and alleged that the impositions on wines had been agreed on at the council table, but this explanation did not satisfy Sir Robert Phelips: "In reformation of grievances, we ought to consider as well the persons who give princes ill advice as the effects which succeed that advice. Therefore, it will be well if the committee deal with the referees. And if it shall appear that any man, to raise his own fortune, hath given the King counsel contrary to the right of the subject let us not spare him, but appeal from the King mis-advised to the King rightly informed." [37]

36. Pym, fol. 46. "This book was printed secretly by Felix Kingston. My Lord Treasurer, understanding we wanted one of them, sent us his own copy, saying that the book was misprinted, expressing some charges which were never intended, but we found it authorized with James Rex." According to Spring, 207, the book of rates was printed on September 5, 1623, and "recalled again the 12th till his Lordship's pleasure were farther known." Tawney (*Cranfield*, 242) alleges that it was necessary for the Commons to use the Duke of Buckingham's influence with the King in order to secure permission to review the account books of the customs farmers. As evidence, he cites Spring, 192, Apr. 8. But the books in question were not those of the customs farmers and indeed had no relation whatsoever to Cranfield. They were the account books of the Merchant Adventurers, which they had been ordered to produce in the Committee of Trade on April 3. See Pym, fols. 48 and 54v (Apr. 8). "Mr. Solicitor, by direction of my Lord of Buckingham, acquainted the House that the merchants had been with the King to be excused for delivery of their book. And his Majesty's answer was . . . that he was pleased the books should be delivered . . . Whereupon there was appointed for this service of the examination of the Merchant Adventurers books a select committee of seven." See also Earle, fol. 123v.

37. Pym, fol. 46v. In an undated letter to James I subsequent to the Parliament of 1624, Cranfield cited the improvement of the King's revenue by thirty thousand pounds per year as a sufficient cause for the remission of the penalties imposed upon him by the Lords. He alleged that the increased income resulted from improved rents in the lease of the great customs and to impositions "which although it were my service I dare not call it so." (Sackville MS. [Kent Archives Office, U 269, Cranfield correspondence 1624].)

Despite Phelips's implied accusation of the Treasurer, the House took no immediate action on the report, and it was not until Fleetwood presented his information that an overt attack began. Had Sandys been a party to a conspiracy against Cranfield, doubtless the grievances he had outlined would have been exacerbated in ensuing debates to form the heart of the charge. But logic dictated that the matter of impositions could not become the central issue. To make it so would have made Cranfield's cause and the King's cause one and the same. If impositions were to be considered at all, it had to be done with a "very tender Hand" or else, as May said, "[It] May open a Gap for him, to lay hold on the Horns of the Altar." [38]

Although it seems doubtful that Sandys was actively intriguing against Cranfield before April 2, 1624, there was sufficient reason for him to oppose the Treasurer. A petition of the Virginia Company, which was delivered to the House of Commons on April 26, charged that Cranfield had sided with the Warwick-Rich faction in the Virginia Company and that "Sir Edwin [Sandys] was commanded by my Lord Treasurer in the King's name to go out of this town where his presence was not then more necessary for the making of his own defense, than for accusing of his predecessors in that government of whose accounts he had been an auditor. And in this hard usage this was very remarkable that the King, being told of it by a great lord, disavowed my Lord Treasurer and gave commandment for Sir Edwin's liberty to return." [39]

38. *CJ*, 764.
39. SP 14/164/46, Sir Francis Nethersole to Sir Dudley Carleton, May 6, 1624. A somewhat different impression of the source of Sandys ill treatment is conveyed in his letter to Middlesex on June 19, 1623. (Sackville MS. ON 6207.) In this letter he thanks Cranfield for "your Lordship's most noble favor toward me unto his Majesty in procuring my liberty to return to the city," and solicits Cranfield's assistance "to restore me again thoroughly to his Majesty's gracious favor." S. M. Kingsbury, ed., *An Introduction to the Records of the Virginia Co. of London* (2 vols., Washington, D.C.: Government Printing Office, 1905), 526, 528, 530, 537–538, 540. The petition was discussed at the Quarter Court of the Virginia Company which met on April 21, 1624. After citing the benefits resulting from the establishment of the company, the petition requested that members of the company who were also members of the House of Commons might be allowed to make a relation of grievances which "they doubt not to make evident had either original or strength from the now Lord Treasurer out of his private and unjust ends." Nicholas Ferrar preferred the petition on April 26. (Nicholas, fol. 177v–178.) Sir Nathaniel Rich equivocally opposed the reception of the petition, but the House ordered its consideration in a Committee in Star Chamber on the afternoon of April 28. The text of Rich's speech is in the Manchester MSS, PRO 30/15/2/410. At a Quarter Court

Although Sandys had good cause to be partisan in his attitude toward Cranfield, he was inclined to be more dispassionate than Sir Edward Coke or Sir Robert Phelips. On April 5 he maintained "The ancient rule is that every man is presumed to be innocent till he be proved to be otherwise." While Coke, on the seventh, stated "The affirmative in accusations is ever presumed, till the negative be proved." More than one contemporary observed that Coke delighted in the prosecution of the Treasurer. "I believe," wrote Sir Edward Conway, Jr., "that if once in seven years he were not to help to ruin a great man he should die himself." [40]

---

held on April 28, the Virginia Company decided to petition the House of Commons to command the presence of Sir Nathaniel Rich at the Star Chamber Committee hearings that afternoon. Lord Cavendish, Sir Edwin Sandys, Sir John Danvers, and Nicholas Ferrar were commissioned to speak about the grievances of the company. Cranfield's reaction to their speeches is recounted in his letter to James on April 29, 1624. (Sackville MS. [Kent Archives Office, U 269, Cranfield correspondence 1624].) "The Lord Cavendish, Sir Edwin Sandys and Deputy Ferrar did yesterday make invective orations against me four hours together about the Virginia business and the proceedings had before your Majesty and your Council about their patent and intended alteration of their government, all which they laid wholly upon me." Further proceedings on the Virginia petition were estopped by James's letter to the Speaker of the House of Commons on April 28, 1624. (SP 14/163/71.)

40. Spring, 174; Holles, fol. 122; Holland, Tanner MS. 392, fol. 80v; SP 14/163/1, Sir Edward Conway, Jr., to Sir Dudley Carleton, Apr. 18, 1624; see also SP 14/163/2, Sir Henry Goodyere to Sir Dudley Carleton, Apr. 18, 1624. In the Parliament of 1625, Coke, Sandys, and Phelips all figured prominently in the action taken by the House of Commons on a petition preferred by the merchants protesting against the continuance of the twenty shillings per tun imposed on French wines. Sir Arthur Ingram, who was on that occasion protecting Cranfield's interests, saw "the petition in Sir Robert Phelips' hands before it was delivered into the House." Phelips refused to suppress the petition saying "If he did not deliver it, some other would." Sandys chaired the select committee appointed to investigate the matter, and the hearing was opened by a tirade from Sir Edward Coke who "spared not to lay the blame of that business wholly upon your Lordship [Cranfield] as an act of your own invention." When the committee rose, Ingram "spoke to Sir Edwin Sandys that he should be tender of your name having suffered too much already." Sandys promised "that he will do it in such sort as it shall not in the least touch you." Coke was absent on a mission to the Lords when Sandys reported from the committee on July 1. This was probably a strategic move to avoid involving Cranfield in the affair: "although Sir Edwin related with his report the proceedings of the House against your Lordship the last Parliament about that matter and concluded that the committee thought fit it should be added to the grievances intended now to be exhibited to his Majesty, no man in the House replied with any invective against your Lordship." Had Cranfield been attacked several prominent parliamentarians had promised to speak in his defense, including Christopher Wandesford, Sir Henry Poole, Sir John Finch, William Noy, and Chancellor of the Exchequer Weston, who even promised "to take off Sir Simon Weston, his uncle." (Sackville MSS [Kent Archives Office, U 269, Cranfield correspondence 1625–1627], George Lowe to Cranfield, June 30, 1625; Nicholas Herman to Cranfield [June 30, 1625]; Sir Arthur Ingram to Cranfield, July 1, 1625; George Lowe to Cranfield, July 1, 1625.) See also

Sir Robert Phelips was even more vitriolic. On April 9, Phelips called attention to two French precedents dealing with finance ministers and noted that an earl had suffered the death penalty. "There was never," he said, "any ill man in this kind but would seek to countenance himself with the King's authority, but he is little less than a traitor that gives the King bad counsel and such as may make a separation betwixt him and his subjects." It was Phelips, likewise, who suggested that Cranfield had procured the dissolution of the Parliament of 1621.[41]

This triumvirate, Coke, Sandys, and Phelips, was a force to be reckoned with in the House of Commons. They were chairmen, respectively, of the grand Committees for Grievances, Trade, and Courts of Justice. It was suspected that two of them had been tampered with before the opening of Parliament.[42] Suspicion of "undertaking" may have been justifiable in the case of Phelips.[43] Next to Fleetwood, he was the most avid advocate of Cranfield's prosecution and the most extreme exponent of severe penalties. No more appropriate instrument for the achievement of Buckingham's purpose could have been found. From his entrance into Parliament Phelips had been vehemently opposed to impositions. He had taken part in impeachment proceedings and had played a significant role in the conviction of Bacon. As chairman of the Committee for Courts of Justice, he was the logical person to direct the investigation of irregularities in the Court of Wards.

Scarcely had Fleetwood laid his charge before the House than Phelips moved the expediting of a trial and suggested a choice

S. R. Gardiner, ed., *Debates in the House of Commons in 1625*, Camden Society, N. S., Volume VI (London, 1873), 35–36.

41. Pym, fol. 56; Spring, 209–210, 225; Holland, Tanner MS, 392, fol. 90.

42. Chamberlain, *Letters*, II, 549, letter of Mar. 20, 1624. "Neither will they be led along by theire old *duces gregis* Sir Edwin Sandes, Sir Dudley Diggs, and Sir Robert Phillips, for they have so litle credit among them that though they speake well and to the purpose sometimes, yet yt is not so well taken at their hands for still they suspect them to prevaricate, and hold them for undertakers."

43. *Cabala*, I, 264–266, Robert Phelips to the Duke of Buckingham, Aug. 21, 1624. This letter shows Phelips to have been in communication with Buckingham during the summer of 1624 and probably before. The Duke had asked Phelips's advice about the possibility of action against the Earl of Bristol and had communicated Bristol's answer to him. In reply Phelips asked him to consider "which of the two waies will most conduce to your Graces purpose, and is likely to receive the best interpretation and success, either to have him dealt with after a quick and round manner, or otherwise to proceed slowly and moderately with him, permitting him for a time to remain where he is, as a man laid aside, and in the way to be forgotten."

committee. But if his intention was to secure leadership of the investigation, he was forestalled by Sir Edwin Sandys, whose judgment was that "This business is fitter for the Committee of Grievances than that of the Courts of Justice for here is no false judgment." Nevertheless, Phelips made a second attempt — this time to split the charge. "This accusation," he said, "consists of two parts: the one concerning the Court of Wards: the other the bribes." The House, however, did not agree with him and the questioning of the Treasurer's activities was referred to the Committee for Grievances, and, incidentally, to the Committee for Trade.[44]

This, however, did not prevent Phelips from giving direction to the movement against Cranfield. It has already been noted that he introduced the "aggravation" of the dissolution of 1621. It was Phelips, likewise, who, on April 12, thought it fit to recommend to the Lords that Cranfield was the "projector" of the new impositions on wines. Phelips did not doubt "the ill-intendment of the Lord Treasurer and that it was suggested by Jacob to him or him to Jacob." He was also convinced that Cranfield was the cause of that "unwarrantable course of benevolence against the King's honor and the liberty of the Commonwealth." If he had had his way, the charges against Cranfield might well have involved capital offenses. The least punishment that he advocated was expulsion from all offices and degradation from the peerage.[45]

As a member of the select committee to prepare the charges against the Treasurer, Phelips undoubtedly worked with the anti-Cranfield clique. In the matter of procedure, when Sir Thomas Hoby moved for a select committee to collect the charge and the proofs for presentation to the Lords, it was Phelips who pointed out that the chairman of the committee was appointed reporter when Bacon was impeached, and he moved that the same course be followed now.[46] The preeminence of Phelips in pursuing the prosecution of Cranfield warrants the conclusion that he was cooperating wholeheartedly with Buckingham and the Prince.

Even before the House of Commons had heard from Cranfield, Sir Richard Yonge wrote to Lord Zouche: "how he will answer it

44. Holles, fol. 119.
45. Earle, fol. 135; Spring, 209, 210; Holland, Rawlinson MS. D 1100, fol. 12–12v.
46. Spring, 209.

[the charge] I know not, but I have many reasons not fit for a pen which make me believe his case is desperate." Two days earlier the Earl of Kellie had written, "it is thought that one of his under-officers does divulge things to his prejudice." [47] When he first came under suspicion on April 2, Cranfield alleged that there was a plot against him "which, if it was suffered, no Man would be in Safety in his Place." With perhaps some tenderness of conscience, the Lords, on April 9, demanded that the Treasurer either name the parties or exonerate the Houses. Despite an effort by the Earl of Arundel to attribute Cranfield's remark to passion, the Treasurer was put in the position where he was compelled to name the Prince and Buckingham or discharge the Lords collectively of any responsibility. The most that Cranfield would say was, "I am questioned here by Informacion of Sir Roberte Pye; in the other House by Mr. Cooke in a buissines concernes neither of themselves." Even though he noted that Sir Miles Fleetwood also had charged him in the Commons, "He cleered bothe Houses. Just proceedings in bothe; craved pardon not to name the parties as yett, and to stande right in their LL[ps] opynion untill [he] be proved faultie." [48]

Of the two Commons members named by Cranfield, Pye seems to have been his most ardent opponent. It was his testimony before the Lords' committee for examining stores and ammunitions of war that initiated the complaint against Cranfield. There is no doubt that he was a Buckingham adherent. Sir James Whitelocke described him as the Duke's servant "who was imployed by him in his most private affayres." [49] Conveniently enough, Pye was

47. SP 14/162/26, Sir Richard Yonge to Lord Zouche, Apr. 7, 1624; HMC, *Mar and Kellie,* 198, Thomas, earl of Kellie, to John, earl of Mar, Apr. 5, 1624.
48. OPH, VI, 127; *Lords Debates 1624 & 1626,* 50, 57, 61, 62; see also *LJ,* III, 328, 336, 337, 338. On May 1, William George petitioned the Lords against two of Cranfield's servants, John Barnes and Richard Colbeck, for scandalous words and affronts when George was examined about the Lord Treasurer. Barnes and Colbeck denied using the words, but Colbeck confessed he told George "that he was too officious; and that Sir Miles Fleetwood had been often to speak with him." Both Barnes and Colbeck were committed to the custody of the serjeant and ordered to be reexamined on the Treasurer's business. Later they acknowledged their offense, apologized to George and were pardoned by the House.
49. Whitelocke, *Liber Famelicus,* 56; see also Chamberlain, *Letters,* II, 283, letter of Jan. 22, 1620; Howell, *State Trials,* II, 1361. In the impeachment proceedings against the Duke of Buckingham in 1626, Christopher Sherland stated "that the Duke, under pretense of secret services, had procured great sums of money to be issued by privy seals to sundry persons named by himself, but afterwards employed

also Auditor of the Exchequer and thus had access to the records of that office. It seems probable that he was the source of information on the two bribes allegedly solicited by Cranfield, even though he was not involved in the presentation of this charge.

As for John Coke, it is difficult to assess his role in the impeachment proceedings. No diarist paid particular attention to anything he said in the House against the King's minister, but, on April 8, Coke was among those appointed to investigate the Treasurer's connection with the extension and enhancement of prerogative taxation on wines, sugars, and grocery ware. Three days previously he had appeared before the Lords as a witness for the prosecution. As a commissioner of the navy, Coke was undoubtedly in the Lord Admiral's confidence. His expert testimony on the deplorable state of England's military preparedness could have shifted the onus of responsibility from Buckingham to Cranfield.[50]

With the exception of Sir Edward Coke, Sir Edwin Sandys, and Sir Robert Phelips, no "leader" of the House ardently supported the impeachment. Those who were instrumental in furthering the prosecution were members who spoke infrequently and who, in this instance, had particular grievances which they wished to see redressed. In the matter of impositions on wines the merchant members of the House almost universally condemned

---

to his own use." Eight thousand pounds was supposedly paid to Sir Robert Pye on August 12, 1620, and disbursed by him for Buckingham's purchase of Burleigh. See also *OPH*, VII, 133. When process was first initiated against Cranfield, Dudley Carleton noted that "Sir Robert Pye is said to work against him." He also contended that "all that hath yet been done against him smells rather of private grudges betwixt my Lord of Buckingham and him, and that they do rather seek for matter against him than allege any sufficient stuff, and the Parliament will judge of all." (SP 14/162/13, Dudley Carleton to Sir Dudley Carleton, Apr. 4, 1624.)

50. *CJ*, I, 760, Apr. 9, 1624. This was a select committee to see who advised the King to lay impositions on wines, sugar, and grocery and to find out who was deterred from complaining to the House and by whom. There were twenty-nine members in this committee, of whom the greater number were opposed to Cranfield. John Coke appeared as a witness against Cranfield on April 5, 1624. See *OPH*, VI, 282–283. See also *Lords Debates 1624 & 1626*, 86, where, in reply to Cranfield's claim of reformation in the government, the Lord Keeper said, "Navy, he not pryvye to those imployments havinge ben otherwise bredd, used the helpe of others, namely of Mr. Cooke, and at last assumed the wholl glory to himselfe." On Coke's activities as a commissioner of the Navy, see HMC, *Twelfth Report*, Appendix, pt. I (London, 1888), MSS of the Earl Cowper, passim. *Cal. S. P. Dom. 1623–1625*, 195. A statement by John Coke alleges a deficiency of 135 lasts of powder and further charges that the King has lost his ratio of 3d in the pound on a large quantity. The date of this document is March 21. Compare with the charges against Cranfield regarding munitions, May 11, 1624. (Howell, *State Trials*, II, 1238–1241.)

Cranfield. On a specific issue, such as composition for grocery, merchants like John Guy and John Barker of Bristol, John Delbridge of Barnstaple, Matthew Pitt and Thomas Gyer of Melcombe Regis, and William Neale of Dartmouth gave testimony or supplied records detrimental to the Treasurer's cause. The London merchants voiced their opposition through Robert Bateman and the recorder.[51]

The sons of two peers joined in the attack. William, Lord Cavendish, was an important member of a faction in the Virginia Company headed by the Earl of Southampton and Sandys, and his attitude toward the King's minister was almost as bitter as that of Phelips.[52] Richard Spencer voiced in the Commons the same sentiments that his father expressed in the Lords. In a lengthy speech in the Committee for Trade, Spencer inveighed against impositions as "against the essence of a free man and subject and against the ancient charter of England, Magna Carta, which provides for freedom in buying and traffic. It overthrows the freedom of the subject and makes him a slave in that it deprives him of the propriety of his goods and makes them subject to his Lord, and so enslaves him." [53]

Spencer maintained that the impositions were for the Lord Treasurer's particular benefit, and he wanted Cranfield's punishment to be commensurate with those meted out in the reign of Edward III. Sir John Eliot, who owed his release from custody to Buckingham's intercession, also moved "that the House would remove this strange and prodigious comet which so fatally hangs over us." [54]

Other members of the House of Commons, who were also crown officers, attempted to substantiate the charges concerning the Court

51. *OPH*, VI, 262–267; Spring, 190, 194–195, 206–208; Pym, fols. 55v–56; Holland, Rawlinson MS. D 1100, fols. 8v, 11–11v.

52. Spring, 196; Holland, Rawlinson MS. D 1100, fol. 28; Chamberlain, *Letters,* II, 492, letter of Apr. 19, 1623, mentions the factions of the Virginia Company in which he lists Cavendish with the Sandys-Southampton-Ferrar group. In July 1623 Cavendish and the Earl of Warwick almost fought a duel because of their disagreements over the management of the company, but Lord Cavendish was prevented from going abroad. See *ibid.*, II, 509, 511, letter of July 26, 1623.

53. Spring, 194. For the opinions of Lord Spencer, see *Lords Debates 1624 & 1626,* 74, 79, 81, 93. For the attitude of "cousin" Richard Knightley, see his letter to the Duke of Buckingham, in S. R. Gardiner, ed., *The Fortescue Papers,* . . . Camden Society, N. S., Volume I (London, 1871), 196–197.

54. Spring, 210.

of Wards. Sir Benjamin Rudyard, the surveyor of the court, admitted that his authority and revenue had been curtailed by the Master's institution of a secretarial office. Sir Miles Fleetwood, the receiver, and Sir Walter Pye, the attorney, confirmed the charge that the Treasurer diminished the ancient perquisites of their offices by his instructions issued in 1622.[55]

None of Cranfield's underofficers castigated him as severely as Fleetwood. From the very first the receiver spearheaded the movement against his superior, and what his charges lacked in substance he supplemented with invective. He seemed intent on gaining the utmost publicity for his accusations. They were not filed in a petition preferred to the appropriate committee; instead, on April 5, he presented them to the whole House with a prefatory speech in which he cited Cranfield as one of those enemies who "under pretense of service to the King do enrich themselves and consume the King's treasure." He spoke of the sale of offices, great New Year's gifts, three or four great bribes, all of which, he said, were undeniable and inexcusable.[56]

55. *OPH*, VI, 289; Spring 175; see also Sackville MS. ON 431, Sir Walter Pye to Cranfield, Mar. 1, 1621/2, which mentions that he has perused the instructions about the Court of Wards and made additions which he submits, leaving all to Cranfield's consideration "for I assure myself your Lordship will be careful that no article be added that may give occasion to any that affect not this work to divulge that these were added or altered to increase charge to the subject or to divert due fees from one officer to another." On August 13 and December 10, 1622, Sir Benjamin Rudyard solicited Cranfield's help in securing the right to nominate two candidates to be made serjeants-at-law as recompense for the three hundred pounds per year that Rudyard claimed he would lose because of the new instructions in the Court of Wards. (Sackville MSS ON 9238, 9239.)

56. Spring, 172; Holland, Tanner MS. 392, fol. 80–80v. See, more particularly, SP 14/165/1, information laid against the Lord Treasurer by Sir Miles Fleetwood. This is calendared erroneously in the printed calendar, *Cal. S. P. Dom. 1623–1625,* 249, under the date May 19, 1624, but it is obviously a copy of the accusations made on April 5. Horne (fol. 65) reports at second hand an incident which helps explain Sir Miles Fleetwood's animosity towards the Lord Treasurer and which also elucidates the connection between Fleetwood and the Prince. "Since this, it is said that the Treasurer, being willed by the Prince to deliver 10,000 pounds speedily to be sent to the King of Denmark, to which the Prince was engaged in promise and credit, made answer and refused, answering that the King's coffers were empty. Upon this the Prince sent for Sir Miles Fleetwood, knight, who receives all, or most part, of the moneys that are paid to the Master of the Wards and Liveries. He had 8,000 [pounds] in esse, and undertook to make up the other 2,000 [pounds] within two days. Therefore the Treasurer, offended herewith, sent for him, and asked him what authority he had to deliver out any moneys without his consent. His answer was, he had the Prince's word for it: and if that were not sufficient, himself would be gage for a greater matter. Hereupon the Treasurer reviled him, which the Prince, hearing of, took in very ill part. It is said, that

When the House had perused Fleetwood's information, some doubt remained as to whether the allegations were sound enough to warrant further proceedings. In the Committee for Grievances that afternoon, Noy summarized Fleetwood's accusations under four headings: the creation of a secretary in the court to take petitions, the double fees resulting from the institution of this office, abbreviating the time for concealed wardships from three years to one, and the use of a stamp bearing his signature. When it was moved that these charges should be transferred to the Lords, the consensus was that they lacked both weight and proof and that further testimony should be taken, particularly from Cranfield's secretary, Nicholas Herman.[57]

When the cause was heard again in the Committee for Grievances on April 7, Fleetwood suddenly shifted his ground. Instead of dwelling on abuses in the Court of Wards (in which he was personally interested), he accused the Treasurer of taking bribes from the customs farmers.[58] Here was a charge that aroused the interest of the House. Few members could get excited about double fees in the Court of Wards when the sum involved was less

---

since this Lord Treasurer's time, this knight hath paid unto him 100,000 pounds in lieu of which he hath not made his audit to the King for 40,000. It is said also he hath purchased 8,000 pounds of land per annum, to him and his heirs in fee. And for his exactions, extortions, and base bribery in the Customs House, many bills are preferred, and much is proved against him: against which, being so weak to stand, he cannot but fall, and well worthy. The Lower House hath bound him over for censure to the Upper." On the identity of Robert Horne and the probable sources for Rawlinson MS. B 151, see *Commons Debates 1621*, I, 100–101. Among the Sackville manuscripts is a letter from Buckingham to Cranfield, March 2, 1622, soliciting furtherance and favor for a suit of Sir Miles Fleetwood in consideration of "his long continued dependence and addresses to me." Buckingham recommends Fleetwood as a person "that I do much affect." (Sackville MS. ON 10.) On April 29, 1624, Cranfield wrote to James I, "I have been this day a full month in such a persecution and prosecution as no story mentions the like; a continual inquisition upon me and all my actions upon oath for the greatest part of my life; men persuaded and entreated (I will not say promised reward) to accuse me and complain of me; all men called in and examined upon oath that had had to do with me either for your Majesty's business or my private; my own secretaries and servants examined upon oath against me; searches made with goldsmiths what plate they have made which was given me, and by whose direction, and those likewise examined by Fleetwood when they gave it and upon what ground." (Sackville MS. [Kent Archives Office, U 269, Cranfield Correspondence 1624].)

57. Pym, fols. 49–49v.

58. HMC, *Twelfth Report*, Appendix, pt. I, (London, 1888), 156, Sir Miles Fleetwood to John Coke, Jan. 19, 1624. "Reminds Coke of his labour in effecting of these instructions for the Court of Wards, producing an increase of 20,000 £. a year to the King. Asks furtherance in his suit for employment."

than five pounds per suitor per year, but two bribes of five hundred pounds each were a different matter. Moreover, Fleetwood's presentation of this accusation differed radically from those he had formerly made. The House conceived that the charge about abuses in the Court of Wards had alleged the possibility of offending. This charge cited bribes already taken, naming names, giving dates with the corroboratory testimony of several witnesses.

Most of the time spent by the Committee for Grievances on the Cranfield affair was concerned with the proofs of these two bribes. A mass of testimony was elicited from witnesses, both eager and reluctant, which satisfied the House that the Treasurer had indeed extorted money from the farmers of the great and petty customs. Despite many inconsistencies in the depositions of the witnesses, the House was influenced by the adverse testimony of men who had frequently been business associates of the Treasurer and were presumed to be his friends. The evidence given by such "friendly" witnesses as Wolstenholm and Garroway was damaging enough, but when an intimate associate, Abraham Jacob, was induced to change his story, thus giving the Treasurer the lie, Cranfield's fate was sealed. The matter of the bribes cannot be considered as a mere adjunct to the case against the Treasurer. As far as the House of Commons was concerned, it was the *sine qua non* of the indictment against him.

The customs farmers maintained that Cranfield had solicited two gratuities: £500 for passing the warrant for an abatement of £9,500 over a nine-year span in the amount due from the petty farm of wines and currants; £500 for accepting the security of the four patentees of the great farm for five shares left unsecured by the withdrawal of some partners. It was alleged that these were two distinct bribes, although paid at the same time, and charged separately to the accounts of the great and the petty farms.

In his defense, Cranfield maintained that the £1,000 was a single payment for four shares of the great farm which he had retained until they were purchased in June 1623.[59] The farmers

---

59. The House of Commons was satisfied by the testimony of Williams, Alan Carey, Simions, and Sir Philip Cary that Cranfield's pretensions to 4/32 parts of the Great Farm were entirely fictitious. "So that Sir Edward Coke observes that the challenge which my Lord pretended for the 4 parts and that he took the 1,000 £ for that is taken away by these men's testimony." (Spring, 208.) Compare with Weston's testimony confirming Cranfield's claim, *OPH*, VI, 249–250.

of the great customs, he said, had defrauded their partners in the petty farm by transferring half of the sum to the latter account. Everything hinged on the testimony of Jacob, who was the messenger who had carried the "bribe," and the agent that the Treasurer had used to effect the alteration in the farmers' accounts. Caught between Scylla and Charybdis, Jacob supported the farmers' statements rather than those of the King's minister. Cranfield's failure to participate in the profits of the great farm for 1622, his failure to order the "correction" of the books before January 1624, and his demand from Jacob of an antedated letter covering the supposed sale of the four shares all told heavily against him.[60] This was sufficient to convince the Commons of his guilt, but presumably the Treasurer felt that, given the proper opportunity, Jacob would still vindicate his reputation. On April 19, Cranfield "stole to Theobalds and carried with him Mr. Jacob and other witnesses hoping by them to have cleared himself to the King, but the Prince having notice of this went after him presently, and his Jacob brought before the King confessed the plain truth of all he had formerly sought to disguise." [61] Even after his conviction Cranfield insisted that Jacob had been guilty of perjury. In a letter to James on May 28, the Treasurer reiterated his innocence of bribery and corruption: "The examinations and inquisitions clear me for I am not touched in those kinds nor any other but those which Jacob hath forsworn me into . . . I have many

60. Pym, fols. 53–53v, 54v, 57; *OPH*, VI, 144. In outlining the first charge before the House of Lords, Coke said, "This Bribe is proved by Hide, Daws, Bishop, and by Abraham Jacob: The last is a Witness with a Witness. For Jacob blanched his Bribe as well as he could, and was taken in three notorious Falsities . . . Here Sir Edward observed, That Jacob was my Lord's necessary creature and petty Chapman." The most notorious example of conflicting testimony occurred when Jacob affirmed that he paid the bribe money to Catchmay on June 27, 1623, while, according to Hide, the farmers did not disburse the money until July 31. This discrepancy was noted by Cranfield in his defense, but the attorney evaded it by saying that Jacob paid the money out of his own pocket and was reimbursed later. See *OPH*, VI, 220–222, 223, 250, 254–255.

61. SP 14/163/50, Sir Francis Nethersole to Sir Dudley Carleton, Apr. 25, 1624. Cranfield was no more fortunate in his nomination of defense witnesses to the House of Lords: On May 3 Dudley Carleton noted, "My Lord Treasurer's business hath little life in it; he having put in his interrogatories and produced his 40 witnesses. But his destiny is such that the very first twelve that were examined, on Saturday afternoon, and should have testified something for him in the expectation of all his judges, deposed directly against him, as if they had been corrupted to do him mischief." (SP 14/164/12, Dudley Carleton to Sir Dudley Carleton, May 3, 1624.)

enemies and great ones, and those who have brought me thus low will do much to perfect their work, which is to ruin me. I have few friends and those dare not appear for me." [62]

The willingness of most courtiers, minor officials, and dependents to abandon the suspect minister leads to the impression that Cranfield had no supporters except the King. Certainly this was not the case. If anything, some of his advocates were an actual embarrassment; the mere rumor of correspondence with the Spanish party increased popular ire against him.[63] In the House of Commons, however, some members did come forward in his defense. Longtime friends and associates, Sir Arthur Ingram and Sir Richard Weston, tried to remove the onus of bribery from his name.[64] Usually the Treasurer's friends were most obvious by their silence. With the exception of Sir Francis Seymour, no one spoke effectively in his defense.

Sir Dudley Digges made an ineffectual attempt to mitigate the seriousness of the charges against him. When Secretary Calvert shifted the blame from the Council to Cranfield as the first promoter of impositions, Digges suggested that "The Treasurer had a 'Dick Lyons' to put this into his head." He wanted to punish those "projectors that are the caterpillars of the Kingdom and are ever buzzing these things [impositions] into great men's heads." He also asserted "that if the charge of my Lord Treasurer had been no more than for taking the two 500 pounds he could have wished it never to have gone to the Lords." [65]

Some important members of the House, like John Glanville

62. Sackville MS. ON 2455, Middlesex to James I, May 28, 1624. Pressure was probably exerted on Jacob to make him change his original testimony. On April 9, Solicitor Heath, a Buckingham client, "informed the House that he had spoken with Jacob who told him he would now discover all, whereupon he was appointed to attend in the afternoon." (Pym, fol. 57.)

63. SP 14/164/12, Dudley Carleton to Sir Dudley Carleton, May 3, 1624. On the attitude toward Cranfield at court, see SP 14/162/56, Dudley Carleton to Sir Dudley Carleton, Apr. 14, 1624, and 14/163/16, Apr. 19, 1624.

64. *OPH*, VI, 244–246, 249–250, the examinations of Ingram and Weston on the Treasurer's behalf.

65. Holles, fol. 127. With reference to Dick Lyons, see William Prynne, ed., *An Exact Abridgement of the Records in the Tower of London . . . Collected by Robert Cotton* (London, 1689), 121, 122. Richard Lyons was a merchant of London accused of various crimes by the Commons in the Parliament held in 50 Edward III. The specific charge which has reference to Digges's allusion is that of procuring new impositions upon staple ware. (See also Earle, fol. 128.) "Latimer's and Lyons' case hits right. Lyons was the projector. Both sentenced for imposing a new found custom. Latimer for the setting the projects on foot." (Spring, 209.)

and Sir Henry Poole, confined their remarks mainly to matters of procedure. Others, like Christopher Brooke, Sir Thomas Wentworth, and Thomas Fanshawe, either commiserated with the plight of the accused, mitigated his offenses, or demanded that the proofs against him be full and clear. When members suggested that the lease of the great farm was let at £1,000 less than it should have been, "Mr. Fanshawe said the King himself was pleased to abate the farmers 1,000 pounds, therefore the Treasurer was not to be charged with it." In addition to testifying for Cranfield before the Lords, the Chancellor of the Exchequer, Weston, excused the Treasurer's failure to answer personally before the Commons committee. Another member, Sir Henry Carey, brought in Cranfield's answer to the charge concerning abuses in the Court of Wards.[66]

However, two burgesses intimately concerned in the matters under consideration remained silent, and neither side called them as witnesses. Maurice Abbot, whose brother, the archbishop of Canterbury, was so active against the Treasurer in the Lords, was one of the four patentees of the great farm and also a lessee of the sugar farm.[67] John Jacob, member for Plimpton, Dorset,

66. Holles, fols. 127v, 128, 129v, 135; Nicholas, fol. 138v; Pym, fols. 53, 59v. It was Weston who on April 5 moved that "the Treasurer may have a particular of the charge to answer it." (Spring, 173.) Sir Henry Carey was the son-in-law of the Earl of Middlesex. He married Martha, the Earl's eldest daughter, early in 1620 (settlement of Feb. 16, 1620). Cranfield seems to have received no overt support from his sometime brother-in-law, Sir John Suckling, Comptroller of the King's Household.

67. *OPH*, VI, 252, 260. The failure of Cranfield to call Abbot as a witness seems inexplicable. Sackville MS. (Kent Archives Office, U 269, Cranfield Correspondence 1624) includes a paper titled "To search." It contains the following notation "Mr. Maurice Abbot never sworn nor examined as yet in parliament and yet he was one of the farm's principal farmers who had one of my 4/32 parts sold Jacob and the rest. To have him examined how many 32 parts he had upon the first division before Mr. Chancellor sold the farmers his 2/32 parts, what was paid Mr. Chancellor for his 2/32 parts, and when they were bought, who had them, and who paid for them, whether they who had the 2/32 or that it was charged to the general account, and whether they put in security to the King for those 2/32 parts before they bought my 4/32 parts or whether they put in security for the 6/32 parts of Mr. Chancellors and mine together, and when they put it in, and who were bound, at how many times they made divisions of the 32 parts and what alterations they made and to whom. What New Years was used to be given to the Lord Treasurer annually for the great farm and what for the petty farms of wines, currants, etc." From the point of view of Buckingham's faction, Abbot's omission may be explained by Glanville's relation of the sixth article against Buckingham in the impeachment proceedings of 1626. It was charged that Buckingham, with the cooperation of Sir Edward Seymour, vice admiral of Devon, had induced the

was the son of Abraham Jacob, a partner with his father in the tobacco farm, and one of the Lord Treasurer's secretaries. When his father was being examined as a witness, and it was moved by Sir John Savile "that Jacob's son, being of the House, should withdraw and not be privy to the counsels of the House, young Jacob answered he was there for his country not for his father, and referred himself to the House." He was allowed to remain, but apparently made no further contribution to the proceedings.[68]

Silence was also the rule for others of Cranfield's "friends" whose sympathies were later evidenced by their activities in his behalf. Early in January 1625, Sir Anthony Maney, Sir Thomas Wentworth, Sir Richard Weston, and Sir Arthur Ingram were all employed in seeking his restoration to favor. Sir Thomas Bludder also seems to have remained on good terms with the Treasurer and was corresponding with him about parliamentary affairs in 1626.[69] The neutrality of Sir Nathaniel Rich and John Pym may perhaps be explained by the favor shown to Rich in the Virginia Company disputes and to Pym in ameliorating the King's displeasure against him in 1622.[70] Generally speaking, the attitude

---

Parliament to prevent the sailing of four East India ships from the first until the twenty-seventh of March 1624 in order to extort ten thousand pounds from the company. Maurice Abbot was elected Governor of the East India Company at a general court held on March 23, 1624. (Howell, *State Trials*, II, 1329, 1335; *Cal. S. P. Colonial, 1622–1624,* IV, 261; see also S. R. Gardiner, ed., *Documents Illustrating the Impeachment of the Duke of Buckingham in 1626,* Camden Society, N. S., Volume XLV (London, 1889), 71–138.

68. Holles, 124v–125; *OPH,* VI, 144; see also Keeler, *Long Parliament,* 231–232. In her biography of Sir John Jacob, Keeler says that his first Parliament was the Short Parliament, when he sat for Harwich, but it is apparent from Holles's diary that he was also the John Jacob who sat for Plimpton, Dorset, in 1624. Whether he was placed by Cranfield's recommendation is problematical. I have discovered only one instance in which the Treasurer tried to influence parliamentary elections. Sackville MS. ON 1177 is a draft of a letter to the borough of Steyning, Sussex, recommending the election of Sir Edward Greville, father-in-law of Sir Arthur Ingram.

69. HMC, *Fourth Report,* Appendix, 288, 306–307.

70. *Ibid.,* 283, 305. Pym was released from house arrest in London on April 20, 1622. (*APC 1621–1623,* 199.) By implication Mrs. Prestwich classifies Pym among the opponents of Cranfield in 1624: "Coke, Bacon, the Marquis of Hamilton, the Duchess of Lennox, and even John Pym were linked in their snobbery towards a mere merchant." (Prestwich, *Cranfield,* 465.) The evidence she cites (pp. 265–266, 488) is an allusion reflecting on merchants as ministers made in a speech concerning Article X of the Duke of Buckingham's impeachment in 1626. Mrs. Prestwich, quoting Rushworth, attributes this speech to Pym, but it was actually delivered by Christopher Sherland deputizing for Edward Whitby. See *CJ,* I, 858; *LJ,* III, 612; *OPH,* VII, 119–123.

of the majority of the Commons seems to have paralleled that expressed by William Noy. On April 5 he was disposed to discount the charges against the Lord Treasurer as matters of small importance, but by April 12 he was convinced that Cranfield had levied impositions for his own particular benefit.[71]

The Treasurer's impolitic handling of his relations with a Commons tender of its privileges certainly helped to swell the tide of opinion against him. It is a matter of no small wonder that such paladins of the Commons as Sir Peter Heyman and Sir Francis Seymour exonerated Cranfield from "aggravations" which had been urged against him by Phelips. On April 15, Heyman said that the Treasurer had not promoted the benevolence, "nor was so forward as other Lords in that business." [72] Seymour went even further in "discharging his conscience." The proofs were plain, he said, "but he would not suffer aggravations without proof, as that he should be an enemy to parliaments; and that he should be a projector of the alterations in the Court of Wards, which was referred to all the officers: and to accuse him of more than can be proved, will do him more right than otherwise." Seymour disliked the protestation concerning impositions, just as he disliked the conjecture that the Treasurer was the "projector" of the illegal duties. He smothered Calvert's argument that the Council had received Cranfield's advice with an "implicit faith." It was no honor, he felt, for any of the Council to say so. As for the benevolence, he maintained, "it were well if we could prove it: but he being one that was called before the Council about the benevolence; he protested he saw no more forwardness in him than the rest." [73]

In the final analysis, the charges sent up to the Lords were not materially affected by the efforts made in Cranfield's behalf. Some of the calumny was deleted, but Sir Edward Coke contrived to

71. Pym, fol. 49; *CJ*, I, 764.
72. Nicholas, fol. 155v. See Tawney, *Cranfield*, 242,n.5, where these speeches are dated April 14, 1624. Both Nicholas and Spring, 223–224, give the date as April 15. Sackville MS. ON 7824 is Cranfield's list of those who were in arrears in contributing to the benevolence, January 8, 1622/3.
73. Holles, fols. 134–134v. See also Spring, 223–224, and Holland, Rawlinson MS. D 1100, fols. 27v–28v for similar reports of these speeches. On the modification of the charge with reference to impositions and the use of the word "propounding" instead of "projecting," see the speech of Sir Thomas Wentworth in Holles, fol. 135. For the recommendations of the Privy Council regarding impositions, see *APC 1621–1623*, 113–114, Jan. 10, 1622, and 115, Jan. 12, 1622.

remedy this defect by magnifying two aggravations he had personally suggested: "(1) Ingratitude to the King who had preferred him to the title of Earl of Middlesex which never subject had before, (2) Perjury by the violation of a three-fold oath as Lord Treasurer, Master of the Wards and Councillor." He then proceeded to indict the Treasurer for taking bribes from the customs farmers and for various offenses in the Court of Wards. Sandys, after protesting that "The House of Commons intended not [at this time] to question the Power of Imposing claimed by the King's Prerogative" followed with charges relating to impositions on wines and sugars, and composition for grocery.[74]

The Commons had been expeditious in assembling their evidence; in less than two weeks they had, by effective use of the committee system, documented the proofs and presented them for trial. During the same time the Lords had failed to complete their committee investigations into the Wardrobe and Ordnance offices.

In the interval before the prosecution began in the upper House, Cranfield had a chance to recoup his fortunes. In the early part of April he scarcely seemed to be aware of the danger he faced, but by the middle of the month he had cause for alarm. Formerly contemporaries had remarked his confident attitude and his vehement assertions of innocence; now they began to comment on his attempts to extricate himself from his predicament by means of the King. That alert observer of court intrigues, John Chamberlain, noted as early as April 7 that Cranfield had been at Theobalds "before seven a clocke in the morning with the King in the parke, and though the Duke of Buckingam were there yet he went away before he could come. Yt shold seeme by all we can guesse that the King gives only the looking on, and leaves him to his fortune which he followes with all industrie, and when he cannot go himself sends his Lady great with child to solicit for him." [75] On April 18, Sir Henry Goodyere mentioned that the Treasurer had "been four or five several times" with the King since he began to be questioned.[76]

If at the outset the King's position on Cranfield's guilt or inno-

74. Pym, fol. 65v; *OPH*, VI, 147–149.
75. Chamberlain, *Letters*, II, 553–554, letter of Apr. 10, 1624.
76. SP 14/163/2, Sir Henry Goodyere writing for Sir Francis Nethersole to Sir Dudley Carleton, Apr. 18, 1624.

cence was not clear, by April 15 it was apparent that James intended to support his minister whenever he felt he was being
unjustly accused. On that very day he wrote a letter to the Speaker
of the Commons specifically absolving the Treasurer of all blame
in connection with the dissolution of the Parliament of 1621. "He
was so far," James said, "from giving any advice in dissolving the
said parliament as we do well remember he was upon his knees
before us humbly desiring us to continue it." [77]

Unfortunately for Cranfield the royal decision to intervene came
too late. By this time the only thing that could save the minister
was the threat of dissolution unless the impeachment was dropped,
and the dangers involved in such a step were too great for the King
to face. The time for effective intervention would have been on or
prior to April 5, but, as usual, the King was at Theobalds and his
privy councillors could not be expected to take immediate action
on their own responsibility. In fact, Fleetwood's ruse of presenting
his accusations while the House was in session effectively forestalled the quashing of the charge. This, coupled with the immediate hearing in the Committee of Grievances that afternoon, seized
the initiative for those who were eager to pillory the Treasurer.

Nevertheless, the King seems to have been in constant touch
with his minister's affairs, either personally or by messenger. On
April 21 Cranfield petitioned James, mentioning the attacks that
had been made upon him in connection with Queen Anne's
funeral expenses and his administration of the Wardrobe. Obviously he expected the King to clear him of these accusations
since, on January 18, 1621, he had received the royal pardon discharging his liability to account for money disbursed to him for
the funeral or the Wardrobe.[78] As late as April 14 the Treasurer

77. Sackville MS. (Kent Archives Office, U 269, Cranfield Correspondence 1624),
James I to the Speaker of the House of Commons, Apr. 15, 1624. Printed in Randall
Davies, *The Greatest House at Chelsey* (London: John Lane The Bodley Head,
1914), 97–98. This letter was prompted by Cranfield's solicitation on April 13, and
it may indeed have been composed by him. A draft was enclosed with Cranfield's
letter to Patrick Maule of April 14, 1624, and accompanied by instructions regarding
its dispatch. (Sackville MS. ON 8826.)

78. HMC, *Fourth Report*, Appendix, 310; *OPH*, VI, 197. On May 11, 1624, the
Earl of Kellie wrote from Theobalds to Cranfield, "This evening at 6 o'clock His
Majesty had your letter and commanded [Kellie] to make this answer that at
Greenwich he told the Prince that he had given you 8,000£ of the Wardrobe, and
yesterday in the morning he did write the same to him again before he parted from

was in regular attendance at Council meetings and apparently had personal conferences with the King. After the twenty-second, James seems to have taken the position that the Treasurer should not be allowed personal access to the throne until he had cleared himself.[79]

Certainly the assumption of royal impartiality was encouraged by the Prince and Buckingham. It has already been noted how, on April 19, Charles followed Cranfield to Theobalds when the latter sought to clear his name. When the order forbidding him to come to court was delivered to the Treasurer on the afternoon of the twenty-fourth, it was transmitted by the Prince, and it was with some justification that Cranfield replied "that if the prince said so by the king's command he would obey, otherwise he would continue as before." [80]

Cranfield's absence from court did not, however, stem the flow of communications between himself and his royal master. On April 26 Conway wrote to Weston ordering him, by the King's command, to ascertain what answer the Treasurer intended to make to the charges laid against him in the Parliament.[81] On the same day Cranfield informed the King that he intended to petition the Lords for additional time in preparing his case. "But because the Prince, his Highnesse, and many of the Principal Lords are now with your Majestie at Windsor, my most humble suit to your Majestie is, That you would be pleased to move them on my behalf, to yield me so much further time, that my Cause may not suffer prejudice for want of time to make my just defence, that which I have propounded being as moderate as is possible." [82]

There is no doubt that the King was active in soliciting support among the Lords. According to Hacket, he "courted many to take side with his Treasurer, and prevailed little." He told

thence." (HMC, *Fourth Report*, 288, Kellie to Middlesex, May 11, 1624.) Note that the King and the Prince were together at Greenwich, presumably on May 6.

79. *APC 1623–1625*, 201; SP 14/162/56 and 14/163/16, letters of Dudley Carleton to Sir Dudley Carleton, Apr. 14 and 19, 1624; SP 14/163/27, Richard Welby to Lord Zouche, Apr. 22, 1624.

80. *Cal. S. P. Venetian*, XVIII, 302, Valaresso to the Doge and Senate, Apr. 30/May 10, 1624.

81. SP 14/163/53, Secretary Conway to Sir Richard Weston, Apr. 26, 1624.

82. *Cabala*, I, 267–268, the Earl of Middlesex to the King, Apr. 26, 1624; also printed in *OPH*, VI, 164–165.

the Lord Keeper that he would not make his minister a public sacrifice, but Williams persuaded him that necessity imperatively obliged him to yield to the wishes of the Commons.[83]

James was dismayed by the partisanship shown by Charles and Buckingham, just as he was appalled by their willingness to involve themselves in a judicial procedure so detrimental to the interests of the crown. "By God, Steenie," he told the Duke, "you are a fool, and will shortly repent this folly, and will find, that, in this fit of popularity, you are making a rod with which you will be scourged yourself." As for the Prince, he said that "he would live to have his belly full of parliaments: and when he should be dead, he would have too much cause to remember, how much he had contributed to the weakening of the crown, by this precedent he was now so fond of." [84]

At the same time he was requesting the King's intervention, Cranfield besieged the Lords with petitions for more time, for copies of the depositions of witnesses, for allowance to appear by attorney, and other favors. As Chamberlain put it: "never hare neere her end made so many doubles as he devises tricks to prolong the busines knowing the proverb that *chi ha tempo ha vita*." [85] Impatience with the failure of the Lords to expedite the prosecution was becoming evident in the House of Commons by the end of

83. Hacket, *Scrinia Reserata*, I, 189–190. According to Dudley Carleton, "the King hath shewed himself very desirous to save my Lord Treasurer harmless and was (as I hear) diverse times in deliberation to turn all into rupture and confusion for his sake." (SP 14/164/72, Dudley Carleton to Sir Dudley Carleton, May 13, 1624.)

84. Clarendon, *History of the Rebellion*, I, 37; see also Arthur Wilson, "The Life and Reign of James the First, King of Great Britain" printed in Kennet, *Complete History of England*, II, 787. "The Prince (that was Buckingham's Right Hand) took Part against him in the House of Lords, where he was Question'd; which the King hearing of, writes to the Prince from New-Market, (whither he often retired to be free and at ease from comber and noise of Business), 'That he should not take Part with any Faction in Parliament against the Earl of Middlesex, but to reserve himself, so that both Sides might seek him; for if he bandied to take away his Servants, the time would come that others would do so much for him.' "

85. Chamberlain, *Letters*, II, 555–556, letter of Apr. 30, 1624. On April 29 Cranfield informed the King, "I have lately understood there is a desire my staff should be taken from me before my trial, which is to condemn me before I am heard. God forbid your Majesty should destroy your poor faithful servant by any such course." James refused to dismiss his minister before judgment, but he was unwilling to concede what Cranfield most desired: "Yet there is nothing can do me good in the first place but your presence at the hearing my cause which will be warranted by many precedents of the best times." (Sackville MS. [Kent Archives Office, U 269, Cranfield Correspondence 1624], Middlesex to James I, Apr. 29, 1624.)

April. Richard Knightley informed the Duke that one of the factors impeding the passage of the subsidy bill was "that the Treasurour's busines should have such a delay, which is interpreted a gapp for an escape if any can be made either by mischeife or money." [86] The more knowledgeable Sir Isaac Wake wrote on April 29, "the decried Great Lord hath time to make his peace with God and man until tomorrow seven-night and it is thought that then he will find that the deferring of his sentence will not turn to his account." [87] Finally, on the Prince's motion, a definite day (May 7) was assigned for Cranfield's personal appearance at the bar in the House of Lords.

Before that day came, James roused himself for his strongest effort on his minister's behalf. On May 4 he informed the peers, by means of the Prince, that he would expect their attendance at the banqueting house at Whitehall on the following day. There, in a sometimes subtle but mainly didactic speech, he spoke to them "of Mercy and of Judgment." He called their attention to the fact that this case differed from that of Lord Chancellor Bacon. Here the charge had been denied, and hence the Lords were to consider not only the greatness of the guilt but also the verity of the fact. He advised them to bound any punishment they meted out with measure and moderation. He described the Treasurer as "an Instrument, under Buckingham, for Reformation of the Houshold, the Navy and the Exchequer." The implication was clear that part of the responsibility for Cranfield's activities must be borne by the favorite who now sought to destroy him. All treasurers, James admitted, were hated men, but this was no reason to punish the defendant in this case. Nor was it any reason to inquire into all of his affairs for "No Man can stand upright before God and Man, if every Act of his should be enquired after and haunted

86. *Fortescue Papers*, 196–197, Richard Knightley to the Duke of Buckingham, undated. From the contents of this letter, it can be dated tentatively in late April, probably around the twenty-eighth, when Buckingham was with the King at Windsor. It was surely written after the petition against recusants had been presented to James on April 23 and after the Spanish ambassador's audience on the twenty-fourth. Gardiner suggests May 1624 as the date, but I think that this is too late. James and Buckingham returned to Westminster on the fifth, but Buckingham had previously been at York House on the first of the month. After May 6 Buckingham was seriously ill. Gardiner also attributes the letter to Sir Richard Knightley, but the Richard Knightley in the House of Commons was an esquire.

87. SP 92/10, Savoy Correspondence, Sir Isaac Wake to Secretary Conway, Apr. 29, 1624, originally calendared 14/163/72.

out by every Man, though it concerns him not." Despite this, the King's defense was equivocal, and he would not, he said, condone corruption: "Errors by mistaking, God forbid that you should be rigorous in censuring them; but Errors that are wilful, spare them not." [88]

Contemporaries thought that James's speech had done the Treasurer small service; some said "yt was so ambiguous that yt might receve a contrarie construction." Nethersole thought that the language was so changeable "that no man could say what color his Majesty laid on his cause, and every man might see that in it which he desired." [89] The King did, nevertheless, make it clear that some of the allegations against his minister involved actions which he himself had condoned. In succeeding days he informed the Lords that he had approved Cranfield's acquisition of the lease of the sugar farm in 1621 at a rent four thousand pounds less than its yearly value. This was the sole instance in which the King's intervention resulted in acquitting the defendant of a major charge. James also did his best to mitigate the accusations concerning the Court of Wards; he wrote to the Lord Keeper acknowledging that the new instructions for that court had been debated before him by the Master and officers of the Court of Wards, and it was his understanding that they were made for the honor and profit of the master.[90]

Although the King had counseled his son not to take part with any faction in Parliament against the Earl of Middlesex, Charles, from the first, had shown himself partisan. In distant Dorset, William Whiteway, Jr., had noted in his diary in early April: "The Duke of Buckingham and my Lord Treasurer are fallen out. The Prince takes the Duke's part." [91] From this position Charles never deviated. On April 17, when Buckingham read a letter in a conference committee from Viscount Falkland, Lord Deputy of Ire-

88. *OPH*, VI, 191–195.

89. Chamberlain, *Letters*, II, 559, letter of May 13, 1624; SP 14/164/46, Sir Francis Nethersole to Sir Dudley Carleton, May 6, 1624.

90. HMC, *Fourth Report*, Appendix, 288, Earl of Kellie to the Earl of Middlesex, May 11, 1624; *OPH*, VI, 289, 301–302. See Rusdorff, *Mémoires*, I, 308, Rusdorff to Frederick, elector Palatine, May 11/21, 1624. "Le procès avec notre Trésorier est sur le point de la détermination, et non obstant que le Roi fait tout en sa faveur, aiant avisé que les impositions des deniers faites par lui étoient faites par son commandement et par son autorité royale, il ne sera pourtant pas exempt de la censure et du châtiment."

91. Egerton MS. 784, fol. 40, British Museum, diary of William Whiteway, Jr.

land, that alleged that the Council had not replied to his requests for men, munitions, and money, "the Prince interposed himself, by affirming that some of their members in the lower House did know that a Lord of the Council undertook to answer my Lord Deputy's letters which was the cause they were not read publicly at the Council table. This pointed at the Treasurer who used to put such letters into his own pocket upon pretense of satisfying them." [92]

Early in May the burden of managing the entire prosecution against Cranfield was placed squarely on Charles's shoulders. Buckingham became seriously ill; for a time his life was despaired of, and he was not out of danger until May 13, the day before the Treasurer was sentenced.[93] Deprived of his "right arm," the Prince intensified his efforts in the prosecution. Late in April the Spanish ambassadors told the King "that they knew of meetings between the prince and members of parliament at night." Hacket alleges that "the Prince . . . accompassed Suffrages to Condemn him." And it is certain that some of the Lords who most actively opposed the Treasurer were under obligation to Charles and the Duke.[94]

Perhaps the Venetian ambassador exaggerated when he reported that the whole credit of the Prince depended upon the Treasurer's downfall, but Charles was assiduous in his attendance in the Lords and made frequent contributions to the debates. On May 11, when the peers were angered by Cranfield's apparent contempt of the House, Charles cautioned them not to be diverted from the main issue. The following day he alleged that "The Treasurer knewe (by his owne wordes) that £14,000 per ann. woulde discharge yt [the Wardrobe]: and yett he demanded £20,000 per ann." He further explained that the King's pardon did not excuse Cranfield from accounting for expenses in the Wardrobe, and he

92. SP 14/163/2, Sir Henry Goodyere (writing for Nethersole) to Sir Dudley Carleton, Apr. 18, 1624. See Nethersole's remark on this statement in SP 14/163/3, "I will not amend anything in my Lord Deputy of Ireland's letter though it be very lame in my father's because I find the great too fully delineated." See also OPH, VI, 154.

93. HMC, Mar and Kellie, 200–201, Thomas, earl of Kellie, to John, earl of Mar, May 13, 1624.

94. Cal. S. P. Venetian, XVIII, 318, Valaresso to the Doge and Senate, May 14/24, 1624; 301, Valaresso to the Doge and Senate, Apr. 30/May 10; Hacket, Scrinia Reserata, I, 189. "And in this Lord's Overthrow, the Prince abetted him [Buckingham], was Privy to the Undertakings of his Adversaries, and accompassed Suffrages to Condemn him."

asked the House to vote immediately on the question of the Treasurer's guilt and respite the punishment until the pardon could be viewed.

When the King removed the onus of profiteering from his minister in reference to the lease of the sugars, the Prince agreed "not to censure any man for a guift gyven by the K[ing]; but I may say he played the extorcioner uppon the K[ing]." In reference to the ordnance officers' claim on Dallison's lands, he noted that the Treasurer could pay arrears when it was for his particular profit, but would pay no money to furnish the King's store of munitions. When Cranfield alleged that he had done the King good service in remitting money to the Palatinate, the Prince retorted that the poor soldiers in Frankendale were as yet unpaid. Finally, when it came to a question of punishment, Charles said that "considering howe he came in uppon reformacion and proved a sharke for himselfe" he thought it proper that the minister should be stripped of his offices. Nevertheless the Prince resisted imposing a penalty which the Commons greatly desired. He was not willing to see Middlesex degraded from the peerage. In the last resort he agreed to a fine of fifty thousand pounds against Cranfield "and to ransome allso, yf he had noe other punnishment." [95]

It is doubtful whether Charles actively supported the bill making Cranfield's lands liable for damages to the parties he had wronged. When the preparation of this act was first suggested by Pembroke on May 13, the Prince wanted to know who would be recompensed under the bill. Nevertheless, on the fourteenth, on the Lord Spencer's motion, the King's counsel was ordered to prepare a bill for making the estates of the Earl of Middlesex liable for his debts, for his fine to the King, and for restitution to those he had injured.[96]

95. *Lords Debates 1624 & 1626*, 73, 75, 76, 77, 80–81, 82, 86, 88, 89.
96. *Ibid.*, 90, 91, 93; see also *LJ*, III, 418, 420–421. The parties who appeared to be pressing for restitution were Sir Thomas Mounson, Sir Thomas Dallison, and Lord Willoughby of Eresby. See also *ibid.*, 326 (Apr. 29), petition of Sir Philip Cary to the Lords concerning the office of Surveyor General of the Customs sold to him by the Treasurer. Sackville MS. ON 5357a is a copy of the petition of Jacob, Abbot, Wolstenholm, and Garroway presented to the House of Lords on May 27 requesting repayment of the alleged bribe of one thousand pounds. Sackville MS. ON 5663 is an undated petition by Cranfield to the Lords requesting the opportunity to be heard by counsel in opposition to the petitioners against him. Oddly enough, the bill to make Cranfield's lands liable for his debts encountered difficulty in the Commons. It was passed only after a division: Yeas, 125 (Sir Francis Barrington and Sir Robert Harley, tellers); Noes, 89 (Sir Francis Fane and Sir Francis

The sentence by which the Treasurer lost his offices, his seat in the Lords, his liberty, his capability of employment in the government, and was fined fifty thousand pounds ended what most contemporaries recognized as a purely political prosecution. However, James did not consider the censure by the Lords to be final, and on the last day of the session pointedly reminded them that not only was the King an integral part of Parliament but that the execution of their judgment depended upon him alone. He noted that he had already partially confirmed the sentence by taking Cranfield's staff and seal from him, but he unequivocally reserved the right to review the Lords' findings. At the same time he made clear his dislike of parliamentary impeachments. "But as it is lawful for grieved men to complain so I would not have an inquisition of Spain raised in England, that men should seek to inquire after faults; but if complaints come to you, judge of them accordingly, but search not for them. You see I have not spared my judges that offend for I have degraded one the last parliament and another this; and if I find that he hath been false to me in my treasure and trust he shall be punished; if not I must be merciful. But I must warn you for the time to come of one thing: Men shall not give informations against my officers without my leave. If there be cause let them first complain to me for I will not have any of my servants and officers, from the greatest Lord to the meanest scullion, complained on by any without my leave first asked; but I will make him smart sorer that complains than he that is complained of." [97]

It was almost universally expected that the King would quickly set Cranfield at liberty and remit all or a large portion of his fine.[98]

---

Seymour, tellers). (*CJ*, I, 797.) On May 25 John Mayle wrote to Cranfield, "The bill in the lower House is put off till 5 of the clock and Sir Arthur [Ingram] will do his best etc." (Sackville MS. ON 7822.)

97. D'Ewes, fols. 135–135v. See also SP 14/165/61, notes on the conclusion of the Parliament.

98. HMC, *Mar and Kellie*, 201, Thomas, earl of Kellie, to John, earl of Mar, May 22, 1624. "I am assured your Lordship has heard of the Treasurer and the course held with him. Those that do best understand it think that his avaricious nature and harsh disposition has well deserved the punishment inflicted to him, and that the grounds of his censure was not such as deserved so great and severe a sentence; for he was ever getting of his Majesty less or more in whatsoever place he had, and in his office of Treasury his carriage was so displeasing to everybody that he displeased every man. So that for him I have no more to say but that I think his Majesty will be favorable to him in his fine, and his imprisonment shall not be so long as the world thinks."

Three days after the Parliament ended he was released from the Tower. It was rumored that six thousand pounds had procured his freedom, and it was predicted that he would be sworn a gentleman of the bedchamber. Before the end of June his name had been included in the commission of the subsidy, but it was expunged by the King himself when the Prince informed him of it.[99]

By July 21 the King had reviewed Cranfield's case. He had read over the charges and answers three times, conferred with his attorney, and resolved to pass over all that concerned the Court of Wards and the merchants. Instead he condemned the amazed Cranfield for peculation in the Wardrobe. James insisted that the office of the Wardrobe was not a fee farm and that Cranfield "ought to have understood it to be accounted for. And that he did not only make this passage of his own want of accounting to abuse the King, but he suffered not the clerk to keep account, by which he destroyed the office, that corruption forever might come in." For a time the King was convinced that Cranfield had robbed him of forty thousand pounds in the Wardrobe. Therefore he demanded that Cranfield pay thirty thousand pounds fine. Moreover, Weston was secretly instructed to inquire into the true worth of his estate, undoubtedly reflecting the King's belief that his former treasurer had amassed a huge fortune.[100]

Through the remainder of 1624 Cranfield's friends and servants worked for the reduction of his fine and the sealing of his pardon. Immediately after his sentence, agents were busy trying to appease the Duke's ire against the Treasurer and to invoke the King's

99. SP 14/167/4, P. Maule to the Duke of Buckingham, June 1, 1624, which indicates that the warrant releasing Middlesex was purchased by his Countess and that neither Buckingham nor the Prince knew anything of it. When questioned by the Prince, James said, "that it was nothing but such as my Lord of St. Albans had and that he intended no farther favor to him but by your [Buckingham's] advice." (Chamberlain, *Letters*, II, 562, 564, letters of June 5 and June 19, 1624; Strafford, *Letters*, I, 21, Sir Thomas Wentworth to Christopher Wandesford, June 17, 1624.)

100. SP 14/170/36, Secretary Conway to Sir Richard Weston, July 21, 1624 (Conway's draft of this letter is SP 14/170/37). See Weston's reply of July 23, 1624, for Cranfield's reaction, SP 14/170/45. See also SP 14/170/82.II, for Cranfield's listing of his assets and liabilities. Among the Sackville MSS (Kent Archives Office, U 269, Cranfield Correspondence 1624) is an undated draft of a letter from Cranfield to James which alludes to the King's review of the impeachment and justifies Cranfield's administration as Master of the Wardrobe. There are also several draft letters to the King which relate to the purchase of Dallison's lands and to Jacob's testimony about the bribes. In still another undated letter Cranfield says "I have sent your Majesty brief accounts of three offices, viz. the Lord Treasurers, the Master of the Wards and the Master of the Wardrobe."

mercy. Ultimately the price for Buckingham's intercession proved to be Cranfield's great house at Chelsea which was resigned to King Charles in May 1625 and immediately bestowed on the Duke. With it went five thousand pounds in cash and the transfer to the King of the lease of the sugar duties which still had sixteen years to run.[101] Cranfield's reaction to the extortion practiced by Buckingham and his mother was chronicled in a letter to Nicholas Herman on May 1, 1626, "The Duke hath in former times been to me most loving and kind, even in excess, but of late to me and mine most cruel and unjust, even to inhumanity, but the old lady hath been ever my enemy. Naboth's vineyard was by Jezebel well and justly gotten in comparison of her getting my Chelsey from me if the matter, the manner, with all the circumstances were rightly understood and equally weighed." [102]

On the day that Middlesex was sent to the Tower, D'Ewes noted that he saw "no man that pitied his fall." But the observant Chamberlain wrote on the same day: "yt is marvailed they proceeded no farther to degrade him upon so many just reasons . . . but seeing they have fayled to crush him low enough when they might he may live to be a pestilent instrument, and to crush some of them hereafter." [103] That prophecy of Chamberlain's might well have come true; in 1626 Cranfield's opportunity to retaliate against his chief enemy presented itself. Nevertheless, he resisted the temptation to join the "Country Party" and the Earl of Bristol in their attack upon Buckingham — perhaps because he believed that the alliance between Charles and the Duke was impregnable. Although his aid was solicited by both camps, he preferred neutrality and remained on his estates. Yet it must have been immensely gratifying to Cranfield to have his services to King James extolled by the redoubtable Sir John Eliot and to receive overtures from the favorite for the renewal of "a loving peace." [104]

101. Prestwich, *Cranfield*, 470–477. It appears that Cranfield's pardon was not finally sealed until early 1627 although two correspondents of the Reverend Joseph Mead reported that it had been granted in August 1626. Birch, *Court and Times of Charles I*, I, 143–145, Anonymous to Mead, Aug. 25, 1626; Pory to Mead, Sept. 2, 1626; see Sackville MS. (Kent Archives Office, U 269, Cranfield Correspondence 1625–1627), Nicholas Herman to Cranfield, Dec. 29, 1626.

102. Sackville MS. (Kent Archives Office, U 269, Cranfield Correspondence 1625–1627), Cranfield to Nicholas Herman, May 1, 1626.

103. D'Ewes, *Autobiography*, I, 245; Chamberlain, *Letters*, II, 560, letter of May 13, 1624.

104. Sackville MSS. (Kent Archives Office, U 269, Cranfield Correspondence 1625–1627), Cranfield to Herman, Apr. 29 and May 1, 1626; Herman to Cranfield

Although he refused to become embroiled in the impeachment of Buckingham, Cranfield was never under any illusions about the identity of the person responsible for his downfall. As late as 1631 he reminded the Duke's widow, "Your dead Lord in the bitterness of his soul told you in bed that he pulled me down, but withal confessed he never had good day after, and did with great vehemency curse all those that had made a misunderstanding between him and me, or that were the cause he did it." [105]

Old enmities against the Treasurer died hard, but within twenty years those who had testified against him agreed that "no man ever suffered for so little as my Lord of Middlesex." [106] But the significance of the trial lies not in the ultimate vindication of Cranfield's reputation but rather in the successful isolation and suppression of his political opposition. As long as triumph or disgrace were the only alternatives presented to men of integrity, the crown continued to be deprived of valuable servants, and the statesman was superseded by the toady. It was Cranfield's personal tragedy, not only that he was the victim of this system, but that he acquiesced in its establishment by his acceptance of defeat.

---

May 3, 1626; Francis White, dean of Carlisle, to Cranfield (May 1626); Cranfield to White (May 1626).

105. Sackville MS. (Kent Archives Office, U 269, Cranfield Correspondence 1624), Cranfield to the Duchess of Buckingham, undated [1631?]. This letter is improperly included with the Cranfield correspondence for 1624, as is evident from the reference to the late Duke of Buckingham.

106. HMC, *Fourth Report*, Appendix, 293, Nicholas Herman to the Earl of Middlesex, Aug. 8, 1637.

# VII  The Stifling of Opposition — Bristol

Allegations of malfeasance and misconduct in the management of domestic affairs justified Cranfield's impeachment, however much it may have been motivated by his opposition to Buckingham's foreign policy. Therefore an open hearing of the case could not prejudice the accomplishment of the Duke's diplomatic aims, but a parliamentary inquiry into the conduct of the Earl of Bristol would have necessitated a critical reappraisal of negotiations with Spain. The ratification of Buckingham's anti-Spanish policy by the Parliament of 1624 was accomplished under the shadow of Bristol's hostility. Indeed, it was the imminence of the ambassador's return that heightened the sense of urgency so characteristic of the breach; it explains Buckingham's sensitivity to charges of ineptitude in the conduct of negotiations in 1623.

From the time of Bristol's recall until his arrival in England, contemporary letter writers frequently referred to his movements and speculated about his future actions, even when there was nothing of significance to report.[1] At court, interpretations of his character and achievements were formed in accordance with factional interests. The partisans of Buckingham considered Bristol a

---

1. Chamberlain, *Letters,* II, 537, 554, and 556, letters of Jan. 3, Apr. 10, and Apr. 30, 1624; HMC, *Mar and Kellie,* 187, 191, 192, 200, Thomas, earl of Kellie, to John, earl of Mar, Jan. 14, Feb. 5, Feb. 11, and May 5, 1624; SP 14/161/36, 14/162/12, 14/163/3, 14/163/50, 14/164/46, Sir Francis Nethersole to Sir Dudley Carleton, Mar. 25, Apr. 3, Apr. 18, Apr. 25, and May 6, 1624; SP 14/160/33, 14/160/89, 14/162/46.2 (84/117), 14/164/12, Dudley Carleton to Sir Dudley Carleton, Mar. 5, Mar. 17, Apr. 11, and May 3, 1624; 14/163/48, Dudley Carleton to the Queen of Bohemia, Apr. 24 (misdated Apr. 15), 1624.

haughty, ambitious, egocentric man — a credulous, temporizing, pedestrian diplomat whose Catholic-Spanish sympathies had predisposed him to promote a course of action dangerous for England. Conversely, Bristol's supporters emphasized his personal dignity, integrity, and high conception of honor, regarding him as a patriotic Englishman and a loyal Anglican whose diplomatic services had been characterized by energy, sagacity, expedition, and precision.[2] The inevitability of a clash between Bristol and Buckingham was accepted by all, and, in some quarters, eagerly anticipated.

No doubts were entertained in England about the nature of Bristol's views; his opposition to the favorite was adamant, vocal, and enduring. Its origins may be traced back to the spring of 1623 when Bristol, negotiating a marriage treaty in Spain, suddenly found himself superseded by two amateur diplomats — Charles and Buckingham. In March 1622 Bristol, as England's most experienced envoy, had been commissioned by James to treat anew for a Spanish match. By the end of that year the treaty was sufficiently advanced to warrant its submission to James for approval, and it was expected that by March or April of 1623 the Pope's dispensation would remove the last major obstacle to the completion of the marriage.

It was at this juncture that Buckingham and Charles began their ill-considered venture. Bristol's advice had not been asked before they set out; Spanish complicity in the arrangements had been contrived through Endymion Porter and Gondomar.[3] Although

2. *Cabala*, I, 30–33, letter of Sir Walter Aston to the Duke of Buckingham, undated [should be Nov. 1, 1623]; *ibid.*, 159–162, L. R. H. to Buckingham, undated; *ibid.*, 209–210, Rochefort to Buckingham, undated; *ibid.*, 316–317, Sir John Hippisley to the Duke of Buckingham, Sept. 1, 1623; SP 14/155/65, Sir Edward Conway to Buckingham, Dec. 20, 1623; Chamberlain, *Letters*, II, 534, 565, letters of Dec. 20, 1623, and June 19, 1624; *Cal. S. P. Venetian*, XVIII, 58, Cornaro to the Doge and Senate, June 30/July 10, 1623; *ibid.*, 130, 177, 273, 301–302, 343–344, Valaresso to the Doge and Senate, Oct. 3/13 and Dec. 19/29, 1623, Apr. 19/29, Apr. 30/May 10, and June 4/14, 1624.

3. PRO 31/8/198, Digby Transcripts #106, Interrogatories to be ministered to Endymion Porter, 1626. It is clear from the questions directed to Porter that Bristol possessed copies of the correspondence between Buckingham and Gondomar relating to the Spanish journey. Moreover, Porter's knowledge of the venture, according to Bristol, was implied in his personal letter to Gondomar of Sept. 18, 1622, written almost three weeks before his departure on his mission to Spain. In 1624 Bristol charged that since 1617 Buckingham had done his utmost to undermine the ambassador's endeavors. He alleged that Buckingham had sent to Gondomar a copy of the advice Bristol tendered to Charles advocating a marriage with a Protestant princess. He also asserted that "this hathe beene usuall upon all

Bristol and the resident ambassador, Sir Walter Aston, were not informed of the projected journey, knowledge of it came to Bristol through court rumor, and he immediately dispatched a courier to England to warn against such an undertaking. James was informed that the Prince's presence in Spain would occasion new delays. The Spanish were apt to take advantage of the situation by introducing harsher conditions in matters of religion, and by lessening the amount of the dowry and protracting the time of its payment.[4] Bristol's dispatch was intercepted by Charles and Buckingham near the Spanish-French border. "We saucily opened your letters, and found nothing either in that or any other, which we could understand without a cipher, that hath made us repent our journey; but, by the contrary, we find nothing but particulars hastened, and your business so slowly advanced, that we think ourselves happy that we have begun it so soon; for yet the temporal articles are not concluded, nor will not be, till the dispensation comes, which may be, God knows when."[5]

Thus Charles and Buckingham optimistically chose to ignore Bristol's warning, confident that their appearance at Madrid would resolve all points of contention. Bristol's reserved attitude toward the advisability of personal diplomacy was attributed to pique at having the treaty removed from his purview at the very moment of its completion. Dismayed by the rashness of the Prince and Buckingham, he was further offended by his virtual exclusion from top-level negotiations. Within a few weeks rumors of his discontent were rife in England, rumors that multiplied and intensified through the remainder of 1623.[6]

---

occasions, firste in England and since in Spayne (as hee can instance in many particulars) to give notice unto the Spanishe ministers of whatsoever the Earl of Bristoll sayd or advertized to the advantage of his Majestie or religion, and the dis-service of Spayne." It was obviously Bristol's intention to prove that Porter was the intermediary through whom Buckingham betrayed state secrets to the Spanish. ("Bristol's Defense," 13.)

4. Halliwell, *Kings' Letters*, II, 177–179, King James to the Prince and Duke, Mar. 15, 1623; Howell, *State Trials*, II, 1406; see also HMC, *Mar and Kellie*, 157, Thomas, earl of Kellie, to John, earl of Mar, Mar. 18, 1623.

5. Halliwell, *Kings' Letters*, II, 173, Prince Charles and the Duke of Buckingham to King James, undated.

6. HMC, *Mar and Kellie*, 157, Thomas, earl of Kellie, to John, earl of Mar, Mar. 18, 1623; see also *ibid.*, 166, 167, 170, 174, 180, letters of May 4, May 9, May 16, July 11, and Sept. 27, 1623; *Cal. S. P. Venetian*, XVIII, 53, Corner to the Doge and Senate, June 21/July 1, 1623; see also *ibid.*, 55, 102, 120, 146, Valaresso to the Doge and Senate, June 27/July 7, Aug. 22/Sept. 1, Sept. 12/22, and Oct. 31/Nov. 10, 1623;

Buckingham noticed the divergence between his views and those of the Earl as early as March 9, 1623, at a time when the camaraderie occasioned by the celebrations and exchange of courtesies at Madrid had not yet given way to the argument and ire resulting from opposing national and religious interests. When Olivares learned there was no hope of the Prince's immediate conversion, he suggested writing to the Pope to expedite the dispensation. Buckingham was dissatisfied with the phraseology of this letter, finding it "verie heavie and ineffectuall." He required the addition of a postscript urging haste, a request which Olivares angrily denied. Later, in attributing to himself the earliest discovery of the insincerity of Spanish intentions, Buckingham claimed that he saw clearly "that theis People never intended either Match or Restitution, and soe wished his Highnes fairlie at Home again." Bristol, however, made a more "benigne Construction" of the letter, and it was sent as originally phrased.[7]

Buckingham's retrospective views distorted the truth about his relations with Bristol at this time. Certainly major policy disagreements did not figure in their personal antipathies as early as mid-March. The joint letters of Charles and Buckingham to James were sanguine, expressing hope for a speedy conclusion of the marriage treaty. Under the aegis of Buckingham the negotiations seemed to be proceeding smoothly, and it was not until the arrival of the dispensation on April 24 that his qualities as a diplomat were put to the test. Even before that time, however, the Earl of Carlisle had noticed that he and Bristol had no voice in the councils of the Prince; Charles and Buckingham alone treated with Olivares.[8]

When the dispensation was published, not merely as a confirmation of treaty articles and an allowance for the nuptials to be performed, but as an instrument demanding more stringent religious conditions, Buckingham was confronted with the fulfillment of Bristol's dire predictions about the results of the journey. No wonder he accused Olivares of breaking his word; no wonder he urged

---

Chamberlain, *Letters*, II, 488, 497, 530–531, letters of Apr. 5, May 17, and Dec. 6, 1623.

7. Rymer, *Foedera*, XVII, 560, Buckingham's relation.

8. *Cal. S. P. Venetian*, XVIII, 28, Valaresso to the Doge and Senate, May 23/June 2, 1623; Chamberlain, *Letters*, II, 497, letter of May 17, 1623; HMC, *Mar and Kellie*, 167, Thomas, earl of Kellie, to John, earl of Mar, May 9, 1623.

the Prince's return to England! [9] Accustomed to demolishing opposition by bursts of temper and threats of rash action, he now
encountered resistance which was both rigid and implacable. The
Spanish commissioners and the papal nuncio refused to make any
concessions and demanded that the terms laid down by the Pope
be fulfilled *in toto*.

The rebuff which Buckingham suffered as the result of the introduction of new conditions into the marriage treaty intensified
the friction between himself and the Earl of Bristol. Matters of
principle now intruded into their personal relationships to complete their estrangement. According to Buckingham, Bristol was
inclined to temporize — to accept the new religious conditions
and the oaths required of James, Charles, and the privy councillors
as articles implied in the intentions of both James and Philip IV.
He tended to view the Spanish insistence upon complete performance of religious conditions as a mere punctilio, a prerequisite to
the completion of the match.[10] Thus Bristol advised the continuation of negotiations, expecting that the give-and-take of diplomatic
exchanges would mitigate the severity of Spanish demands.

Buckingham was diametrically opposed to conciliation. He
quarreled violently with Olivares, and for days the two favorites
would not speak to each other. In the councils of the Prince, the
Duke urged a rupture in the negotiations.[11] Writing to Williams
on August 20, 1623, Bristol recounted the incident as a climactic
point in his relations with the favorite.

And my Lord, this is the truth, whatsoever may be said or written to
the contrary: It is true, that some four moneths since in a businesse
that no lesse concerned his Majestie and the Prince's service, then
abruptly to have broken off all our Treaty, I was far differing from my
Lords opinion; And thereupon happened betwixt us some dispute in
debate of the businesse, but without any thing that was personal, and
there was no creature living at it but the Prince, to whose Censure I
shall willingly refer my self. In me I protest it unto your Lordship,
it made no alteration, but within half an hour I came to him with the
same reverence and respect that I was wont to do, the which I have

9. *Cal. S. P. Venetian*, XVIII, 20, Corner to the Doge and Senate, May 14/24,
1623.

10. Rymer, *Foedera*, XVII, 561, Buckingham's relation.

11. *Cal. S. P. Venetian*, XVIII, 20–22, Corner to the Doge and Senate, May
14/24, 1623; *ibid.*, 40–42, Valaresso to the Doge and Senate, June 6/16, 1623.

continued ever since, so that I have much wondered how it cometh to be so much spoken of in England, that my Lord Duke and my self should live here at too much distance. And I cannot find any other reason for it, but that every body hath taken so much notice of my ill, and contemptible usage, that they think it unpossible for any Gentleman, but to be sensible of it.[12]

The nature of this ill-usage was graphically illustrated in the rumors that abounded in England. On May 16 the Earl of Kellie wrote:

My Lord of Bristol is not well pleased. One particular I have heard which I think no marvel if it do trouble him, and that is this; he being one day in the coach with the Prince and my Lord of Buckingham, at the very instant comes the Count D'Olivares, whereupon Buckingham says to Bristol, My Lord, you shall do well to take your horse, for the Prince has something to confer with the Count D'Olivares privately. The other answered, My Lord, I am in the commission of this business, and have dealt most of any man in it; I think, my Lord, I must have the commandment of some other man than your Lordship. Upon which the Prince answered, If that shall serve, then my Lord I think it good that your Lordship go to your horse. Whereupon he did take his horse immediately, and then Porter, the Prince his servant, was called on, and did interpret betwixt them. Which I think could not but much move Bristol, for it is true that he has done the most service of that business, and yet the world thinks he was insolent enough and would have done all, and now he is shifted quite off all, because he would admit of no fellow.[13]

The pattern of the Prince's diplomacy in Spain demonstrates that he was not entirely guided by Buckingham's wishes. In fact, he seems to have vacillated between the policies advocated by Bristol and the Duke. Several times in the course of the summer Charles threatened to go home unless the Spanish made concessions, and yet within a relatively short time of each incident he submitted to Olivares's demands and remained at Madrid. A typical occasion occurred on May 23, when the junta of theologians rendered a decision that the King of Spain could not take the oath to guarantee English performance of the conditions demanded by

12. *Cabala*, I, 20–22, Earl of Bristol to Lord Keeper Williams, Aug. 20, 1623.
13. HMC, *Mar and Kellie*, 170, Thomas, earl of Kellie, to John, earl of Mar, May 16, 1623. This same incident is reported in Birch, *Court and Times of James I*, II, 399–400, Rev. Joseph Mead to Sir Martin Stuteville, May 24, 1623.

the pope unless the utmost security was offered by James. The Infanta was to remain in Spain for at least a year after the marriage ceremony had been performed; within this time the suspension of the penal laws and the concession to English Catholics of free exercise of their religion in private houses was to be publicly proclaimed. In addition, the King, the Prince, and the Privy Council were to swear that these concessions would never be withdrawn, and they were to do their best to secure parliamentary endorsement of the favors already granted.[14]

When this decision was communicated to Charles, it occasioned a heated dispute between Buckingham and Olivares. "Buckingham in particular blazed forth, without restraining his expressions, declaring that it was all a plot to mock and betray them. He went so far that they exchanged stinging remarks, the Count replying sharply and upbraiding Buckingham, saying it would have been better for carrying the affair to a successful issue if he had never meddled with it, but had allowed Digby to guide the business, as he had done up to that time. The Prince subsequently remonstrated so bitterly that he could not restrain his tears, because he professes himself deeply in love with the Infanta." [15] The following day Cottington was sent to request permission for the Prince to return to England. But Charles was dissuaded from his intention; Bristol interceded with the nuncio, promising marvelous results if the Infanta were to accompany the Prince, and Buckingham gradually yielded on the subject of concessions. By June 21 it was reported that the Prince was critical of the Duke's harshness and that "by his command, the negotiations are especially under the guidance of Digby." [16]

As the negotiations entered the doldrums, pressures on Buckingham began to mount. Hopes for a brilliant diplomatic coup had now given way to fears for his own security. His disputes with Olivares were reported in England, and he, in turn, received news of intrigues against him at Westminster. The Spanish were increasingly alienated by his personality, his morals, and his excessive familiarity with the Prince. The Duke's quarrel with Bristol

14. *Spanish Marriage Treaty*, 236–242.
15. *Cal. S. P. Venetian*, XVIII, 37–38, Corner to the Doge and Senate, June 3/13, 1623; see also SP 14/169/42, Bristol's interrogatories and his answers, question 13.
16. *Cal. S. P. Venetian*, XVIII, 53, Corner to the Doge and Senate, June 21/July 1, 1623.

was notorious, and, at this juncture, he seemed in danger of losing his most important advantage — the Prince's favor. Yet, when overtures were made for a reconciliation with Bristol, they were contemptuously rejected. In July the Lord Keeper wrote to Buckingham exhorting him: "to observe his Highnesse with all lowlinesse, humility, and dutiful obedience, and to piece up any the least seam-rent, that heat, and earnestnesse might, peradventure, seem to produce . . . And for Gods sake I beg it, as you regard the prayers of a poor friend, if the great negotiation be well concluded, let all private disagreements be wrapped up in the same, and never accompany your Lordships into England, to the joy and exultation of your enemies, if any such ingrateful Divels are here to be found." [17] As Bristol had anticipated, Williams's suggestions were "despised rather then received with any thankfulnesse." [18]

As the rift between Buckingham and Bristol widened, so did the implications of their dispute. Inevitably reports of the quarrel came to the King's attention. It was suspected that Buckingham complained in private letters to James about Bristol's conduct, but few hints of disharmony appeared in the joint letters of the Prince and the Duke. By July 29, however, there was a veiled allusion to the Earl's intransigence: "we are very confident, when we see your majesty, to give you very good satisfaction for all we have done; and had we had less help, we had done it both sooner and better; but we leave that till our meeting." [19] Exactly a month later Bristol openly criticized Buckingham in a letter to the King:

although I conceive it not to be doubted that the match will, in the end, proceed, — yet your Majesty will find yourself frustrated of those effects of amity and friendship which by this alliance you expected. For the truth is, that this King and his ministers are grown to have so high a dislike against my lord Duke of Buckingham, and, on the one side to judge him to have so much power with your Majesty and the Prince, and, on the other side, to be so ill affected to them and their affairs, that if your Majesty shall not be pleased in your wisdom either to find some means of reconciliation, or else to let them see and be assured that it shall no way be in my lord Duke of Buckingham's

17. *Cabala*, I, 78–79, Williams to the Duke of Buckingham, undated, probably in July 1623. Bristol makes mention of a letter of Williams of July 23 referring to a reconciliation.

18. *Ibid.*, 20–22, Bristol to Williams, Aug. 20, 1623.

19. Halliwell, *Kings' Letters*, II, 217–218, the Prince and Buckingham to the King, July 29, 1623.

power to make the Infanta's life less happy unto her, or any way to cross and embroil the affairs betwixt your Majesties and your kingdoms, I am afraid your Majesty will see the effects which you have just cause to expect from this alliance to follow but slowly, and all the great businesses now in treaty prosper but ill. For I must, for the discharge of my conscience and duty, without descending to particulars, let your Majesty truly know that suspicions and distastes betwixt them all here and my Lord of Buckingham cannot be at a greater height.[20]

At his trial in 1626 Bristol stated that his dispatches, which reflected on the reprehensible conduct of the Duke, were submitted to Charles before they were sent to England. The Prince had not prohibited their transmission, however displeased he was that discords in Spain were reported to his father. In fact, Bristol maintained: "At the Prince's coming out of Spain, I was in favor with his Highness," [21] and there is no reason to doubt the truth of this assertion. Certainly Charles was dismayed by the reluctance of the Spanish junta to allow the Infanta's journey before the following spring. He felt that he had exceeded the requirements of courtesy by remaining at Madrid throughout the summer. Indubitably Bristol had been instrumental in delaying the Prince's return, but his counsel had been given in good faith, and it was Charles's option to accept or reject it. The continuation of Bristol as prime negotiator for the match, and the deposit of the Prince's proxy in his hands indicated that as yet Charles was not committed to Buckingham's views. Consequently his adoption of a partisan attitude was contingent upon events subsequent to his departure from Madrid.

The Prince's abandonment of neutrality can be explained partially on the basis of his friendship with the Duke, but it is significant that for some months there was no point of view presented to him which could counterbalance Buckingham's antipathy to-

20. Gardiner, *History of England*, V, 114–115, Bristol to the King, Aug. 29, 1623.

21. Howell, *State Trials*, II, 1295; *Lords Debates 1624 & 1626*, 174; see also the letter of Kenelm Digby to Bristol, May 27, 1625, printed in "Bristol's Defense," xxvi–xxvii, where the Prince's version of the event is recounted. "Your Lordship shewed him a little before his goeing out of Spayne a letter, wherein yow writt of the Duke of Buckingham, which he misliked, and told your Lordship yow expressed much spleen against the Duke, and therefore would have yow alter it. The letter yow sent away, without first shewing it unto him; but when he returned to England he saw it, and found yow had altered it much after the manner that he badd yow." Also printed in HMC, *Eighth Report*, Appendix, pt. I (London, 1907–1909), 217, Digby MSS.

ward Bristol and the Spanish. Thus, when the Earl announced his intention to deliver the proxy, disregarding the Prince's demands for the restoration of the Palatinate, his actions seemed to confirm the suspicions which Buckingham had inculcated into Charles's mind. By mid-November, when a host of couriers was sent to prevent the marriage, Charles was firmly committed to Buckingham's policy and estranged from Bristol. Henceforth the Earl's revelations and criticisms would tend to inculpate the Prince as well as the Duke and endanger their program.

There is no reason to believe that Buckingham's animosity toward Bristol ever wavered in the autumn of 1623. Had the ambassador acquiesced in the favorite's policy, he might not have been subjected to a searching inquisition into his actions, but his complaints against the Duke in August were tantamount to an open declaration of war. Buckingham, too, had carried his case to England, and, through Sir John Hippisley, had informed the court of Bristol's "high carriage" in Spain. In his letter of September 1, Hippisley indicated that he had canvassed the leading courtiers and found "that all my Lord of Bristols actions are so much extolled, that what you command me to say is hardly believed." [22] For those in England who pretended to neutrality, Hippisley's lobbying emphasized the necessity of choosing sides. In the case of Williams, for instance, his efforts as a mediator were superseded by his commitment to the Duke's party: "Now that I understand by Sir John Hipsley how things stand between your Grace and the Earl of Bristol; I have done with that Lord, and will never think of him otherwise, then as your Grace shall direct." [23]

Bristol adopted similar tactics: in October his emissary, Simon Digby, was in England encouraging the ambassador's partisans and observing the actions of the favorite and his sycophants. Aware of the consternation which the journey to Spain had caused in England, Bristol emphasized its futility, and, by laying the onus of a dangerous and costly embassy on Buckingham, hoped to discredit him.[24] By December it was apparent that the favor which the Duke enjoyed was not materially lessened and that the King

22. *Cabala*, I, 316–317, Sir John Hippisley to the Duke of Buckingham, Sept. 1, 1623.

23. *Ibid.*, 84–85, Williams to Buckingham, undated, probably Sept. 1623.

24. *Cal. S. P. Venetian*, XVIII, 130, Valaresso to the Doge and Senate, Oct. 3/13, 1623.

and Prince were not apt to be influenced against him by representations from Spain. Thus, on December 6, Bristol made dignified overtures for a reconciliation: "The present estate of the
Kings affairs requireth the concurrencie of all his servants, and the
Co-operation of all his Ministers, which maketh me desirous to
make unto your Grace this tender of my service, that if there have
happened any errours, or misunderstandings your Grace would
for that regard passe them over: and for any thing that may personally concern my particular, I shall labour to give you that satisfaction as may deserve your friendship. And if that shall not serve
the turn, I shall not be found unarmed with patience against any
thing that can happen unto me. And so wishing, that this humble
offer of my service may find that acceptation as I humbly desire,
I rest." [25]

This letter, lacking the abject submission which Buckingham
regularly extorted from his opponents, was not favorably construed by the Duke, and Bristol's subsequent behavior in Spain
confirmed the belief that he was still laboring for the completion
of the match. Buckingham was willing to forgive Sir Walter
Aston's involvement in a course of action that was considered
irreconcilable with the new policy adopted in England, but he
was not willing to overlook Bristol's mistakes.[26] On December 30
the extraordinary ambassador was officially recalled, a revocation
conceived to be both necessary and perilous. Convinced that Bristol had intended to exceed his instructions, James summoned him
home to answer for his conduct although it was a foregone conclusion that Bristol, as a peer, would demand his trial in the forthcoming Parliament.

On January 14 Bristol notified Olivares of his recall and received in return assurances of support and large offers of preferment. Rejecting these, the ambassador said: "that howsoever he
might have reason to fear the power of his enemies, yet he trusted
much upon the innocency of his own Cause, and the Justice of the
King, and that he could not understand himself in any danger:
but were he sure to lose his head at his arrival there, he would go
to throw down himself at his Majesties feet and mercy, and rather

25. *Cabala*, I, 28, Bristol to Buckingham, Dec. 6, 1623.
26. *Ibid.*, 30–33, Sir Walter Aston to Buckingham, undated; *ibid.*, 34–36, Buckingham to Aston, undated; *ibid.*, 37–39, Aston to Buckingham, Dec. 22, 1623.

there die upon a Scaffold, then be Duke of Infantada in Spain." [27] Subsequently Bristol gave evidence of his reliance upon James by suing for the performance of the King's promise "that I shoulde never be condemned by you or cast out of your favour, untill I should have appeared in your presence, and had a gratious hearing." [28] Concurrently he notified Secretary Calvert of the difficulties involved in his return, alleging that he had not one penny although six thousand pounds were due to him from the exchequer. Whether for lack of money or for fear of Buckingham's enmity, Bristol remained at Madrid for an unduly long time. By January 29 he had taken leave of Philip IV and had received from him twenty thousand crowns worth of silver plate, diamonds valued at two thousand crowns, and a ring which the King took from his own finger. Although Bristol's need for money to finance his return was known in England by February 13, it was not until the latter part of March that six thousand pounds were remitted to him. Consequently, it was only by pawning his plate that he was able to set out on March 17. Meanwhile, it was rumored in England that his delay was occasioned by a secret order forbidding him to make haste in his departure.[29]

Before he left Madrid, Bristol paid a farewell call on the Venetian ambassador to Spain. In the course of a long conference he confided his distress concerning recent events in England and reaffirmed his belief that the marriage negotiations would ultimately be concluded. He also predicted the nature of the charge that would be laid against him and outlined the heart of his defense.

I perceive, however, that he puts his trust in the parliament, saying

27. *Ibid.*, 40–44, Aston to Conway, Jan. 22, 1624; SP 14/161/36, Sir Francis Nethersole to Sir Dudley Carleton, Mar. 25, 1624; PRO 31/8/198, Digby Transcripts, #65, Olivares's offer to Bristol, Jan. 14/24, 1624. In his speech to the Lords on May 19, 1626, Bristol not only alluded to the offer made by Olivares, but said "he had another offer made him in private of 100,000 ducats to take with him in his purse, that so if haply his own estate was seized on he might have means to make his way and go through with his troubles." (Stowe MS. 365, fols. 65v–66, British Museum.)

28. "Bristol's Defense," iii, Bristol to James, Jan. 22, 1624.

29. *Ibid.*, ii–iii; *Cal. S. P. Venetian,* XVIII, 272–273, Corner to the Doge and Senate, Apr. 7/17, 1624; *ibid.*, 219, Valaresso to the Doge and Senate, Feb. 13/23, 1624; *ibid.*, 263, Valaresso to the Doge and Senate, Mar. 26/Apr. 5, 1624; SP 14/161/36, Sir Francis Nethersole to Sir Dudley Carleton, Mar. 25, 1624; "Bristol's Defense," iii–iv; SP 84/117, Dudley Carleton to Sir Dudley Carleton, Apr. 11, 1624, calendared as SP 14/162/46.2. See also Howell, *State Trials,* II, 1296, for Bristol's assertion that he was urged to delay his return.

that he will prove that he is wrongly accused of disobeying his orders to delay the espousals, as by arrangement made between the Catholic King and the Prince of Wales, he had powers to have these concluded 10 days only after the arrival from Rome of the confirmation of the dispensation, wherefore in this he was not an ambassador who could immediately change his conduct at any order soever from his King, but a neutral, in the confidence of both parties. He could not honourably execute immediately the order for delay without previously protesting and declaring that his Majesty had simply compelled his obedience as a subject. Upon this he enlarged fully, charging Buckingham with endless falseness and duplicity.[30]

Despite Bristol's confidence in Parliament, he chose to return to England overland, rather than by sea, and his progress appeared to be leisurely. His partisans at home eagerly awaited his coming. He could count on the support of a number of peers with Catholic leanings and those with Spanish sympathies. But because feverish anti-Spanish prejudice prevailed generally in England, that support would be largely sub rosa and dependent on the King's attitude for its effectiveness. Judging by James's character, there was every likelihood that he would not openly avow Bristol's proceedings to have been in accord with his own intentions. Given this situation, the best that could be hoped for, from Bristol's point of view, was postponement of his trial until popular hysteria had subsided. The worst that could be feared was that he might be discountenanced by the King and left to defend himself as best he could. This would have put him in the position of accusing the King of being an accessory to his "crimes."

By April 15, Bristol had traveled no further than Poitiers, where he despatched a letter to Cottington. Implied in his message was his belief that the King had been won over to the policy advocated by the Prince and the Duke. "If his Majestie and the Prince will have a war, I will spend my life and fortunes in it, without so much as replying in what quarrel soever it be. And of thus much I entreat you let his Highnesse be informed by you." Promising all manner of conformity to the Prince's directions, he asked for instructions "how to behave my self . . . to the end that understanding his pleasure, I may commit no errour." [31]

30. *Cal. S. P. Venetian*, XVIII, 272–273, Corner to the Doge and Senate, Apr. 7/17, 1624.
31. *Cabala*, I, 28–29, Bristol to Cottington, Apr. 15, 1624. In his speech to the

The Prince's pleasure was not immediately apparent; no method of proceeding against Bristol had been worked out. Buckingham wanted him committed to the Tower without delay and, for that purpose, solicited the complicity of the Duke of Richmond, the Earl of Pembroke, and the Marquess Hamilton. Two years later he gave the reason for this precaution: "I dyd feare that yf Br[istol] should but gett the eare of my M[aste]r, he myght by some words he would use to him subverte all." [32] Buckingham's conviction was shared by others to whom it was cause for hope. The Spanish ambassadors were ostensibly remaining in England for the sole purpose of combining their influence with Bristol's to undermine the plans of the Duke and the Parliament. [33]

On or about April 18, James, with his usual subtlety, indicated that he was not entirely antipathetic to the Earl. On that date a petition was presented to the King asking that Bristol's manor of Sherborne be secured against any legal claims filed on behalf of the heirs of Sir Walter Raleigh. James answered the request by sending a note to the House of Lords advocating the insertion of an amendment in Carew Raleigh's bill to that effect. [34]

Despite this mark of royal favor, Bristol, according to his own testimony, felt the effects of Buckingham's displeasure before he arrived in England. With crown jewels valued at forty thousand pounds in his possession, he came to Calais fully expecting a quick and easy passage to Dover. "I could not procure shipping from hence to pass me over: but was enforced to venture in a boat with six oars: I making haste to come before the parliament should end, and the Duke using all the means he could to put off my

---

Lords on May 6, 1626, Bristol stated that he was proceeding toward England at a leisurely pace (on Conway's instructions) when he learned at Bordeaux of the "many great and sinister aspersions" laid upon him in the Duke of Buckingham's narration to Parliament. Thereafter he made haste "for that he hoped to clear his honor in parliament before it should break up." Bristol interpreted Buckingham's speech as a plot "to terrify him that he should not return, saying publicly and ordinarily that the Earl was not so wise as he took him to be if he kept not himself where he was and laid hold of those great offers which he had heard were made unto him in Spain." (Stowe MS. 365, fols. 38v–42.)

32. *Lords Debates 1624 & 1626*, 154–155, 176, 178. Note that the Duke of Richmond died on Feb. 16, 1624.

33. *Cal. S. P. Venetian*, XVIII, 263, Valaresso to the Doge and Senate, Mar. 26/Apr. 5, 1624.

34. SP 14/163/5 and 6; SP 14/164/86, Sir Francis Nethersole to Sir Dudley Carleton, May 15, 1624.

coming until the parliament was ended." [35] Some observers thought that Bristol was purposely delaying his arrival, and that he would lose his reputation, "if not himself if he appeared under the planet [that] now reigneth in parliament." Friends and foes alike expected him to go directly to the King, and no one doubted that, if he were allowed access, the effects would be detrimental to the favorite.[36]

By April 24, Buckingham had procured a royal command preventing Bristol from coming to court. To make sure that this order would not miscarry, it was sent to Dover by two different messengers, and it was awaiting Bristol upon his arrival. Ordered to remain in his lodgings pending signification of the King's further pleasure, Bristol again appealed to James's better instincts. From Canterbury, on May 3, he reminded the King of his promise of a personal hearing, claiming that favor in respect of twenty years of faithful service. And shortly thereafter he solicited permission to attend the Prince in order to vindicate his conduct and to learn "what your Highness would have me do [so that] I may be sure not [to] err." [37]

On May 4, Bristol arrived at his London residence in St. Giles Fields. By that time the Spanish ambassadors had virtually eliminated themselves as useful allies. English military preparations and the impending persecution of Catholics had prompted them to commence their attack on Buckingham prematurely. On May 2 the favorite was vindicated by the sworn testimony of the Privy Council, and, henceforth, the ambassadors were denied access to the King. Subsequent attempts by Inojosa and Coloma to recoup their fortunes by concerted action with Bristol merely embarrassed the Earl, identified him with Spanish intrigue, and intensified the surveillance of his activities.[38]

35. Howell, *State Trials*, II, 1296; see also SP 14/214, Conway's letterbook, 117, for entry under date of Apr. 23, 1624, for a ship appointed to bring him over.
36. SP 14/163/3, Sir Francis Nethersole to Sir Dudley Carleton, Apr. 18, 1624, and 14/163/50, Sir Francis Nethersole to Sir Dudley Carleton, Apr. 25, 1624; SP 92/10, Wake to Conway, Apr. 29, 1624. "The Lord that is lately come out of Spain doth intend (as his followers say) to go directly to the court; if he do so I shall see a solecism of state committed here which I should never have seen in any court of Italy." This letter is calendared 14/163/72.3.
37. SP 14/163/44, Conway to Bristol, Apr. 24, 1624; SP 14/164/13, Bristol to the King, May 3, 1624; PRO 31/8/198, Digby Transcripts, #66, Bristol to Charles, May [?] 1624.
38. See chap. v, n. 52.

Immediately prior to Bristol's arrival, Buckingham had stayed at court so that nothing could pass between the King and the Earl without his intervention and privity. But, on May 5, the Duke contracted a serious illness and for some weeks took no active part in affairs. The burden of maintaining the King's resolution devolved upon Charles. To James it appeared that the way was now open for a reconciliation. Consequently, he sent kind messages to Bristol and "let him understand that within a day or two he will speak with him." He denied Bristol's request for a trial in the House of Lords on the grounds that Parliament was too incensed against him to render a fair verdict. Then, on May 6, the King visited Buckingham and "dealt earnestly to reconcile him and the earle of Bristowe." Although a rumor was circulating that peace could have been made between the two antagonists in the preceding autumn if the Earl had joined in the attack on Spain, it was evident that these terms were no longer a sufficient basis for the restoration of amicable relations.[39]

Some courtiers, not fully in accord with Buckingham, went to St. Giles to hear a variant account of proceedings in Spain. Foremost among them were the Marquess Hamilton and the Earl of Pembroke. Following their lead, the Elector's representative, Rusdorff, went to see Bristol and was entertained with a prolix relation of the services he had rendered to the Palsgrave. Seemingly confident of his own innocence, the Earl maintained that his memoirs, letters, and actions would acquit him of all charges and testify to the world that James had no more faithful servant.[40]

In lieu of a trial before Parliament, it was expected that Bristol would be summoned before the King and Council, and throughout May there were rumors that charges were being prepared, or had actually been completed. Such, however, does not seem to have been the case; it was not until May 25 that Conway wrote to Phelips demanding the return of Bristol's dispatches, transcripts of which had been distributed to members of the House

39. Rusdorff, *Mémoires*, I, 295–297, Rusdorff to Frederick, elector Palatine, May 2/12, 1624; *Cal. S. P. Venetian*, XVIII, 364, Valaresso to the Doge and Senate, June 18/28, 1624; SP 14/164/44, Dudley Carleton to Sir Dudley Carleton, May 6, 1624; Chamberlain, *Letters*, II, 558, letter of May 13, 1624; Howell, *State Trials*, II, 1296; SP 14/163/3, Sir Francis Nethersole to Sir Dudley Carleton, Apr. 18, 1624; SP 14/163/50, Apr. 25, 1624.

40. Rusdorff, *Mémoires*, I, 303–306, Rusdorff to Frederick, elector Palatine, May 11/21, 1624.

of Commons.[41] On May 28, Bristol wrote to Conway requesting a copy of the King's order for his examination. When he learned that James would not be present at his hearing, Bristol petitioned "that all [that] was done might be set in writing for his Majesty's better information; and this his Majesty has found to be agreeable to reason." [42]

As the time for the trial approached, the dread of damaging revelations evoked positive action from Charles. "The prince sent some hint to the Earl of Bristol that he would like to end his business by silence and by his absenting himself from the Court for some time. But Bristol replied boldly that he desired either justification or death, and wherever he went he wished to go with honour." [43] On June 1, Bristol wrote to Sir Francis Cottington, secretary to the Prince, claiming the performance of a royal promise of favor and assistance if he should ever fall into trouble. Now Charles had told him "that if I will not follow his advice I must not hereafter looke for his assistance." Lacking His Highness's favor, all that Bristol asked "is that I may be hearde, and that he will trewly understande my cause, and then he will see in what sorte I am capable of his grace." [44] Alarmed at Bristol's recalcitrance, the Prince notified Buckingham: "Bristol stands upon his justification, and will by no means accept of my counsels; the King does haste to have him come to his trial, and I am afraid that if you be not with us, to help to charge him, and to set the King right, he may escape with too light a sentence: therefore, I would have you send to the King to put off Bristol's trial until you might wait on him: but for God's sake do not venture to come sooner than you may with safety of your health, and with that condition the sooner the better." [45]

The conversion of the Prince from a possible ally into an active antagonist must have been a source of dismay to the Earl of

41. SP 14/165/41, Secretary Conway to Sir Robert Phelips, May 25, 1624.
42. SP 15/43/60, Bristol to Conway, May 28, 1624; HMC, *Mar and Kellie,* 204, Thomas, earl of Kellie, to John, earl of Mar, May 30, 1624.
43. *Cal. S. P. Venetian,* XVIII, 343–344, Valaresso to the Doge and Senate, June 4/14, 1624; see also HMC, *Mar and Kellie,* 204–205, Thomas, earl of Kellie, to John, earl of Mar, May 30, 1624; SP 14/167/10, Sir Francis Nethersole to Sir Dudley Carleton, June 2, 1624.
44. "Bristol's Defense," ix, Bristol to Cottington, June 1, 1624.
45. Harl. MS. 6987, fol. 207, undated letter of Charles to Buckingham, probably June 1 or 2, 1624.

Bristol, but it was scarcely a surprising development. If Bristol's honor was involved in the vindication of his conduct, no less was Charles's honor involved in maintaining the veracity of Buckingham's parliamentary narrative, which the ambassador sought to falsify. Before the Lords and the Commons the Prince had attested to the truth of Buckingham's relation and had assisted in the denigration of the Earl's proceedings. To impeach Buckingham's narrative, therefore, was to give the lie to Charles and to asperse his royal honor — an intolerable outcome. The Prince was prepared to be benevolent so long as Bristol remained silent, but, when a direct confrontation between Buckingham and Bristol became inevitable, there could be no doubt about his commitment. In fact, before the final settlement of the Bristol affair, Charles had become his principal adversary.

By June 2, there had been "something hammering for the naming of a commission," and by the fourth of the month it was known that Bristol's case would be referred to the Lords of the Council who had charge of Spanish affairs. By the King's order, they were to review the negotiations with Spain and submit a series of questions on which a charge of misconduct could be built. Then, if Bristol failed to justify his proceedings, he would be brought to public trial. Some of the Earl's friends protested against this inquisition, "saying it is too great an injustice to punish a man with confinement first, and afterwards to seek for matter against him." [46]

How strictly the Lords of the junta would call Bristol to account certainly was not known. He did not lack for friends on the board, "including the Earl of Arundel, who seems to rise hourly in the King's favor." Hamilton and Pembroke had already prevented Bristol's imprisonment in the Tower. Weston had divided loyalties. His sympathies were Catholic and pro-Spanish, but he had hopes of becoming Lord Treasurer. [47] Calvert, too, was popishly inclined, but he had been excluded from important state business and was considering retirement from office. Middlesex had been deprived of political power by the judgment of Parlia-

46. SP 14/167/10, Sir Francis Nethersole to Sir Dudley Carleton, June 2, 1624; *Cal. S. P. Venetian*, XVIII, 343–344, Valaresso to the Doge and Senate, June 4/14, 1624; SP 14/167/26, Dudley Carleton to Sir Dudley Carleton, June 7, 1624.
47. *Cal. S. P. Venetian*, XVIII, 343–344, Valaresso to the Doge and Senate, June 4/14, 1624; *Cabala*, I, 93–94, Lord Keeper Williams to the Duke of Buckingham, May 24, 1624.

ment. Belfast and Williams had been coerced into agreement with Buckingham. The remaining members, Conway and Carlisle, unswervingly followed the Duke's lead.

The gravity of Buckingham's charges against Bristol left no doubt that he wished the Earl to be severely censured. Some of his allegations had already been publicized in Parliament in his relation to a committee of both Houses on February 24. Now, in addition to insisting that Bristol had deliberately misinterpreted his instructions, Buckingham emphasized his credulity, personal ambition, and Catholic sympathies. The Duke introduced as evidence the discourse of one Lassells who had purportedly told Bristol at Brussels that the Spanish had no intention of concluding a match with England without an absolute toleration and had warned him of a Catholic undertaking for the reconquest of Ireland. Moreover, every conversation in which Bristol had magnified the might of Spain or the power of the Catholic religion was cited as proof of his popish predilections. He was charged with having consented to "the breeding of the King's grandchild in the Emperor's court which implied a conversion." Finally, it was alleged that Bristol had done everything possible to bring the match to a conclusion, even to the point of depriving the Prince of all hopes of posterity and preventing the King "from relieving the Low Countries or being so powerful an instrument as he now is in the peace of Christendom." Crossed in his designs, Bristol "directly did all that lay in him to make the breach fall upon his Majesty and the Prince." [48]

In their observations upon Bristol's proceedings, the Lords of

---

48. SP 14/168/68, Lassells's discourse; SP 14/180/103, Buckingham's notes for questioning Bristol. This paper is not attributed in the *Calendar* to Buckingham, but internal evidence warrants that conclusion. See also SP 14/168/69 for another draft of the charges against Bristol. Authorship of this document cannot be established definitely, but it contains many points of correspondence with the questions that were later submitted to Bristol. The opening paragraph of this document reads: "That it could not be unknown to the Earl that the King of Spain pretended to a monarchy, and his chief instruments to that were the Jesuits who labored the propagation of the Roman Catholic faith, which had reflection, dependence and support to and from the Catholic King." In a draft of the questions submitted to Bristol (SP 14/168/71) the second question reads, "Whether did you find by your observation during the time of your negotiation in Germany or in Spain that the King of Spain pretended to a general monarchy in Christendom?" This question was deleted in the final draft. There are notes in Conway's handwriting at the bottom of this State Paper which indicate not only that he was engaged in drafting the questions but that they were at least partially formulated on the basis of 14/168/69. The questions in their final form are found in 14/168/70.1.

the Council were vague as to the ambassador's culpability. They noticed:

His long delays; his fair promises; acceptation of loose answers; his acts contrary to directions, contrary to his own conception; his pointing of a day, by which he hath multiplied the cause of mislike on the King of Spain's part; the dangerous desperate evil he had committed if by fast riding it had not been prevented, and many accidents that might have prevented the timely arrival of that dispatch . . .

But above all, that he had (contrary to his own declared interpretation of his Majesty's words) taken the boldness to frame an argument to do an act which had been so directly waived by his Majesty and the Prince, and contrary to all intentions, and the direct words of the articles mentioned in the powers of the Prince's direction touching the delivery. And in his own letters repeated the delivery of the power to be when the approbation of the dispensation should come clear from Rome, which did not, nor yet is cleared.[49]

Evidently the Lords felt that the primary charge against Bristol was his intention to complete the marriage despite instructions to the contrary. They were willing to delegate the responsibility for drawing up the interrogatories, and it seems that they assigned the task to Conway. On June 7, Conway wrote to Bristol informing him of "The cause of the delay in his business, and the course it is now put into." But, disliking sole responsibility for framing the questions, Conway apparently applied to the King and secured his command to transfer the work to Weston and Calvert. These two councillors were at Whitehall arranging for the transportation of the Spanish ambassadors, and they pleaded this urgent employment as an excuse for evading the obligation. They were under the impression that "the business was done already by yourself. For better questions cannot be demanded of my Lord of Bristol than those which you drew out of the letters and presented to the committee, and were allowed by their Lordships." [50] This answer scarcely satisfied Conway: "His Majesty knowing what em-

49. SP 14/180/104. In the *Calendar*, this paper is described as "Observations deduced from the examination conducted by the Lords, on the King's direction, into the proceedings of the Earl of Bristol, giving the general nature of the charges against him, and his explanations thereon."

50. *Cal. S. P. Dom. 1623–1625*, 270, June 7, 1624, minute of a letter from Conway's letterbook, 126; SP 14/167/35, Conway to Weston and Calvert, June 8, 1624; SP 14/167/37.1, Calvert and Weston to Conway, June 8, 1624.

ployments he hath presently for me commanded me in the presence of the Prince three times to write to you both to undertake the work presently, and to finish it with expedition; adding that Mr. Secretary Calvert knew the whole business [and] that Sir Richard Weston was most fit to direct that work by reason of your negotiations abroad in a great part of this business." [51] James also commanded Conway to collaborate with them so "you could have no color to refuse it." Conway even volunteered to accommodate his schedule to that of the other ministers in order "to form and polish" the charge.

On June 14, Conway informed Buckingham that the interrogatories were being drafted and would be submitted to his Grace before they were presented to Bristol.[52] Because of the Duke's illness, delay seemed unavoidable, but not all observers were convinced that this was the only factor impeding the process. "My Lord of Bristol is still in Town pressing to have his Charge, and to be admitted to his Defence; wherein for Fashion Sake, the two Secretaries and Mr. Chancellor of the Exchequer meet for drawing of the Interrogatories; but it moves so slowly, as if now being come to a full and compleat Time of Birth, they had not Strength to bring forth any well-form'd or solid Matter, no not so much as in Idea. For sure, I conceive, it is not any good Nature or Tenderness to the Nobleman, that causeth this leaden heavy March, so as in good Faith I do begin almost to think, there was no Ground for their Opinions, who thought his Offences so great as he never would, nay never durst, return home hither into England." [53]

Day by day Bristol's impatience was mounting. On June 16, the very day that Buckingham returned to court after a long illness, Bristol solicited anew for the dispatch of his business. He complained to Conway:

You were pleased by your letter of the 7th of this month to signify the command you had received from his Majesty to put my business into a speedy way, and wished me to rest upon his Majesty's care of expedition, and continue my patience a day or two and excuse the past.

It is now nine or ten days since, and I have heard nothing from his

51. SP 14/167/38, Conway to Calvert and Weston, June 9, 1624.
52. SP 14/167/59, Conway to Buckingham, June 14, 1624.
53. Strafford, *Letters*, I, 21, Sir Thomas Wentworth to Christopher Wandesford, June 17, 1624.

Majesty or yourself. I confess unto you it seemeth very long unto me that have never been used to any restraint to be so long debarred from his Majesty's presence, and an example hardly to be paralleled in Christendom, I am sure it never was since his Majesty's gracious reign, that a councillor should be imprisoned two months and neither heard, nor question asked him.

I do therefore now desire you to represent unto his Majesty my humble request to be admitted to his presence and that he will hear me.[54]

There was no other alternative than complete reliance on James's justice if Bristol was to be vindicated. The possibility of appealing directly to Parliament no longer existed; it had been prorogued on May 29. It was expected to meet again at Michaelmas, but there was no certainty that the King would keep his promise to reconvene it. With the Duke back at court, moreover, there was every likelihood that James would be persuaded to exile Bristol to political oblivion in the country.

The course of action least attractive to the Earl entailed complete submission and implied an admission of guilt. His reluctance to accept this mode of accommodation explains his almost frenetic attempts to have his defense heard before the King went on his summer progress. Conversely, apprehension about the revelations expected from Bristol explains the delicacy with which his case was handled. On June 24, after earnest solicitation, the Earl received permission to visit his sick mother, but the fear that he might take advantage of the situation to rally a party behind him was all too evident in the limiting clause inserted in Conway's letter: "In the meane tyme, because his Majesty knowes not the extreamity of your noble mother's sicknes, nor what comfort may be denied to you both bye restraint of visiting her, his Majesty hath commanded me to signifie his pleasure to you (his Majesty conceiving that your mother lies in London or Westminster, or neare there,) that you visitt your mother with this caution and advice, that in time and manner you use it as privately as conveniently as you may." [55]

54. SP 15/43/66, Bristol to Conway, June 16, 1624.

55. SP 14/168/32, Conway to Bristol, June 24, 1624; cited by Gardiner, "Bristol's Defence," xi, n. 5. Bristol referred to this episode in 1626, "whereupon the Earl wrote to the said Lord Conway, to desire him to move the King for his leave; which he putting off from day to day told the person employed that, by reason of the Duke's sickness, he could not find opportunity to get the Duke's leave to move the King, and having spoken with the Duke, he made a negative answer in the King's

At last, on June 30, Conway sent twenty interrogatories to Bristol. They were conveyed by Sir William Beecher, Clerk of the Council, "but sealed up in a paper so as the bearer knew not the contents." Although he refused to accept them because they were not signed, Bristol must have retained them long enough to make a copy. On July 1, and again on the third, he wrote to Conway informing him that he was in the process of framing his answers, but he wanted the questions signed so that they might be avowed in judicial proceedings. Although he thought that some of them involved capital offenses, he conceived Conway's signature alone to be sufficient for their authentication.[56]

At approximately the same time that the questions were delivered, Bristol was advised to seek a reconciliation with Buckingham. At his trial in 1626 the Earl recalled that "his late Majesty being desirous that the business should have been accomodated sent secretly unto him a gentleman, who is ready to depose it, with this message: that he should write a fair letter to the Duke and leave the rest unto him." By July 3 Bristol had resolved to follow the King's advice; on that day he wrote to Conway, "God well knoweth how much I have and do desire to have these businesses fairly passed over, and shall not fail on my part to contribute all that possibly can be expected from a man of honesty and honor, as you shall find by me, if by the King's permission, I might receive so much honor as to see you on Monday next at your coming to town." Simultaneously Bristol seems to have commissioned the Marquess Hamilton to intercede with Buckingham.[57]

---

name; wherewith the Earl acquainting the King by some of his bedchamber, his Majesty was in a very great anger, swearing the secretary had never moved him, and that to deny the said Earl leave was a barbarous part, and thereupon sent him presently free leave; which the secretary hearing of, sent likewise afterwards a letter of leave, but with divers clauses and limitations, differing from the leave sent him from the King's own mouth." (Howell, *State Trials,* II, 1291.) This is the fifth article in the charges which Bristol filed against Conway on May 1, 1626. Doubtless Conway's malignity was exaggerated, for no letters of Bristol to the Secretary in 1624 imply such biased intervention on Conway's part. In fact, it was through Conway, and at his suggestion, that Bristol sought an accommodation with the Duke, and more than once, as he did on July 3, Bristol thanked Conway for your "friendly and noble care" of me. (SP 15/43/69, July 3, 1624.)

56. SP 14/168/70.1, Interrogatories to be put to the Earl of Bristol, June 30, 1624; SP 14/169/35, Sir Francis Nethersole to Sir Dudley Carleton, July 10, 1624; SP 15/43/70, Bristol to Conway, July 1, 1624. (This letter is erroneously calendared in the *Cal. S. P. Dom Addenda 1580–1625,* 668, under the date July 5, 1624.)

57. Stowe MS. 365, fols. 38v–42, Bristol's speech, May 6, 1626; SP 15/43/69, Bristol to Conway, July 3, 1624.

The Duke's response to these overtures was the dispatch of his personal servant, Edward Clark, to Bristol's residence. Clark carried "fair propositions offering to procure him whatsoever he could reasonably pretend, only he must not be admitted to come to the King's presence for some time, and the Duke would have the disposing of his Vice-Chamberlain's place having been therein formerly engaged." Bristol replied, "that to condescend to any such course were tacitly to confess himself faulty in some kind, which he would not do for any respect in the world."

In the course of their discussion, Bristol showed Clark "a paper that he had made ready for the King containing the particulars wherein the Duke had disserved him." When Buckingham learned of this, he "wrote a letter the next day unto the Earl, bearing date the 7th of July, telling him that he had willingly intended the accomodation of his affairs, but by what he had now said unto Mr. Clark, he was disobliged unless he should be pleased to retract it." Whatever concessions Bristol offered in reply failed to mollify Buckingham. He refused to engage in what he termed a "paper process between us." He alleged that his report of the Spanish negotiations "was a true relation without calling for a comparison from you." He insisted that Bristol was charged because of the King's interpretation of his proceedings, and he informed the Earl that he personally gave way to his trial "which I have assurance will be equal and just and tending your own justification and with no consideration of what may reflect upon me." Bristol later interpreted Buckingham's reaction in an entirely different manner: "The course of mediation was interrupted, and the Duke so far incensed that he swore he would have him questioned for his life." [58]

58. Stowe MS. 365, fols. 38v–42, Bristol's speech, May 6, 1626; SP 14/169/49, Buckingham to Bristol, July 11 (?), 1624. Buckingham's letter exists only as an undated draft by Conway. I suggest that it was written before July 11 and possibly as early as July 8. SP 16/523/78 is a modern transcription of Conway's draft and has been erroneously calendared with the probable date of March 1626. The report of the Earl of Bristol's speech (May 6, 1626) contained in Stowe MS. 365 makes it possible to determine the exact date of Clark's conference with the Earl. Clark reported to Buckingham on July 6. On the seventh, Buckingham wrote to Bristol demanding his retraction, which Bristol refused. SP 14/169/49 is Buckingham's rejoinder and begins with the statement "I have received yours in answer of mine of the 7th." Neither Buckingham's letter of the seventh nor Bristol's reply seem to have survived. See also *Cal. S. P. Venetian*, XVIII, 400–401, Valaresso to the Doge and Senate, July 16/26, 1624; HMC, *Mar and Kellie*, 207–208, Thomas, earl of Kellie, to John, earl of Mar, July 17, 1624.

Meanwhile Bristol was drafting his answers to the twenty questions. Formerly he had told Conway, "I hope mine answer shall in no kind exasperate or offend any, it tending only to mine own justification, and not to the wronging or blaming of any, unless by their criminating or charging of me I shall be forced unto it for mine own just defense." However, the disclosure to Clark of the charges which Bristol had prepared against Buckingham warned the Duke of an impending change in the Earl's tactics. By July 7 Bristol accepted the inevitability of a trial. He informed Conway that his answers were ready for submission but that he had "reserved many things in them to be delivered unto his Majesty by word of mouth." Therefore he had renewed his petition to James for personal access, if not as a councillor and faithful servant, "at least as a supposed delinquent and examinate." By requesting to be heard as a defendant, Bristol obviously hoped to force the issue of a personal hearing. Only by his presence could he hope to nullify Buckingham's influence and refute his accusations. James, however, saw through the stratagem and refused to grant the plea. Later, in excusing his conduct, Bristol wrote: "The truth of it is I moved your Majesty not primarily to be admitted as a delinquent, but conceiving it so highly to import my justice, I rather moved to have it in that nature than not at all, but I must needs think myself a most unfortunate man both to be debarred as a servant and not to be admitted as a delinquent." [59]

Refused personal access to the throne, Bristol employed another device. At the same time he complied with the King's command to present his answers to the twenty interrogatories, he submitted an abstract which he begged James to allow Simon Digby to read to him. What happened to these papers was described by the Earl of Kellie: "One of his answers was more shorter than the other and yet it was some 5 or 6 sheets of paper, but the other was above a dozen of sheets. The King read the shortest himself every word, and commanded me to give the other to Secretary Conway, of whom the King is as weary as ever you were of the school. Since the delivery of these answers there has not been anything either done or said that I can hear of since that time, but it is true that

59. SP 15/43/69, Bristol to Conway, July 3, 1624; SP 15/43/73, Bristol to Conway, July 7, 1624; SP 15/43/74, Bristol to James I, July 10, 1624; see also PRO 31/8/198, Digby Transcripts, #69, Bristol to Charles, July 10, 1624.

matters are very ill betwixt Buckingham and Bristol, and if the Prince were free of the matter, I think Bristol would speak strange discourse." [60]

The twenty interrogatories which had been submitted to the Earl were not of equal importance in the admissions they sought or the charges they implied. Some of them were based on common fame, some on hearsay evidence, and only a few on documents or direct testimony. In general they were designed to elicit proof of Bristol's complicity in the promotion of Spanish diplomatic aims. Two charges were particularly serious: that he had consented to the rearing of the Elector Palatine's heir at the Catholic imperial court, and that he had agreed to deliver the Prince's proxy on November 29, 1623, despite instructions to the contrary.

To these accusations Bristol devoted most of his attention, being careful not to cast aspersions upon either James or Charles. He pointed out that the project to educate the Palsgrave's son at Vienna did not, in his estimation, imply his conversion, indeed, all historical precedent contradicted such a conclusion. In his defense against the charge of deliberately disobeying explicit instructions, Bristol alleged that all of the commands received by him expressly enjoined the completion of the match, or implied as much. The restitution of the Palatinate, he maintained, had never been demanded as a necessary prerequisite for the marriage, and he could not be expected to destroy the match on the basis of inferences drawn from dispatches from England. Only after he had been specifically commanded to prevent the espousals could the question of his obedience be raised, and, in this instance, he had immediately carried out the King's directives. In the matter of the desponsories, moreover, Bristol conceived himself to be bound by the articles of the marriage treaty. Being sworn to its terms, he was not at liberty to defer the completion of the ceremony unless he was commanded to do so in his private capacity as a subject of the British crown. In the absence of such an order he considered himself a neutral trustee responsible to both contracting parties.

Considering his animosity toward Buckingham, it is surprising how little of Bristol's narrative reflects discredit on the Duke.

60. SP 15/43/74, Bristol to James I, July 10, 1624; HMC, *Mar and Kellie*, 207–208, Thomas, earl of Kellie, to John, earl of Mar, July 17, 1624.

When asked how the Prince's journey had affected Spanish intentions toward the treaty, the Earl replied that they were well disposed to negotiate before the Prince's coming, even more so while
he was there "despite personal distastes" and most favorable after
he had departed, for then the distractions and disgusts of ministers
had been removed. Asked if he had supported the idea of the
Prince's conversion, Bristol offered to prove his loyalty to the
Anglican Church by witnesses, two of whom were the Prince's
chaplains. He asserted that he had neither advised nor invited the
Prince's conversion as "others" had done by procuring conferences with Catholic divines. Neither did he think that a conversion was expedient.

With Buckingham's minions Bristol was less gentle. Endymion
Porter's deposition had been used to demonstrate the necessity of
the Spanish journey, but his assertion that Olivares was ignorant
of the match negotiations in the autumn of 1622 was proved, by
Bristol, to be a tissue of lies. Porter's perjury was revealed by quotations from letters of James, Charles, and Buckingham written
in January 1623. Likewise, Lassells's testimony that he had informed Bristol of the insincerity of Spanish proceedings was dev-
astated by the statement that his information had been referred
to James who refused permission to pay the informer on the
grounds that he was an idle, cozening fellow.[61]

Although Bristol's replies skillfully avoided giving further offense, they were unsatisfactory, even to James. Undoubtedly the
King did not seek the Earl's downfall as avidly as did the Prince
and the Duke, but, being conscious of his reputation abroad, he
needed someone to assume the blame for the Spanish debacle. This
Bristol refused to do; his whole answer was a protest of injured
innocence. Thus, even before Buckingham was informed that
Bristol had submitted his defense, the King had expressed his
dissatisfaction with it.[62] On July 12 Bristol heard that he was to
be questioned further; within a day or two he would receive ad-

---

61. SP 14/169/42, the charges against the Earl of Bristol and his replies. Printed
in *Hardwicke State Papers*, I, 494–522.
62. SP 14/169/50, Secretary Conway to the Duke of Buckingham, July 12, 1624. In
this letter Conway informed Buckingham of the receipt of Bristol's answers. By the
same day James had informed Bristol that he was to be questioned further. (SP
14/170/6, Bristol to Conway, July 15, 1624; see also PRO 31/8/198, Digby Transcripts, #70, Bristol's petition to James I, July 13, 1624.)

ditional questions from the King. On the fifteenth he asked Conway for the dispatch of the new interrogatories and again entreated his assistance in arranging an accommodation. Simultaneously, the Earl's wife, Beatrice, was attending at Wanstead, trying, among other things to secure leave for him to deal with his private affairs in the country. Although James refused to see Lady Bristol, he did give permission for her husband to go to Sherborne until August 31, 1624.[63]

This order signified the King's intention to keep the whole matter in abeyance, especially since Bristol was enjoined from coming into his presence. It is no wonder that the Earl construed it as a "sad message," for it meant that a reconciliation with Buckingham was the only alternative.

Although Bristol continued to petition for the additions to the questions and although he continued to assert his innocence, he also reiterated his desire for an accommodation, blaming Clark for previous misunderstandings and offering to meet with Buckingham in order to rectify mistakes.[64] These overtures were duly communicated by Conway to Buckingham, but the Duke exhibited no inclination to receive Bristol into favor again. To all intents and purposes the failure of Bristol to secure access to the King had accomplished precisely what the Prince and the Duke had desired — it had isolated him and rendered him harmless. Nevertheless, Buckingham submitted Bristol's answers to Sir Robert Phelips and received in reply some very cogent advice:

First, that it may be maturely considered, Whether the tendring him any further charge, unto which he may be able to frame a probable satisfactorie answer, will not rather serve to declare his innocencie, then to prepare his Condemnation, and so instead of pressing him, reflect back with disadvantage upon the proceeding against him.

Secondly, That your Grace would be pleased to consult with your self, whether you may not desist from having him further questioned, without either blemish to your Honour, or manifest prejudice to the service: Considering that you have (to your perpetual glory) already

63. SP 14/170/6, Bristol to Conway, July 15, 1624; SP 15/43/76, Bristol to Conway, July 21, 1624; *Cal. S. P. Dom. 1623–1625,* 309, under date of July 21 is a notice of a minute in Conway's letterbook of a letter from Conway to Bristol, 138.

64. SP 14/170/68, Bristol to Conway, July 27, 1624; see also *Cabala,* I, 30, Bristol to the King, July 27, 1624. Bristol's petition to the King, Aug. 11, 1624, is printed in "Bristol's Defense," xvi.

dissolved and broken the Spanish partie, and rendred them without either the means, or the hope of ever conjoyning in such sort together again, as may probably give the least disturbance or impediment to your Graces waies and designs.

And lastly, Although his Lordship in sundry places of his answer, especially in the latter part, doth seem directly to violate the rule of the prudent Marriner, who in foul weather, and in a storm, is accustomed (to prevent shipwrack) rather to pull down, then to set up his sailes. Neverthelesse as this case stands, it deserves to be thorowly pondered, which of the two waies will most conduce to your Graces purpose, and is likely to receive the best interpretation and success, either to have him dealt with after a quick and round manner, or otherwise to proceed slowly and moderately with him, permitting him for a time to remain where he is, as a man laid aside, and in the way to be forgotten. A state of being (if I mistake not his complexion) which will be by him apprehended equivalent to the severest and sharpest censure, that possibly can be inflicted on him.[65]

In the autumn and early winter of 1624 it seemed as if Phelips's advice to let sleeping dogs lie would be followed. However, on January 13, 1625, Bristol again sought permission, through Buckingham, to approach the court. He was allowed to come to London, but on February 2 the Duke submitted five propositions to Bristol, expecting in answer an acknowledgement of "errors in judgment and confidence." Although Buckingham tacitly conceded that no legal charge could be maintained against him, he nevertheless continued to demand admissions of error from the Earl — errors which proceeded "not from malice nor want of faith, but from an earnest and misled zeal to endeavor by all means his master's ends." Without this confession, Buckingham was not prepared to secure Bristol's readmission to royal favor.[66]

Instead of subscribing an acknowledgement of guilt, Bristol again argued his case, attempting to prove the integrity of his proceedings in Spain.[67] This unyielding reply was no more to Buckingham's liking than previous responses had been. It not only disrupted his plans to dispose of the vice-chamberlainship to Sir

65. *Cabala,* I, 264–266, Sir Robert Phelips to the Duke of Buckingham, Aug. 21, 1624.

66. PRO 31/8/198, Digby Transcripts #76, Bristol to Buckingham, Jan. 13, 1625, printed in "Bristol's Defense," xviii; Stowe MS. 365, fol. 12, Buckingham to Bristol, Feb. 2, 1625; Stowe MS. 365, fols. 24–24v.

67. Stowe MS. 365, fols. 24–32, Buckingham's five propositions with Bristol's answers, printed in "Bristol's Defense," xix–xx, 30–54.

Dudley Carleton, but it also deprived him of the indispensable weapon he needed to insure Bristol's silence and complaisance. Lacking such an instrument, it was essential that Bristol be denied access to either King or Parliament. Although the Earl received his writ of summons to the Parliament of 1625, he was refused permission to attend when he asked for royal instructions regarding its use. All that Charles demanded for Bristol's return to favor was "the least acknowledgement" of his error.[68] When he had answered Buckingham's five propositions, Bristol had coupled his plea for relief with an entreaty to "his Grace, not to insist or presse mee to those thinges which would make mee for the future incapable of his Majestyies favour and unworthy of his friendshipp." [69] Now, to the Earl's great chagrin, the new King was asking for a similar confession. Bristol was no more prepared to comply with this royal request than he had been to yield to the favorite's demands. He was determined that his return to favor should be based upon an unconditional act of grace which should not in any way imply his culpability.

Charles's demands, combined with a new order for restraint issued on June 10th, 1625, undoubtedly convinced Bristol that petitions to Buckingham and the King would not secure the vindication of his reputation. However, in January 1626, with the approach of the coronation and the convention of Charles's second Parliament, Bristol dispatched letters to the King, Buckingham, and Conway requesting a more precise definition of the confinement which had been imposed upon him. By his restraining order Charles had undoubtedly intended to keep Bristol in the country, but, due to an oversight, his command merely confirmed the conditions previously defined by his father. Before his death James had allowed Bristol liberty to come to London if he pleased — a potentially dangerous concession.

Since 1624 Bristol's legal position had been strengthened; he had been excepted from neither the general pardon of that year nor the coronation pardon of Charles I.[70] Moreover, Buckingham's

68. "Bristol's Defense," xxv–xxvii, letter of Kenelm Digby to the Earl of Bristol, May 27, 1625; See also HMC, *Eighth Report,* Appendix, pt. I, 217.
69. "Bristol's Defense," xxii–xxiii, Earl of Bristol to Sir Kenelm Digby, Mar. 16, 1625.
70. SP 16/524/95, Bristol to Charles I, Aug. 16, 1626. Bristol stated "I desired to lay hold thereof by suing forth your Majesty's general pardon granted at your

popularity had declined appreciably and this provided an opportunity which could be exploited. The King and the Duke were
already convinced that in 1625 Bristol had plotted and combined
with some Parliament men "that seemed adverse to his Grace at
Oxford." [71] Thus, even if his writ of summons were denied him,
Bristol's presence in the environs of Westminster would most assuredly strengthen his party and have a disruptive effect on the
new Parliament. This was, indeed, precisely what happened; the
issue was forced by the change in Bristol's tactics.

In 1625 he had complied with a royal command prohibiting his
attendance in Parliament, but now he sued for his writ and asserted that he could only be discharged from obeying it by an
order from the House of Lords.[72] By April 19 Bristol had received
his summons and was petitioning the Lords for permission to indict the Duke of Buckingham. Although Charles was, in every
sense of the word, a defendant in the action, it was impossible for
Bristol to prefer charges against him; his only recourse was to
accuse Buckingham and Conway. This resulted in a counterindict-
ment of high treason against Bristol, instigated by Buckingham
but prosecuted by the King. It was the Earl's misfortune to be
unable to separate the King's interests from those of the Duke,
just as it was his good fortune to present his charges against Buck-

---

coronation (which was not at the same time denied to diverse of mine own servants)
yet held back from me, whereupon I petitioned my Lord Keeper to become a
suitor for me unto your Majesty in that behalf, but received answer that he had
express order not to suffer any pardon for me to pass."

71. "Bristol's Defense," xxxi, Bristol to Conway, Feb. 6, 1626. In his apology to
the Oxford Parliament, Buckingham defended himself against the charge that he
had broken the Spanish treaties because of personal enmity toward Olivares. "I will
leaue that business a sleep, w^ch if it be wakned will prove a lion to devour him
that was the author of it. I meane one of myne owne nation who did cooperate
w^th him." (Eliot, *Negotium Posterorum*, II, 70.)

72. Stowe MS. 365, fols. 38v–42, Bristol's speech, May 6, 1626. In 1625, Bristol
received his writ of summons and asked instructions regarding its use. On May 2
Buckingham replied "I have acquainted his Majesty with your respect towards
him touching your summons to the parliament, which he taketh very well, and
would have you rather make some excuse for your absence notwithstanding your
writ than to come yourself in person." Thereupon Bristol "sent humbly to desire
a letter of leave under his Majesty's hand for his warrant, but instead thereof he
received from the Lord Conway a letter of absolute prohibition and to restrain
him and confine him in such sort as he had been in the late King's time." However, in 1626 Bristol raised the question whether a "missive letter" was a sufficient
discharge against the great seal of England. (Bristol to Lord Keeper Coventry, Apr.
12, 1626, printed in *OPH*, VI, 479–481; see also SP 16/524/95, Bristol to Charles I,
Aug. 16, 1626.

ingham at the very moment when the Commons, spurred on by Pembroke's satellites, were most incensed against the favorite. The King's reluctance to desert Buckingham induced him to dissolve Parliament, and once again Bristol's attempts to vindicate his honor proved abortive.[73]

The acrimony implicit in the charges and countercharges filed in the Parliament of 1626 was remarkable, not because it indicated any significant change in the Buckingham-Bristol dispute, but rather because it exhibited the intensified hatred between the rivals and led to exaggerated accusations. Bristol, for instance, was not content with retorting upon the Duke those allegations which had previously been leveled against himself, but he claimed, in addition, that the Pope had sent a special brief to Buckingham encouraging him to pervert the Prince from his religion and embrace Catholicism.[74]

73. The change in attitude toward Bristol between 1624 and 1626 is graphically illustrated by the Salvetti correspondence. On May 12/22, 1626, he described Bristol's delivery of his accusation against Buckingham: "The Earl spoke so calmly and modestly that he made a very favourable impression upon the greater number of the Members." HMC, *Eleventh Report,* Appendix, pt. I (London, 1887), Skrine MSS, 63. Of the Lords' attitude, Salvetti says, "They desire to maintain all their privileges intact, and they also wish to lighten the case against the Earl, as much as possible, probably being inwardly convinced of his innocence, whilst they oppose the Duke who takes so strong a part against him." (*Ibid.,* 64.) On May 19/29, 1626, Salvetti reported, "Meanwhile public opinion is in favour of the Earl, and the people will rejoice in his acquittal, such is the odium with which his opponent is regarded." (*Ibid.,* 66.) On May 26/June 5, after Bristol had made his defense, Salvetti noted, "The House would then and there have acquitted him, but that it was bound by the usual precedent which required it to hear the Attorney-General in reply . . . The prevalent disposition is in his favour, and the desire is to absolve him at once, if the powerful party which is opposed to him does not bring forward new charges or throw impediments in the way." (*Ibid.,* 68.) Immediately after the Parliament on June 16/26, he wrote, "The Earl of Bristol has special cause of complaint, this break up having taken place before the termination of his case; for he now remains without protection in the power of those who do not love him, or he must depend on the compassion of the King." (*Ibid.,* 75.)

74. Bristol's articles against Buckingham and Conway are printed in *OPH,* VII, 12–19. Notice the bitter sarcasm employed by Bristol in his remarks in answer to the charge against him on May 6. "I expected a Remonstrance of some Practice, with Spain, against the State; or to be charged with the Receipt of Ten or Twenty Thousand Pounds, for the persuading and procuring the Delivering up of some Town, that the Crown was in Possession of, as might be the Brill or Flushing, or the like; or for being the Means of the Delivery of the King's Ships to serve a foreign Nation against those of our own Religion; or for the Revealing of his Majesty's highest Secrets, which none but two or three did know of; or for treating of the greatest Affairs, as it were by my own Authority, without formal Instructions in the Point; or, as the Law calls it, to have committed some Overt Act of Disloyalty, and not to be charg'd, after seven Ambassages, with Discouragements and Inferences." (*OPH,* VII, 22–23.)

On the opposing side, the personal intervention of Charles was a noteworthy factor. Throughout 1624 he had been an interested partisan in a dispute in which Buckingham and Bristol had played the leading roles. His discussions with Kenelm Digby in 1625 indicated that he would have been satisfied with a private admission of error on the Earl's part and that he was more sensitive over affronts to Buckingham than over injuries to his own reputation. By January 21, 1626, however, his attitude had altered completely, and he not only accused Bristol of attempting to convert him to Catholicism, but also charged him with magnifying the power of Spain, derogating the prestige of England, delaying his return from Madrid, neglecting the interests of the Palsgrave, and consenting to the education of the Elector's son in the imperial court at Vienna.[75]

It was with some justification that Bristol, in his defense, maintained that Charles appeared against him as relator, prosecutor, witness, judge, and beneficiary of his sentence, because the King went to extreme lengths in his efforts to insure the Earl's conviction. Certainly the King's reluctance to accede to the Lords' demands for the release of the Earl of Arundel from the Tower was partially motivated by his fear that the five proxies held by Arundel would be used in favor of Bristol and against Buckingham.[76] This apprehension, however, could not explain his adamant refusal to allow counsel to the Earl of Bristol — resistance which was not overcome until it was shown that he had been present in the House of Lords on May 28, 1624, when an order was made

75. "Bristol's Defense," xxx, Charles to Bristol, Jan. 20, 1626. In the *Cal. S. P. Dom., Addenda, 1625–1649*, 98–99, this letter is printed with Charles's corrections indicated in italics.

76. SP 16/524/9, Edmund Bolton to the Duke of Buckingham, May 29, 1626. "As for the proxies which the Earl of Arundel hath, if they be freed, one of them if no more shall certainly be yours . . . for I have the nobleman's free promise for that purpose." (PRO 31/8/198, Digby Transcripts, #88, Bristol's list of the Lords' proxies in the Parliament of 1626.) According to this list Arundel held four proxies and Pembroke five. On March 17/27, 1626, Salvetti wrote that the Duke had eleven proxies. (HMC, *Eleventh Report*, Appendix, pt. I, 53.) This perhaps explains the attempts of both the Commons and the Earl of Bristol to have Buckingham sequestered from the House of Lords while the charges against him were heard. Chamberlain (*Letters*, II, 630, letter of Mar. 7, 1626) says that the Duke had eleven proxies and the Earl of Pembroke had eight proxies. On the question of limiting the number of proxies to one per peer, Pembroke gave four in favor of the motion and four against it, but Montgomery voted with the Duke. The motion was defeated.

that allowed counsel to defendants in the upper House. Again, when the peers wished to hear the opinions of the judges on the admissibility of the King's testimony in cases of treason or felony, Charles stayed the delivery of their resolution on the grounds that it concerned the rights of the crown and might prove a dangerous precedent for the future.[77]

Doubtless Buckingham would have preferred to consign Bristol's prosecution to the King's courts where a directed verdict was not beyond the realm of possibility. That Charles concurred is evident from the proceedings that followed the dissolution of the Parliament. On July 24, 1626, Attorney General Heath and Solicitor Shelton laid an information against Bristol and requested the issuance of a subpoena directing him to answer in the Star Chamber. Eleven charges were specified, the majority of which recapitulated Bristol's "crimes" during his embassy to Spain. The Earl immediately countered with a demurrer and, from his cell in the Tower, began to prepare his defense. Since the accusations against him no longer involved capital punishment, he petitioned to be admitted to bail, which was denied. Thereafter he continually solicited for temporary liberty in order to recover his health, consult his counsel, and search his diplomatic records. Concomitantly he reiterated his desire for a personal hearing before the King and for his restoration to favor as a free act of royal grace.

---

77. *Lords Debates 1624 & 1626*, 178, 185–187, 191, 203–204. There were other proceedings against Bristol outside of Parliament that were both humiliating and annoying. For instance, in January 1625 Bristol was ordered to render an exact account of all the jewels taken to Spain. (*Cal. S. P. Venetian*, XVIII, 575, Rosso to the Doge and Senate, Jan. 28/Feb. 7, 1625.) On another occasion Charles demanded the return of a valuable portrait of himself which he had given Bristol. (SP 14/171/9, T. Locke to Sir Dudley Carleton, Aug. 2, 1624.) The embassy to Spain also proved a heavy drain on Bristol's financial resources. To undertake it in 1622, twenty thousand pounds was required, of which Bristol supplied thirteen thousand, taking a short-term mortgage on crown lands at 10 percent. F. C. Dietz, *English Public Finance, 1558–1641* (New York, 1932), II, 174–175. Bristol himself gives the figure at twelve thousand pounds. ("Bristol's Defense," 37.) While in Spain, Bristol provided the Prince with fifteen thousand pounds upon his own credit and an additional six thousand pounds were charged upon him from Santander. (*Ibid.*, 49.) Just before he left Madrid, Bristol wrote to the King that he was engaged for more than fifty thousand crowns for the Prince. (*Hardwicke State Papers*, I, 489, Bristol to the King, Nov. 26, 1623.) Bristol frequently complained about delay in the repayment of this money, pointing out that he was responsible for the interest on it. On July 15, 1626, Bristol listed the lands he had sold since his return from Spain. The total realized was £15,446. He paid out £14,966 for debts. The remaining indebtedness amounted to £13,028. *Cal. S. P. Dom., Addenda, 1625–1649*, 140.

In the last analysis it was Bristol's legal tactics that prevented his condemnation. He took care to inform the Attorney General that he had reserved, in his parliamentary defense, some state secrets that might reflect discredit on Buckingham and Charles. He took advantage of the imprecision of the indictment against him to involve, as codefendants by implication, all commissioners who had participated in the drafting of his diplomatic instructions and all ambassadors who had served with him in joint embassies. Above all, he refused to waive the immunity which he had acquired by means of the general pardon issued in 1624. Since virtually all of his offenses had been committed prior to that time, the efforts of the prosecution were effectively thwarted.[78]

Month after month Bristol's case was deferred while the two Chief Justices and the Chief Baron of the Exchequer sought a solution to the legal dilemma. Meanwhile, periodic imprisonment and increasing financial distress made the Earl more receptive to an accommodation, and by October 19, 1627, he informed the judges of his willingness to make submission in open court. Ill health prevented Bristol's personal appearance, but his attorney was instructed to act on his behalf. This procedure, however, failed to satisfy Charles and Buckingham, and on February 17, 1628, Lord Savage was sent with two draft letters of submission which required the Earl to acknowledge his guilt. Bristol was expected to beg forgiveness for having contradicted "your Majesty's speeches and former relations" and for having committed "notable errors and dangerous mistakes." "Therefore, with all humility lying prostrate at your Majesty's feet, I condemn myself and likewise confess to have been over-credulous of the many vowed protestations of the court of Spain, and do believe that fearful effects might have ensued thereupon had not God in his divine providence, and your Majesty in your great wisdom diverted it." Simultaneously Buckingham was to be entreated to forgive and forget those public aspersions which "my heart never could accuse you of" and to act as mediator in assuaging the King's displeasure.[79]

78. Stowe MS. 365, fols. 73–78v, information laid by Heath and Shelton against Bristol, July 24, 1626; *ibid.*, fols. 79–89v, Bristol's demurrer to the charge. For Bristol's petitions and legal maneuvers, see PRO 31/8/198, Digby Transcripts, #95–98, 100, 104–106, 108.

79. Stowe MS. 365, fol. 98v, Bristol to Sir Nicholas Hide, Sir Thomas Richardson, and Sir John Walter, Oct. 19, 1627; *ibid.*, fol. 99, Bristol to Charles I (draft) Feb. 17, 1628; *ibid.*, fol. 100, Bristol to Buckingham (draft), Feb. 17, 1628.

Bristol ignored these obsequious letters of submission and substituted compositions of his own. He made no references to "errors" or "aspersions." Buckingham's intercession was requited
with grateful acknowledgement, and the ending of Bristol's ordeal
was termed a gracious act of the King's piety and goodness. In fact,
on March 13, 1628, Bristol wrote to Attorney General Heath
threatening to reopen his case in Parliament if the Star Chamber
information against him was not removed from the file. On the
nineteenth, Heath assured Bristol that there would be no further
proceedings because he had sent for the original documents and
had them in his custody.[80]

By 1628, war with France had directed English attention away
from revelations about the breach with Spain, and the issues involved in Bristol's prosecution had been reduced to insignificance.
Moreover, the King's desire for the restoration of harmonious relations with Parliament induced him to restore the Earl to his
seat in the Lords. Bristol's subsequent attempts to reconcile the
royal prerogative with the liberties of the subject were sufficiently
appreciated to insure his future immunity from prosecution, but
undoubtedly the death of the Duke of Buckingham was the critical factor in the consignment of the Bristol affair to oblivion.

Despite Sir Robert Phelips's conviction that Spanish partisans
in 1624 were devoid of the hope or means of conjoining together
again, some remnants of the "party" survived the demise of Buckingham. Indeed, Weston assumed his mantle, and Cottington, too,
climbed to positions of trust and power,[81] but they had never been
subjected to the full force of Buckingham's wrath or assaulted by
the power that had ruined Cranfield and neutralized Bristol.

Nevertheless, the mere political survival of the Earl of Bristol
disclosed the limitations on the favorite's arbitrary authority. It
was fortunate for him that those councillors who opposed the new
policy were impelled by motives too diverse to unite them into

80. Stowe MS. 365, fol. 99v, Bristol to Charles I, Feb. 19, 1628; *ibid.*, fol. 100v,
Bristol to Buckingham, Feb. 19, 1628; *ibid.*, fol. 101, Bristol to Heath, Mar. 13,
1628, and Heath to Bristol, Mar. 19, 1628.

81. Immediately after the assassination of the Duke of Buckingham, Henry, Lord
Percy, wrote to the Earl of Carlisle, "It is thought the treasurer [Weston] will have
the greatest power with the King. Then consequently the popish faction will be
much exalted (for he will bring in Arundel, Bristol, and Sir Francis Cottington,
his great friend) without they have great resistance." (SP 16/529/15, Lord Percy
to the Earl of Carlisle, Sept. 3, 1628.)

a cohesive faction. Between Cranfield with his "pedlar's blood" and Bristol with his "traitor's blood," there was no community of interest and no bond of action except loyalty to the King, and the King allowed his policy to be swayed by his affections.

Certainly Buckingham's actions suggest little more than opportunism. As each crisis developed, he forestalled or frustrated his opponents with the methods most expedient at the time. If there was a principle governing his conduct, it dictated the absolute necessity of retaining the King's favor. In Spain he learned one lesson and learned it well: to lay hold of the royal bedpost and never to quit it.[82] Since his power depended so much on personal appeal, he seemed incapable of understanding an honest conflict of interests or principles, and his tendency was always to personalize a quarrel. Thus it frequently happened that a dispute continued long after the significant issues that had occasioned it became irrelevant. From his enemies Buckingham demanded either silent acquiescence or unconditional surrender which often entailed disgrace or removal from office. However effective these tactics may have been in quelling opposition on the ministerial level, they were scarcely suited to the implementation of a policy that required the full utilization of all political talents and the expression of all varieties of opinion and advice.

82. Halliwell, *Kings' Letters*, II, 225–226, Charles and Buckingham to James, Aug. 20, 1623.

# VIII Conclusion and Disillusion

Facing his critics in the Oxford Parliament of 1625, the Duke of Buckingham reviewed the change in European affairs since the session of 1624. The contrast, he asserted, was little less than miraculous: then "the K[ing] of Spaine went conquering on, & was sought to by all the world"; now the Valtelline was liberated, France and Spain were at war, Sweden and Denmark were engaged in the Protestant cause, and the German princes were revitalized. All of these beneficial effects were directly attributable to the counsels and resolutions which the Lords and Commons in 1624 had initiated at the Duke's behest. To complete the grand design, it was incumbent upon Parliament to make Charles the "chiefe of the warr" by outfitting a fleet to strike at the vitals of the Spanish imperial system and thereby reduce that kingdom to impotence.[1]

Unfortunately for the Duke, his auditors did not concur in his analysis of the European situation. They had reviewed the statement of accounts presented by their treasurers on June 30, 1625, and saw little cause for elation.[2] Their money had been squandered in support of fruitless continental adventures, and it was impossible for the members to believe that Buckingham's optimism was warranted. Now they were informed that they were engaged to finance a policy which they had supposedly initiated, but with which they alleged themselves to be totally unfamiliar.

1. Eliot, *Negotium Posterorum*, II, 61–71.
2. Harl. MS. 354, fols. 206–207, account of the Commons' treasurers of the subsidies to June 30, 1625; see also SP 16/521/83, a collection of all the warrants directed to be paid by the treasurers of the subsidy money, June 28, 1625.

It was not their doing that thirty thousand pounds a month were consigned to the King of Denmark and twenty thousand pounds per month to Mansfeldt's army. What they had wanted was a diversionary naval campaign against Spain; what they got was the endless prospect of subsidizing continental mercenaries to attempt the recovery of the Palatinate. When Buckingham played the devil's advocate and asked himself "Where is the enemy?" he was asking the question that had perplexed all parliamentarians since they had resolved to break with Spain. And when, in his master's name, he invited Parliament to designate the enemy, he was conceding a prerogative which the Parliament had hoped to seize in 1624.

Historians who adopt Gardiner's interpretation allege that, after 1622, James rapidly declined into senility and virtually lost control of the government. Under pressure from the Prince and Buckingham after they returned from Spain, he abjectly surrendered his prerogative by agreeing to summon a Parliament empowered to discuss foreign affairs — a Parliament which he knew full well would be hostile to Spain and vehemently opposed to his own pacific policy.[3] On the other hand, Hulme has maintained that James looked on Parliament as the last possible refuge of regal authority and that, unable to resist the concerted pressure of Charles, Buckingham, and their cohorts, he made a last desperate effort to save the peace by submitting the issue to Parliament.

In either event, the result was the same; James relinquished, by default, his control over foreign policy. "The king had indeed enlarged and amplified the Commons' privilege of freedom of speech. He now permitted them, nay urged them, to speak freely on all those vital subjects, foreign affairs, religion, and the prince's marriage, which he had declared in the last parliament to be under his prerogative and not even to be mentioned by the Commons. They were now free to speak on any subject. They had freedom of speech in practice. That is what they wanted. James had established such a powerful precedent, without realizing what he was doing, that the Commons could never again be stopped by the king from discussing any topic they pleased."[4]

These interpretations rely upon weaknesses inherent in the

3. Gardiner, *History of England*, V, 159.
4. Harold Hulme, "The Winning of Freedom of Speech by the House of Commons," *American Historical Review*, XLI (July, 1956), 825–853, esp. 851.

King's character, and insist upon the progressive deterioration of his authority after 1622. He is described as a broken, debauched, and repulsive old man, suspicious and fearful, perplexed and disillusioned, timorous and maudlin, drunken and profane, feeble in mind and body.[5] It is assumed that James had nothing to gain by assembling Parliament, but it is quite clear from the evidence that he was not of this opinion. Admittedly he disliked popular assemblies and their attacks upon his prerogative; admittedly he abhorred the idea of war with Spain as advocated by Buckingham and Charles; but even the "wisest fool in Christendom" was not fool enough to create an antimonarchical precedent implying parliamentary determination of foreign affairs without good cause.

James was persuaded that Parliament could be used as a weapon in diplomatic negotiations, and it was for this reason that questions of foreign policy were submitted to it. Unlike his son and favorite who wanted to engage Parliament to finance a war against Spain, James wished to use its aggressive designs to extort better conditions for the peaceful restitution of the Palatinate. And, if in the last resort negotiations proved impossible, he felt confident of his power to direct the war to the ultimate realization of his longtime ambition, the restoration of the Palatinate.

Never during the course of the Parliament did James meet the Spanish ambassadors without raising the German question. Even after he had discarded the idea of a Spanish match for his son, he continued to press for Spanish assistance to recover the Palatinate. Each graceful concession he made to Parliament was designed to put additional pressure on the Spanish envoys so that they would come to regard the King as the only bulwark against a declaration of war. It was unfortunate for James that he could not play this role convincingly. Most of the diplomatic corps analyzed his character correctly when they assumed that his peaceful and pro-Spanish attitudes could not be discarded overnight. And his dispatches to Spain reinforced this conviction at Madrid, so that it was possible to view with equanimity the military preparations in England and hope to neutralize them by dangling the lure of impending concessions.

5. D. H. Willson, *James VI and I* (New York: Henry Holt and Co., 1956), chap. xxii, passim. Compare this with C. H. Carter, *The Secret Diplomacy of the Habsburgs 1598–1625* (New York: Columbia University Press, 1964), chap. ix.

Once resolved to consult his people in Parliament, did James realize that he was creating a precedent for parliamentary determination of foreign policy? I think not. Discussion and determination were distinct and separate functions so far as the King was concerned; however much the members of the House of Commons wanted to combine the two, they were well aware that in so doing they were proceeding beyond constitutional precedent. Mere discussion of foreign affairs in Parliament was no significant departure from tradition; precedents dating from the Middle Ages convinced court and country alike that on occasion Parliament had dealt with such high prerogative issues as treaties and alliances, war and peace, marriage and succession.

In James's view the function of Parliament on prerogative matters was consultative, but parliament men wanted to make their advice mandatory. From the very moment that he opened the session of 1624 the King did not deviate from his convictions. In his initial address he asked for advice without committing himself and delegated to his son and favorite the task of informing Parliament about the matters to be considered. Thereafter, he qualified his acceptance of their resolutions to accord with his own understanding of the diplomatic necessities of the day. He accepted Parliament's advice to annul the two treaties, but he rejected every suggestion and coercive device designed to force a declaration of war against Spain. He insisted that the recovery of the Palatinate was the only justifiable reason for the commencement of hostilities, and, when the Commons refused his request to have this specifically included in the subsidy bill, he asserted his right to "alter it and set his marginal note upon it." [6]

Throughout the remainder of his reign James's actions were consistent with this attitude. Diplomatic relations with Spain were not severed; Aston remained at Madrid, and new Spanish envoys negotiated in England. Although English merchants were warned of possible peril in continuing to trade with Spain, commercial

---

6. SP 14/165/51, notes of what passed in Parliament on May 28 and 29, 1624. This separate which contains the King's speech on May 28 and the proceedings which concluded the Parliament on May 29 has been attributed to Edward Nicholas. Although his marginal notes appear on the manuscript, the text is not in his handwriting. Moreover, during the time that the committee attended the King on May 28, Nicholas was recording the debates in the House of Commons in his diary.

contacts were not ended and representations continued to be made against Spanish restrictions on English merchandise. Most of the subsidies granted by Parliament were devoted to the financing of Mansfeldt's ill-fated German expedition, and he was specifically enjoined from using his troops against the Spanish in the Low Countries. Elements of the Spanish fleet based at Dunkirk were protected from the depredations of the Dutch when they sought sanctuary in English waters. Recruitment for Lord Vaux's regiment, which was serving the Archduchess Isabella, was authorized at the same time as soldiers were being enlisted in the service of the United Provinces, and, indeed, those who sought volunteers for the Dutch were ordered not to mention the King of Spain or the Archduchess in their proclamations. The very alliance concluded with the United Provinces was manifestly defensive, and plans for a joint naval expedition against the Spanish treasure fleet were abandoned. The fitting out of the royal navy, which was conceived by parliamentarians to portend the implementation of their policy, was restricted to the equipment of six ships: two for Irish waters, two for the western seas, one for the Downs, and one to bring back from Spain the jewels which the luckless Lothario had bestowed upon his prospective bride. So careful was the King to avoid offense that the production of Thomas Middleton's anti-Spanish drama, *A Game of Chess,* was prohibited by royal command, and the players were haled before the Privy Council.[7]

But it must not be concluded that James's tenderness toward Spain was based on nothing more than a maudlin attachment to a vanished dream of a Pax Europa arranged through Anglo-Spanish cooperation. The recovery of the Palatinate had become his obsession, and he was aware that the difficulties involved in its restitution would be compounded if Spain became an active belliger-

7. SP 94/30, fols. 202–204, Sir Walter Aston to Secretary Conway, Apr. 25, 1624; Harl. MS. 1580, fols. 54–56, Sir Walter Aston to the Duke of Buckingham, Dec. 10, 1624, printed in *Cabala,* I, 165–168; SP 94/30, fols. 280–281, Secretary Conway to Sir Walter Aston, May 27, 1624; SP 14/167/28, 14/168/7, 14/169/14, and 14/171/49, Sir Francis Nethersole to Sir Dudley Carleton, June 7, June 19, July 3, and Aug. 14, 1624; SP 14/165/12, 14/167/26, 14/167/65, 14/168/48, Dudley Carleton to Sir Dudley Carleton, May 21, June 7, June 14, and June 26, 1624; SP 14/171/39, Secretary Conway to the Council, Aug. 12, 1624; Harl. MS. 6987, fols. 203–204, Charles to Buckingham, Jan. 24, 1625; *Cal. S. P. Venetian,* XVIII, 345–347, Corner to the Doge and Senate, June 8/18, 1624, *ibid.,* 364–366, Valaresso to the Doge and Senate, June 18/28, 1624.

ent. Unlike his Commons, who tended to identify Spanish and Hapsburg interests and divided Europe into Protestant and Catholic camps, James recognized that reason of state did not always coincide with religious persuasion. Consequently, he sent his ambassadors first to the Catholic powers — France, Savoy and Venice — to solicit their intervention on behalf of the Palsgrave by appealing to their political ambitions. Subsequent missions to Protestant princes were less critical for the achievement of his purpose; it could be assumed that the maintenance of their religion would supplement reason of state as a motive for their engagement in a war against the Emperor. Thus James's conciliatory attitude toward Spain reflected his desire to neutralize that power, isolate the imperial forces, and facilitate the restoration of the Palatinate.

Complete responsibility for the failure of this grand design cannot be attributed to James alone. Partially it was due to the reluctance of the Catholic powers to commit themselves unreservedly to the achievement of a goal alien to their own interests: the recovery of the Palatinate. More particularly, the failure was due to the diversion of England's main effort away from the Empire and toward Spain. This change in strategy must be attributed to Charles and Buckingham acting in conjunction with Parliament. Furthermore, even if the King's original plan had been retained, lack of financial support would have forced its abandonment. "The greatest aid which was ever granted in parliament to be levied in so short a time" only yielded £253,139 12 s. 2d. and 3 farthings.[8] By the spring of 1625, England was committed to annual military expenditures of £720,000, exclusive of naval disbursements. An expenditure of £360,000 subsidized the armies of Denmark, £240,000 were consigned to Mansfeldt, £96,000 were reserved for the Dutch, and £24,000 were appropriated for Ireland. It is inconceivable that the Commons, who had grudgingly granted three subsidies and three fifteenths, would have regarded such expenses as warranted by their general engagement to support a war.

The mere fact that Parliament's recommendations were nullified, amended, or reinterpreted does not invalidate the contention that a powerful precedent for free discussion of foreign affairs had been created. But a precedent in isolation is of little worth; it is

8. Harl. MS. 159, fol. 33, "The Resolution of the Houses to the King the 2 and 20th Day of March, 1623 [*sic*]"; Harl. MS. 354, fols. 206–207.

through continuous reinforcement that the exceptional becomes the rule.[9] The Parliaments of the decade between 1620 and 1630 were all intimately concerned with foreign affairs. Despite prohibitions, recommendations were made and resolutions were passed in the sessions of 1621. The cleavage between the royal foreign policy and that preferred by Parliament at this point was virtually complete. The King was resolved to negotiate for the Palatinate and was intent on securing a Spanish bride for his son. With this policy Charles and Buckingham were in complete agreement. When they went to Madrid in 1623 the German question was shunted aside because, as the Duke put it, they came "to woe and make love, and not to make warr." [10]

By the beginning of 1624 the worsening fortunes of the Pals-

9. By 1630, Charles was prepared to admit that "experience hath shown us that to beat the King of Spain until he bring the Emperor to reason is not the next way to gain our desires; besides, it is impossible for us alone to effectuate this great work, except our friends and allies join with us more heartily than hitherto they have done." (Gardiner, *History of England*, VII, 173.) Perhaps this explains why a Parliament was not summoned to ratify the unpopular Treaty of Madrid (November/December 1630) by which England secured little more than the reiteration of Spanish promises of "good offices" for the recovery of the Palatinate. However, the royal promise to consult Parliament before concluding peace was not forgotten, and in the "Grand Remonstrance" it was charged that the King had broken his word and deserted the Palatine cause. ("A Remonstrance of the State of the Kingdom, 15 December 1641," in *An Exact Collection of all Remonstrances . . . December 1641 . . . until March the 21, 1643* [London, 1643], 3–21.) In the Short Parliament Mr. Jones "Urged the 21st of King James, where a declaration was made of the intentions of the House to the King though no subsidy passed and wished the House to look thereunto," but Pym "Dissented from Mr. Jones in shewing a great difference between the present case and that in the 21st of King James for then, he said, the King declared the business to the House and desired their advice concerning the Palatinate. The House after consideration had delivered their opinions with a declaration to assist him with money for supply if he pleased to follow their advice, but now, he said, the King hath not pleased so far to impart his affairs to the House, or to demand any counsel from them." (Finch-Hatton MS. 50, p. 58, Northhamptonshire Record Office, an anonymous diary of the Short Parliament.) Prior to the commencement of the war with the Dutch in 1665, the Earl of Clarendon tried to dissuade James, Duke of York, from promoting hostilities by reminding him that "he was old enough to remember when a parliament did advise, and upon the matter compel, his grandfather king James to enter into a war with Spain, upon promise of ample supplies; and yet when he was engaged in it, they gave him no more supplies; so that at last the crown was compelled to accept of a peace not very honourable." (Edward Hyde, *The Life of Edward Earl of Clarendon, Lord High Chancellor of England, and Chancellor of the University of Oxford* . . . (3 vols., Oxford, 1827), II, 241–242. In financing the Dutch war, Parliament revived the principles of specific appropriation and accountability that had been initiated in the subsidy bill of 1624. See Caroline Robbins, ed., *The Diary of John Milward, Esq. Member of Parliament for Derbyshire, September, 1666 to May, 1668* (Cambridge: Cambridge University Press, 1938), passim.

10. "Bristol's Defense," 41.

grave and the disenchantment of the Prince and the Duke with the Spanish match had brought the divergent policies of the King and Parliament into closer relation. Three years of fruitless negotiations on the German problem had induced the King to take a firmer stand and to consider the possibility of treating with arms in hand. The defection of the Prince and Buckingham to the anti-Spanish camp acted as a catalyst in this development. Foreign policy could now be discussed by royal permission, but as yet there was no identity between the aims of King and Parliament. Agreement was possible on the means to be employed, but where, how, and against whom were subjects of dispute.

In the first Parliament of Charles I these difficulties were resolved; the King and his people agreed on the enemy and the methods by which he should be attacked. When England became an active belligerent against Spain instead of paymaster for levies under foreign command, it was no longer possible to prohibit discussion of foreign affairs. Fundamental policy differences were submerged in debate concerned primarily with the prosecution of a war which all parties supported in principle. Constitutional issues between the King and Parliament, therefore, were focused on the right of the monarch to compel his subjects to fulfill the general financial obligations which they had solemnly undertaken in 1624.

It is obvious that Charles and Buckingham believed that discussion of foreign policy bound Parliament to support the course it had advocated. This implied that the two Houses, at the King's request, could initiate policy changes which the crown would put into practice. Undoubtedly many in the Parliament of 1624 wanted the initiative to reside with the Commons. Consistently throughout the session they pressed James to implement their decisions. At the outset they interpreted the King's request for advice as carte blanche to determine future policy. If the King was suspicious that his Commons would engage him in a war and then leave him "Naked to his enemies," the Commons were equally suspicious that James would accept their subsidy grants and refuse to follow their directives. They found it difficult to overcome the constitutional tradition that war and peace were the King's undoubted prerogative. Collectively, they proceeded as far as they had warrant in advising the dissolution of the treaties, and their continual references to the "war likely to ensue" made it abundantly clear that they wanted war with Spain. Individually, on the floor of the Commons, they went beyond constitutional precedent and a powerful movement developed in support of a declaration of war indicating a specific enemy and a definite theater of operations.

The conservatism of the majority, the persuasiveness of the privy councillors, and, most of all, the difficulties inherent in the policy prevented the implementation of the radical program. But the drafting of a declaration which the King would proclaim and the enactment of the breach of the treaties in the subsidy bill revealed the strength of the movement. In fact, extremist tendencies were more apparent in the subsidy bill than in any resolution of advice tendered by Parliament to the King in 1624. Not only was the breach of the treaties certified in a public instrument, but a greater threat to the royal prerogative lurked in the legalistic sections of the act.

Potentially James had made dangerous concessions when he outlined the purposes for which money was required and allowed the Commons to name the treasurers of the subsidies. The implications of specific appropriation and accountability to the lower House were eagerly seized upon by those who distrusted royal intentions and subsequently incorporated into the revenue act. Although war with Spain was not mentioned, neither was the recovery of the Palatinate; hence, the King asserted his right to amend the bill after passage. Moreover, it required an opinion of the judges to satisfy the Council of War concerning their powers of disbursement under the terms of the act.

Had the Commons in future Parliaments continued to insist upon this financial procedure, it would have hastened the advent of parliamentary sovereignty. It was fortunate for the crown that the difficulties of arranging for parliamentary disbursement of money were so acute. Instead of constructing a financial institution dependent upon itself, future Parliaments preferred to establish the general principle that all revenue must be warranted by legislative grant and leave receipt, expenditure, and account in the hands of the King. Thus it was not until the revolutionary years that Parliament, under the pressure of necessity, again concerned itself with financial administration.

The King's control over his officers was also threatened by the subsidy bill. Although the personnel he had nominated and the procedures he had commanded were not altered by parliamentary action, some significant additions were made. The accountability of councillors of war was, in the first instance, to the House of Commons, and, if occasion warranted, Lords would be referred to the upper House for trial. Even this slight infringement of their privileges was sufficient to cause the peers to register a protest, but nothing was mentioned about the threat to the royal prerogative. Moreover, the very fact that the names of the councillors were incorporated into the subsidy bill implied that they could not be removed or increased without parliamentary approval. Had this principle been insisted upon, King and Parliament would have been irreconcilably opposed.

In both of these instances (financial and appointive) a precedent had been established, but its value was nullified by desuetude. The opportunity to acquire still another prerogative was ignored by Parliament when the royal concession promising consultation before the conclusion of a treaty of peace was not exploited. Perhaps Charles did not consider himself bound by the promise of his father; perhaps a general desire for peace silenced all protests; perhaps the fact that Parliament was not in session influenced the decision. In any event, performance of the vow was not insisted upon and, consequently, the opportunity to enlarge Parliament's sphere of policy control was lost.

In view of the mutual distrust between the King and his Commons which persisted throughout the Parliament of 1624, it is surprising that it did not end in dissolution. Certainly one of the reasons for the successful completion of the session was the universal fear of a breach that induced both the King and the members to practice forbearance, conciliation, and compromise. If James desired "to be in love with parliaments," his people desired no less to have good laws enacted and grievances redressed. But, if one factor was fundamentally responsible for the completion of the "Happy Parliament," it was the political activity of the Prince and Buckingham. The solidity of their partnership was such that it was difficult for contemporaries to assign primacy to either of them. They played complementary roles in attempting to achieve the adoption of a policy which, in their estimation, would be beneficial to English interests and, incidentally, redemptive of their honor. In the final analysis, their desires for vengeance were temporarily thwarted by the King's insistence upon regarding the recovery of the Palatinate as the primary objective, but this was probably less abhorrent to them than to the Puritan patriots in the House of Commons who would be contented with nothing less than war with Spain.

Lack of management has been frequently cited as a cause for the failure of many Jacobean Parliaments, but certainly it was not wanting in 1624. From the outset, the members were predisposed to follow the lead of the Prince and the Duke — not only because they agreed with their policy, but because they realized how much the issuance of the writs of summons had been resisted by the King and his Hispanophile councillors. Princely and ducal condescension confirmed the paramount position of Charles and Buckingham even before the opening of Parliament; popular peers were courted, consultations held, and old rivalries salved. Patronage perquisites were exploited to the fullest extent, and leaders of the House of Commons were converted into willing allies by favors or flattery. The Speaker was carefully chosen, and even the King's councillors seemed disposed to serve the alliance of the Prince and the favorite.

Once the session had commenced, the managerial ability of Charles and Buckingham was put to the test. All possible deference was paid to the wishes of Parliament, and both became the willing servants of the Houses. They were assiduous in attendance and extremely sensitive to disruptive influences. They were willing to forgo their own desires when Parliament seemed unresponsive or antagonistic, as had happened with the plan to borrow against future subsidies. They gratified the Commons by procuring royal concessions such as the promise of additional sessions at Michaelmas and in the following spring. Through persuasion and pressure they secured authorization to reinterpret royal pronouncements and mitigate the King's demands. The Prince even promised no future remission of penalties against Catholics as the result of a French marriage and gave evidence of his sincerity by expediting the petition against recusants. The prosecution of "corrupt ministers" was encouraged, and the passage of good laws was facilitated. And, finally, a week's extension to the term of the session was obtained through the Prince's mediation.

So completely were the Prince and Buckingham immersed in parliamentary business that the King complained bitterly of their popularity and their willingness to sacrifice the royal prerogative, particularly in matters of revenue. He also castigated his secretaries for their failure to keep him informed about the disposition of the lower House, and he was told by Calvert that "all things have gone so fairly and well as I saw no cause for my part to advertise anything hitherto." [11]

It cannot be said that Parliament was not managed, but, rather, that the guidance of its affairs was taken out of the hands of the privy councillors in the House of Commons and vested in the Prince, the Duke, and their confidants. True, councillors in the Commons did play their role; Heath, particularly, as a royal official, did yeoman service in connection with the subsidy bill and the petition on religion. Conway, too, had brief moments of glory in allaying the jealousies of the House, but it is noteworthy that unpopular duties were also consigned to individual privy councillors. Thus the strictures placed upon hearing petitions against the Lord Keeper, and the denial of permission to deal with disputes in the Virginia Company redounded to the detriment of the King and his councillors, but not to Buckingham and the Prince.

Not all services rendered by Charles and Buckingham were intended to gratify Parliament. It was the essence of their diplomacy that they were able to placate the King and convince him that they were furthering his interests. Thus Buckingham's continual requests for relief of the King's necessities were made in response to royal promptings, and he did not hesitate to promise, on behalf of Parliament, that the next session would replenish the King's coffers. Charles, too, did his bit in mitigating the severity of the Commons' petition against papists and in meeting their challenge to the King's right to levy impositions upon wines. Incidents which could have led to a dissolution were thereby minimized.

On only two occasions was there real danger that Parliament would be dissolved. Had the King insisted upon his original demands (five subsidies and ten fifteenths for the war and one subsidy and two fifteenths annually for payment of his debts) before annulling the treaties, it is probable that Parliament would have

11. SP 14/165/4, Secretary Conway to Secretary Calvert and Chancellor of the Exchequer Weston, May 20, 1624; SP 14/165/11, Secretary Calvert to Secretary Conway, May 21, 1624.

revolted. The persuasiveness of the Prince and Duke averted that contingency. A dissolution may also have been meditated by James as a means of saving Cranfield. In this case, due to the implication of Charles and Buckingham in the prosecution, there was no place for explanations or compromise, but circumstances favored the continuance of Parliament. By the time Cranfield's trial was under way, the primary objective of the Parliament had been accomplished: the breach of the treaties. However, the subsidy bill had not yet been passed. In view of the diplomatic situation a dissolution in early May would have been strategically unwise, and, when considered in conjunction with the domestic public reaction, it would have been asinine.

Perhaps Buckingham was the chief beneficiary of parliamentary popularity, even though the session was sometimes called the "Prince's Parliament." True, Charles reaped a harvest of applause that continued until after his accession to the throne, but he earned it by encouraging the diminution of the royal prerogative. Throughout his reign, the precedents which he had helped to create came back to haunt him and to give him, as James had predicted, his "belly full of parliaments." Buckingham, too, helped forge the weapon designed to pierce him, but he was saved by the fidelity of his master at considerable cost to royal dignity. In short-term gains, however, the Duke profited by his alliance with the Parliament of 1624. Not only was he lionized as the savior of the nation, but his reputation was vindicated by votes of the Lords and Commons when he was attacked by the Spanish ambassadors. For a brief period he enjoyed a double security as a favorite of both King and nation. Padre Maestro's accusation of collusion between Buckingham and Parliament redounded to the discredit of its author and prevented the consolidation of effective opposition to an anti-Spanish policy. Indeed, Parliament willingly cooperated in the destruction of the Duke's enemies and consequently afforded him a golden opportunity to increase his patronage empire through the distribution of vacated offices.

Cost as well as gain was involved in the achievement of a successful Parliament, and the King paid most heavily of all. Prior to the annulment of the treaties with Spain, virtually the only concession demanded by the House of Commons was the right to devote all subsidy grants to military purposes. Until the Easter recess a "happy" Parliament was in prospect if the King merely dissolved the treaties and claimed no relief for his necessities. Thereafter the costs mounted rapidly; the subsidy bill proceeded at a snail's pace, while demands for redress of grievances, limitations on patents, investigations of crown officers, action against recusants, interference in church government, a liberal general pardon, and the passage of good laws followed each other with lightning rapidity.

By the end of the session the King felt compelled to remind his Commons of the cause of their summons and to tell them bluntly, "Kings do not use to call their people to rob them . . . It hath been common for courtiers to be begging and getting from their King; but it is a popular humor which I shall loath to see in the Commons to be too forward in taking from me to ease the people." The refusal of the House to enter this speech upon the record or to allow the circulation of copies must have confirmed the King in his conviction that he was being exploited. No part of his authority, no type of revenue seemed above question, and, as he complained half seriously, half facetiously, "if I should make a patent to say the Lord's prayer you will call it in." [12]

But the Commons also paid in their way. With considerable murmuring they obeyed the King's commands to forbear investigation of the Virginia Company, even though they were convinced that it created a precedent for royal revocation of any cause. They agreed not to proceed against the Lord Keeper except for manifest corruption. They ameliorated their charges against Cranfield in response to the King's letters. They soft-pedaled categorical assertions of the illegality of impositions. They accepted the attenuation of their declarations on the treaties and their petition on religion in order to "spare" the King's conscience and honor. They witnessed the veto of several of their most cherished bills on what they considered to be unjustified pretexts. Most importantly, they smothered the issue of parliamentary privilege, even to the point

12. SP 14/165/51. In 1628, Laud noted: "the last parliament of King James they gave 3 subsidies, and had that from the King that was worth 6 if not 10 to be bought and sold." (SP 16/94/89, "Considerations whether a parliament or not, 1627 by Lord Canterbury.") Peter Heylin cites Justice Dodderidge's authority for the statement "That his Majesty had bought those Fifteenths and Subsidies at ten years purchase." (Peter Heylin, *Cyprianus Anglicus or the History of the Life and Death . . . of William Laud* [London, 1671], 114.)

of interrupting speakers and burying in committee a bill designed to define the legal privileges of Parliament. Thus they preferred de facto exercise of the right to free speech to de jure recognition of it, believing that debate and determination were synonymous words.

The unanimity of the House of Commons in 1624 was strikingly apparent on issues of national importance. Dissent during the foreign policy debates was virtually nonexistent. It is interesting, however, to note that the French match was not subjected to the searching criticism reserved for the Spanish marriage although identical objections could have been offered regarding concessions to Catholics. Certainly the tests applied to the members — the oaths of supremacy and allegiance and the reception of communion according to the Anglican rite — contributed to the homogeneity of opinion on any issue involving religious convictions.

Patronage was practiced on a wide scale, but it had little discernible significance in reference to the treaty debates in the House of Commons. Action on the floor was far more consequential. Scarcely more than 10 percent of the members were mentioned by contemporary diarists as having voiced their opinions on any issue. The most striking distinction apparent in the House was between speakers and listeners. The nomination of one persuasive orator, therefore, was potentially of more significance than the seating of ten silent placemen. As a result of their forensic training, their skill in drafting legislation, and their acquaintance with past precedent, lawyers were the natural leaders of the House, despite the numerical majority enjoyed by country gentlemen. Inasmuch as legal fortunes tended to migrate to country estates, even the distinction between professional and landed interests was blurred. Perhaps the ideal parliamentary "type" in 1624 was the Speaker of the Commons, Sir Thomas Crew, an accomplished lawyer who was Puritanically inclined and established among the gentry of Buckinghamshire.

It was to men like Crew, Coke, Selden, Pym, Hakewill and Alford and to their confreres among the gentry, Phelips, Digges, Sandys, Cotton, and Eliot, that the Commons entrusted the consolidation of their gains and the defense of their liberties. But on May 29, 1624, the conflict with the prerogative was still very much in doubt, and a perceptive contemporary analyzed the situation in a pessimistic commentary on the proceedings that ended the session. He regarded the King's decision to "set his marginal note" upon the preamble of the subsidy bill as an ominous portent of the tyranny to come: "For by this conclusion we apparently found that the King was bent to run the ends of his own will, both for matter of government by proclamation, patent and commission; that for matter of religion he was resolved to abet his clergy against the laity and . . . would by degrees alter the face of the church government under color of protecting them from supposed Puritans . . . That he would keep some things to be passed at [the next session], as if he would draw us to buy our bills and good laws for money from him; and lastly we found ourselves in high terms concluded by the King to meddle with nothing that did concern any servant, officer or business belonging to him or the meddling with any offense of the clergy as not belonging to us, but out of our power and jurisdiction of our House." [13]

Disillusionment and disappointment were rendered doubly bitter by contrast with the "bright promise" of what might have been: "And thus with menacing we parted from his presence and concluded this (*happy*) parliament wherein the King had so much protested . . . what he would do, both for religion, government of the commonwealth, recovery of the Palatinate, assisting his friends and allies, revenging the wrongs and indignities put upon him and the Kingdom, and the rectifying of all abuses both in church and commonwealth, *which he referred solely and wholly to both Houses to consider and determine of, and unto which he (for redress) would apply himself as an helper unto us.*" [14]

13. SP 14/165/51; see also Strafford, *Letters*, 21–23, Sir Thomas Wentworth to Christopher Wandesford, June 17, 1624.

14. SP 14/165/51. (Italics mine.) For a vivacious and somewhat facetious appraisal of the effects of Charles's and Buckingham's foreign policy on the west of England, see Strafford, *Letters*, I, 40–41, Denzil Holles to Sir Thomas Wentworth, Aug. 9, 1627.

Appendixes and Index

# Appendix A: Full Citations for Abbreviated References

| | |
|---|---|
| *Add. MSS* | Additional Manuscripts, British Museum. |
| *JHC* | Acts of the Privy Council of England. |
| *Bacon, Works* | Bacon, Francis. The Works of Francis Bacon, Baron of Verulam, Viscount St. Alban, Lord High Chancellor of England, James Spedding, R. L. Ellis, and D. D. Heath, eds. 14 vols. London, 1857. |
| *Birch, Court and Times of Charles the First* | Birch, Thomas. The Court and Times of Charles the First. Illustrated by Authentic and Confidential Letters from Various Public and Private Collections, 2 vols. London, 1848. |
| *Birch, Court and Times of James the First* | Birch, Thomas. The Court and Times of James the First. Illustrated by Authentic and Confidential Letters from Various Public and Private Collections, 2 vols. London, 1848. |
| *Braye MS. 73* | Third session of Commons Journal. See Appendix B under Wright, John. |
| *"Bristol's Defense"* | Digby, John, earl of Bristol. "The Earl of Bristol's Defense of his Negotiations in Spain," S. R. Gardiner, ed. In The Camden Miscellany Volume VI, Camden Society, Volume CIV. London, 1870. |
| *Cabala* | Cabala Sive Scrinia Sacra, Mysteries of State and Government in Letters of Illustrious Persons. London, 1654. |
| *Cal. S. P. Dom.* | Calendar of State Papers Domestic Series. |
| *Cal. S. P. Venetian* | Calendar of State Papers and Manuscripts, Relating to English Affairs, Existing in the Archives and Collections of Venice and in the Other Libraries of Northern Italy. |
| *Chamberlain, Letters* | Chamberlain, John. The Letters of John Chamberlain, N. E. McClure ed. 2 vols. Philadelphia: The American Philosophical Society, 1939. |
| *CJ* | Journals of the House of Commons. |
| *Cobbett, Parliamentary History* | Cobbett, William. The Parliamentary History of England, from the Earliest Period to the Year 1803. London, 1806–20. |

# Appendix A    Full Citations for
# Abbreviated References

| | |
|---|---|
| Add. MSS | Additional Manuscripts, British Museum, London. |
| *APC* | *Acts of the Privy Council of England.* |
| Bacon, *Works* | Bacon, Francis. *The Works of Francis Bacon, Baron of Verulam, Viscount St. Alban, Lord High Chancellor of England.* James Spedding, R. L. Ellis, and D. D. Heath, eds. 14 vols., London, 1874. |
| Birch, *Court and Times of Charles the First* | Birch, Thomas. *The Court and Times of Charles the First: Illustrated by Authentic and Confidential Letters from Various Public and Private Collections,* 2 vols., London, 1848. |
| Birch, *Court and Times of James the First* | Birch, Thomas. *The Court and Times of James the First: Illustrated by Authentic and Confidential Letters from Various Public and Private Collections,* 2 vols., London, 1848. |
| Braye MS. 73 | Third version of *Commons Journal.* See Appendix B under Wright, John. |
| "Bristol's Defense" | Digby, John, earl of Bristol. "The Earl of Bristol's Defense of his Negotiations in Spain." S. R. Gardiner, ed. In *The Camden Miscellany,* Volume VI, Camden Society, Volume CIV. London, 1870. |
| *Cabala* | *Cabala Sive Scrinia Sacra: Mysteries of State and Government in Letters of Illustrious Persons.* London, 1654. |
| Cal. S. P. Dom. | *Calendar of State Papers: Domestic Series.* |
| Cal. S. P. Venetian | *Calendar of State Papers and Manuscripts, Relating to English Affairs, Existing in the Archives and Collections of Venice and in the Other Libraries of Northern Italy.* |
| Chamberlain, *Letters* | Chamberlain, John. *The Letters of John Chamberlain.* N. E. McClure, ed. 2 vols., Philadelphia: The American Philosophical Society, 1939. |
| *CJ* | *Journals of the House of Commons.* |
| Cobbett, *Parliamentary History* | Cobbett, William. *The Parliamentary History of England, from the Earliest Period to the Year 1803.* 36 vols., London, 1806–20. |

| | |
|---|---|
| *Commons Debates 1621* | Notestein, W.; Relf, F. H.; and Simpson, H., eds. *Commons Debates 1621*. 7 vols., New Haven: Yale University Press, 1935. |
| *Cottoni Posthuma* | Cotton, Sir Robert. *Cottoni Posthuma: Divers Choice Pieces of that Renowned Antquary Sir Robert Cotton, Knight and Baronet, Preserved from the Injury of Time and Exposed to Public Light, for the Benefit of Posterity*. London, 1651. |
| D'Ewes | Harleian MS. 159. See Appendix B under D'Ewes, Si: Simonds. |
| *DNB* | *The Dictionary of National Biography Founded in 1882 by George Smith*. Sir Leslie Stephen and Sir Sidney Lee, eds. Oxford: Oxford University Press, 1921–1922. |
| Dyott | Staffordshire County Record Office MS. D 661/11/1/2. See Appendix B under Dyott, Richard. |
| Earle | Additional MS. 18,597. See Appendix B under Earle, Sir Walter. |
| Eliot, *Negotium Posterorum* | Eliot, Sir John. *An Apology for Socrates and Negotium Posterorum: By Sir John Eliot*. Rev. A. B. Grosart, ed. 2 vols., London, 1881. |
| Gardiner, *History of England* | Gardiner, S. R. *History of England from the Accession of James I to the Outbreak of the Civil War 1603–1642*. 10 vols., London, 1886. |
| Glanville, *Reports* | Glanville, John. *Reports of Certain Cases, Determined and Adjudged by the Commons in Parliament, in the Twenty-first and Twenty-second Years of the Reign of King James the First*. London, 1775. |
| Goodman, *Court of James I* | Goodman, Godfrey (Dr.), bishop of Gloucester. *The Court of King James the First*. 2 vols., London, 1839. |
| Hacket, *Scrinia Reserata* | Hacket, John. *Scrinia Reserata: A Memorial Offered to the Great Deservings of John Williams, D. D. Who Some Time Held the Places of L$^d$ Keeper of the Great Seal of England, L$^d$ Bishop of Lincoln, and L$^d$ Archbishop of York*. London, 1692. |
| Halliwell, *Kings' Letters* | Halliwell, J. O. *Letters of the Kings of England, Now First Collected from Royal Archives, and Other Authentic Sources, Private as well as Public*. 2 vols., London, 1848. |
| *Hardwicke State Papers* | York, Philip, earl of Hardwicke. *Miscellaneous State Papers from 1501 to 1726*, 2 vols., London, 1778. |
| Harl. MSS | Harleian Manuscripts, British Museum, London. |
| Hawarde | Wiltshire County Record Office, unnumbered manuscript. See Appendix B under Hawarde, John. |
| HMC *Mar and Kellie* | Historical Manuscripts Commission. *Supplementary Report on the Manuscripts of the Earl of Mar and Kellie Preserved at Alloa House, Clacmannanshire*. Henry Paton, ed. London: H.M. Stationery Office, 1930. |
| Holland | I. Tanner MS. 392; II. Rawlinson MS. D 1100. See Appendix B under Holland, Sir Thomas. |
| Holles | Harl. MS. 6383. See Appendix B under Holles, John. |

| | |
|---|---|
| Horne | Rawlinson MS. B 151. See Appendix B under Horne, Robert. |
| Howell, *State Trials* | Howell, T. B., Esq. *A Complete Collection of State Trials and Proceedings for High Treason and Other Crimes and Misdemeanors.* 21 vols., London, 1816. |
| Jervoise | Jervoise family manuscript. See Appendix B under Jervoise, Sir Thomas. |
| Keeler, *Long Parliament* | Keeler, M. F. *The Long Parliament, 1640–1641: A Biographical Study of Its Members.* Philadelphia: American Philosophical Society, 1954. |
| Kennett, *Complete History of England* | Kennett, White. *A Complete History of England: With the Lives of All the Kings and Queens Thereof.* 3 vols., London, 1706. |
| *LJ* | *Journals of the House of Lords Beginning Anno Primo Henrici Octavi.* |
| *Lords Debates 1624 & 1626* | *Notes of the Debates in the House of Lords, Officially Taken by Henry Elsing, Clerk of the Parliaments, A.D. 1624 and 1626.* S. R. Gardiner, ed. Camden Society, New Series, Volume XXIV, London, 1879. |
| Nicholas | SP 14/166. See Appendix B under Nicholas, Edward. |
| *Official Return* | *Return of the Names of Every Member of the Lower House of Parliament of England, Scotland and Ireland, with Name of Constituency Represented, and Date of Return from 1213–1874.* Parliamentary Papers, Volume LXII, Part I, Session 1878. |
| *OPH* | *The Parliamentary or Constitutional History of England: Being a Faithful Account of All the Most Remarkable Transactions in Parliament, from the Earliest Times, to the Restoration of King Charles II . . . .* 24 vols., 2d ed., London, 1761–1763. |
| Pym | Finch-Hatton 50. See Appendix B under Pym, John. |
| PRO | Public Record Office, London. |
| Rich | Add. MS. 46,191 and PRO, 30/15/Box I, Part II, 168. See Appendix B under Rich, Sir Nathaniel. |
| Rusdorff, *Mémoires* | Rusdorff, John. *Mémoires et Négociations Secrètes de M$^r$. de Rusdorff.* 2 vols., Leipzig, 1789. |
| Rushworth, *Historical Collections* | Rushworth, John. *Historical Collections of Private Passages of State, Weighty Matters in Law, Remarkable Proceedings in Five Parliaments.* London, 1659. |
| Rymer, *Foedera* | Rymer, Thomas, and Sanderson, Robert, eds. *Foedera, Conventiones, Litterae, et cujuscunque generis acta publica inter reges Angliae et alios quosvis imperatores, reges, pontifices, principes, vel communitates* (Volumes I–XV edited by Thomas Rymer and Volumes XVI–XX, by Robert Sanderson), 20 vols., 2d ed., London, 1727–1729; 3d ed., The Hague, 1739–1740. |
| SP 14 | State Papers Domestic, James I. PRO. |
| SP 15 | State Papers Domestic, Elizabeth and James I, Addenda: 1580–1625. PRO. |
| SP 16 | State Papers Domestic, Charles I. PRO. |

| | |
|---|---|
| *Spanish Marriage Treaty* | Gardiner, S. R., ed. and trans. *El hecho de los tratados del matrimonio pretendido por el principe de Gales con la serenissima infante de España Maria, tomado desde sus principios para maior demonstración de la verdad, y ajustado con los papeles originales desde consta por el maestro F. Francisco de Jesus, predicador del rey nuestro señor.* Camden Society, Volume CI. London, 1869. |
| Spring | Harvard English MS. 980. See Appendix B under Spring, Sir William. |
| *Statutes of the Realm* | Luders, A., *et al.*, eds., *Statutes of the Realm.* 11 vols., London, 1810–1828. |
| Strafford, *Letters* | Wentworth, Sir Thomas. *The Earl of Strafforde's Letters and Dispatches.* William Knowler, ed. 2 vols., London, 1739. |
| Tanner, *Constitutional Documents James I* | Tanner, J. R., ed. *Constitutional Documents of the Reign of James I A.D. 1603–1625 with an Historical Commentary.* Cambridge: Cambridge University Press, 1930. |
| Tawney, *Cranfield* | Tawney, R. H. *Business and Politics under James I: Lionel Cranfield as Merchant and Minister.* Cambridge: Cambridge University Press, 1958. |
| Whitelocke, *Liber Famelicus* | Whitelocke, Sir James. *Liber Famelicus of Sir James Whitelocke, a Judge of the Court of King's Bench in the Reigns of James I and Charles I.* John Bruce, ed., Camden Society, Volume LXX. London, 1858. |
| *Walter Yonge's Diary* | Yonge, Walter, *Diary of Walter Yonge, Esq., Justice of the Peace, and M. P. for Honiton, Written at Colyton and Axminster, Co. Devon, From 1604 to 1628.* George Roberts, ed. Camden Society, Volume XLI. London, 1848. |

# Appendix B  Parliamentary Diaries: 1624

D'Ewes, Sir Simonds. Diary of proceedings in the House of Commons, February 12 to May 29, 1624 (compiled from the manuscript Journals of the House of Commons and from unidentified private diaries and separates), British Museum, Harleian MS. 159, fols. 59–136v.

Dyott, Richard, M.P. for Stafford, Staffordshire. Diary of proceedings in the House of Commons, March 5 to March 15 and April 20 to May 29, 1624, Staffordshire County Record Office, MS. D 661/11/1/2 (deposited by the Dyott family).

Earle, Sir Walter, M.P. for Poole, Dorset. Diary of proceedings in the House of Commons, February 19 to May 29, 1624, British Museum, Add. MS. 18,597.

Hawarde, John, M.P. for Bletchingly, Surrey. Diary of proceedings in the House of Commons, February 12 to May 29, 1624. Wiltshire County Record Office, unnumbered manuscript (deposited by the Marquess of Ailesbury), pp. 143–307.

Holland, Sir Thomas, M.P. for Norfolk County. Diary of proceedings in the House of Commons, February 25 to April 9, 1624, Bodleian Library, Tanner MS. 392; diary of proceedings in the House of Commons, April 10 to May 15, 1624; Bodleian Library, Rawlinson MS. D 1100.

Holles, John, M.P. for East Retford, Nottinghamshire. Diary of proceedings in the House of Commons, February 23 to May 19, 1624, British Museum, Harleian MS. 6383, fols. 80v–141.

Horne, Robert. Synopsis of proceedings in the House of Commons, February 19 to May 29, 1624 (compiled from separates and newsletters), Bodleian Library, Rawlinson MS. B 151, fols. 58–70 and 103v.

Jervoise, Sir Thomas, M.P. for Whitchurch, Hampshire. Diary of proceedings in the House of Commons, February 23 to April 28, 1624, Jervoise family manuscript, Herriard Park, Hampshire.

Nethersole, Sir Francis, M.P. for Corfe Castle, Dorset. Parliamentary newsletters to Sir Dudley Carleton, PRO, SP 81/30 (German); SP 14/161, 162, 163, 164, 165, 167 passim.

Nicholas, Edward, M.P. for Winchelsea, Cinque Ports. Diary of proceedings in the House of Commons, February 19 to May 29, 1624, PRO, SP 14/166.

Pym, John, M.P. for Tavistock, Devon. Diary of proceedings in the House of Commons, February 19 to May 7, 1624, Northamptonshire Record Office,

Finch-Hatton MS. 50 (deposited by the Earl of Winchilsea, sometimes cited as the Winchilsea diary); diary of procedings in the House of Commons, April 13 to May 10, 1624 (another version of the Pym diary, somewhat abridged), British Museum, Add. MS. 26,639, fols. 1–37v; fragment of the Pym diary, February 23 to February 26, 1624, Brtish Museum, Harleian MS. 6799, fols. 131–133.

Rich, Sir Nathaniel, M.P. for Harwich, Essex. Diary of proceedings in the House of Commons, February 23 to March 6, 1624, British Museum, Add. MS. 46,191 (formerly in the library of Robert Devereux, third earl of Essex); proceedings in the House of Commons (Committee on Religion), April 2, 1624, PRO, 30/15/Box I/Part II, 168 (Manchester MSS).

Spring, Sir William, M.P. for Suffolk County. Diary of proceedings in the House of Commons, February 19 to May 27, 1624, Harvard University, Houghton Library, MS. English 980 (formerly in the possession of the Gurney family, Keswick Hall, Norfolk, and frequently cited as the Gurney fragment).

Wright, John, Clerk of the House of Commons. Third version of the Commons Journal, February 12 to February 25, 1624, House of Lords Record Office, Braye MS. 73 (sometimes referred to as the Braye diary or the Stanford manuscript, formerly in the possession of Lord Braye of Stanford Hall); proceedings in the Committee of Grievances, May 21 and May 24, 1624, House of Lords Record Office, Commons journal MS., first version, vol. II, fols. 49–50v.

Anonymous. Diary of proceedings in the House of Commons, February 19 to February 24, 1624, Bodleian Library, Rawlinson MS. D 723, fols. 84–90v.

The nomenclature of some of the 1624 parliamentary diaries has varied considerably since they became available for study by scholars several decades ago. It is in the interest of resolving any doubts about the sources of my citations and to suggest a uniform method of reference that this list has been compiled.

The identification of John Wright as the author of the Braye diary or Stanford manuscript was made by Maurice Bond, Clerk of the Records in the House of Lords (Record Office Memorandum No. 24, Item 15). The Dyott diary was found by the late Major R. A. Dyott at his residence, Freeford Manor, and was deposited in the Stafford County Record Office after World War II. The identification of the Rich diary and fragment for 1624 is my responsibility, as is the attribution of the Wiltshire manuscript to John Hawarde. Concurrently the late Professor Hartley Simpson and I independently ascribed the so-called Gurney fragment (Harvard MS. English 980) to Sir William Spring.

In the cases of doubtful authorship, wherever possible, I have made my ascriptions on the basis of internal evidence, handwriting comparisons, and the analysis of shorthand systems.

# Appendix C

Alphabetical List of the Members Returned to the House of Commons from the Issuance of the Writs, December 28, 1623, to the Dissolution of the Parliament, March 27, 1625.*

| | |
|---|---|
| Abbot, Maurice, Esq. | Kingston-on-Hull, Yorkshire |
| Aglionby, Edward, Esq. | Carlisle, Cumberland |
| Alford, Edward, Esq. | Colchester, Essex |
| Anderson, Henry, Kt. | Newcastle-on-Tyne, Northumberland |
| Angell, John, Esq. | Rye, Sussex |
| Armine, William, Kt. & Bart. | Boston, Lincolnshire (vice Clement Cotterell, Kt.; returned March 8, 1624) |
| Arundel, John, Esq. | St. Mawes, Cornwall |
| Ashton, William, Esq. | Hertford, Hertfordshire (borough restored May 4; returned May 17, 1624) |
| Ayscough, Edward, Esq. | Stamford, Lincolnshire |
| Bagg, James, Esq. | West Looe, Cornwall |
| Bancroft, Thomas, Esq. | Castle Rising, Norfolk |
| Bankes, John, Esq. | Wootton Bassett, Wiltshire |
| Barker, John, Alderman | Bristol, Gloucestershire |
| Barnham, Francis, Kt. | Maidstone, Kent |
| Barrington, Francis, Kt. & Bart. | Essex |
| Barrington, Thomas, Kt. | Newtown, Hampshire (vice Gilbert Gerard, Bart.; returned March 22, 1624) |
| Bateman, Robert, Skinner | London |
| Baynton, Edward, Kt. | Devizes, Wiltshire |
| Beaumont, Richard, Kt. | Pontefract, Yorkshire (vice Henry Holcroft, Kt.; returned March 11; return voided May 28, 1624) |

* In cases of multiple returns, preferred constituencies are italicized.

| | |
|---|---|
| Beecher, William, Kt. | Leominster, Herefordshire |
| Beeston, William, Esq. | Yarmouth, Hampshire |
| Belasyse, Thomas, Kt. | Thirsk, Yorkshire |
| Bence, John, Gent. | Aldeburgh, Suffolk |
| Berkeley, Charles, Kt. | Bodmin, Cornwall |
| Berkeley, Maurice, Kt. | Gloucestershire (vice Thomas Estcourt, Kt., deceased; returned October 20, 1624) |
| Berkeley, Robert, Esq. | Worcester, Worcestershire |
| Berkley, Francis, Esq. | Shrewsbury, Shropshire |
| Bertie, Montague, Kt. | Lincolnshire |
| Blount, Walter, Esq. | Droitwich, Worcestershire |
| Bludder, Thomas, Kt. | Reigate, Surrey |
| Bond, Martin, Haberdasher | London |
| Bond, Thomas, Esq. | Southampton, Hampshire (vice Henry Sherfield, Esq.; returned March 9, 1624) |
| Booth, William, Esq. | Cheshire |
| Borlace, Henry, Esq. | Great Marlow, Buckinghamshire (borough restored May 4, 1624) |
| Borough, John, Esq. | Horsham, Sussex |
| Boswell, William, Esq. | Boston, Lincolnshire |
| Bowyer, Edmund, Kt. | Gatton, Surrey |
| Bowyer, Thomas, Esq. | Bramber, Sussex |
| Bowyer, William, Kt. | Staffordshire |
| Brakyn, Francis, Esq. | Cambridge, Cambridgeshire |
| Brandling, Francis, Kt. | Northumberland |
| Breres, Edmund, Esq. | Newton in Makerfield, Lancashire |
| Brereton, Thomas, Esq. | Taunton, Somerset |
| Brereton, William, Esq. | Cheshire |
| Brooke, Christopher, Esq. | *York, Yorkshire;* Newport, Hampshire |
| Brooke, Robert, Kt. | Dunwich, Suffolk |
| Bromfield, Robert, Esq. | Southwark, Surrey (return voided March 2, 1624; reelected) |
| Browne, John, Esq. | Gloucester, Gloucestershire |
| Browne, Robert, Esq. | Bridport, Dorset |
| Buller, Francis, Esq. | Saltash, Cornwall |
| Bulstrode, William, Kt. | Rutland |
| Burges, Thomas, Gent. | Truro, Cornwall |
| Bushrode, Richard, Merchant | Dorchester, Dorset |
| Byron, John, Esq. | Nottingham, Nottinghamshire |
| Bysshe, Edward, Esq. | Bletchingly, Surrey (vice Miles Fleetwood, Kt.; writ dated March 3, 1624) |
| Cage, William, Gent. | Ipswich, Suffolk |
| Caldicot, Matthew, Esq. | East Grinstead, Sussex |
| Calvert, George, Kt. | Oxford University |
| Capel, Arthur Jr., Kt. | St. Albans, Hertfordshire |
| Carew, Francis, Esq. | Helston, Cornwall |

Carew (alias Throckmorton), Francis, Esq.    Haslemere, Surrey

Carey, Henry, Kt.    Beverley, Yorkshire (vice Henry Vane, Kt.; returned March 3, 1624)

Carey, Thomas, Esq.    Helston, Cornwall

Carnaby, William, Kt.    Morpeth, Northumberland

Carr, Edward, Esq.    Camelford, Cornwall

Carr, Robert, Kt.    Aylesbury, Buckinghamshire (vice John Packington, Jr., Bart., deceased; returned January 27, 1625)

Carvill, John, Esq.    Aldborough, Yorkshire

Cary, Philip, Kt.    New Woodstock, Oxfordshire

Cavendish, Charles, Kt.    Nottingham, Nottinghamshire

Cavendish, William, Lord    Derbyshire

Cecil, Edward, Kt.    Dover, Kent (return voided March 24, 1624; reelected)

Champernowne, Arthur, Esq.    Totness, Devonshire

Charnock, Thomas, Esq.    Newton in Makerfield, Lancashire

Chaworth, George, Kt.    Arundel, Sussex (return voided March 24, 1624)

Cheeke, Thomas, Kt.    *Essex;* Berealston, Devonshire

Chichester, John, Esq.    Lostwithiel, Cornwall

Cholmeley, William, Esq.    Great Bedwin, Wiltshire

Cholmley, Hugh, Esq.    Scarborough, Yorkshire

Chudleigh, George, Kt. & Bart.    Tiverton, Devonshire

Clare, Ralph, Esq.    Bewdley, Worcestershire

Clarke, James, Esq.    Hereford, Herefordshire

Clifton, Gervase, Kt. & Bart.    Nottinghamshire

Coke, Edward, Kt.    Coventry, Warwickshire

Coke, Henry, Esq.    Chipping Wycombe, Buckinghamshire

Coke, John, Esq.    St. Germans, Cornwall

Conway, Edward, Jr., Kt.    *Warwick, Warwickshire;* Rye, Sussex

Conway, Edward, Sr., Kt.    Evesham, Worcestershire

Conway, Thomas, Esq.    Rye, Sussex (vice Edward Conway, Jr., Kt.; writ dated February 24, 1624)

Conyers, William, Gent.    Scarborough, Yorkshire

Cooke, Robert, Kt.    Fowey, Cornwall

Cope, William, Kt. & Bart.    Oxfordshire

Corbet, Andrew, Kt.    Shropshire

Corbet, John, Bart.    Norfolk

Coryton, William, Esq.    Cornwall

Cotterell, Clement, Kt.    *Grantham, Lincolnshire;* Boston, Lincolnshire

Cottington, Francis, Kt. & Bart.    Camelford, Cornwall

Cotton, Robert, Kt. & Bart.    Old Sarum, Wiltshire (vice Arthur Ingram, Sr., Kt.; writ dated March 2, 1624)

Cotton, Thomas, Esq.    Great Marlow, Buckinghamshire (borough restored May 4, 1624)

Cowcher, John, Gent. — Worcester, Worcestershire

Cowper, Benjamin, Alderman — Great Yarmouth, Norfolk

Craddock, Matthew, Esq. — Stafford, Staffordshire (return voided March 22, 1624; reelected April 1, 1624)

Crane, Francis, Kt. — Launceston, Cornwall

Crane, Robert, Kt. — Sudbury, Suffolk

Cresheld, Richard, Esq. — Evesham, Worcestershire

Crew, Clipsby, Kt. — Downton, Wiltshire

Crew, John, Esq. — Amersham, Buckinghamshire (borough restored May 4, 1624)

Crew, Thomas, Kt., Sjt.-at-Law — Aylesbury, Buckinghamshire

Crofts, Anthony, Esq. — Bury St. Edmunds, Suffolk

Crofts, Henry, Kt. — Eye, Suffolk

Crompton, Hugh, Esq. — Great Bedwin, Wiltshire

Cromwell (alias Williams), Oliver, Kt. — Huntingdonshire

Cuts, John, Kt. — Cambridgeshire (vice Simeon Steward, Kt.; returned March 18, 1624)

Dallison, Maximillian, Kt. — Rochester, Kent

Dalston, George, Kt. — Cumberland

Daniel, Richard, Gent. — Truro, Cornwall

Danvers, John, Kt. — Newport, Hampshire (vice Christopher Brooke, Esq.; returned March 9, 1624)

Darcy, John, Esq. — East Retford, Nottinghamshire (vice Nathaniel Rich, Kt.; returned March 9, deceased April 21, 1624)

Davies, Matthew, Gent. — Hindon, Wiltshire

Delbridge, John, Merchant — Barnstaple, Devonshire

Denne, Thomas, Esq. — Canterbury, Kent

Denny, William, Esq. — Norwich, Norfolk

Denton, Thomas, Kt. — Buckinghamshire

Devereux, Walter, Kt. — Pembroke, Pembrokeshire

Devereux, Walter, Kt. & Bart. — Worcestershire

Digges, Dudley, Kt. — Tewkesbury, Gloucestershire

Digges, Richard, Sjt.-at-Law — Marlborough, Wiltshire

Doddridge, Pentecost, Merchant — Barnstaple, Devonshire

Dodington, William, Jr., Kt. — Downton, Wiltshire (deceased December 1624)

Doughty, William, Alderman — King's Lynn, Norfolk

Downes, Francis, Esq. — Wigan, Lancashire

Drake, Francis, Bart. — Plympton, Devonshire

Drake, Francis, Esq. — Sandwich, Kent

Drake, John, Esq. — Devonshire

Drake, John, Kt. — Lyme Regis, Dorset

Drury, Drew, Esq. — Thetford, Norfolk

Dryden, Erasmus, Bart. — Banbury, Oxfordshire

Duck, Arthur, LL.D. — Minehead, Somerset

Duck, Nicholas, Esq. — Exeter, Devonshire

Duckett, John, Esq. — Calne, Wiltshire

Dunch, Edmund, Esq. — Berkshire

Dutton, John, Esq. — Gloucestershire

Dyott, Richard, Esq. — Stafford, Staffordshire (return voided March 22; reelected April 1, 1624)

Earle, Walter, Kt. — Poole, Dorset

Edgcombe, Richard, Kt. — Grampound, Cornwall

Edmondes, Thomas, Kt. — Chichester, Sussex

Egerton, Rowland, Kt. & Bart. — Wootton Bassett, Wiltshire

Eliot, John, Kt. — Newport, Cornwall

Escott, Richard, Esq. — Newport, Cornwall

Estcourt, Thomas, Kt. — Gloucestershire (deceased July 4, 1624)

Eversfield, Nicholas, Esq. — Hastings, Sussex

Fairfax, Ferdinand, Kt. — Boroughbridge, Yorkshire

Fairfax, Thomas, Kt. — Hedon-in-Holderness, Yorkshire

Fane, Francis, Kt. — Peterborough, Northamptonshire (created Earl of Westmorland December 29, 1624)

Fane, George, Kt. — Maidstone, Kent

Fanshawe, Thomas, Esq. — Hertford, Hertfordshire (borough restored May 4; returned May 17, 1624)

Fanshawe, Thomas, Esq. — Lancaster, Lancashire

Fanshawe, William, Esq. — Clitheroe, Lancashire

Farnefold, Thomas, Kt. — Steyning, Sussex

Fenwick, John, Kt. — Northumberland (vice William Grey, Bart.; writ dated February 27, 1624)

Ferrar, Nicholas, Esq. — Lymington, Hampshire

Fetherstonhaugh, Francis, Gent. — New Romney, Kent

Finch, Francis, Esq. — Eye, Suffolk

Finch, Heneage, Kt. — London

Finch, John, Esq. — Winchelsea, Sussex (return voided March 18, 1624; reelected)

Fleetwood, Miles, Kt. — *Launceston, Cornwall;* Bletchingly, Surrey

Fleetwood, William, Kt. — Buckinghamshire

Fleming, Philip, Esq. — Newport, Hampshire

Forest, Anthony, Kt. — Wallingford, Berkshire (vice Edward Howard, Kt.; returned March 7, 1624)

Francis, Edward, Kt. — Steyning, Sussex

Freake, John, Esq. — Weymouth & Melcombe Regis, Dorset

Gauntlet, Roger, Gent. — Salisbury, Wiltshire

Gawdy, Framlingham, Esq. — Thetford, Norfolk

Gerard, George, Gent. — Newtown, Hampshire

Gerard, Gilbert, Bart. — *Middlesex;* Newtown, Hampshire

Gerrard, Thomas, Kt. & Bart. — Liverpool, Lancashire (ordered to Tower for contempt April 3, 1624)

Gewen, Thomas, Esq. — Bossiney, Cornwall

Gifford, Richard, Kt. — Stockbridge, Hampshire

Giles, Edward, Kt. — Totness, Devonshire

Glanville, John, Esq. — Plymouth, Devonshire

Glemham, Charles, Esq. — Newcastle-Under-Lyme, Staffordshire (vice Edward Vere, Kt.; returned April 28, 1624)

Glover, William, Esq. — Orford, Suffolk

Glynne, Thomas, Esq. — Carnarvonshire

Godfrey, Richard, Gent. — New Romney, Kent

Godolphin, Francis, Kt. — St. Ives, Cornwall

Gooch, Barnabas, LL.D. — Cambridge University

Goodwin, Arthur, Esq. — Chipping Wycombe, Buckinghamshire

Goodwin, Ralph, Esq. — Ludlow, Shropshire

Goring, George, Kt. — *Lewes, Sussex;* Stamford, Lincolnshire

Grantham, Thomas, Kt. — Lincolnshire

Grenville, Bevil, Esq. — Cornwall

Grey, William, Bart. — Northumberland (created Lord Grey of Wark February 11, 1624)

Grymes, Thomas, Kt. — Surrey

Guy, John, Alderman — Bristol, Gloucestershire

Gyer, Thomas, Alderman — Weymouth & Melcombe Regis, Dorset

Hakewill, William, Esq. — Amersham, Buckinghamshire (borough restored May 4, 1624)

Hampden, John, Esq. — Wendover, Buckinghamshire (borough restored May 4, 1624)

Hanmer, John, Bart. — Flintshire (deceased June 29, 1624)

Hardware, George, Alderman — Great Yarmouth, Norfolk

Harley, Robert, Kt. — Herefordshire

Harrison, Richard, Kt. — Berkshire

Harvey, William, Kt. — Preston, Lancashire (vice Francis Nicholls, Esq., deceased; writ dated February 25, 1625)

Harwell, Henry, Merchant — Coventry, Warwickshire

Haselrig, Thomas, Kt. & Bart. — Leicestershire

Hassard, Robert, Jr., Gent. — Lyme Regis, Dorset (deceased)

Hastings, George, Kt. — Christchurch, Hampshire

Hastings, Henry, Kt. — Leicestershire

Hatcher, Thomas, Esq. — Lincoln, Lincolnshire

Hatton, Christopher, Esq. — Peterborough, Northamptonshire (vice Francis Fane, Kt.; returned January 18, 1625)

Hatton, Robert, Kt. — Sandwich, Kent

Hatton, Thomas, Kt. — Malmesbury, Wiltshire

Hawarde, John, Esq. — Bletchingly, Surrey

Heath, Robert, Kt.  East Grinstead, Sussex

Hele, Nicholas, Esq.  Liskeard, Cornwall

Hele, Sampson, Esq.  Tavistock, Devonshire

Herbert, Edward, Esq.  Downton, Wiltshire (vice William Dodington, Jr., Kt., deceased; returned January 3, 1625)

Herbert, George, Gent.  Montgomery, Montgomeryshire

Herbert, Percy, Kt. & Bart.  Wilton, Wiltshire

Herbert, William, Kt.  Montgomeryshire

Herris, Arthur, Kt.  Maldon, Essex

Herris, Christopher, Esq.  Harwich, Essex

Hewett, William, Kt.  New Windsor, Berkshire (vice Thomas Woodward, Esq., deceased; returned September 14, 1624)

Heyman, Peter, Kt.  Hythe, Kent

Hicks, Baptist, Kt. & Bart.  Tewkesbury, Gloucestershire

Hilliard, Christopher, Kt.  Hedon-in-Holderness, Yorkshire

Hippisley, John, Kt.  Petersfield, Hampshire

Hirne, Thomas, Kt.  Norwich, Norfolk

Hitcham, Robert, Kt., Sjt.-at-Law  Orford, Suffolk

Hobart, John, Kt.  Lostwithiel, Cornwall

Hoby, Thomas Posthumus, Kt.  Ripon, Yorkshire

Hockmore, William, Esq.  St. Mawes, Cornwall

Holcroft, Henry, Kt.  *Stockbridge, Hampshire;* Pontefract, Yorkshire

Holland, Thomas, Kt.  Norfolk

Holles, Denzil, Esq.  Michael, Cornwall (vice John Holles, Esq.; returned March 3, 1624)

Holles, John, Esq.  *East Retford, Nottinghamshire;* Michael, Cornwall

Horsey, George, Kt.  Dorset

Howard, Edward, Kt.  *Calne, Wiltshire;* Wallingford, Berkshire

Howard, Robert, Kt.  Bishop's Castle, Shropshire

Howard, William, Kt.  Cricklade, Wiltshire

Huddleston, Ferdinand, Esq.  Cumberland

Hughes, Thomas, Esq.  Appleby, Westmoreland

Hungerford, Edward, Esq.  Wiltshire

Hutton, Richard, Esq.  Knaresborough, Yorkshire

Hyde, Lawrence, Esq.  Hindon, Wiltshire

Ingram, Arthur, Jr., Kt.  Appleby, Westmoreland

Ingram, Arthur, Sr., Kt.  *York, Yorkshire;* Old Sarum, Wiltshire

Ireland, George, Esq.  Liverpool, Lancashire

Ive, William, Gent.  Leicester, Leicestershire

Jackson, John, Kt.  Pontefract, Yorkshire (vice Henry Holcroft, Kt.; returned March 11, return voided May 28, 1624)

Jackson, Robert, Kt. — Berwick-on-Tweed, Northumberland
Jacob, John, Esq. — Plympton, Devonshire
Jephson, John, Kt. — Petersfield, Hampshire
Jermyn, Thomas, Jr., Esq. — Berealston, Devonshire (vice Thomas Cheeke, Kt.; returned February 28, 1624)

Jermyn, Thomas, Sr., Kt. — Bury St. Edmunds, Suffolk
Jervoise, Thomas, Kt. — Whitchurch, Hampshire
Jones, Charles, Esq. — Beaumaris, Anglesey

Kent, John, Gent. — Devizes, Wiltshire
Killigrew, Robert, Kt. — Penryn, Cornwall
Kirton, Edward, Esq. — Ludgershall, Wiltshire
Knightley, Richard, Esq. — Northamptonshire
Knollys, Francis, Jr., Kt. — Reading, Berkshire
Knollys, Robert, Kt. — Abingdon, Berkshire

Lake, Arthur, Kt. — Minehead, Somerset
Lakes, William, Esq. — St. Ives, Cornwall
Leech, Edward, Kt. — Derby, Derbyshire
Leeving, Timothy, Esq. — Derby, Derbyshire
Lenthall, William, Esq. — New Woodstock, Oxfordshire
Leveson, Richard, Esq. — Newcastle-Under-Lyme, Staffordshire
Lewis, James, Esq. — Cardiganshire
Lewis, Robert, Esq. — Reigate, Surrey
Lewknor, Richard, Esq. — Midhurst, Sussex
Ley, Henry, Kt. — Westbury, Wiltshire
Lister, John, Esq. — Kingston-on-Hull, Yorkshire (vice John Suckling, Kt.; returned March 15, 1624)

Littleton, Edward, Kt. — Staffordshire
Littleton, Thomas, Kt. — Worcestershire
Lively, Edward, Gent. — Berwick-on-Tweed, Northumberland
Lovell, Henry, Gent. — Bletchingly, Surrey (fraudulent return February 9; return voided March 22, 1624)

Lowther, John, Esq. — Westmoreland
Lucy, Francis, Esq. — Warwick, Warwickshire
Lucy, Thomas, Kt. — Warwickshire
Ludlow, Henry, Kt. — Heytesbury, Wiltshire
Luke, John, Kt. — St. Albans, Hertfordshire
Luke, Oliver, Kt. — Bedfordshire
Lukyn, Robert, Gent. — Cambridge, Cambridgeshire
Lytton, William, Esq. — Hertfordshire

Mainwaring, Arthur, Kt. — Huntingdon, Huntingdonshire
Mainwaring, Philip, Esq. — Boroughbridge, Yorkshire
Mallet, John, Esq. — Bath, Somerset
Mallory, William, Esq. — Ripon, Yorkshire
Man, William, Esq. — Westminster, Middlesex

Manaton, Ambrose, Esq. — Tregony, Cornwall

Maney, Anthony, Kt. — Midhurst, Sussex

Manners, George, Kt. — Grantham, Lincolnshire

Mansell, Robert, Kt. — Glamorganshire

Marlot, William, Gent. — Shoreham, Sussex

Masham, William, Bart. — Maldon, Essex

Master, William, Kt. — Cirencester, Gloucestershire

Matthew, Roger, Merchant — Dartmouth, Devonshire (vice William Neale, Esq., deceased)

May, Humphrey, Kt. — *Leicester, Leicestershire;* Lancaster, Lancashire

Maynard, Charles, Esq. — Chippenham, Wiltshire (return voided March 11, 1624)

Maynard, John, Esq. — Chippenham, Wiltshire (admitted March 11, 1624)

Middleton, Hugh, Bart. — Denbigh, Denbighshire

Middleton, John, Esq. — Horsham, Sussex

Middleton, Thomas, Jr., Kt. — Weymouth & Melcombe Regis, Dorset (vice Matthew Pitt, Alderman, deceased; returned May 10, 1624)

Middleton, Thomas, Sr., Kt. — London

Mildmay, Henry, Kt. — Westbury, Wiltshire

Mill, John, Bart. — Southampton, Hampshire

Mills, William, Esq. — Arundel, Sussex (vice George Chaworth, Kt.; admitted March 24, 1624)

Mingay, Francis, Esq. — Southwark, Surrey (return voided March 2, 1624)

Mitton, Henry, Esq. — Much Wenlock, Shropshire

Mohun, John, Esq. — Grampound, Cornwall

Montagu, Charles, Kt. — Higham Ferrers, Northamptonshire

Montagu, Edward, Esq. — Huntingdonshire

More, George, Kt. — Guildford, Surrey

More, John, Esq. — Lymington, Hampshire

More, Poynings, Esq. — Haslemere, Surrey

More, Robert, Kt. — Surrey

More, Samuel, Esq. — Hastings, Sussex

Morgan, Thomas, Kt. — Wilton, Wiltshire

Morgan, William, Kt. — Monmouthshire

Morley, Robert, Esq. — Bramber, Sussex

Morrison, Charles, Kt. & Bart. — Hertfordshire

Mosely, Edward, Kt. — Preston, Lancashire

Mostyn, John, Esq. — Anglesey

Muschamp, William, Esq. — Bridport, Dorset

Mutton, Peter, Kt. — Carnarvon, Carnarvonshire

Mynne, George, Esq. — West Looe, Cornwall

Naunton, Robert, Kt. — Cambridge University

Neale, William, Merchant — Dartmouth, Devonshire (deceased)

Nethersole, Francis, Kt. — Corfe Castle, Dorset

Nevill, Christopher, Esq. — Lewes, Sussex
Newport, Richard, Kt. — Shropshire
Nicholas, Edward, Esq. — Winchelsea, Kent
Nicholls, Francis, Esq. — Preston, Lancashire (vice William Poley, Kt.; returned March 2, 1624, deceased February [?] 1625)

North, Roger, Kt. — Suffolk
Norton, Daniel, Kt. — Hampshire
Noy, William, Esq. — Fowey, Cornwall

Oakley, Richard, Esq. — Bishop's Castle, Shropshire
Oldisworth, Michael, Esq. — Old Sarum, Wiltshire
Oliver, Richard, Esq. — Buckingham, Buckinghamshire
Osborne, Peter, Kt. — Corfe Castle, Dorset
Owen, Thomas, Esq. — Shrewsbury, Shropshire
Owfield, Samuel, Esq. — Gatton, Surrey
Oxenbridge, Robert, Kt. — Hampshire

Packington, John, Jr., Bart. — Aylesbury, Buckinghamshire (deceased October 1624)

Palmer, Roger, Esq. — Queenborough, Kent
Palmes, Guy, Kt. — Rutland
Pelham, Henry, Esq. — Great Grimsby, Lincolnshire
Pelham, Thomas, Esq. — Sussex
Pepper, Christopher, Esq. — Richmond, Yorkshire
Percy, Algernon, Lord — Sussex
Perrot, James, Kt. — Pembrokeshire
Peyton, Edward, Kt. & Bart. — Cambridgeshire (return voided March 5; reelected March 18, 1624)

Phelips, Robert, Kt. — Somerset
Pitt, Edward, Esq. — Poole, Dorset
Pitt, Matthew, Alderman — Weymouth & Melcombe Regis, Dorset (deceased April 18, 1624)

Pitt, William, Kt. — Wareham, Dorset
Plumleigh, William, Merchant — Dartmouth, Devonshire
Poley, William, Kt. — *Sudbury, Suffolk;* Preston, Lancashire
Poole, Henry, Esq. — Cirencester, Gloucestershire
Poole, Henry, Kt. — Oxfordshire
Poole, Neville, Kt. — Cricklade, Wiltshire
Pooley, Robert, Esq. — Queenborough, Kent
Popham, Edward, Esq. — Bridgwater, Somerset
Popham, Francis, Kt. — Chippenham, Wiltshire (returned January 23; admitted April 9, 1624)

Powell, Lewis, Gent. — Haverfordwest, Pembrokeshire
Price, Charles, Gent. — Radnor, Radnorshire
Price, James, Esq. — Radnorshire
Price, William, Esq. — Cardiff, Glamorganshire
Prowse, John, Esq. — Exeter, Devonshire
Prowse, Roger, Gent. — Taunton, Somerset
Pugh, Rowland, Esq. — Cardigan, Cardiganshire

Pye, Robert, Kt. — Bath, Somerset
Pye, Walter, Kt. — Brecon, Brecon County
Pym, John, Esq. — *Tavistock, Devonshire;* Chippenham, Wiltshire
Pyne, Arthur, Esq. — Weymouth & Melcombe Regis, Dorset

Ratcliffe, John, Kt. — Lancashire
Ravenscroft, William, Esq. — Flint, Flintshire
Reynell, Thomas, Esq. — Morpeth, Northumberland
Rich, Nathaniel, Kt. — *Harwich, Essex;* East Retford, Nottinghamshire
Riddell, Peter, Kt. — Newcastle-on-Tyne, Northumberland
Rivet, Nicholas, Esq. — Aldeburgh, Suffolk
Roberts, Edward, Esq. — Penryn, Cornwall
Robinson, Anthony, Gent. — Gloucester, Gloucestershire
Rodney, Edward, Kt. — Wells, Somerset
Rolle, Henry, Esq. — Callington, Cornwall
Rowse, John, Kt. — Dunwich, Suffolk
Rudyard, Benjamin, Kt. — Portsmouth, Hampshire

St. Amand, John, Esq. — Stamford, Lincolnshire (vice George Goring, Kt.; returned March 1, 1624)
St. John, Alexander, Kt. — Bedford, Bedfordshire
St. John, Anthony, Kt. — Wigan, Lancashire
St. John, Henry, Kt. — Huntingdon, Huntingdonshire
St. John, John, Kt. & **Bart.** — Wiltshire
St. John, Oliver, Esq. — Bedfordshire
Sandys, Edwin, Kt. — Kent
Saunders, John, Esq. — Reading, Berkshire
Savage, John, Esq. — Chester, Cheshire
Savage, William, Esq. — Winchester, Hampshire
Savile, John, Kt. — Yorkshire
Savile, Thomas, Kt. — Yorkshire
Sawle, John, Esq. — Michael, Cornwall
Sawyer, Edmund, Esq. — New Windsor, Berkshire
Scot, Edmund, Esq. — Beverley, Yorkshire
Scott, Thomas, Esq. — Canterbury, Kent
Scudamore, John, Bart. — Herefordshire
Selden, John, Esq. — Lancaster, Lancashire (vice Humphrey May, Kt.; returned March 2, 1624)
Semons, George, Kt. — Wallingford, Berkshire
Seymour, Edward, Kt. & Bart. — Callington, Cornwall
Seymour, Francis, Kt. — Marlborough, Wiltshire
Sheffield, William, Kt. — Thirsk, Yorkshire
Sherfield, Henry, Esq. — *Salisbury, Wiltshire;* Southampton, Hampshire
Sherland, Christopher, Esq. — Northampton, Northamptonshire
Sherwill, Thomas, Merchant — Plymouth, Devonshire
Shuter, John, Esq. — Andover, Hampshire

Sidney, Robert, Viscount Lisle — Monmouthshire
Slingsby, Henry, Kt. — Knaresborough, Yorkshire
Smith, George, Esq. — Bridgnorth, Shropshire
Snelling, Robert, Gent. — Ipswich, Suffolk
Sotwell, William, Esq. — Ludgershall, Wiltshire
Southworth, Thomas, Esq. — Wells, Somerset
Speccott, Paul, Esq. — East Looe, Cornwall
Speccott, Peter, Esq. — Tregony, Cornwall
Spencer, Edward, Esq. — Brackley, Northamptonshire
Spencer, Richard, Esq. — Northampton, Northamptonshire
Spencer, William, Kt. — Northamptonshire
Spiller, Henry, Kt. — Arundel, Sussex
Spiller, Robert, Kt. — Castle Rising, Norfolk
Spring, William, Kt. — Suffolk
Stafford, Thomas, Kt. — Bodmin, Cornwall
Stanhope, John, Kt. — Derbyshire
Stapley, Anthony, Esq. — Shoreham, Sussex
Steward, Simeon, Kt. — Cambridgeshire (return voided March 5, 1624)
Steward, Walter, Esq. — Monmouth, Monmouthshire (sequestered March 10; return voided May 28, 1624)
Stoughton, Nicholas, Esq. — Guildford, Surrey
Stradling, John, Kt. & Bart. — St. Germans, Cornwall
Strangways, John, Kt. — Dorset
Strickland, Robert, Esq. — Westmoreland
Strode, William, Jr., Gent. — Berealston, Devonshire
Strode, William, Sr., Kt. — Devonshire
Suckling, John, Kt. — *Middlesex;* Kingston-on-Hull, Yorkshire; Lichfield, Staffordshire
Sutton, Robert, Esq. — Nottinghamshire
Symes, John, Esq. — Somerset
Taylor, Richard, Esq. — Bedford, Bedfordshire
Thelwall, Eubule, Kt. — Denbighshire
Thoroughgood, John, Esq. — Shaftesbury, Dorset
Throckmorton, Clement, Kt. — Warwickshire
Thynne, Thomas, Kt. — Heytesbury, Wiltshire
Tichborne, Richard, Kt. — Winchester, Hampshire (vice James, Lord Wriothesley, deceased November 5, 1624)
Tomkins, James, Esq. — Leominster, Herefordshire
Tomkins, Nathaniel, Gent. — *Christchurch, Hampshire;* Ilchester, Somerset
Tomlyns, Richard, Esq. — Ludlow, Shropshire
Towse, William, Sjt.-at-Law — Colchester, Essex
Trenchard, John, Esq. — Wareham, Dorset
Trevor, John, Jr., Kt. — Flintshire (vice John Hanmer, Bart., deceased; returned December 6, 1624)

Trevor, Thomas, Kt.                                   Saltash, Cornwall
Tufton, Nicholas, Kt.                                 Kent

Unton, Alexander, Kt.                                 Wendover, Buckinghamshire
                                                      (borough restored May 4, 1624)
Uvedale, William, Kt.                                 Portsmouth, Hampshire

Vane, Henry, Kt.                                      *Carlisle, Cumberland;* Beverley,
                                                      Yorkshire
Vaughan, Henry, Esq.                                  Carmarthen, Carmarthenshire
Vaughan, Richard, Esq.                                Carmarthenshire
Vere, Edward, Kt.                                     Newcastle-Under-Lyme, Staffordshire
                                                      (return voided April 9, 1624)
Verney, Edmund, Kt.                                   Buckingham, Buckinghamshire
Villiers, Edward, Kt.                                 Westminster, Middlesex

Wake, Isaac, Kt.                                      Oxford University
Waller, Edmund, Esq.                                  Ilchester, Somerset (vice Nathaniel
                                                      Tomkins, Esq.)
Wallis, John, Alderman                                King's Lynn, Norfolk
Wallop, Henry, Kt.                                    Whitchurch, Hampshire
Wallop, Robert, Esq.                                  Andover, Hampshire
Walmesley, Thomas, Kt.                                Lancashire
Walsingham, Thomas, Kt.                               Rochester, Kent
Walter, John, Kt.                                     East Looe, Cornwall
Wandesford, Christopher, Esq.                         Aldborough, Yorkshire
Wandesford, John, Esq.                                Richmond, Yorkshire
Wardour, Edward, Kt.                                  Malmesbury, Wiltshire
Warre, Roger, Esq.                                    Bridgwater, Somerset
Watson, Lewis, Kt. & Bart.                            Lincoln, Lincolnshire
Weare, Humphrey, Esq.                                 Tiverton, Devonshire
Weaver, Richard, Gent.                                Hereford, Herefordshire
Wenman, Thomas, Kt.                                   Brackley, Northamptonshire
Wentworth, Thomas, Esq.                               Oxford, Oxfordshire
Wentworth, Thomas, Kt. & Bart.                        Pontefract, Yorkshire
Weston, Richard, Kt.                                  Bossiney, Cornwall
Weston, Simon, Kt.                                    Lichfield, Staffordshire (vice John
                                                      Suckling, Kt.; returned April 15,
                                                      1624)

Whatman, Thomas, Esq.                                 Chichester, Sussex
Whistler, John, Esq.                                  Oxford, Oxfordshire
Whitaker, Lawrence, Esq.                              Peterborough, Northamptonshire
Whitaker, William, Esq.                               Shaftesbury, Dorset
Whitby, Edward, Esq.                                  Chester, Cheshire
Whiteway, William, Sr., Merchant                      Dorchester, Dorset
Whitfield, Ralph, Esq.                                Clitheroe, Lancashire
Whitmore, William, Kt.                                Bridgnorth, Shropshire
Wightwick, John, Esq.                                 Tamworth, Staffordshire
Wilde, John, Esq.                                     Droitwich, Worcestershire

Williams, Henry, Kt. — Brecon County
Wingfield, William, Esq. — Lichfield, Staffordshire
Wolrich, Thomas, Esq. — Much Wenlock, Shropshire
Woodford, John, Esq. — Tamworth, Staffordshire
Woodward, Thomas, Esq. — New Windsor, Berkshire (deceased September [?] 1624)

Wortley, Francis, Kt. & Bart. — East Retford, Nottinghamshire (vice John Darcy, Esq., deceased April 21, 1624)

Wray, Christopher, Kt. — Great Grimsby, Lincolnshire
Wrey, William, Esq. — Liskeard, Cornwall
Wriothesley, James, Lord — Winchester, Hampshire (deceased November 5, 1624)

Wriothesley, Thomas, Esq. — Yarmouth, Hampshire
Wynn, Henry, Esq. — Merionethshire
Wynn, Richard, Kt. — Ilchester, Somerset
Wynn, William, Esq. — Lyme Regis, Dorset (vice Robert Hassard, Jr., Gent., deceased)

Yarwood, Richard, Esq. — Southwark, Surrey
Yonge, Richard, Kt. — Dover, Kent (return voided March 24, 1624; reelected)

Zouche, Richard, LL.D. — Hythe, Kent

This list was compiled from the following sources: C 219, bundle #38, original writs and returns; C 193/32, Crown Office List; SP 14/159/53, variant copy of Crown Office List; SP 14/159/54, variant copy of Crown Office List; Westminster Abbey Muniments 12271, variant copy of Crown Office List; Society of Antiquaries MS. 253, manuscript list of members compiled by William Yonger, Jr.; *A True Platforme and Manner of the Sitting in the Lower House of Parliament: Together with the Names of Knights, Citizens, Burgesses, of the Counties, Cities and Borrow-townes of England and Wales, with the Baronry of the Ports, Comming to the Parliament Holden at the Citie of Westminster, February 12, 1623* (3d ed., 1624). Copies of the *True Platforme* are available in SP 14/159/61; Harleian MS. 159.

# Index

358–359; diplomatic activity in
Spain, 13, 20, 24–25, 26–27, 28, 37,
163, 165, 346, 347, 348, 349–350, 351,
354, 355–356; relations with James,
20, 26–27, 37, 287, 290, 356, 359,
360–361, 366, 369, 373; opposition
to Buckingham, 140, 264, 265, 292,
345, 347, 349–350, 352–353, 355, 356–
357, 367, 368, 372, 375, 376, 379–380;
relations with Spanish party, 262;
intermediary for Spanish ambassadors, 297–298, 359; and Cranfield,
307; estimate of his diplomatic
abilities, 345–346, 366; relations
with Charles, 346–347, 348, 357, 359,
361–362, 374, 375, 378–380; and
Parliament, 360, 374, 375–376, 380;
proceedings against, 362–366, 367,
373, 379–380; replies to accusations,
370–371, 373–374, 376, 378–380;
Phelips's advice concerning, 372–
373
Digby, Kenelm, 377
Digby, Simon, 354
Digges, Sir Dudley, 10, 74, 182, 185, 194,
207, 223, 251, 329
Digges, Richard, 109
Dodington, Sir William, Jr., 128
Dorset, Earl of, *see* Sackville, Richard
Dover, 132
Drake, John, 71, 88, 169
Drury, Drew, 45
Duchy of Lancaster, 51–52, 66, 119–120
Duck, Arthur, LL.D., 54
Duckett, John, 100, 102
Durham, Bishop of, *see* Neile, Richard
Dutch, *see* United Provinces of the
Netherlands
Dyott, Richard, 169

East India Company, 82, 185–186
Edgcombe, Sir Richard, 60
Edmondes, Sir Thomas, 47, 48, 49, 63,
208, 219, 224
Egerton, John, earl of Bridgewater,
115, 188
Elections: James's attitude toward, 8;
proclamations preceding, 8, 45–46;
advice of Williams, 46–47; gentry
attitudes, 91, 92–95; tactics in counties, 95, 105–106; tactics in boroughs, 95–97, 100–102; attitude of
lawyers, 109–110; issues in, 121
Elections, boroughs (alphabetical arrangement): Abingdon, 116–117;
Aldborough, 61–62; Amersham,

110; Andover, 126; Appleby, 56;
Arundel, 53, 101–102; Aylesbury,
59, 66, 110; Bath, 79; Bedford, 106;
Berealston, 67, 102; Beverley, 61,
65; Bewdley, 63, 66; Bishop's Castle,
102, 145; Boroughbridge, 61–62;
Bossiney, 48, 58, 60; Boston, 87,
144; Brackley, 106–107, 115; Brecon,
79; Bridgnorth, 102; Buckingham,
66, 72; Bury St. Edmunds, 63, 68;
Callington, 82; Calne, 87, 102, 117;
Camelford, 58–59; Cardiff, 128;
Carlisle, 61, 65; Carmarthen, 65;
Carnarvon, 145; Castle Rising, 53,
101–102; Chester, 60, 63, 64; Chichester, 47; Chippenham, 86;
Christchurch, 65; Cirencester, 110;
Clitheroe, 52; Corfe Castle, 82–83;
Coventry, 63, 109; Cricklade, 65,
66, 110; Denbigh, 56; Derby, 54, 146;
Dover, 133, 134–135; Downton, 110,
128–129; Droitwich, 107; East
Grinstead, 52, 84; East Looe, 58; Eve-
sham, 47, 84; Eye, 63, 110; Flint,
91; Fowey, 58; Gaton, 98–100;
Grampound, 60; Grantham, 87;
Great Bedwin, 53; Great Grimsby,
85, 102; Guildford, 113; Haslemere,
113; Hastings, 133; Helston, 58,
59, 85; Hertford, 52–53, 119–120;
Higham Ferrers, 115; Horsham, 53,
101; Huntingdon, 52; Hythe, 55,
133; Ilchester, 65, 66, 111, 145;
Kingston-upon-Hull, 47; Knaresborough, 61–62; Lancaster, 51;
Launceston, 58, 79–80; Leicester, 51,
92; Leominster, 84; Lewes, 78;
Lichfield, 47–48; Lincoln, 88, 114;
Liverpool, 89; London, 110; Lostwithiel, 58; Lyme Regis, 52, 111,
145; Lymington, 124; Maldon, 112;
Malmesbury, 53; Marlborough,
109; Minehead, 54; Monmouth, 52;
Montgomery, 130; Morpeth, 67;
Newcastle-under-Lyme, 52, 66;
Newport, 81; Newport I.W., 124;
Newtown I.W., 112; Northampton,
109, 115; Old Sarum, 56, 86, 118,
128; Orford, 55, 109; Oxford, 109;
Penryn, 60; Peterborough, 114–
56; Plymouth, 63, 109; Pontefract,
56, Plymouth, 63, 109; Pontefract,
60, 61, 103–105; Poole, 82; Portsmouth, 54, 129; Preston, 51–52, 66;
Queenborough, 130–131; Reading,
116; Reigate, 87; Ripon, 102; Rom-

# HARVARD HISTORICAL STUDIES

OUT OF PRINT TITLES ARE OMITTED

33. *Lewis George Vander Velde*. The Presbyterian Churches and the Federal Union, 1861–1869. 1932.

35. *Donald C. McKay*. The National Workshops: A Study in the French Revolution of 1848. 1933.

38. *Dwight Erwin Lee*. Great Britain and the Cyprus Convention Policy of 1878. 1934.

48. *Jack H. Hexter*. The Reign of King Pym. 1941.

58. *Charles C. Gillispie*. Genesis and Geology: A Study in the Relations of Scientific Thought, Natural Theology, and Social Opinion in Great Britain, 1790–1850. 1951.

62, 63. *John King Fairbank*. Trade and Diplomacy on the China Coast: The Opening of the Treaty Ports, 1842–1854. One-volume edition. 1953.

64. *Franklin L. Ford*. Robe and Sword: The Regrouping of the French Aristocracy after Louis XIV. 1953.

66. *Wallace Evan Davies*. Patriotism on Parade: The Story of Veterans' and Hereditary Organizations in America, 1783–1900. 1955.

67. *Harold Schwartz*. Samuel Gridley Howe: Social Reformer, 1801–1876. 1956.

69. *Stanley J. Stein*. Vassouras: A Brazilian Coffee County, 1850–1900. 1957.

71. *Ernest R. May*. The World War and American Isolation, 1914–1917. 1959.

72. *John B. Blake*. Public Health in the Town of Boston, 1630–1822. 1959.

73. *Benjamin W. Labaree*. Patriots and Partisans: The Merchants of Newburyport, 1764–1815. 1962.

74. *Alexander Sedgwick*. The Ralliement in French Politics, 1890–1898. 1965.

75. *E. Ann Pottinger*. Napoleon III and the German Crisis, 1865–1866. 1966.

76. *Walter Goffart*. The Le Mans Forgeries: A Chapter from the History of Church Property in the Ninth Century. 1966.

77. *Daniel P. Resnick*. The White Terror and the Political Reaction after Waterloo. 1966.

78. *Giles Constable*. The Letters of Peter the Venerable. 1967.

79. *Lloyd E. Eastman*. Throne and Mandarins: China's Search for a Policy during the Sino-French Controversy, 1880–1885. 1967.

80. *Allen J. Matusow*. Farm Policies and Politics in the Truman Years. 1967.

81. *Philip Charles Farwell Bankwitz*. Maxime Weygand and Civil-Military Relations in Modern France. 1967.

82. *Donald J. Wilcox*. The Development of Florentine Humanist Historiography in the Fifteenth Century. 1969.

83. *John W. Padberg, S.J.* Colleges in Controversy: The Jesuit Schools in France from Revival to Suppression, 1813–1880. 1969.

84. *Marvin Arthur Breslow*. A Mirror of England: English Puritan Views of Foreign Nations, 1618–1640. 1970.

85. *Patrice L.-R. Higonnet*. Pont-de-Montvert: Social Structure and Politics in a French Village, 1700–1914. 1971.

86. *Paul G. Halpern*. The Mediterranean Naval Situation, 1908–1914. 1971.

87. *Robert E. Ruigh*. The Parliament of 1624: Politics and Foreign Policy. 1971.